2495

SHAMANS AND ELDERS

D1614082

OXFORD STUDIES IN SOCIAL AND
CULTURAL ANTHROPOLOGY

Oxford Studies in Social and Cultural Anthropology represents the work of authors, new and established, which will set the criteria of excellence in ethnographic description and innovation in analysis. The series serves as an essential source of information about the world and the discipline.

SHAMANS AND ELDERS

EXPERIENCE, KNOWLEDGE, AND POWER AMONG THE DAUR MONGOLS

CAROLINE HUMPHREY

with

URGUNGE ONON

CLARENDON PRESS · OXFORD
1996

Oxford University Press, Walton Street, Oxford OX2 6DP

Oxford New York
Athens Auckland Bangkok Bombay
Calcutta Cape Town Dar es Salaam Delhi
Florence Hong Kong Istanbul Karachi
Kuala Lumpur Madras Madrid Melbourne
Mexico City Nairobi Paris Singapore
Taipei Tokyo Toronto
and associated companies in
Berlin Ibadan

Oxford is a trade mark of Oxford University Press

Published in the United States
by Oxford University Press Inc., New York

British Library Cataloguing in Publication Data
Data available

Library of Congress Cataloging in Publication Data
Data available

ISBN 0–19–827941–8
ISBN 0–19–828068–8(Pbk)

Typeset by Best-set Typesetter Ltd., Hong Kong
Printed in Great Britain
on acid-free paper by
Biddles Ltd., Guildford and King's Lynn

For Martin Rees and Narangerel Eltüd

ACKNOWLEDGEMENTS

Our book was conceived jointly and its whole central body derives from a long series of conversations between Urgunge Onon and Caroline Humphrey. This produced an enormous amount of information which we could not include here directly, and it was supplemented by Urgunge's translations of Japanese and Chinese sources. In the contextualizing of all this material, the writing of the manuscript, and the production of the book Caroline has a great many people to whom she owes sincere thanks. The acknowledgements are therefore written in the first person from Caroline Humphrey.

My gratitude goes first to the many Daurs of Hohhot, Hailar, Morin Dawaa (Molidawa), and Tengke who were so sympathetic to my endeavours and generously gave me so many insights into their culture. Among them I must single out Mr and Mrs Adiya and Mrs Odongowa for their vivid and wise memories of Huangge Shaman and for their hospitality, Mrs Høyün for sharing with me her hard-won experiences and her reminiscences, and Professor Mendüsürüng for his endlessly patient and knowledgeable discussions of Daur shamanic practice.

I am very much indebted to many people who have helped me by providing materials, translations, references, illustrations, and maps, and discussing points about shamanism: Christopher Atwood, Professor Badamhatan, Professor Bulag, Mark Chopping, Mrs Chechendelger, Mr Chu Jien, Chun Ying, Professor B. Damdin, Professor S. Dulam, Mrs Bayarmandah Gaunt, John Gaunt, Dr K. M. Gerasimova, Mrs Sechin Goa, Mrs E. Guoliang, Professor Walther Heissig, Mrs Hüseløø, Tim Ingold, John Lindgren, Li Lisha, Professor Choi Lubsangjab, Mr Myahdadav, Professor Mergendi, Mrs Naran, Dr Naran Bilik, Mr Nima, Dr H. Nyambuu, Mrs Oyun, Mrs Oyundelger, Mrs Pagma, Carole Pegg, Mr Qi Bao-shan, Mrs Qi Xiao-hong, Mr Sheler, Professor Sain Tanaa, Tony Tanner, David Sneath, Vinay Srivastava, Kevin Stuart, Mr Tergüng, Tseren P. Buhan, Tsui Yen-hu, Ms Uran, Wen Hao, Harvey Whitehouse, Balzhan Zhimbiev, and Natasha Zhukovskaya.

Many anthropologist friends read the whole or parts of the manuscript and offered me the gift of their knowledge and insight: Barabara Bodenhorn, Alfred Gell, Stephen Gudeman, Stephen Hugh-Jones, Heonik Kwon, Marilyn Strathern, and Piers Vitebsky (I especially thank Piers for his help with my quandaries over a title). I also acknowledge the helpful comments on earlier drafts made by anonymous reviewers as the book was going to press. I am particularly grateful to Pascal Boyer, whose innovative investigations of the anthropology of cognition were an inspiration to me, and who was patient enough to make comments on two drafts of the book.

Three people were helpful beyond the call of friendship while I was struggling with the manuscript of the second draft. Their perceptive comments, criticism, new information and encouragement helped me focus my thoughts and deepen my understanding: Uradyn Erden Bulag, A. Hürelbaatar, and James Laidlaw.

I gratefully acknowledge the administrative assistance in Inner Mongolia of: Dou Bo-ju, President of Inner Mongolia Normal University, Professor Chen Shan, Vice-President of Inner Mongolia Normal University, Chen Yue, Lan Shi-bi, and the officials of the Hulun Buir Aimag Government. I also acknowledge the financial support of King's College, Cambridge, the MacArthur Foundation, the University of Cambridge, and the British Academy, which gave me a grant to cover fieldwork expenses and also awarded me the inestimable benefit of a research readership. My thanks go too to Anita Herle for her unfailing helpfulness, to Gwyl Owen, and to the Museum of Archaeology and Anthropology of the University of Cambridge for allowing me to use photographs from the Lindgren collection. Peter Momtchiloff has been a most understanding and encouraging editor at Oxford University Press; and for their knowledgeable assistance and patience with such a long and complex typescript I am very much indebted to Hilary Walford, Jenni Scott, Susan Ranson, and Robert Ritter.

CONTENTS

LIST OF PLATES

MAP 1. Inner Asia

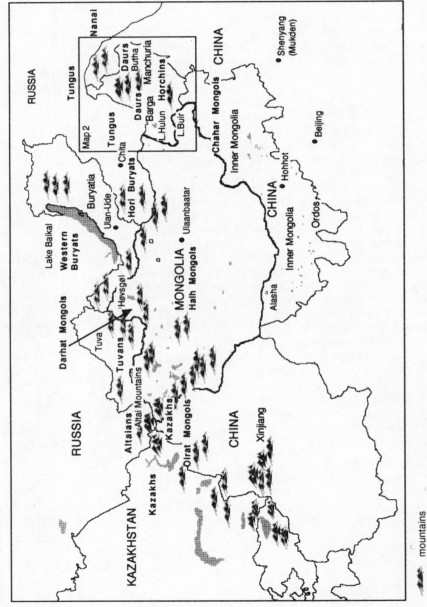

scale = ⟋ mountains

500 km (approx.)

MAP 2. The North-Western Part of Manchuria

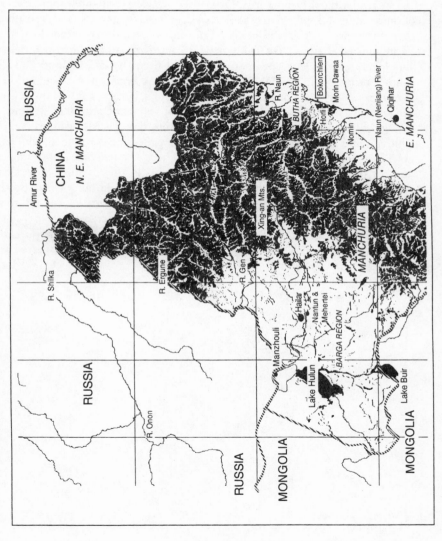

SCALE: |————| 150 miles approx.

A NOTE ON THE TEXT

THE variety of conventions for transliterating Daur and Mongolian, and the problem of whether to follow the sources or work with a unified system, was one of the reasons why I have given relatively few texts in native language here (the other being the amount of space original texts would take up).

For rendering of Daur words, I have used the closest possible approximation of the spelling in Engkebatu (1984), reducing the sixty-three sounds recognized there to the ordinary Latin alphabet. For some spoken words, which I could not locate in Engkebatu, I have had to make an approximation of my own. Readers should note that Daur does not have vowel harmony as in Mongolian. For sources originally in the Mongolian script, I have based my transliteration on Lessing *et al.* (1982) though with ch for c, sh for š, h for x, g for Γ, and ü for Y. For the sake of both recognizability and relatively close approximation to the Mongol I have spelled the names of the two most famous Mongolian emperors Chinggis and Khubilai, rather than Genghiz, Chingghis, or Kublai, etc., and I have used Khan for their title, rather than Haan, Qaghan, Khaan, or one of a number of other possible spellings. For sources in the Cyrillic script I have used the same transliteration as for Russian with the addition of ü and ø. For Chinese I have used Pinyin. The original spelling has been kept in all quotations. I would beg readers' indulgence for any inconsistencies.

I have normally used the past tense for information referring to an earlier period and the present to refer to contemporary materials (those gathered after 1990, e.g. citations from Dulam 1992).

Introduction

IT was when he had become an elder, mettlesome and with every shining black hair in place but approaching the age of seventy, that Urgunge Onon suggested we explore his memories. He wanted a book to be written about the shamanism of his youth, a book which would explain shamanism both as an anthropological subject and 'from inside'. Urgunge is a Daur Mongol who was born in Manchuria in far Northern China and now lives in England. Our book is based largely on his recollections of his youth, up to the time when he left China in 1948. It therefore grounds the magical and difficult-to-grasp topic of shamanism in a specific region, period, and set of historical circumstances. But we hope also to explain shamanism in a more general sense, in particular to explain the holding of the practical understandings, the metaphorical ideas, the fears, and the defiance that give rise to it. Existing studies of North Asian shamanism are virtually all written in the unsatisfactory idiom of general cultural models, neglecting history, singular views, contexts, and disagreements, and above all ignoring *how* people hold religious ideas, their salience, and the extent to which people really hold to them in particular situations.

Urgunge was expectant and engrossed with his memories when we began our conversations. He wanted our talks to uncover his recollections and somehow make them meaningful for English-speaking people, because he holds shamanism to represent the best orientation for living in our times. Caroline Humphrey, an anthropologist who had worked in many regions of Inner Asia, had long wanted to delve further into the enigma of shamanism, which had so often been described to her as 'lying below' the cultural practices of Mongols, Buryats, Tuvans, and others. It had been difficult to carry out research on shamanism for many reasons, one of which was that people in the 1960s–1980s were—at one level at least—ashamed of it and frightened to acknowledge it. Shamans in Siberia, Mongolia, and Manchuria were imprisoned and killed by Communist governments; this fate was escaped only by some who made a more or less public recantation. From the 1930s onwards repressive propaganda campaigns had informed people that shamanism was a primitive superstition and must be abandoned. By the 1960s–1970s, when I (Caroline Humphrey) was working in the Buryat region of the USSR, a grimly familiar cloud would immediately descend if I brought up the subject, together with the sense that personal jeopardy attached to the smallest remarks; my questions died away. The great difference of talking to Urgunge was

that during his youth shamanism was practised unhindered in his remote
village, and though the Chinese authorities condemned it from afar, no one
cared much about that.[1]

Perhaps it may be difficult for our readers to believe that shamanism could
ever have been seriously regarded as a threat by the great states of Inner Asia.
But for the central decades of our century shamanism in these regions was
not exotic, nor extraneous and unearthly, least of all a cult of New Age
self-discovery; rather, it was pervasive in the form of undercurrents that could
be present in anyone's consciousness, posing alternative ways of thinking
about the actual difficulties facing people at the moment. Socialist ideology may
even have perversely encouraged this, as its heroic construction of positive
achievements left many gaps, usually disasters, for people somehow to understand. So in the public inertia of fear there was nevertheless an inner shiver.
Once at a party in the 1960s a Buryat teacher lurched close to my ear and said,
'It is true what they told you: there are no shamans. But we are all a little bit
shamans,' and I glimpsed a defiant grin before he disappeared into the crowd.
This book will show that shamanism always involved ways of thinking that ran
alongside other ideologies, notably, during Urgunge's youth, the bulwark of
institutionalized Buddhism. Heissig has indeed argued (1992: 198–214) that
shamanism in Inner Asia was always persecuted by the state from the ninth
century onwards and that it became an intrinsically oppositional form of
religion.

We do not take this view, because shamanism has sometimes been a central
practice of the rulers of states (Jian 1993; Humphrey 1994*a*). Shamanism did
not define itself in relation to a dominant polity so much as create its own way
of operating in the world in all its facets, reacting to stones and stars as well as
to monasteries, emperors, and wars. However, shamanism was concerned with
the manipulation of the diverse energies or powers in the world, and political
domination was one of these. In the process of acting amongst these various
powers, shamanism, which was anyway de-centred, splintered into many cults,
some of which were dark and hidden because they dealt with forces that were
repressed and squeezed into the secret crannies of social life. How does one find
out about something that is condemned from outside and has also hived off
parts of itself as dangerous and secret? The question has been central to the way
this book has come to have the form it does, not simply as a practical question
of discovery, but also as an attempt to reflect in the text itself, in its many
different and counterposed sections, the kind of phenomenon shamanism has
been in twentieth-century Inner Asia.

This book suggests that shamanism can be seen as a 'whole' only by recognizing and moving between its several inconsistent parts. Later chapters show
that the separate parts too construct themes of internal divisibility and difference. In Urgunge's youth, something like a distinction between shamanism and

other authoritative external belief-systems was reproduced *within* shamanism by a central division between cults conducted by ritualists on behalf of patriarchal elders and those conducted by a variety of shamans. In Section 1.3, after introducing Urgunge and the village of his youth (1.1 and 1.2), we provide an initial explanation of this distinction in his community. However, to show that this was not an inevitable and timeless structural fault-line, the following section entitled 'Bandits' (1.4) describes the fragility of the clan-village in the war-torn Manchuria of the 1920s–1930s. In this episode, in which Urgunge was captured and taken away for ransom, we see how elders were usurped and shamans confounded, and it is later argued (2.1 and 7.1) that such historical upheavals gave rise to further divisions within the conglomeration of shamanic practices.

The de-centred and variable nature of shamanism is addressed at a theoretical level in 1.5. Here the central questions are asked: what is shamanism and why does it have this fragmentary character? Probably many answers could be given to these questions, and the solution suggested here, which is based on cognitive psychology, is only one of a number of possible explanations. It is argued that the diversity within shamanism rests on cultural acknowledgement that different *kinds* of intuitive knowledge are involved in understanding the objects and people in the world. Thus 'plants', or 'mountains', or 'wild animals' are thought of as exemplars of their own particular types of existence, implying different ontologies in each case, and different causal explanations of natural processes. All types of being are attributed with their own energy or force. It is necessary to understand the various ways of being in the world in order actively to live one's own life in it. A crucial premiss here is that 'knowledge' in these cultures implies the ability to control the thing known. It comprises both everyday understandings and the comprehension of whatever is occult about the object. The various kinds of shaman, ritualist, and other practitioners are the people with the specialized and inspirational knowledge to deal with those objects in the world which are culturally important at a given time.

The social and economic character of the vast region of Inner Asia was highly diverse in Urgunge's day. It included hunter-gatherers, nomadic and settled pastoralists, reindeer-herders, fishing communities, traders, and peasant farmers like the Daurs. Politically there were wandering bands, relatively egalitarian clans, patron–client networks, princedoms, military cantonments, and theocratic Buddhist states, all to a greater or lesser extent under the quasi-neglectful—and then deeply intrusive—eyes of the Russian and Chinese Empires in their imperial, republican, and communist forms. Now shamanism, however we like to define it, did not have such variety, or at least nothing like as much as one would expect if it were only an expression of social forms. The diversity of shamanism was of a different order, and its divisions were reproduced, with relatively minor differences, in one place after another. A functional analysis could not explain the extraordinary similarity one finds between certain shamanic practices in different kinds of societies thousands of miles apart. This implies two things. First, we have to abandon analysis in terms of discrete 'societies' and 'cultures'. This book refers to the Daurs only as a shorthand way of talking about a generally recognized identity people could assume, and, in fact, the population of Daurs in China was highly uncertain (see note 1, Section 1.1). Second, we cannot derive shamanism as a type of religious activity simply from particular social institutions, or indeed from 'society' in general. It is necessary to look, as we have done, at other phenomena, and we suggest these should be the recognized forms and distribution of knowledge.

The major anthropological studies of Siberian shamanism have constructed 'it' by comprehensive theories: as a system for regulating psychological–social tensions (Shirokogoroff 1935), as the archaic origin of all religion (Eliade [1951] 1964), as an experience of transcendence which compensates for social insecurities (Lewis 1971), as the changing ideology of stages of social evolution (Mikhailov 1980), as a pan-Siberian ritual structure (Novik 1984; Siikala 1987), and as a magnificent symbolic system of exchange between humanity and nature (Hamayon 1990). This book attempts something different because it starts from the position that shamanism may not be an 'it' at all. Among practitioners there was no name for the various activities that outsiders have called 'shamanism' and these practices were not thought of as all one thing. Urgunge and I decided reluctantly that we would have to use the word 'shamanism' (see discussion in 1.5), but our subject is something else: the ways of being in the world which suggest quite simply that 'we need to have shamans'. This book therefore has common ground with studies of native conceptualizations of the world, such as the three-volume study of the *Traditional World View of the Turks of Southern Siberia* edited by Gemuyev, (1988, 1989, 1990). Just to continue with the genealogy of this book, I would mention that it has been influenced by Boyer's work (1994) on the psychological basis of religious concepts, by Gudeman and Rivera's idea (1990) of the anthropological conversation, and by Taussig's study (1987) of shamanism and colonialism.

Sections 2.1 and 2.2 use ideas from cognitive psychology which enable us to think about the relation between everyday intuitive concepts and religious representations. However, the aim is not to reduce culture to psychology, but to see what psychological advances we need to know about to talk realistically about culture. This is especially important in shamanism, because, if we look at all of what Urgunge recognized by this term and not just the shaman's performances, we can see that it often achieved its effects without language and without ritualization. So this book takes a wider view of what comprises 'religion' than is common in much of anthropology, and it does this because it is argued here that the most important validation of shamanic practice in all its varieties derived from the direct intuitive experiences of the participants, rather than from the authoritative social status of shamans or their pronouncements. This is why there was a constant slippage between elaborate, symbolic, and metaphorical visions of the world and commonsense, agnostic, or idiosyncratic versions. In fact, trance shamans had to embody this very distinction in themselves. They were at the same time ordinary people (farmers, parents, players of *mah-jong*) and people with special occult abilities and visions. The experiences and emotions of their own lives were like tuning-forks for the trueness of the mythic accounts they told the people. This 'trueness', if it was present, lay in the shaman's expression of the immediately recognizable psychology of real human relations—such as shame, attachment, revenge, or domination—not in their accounts of the physical world, which were very often quite fantastic.

The kind of shamans just mentioned were not the only practitioners of religion or authors of cosmologies. This does not mean that Inner Asian shamanism was a matter of constant deconstruction of categories, as seems to have been the case, according to Taussig's account (1987), in Colombia. The several kinds of shaman acted within their own relatively constant perspectives on power. Another way of putting this is that these were relatively stable preoccupations linking processes in the external world with human processes. One or another perspective was more attractive, or suitable, or useful, to individual people at given moments, according to their concerns and predicaments. There certainly was a social element in this, even if the cosmologies themselves did not derive from particular social statuses. The point is that these visions were inconsistent with one another, if not conflicting. For this kind of religious practice we therefore cannot speak of 'a system' of knowledge, but have to deal rather with the social distribution of knowledge (see Barth 1993). And what this means is that any account of shamanism from inside (and maybe from outside too) is bound to be partial. It can only be authentic if it is partial, both in the sense of explaining only a part and in the sense of taking its values, its 'prejudices' and its disagreements from this part. Urgunge's is the voice we shall be working with in this book, and I (Caroline Humphrey) have taken my role as the writer to be to convey his ideas as clearly as I can, and also to circle around and collect other facts and other Daur voices, so that his single, genuine utterance can be understood for what it is.

What this has in common with Gudeman and Rivera's 'long conversations' is that it attempts to create, out of the collaboration between natives of two different countries, an understanding of a type of religious practice that has had relevance in many places and times. Like Gudeman and Rivera we also emphasize the immediacy and transience of the spoken word (of the conversation, of the memory, of the shaman's song) as opposed to seeing cultures as 'texts' to be subjected to critique. As a result—perhaps to the annoyance of readers who would prefer a neat general summary—this book discusses individual shamans, as opposed to 'the shaman'. Since shamans memorized and acted upon their own idiosyncratic histories the identity and forcefulness of particular shamans varied greatly (see 5.1), and therefore a lot more can be said about each shaman than about 'the shaman' in general.

In their performances of control over the energies of the world Inner Asian shamans were locally renowned actors in their times. This rarely came to the attention of historians, because of the oral, folk-based, and non-documented nature of shamans' activities, but it was very important as a weapon for the people. Taussig (1987) is right therefore to locate shamanism among the orders of political and colonial power. In the case of Daurs in Urgunge's time, they were beset by competing imperialisms on all sides: by the Republic of China and war-lords, by the Russians looming from the north, by the Japanese advancing from the east, and by the Mongolian communists to the west (see Map 1). All of these exercised their own kinds of economic, military, and propagandistic might. It has not been possible to do full justice to the complexities of these clashing relations here, but we hope our book provides an understanding of how the Daurs were entangled among them, and in particular of their seemingly devastating predicament as they were left bereft of their centuries-old identity as Bannermen (hereditary soldiers) after the collapse of the Manchu Empire in 1911. However, unlike Taussig's depiction of terror and despair ('the politics of epistemic murk'), Urgunge's view is that the practice of shamanism provided strength, resilience, and far-sightedness. The revolutionary leaders in Inner Mongolia came largely from shamanic rather than Buddhist regions. At the end of the book we show how intricately and intimately revolutionary activism could be related to a shaman's practice (7.3). The argument here is that individuals were adept in negotiating the inconsistent cosmologies of shamanism, and this gave them mental boldness to operate in the anarchic violence of Manchurian political life. It was not, of course, that they always succeeded in their aims, but that, even in Urgunge's remote village sleeping by its great river and surrounded by forests, the shamanic way of life prepared one for surprise and provided vast mythic landscapes that effortlessly encompassed the Imperial state.

Such a resonant statement has perhaps an over-authoritative sound. In fact, our book has had to be made up of bits and pieces, of incomplete sketches, because that was the way cosmologies were experienced and the way our materials were put together. I shall attempt some systematization at various points in this book, but meanwhile let me end this introduction with three snapshots, to let our readers' imaginations flow. The first is a note about Urgunge's fascination with shamanism as a boy.

In far north-eastern Manchuria there was a valley where small villages of mud-built houses clustered along the river Naun. The snow lay for more than six months in the winter, and in the dry, bright air sounds would become extraordinarily clear. Often Urgunge would hear the preparatory clang of great bronze mirrors as the shaman, Du Yadgan, got ready for his curing ceremonies. He would rush to the house, along with everyone else, waiting expectantly for the boom of the drum, the whirling dance and the chanting which became faster and faster until the shaman gave a shrill whistle and fell to the ground, united with his spirits. Urgunge wanted to be a shaman; he was convinced he had been a shaman in a previous life.[2] In secret, he turned one of his coats into a shaman's gown, sewed on scrap metal, made a drum, and with his friends used to go into the forest to play shamanizing. He stole chickens from a neighbour and made offerings of their blood at a stone, which he named Bayin Achaa, the spirit of hunting. He did not know if he believed in shamanism, but he very much wanted to do it.

Urgunge as a child did not realize that such innocent scenes were regarded as dangerous: he could have called forth 'real' spirits which would have caused misfortune to anyone. When Urgunge's uncle discovered him one day, he was beaten till he could barely move.

Another image of this region is provided by a carefree American traveller in the 1920s:

One of the most curious of the many strange sensations you can experience in Siberia is to sprawl on the turfy bank of a woodland stream just like any place that you know so well in New Jersey or the south of England, and to realise, as you watch the English butterflies flitting from flower to flower of precisely the same species that flourish in every English country lane, that instead of a perky little moor-hen coming out of yonder patch of reeds upwind, it may part to reveal an enormous tiger. . . . They reach the length of fourteen feet, more than twice the length of a tall man—but that includes, of course, the tail. The big, thick-coated, vividly-striped fellow made a great nuisance of himself when the railway was being built, raiding the Chinese coolies' camps so often that they struck and troops had to be fetched to clear the area. . . . He has an uncatlike way of taking to the water at times. On several occasions he has been seen swimming the two- or three-mile-wide Amur, in the region of Blagovestchensk. (Digby 1928: 193–5).

Why do I introduce this seemingly irrelevant piece? Tigers, or more precisely a tiger's snarl, and birds like 'perky little moor-hens', were forms taken by the ancestral shaman's spirit of the Daurs (see 6.2). What kind of weapons were these in the dark turmoil of early twentieth-century Manchuria? What kind of viewpoint did people have who took these as any kind of weapon at all?

One of the first things Urgunge told me was the following story and he returned to it many times. I understood from him that it represented the essence of shamanic ability, situated in the paradigmatic Empire where the Daur ancestors had always lived. The story is also archetypal in the sense that it is found all over the place in Asia, among many different peoples. For this reason it is interesting to discover in what ways Urgunge actually holds to the story.

The Emperor in the capital city fell ill, but none of his Buddhist lamas' remedies worked, try as they might. The Emperor called a famous Daur shaman to cure him. Now around the empire there was the Great Wall and the Daurs were outside it. How could the shaman get through the wall? His ordinary human body could go, but an Imperial edict forbade the entry of shamans' spirits, even though on this occasion the Emperor himself needed them. The shaman journeyed for many days and arrived at the great gate of the wall. He stopped and concentrated all his spirits [*onggor*] and transformed them into a small bird. At this moment a carter was trundling through and in his right hand he was holding up a long whip with a leather tip. The bird perched joyfully on the top of this whip and rode through the gate. It flew straight to Beijing and into the palace. There was a hell of a fight and the Emperor was cured.

Once I asked Urgunge if he believed this. 'Of course, of course,' he replied. 'My father told me that story, and he believed it one hundred per cent.' To persuade me he added, 'I know the name of the gate too, it was the Shang Hai Guan, and all the roads from north went through it. On the gate were five Chinese characters, saying "This is the Number One gate in the world." In those days you needed permission to go through. If you ask me when all this happened, it happened in the Qing Dynasty of the Manchus.' Feeling somewhat foolish because to me the story was clearly a myth, I reminded him that earlier he had said that it happened at the time of Khubilai Khan, in the much earlier Yuan Dynasty. Naturally irritated, he replied, 'How the heck can we know those details? . . . I'll tell you what we thought: there was shaman's power and there was the Emperor's edict, and one was stronger than the other. That's all you need to understand.' Here we see that Urgunge could hold this story in three ways: as deriving from an authoritative source (his father), as quasi-authenticated by a real place and historical time, and, most strongly, as demonstrating a cultural value (shamanic, as against state power). None of these quite amounts to 'belief in the story', but it is exactly such qualified beliefs that we shall have to deal with in shamanism.

Anthropologists always engage in a number of ways of understanding their subjects and in this book, rather than trying to hide this fact in a seamless narrative, it is intended to make it evident. In this case we shall be engaging with Daur shamanism on different planes, putting together Urgunge's memories, his views on life in England, Caroline's fieldwork experiences in Asia, descriptive reports about the Daurs, discussions of cognition, shamans' songs, histories of the region, photographs, stories and observations from other Daurs and people living near them, and so forth. The result is perhaps a new way of doing anthropology, and it is different from the 'single ethnographer in a field-site' approach. The author is the one who makes a unique combination of all this, but by allowing the varied inputs their own expressions and slants as far as possible it is hoped to give the lie to those who claim that the anthropologist inevitably has an 'imperialist' view or that doing anthropology implies that a single view is the best method of explanation. Much recent anthropology has pointed in a similar direction.[3] Such approaches fully acknowledge the intellectual and practical force of indigenous understandings of the topic at hand and they thereby destabilize the concept of separate and hierarchically opposed 'cultures'. I can scarcely convey to our readers Urgunge's anger at the idea that he might be a 'Daur informant' for this book, though he was equally insistent that I should write it.

The approach does suggest new perspectives for anthropology. It is true that certain classic 'anthropological issues' would not gain by being answered in this way, the questions set up within academic disciplines. For example, if 'feudalism' is defined in some particular way by anthropologists, who then try to work out what causes its collapse, then no person from a society considered to be feudal can have, in that capacity, anything useful to say, since the category 'feudalism' as academically defined does not exist for him or her. Such questions are not necessarily invalid or unimportant, but they are different from an investigation of particular cultural phenomena which yet have an abiding interest for people in general. In this book we have taken a step back from academic theories of shamanism to look at the phenomenon itself in history, and the emphasis given to its diversity is not to create a deconstructivist text but an attempt to show what shamanism was actually like. It was a dispersed religion. Here the anthropologist can best be chameleon-like. Daurs, Manchus, and Japanese, soldiers, midwives, and teachers understood shamanic activities in their own ways, and carried them with them when they travelled and even after they left the shamans behind for good. This is why Urgunge's memorizing of shamanism through his life in Asia, America, and England is part of our story, and it is why, like a shaman, I have tried out these different voices for the reader, placing them in the 'journey' that is the book.

Notes

1. This changed after Urgunge left China. During and after the land reform of 1952 Daur shamans were prevented from shamanizing and their spirit-representations were burnt. An official study undertaken in 1956 revealed that beliefs were nevertheless still strong and rituals carried out secretly. One man, aged 50, said to the researchers, 'Would it not be possible for you to send a report to Chairman Mao and ask him to order the spirits not to haunt us, not to make us ill? If you could do that, then we would have no need to employ the *yadgan* or *bagchi* [types of shaman].' The researcher commented that the man's meaning was: if you do not do this, then you must allow us to worship the spirits (*DSHI* 1985: 265). The Cultural Revolution in the late 1960s and early 1970s unleashed a further violent campaign against shamanism.

2. Urgunge does not come from a family with a tradition of having shamans. On the 'inheritance' of shamanic ability, see 5.1.
3. For example, there is the exposé of contradictory interpretations of an event in Sahlins (1985) or Wolf (1992), the aim of synthesizing native and non-native views by conversation in Gudeman and Rivera (1990), and the acknowledgement of the cross-global nature of individual imagination and its engagement with 'realisms' in Appadurai (1991).

1

Sketches of the World of Youth

1.1 Urgunge Onon

Urgunge[1] felt his recollections were not just memories of his own, but that they encapsulated a view on life that all the world, particularly the contemporary Western world, should share. He urged me to imagine myself into the archaic images of those long past times, so that they could become no longer simply his memories but exemplars of a vigorous way of life, which only chanced to have occurred when they did in history. My assumption of the irrevocable pastness of Daur shamanism was thus abruptly faced with this living person, this friend with me in the room, who through our conversations was expressing the continuous vitality of something that happened long ago.

Urgunge wanted me to help him go backwards into his past, to retrieve his memories of childhood. 'I can't do it by myself,' he said. 'Ask me your questions, dig deeper, ask me about everything you don't understand.' Urgunge is convinced that shamanism is the religion of the future, for everyone. 'It is the best, most beautiful religion. Most balanced. Most bright, most free.' I asked him, 'What do you mean by "most bright"?' He replied, 'You know when you have been sitting in a Mongol yurt about noon, reading in the shade, and then suddenly you open the door and step outside, what do you feel? Vast, bright. . . . The sky and the earth, they are balanced, you see. Now, I wish us to have our readers taken to Mongolia, put them in the yurt, then ask them to take a walk, a walk out from the yurt. What will they feel?'

Nevertheless, Urgunge could not describe what happened as it really happened, and, even if he had, I could not have made sense of it in this form as anthropology. It was because of his acquisition of new forms of language from his life in Inner Mongolia, Japan, America, and England that Urgunge talked about the religion of his youth in the way he did. Similarly, our combined production of this account of shamanism drew upon the countless delineations of shamanism in European literature known to me. References to this literature will appear throughout this book, but my first task must be to tell our readers the remarkable story of Urgunge himself. I wish in this way to provide an account of the historicity of his memories, and at the same time to convey some understanding of his continued attachment to shamanism (taken up again at the very end of the book). This will enable us to see why, in contrast to the anthropological informant conventionally taken to be the bland representative of culture as a whole, Urgunge's views bore a distinctive slant, something I consider to be inevitable and a sign of the genuineness of any individual's convictions.

First let me say a little about Urgunge's people, the Daur Mongols,[2] who live on a remote stretch of the Naun River[3] in northern Manchuria (see Map 1). This region is within the heartland of classic North Asian shamanism. Indeed the term 'shaman' originates from Tungus-Manchu languages of this area and the Daurs also use it.[4] The Daurs are not traditionally nomadic pastoralists like most Mongols but have a mixed economy based on farming, herding, hunting, and fishing. Cut off by the Xing-an Mountains from the grasslands in Inner Mongolia, their neighbours were various groups of reindeer-herding and hunting Tungus to the north, and the Manchus to the south.[5] A more distant circle of contacts were the peoples of the Amur and the Horchin and Harchin Mongols (see Map 2). Some scholars say that the Daurs are a separate people, probably descended from the Khitan,[6] but many ordinary Daurs hold firmly to a Mongol identity. Urgunge insists that his people are Mongols, and not just any Mongols but the 'original ones'. He bases this assertion on the scholarly argument that the present Daur dialect is closer than any other to the language of the thirteenth-century *Secret History of the Mongols*, the great history of Chinggis [Genghis] Khan and his conquests.[7] However, he also told me that the villagers of his childhood had never heard of Chinggis Khan and saw themselves primarily in non-ethnic terms, as bannermen (hereditary soldiers) of the Manchus. Thus, the Mongolness of the Daurs is a matter of a shifting relational identity, something which has preoccupied Urgunge, and, as we shall see, emerged in shamanism too.

It is clear that most of the Daurs separated from other Mongols before the rise of Chinggis and were peripheral in his empire. By the early thirteenth century they had already moved far to the north, along the rivers which cut through the great dark forests of eastern Siberia, north-west of the Xing-an Mountains and in the upper reaches of the Amur River. When Russians invaded this region in the 1640s, they found a prosperous people with fortified small towns, wooden houses, writing, fields, herds, and a trade in silver, silks, and furs with the Chinese. The Daurs lived in clan groups attached to a number of chiefdoms, and their headmen were recipients of tribute from Tungus subjects.[8] In the 1630s they themselves began to pay a tribute in furs to the Jurchen-Manchus, who were rapidly expanding from the south. The Daurs put up a sporadic armed resistance against both Manchus and Russians, but after heavy losses of life to the Cossaks they were unable to maintain even a limited autonomy. By the 1650s one small group of Daurs and Tungus, under Gangtemur, had joined the Russians and moved westwards to the Lake Baikal area, while virtually all the others burned their villages and fled south-east-wards, across the 'Black River' (the Amur) and down the Naun River into Manchurian territory on its middle reaches.[9] This historic move of the Daurs into their present lands is foundational in the present Daurs' sense of their identity, in the idea that they were formed as a people by a savage attack and a journey, a mythicized transition from a world of scattered clans to a defined status within the huge Manchu Empire.

By the Emperor's orders the Daurs were instructed to practise agriculture and live in military settlements called Banners (Baranov 1907 and 1911: 58).[10] The Daurs joined the Manchus to repel further Russian attacks and soon were regarded as some of the most loyal troops of the Qing Empire. In 1732 the Manchu authorities sent twenty-six companies of Daur soldiers to Hulun Buir, also known as Barga, to guard the frontier with Russia. There they were organized into the four Left Wing Solon Banners.[11] These Hailar Daurs, whom we shall meet often in this book, arrived in a rich and well-watered pastureland at the cosmopolitan frontier of Mongol, Russian, Chinese, Buryat, and Tungus cultures. By contrast, the Naun River valley of Urgunge's own people was maintained by the Manchus as a reserve, in effect a dormant hinterland, until the tremendous changes of the twentieth century.

Urgunge was born in 1919, the youngest of five brothers. He also had four older sisters, all of whom died in childhood. His father was a prosperous farmer and the headman of a village called Bokorchien, which was one of seven dominated by the Onon clan. These villages, together with those of other Daur clans and some settlements and nomadic camps of Tungus, comprised the district known as Butha.[12] Butha, which means 'hunting-grounds' in Manchu, had been one of the most remote of the recruiting reserves for the élite Banner regiments. Through the eighteenth and nineteenth centuries the Manchus, who wanted to preserve the purity of their warriors, kept Butha largely sealed off from outside influences and contacts. Urgunge first saw 'white people' (Russian refugees) around the age of 8, and he did not meet a Buddhist lama until much later when he left Butha. He remembers only a handful of Chinese families living peacefully in the village as traders and servants.

However, in Urgunge's lifetime Manchuria again entered world politics and his childhood home was ravaged and transformed. After the fall of the Manchu Qing Empire in 1911, the surrounding region had been subject to disruptive changes. In this period there was a massive increase in the Chinese population. Penetrating to the Butha region, Chinese peasant farmer settlement forced tens of Daur villages to move lock, stock, and barrel from the east to the west bank of the Naun River. In 1931, when Urgunge was 12, his third brother joined an uprising against the Chinese at Morin Dawaa. In the same year Urgunge himself was captured by bandits and taken away for ransom. It was this lawless but potentially rich and prosperous land that the Japanese invaded in 1931–2. Establishing the Manchukuo regime they rapidly set about eliminating banditry, modernizing and 'rationalizing' the entire population (around 1936 Urgunge's entire village was moved across the Naun River to Horli to form a Daur zone separate from the Chinese). Urgunge thinks that it was his return from the bandits, when his family had given him up for dead, which prompted his father to seek in this new world a different kind of life for his youngest son.

Urgunge was sent to a Mongol school in the city of Qiqihar in 1932. He refused to wear a pig-tail, sign of nostalgic loyalty to the Manchus, and he lost his desire to become a shaman. When he was 17, to his parents' dismay, he went to join the Mongolian freedom movement under Prince De,[13] away to the south in the sandy steppelands of Inner Mongolia. For twelve years, from 1936 to 1948, Urgunge's life was closely tied to the Prince and his fate. A descendant of Chinggis Khan, Prince De was attempting to wrest some form of Mongol autonomy from the massive Chinese presence in Inner Mongolia. At the same time, he saw the need to unite the disparate Mongol groups against the threat of Japanese incursion from Manchuria. He formed a government based at Kalgan (Zhang Jia Kou) in 1937. Among other projects designed to educate the Mongols, he set up a Military Academy near his palace at Sunit and offered Urgunge a position there. Prince De was no Communist, and, lacking firm support from Mongolia, in the end he had no alternative but to accept Japanese backing for his government. In the early 1940s the Prince sent Urgunge to university in Japan for three years. Here Urgunge had the alienating experience of being present during the military defeat of the people who had been both saviours and conquerors of his own country. After graduation (and near starvation) Urgunge returned to Inner Mongolia, to the West Sunit Banner in Shilingol, to teach in a new model girls' school. This idyllic encampment in the steppe, with its herds and its daily lessons, was another project of the idealistic Prince De, who wished Mongol women to be skilled in the old pastoral occupations but also to be educated and outward looking.

During all of this time, 1936 onwards, Urgunge had gone to stay in his village for several months each summer and winter. He did every kind of work, cleaning out the animal pens, threshing, wood-chopping. His last dangerous return home, in a chaos of Maoist, Nationalist, and retreating Russian armies, was in 1946. He had intended to look after his beloved mother for the rest of her life.[14] But soon after setting out Urgunge received the news that she had died. His sadness was tinged with exhilaration: he felt an essential tie was broken and he was free to cut loose.

Urgunge's life now took him further and further from his roots. With the Japanese surrender in 1945, he had fled to Beijing together with Prince De to avoid the Chinese Communists. He had become a captain of the Prince's bodyguard, though everyone knew that the movement was doomed. After returning from his last visit home, he was appointed, with the Prince's approval, an officer of the Control Yuan in the Chinese Nationalist Government under Chiang Kai-shek (Jiang Jie-shi) in Nanking (Nanjing). Here he married Narangerel, the beautiful and intelligent daughter of a Mongol professor from Harchin. But the fate of his prince, the corruption of the Chinese Nationalists, and the growing power of the Communists made him despair of a future in

1. (*Left*) There are no extant photographs of Urgunge's early life, but this and the following picture show young men of his time. A Daur boy with a sheep, Hailar region. Photo: 1931, O. Mamen. [1.1]

2. (*Right*) Dugarsüren, eldest son of Prince De and Urgunge's friend. Dugarsüren used to bring Urgunge presents of cigarettes while he was working as a teacher in Chahar. Photo: 1930s, O. Mamen. [1.1]

China, and increasingly his thoughts turned to further horizons. In Japan Urgunge had loved to watch cowboy movies. This was his first encounter with what he took to be the American way of life. Urgunge had only just left a world of cavalry and galloping horses in Inner Mongolia; indeed he had seen its wretched defeat. But those films, he said, 'with their brave and honest message represented my own lost boyhood, only more glamorous'. Urgunge had also loved Samurai films, and for a time thought half-seriously of becoming an actor. But the war swept that aside. The cowboy films remained in his mind, and encouraged in him a desire to leave Asia altogether. In 1948 he approached the American Embassy and soon accepted Owen Lattimore's invitation to teach Mongolian at the Johns Hopkins University in Baltimore. After a last farewell with Prince De in Beijing in 1948, Urgunge flew to America just before the Communists closed in.

He landed at Seattle, where he was amazed to find the reality: crowds, noise, huge cars, great buildings, and not a horse in sight. He travelled to Baltimore to meet Lattimore with just US 25 cents in his pocket. Unable to speak English, he felt lost and humiliated, and he was shocked by the absence of clear relations of respect between people and the openness of sexual contacts between men and women. He had no idea how to behave. It was Lattimore who saved him, taking great trouble to rescue Urgunge's wife and baby from China, to provide money, work, and an ambience in which Urgunge's knowledge of Mongol and its dialects was valued. But this security was short-lived. The McCarthy trial, in which Lattimore, together with Urgunge and Lattimore's other Mongol assistants, was unjustly accused of being a Communist spy, was a devastating experience. Although their names were cleared, Lattimore's group lost its research grant and therefore Urgunge was forced to leave the university and work for a time in factories and other places. Around this time Urgunge's entire family in Manchuria was put to death by the Communists. He was left with a deep hatred of the Chinese.

When Lattimore left America for Leeds University in England in 1963, Urgunge came too. He taught Chinese and Mongolian. This is where I first met him, when I became one of the first students on the new course in Mongolian Studies in 1969–70. Through the 1960s and 1970s Urgunge's thoughts turned increasingly to Mongolia, and it was a great moment for him when in 1966 he was able to visit the Onon River in the People's Republic, the home of his ancestors. Now he lives in Leeds and makes frequent visits to Japan and Mongolia. This in brief is his life's journey—a journey through many different cultures, a journey from an early modern world to a global present, and the first of those which will emerge in the narrative of this book.

Urgunge is a citizen of the twentieth-century world and nothing like the localized, historically unselfconscious 'informant' of earlier anthropology. Now he says that he does not know where his real home is, and his childhood Daur is no longer his first language. These changes are indicated by the many names he has borne in his life which mark different points in his social personhood. He does not know his first name as a young child. At the age of about 5 he received a new name, Gadaa (itself with no meaning); after a ritual at which he was consecrated to the Sky as protection against a chronic weakness and illness. He was also nicknamed 'Wolf'. During his captivity with the bandits he was called Caishen (the Chinese God of Money) in the expectation that he would bring in a good ransom. It was not until he went to school at Qiqihar that he received the Manchu name, *Urgungge*, which means 'happiness'. Back at home in the village he was called Boigon Daa (Lord of the Property), as, being the youngest son, he could expect to inherit his father's farm. While he was with the Mongolian Prince De, Urgunge liked to use his clan name Onon, as this is also the name of one of Mongolia's great rivers, so he was known at this time as Onony Urgungge (Urgungge of the Onons). In America, however, 'Urgungge' sounded too foreign and he took the name Peter Onon. But he hated the 'Peter' and after he became an American citizen he adopted the name and spelling he now uses, Urgunge Onon.

Increasingly, anthropology will require the understanding of 'the deterritorialized world that many persons inhabit and the possible lives that many persons today are able to envision' (Appadurai 1991: 196). Conventionally in anthropology, such subjects have been avoided and de-racination is seen as loss. But this need not be the case. Despite the tragedies in his life, Urgunge is a happy, confident, successful person. Behind him he has more varied experience and broader, bolder dreams than almost any anthropologist (Clifford 1992). The reader will discover our two very different imaginative inputs, and in this way I (as the writer) hope to avoid attributing a bounded, object-like, quality to Daur culture, and to provide at least a glimmer of an alternative to Western categories. One of the things I hope this book will show is that Urgunge's views of shamanism are as intellectually 'worked upon' as are mine. His sense of his identity as a Mongol, his travels in China, Japan, and Mongolia, his poetry and calligraphy, and his research work on *The Secret History of the Mongols* are as powerful orienting factors in his imagination as is my training as an anthropologist and my experiences of Buryatia and Mongolia.

Urgunge's 'ethnoscape' (Appadurai 1991)—the cultural influences which have shaped his thinking—are not to be confused with the historical record of what happened to him. He has chosen what aspects of this history to accept and incorporate and what to reject. In the West he could have merged himself into Americanness, or called himself 'Chinese' and no one would have been the wiser; or he might have stressed the backwoods uniqueness of the Daurs; but the identity he has chosen is Mongol, and as we shall see later it deeply affects his views of the world and his memories.[15]

Maybe Urgunge wanted me to write this book because I already knew a lot, in a way, about shamanism. I had travelled widely in Buryatia, Mongolia, and Tuva, I had talked at length with people who practised this religion, and I had written a Ph.D. thesis on magical drawings in Buryat shamanism. The walls of my office in Cambridge are lined with books, including histories and theories of 'shamanism', ethnographies of the Mongols, the Tungus, the Yakut, the Manchu, the Tuvinians, the Buryat, the Nivkh, the Altaians—all those cultures from which the theories of classic 'Siberian shamanism' were drawn. Urgunge had read none of this corpus. I had never been to the Daur country on the Naun River, a region in China which was and still is closed to foreigners. Through our conversations, the plan was, I was to come to understand what the experience of shamanism felt like for a child and a young man; and he was to dredge up his deepest memories and compare them with the more anthropological knowledge I had. Together we would discover what they 'meant'. Admittedly, Urgunge, who has a deep respect for the idea of books and libraries in general, had a good deal of scepticism about the contents of ethnographies of North Asia.

The very question-and-answer format of our discussions had the effect of producing dissonance as far as Urgunge was concerned. I was aware that questions which almost involuntarily occurred to me forced Urgunge to provide 'answers' he never would have thought of on his own. We both noticed how conversations, in order simply to conclude a topic, in effect tidy up and decontextualize things which were in actuality known by the Daurs in other (non-conversational) ways. The only way round this seemed to be to hold further conversations on the same topic, coming perhaps to different conclusions, but this labyrinthine procedure and the inevitable absence of immediate lived experience of shamanic activity made me feel at one time that the whole project was fatally flawed. But then I thought about the generosity of Urgunge's offer to explore shamanism with me, his patience, and his willingness to address any question; I knew that Daur shamanism was, and still is, subject to repression and disdain in China, and I resolved to write the book.

Soon Urgunge and I found ourselves disagreeing on certain points. Sometimes I could not quite believe what he said, if it did not 'fit' with what I thought I knew already. Sometimes there were misunderstandings, when I could not grasp the meaning expressed in an elliptical way. Often Urgunge could make no sense of questions anthropology suggested to me as important. An early idea was to allow these differences of view to appear through verbatim dialogue, from transcripts of tape-recordings of our conversations. But colleagues who were shown these dialogues said they were quite unreadable. We had spoken mostly in English, with plentiful phrases in Mongolian, and long discussions of Daur, Buryat, and Chinese expressions. This made the transcripts difficult to read, but the main trouble was that any verbatim conversation is actually understood through pragmatic information derived from physical co-presence (tone of voice, expression, gesture, and so on). A transcript not only omits this but it also gives undue prominence to verbal hesitations, repetitions, and irrelevancies which one is hardly conscious of while talking. Furthermore, Urgunge's idiosyncratic speech emerged on the page as a kind of pidgin English, which quite misleadingly had the effect of diminishing his lively intelligence. I came to the conclusion that a literal transcript is in fact a distortion of a lived encounter. Therefore, with some regret, I have used relatively few examples of dialogue and these have been translated into regular English.[16]

After the first year of our conversations, and later when I wanted to clarify some point, I found that Urgunge's memories returned to a bedrock of solidly remembered people, events, and places.[17] But they very rarely went further. Mostly these were memories from his childhood, up to the age of 15–16, before his village of Bokorchien was moved across the river to Horli. I became familiar in a way with this world so that I could almost predict Urgunge's responses. He was always very definite about what he knew, and he was able to date it by key events, like his seizure by the bandits, the resettlement of his village, or his leaving to work for Prince De. Because recapturing a vivid 'true' image and feeling of his own was what interested him, he never minded saying about some extraneous proposition of mine, 'I can't remember now,' or something like, 'How can you expect me to know about that? I was only a boy, and that was a matter for women.' He wanted my questions to ignite *his memories*, not some abstract 'knowledge' about the Daurs.[18]

There is a substantial literature written by Daur scholars in Mongolian and Chinese, and a smaller one in Daur (that is, in various renderings of the Daur language in the Latin script). We explored this body of texts during our own conversations. The result was something like overlapping pools of 'information' of different kinds and status. The major ethnography, the *Daur Social History Investigations* (*DSHI*), was gathered in 1956 by an anonymous team and presents its material as factual, but with few of the scholarly underpinnings (dates, places, names of informants, etc.) used in Western anthropology. The *DSHI* describes certain rituals and stories which Urgunge either did not know or had only dimly heard about. Nevertheless, when these accounts tally with the descriptions given by other Daur authors, such as Engkebatu, Batubayin, and Mergendi, I have made use of them in this book. Urgunge was extremely sensitive to the 'genuineness' of these publications—that is, the extent to which they resonated or jarred with his own memories. He always knew if an account referred to Daurs of the Hailar region, even if the author did not say so. He rejected a few of the writings, especially stories rendered in Chinese, saying that they were sinified and artificially literary. But most of these accounts, partially 'authenticated' by things he remembered, came to have a bracketed status for us. Urgunge could not remember certain points recounted in them, but he felt there was no reason to doubt them.

Urgunge's recollections during our conversations were not distanced by the act of thinking them into history or anthropology. That task was for me. He was not trying to see himself as an exemplar of an idea, or posit himself as a subject in history. His memories were fluid, turned hither and thither by our conversations. He never prepared, or had an agenda, for our talks. If this book has a shape, it is mine alone. Since one of the aims of this book is to show how shamanism was produced from within everyday life, it is to that subject, the life of the Onons in the 1920s and 1930s, that I now turn. Fairly early on I composed the following account of Urgunge's village and family. Based on our conversations, it tries to render Urgunge's own preoccupations and viewpoint.

1.2 The Village of Bokorchien

A long way from the river, as the boy Urgunge imagined, though perhaps it was only one or two miles, was a bare mountain. Cart tracks wound there through scrub covered valleys. Climbing to the summit one discovered a large cairn of stones, perhaps the height of two men. Young cut willow trees had been pushed into the top and their withered branches blew sideways in the wind. This was the *oboo*, the place for worship of the sky, mountain, and forests. At the foot of the hill on the sunny sheltered side was a grove of tall and beautiful pine-trees, whose dark glossy foliage was the only green in the entire landscape during the snowy months of winter. But signal of life though the pine-trees were, they marked the village graveyard. The resting-places of the ancestors were rows of grassy hummocks. They were unmarked except for the stone plinth resting on a carved turtle which had been erected to the memory of a famous Daur general who had served with the Manchu army (see Plate 12). On either side of the graveyard lay the village (*ail*) of Bokorchien.[19] It was divided into two parts. The northern and larger part was where the richer people lived, and in the south, past the graveyard, was the house of the shaman, Du Yadgan.

Urgunge's family lived in the north and was by far the wealthiest in the village. All of the fifty or so families of Bokorchien, apart from three or four Chinese households, were members of the same Onon clan. Bokorchien was a quiet place, centred on its own events and festivals. A dusty road led between the two parts of the village, skirting the graveyard, and it then turned into several branches so that all the houses could face southwards. They were single-storied and made of logs with mud facing, usually with two rooms opening to either side of a central door.[20] Wooden lattice windows lined with paper faced south and west. Each house was set in a compound with a high wooden fence and a gateway to the road. Inside the yard there were storehouses and animal sheds, and a vegetable patch behind the house.[21]

Urgunge remembered one of these storehouses with a mixture of dread and amusement: here were kept the *barkan*s, images of shamanic spirits (see Plate 3). The place was out of bounds to women.[22] On a shelf above the grain and meat was a row of about ten wooden boxes, each with its own door and a ledge in front for offerings. Inside were paintings on paper (*nuwargan*)[23] of groups of people, with foxes, snakes, or other creatures drawn underneath. Blood was smeared on the mouth and eyes of the images.[24] Grass was strewn in some boxes as a nest for the fox, and feathers were there too, 'to help the spirits fly'. His parents refused to tell Urgunge the names of the spirits and as a young boy he was not as deadly afraid of them as the adults were. In face, he used to steal the cake offerings. He told me:

They had human faces, but behind the faces were devil animals. Originally they were evil spirits and only became *barkan*s when their pictures were made. When I went in I reminded myself of wolves and bears: you know if you look directly in their eyes they won't attack you. So I looked at the *barkan*s' eyes. But they were looking at me! And their eyes turned to follow me. I grabbed them [the cakes] and dashed to the door and slammed it shut.

3. Wooden house on legs with *barkan* figures inside. Just such pictures half-frightened Urgunge as a child. Photograph taken in the region of Mergen on the Naun River, just north of Urgunge's village. Photo: 1927–9, Stötzner. [1.2]

A small neglected Chinese temple lay on the outskirts of the village.[25] There was a one-roomed primary school, with a Daur and a Chinese teacher.[26] The single shop was run by a Chinese family in their house. Water came from wells shared by ten or fifteen families. There was no electricity, radio, doctor, inn, or post office, and a small militia post was set up only when the bandits began to roam closer in the late 1920s. No one owned a car, tractor, or boat. Indeed the villagers employed a ferryman to take them across the wide river Naun (like many Mongols the Daurs were nervous of water). The richer people got around in two-wheeled carts or rode their shaggy, hardy ponies, and everyone else walked.

Men and boys wore long gowns of dark cotton with a sash-like belt of black material. For festivals people had silk gowns, worn with a short, dark 'horse-jacket' of the Manchu type. Some men wore round silk hats, like skull-caps, and all men plaited their hair in a long pig-tail as had been required by the Manchus (see Plates 1, 2, and 10). In winter men and boys wore gowns of deerskin, with the hair inside, and fur-hats with ear-flaps. Women, who rarely went out of doors in winter, had dark-blue beltless cotton gowns which they wore all year round. Everyone had soft reindeer-skin boots, highly valued because they trod soundlessly when the men went hunting. Only the young girls' embroidered dresses broke the colourless monotony—that and the elaborate glittering costume of the shaman when he performed.

Bokorchien was one of a series of villages on the east side of the Naun.[27] The Daur villages on both sides of the river, some forty in all, were known locally as the Naunchien. Each had its own *oboo* cairn for worship, and they were also separated from the next by another kind of smaller *oboo* which marked the boundary. The farmers' fields were some miles from the village, wherever flat and fertile land was found.[28] Scrub extended further, some days' cart ride, this being the grazing area in which all large trees had been cut down. Beyond this swathe along the river was trackless forest extending for hundreds of miles, the *hoi shibe*, rising in the west to the wilderness of the Xing-an Mountains. In the forest lived Tungus hunters and reindeer-herders, whom the Daur called Hongkor and Orochen.[29] Downriver to the south lay two small towns, Nirgi and Bwordo, and upriver was Mergen, all three having been Manchu garrisons.[30] The provincial capital was a hundred miles to the south, the industrial and mainly Chinese town of Qiqihar, called by the villagers simply *Kotong* (city).

Farming land was in plentiful supply. The territory of each village belonged to the members jointly, and while households had exclusive use-rights of their fields, land was customarily not bought or sold. Bokorchien farmers used their own domestic household labour and only a few poor families hired out men for work on a temporary basis. Farming and vegetable growing was essentially for subsistence and produce was not taken to market. The basic grain diet was supplemented by hunting, gathering fruits, berries, and mushrooms, and a little fishing in winter. Domestic livestock were killed only at rare and exceptionally lavish sacrifices. Bokorchien was a place in which even the poorest families never went hungry. But it was hard-working, in-turned, and literally hide-bound (see 5.8 for a description of the ritual in which the villagers were bound together with a leather thong). The only two activities carried out for the purposes of sale, and then only by the richer families, were hunting for furs and logging. Drinking, gambling, and opium smoking were frowned upon, except at festivals.[31]

A curious fact about the Daurs is that, though every family had a farm, agriculture seems hardly to have figured in their imagination. The annual round was ploughing, hoeing, weeding, and harvesting, and the routine was lumbering to and from the fields in sagging carts. But it was hunting in the forest that was exciting, daring, and always varied. The heroes of Daur myths were virtually all hunters. They were entitled *mergen*, which means both 'hunter' and 'wise'. In the village the more prosperous families hastened to acquire guns, and they alone could spare the labour to send men on the hunt. The most prestigious hunt of all, with falcons, required devoting great amounts of time to training the birds and keeping them primed for attack. Hunting was both a sport and a need (it supplied much of the meat eaten in the village and was shared out from the richer to the poorer families).[32] But above all it had connotations of aristocratic valour and recalled the historical and legendary use of the *battue* as a preparation for campaigns of war (remember also that Urgunge's entire region, Butha, had been designated as an imperial hunting-ground of the Qing Manchus).[33] Even at Urgunge's time no one forgot that the Daur Banners had produced élite troops and military stars who served in the capital and travelled the Empire. To convey the romance of these imperial hunts, whose history goes back at least to the period of the Mongolian Empire (12th–14th centuries), I can do no better than quote a Manchu poem:

At the palace with his leopard's tail pennon, easily he sits his prancing horse, a wonderful hero. He is all the more so when he approaches the Sang-kan River, on that endless expanse of sand, when he has just loosed the falcon that will swoop down to the ground.
Ten thousand horsemen, returning to the camp from the hunt, drink their wine while the evening sun flickers and fades.
Jade bridle in the wind's roar, engraved bows in the night's cry. The cold soaks his wind-blown hair. Beating the whip while composing a poem, he startles a crow into wheeling away under the frosty moon.

(Chiang Ching-ch'i, quoted in Spence [1966] 1988: 52)

Archaic images by the twentieth century—the pennant, the bow and arrow, the falcon, the whip, the startled bird—all were to be found in shamanism.

At home, life was strictly regulated in a number of cross-cutting ways, by social rank, by the subordination of women to men, by the respect accorded to old age, and by genealogical seniority in the clan system. The Onons were one of the great clans or surname groups (*hala*) of the Daurs. A *hala* was a patrilineal and strictly exogamous entity tracing its history back to one of the clans living in the tributary valleys of the Amur River in the seventeenth century.[34] By Urgunge's time, although the *hala* remained exogamous, it was far too large and scattered for its members to meet. The operative patrilineal group was the *mokon* (clan, lineage), a term which was used both for a grouping like the seven villages of Onons and for each village-based subgroup on its own.[35] The local Onon villages were said to have descended from seven brothers, and they had a written genealogy that was updated every three years.[36] But even so, since only around 10 per cent of men could read (1920s–early 1930s) and there was only one copy of the genealogy which was kept in another village, there was some uncertainty in Bokorchien about the lines of seniority between villages. The relationships everyone did know were those of the local lineage (*mokon*) based in a single village (*ail*).

Urgunge thought of the village as 'all Onons'. He excluded not only the

Chinese and a large bondsman family[37] but also all of the married women. According to the rules of exogamy, wives had to come from a different *hala* and *mokon*, which meant from another village. By the same token, all daughters and sisters of the Onons had to marry outside, about which people remarked dismissively, 'Those [girls] are not our village's devils.'[38] Betrothal and marriage were long-drawn-out and serious affairs, like a diplomatic treaty between rival chiefdoms, and they were arranged by elders through a male matchmaker (*jauchi*) from the man's side.[39] Divorce was virtually unknown, though men could take second wives or concubines, especially if the first wife failed to have children. It seems that clusters of lineages used to pair with groups within other clans to exchange women (Vreeland 1954: 303–5), or that one lineage regularly went to another to find wives in a matrilateral cross-cousin marriage pattern (Batubayin 1990: 154), but by Urgunge's time there was no clear marriage system. Nevertheless, one thing was evident to him: women passed between lineages, always either preparing to leave one, or not completely assimilated to another.

As he grew up, Urgunge had little to do with the women of the household. Girls in their embroidered dresses and headpieces devoted themselves to artistic sewing and 'fun', as Urgunge put it, while the heavy housework was done by the married women.[40] Women rarely went beyond their home compounds in winter, and they were strictly excluded from hunting and from the killing of animals in general. Daughters were released from hard work in the fields because they were 'favourites' and shortly to leave home for ever. But they had to sew. Their intricate, jewel-like designs created imaginative worlds like that of myth. Over several years it was intended to build up a dowry. At marriage a great collection of decorated clothing, pillow-cases, tobacco-pouches, etc. was taken to the groom's house and displayed. There it was judged like an exhibition, which revealed by its wit, subtlety, and inventiveness the mental qualities and cultivation of the girl herself.

Urgunge lived in a large family (*boigon*)[41] in which three of his older brothers with their wives and children shared the house with his parents and himself. Though all the men worked a common farm, relations were strictly hierarchized at home. The brothers were not on easy terms of friendship, since juniors had to defer to seniors and could be physically punished by them. A senior brother could not remain alone in a room with a junior brother's wife, nor even enter a room where a junior brother and his wife were the only people present. Relations were more relaxed with older brothers' wives, but, even so, these sisters-in-law had the right to punish a junior brother-in-law. Meals were taken in relays according to a strict protocol by age. Urgunge ate first with his father and mother, sitting cross-legged at a low table on the raised heated bed on the south side (see Plate 13). This was his privilege as the youngest son, destined to inherit the family home when the older brothers would have separated off. His older brothers sat at another table and were served later.

Their wives would do the cooking and serving and eat last when the males had finished. It was a hurtful punishment to be demoted from one's designated place in the order of eating. The fount of all authority was Urgunge's father, whose word was unquestionably obeyed. Even Urgunge's mother could not go against her husband's order. Urgunge behaved towards his father with utmost respect. His father died when Urgunge was 22, but in all that time Urgunge never once raised his eyes to look his father directly in the face. Because it was forbidden to use the name of a senior, and Urgunge's father was the head of the whole village, to this day Urgunge is not sure of his father's full name.[42]

Even minor breaches of etiquette were punished sharply. Urgunge recalls a boyhood friend who inadvertently handed his uncle a knife using his left hand. The uncle was so angered by this that he slashed the boy's hand, cutting it deeply. When he ran home, the boy received no sympathy from his own father. 'If you ever hand me a knife with your left hand, I'll cut both your hands,' he said. Urgunge insists that rebelliousness inside the village was extremely rare and Batubayin (1990) confirms that outbursts of violence were regarded as deeply shocking and remembered even a century later.

As well as their veneration for sheer old age, the villagers acknowledged genealogical seniority in the patrilineage. Occasionally this meant deferring to people younger than themselves. Thus Urgunge's entire family, including his father, paid respect to all the members of the *shihe geri* (the senior household). By the same token Urgunge himself was deferred to by his nephews and nieces, even though they were considerably older than him. Formal deference was marked by a genuflection, something between a bow and a curtsey, called *sain hasso*.[43] In his childhood Urgunge was given such bows only on ritual occasions, but when he was around 15 he began to sense a change in attitude: he was now an adult member of a senior generation and the heir of the headman. His older nephews and nieces began to accord him respect at all times.

Seniority was power, and not only in a mundane sense. There was a man in the village who was greatly afraid of Urgunge's father. This man also suffered from spirit attacks and was more or less constantly ill. 'But whenever my father went over there,' Urgunge said, 'the man got better. When he went away, the chap got worse again. What does this mean? My father's power was stronger than that man's devil (*shurkul*). That's the name of the game.'

The shaman's performance was an exception to all the otherwise constant social observances. An invited shaman was accorded the greatest honour, however young or old, whether male or female, and notwithstanding the fact that he belonged to a junior and poor branch of the clan like Du Yadgan. The shaman was placed in the most respected seat, begged to smoke and drink, and given deep bows even by the oldest people. 'Why? If you want to deal with devils, you must be a super-devil,' Urgunge said. 'A beautiful Buddha is not going to scare a devil away—he is just merciful to everybody, even to devils. A shaman has to be more powerful than any spirit. The *yadgan* (shaman) is the best species of human being.'

More of this later. Meanwhile let us return to Urgunge's account of village affairs. A group of experienced older men was in charge. They chose a headman (*mokon-daa*), who for many years was Urgunge's father.[44] They mediated in quarrels, organized help for unfortunate or poor members of the *mokon*, authorized the adoption of children, regulated inheritance by male relatives if a man died with no sons, punished people who commited misdemeanours, and decided who should be buried in the village graveyard. The main task of the *mokon* seniors was the regulation of the economy. They decided when plough-ing and harvesting should take place, allocated pastures, and made sure that outsiders did not use *mokon* fishing reaches or hunting areas in the forest.[45] Each *mokon* had its own willow plantation, which was used for building, making carts, and so forth. The elders decided when the plantations could be cut and punished people who broke the rule. They also decided which part of the woods should be replanted every year.

The elders had charge not only of the practical overseeing of the village economy but also of the clan's vigour, success, and on-going reproduction of itself. They saw to it that the *mokon* had a shaman (*yadgan*) who could com-municate with the 'root spirit' (*hojoor barkan*) of the clan. They also organized the ritual of the *oboo*, the mountain-top cairn mentioned earlier. Twice yearly, in spring and autumn, sacrifices were made at the *oboo* with a ritual to 'beckon down' good fortune—namely rain at suitable times, good weather, abundant crops, healthy livestock, and numerous male offspring. The powers of the wide universe were called upon at these times, the Sky, the Earth, the mountains, rivers, and the wild forest. The rites were followed in many areas by games to promote and celebrate male strength: wrestling, horse-races, archery, and field-hockey (Batubayin 1990). Meanwhile Urgunge told me of one crucial and puzzling point: women could not attend, and shamans were not permitted to officiate at, the *oboo*. That is, they could not attend *as shamans*, though male shamans could be present as ordinary clan members. Investigating this puzzle (see 1.3) will take us some way towards elucidating the social context of shamanism.

It was the graveyard, with which this section started, that summed up the overt social principles important to the Daurs. Urgunge's family was somewhat unusual in having its own burial-ground (*geri monggong*) separate from the village graveyard (*aili monggong*). This was because they felt, and were acknowledged to be, wealthy and superior ('it was like the private and commu-nal wards in American hospitals,' Urgunge said).[46] Only men and women who had lived long successful lives with plenty of offspring qualified to be buried there. All the people who did not make the grade for a family burial were relegated to the village burial-ground. This included unmarried boys, wives who died before they had children, and the clanspeople from less distinguished

Onon families. The family graveyard was a long way from the village and very little frequented.[47] People were a little in awe of the ancestors and certainly did not wish to disturb them (Urgunge once told me: 'I hate the Russians for one thing—they moved the body of Stalin'). However, Urgunge remembers one visit with his father and brother, when they passed by on the way back from hunting partridges. The graves were grassy mounds arranged in rows like a chart, with the great-great-grandfather generation to the north, and their descendants in order below. The little group made a smoke offering to Urgunge's father's father: a pipe was taken out, filled, lit by taking a few puffs, and then it was laid beside the grave. Urgunge's older brother pointed to a spot, and, looking at him as the heir, said, 'I want to be buried here!'

The village graveyard too was fairly exclusive, since only people destined to become regular clan ancestors were buried there. The exceptions are significant. The bodies of shamans and very young children were not buried in the ground at all but exposed in the branches of trees, the idea being that this would enable their souls to return quickly to this world. Then there were other people not destined to become normal ancestors: illegitimate children, unmarried girls, suicides, men and women sentenced to death, people excluded from the *mokon*,[48] pregnant women,[49] and those who died of infectious diseases. All of these people were buried in unmarked wasteland some distance from the village. Finally, outsiders (non-Daurs or the members of other clans) were returned to their own places for burial.

All this shows that avoidance of social ambiguity was a matter of utmost concern. In 1953 a man called Bangaladis, who had insisted on marrying a woman of the same *mokon*, citing the Chinese state marriage laws, attempted to attend the funeral of a relative. But the clanspeople jeered at Bangaladis and his wife, saying to her: 'Hey, what status are you to attend the funeral? If you were a girl of our clan you could be given a place on the *kang* (brick bed). But if you were a daughter-in-law of our clan, then you would be giving a hand with the kitchen-work and not allowed near the *kang*!' And they said to Bangaladis, 'Hey, shall we look upon you as a member of our clan or as a son-in-law of our clan?' The couple had no reply and had to leave in disgrace. The villagers would not speak to them. In the end, driven to despair, they left the village altogether (Batubayin 1990).

This in brief was the picture I received from Urgunge: an in-turned 'old-fashioned' community, following the annual round of the seasons and obedient to the rankings of patrilineal seniority. A cycle of rituals existed to ensure the exclusive perpetuity of the clan, which, as it were, laid out its own future—notably in the order constructed in the graveyards, so a person could look there and know exactly his place. The clan did not have a single hereditary powerful leader, but rather each man submitted to internalized rules which allotted him a place and kept him subservient until late middle age or until the entire older generation of male relatives had died off. It was as though volition and extravagance were repressed in the interests of communal harmony (though, as we shall see, this was not really the case). There were no concepts of absolute 'right' and 'wrong', Urgunge said.[50] Rather, people talked only of whether an action was fitting (*jukin*) or not fitting, like a key in a lock. 'There was a feeling of togetherness, like the five fingers of your hand. Your fist, your root, those words in Daur have the same origin. Everyone knew from childhood what was fitting, and that is what they did. It was organic, like your body.'

My account so far of Bokorchien no doubt has a familiar ring to anthropologists, since what Urgunge said resonates so closely with mid-century studies of patrilineal clanship. And indeed my years as a student of Meyer Fortes and Edmund Leach are part of my formation as a writer, and one I have no wish to repudiate. But since that time anthropology has become increasingly aware of historicity and its own role in making its object (Fabian 1983; Thomas 1989), and of the need to account for the ways in which cultural meaning and subjectivities are produced (O'Hanlon 1988; Gudeman and Rivera 1990). We therefore cannot understand Urgunge's ideas only as the views of an unchanging and sovereign subject, informing us simply about the society of his childhood. Alongside his unique personality which composed the fragments of his experiences, we have to explain how his kind of positional view of the world was produced by this society and culture. His views were dynamic and changing even within the course of his conversations with me; however, we can also perceive relatively stable parts of Daur subjectivities,[51] not only Urgunge's but also those of other Daur people, and these were located within social practices associated with discursive fields. Urgunge was the youngest son due to inherit, in a world of hierarchically ordered men. A fuller account of this will involve understanding Daur gender concepts (see Ch. 4) and the native terms used in the production of particular cultural categories. In the past anthropology tended to depict men and women as situated in the family, as I have done above and as, indeed, was Urgunge's own view. But, as Cowie (1978) and Barlow (1994) have argued about gender, we need also to think about how 'it is within the family—as the effect of kinship structures—that women as women are produced'. Barlow (1994: 256) remarks that this is to see kinship 'as a production line for subjectivities'. I find this approach useful, since on the one hand it enables me to give an account of the differentiation of categories of persons as subject-agents, and on the other it allows us to see a kinship-generated dimension whereby people may differ in their religious attitudes to the world (not that the attitudes attached to these subject positions are the only ones any given individual will have). So, to continue the story approximately according to the chronology of my conversations with Urgunge, the next section discusses the Daur category of 'old man', which I contrast with 'shaman'. Here I shall attempt to go beyond a description of social organization and begin an account of how these categories were produced.

1.3 Old Men and Shamans

Some way into our conversations Urgunge presented me with an enigma that led me to ponder the relation of the elders with shamans. He had remarked that *yadgan* shamans never went hunting like other men. I could not make much sense of his explanation. 'A shaman is part of the sky and wild animals are cousins of the sky, so a shaman and animals are relatives. Perhaps, what do you call it, cross-cousins. Therefore, of course, he should not kill them.' I decided to look beyond the Daurs. Things started to become clear when it appeared that the 'old man', who goes hunting, and 'the shaman', who does not, are very different, though linked, cultural constructions in many regions of Inner Asia.[52]

In the patriarchal way of looking at the world, the morality was clear: the right and the achievement of each man was to have male descendants, and his duty was to revere his own parents.[53] The appearance of grandchildren, and even more so of great-grandchildren, was a sign that a man's life was approaching its end. One had reached the last living generation (*uye*, literally 'joint of the bones') in a vertical line of time reaching back into the past. Sagalayev and Oktyabr'skaya have written:

Now there approached the unseen and frightening other existence, which made itself known ever more frequently by terrible dreams or grave illness. The acquisition of a new status occurred gradually and was formulated in both substances and activities. Among the Tuvinians people over the age of fifty cut their hair short. Women took off their hair ornaments and handed them on to their daughters. Gradually the signs of sexual difference in clothing were relinquished. People began to give back to society those signs of the social norm, the signs of [social] full value that they had been collecting all their lives, as if they were preparing themselves to go away into the world of Nature. (1990: 78)

Among the Daurs, as men moved gradually from maturity into old age they stopped shaving and allowed their beards and moustaches to grow. They entered a liminal status that was at once 'above' daily life and at the same time 'closer' to the ancestors. Urgunge said that the word for old man (*utaachi*) made him think somehow also of ancestral old men beyond the grave; both were held responsible for the well-being of their descendants. The old man was a repository of knowledge, not the compromised and contingent knowledge of the middle years, but a purified wisdom crystallized from many experiences. This also fitted him for ritual, for the sacralized activity of interaction with the ancestors and deifications of nature. In Urgunge's village it was 'old men' who led the worship of the Sky, of mountains, stars, cliffs, rivers, the forest, individual trees, and the domestic fire. They also had charge of regular offerings to the pictures of *barkan*s (vessels for spirits) kept at home. Indeed, Urgunge agreed with what Sagalayev and Oktyabr'skaya wrote about the Altaians, 'the spectrum of the ritual role of the "old man" in the past was considerably wider and more varied than that of the "shaman"' (1990: 86).[54]

In Bokorchien the elder most specifically concerned with ritual was known as the *bagchi*.[55] Urgunge insisted that the *bagchi* (ritualist) was quite different from spirit-inducing shamans like the *yadgan* or *otoshi*. The *bagchi*'s job was to know the rituals and say prayers. A *bagchi* did not undergo any initiation, nor wear special clothes, but he had to be old and could never under any circumstances be a woman. He would make sacrifices and offerings, consecrate horses to spirits,[56] pronounce banishing spells, and make divinations by reading the cracks in a sheep's shoulder-blade heated on the fire. The *bagchi* often acted as ritual adviser and helper to shamans. The *bagchi* was considered better than shamans at oratory and prayers, and such performances could be exalted (Mendüsürüng 1983: 263), but the crucial difference was simply that he *was not* a shaman. He had a lot to do with spirits, but this was action towards them, preserving a difference of identity, and he was normally not able to embody them. In fact, all of the rituals conducted by the *bagchi* could be carried out by other old men. He was like the quintessence of 'the old man', someone who emerged from the others by virtue of his knowledge of ritual and oratorical skills.

From this we can see two things. First, it is clear that having to do with spirits, ancestors, and so on was not the prerogative of shamans alone. Second, we can take this opportunity to question the continued use in anthropology of terms like 'trance' or 'ecstasy' as the defining characteristic of the shaman. Hamayon (1993) has rightly argued that such terms, used by Eliade ([1951] 1964) and Lewis (1971), have not been helpful and reflect Western traditions of demonizing or romanticizing shamanic practice. For a start, there is no psychological state that we can definitely identify with 'trance', and it is impossible either to prove or to deny its presence. Then, ethnographically, we find that in Inner Asia states describable by this term are entered by many people, such as singers, diviners, midwives, lamas, hunters, or children while playing. Finally, there does not seem to be a native word corresponding to the academic use of 'trance' in North Asia.

In the case of the Daurs and Mongolians, people commonly use verbs deriving from the term for the practitioner, like the English 'to shamanize' (for example, the Daur *yadgalji-* from *yadgan*, or the Mongolian *boole-* from the type of shaman called *boo*). Poppe (1930: 29) mentions the Daur expression 'singing to frenzy' (*chorkirtal*).[57] Such words refer to a range of behaviours such as trembling, dancing, falling to the ground, croaking, foaming at the mouth, etc., which are cultural representations of being in contact with occult forces. But the behaviour does not itself constitute such contact (Hamayon 1994: 10–15). More or less anyone can shamanize (*yadgalji-*), as Urgunge himself did as a boy.

What we in fact have to deal with is a range of states of mind (different kinds of dreaming, assumption of other identities, having visions, the exaltation of calling for blessings, various states of dissociation achieved by shamans, and even fever-induced delirium or drunkenness) that were considered to promote access to different kinds of knowledge and experience, or to aid in certain ritual actions. From the native point of view, different states of mind were means to various ends. Their appearances were signs of what was going on, and therefore they were not in themselves so important, much less so than what people thought was actually happening.

What was essential to someone being a *yadgan* shaman was the ability to become at one with a spirit, and consequently able to journey in the cosmos, and come to know what ordinary people could not know. The joining with a spirit was represented physically in a cultural repertoire of shuddering, 'falling unconscious', making inarticulate noises, foaming at the mouth, etc., but there were also established shamanic routines of contact with spirits that did not involve such 'ecstatic' behaviour.[58] Thus, it seems unlikely that any one definable mental state was involved. This may explain why Daurs seem to have no term for the mental state, but could quite clearly say what was happening, e.g. by the expression *onggor buulga-* (to make a spirit descend).[59] Therefore, when the word 'trance' is used in this book it refers to a conventional set of behaviours, not to a mental state, and what is important is that these behaviours were a sign that the shaman had now activated one or another of his or her special means of engaging with unseen forces (for further discussion see 5.1, 5.5, and 5.7).

The shaman was someone, male or female, who was differently constituted as a person from ordinary people by this very ability. This meant not simply undergoing a public consecration ritual, though most shamans did this, but experiencing an inner metamorphosis. A young man or woman would fall ill, experiencing disorientation and mental and physical suffering which might last for several years. This apparently incurable state culminated in a terrible vision or dream: one might see oneself as dying, as being eaten by spirits, or taken apart limb by limb, and being forced by the spirits to accept a shaman ancestor spirit (*onggor*) as a new soul. Reconstituted physically by the spirits, or at least acknowledging that the suffering was spirit-caused, and consciously accepting the *onggor*, the initiate recovered and took on a new existence as a shaman. Thereafter the neophyte was given intensive training by an older shaman teacher. This whole area of experience was conceived in different ways by various people as will become clear later, but for the time being we can say that after some kind of spiritual death the shaman was considered an artefact of the spirits and a human vessel for their power. He or she was not construed as getting closer to death like the old man, but had already in spirit crossed the frontier and returned to an ontologically new existence. The *yadgan* ventured over the boundary of death at each occasion when he or she 'became' or 'called down' an *onggor*.

4. Old Daur man from Butha who had travelled to the Gangjuur fair near Hailar. Photo: 1931, O. Mamen. [1.3]

5. Saime Shaman, a Solon, conducting a ritual by the banks of the frozen Imen River to the south of Hailar in the Barga region. Photo: 1932, O. Mamen. [1.3]

This is how the initiatory spiritual death and rebirth are described from the subjective position of shaman (see note 51 in 1.2) in an epic popular in Urgunge's time.[60] The female Nishan Shaman is addressing a client who had begged her to rescue his son's soul:

At a time when I was seventeen years old,
together with all the women,

ikule ekule	having set out to the steppes and valleys
ikule ekule	having gathered vegetable plants [there]
ikule ekule	[we] were returning home,
ikule ekule	when suddenly with a dazzle arising in my eyes
ikule ekule	[I] stopped understanding anything.
ikule ekule	[I] hardly managed to get home.
ikule ekule	Not knowing why
ikule ekule	[I] myself, weak, knowing nothing,
ikule ekule	fell backwards.
ikule ekule	Since [you] have come to search, I'll tell [you] the communication of the great source.
ikule ekule	[My] physical sensations dimmed,
ikule ekule	and suddenly from the tie-beam like the sun in the sky a huge mirror descended.
ikule ekule	Only just coming to
ikule ekule	[I] took [the mirror], and, it seems,
ikule ekule	in purity and solitude [my] whole body turned into powder.
ikule ekule	With a breaking of eighty bones
ikule ekule	ninety bones were twisted.
ikule ekule	And thus [I] myself, becoming radiant,
ikule ekule	in unity with the great spirit,
ikule ekule	[I] myself became glorious, legendary and elevated!

(Yakhontova 1992: 102–3)

It is significant that the shaman's initiatory experience broke and twisted her bones. In the make-up of the human body, bones were given by the father, blood and flesh by the mother, and the 'bone joint' (*uye*) was at the same time the word for the patrilineal generation. Shamanic initiation thus shattered the very line of joints-generations in which the 'old man' was the crucial link with the ancestors. As Sagalayev and Oktyabr'skaya observe (1990: 30): 'This vertical line of descendants—ancestors was more than a "cult of ancestors." It was a means of understanding one's place in the space-time and cause-result coordinates of the world.'

Before taking up this point again let me describe the situation in Bokorchien. The one shaman, Du Yadgan, was getting on in years and had protected the village for many decades. His main duties were curative, putting right physical and mental suffering thought to be caused by soul-loss or attacks by spirits. He also explained people's dreams, foretold the future, and 'enlivened' pictures of spirits, but most minor rites, such as purifying animals or houses by smoke, were left to the *bagchi*. Du Yadgan took no part in birth, marriage, or funeral rites.

By the time Urgunge knew him, Du Yadgan's wife had died, but he had three sons and so he was freed from farming and could practise shamanizing at any time. It would have been considered quite wrong for such a respected person to do much hard physical work. The family was not rich. 'They were too poor to have a kerosene lamp,' said Urgunge. Du Yadgan was a small man, precise in his movements, and neat in his dress, which he always kept tightly buttoned up. To the end of his life he wore his hair in a long pig-tail, which was accurately wound round his head under his hat. By Urgunge's young manhood this Manchu style was beginning to seem old-fashioned, but he remembers that a pig-tail was thought to be attractive to girls. Rumour had it that, despite his small stature, Du Yadgan had preternatural strength. He had been a wrestler in his youth, people said, and even in old age he could dance for hours laden with the huge bronze mirrors of his shaman's costume. Du Yadgan could not read or write, nor was he in any way involved in politics. But he was highly knowledgeable about shamanism, and he knew the intimate secrets of everyone in the village. He was a kindly, sincere man, to whom everyone turned if they were in inexplicable trouble. There was a sense therefore in which Du Yadgan was 'ordinary', except that everyone knew that inside him there was the uncanny faculty of becoming at one with spirits and influencing their power.

However, as he became older Du Yadgan's abilities began to fail. The boys' attention at his performances began to wander, and Urgunge and his friends dared to whisper, '*Du Yadgan sain indeesen!*', a joke that caused gales of suppressed mirth. This literally means 'Du Yadgan is grinding well,' referring to the donkey pulling the corn-grinding stone which circled a central spike. The donkey, like the shaman, wore a fringe over its eyes to prevent it from getting dizzy from the endless circling. But *indeesen* had another meaning: grinding was slang for sex. This sacrilegious joke is something that even now Urgunge is rather ashamed of. The time had come to get another shaman, and Urgunge's father invited a young man from another village to become Du Yadgan's successor.[61] This young shaman was not yet well known, but he was handsome, strong, lucky, and dominating in performance. He had a beautiful bright new costume. The girls loved him, and he seemed to sing with a particular lilt when he danced towards them.

All this suggests that, on the one hand, the shaman was in a sense a constructed person, one defined by a socially recognized transformation determined by the idea of spirits. On the other, he or she quite simply had to be physically and mentally strong, and old age was understood to bring failing powers. This was different from the 'old man', who entered such a status gradually, as a result of the ritually unmediated, though socially acknowledged, process of turning experience into knowledge. Sagalayev and Oktyabr'skaya write, 'Maybe the old man is the custodian not so much of sacral knowledge, but primarily of the rational, socially-significant *experience* of the collective. The defining moment in the formation of the role is the age of the person, and thus its parameters are given by life itself. . . . As such, the old man was *older* than any shaman' (1990: 86).

An 'old man' had to accompany Daur hunters to the forest. He was called *aanag-daa*, chief of the nomadic hunting-camp. Urgunge said that an *aanag-daa* would usually be long past it as far as active hunting was concerned. His duty was to bestow his wisdom and knowledge of the way. Hunting, whether it was the four-month long winter hunt or the shorter summer hunt, was conceived as a journey (*ayin*). This kind of journey had the connotations of a campaign (military expeditions, logging trips, trading-caravans, and shamans' journeys to other worlds were all *ayin*). The winter hunt (*pentumen*) was primarily for deer horns filled with blood (*pentu*) and the sexual organs of male deer, which were traded to the Chinese as an aphrodisiac. Daurs also hunted for bears, tigers, boar, lynx, antelope, squirrels, foxes, and wolves, but getting *pentu* was the real goal, though it was rare and considered to bring luck to the whole community. The *aanag-daa* was the driver of the lead cart because he knew the tracks (*mør* (spoor, trace, track)) through the forest to the places where the animals would be found. First, he organized the ritual of 'opening the way'.[62] This involved a dummy journey, setting out and stopping only a little way from the village, shooting a few shots and eating a meal, returning home, and only then starting on the real campaign. This was said to 'open up the lucky road'. Once in the forest, the old man would preside over the camp and make sure that hunting etiquette was followed. He would skin the animals, cut the meat into strips for freezing and distribution into equal shares, and make an offering to the fire. At each stopping-place he would make a man-shaped image of snow, or slice the bark off a living tree to draw a face on the trunk (see Plate 6). This was Bayin Achaa ('rich father'), the master-deity of the forest. Here each night the *aanag-daa* would make meat offerings, without which the hunt could not be successful.

It was not only among the Daur that shamans as shamans did not take part in hunting.[63] Among the Nanai of the Amur region, shamanizing on the hunt was strictly forbidden on the grounds that it would frighten away the animals and keep them from falling into traps; hunters who had set traps were forbidden from taking part in shamanic performances on their return home (Smolyak 1976: 129). The forest was full of unseen demonic spirits, it was said. The mysterious sounds of the forest were the whispers of spirits and shamanizing would inevitably draw these forth. Human souls too might harm the hunting. 'If my son goes away hunting and I think about him, my soul wanders around him and frightens the animals' (Smolyak 1976: 154).[64]

Urgunge described something similar for the Daur, where demonic spirits (*shurkul*) also roamed in the wilderness; these souls and spirits were different from the 'masters' of mountains and the forest to which the *aanag-daa* made his offerings.

By contrast with shamans, an old man's speech did not frighten away animals but could attract them in. Nanai old men spoke directly to fishes. 'Your head is dizzy, don't know anything, forgotten everything, feeling bad. You are going across and I make you submit, you are going round [the net] and I drive you in.' There were particular things to be said to each kind of animal and fish (Smolyak 1976: 144). Some old men had a special ability in talking to animals and a host of practical and magical actions directly performed on them. The *aanag-daa* told Urgunge about reading animal tracks, the importance of wind-direction, the training of sight, hearing, and the sense of smell. All of this was absolutely essential, as were the offerings made by old men as mediators between the hunters and the master-deity of the mountains and forests.[65] Quite apart from talking directly to animals, Daur hunters would tell stories in the evenings, and, as with the same practice among Buryats, where it was virtually obligatory, this story-telling was designed to entertain the forest master, encouraging him to give more animals to the hunters who had given him such pleasure.

Accounts of hunting give us repeated pictures of a world that was both practical and sacralized, and from which the shamans were excluded. Hunting was one of the main occasions for the training of young boys in valour, skills, and cultural traditions. The hunt, especially the large quasi-military communal *battue* hunt, established its own male micro-world. Zhambalova has observed about Buryats, 'Old people today emphasize that the communal hunt (*aba*) was carried out not so much for the sake of getting game, but to observe the custom set down by the ancestors. The *aba*, they say, was the "festival of men"' (1991: 105). In other words, the hunt was as much an ideological and social activity as an economic one. However, the shaman's relation to this is still not entirely clear.

Let us explore further what Urgunge said about the shaman and his 'cross-cousins', the wild animals. A certain complexity arises unavoidably in conversations. Perhaps to tease me, Urgunge had continued: 'Aha, I see you are wondering how I know this word cross-cousin in English. By now at least maybe I've become a second-class anthropologist. And maybe, those game animals are double-crossing cousins!' For us even to begin to understand these double-crossing cross-cousins one has to know that not only demonic spirits (*shurkul*) but also shaman's spirits (*onggor*) often took the form of wild animals and birds and could be helpful to humans or very harmful indeed. Further, *onggor* spirits were 'ancestral' in a different sense from the old man's ancestors. Shamanic spirits had previously belonged to an earlier shaman, but they were not inherited in the male line. So the connection between shamans was in principle not a patrilineal affair, unlike Daur male-oriented society in general. The link could zig-zag from women to men and vice versa, or branch off into temporary animal existence. In other words, the metaphor of the line stretching 'vertically' into the past did not apply. So perhaps *onggor* spirits could in a sense be 'cross-cousins'. But kinship terminology, which designates definite categories of people, was not normally used for spirits, for they had an uncertain nature and existed in a nebulous relation to living people. In fact present-day Mongols often call spirits *yum*, which means 'thing', suggesting that even the word 'spirits' may be too exact.[66] I think that Urgunge wanted to dazzle me with his pun from the first and that his cross-cousin metaphor should not be taken literally; he meant only that shamans, in the religious dimension denoted by the overall and distant ancestorhood of the Sky, had some kin-like identity with wild animals, and that this was especially 'crossed' or tricky because the animals might turn out to be spirits. The shaman should not kill these spirit-animal kin. Just as important, he should not, by shamanizing (calling up spirits) in the forest, confuse the idiom of the hunt, which concerned animals as animals.

Now spirit-animals were not the same as ordinary animals, and yet could appear as them. There are several dimensions to the cognitive complexity or 'trickyness' this statement involves. One is very fundamental. Urgunge told me: shamans were as observant as anyone else, maybe more so, but the way they knew these spirit-filled wild creatures could not be by the training of straightforward vision, hearing, or smell, like the hunters. 'Of course not,' he said. 'After all, were we even sure they existed or not?'

Shamans' songs presume the existence of spirit-animals, and as we return to Urgunge's essential doubt later (5.7), let us briefly look at how such songs represent this existence. In the following song and accompanying story, we shall begin to glimpse the nature of shamanic spirits and see how the ability to control them differed from the ability of old men.[67] From this foundational story of Darhat Mongol shamanism, it is clear that extreme physical and mental old age are incompatible with shamanic ability. The *senile shaman* is a concept which disastrously combines the shaman with the old man.

The original shaman, who lived long ago, was Zønøk Hairhan (Senile 'Dear-one').[68] Zønøk Hairhan in his idiocy made a dreadful mistake. He let out of their nine graves buried below the River Tenggis the 'uncontrollably evil things' which generations of people had been keeping blocked in their holes. Zønøk dug up all nine graves, and out came infants, bloody parts, dead people's ears and limbs, ghosts, genies, and other disgusting and dangerous things. The Darhat call these *ozuur yum*,[69] which can be roughly translated as 'root things', a term which we shall have occasion to discuss later (5.1) in relation to the Daur. These began to attack people. Controlled by subsequent generations of shamans, the 'root things' became shamanic ancestral spirits (*onggod*) and today sing through shamans of the nine forms or transformations they take:

Hu-hug, hu-hig, . . . [nine times making the gruff, reedy sound of the common owl]
Hooi . . . Abandoning the resting-place of Tenggis River,
Heei . . . Transmitting the *onggod* of Tergelik and Huurta [place-names]
Heei . . . Transmitting the *onggod* of Toj and Tolbo [place-names]
Heei . . . Toya and Baya are the places we haunt.
Hooi . . . The great black boulder tumbling is my coffin.
Heei . . . The black bull wild-beast is my mount
Heei . . . The vulture black bear is my rolling [manifestation]
Heei . . . The black and spotted snakes form my tightly entangled [manifestation]
Heei . . . The velvet black eagle is my flapping [manifestation]
Heei . . . The owl at night is my haunt,
Heei . . . By the blind lynx at night [I take] my aimed-at direction
Heei . . . I have eighty-one metamorphoses
Heei . . . I have eighty thousand invisible tracks across the earth!

This song in several places makes a point of negating straightforward ordinary understanding of objects and creatures in the world. It turns them into mysteries. It is very important to understand that the expressions in shamanic songs are not mere tropes or figurative expressions, but denote the nature of the existence of this type of spirit. So we are led to ask: How could the black boulder tumble? How can a bull be a wild beast? How is the bear also a vulture? What is the direction taken by the blind lynx? The understanding of impossible existences is the understanding of the shaman. These images are not symbolic; that is, they do not stand for something else. Rather, the point of them is that they contradict in different ways people's most fundamental knowledge of ordinary things. A boulder does not tumble of its own accord, a domestic bull is not a wild-beast, the lynx is known above all as having sharp sight, and the most visible traces left on the earth are the tracks of animals and humans. These shamanic images contrast radically with the knowledge of old men and hunters, for whom the eyesight of the lynx was something they had to deal with in a practical way. It will be described in 1.5 how the religious cults of the old men involved, above all, ontological plainness.

The story of Zønøk Hairhan repeatedly shows naturally occurring decrepitude entering to trip up the status of shaman. In the story, which is a very long one, one learns how Zønøk carelessly allowed his shamanic horse to drink and eat so much that it got too heavy to fly to other worlds. At last he decided that the time had come to die. 'Now I really cannot fly, you lot can kill me,' he said. people tried to kill him, but all normal means (beating, shooting, burning, etc.) would not work, and in the end Zønøk had to tell them how to do it, by wrapping his head in dog's intestinal fat and in the underpants of a woman who had given birth three times.[70] In other words, a shaman does not die an ordinary human death. Acquiring spirits inspirationally in youth, he or she should 'die' by magically banishing them, ideally while still in vigour. Ordinary people, on the other hand, have a human span of life measured physically from conception to biological death, and to die earlier is harmful to the clan. As was noted in the last section, people who died young were not buried in the Daur clan grave-yard: their souls became vengeful spirits.[71] A shaman's life as a shaman, how-ever, was not measured in the span of physical existence, but by the intersection of this with the presence of spirit power. A shaman, in effect, should not be an old man.

Thus, although each clan had its own *yadgan* for protection against spirits and although he was an admired figure, this appearance of being 'on the staff' of the clan only masked a mode of operation which was radically different and indeed subversive of patrilineal values. The shaman's special ability, spirit genealogy, relationship to life in this world, and mode of death and burial all differentiated him or her from the ranks of soldier-clansmen. A shaman did not go hunting to kill wild animals, because the very spirit power that made him or her a shaman was imagined as present among the beings of the wilderness. A shaman did not make offerings *to* spirits like the old man, because as a shaman he or she *was* (in part) a spirit. The shamanic construction of causality was to a great extent different from that employed by old men, in that it was founded on a particular, flagrantly non-realist, premiss. The very supposition of shamanic spirits proposed the existence of an 'impossibility': the persistence of human personalities after death and their location in diverse objects and ani-mals. Urgunge's remark, 'Were we even sure they existed or not?', indicates that a certain realism was not foreign to Daurs. But with shamanic spirits we are faced also with 'things' the old men preferred not to deal with (the uncanny, the painful, the disgusting), and their existence was also 'contrary to reason' in that sense. The main religious activity of the old men did not deny the presence of shamanic spirits but ignored it, and as we shall see (1.5) the elders themselves construed the objects and creatures in the world in a different way.

Perhaps it could be said that the cultural constructions of 'shaman' and 'old man' were in a sense complementary; but the idea of 'the shaman' also opened up an area of ambiguity which came to be the subject of different socio-political processes among various societies in Inner Asia. This ambiguity or duality lies in the fact that shamans were also people who were members of clans, with households, farms and livestock, relatives and patrons, and who got old and died like anyone else. This aspect of a shaman's identity cannot be ignored. It not only gave the shaman a means of acting to help people, i.e. the intimate knowledge required to create a causal scenario of the trouble affecting them, but it also determined the political question of who the shaman was acting for. This becomes a crucial question when we look at the relations between Daur clans, and between them and the turbulent world outside.

1.4 'Bandits'

The following is Urgunge's story of how he was captured by bandits at the age of 12, was taken on their campaigns of pillage, and returned to his family changed by his experience. We cannot read this story as a straightforward memory. Its narrative shape is the product of many tellings, and perhaps there are echoes in it also of a mythicized self, such as those we all narrate about ourselves. The style I have used is intended to reflect this worked-upon quality. It is impossible not to notice how closely this account parallels the archetypal shamanic narrative of soul capture and rescue. At the same time, it tells us something of the real world with which shamans had to contend.

Let me very briefly outline the historical situation. At the end of the nineteenth century Japan and Russia vied for control of northern China and obtained concessions to trade and build railways there. The Manchus, clinging to imperial control, decided they would have to strengthen the underpopulated frontier and to this end they proposed a new policy of settling Chinese farmers in Mongol lands. To weaken Mongol opposition they replaced elected and hereditary local officials by appointed Manchus and Chinese. Land-hungry Chinese peasants surged north. At the very end of the nineteenth century the xenophobic Boxer rebellions of Chinese against European missionaries in North China attracted some Manchurian Mongols to their side, while others fought against them (Jagchid 1988*a*: 211–12). The Boxer rebellion was the excuse for Russia to occupy Manchuria in 1900–2, with thousands of troops stationed along the new railways. The Japanese counter-attack culminated in the defeat of Russia in 1904 and increased Japanese influence in the north. As the Manchu empire disintegrated, armies were disbanded and banditry became endemic. Most significant from our point of view, the Daurs had lost their privileged status as Bannermen with inviolate lands. In the anarchic period which ensued, they cast around for alternative paths to follow.

In 1911 Outer Mongolia declared independence from China, and from this time well into the 1920s there were groups of Daurs who were eager to join Mongolia. Daurs in the region of Hulun Buir were active in setting up short-lived nationalist autonomous governments at Hailar in 1912 and again in 1915.[72] From 1917 to 1930 rival war-lords, Zhang Zuo-lin in Manchuria and Feng Yu-xiang in Inner Mongolia, fought for control. The various Mongol groups were divided. They veered between maintaining conservative prince-doms, joining nationalist movements, setting up revolutionary parties inspired from Russia, supporting one or another Chinese war-lord, working with the Japanese, or just lying low. Here is Urgunge's story of what happened to him in these times.

Suddenly bandit gangs appeared in the vicinity of Bokorchien. People were in panic everywhere and my father began to take precautions. Each day, with the approach of evening, I and my brothers were told to round up the herds and hide them far away in the steppes, where we used to spend the night. But it was the time for the deer-horn hunt, which no family wanted to miss. My three older brothers saddled their horses and left for the forest, as did all the other strong young men. Day by day, the defensive strength of the village dwindled, an open invitation to the bandits.

Seeing this, my father ordered my mother to take the children and other women and go to Kwamatai. This was a nearby village where a relative called Lakantai had a large house surrounded by a high, stout wall. But one day when Lakantai was absent a troop of Chinese soldiers appeared on the horizon. The frightened people inside did not know what to do: some wanted to open the gates at once before a bombardment could begin, others were determined to fight it out. In the end, they opened the gates and the soldiers poured in. They seized Lakantai's son and beat him, demanding to know where the family's silver and gold had been buried. For three days the boy refused to say a word. The soldiers ruled the village, plundering the inhabitants, and I was ordered around like a servant, cooking their food and cutting firewood. Suddenly, the soldiers departed in search of another defenceless village. My family had no choice but to return to Bokorchien on foot. It rained all the way. We returned exhausted and famished.

We had just rested when my father ordered everyone to pack all their possessions. The family and virtually all of the clan made their way across the scrubland and up the slopes of a wooded mountain in search of a secure hiding-place. For four days we remained hidden on the hillside, watching the plains below for signs of raiders. Then one day, a villager came running up the trail, shouting, 'The bandits have taken Bokorchien!' But the people felt secure in their mountain refuge, and they unrolled their blankets and prepared for sleep as usual. During the night thick fog descended on the mountain. Early in the morning one of my nephews groped his way to fill his water-buckets at a mountain stream. Suddenly he heard hoof-beats. Riders loomed out of the fog. The boy sped back to the camp, shouting, 'The bandits are coming! Run!' But we were hardly awake. I was startled by a rifle poked in my ribs, and staring about saw strange, wild-looking men everywhere in the camp, stabbing with their rifles in the bushes and dragging people from their hiding-places. One man was lashed to a wheel. 'Point out the son of a rich man or we'll beat you to death,' the bandits threatened. The unfortunate man glanced wildly from side to side. His eyes fell on one of my nephews. 'He is the grandson of the richest man in our village,' he muttered. But my honest mother was troubled. She pushed me forward and said, 'This is my child. If you must have the son of a rich man, take him.' Quickly the bandits asked the man tied to the wheel, 'Is this the son of a rich man?' and the unhappy man nodded, 'Yes, yes, he is . . .'. Smiling, the bandits pulled me from my mother's arms.

I could not help asking Urgunge, 'Why did your own mother give you up?' He replied that this was due to her upright character and sense of fate. She thought, 'The bandits have asked for my son, therefore it is his destiny (*jiya*) to be taken.' Also, she knew that the other boy's father was away, and in his absence it would not be right for her to let him be taken.

Pushing aside my father, the bandits made a quick raid on what few possessions remained among our little band. I was mounted on a bandit horse, and everyone stumbled back down the trail to Bokorchien. The bandit chief called to my father, 'I know you have gold, silver, and guns. Give them to us, and you shall have your son.' He replied, 'The guns are with my older sons who have gone deer-hunting, and all my gold and silver were lost at Kwamatai.' The bandit chief said, 'In that case, we shall take your son.' Resolving not to cry, I turned to my father and said, 'Don't worry about me, I'll be back . . .', and rode away with my bandit captors.

That very night the bandits carried out a raid on another village. Fanning out in the practised pattern, they closed in from all sides, yelling and shouting wildly. I glimpsed startled faces as we thundered into the village. That night I feasted on fresh-killed beef. Exhausted and frightened I hardly slept. I kept waking, only to see the moonlight glinting on the gun-barrel of the guard posted to prevent my escape.

Next day my hopes were raised high as I saw the familiar face of Du Yadgan, the shaman, sent to negotiate my return. From gestures and glances in my direction I knew they were debating my fate. The voices grew high and then ceased abruptly. As Du Yadgan walked away, I called to him, but he strode past without a word. His grim face told me that his efforts had failed.

Soon the horses were packed with loot and the band set out again, in a direction which took us further and further from Bokorchien. Another hapless village came into sight, and the swift assault of the day before was repeated. The bandits helped themselves to the villagers' most precious belongings, calmly settled down for the night, and in the morning were off again. So we went from village to village across the plains until we reached a region inhabited by Chinese. Now my captors relaxed their guard, reckoning that it would be hard for me to escape and that no one would be able to rescue me. I began to adapt to their ways. It was not difficult to converse with them, as I had already learned Chinese, but they had a strange jargon. They referred to me as their 'ace in the hole' (source of ransom) and they also called me Caishen, the Money God. They would talk of burning incense in honour of 'Caishen' so that he might bless them with a rich bounty, but they also hinted that it might be a good idea to give the 'money god' a beating when his father came to discuss the ransom. I hid my apprehension by laughing.

I quite liked the man assigned to guard me, who was a Daur. We slept alongside, ate together, and rode close on the march. Like many of the bandits, this man was an inveterate opium-smoker. Sometimes the rumour would circulate that regular Chinese troops were in the vicinity and we hastened in another direction without stopping. Then my guard would have no chance to smoke, and he would lag behind with dull eyes, yawning, the tears streaming down his dirty cheeks. The bandits had a rough code of honour of their own. They would not rob a fellow-bandit. Nor did they molest women, as this was said to bring bad luck. One of our gang was shot in the back for raping a woman. There were special signs used for recognition, such as placing two hands over one's heart. After a time I began to wear a red band on my left arm, which identified me as a boy bandit. One day we were scouring a village for eggs and salt. I was much more energetic than my drowsy companion. I came proudly back with a bowl of two dozen eggs, and thereupon I was dubbed 'Egg' along with my other nicknames. But the bandits could be suddenly cruel. I remember that enemies of theirs were strung up, terribly beaten, and subjected to various tortures.

I found out later that the Japanese had recently invaded Manchuria. They made it one of their first tasks to clear up the bandits and were remarkably efficient in doing so. With their steady advance banditry became less attractive, and perhaps this was why my own gang dwindled in size as the more half-hearted returned home. Word was sent to my family that I would be released to anyone sent to get me, on the understanding that a payment of guns and opium would be made at a later date. While these negotiations were going on, it was rumoured that my brother was coming to get me accompanied by a troop of regular soldiers. Suddenly the bandits were eager to get rid of me. But another fortnight passed and no one came. In the mean time I reigned supreme among the bandit boys, fighting anyone who challenged me, taking revenge for earlier humiliations.

At last my long-awaited relative appeared. It was decided that I should return home by river, as the roads were still infested with roving bands of marauders. Arrangements were made to hire a man with a boat to take me down the Naun River. We left on a clear moonlit night. The air was still, the waters slid quietly by. Elated at the prospect of returning to my family, I sang cheerfully as we paddled. The bright stars above and the calm beauty of the night dispelled the tensions and fears of the weeks past. Suddenly we heard gunfire from a village on the shore, and a voice called out loudly in Chinese, 'Halt!' My song choked in my throat. Crouching low in the boat, we paddled with all our might to the opposite shore. The voices died away. Now, with heads low, we paddled hard, returning to the centre current of the river as the village disappeared behind us. On and on through the night we moved silently. With dawn, we caught a glimpse of Kwamatai far down the river and soon it was clearly lit in the sun's rays. By noon there was the familiar outline of the hills I knew so well. We beached the boat and walked the mile or so to Bokorchien. Leaving my companion behind, I pressed ahead. As I approached the village gate I broke into a run, calling out joyfully, 'I'm back! I'm back!' My father and mother burst out of the house. My mother swept me into her arms. I felt my father's hand stroke my head and heard his voice saying, 'My son, you have grown up.'

I am quite sure that Urgunge was not thinking about shamanic analogies when he retold me this story. The capture by alien marauders, being taken away to a distant land, the predatory and cruel images of the outlaw existence, the demand for a ransom, the shaman sent as negotiator, the return on the current of the river by night—all these just happen to be repeated themes in the shamanic repertoire. Just as significant are Urgunge's comments on how the adventure changed him. He learnt how he was categorized in society, that he had a value (to be weighed against other values), that he could be 'Egg' and 'Money God', that he could even find himself with an enemy's point of view, and that his identity continued throughout. These themes of identity and metamorphosis will appear again in regard to shamanic spirits, and the reader can make of that what they like.

The nature of banditry in Manchuria allows it to be seen in several different ways. Urgunge's account depicts bandits (*chan-du*) as an outside, foreign scourge. However, Billingsley's study (1988) shows bandits also to have been generated from within local society, including the insular, tightly knit, and isolated village communities of the kind Urgunge came from. We are led to ask, who in fact were 'bandits'?

It is possible to trace the seasonality of banditry in North China, beginning in the spring when many people's previous year's stocks of food were exhausted. They took to raiding to avoid starvation. But only temporarily. In May they went home to get in the wheat harvest and plant the soya bean crop. By midsummer the sorghum had grown up, its towering ten-foot stands providing convenient cover for outlaw gangs. Early autumn saw the bandits return home for harvest, but the long empty months of winter and the traditional paying of debts at the New Year made robbery again a logical path to follow in December and January (Billingsley 1988: 20–3). Banditry had been seasonal in China for centuries, but it increased exponentially with the political chaos of the demise of the Manchu Qing Empire. Permanent banditry was a new phenomenon. Bandit leaders could gain power over whole regions, becoming powerful war-lords with standing armies. War-lords existed by extraction from the exhausted peasants. War itself destroyed lives, crops, and villages. The agricultural de-cline caused unendurable poverty.

Urgunge's village seems to have clung on to the remnants of a political order established under the Manchus, never becoming resigned to the new land-settlement policies. However, the influx of Chinese peasants, which was the main Daur grievance in the 1910s–early 1930s, had in part been initiated by Daur leaders themselves. As early as 1900 Ye Pu-chun, the vice-governor of Butha, had requested the Manchus to allow Daur-owned land to be cultivated by Chinese farmers (Ikeshiri [1943] 1982: 90). Not surprisingly the emperor granted this request, as it conformed to the new state policy. (Perhaps we can see here an example of 'anticipating' orders from above by those below, later to become characteristic of Communist state regimes.)[73] However, when the land was allocated the Daurs discovered to their dismay that the state had granted full ownership to the incomers.[74] Throughout the 1910s and 1920s further land was alienated at very low prices. Meanwhile, in North China poverty-stricken peasants were exhorted, 'Go to North Manchuria!' According to Ikeshiri ([1943] 1982: 92), the Daurs discovered too late that their 'primitive plundering' farming methods, in effect virtually shifting cultivation, required more land than they had reckoned. Because they had never been interested in land, they were victims to cheats and middlemen. War-lord taxation was heavy, and many families resorted to selling livestock. To add to this misery there were frequent cattle plagues, especially in 1931–2. In this situation, Daurs were not only victims of bandits but became bandits themselves. The Chinese called them *ching-lung zhueze* (blue-dragon pig-tail people) (*DSHI* 1985: 19).

I decided to ask Urgunge more about the people who captured him. It turned out that they were 'not real bandits', as he put it. They were a rich Chinese group of brothers who lived in a village north of Bokorchien together with some Daurs. Furthermore, perhaps fearing to spoil the story, he had failed to men-tion that these Daurs were his own family's affinal relatives. The gang thus included several of Urgunge's kinsmen through his mother. 'So what I can never understand is why they took me,' Urgunge said. 'They must have got greedy and turned into bandits on the way.'[75]

This revelation reminded me that the archetypal wicked grabber of souls in the Nishan Shaman epic was Mongoldai Nagchu ('Mongol mother's brother'), adding another twist to the curious interpenetration of shamanic themes with Urgunge's story (see 6.5). However, if we remain with historical descriptions of who became a bandit, it seems that it was closely related to inability or unwillingness to sustain the patriarchal life. The reasons for taking up outlawry were only partly economic. Young men who could not afford a wife, the landless younger sons, cripples, orphans, people who hated and resented the rich, boys who could not get along with a stepmother, peddlars, servants, cooks, ex-soldiers, and others with no settled home, men humiliated by an unhappy marriage, the early revolutionaries, all these were attracted to the bandit life. Bandit society provided kinship-like security. Many groups created blood-brother type initiations, worshipped founders as ancestors, and had rules for the respectful burial of members. Some outlaw groups were more resilient than families or village communities (Billingsley 1988: 79).

Thus bandits were produced (or ejected) from the faults between and within patriarchal families. The placid, circumscribed village community looks different in this light. As Urgunge's account somehow indicates, 'bandits' were terrifying outsiders but also understandable. Once captured, Urgunge himself became a bandit for a time. As mentioned earlier, such a dual perception applied also to marauding spirits, who were 'not ours' and yet 'ours'. The antagonistic relation with affines, the fear of foreign incursion, and the paying of ransom for the return of a soul, all occurred in shamanistic ritual constructions (5.1; 6.6). It seems fitting that the shaman Du Yadgan was employed by the clan as negotiator with Urgunge's captors.

Yet, Du Yadgan failed. Sending the shaman with his extra abilities was perhaps the best the village could see itself doing, and it was not enough. This reminds us of the more general fact that shamanism was not just a 'system of thought' pervading culture, as depicted by some anthropologists, but a practice in the real world of misery, poverty, and violence. Recent writing has provided several accounts of the relation between shamanship and politics, and it has described several examples of the resurgence of shamans coinciding with a weakening of political structures (Atkinson 1989; Thomas 1988; Balzer 1993; Thomas and Humphrey (eds.) 1994). However, in North Asia the relation between shamanship and political leadership has not been a simple one of oscillation. The Daurs in Urgunge's youth faced not only a dismantling of the old Banner leadership, but the abrupt emergence of new and unpredictable forms of political and military power. Shamanic practice was willy-nilly deeply involved in this, as I shall later show (7.1 and 7.2). Pursuing the theme of bandits a little further provides a glimpse of what reality it was that shamans had to deal with.

I shall argue (5.1) that shamans of Du Yadgan's type were expected by the clients to acquire new knowledge and skills, but at this historical juncture very few of them reacted fast enough. We shall have to do here with the limits of certain traditions, and their partial replacement by others (which could also be called 'shamanistic'). Some of the reasons for this are revealed when we see that the perceived causes of disaster in the socio-political landscape were changing chaotically, that is, in ways beyond any possible prediction from existing dynamic trends within Manchurian society. A crucial element of this was a sudden globalization in understandings of 'banditry'. Local skirmishes were transformed into resistance to state and ethnic hegemony, and became involved even with international wars.

In an essay describing the Chinese colonization of Mongol lands, Jagchid (1988*b*) documents the many different types of robbers, outlaws, and rebels, all labelled *Meng-Fei* (Mongol Bandits) by the Chinese.[76] From the mid-nineteenth century until the 1940s the category of 'bandit' was used to condemn what were in fact numerous popular uprisings, against corrupt administration and misrule by Mongol princes, but increasingly above all against Chinese colonization. At the very time when Urgunge was captured, one of his older brothers was fighting in an uprising of this kind, based in the hills south of Bokorchien at Morin Dawaa. Called 'bandits' at the time, the group was described in later history as a 'self-defence brigade', struggling against feudal war-lords and national oppression (Daur History Writing Team 1986: 162). Urgunge always disliked grandiose words, and says they simply wanted to drive out the Chinese.[77] But such a comprehensible aim was blotted out by the turn of events, which swept the Daurs into world history. The fighters had got some arms from the Japanese. With the full-scale Japanese occupation of Manchuria in 1932, the band was demilitarized and found itself on the Japanese side. Suddenly it now became a symbol of the native welcome of the new state of Manchukuo and 'the friendly neighbour Japan' (Ikeshiri [1943] 1982: 93).

With luck, and astute adaptation to the dizzying changes on the power scene, bandit leaders could in a few years become governors of huge provinces. This can be seen even from a highly simplified version of the career of Zhang Zuolin. After working as an errand-boy at an inn near Mukden, Zhang 'entered the greenwood' (i.e. became a bandit) in 1896 aged 22. Rapidly his band of 'Red Beards' acquired local power, since the weakened Manchu prefecture was forced to woo the bandits in order to counteract the Russians then in virtual occupation of north-east Manchuria (McCormack 1977: 16–17). Made commander of the local garrison, Zhang was soon, however, helping the Russians in the war against Japan. When Russia was defeated, evidence that he had also co-operated with the Japanese, plus the belief that he could still be of some use to the victorious side, saved his life. The flexible Zhang now acquired control over an increasing number of battalions, murdering rival leaders along the way, and by 1915 he was in effective control of Southern Manchuria. He took part in Japanese plots to restore the Manchu dynasty in Manchuria, Mongolia, and Northern China, a move which also involved the Mongolian 'bandit' leader Bavuujav (Babujab), who had an army of cavalrymen based in Hailar (McCormack 1977: 16–17). At this point, Hailar was a quasi-independent polity, led largely by Daurs. However, Bavuujav's army was defeated by the Chinese and Japan withdrew its support. Zhang now came under attack from his former bandit comrades, but he made an astute turnabout yet again, and the outcome was the collapse of their challenge and the expansion of Zhang's direct military power. After 1916 he quickly established control over the whole vast region of Northern Manchuria (McCormack 1977: 17–34). The village of Urgunge's childhood, with all its nostalgia for the days of the Manchu Banners, lay in fact within the mega-bandit's domain.

Among the various groups struggling for power, there were Mongolian nationalists and revolutionaries. We now come to someone who will have an important role in this book, the activist Merse (Guo Dao-fu), who was born in a wealthy Daur family in Hailar (see also 7.3). In the 1920s Merse was the main founder of the Hulunbuir Youth Party, which was inspired by the revolutions in Mongolia and Buryatia. As a Comintern agent he organized military and underground activities in several parts of north-west China. In 1928 his Hulunbuir Youth Party led a coup which took Hailar. A few years later he disappeared in mysterious circumstances (see 7.3). Merse was an educator and a far-sighted political thinker—perhaps too far-sighted for the times. Unlikely as it may seem, he was also intimately connected with shamanism, and we shall meet him again several times in these pages.

I now return the narrative of this book to shamanism. It is time for me to explain my use of this term and to address the issue of the multiplicity of ideas and practitioners which come under this name.

1.5 'Shamanism'

From the beginning of our conversations there was a problem with English words, the term 'shamanism', for example. If we were talking about 'shaman-ism', what were our conversations actually about? The Daurs had no word for their religion. Urgunge considered all the words used by other Mongol groups for 'shamanism'.

Not *üzel* [view, ideology, creed], that is a Buddhist idea; not *har shashin* [black religion], we Daurs do not have the word *shashin*;[78] not *itgel* [faith], that is really Buddhist. Not *shüteen*[79] [worship], I never heard Daurs use this word. No, there is no word for 'religion' in Daur language. In the old days I think people in our village sometimes used a Chinese word to talk about shamanism, *lun*.[80] It means notable pronouncements.

Urgunge's view, that the Naun River Daurs represented an totally uncontaminated tradition of 'shamanism', cannot be accepted, since constant interactions during the course of Inner Asian history make such an idea unfeasible. However, his implicit claim that his group of Daurs was relatively uninfluenced by Buddhism is justified. It is important for us to see that this was not entirely a default state of affairs, to be explained by geographical isolation, but a position deliberately maintained *vis-à-vis* other peoples' beliefs. If the Daurs did descend from the Khitan, then their ancestors must have been aware of, or even taken on, Buddhism in the tenth and eleventh centuries (Cheng 1987: 47). However, in recent centuries the Daurs have practised their nameless religion as distinct from Buddhism. When they moved south from the Amur region in the seventeenth century they were people to be converted, though the mission of the famous Buddhist, Neyichi Toyin, in Eastern Mongolia stopped just before the Daurs arrived (Heissig 1992: 79, 81).[81] Thereafter neither the Naun Daurs, nor even those of Hailar, were converted, even though the latter were exposed to the Buddhism of their Mongol, Barga, and Buryat neighbours. In other words, it was not for lack of opportunity that the Daurs failed to become Buddhists. The attitude of Naun people to that religion, an ironically contemptuous wonder, emerges from the traveller's tale recounted in 3.3.

Many European theories of Siberian shamanism focus on the shaman (Shternberg 1893; Eliade [1951] 1964; Lewis 1971). Shamanism then becomes a metaphysical elaboration on the basis of the shaman's experiences (the 'wounded healer'; the ecstatic trance; the 'ascent to heaven', etc.). More recent theories see shamanism as a structure of symbolic action (Hamayon 1990) or as characterized by specific ritual sequences (Siikala 1978), but they still focus on the place of the shaman in these structures. By contrast, the most famous native exposition of 'the black faith', by the nineteenth-century Buryat scholar Banzarov ([1846] 1955), describes a heterogeneous variety of religious practices and a cosmology, and mentions shamans only at the end of the book.[82] Thinking about the minor place given to shamans in this account, I asked Urgunge if he thought shamanism was the abilities and techniques of shamans or whether it was the expression of a whole religion and view of the world.

I don't know what you are talking about [he replied]. This is maybe a very technical question you are asking me, because I have no idea what you are asking me. Whether shamanism is a religion . . . well, of course it is, I have to say yes. But you have to define what religion is. How do you define religion?

   In Christianity the God created everything, isn't that so? But for us [Daurs] there is nothing greater than heaven and earth. So how can you ask who created them? In our own way, I think we [the Daurs] were advanced. We understood that no one created the sky and earth. They just are. There is balance in the world, but no cause. What is the reason for it [being like it is]? That question is as if I were to ask the white man, Why is your nose so big?

Beyond this, I could never get Urgunge to define what 'shamanism' is, and even less to focus on 'religion' in the abstract. The question did not interest him. For him, supernatural forces interpenetrated with reality or 'what is' (*baidah yum*). Although reality included intangible, invisible beings and energies, any metaphysical notion could be shed if it was discovered to be wrong, i.e. not to be practically effective. This happened in Urgunge's lifetime with the explanations for certain illnesses.[83] Inoculation and Chinese medicine removed a range of diseases from the catalogue of those initially assumed to be caused by spirits. Urgunge said that the Daurs were not a 'religious' people, meaning credulous or superstitious. Whatever dangers and misfortunes there are in the world are real. Since I was writing the book, deciding what words to use was my problem.

For a time it seemed to me best to write the book somehow without the words 'religion' or 'shamanism'. 'Religion' seemed wrong for ideas and beliefs which are never set out as a general theory and make use of relatively few abstract concepts, for which there is no holy founder, no organized institution, no moral dogmas, and no authoritative corpus of books. Above all, there is no tortuous justification of earlier beliefs enshrined in sacred texts. As for 'shamanism', if its rituals were done differently from place to place, and there were always several kinds of 'shaman', what use did the term have? Perhaps, I thought, we should stick with what the shaman does, with an idea such as 'shamanship' (Atkinson 1989), the shaman's techniques and ability to convince people he could contact spirits and use their powers to human benefit.

But as Urgunge talked it became clear that this alone would not do. 'Shamanship' does not account for everything that the Daurs practised and believed in respect of the mysteries and dangers of the world. Soon it emerged that it explained very little of it.

You are looking from a European point of view [said Urgunge]. Here in the West there are priests, and they have too much influence. But it is most important that we point out in our book how much influence the shaman had in the Daurs' life. In my opinion, not much at all. The shaman is just like your GP [general practitioner, family doctor]. You go to him if you are ill, especially mentally ill or depressed, if you can't cure yourself. Otherwise what can he do for us? Nothing. This is good, you see. It means that the shamanists have a much better religion, a religion without dogma. They are free, each person rules their own life.

For weeks I was suspicious of this statement, and could only just bring myself to write it in my notebook. Surely this was too prosaic. Or perhaps Urgunge was at the tail-end of a process of historical decline, when shamanism had ceased to be socially important or widely believed? But he also described the intensity of the shaman's seance in his boyhood, when every movement would be watched anxiously for its outcome; and as he talked of the mountains, wild fire in the prairies, the moon, or tigers in the forest, it seemed to me that religious awe was not far away. When he mentioned the sky (*tengger*) his voice changed, as many English-speakers' voices do when they talk about God. The sky was the one who (which) destines, who is the regulator of all birth, growth, decay, death, and rebirth. But the problem, with regard to 'shamanism', was that a shaman's presence was quite unnecessary for the worship of the sky. There were many other rituals too, sacrifices to mountain spirits at the *oboo* for example, where other ritual practitioners were dominant and shamans were even excluded. This led me to think for a time that perhaps there were two religious spheres, one which centred on the shaman and one which did not. But how could this be, if the very world in which the shaman undertook his ritual activities, in which he exercised his power, was the same as that conceptualized by the ideas of 'the sky' and 'the mountain spirits', and if shamanship could have a more extensive or more restricted part in its worship? Gradually I became aware that what we were talking about, the subject of our conversations, was not so much the shaman as a person, or as a role, or as having certain abilities, and what stems from that, but Daur views, quite simply, of the nature of human life in the world, and it was these that the book would have to be about. These suppositions about humanity and the world made the shaman possible. Or rather, people, objects, animals being like this made a compelling reason, even an imperative one, for human beings to have a shaman. However, shamans, varied and shifting as the ranges of their activities were in different times and places, could never do everything. Theirs was never the only response to Daurs' views of existence, and shamans were never the masters of all religious life.

Nevertheless, in the end we decided to keep the term 'shamanism' to refer to the entire conglomeration of ideas about beings in the world which includes the shaman, and to use 'shamanship' for the shaman's practice.[84] I retained 'religion' not as a theoretical term but because it is a word in our language which respects other people's sense of the sacred and takes their beliefs seriously in the sense of supposing that they at least believe them to be true.

The major recent study of Siberian shamanism, Roberte Hamayon's *La Chasse à l'âme* (1990), is a grand Lévi-Straussian theory of the shaman as the mediator of an integrated system of symbolic exchange and alliance between humans and spirits of the natural world. My approach differs from this in that I do not think 'shamanism' is a coherent, lasting symbolic structure. A great deal of it does not involve symbols (things standing for something else) but consists of sensuous and magical actions in the world. Parts of it can change quite fast, as can the relations between different religious activities. Also, shamanists in Inner Asia have been very susceptible to ideas and cults from outside. Only taking account of these facts can we explain why all Inner Asian societies seem to have other religious practitioners alongside shamans and several types of shamans, and why shamans' range of effective agency changes in different historical circumstances. The word 'shamanism' is retained here as a matter of convenience and because I am writing about a broad area of religious life which is normally referred to by this term. However, because the term 'shamanism' gives a misleading impression of a single unified system I shall use it as little as possible and henceforth always in inverted commas. So, unlike most other studies, I focus not on the figure of the shaman but on the cosmologies that 'call for' the shaman as well as other religious practitioners.

There is no society in North Asia which has only the classic spirit-managing shaman as religious specialist. We have already seen that Daur clan elders and the ritual specialist *bagchi* were active in religious matters separately from the *yadgan* shaman. The Daurs also had a variety of other specialists in dealing with invisible powers. In Butha these were: (1) *otoshi* (curer); (2) *barishi* (bonesetter); (3) *bariyachi* (midwife); and (4) *kianchi* (sorcerer). Batubayin (1990) writes that these practitioners were called *bumian yadgan* (special ability shamans) and ethnographers mention further shamanic specialists in other districts.[85] It will be seen that the practical activities of midwifery, bone-setting, etc. were not separate in Daur ideas from religious life. All of these specialists, according at least to some accounts, had the ability to embody spirits, and all of them, in some way or another, used mentally dissociative states in their prac- tice. Most Naun Daur villages used to have at least one of each of the specialists. Bokorchien in Urgunge's childhood had all of them apart from the *kianchi* (see Sections 2.1, 7.1, and 7.2, which discuss the historical emergence of the *kianchi* cults).

This book suggests that having all these various religious specialists was a corollary of the Daur apprehension of a number of *different* causal processes pertaining to beings, or kinds of existence, in the world. This was direct, phenomenal perception, not necessarily expressed in language. However, certain of these processes were culturally emphasized by the selection of particular categories of objects that were held to exemplify them, and by making these objects the focus of different kinds of ritualization. Thus mountains, for example, exemplified the existence of large inanimate geophysical entities and had their own rituals. These were different from the rituals for trees or rivers or human ancestors. The selection of a few exemplars from the myriad experiences of the world and the creation of different kinds of ritual for them was accompanied by a division of labour among specialists. In other words, within the conglomeration of 'shamanism' the divisions between the various ritual practitioners had their basis in the idea that there were different kinds of occult ability related to different kinds of religious knowledge. This 'knowledge' (more precisely constructed techniques of relating mundane understanding of the nature of things with an imaginative reaching out to processes that were not known in an ordinary commonsense way) was based on the cultural representations of different basic ontological categories implying processes in nature.

Let us see how different categories of existence were found in the world. According to Urgunge the Daurs had no linguistic terms for nature or culture. Urgunge said that the Halh Mongol terms *baigal* (nature) and *soyol* (culture, civilization) 'were too sophisticated for us'. However, Daurs did have a concept of 'nature' as objects, beings, and processes that were uncreated, spontaneous, or innate. Aspects of human biological, social, and psychological life were included in this idea. Nature in this sense was distinct from a much weaker concept of intentionally created artefacts and social institutions, and in fact most of the latter could on occasion be subsumed in it, so that almost anything could be seen as natural. At the same time Daurs often contrasted the wild (non-human nature, found in the forests and mountains) with the domestic (human, found in the village). However I shall henceforth use the terms 'nature'/'natural' for the large and general idea of innate being. Within it, Daurs used two different verbs 'to be' to differentiate between inanimate *baidah yum* (things which 'are' in a static way) and animate *aasen yum* (beings which 'are' in an animate way).

Now all objects and beings in nature, including the sky, humans, sticks and stones, the wind, and social institutions and human-made artefacts,[86] were attributed with their own kinds of causal force or energy. Sometimes, especially in ritual contexts, people anthropomorphized these energies, attributing them with a few limited human characteristics, such as intention or consciousness. In this case the genius or spirit of the object was often called master (*ejin*, pl. *ejed*). The main specialized agency of shamans (*yadgan*s and others) was in dealing with the forces of animate, especially human, nature, while that of the *bagchi* or old man dealt with the energies of inanimate nature.

Let us turn to religious ideas about the inanimate domain of nature. Daurs and other Mongol peoples focused culturally on certain relatively inclusive natural categories as exemplars of causal processes (*üildel*) implied by that kind of existence.[87] For example, the tree (*mood*) exemplified the existence of plants, and the mountain (*aul*) exemplified the kind of existence of geophysical entities. Whether the idea of master-spirits was present or not, the forces of these types of existence were what people felt they had to deal with. Evidence for this way of thinking appears in many different discursive situations, from practical activity and everyday talk to ritual speech. It is striking that ritual language addressed to natural objects did not disguise such basic ideas but revealed them in set formulae. I discuss more ordinary situations in the following section and here focus on the ritual invocations, since these lay bare the qualities of the objects considered religiously relevant. In the rest of this chapter I shall use non-Daur texts because they exemplify most clearly what I see as characteristic attitudes found throughout Inner Asia. As Even (1992: 80) notes, the same formulae, or closely similar images, are used by religious specialists among different Mongolian groups often located thousands of miles apart. Here is an example of an address to inanimate forces, translated from a Halh Mongol invocation to the starry sky.[88] Such a speech would not be made by a shaman, but by an elder or ritualist.

Dardayin bayigci agula-yin ejed	Stiffly projecting standing mountain masters
Darkiran urusugci usun-u ejed	Noisily rushing flowing water masters
Arbayin bayigci agula-yin ejed	Spread-out standing mountain masters
Sarbayin urugsan ebesün modon-u ejed-ece xutug guyuna	Dishevelled growing grass and tree masters (we) ask blessing from (you)
Urusxu usun-u ejed	Flowing water masters
Uyiltu toxui-yin ejed	Whirling river-bend masters
Keyiskü salkin-u ejed	Airily blowing wind masters
Kebtege cilagun-u ejed-ece xutug guyunam	Lying down stone masters we ask blessing from (you)

(Dulam 1989: 20)

Dulam, a Mongolian anthropologist, sees here a typically Mongolian cultural structure, which he describes as 'quality—process—subject—idea'. This specifies the characteristics of existence proper to each natural object (see Table 1.1). There is nothing strange or mysterious about this. Nevertheless, its very plainness requires explanation. What is curious here is the lack of symbolism or metaphor, when we know that Mongols do also have diverse imaginative ideas about mountains, trees, etc. (see Section 2.1). It seems the ritual formulae bleach out such fantasies in order to insist on their own 'straightforward' images. This speech of the elders is quite different from the shaman's song, which readers may remember consists of counter-intuitive, 'twisted' images (1.3). The elders' invocation presents images evoking the kind of knowledge the elder is supposed to have, that is, 'plain' knowledge about this world around us, while the shaman's song presents figures evoking another world, hidden behind appearances. As Boyer (1980) has written about comparable contrasting types of ritual language in African initiations, it is clear that such ritual speeches do not convey information to the participants. Everyone knows that wind blows, and so forth. What they present is the question of 'knowledge' as such. Thus the effect of the elders' speech, in the circumstances of a ritual calling for blessings, is to put into focus not so much the world itself as a particular kind

TABLE 1.1.

Quality	Process	Subject	Idea
stiffly projecting	standing	mountain	masters
noisily rushing	flowing	water	masters
dishevelled	growing	grass/tree	masters, etc.

of 'straightforward' knowledge of the world. I shall expand on this point, as this is the wider religious context in which shamans' invocations construct a very different configuration of what knowledge is.

Research in developmental psychology has shown that the identification of objects as examples of particular ontological categories seems to be an intuitive, largely unconscious process that is based in part on complex inferences from perceptual clues. 'Animate'/'inanimate' is one such distinction, as are the physical differentiations between solid, watery, and airy in this invocation. Long before they can speak, children are aware of the distinction between animate and inanimate, which seems to be founded on an early sensitivity to the difference between self-generated and non-self-generated movement (R. Gelman 1990). But ontological categories are not just a way of sorting out objects: they have conceptual consequences. Keil has argued (1979) that onto-logical categories imply intuitive expectations, and that this can be seen from the predicate restrictions that people, even very young children, spontaneously make in language. The predicate 'stiffly projecting standing' can apply to mountains in a way that 'noisily rushing flowing' cannot (not to mention a host of other inappropriate predicates for mountains, such as 'was late' or 'needs mending').[89] The elders' invocation to the starry sky seems to evoke just this spontaneously appropriate knowledge about the world.

However, intuitive expectations about mountains or rivers should not be confused with explicit concepts expressed in language (Lloyd 1990: 419; Bloch 1991).[90] The simplicity of the elders' invocation is thus deliberate, a point which will be clear when we see the much more imaginatively contrived thoughts of ordinary people about natural objects in 2.2. Nor is it the case that explicit ideas, elaborated in particular historical and religious contexts, actually govern people's intuitive assumptions. In fact the reverse may be true. As Boyer writes (1994: 36): 'People's expectations about events are only weakly constrained by explicit theories; however, their explicit theories generally constitute attempts to extract general principles from the range of situations or events they would intuitively find "natural".' The elders' verses quoted above are not theories of course, but they are highly condensed images rep-resenting intuitive and experiential knowledge. They are unusual, not only because anthropologists usually seek (and find) the peculiar and the symbolic in other people's religions, but because these verses bring up and put into ritualized language what is usually apprehended outside language, even unconsciously.

It seems to me possible that this cultural focus on the plain intuitive expec-tations of the processes associated with ways of being in the natural world may be based on universal (or very widespread) cognitive predispositions.[91] Re-search in developmental psychology suggests that cognitive principles and cognitive development vary according to the ontological domain being rep-resented, notably the domains of physical objects, persons, plants, events, artefacts, etc. This is in contrast to the earlier Piagetian view according to which developmental stages of cognition apply across the board to all domains. The more recent research shows how each of these domains seems to be understood by presumptions which develop in early childhood and is relatively independent from the principles used for other domains. In general these domains are not fundamentally contradicted by more complex 'folk' notions developing later in life (for reviews of the research on 'domain-specificity', see Atran 1989; Wellman and Gelman 1992; and Boyer 1994). Of course, it is also possible to violate these basic assumptions, to apply surprising or metaphorical predicates to natural categories, and the Mongols do this too, but I wish to point out here the cultural precedence given by elders to straightforward ontological processes even in religious contexts. As Dulam writes, discussing the verses above, these are to the Mongols both evident and as wonderful as the natural existence of humankind in this world (1989: 23). The unfathomable aspect of ordinary being, or rather the processes implied by it, was the province of an important strand of religious knowledge.

In Daur religious life, natural objects like the sky or mountains were worshipped in themselves. However, especially in ritual, the various kinds of processes associated with natural categories were also made to stand symbolically for social processes. In this connection, rather than seeing natural categories as inherently metaphoric or symbolic, being generated by 'society', and thus seeing their appearance in the form of symbols as primary, in the tradition of Durkheim and Mauss (1963), I think that the reverse was the case: perceptual understandings of straightforward, non-symbolic natural processes were the basis for conceptualizations of the dynamics of society (see Rival 1993). The effect of this was to mystify not nature but society. The solidity of the mountain stood for the 'solidity' of the clan (see discussion in 4.1).

The Daurs had many fewer types of specialist than even the main causal processes engaged with in rituals. Apart from the _bagchi_ who addressed external nature, there were named expert roles, like 'midwife', really only for the culturally important aspects of human nature. However, more sporadically, and not in every village, there were people who had abilities to deal with other energies, like those of stars or medicinal plants. Thus, although only certain natural categories were chosen for ritualization, we can observe nevertheless the tendency to divide up religious activities in accordance with ontological domains conceptualized as existing naturally in the world. The number and type of specialists corresponded with the domains of nature picked out as most salient in their connotations, given the interests and preoccupations prevailing at the period of Urgunge's youth.

Considering now this whole sphere of animate and inanimate natural (uncreated, innate) being, I give below a list of some important categories, processes, symbolic usages, and specialists (see Table 1.2). This is intended to give an initial idea of the disparate and discrete causal processes Daurs empha-

TABLE 1.2.

Category	Process	Symbolic usage	Practitioner[a]
sky, weather	weather, seasons	'balancing' nature	*bagchi*, old man
mountain, cliff	standing solidity	permanence of male groups	*bagchi*, old man
river	flow	movement between social groups	women, *bagchi*
fire	warmth, light	patriarchal continuity	old man, *bagchi*, lama (Hailar)
tree	growth, maturation, decay, regeneration	fertility and health	whole community *yadgan*
wild animals, birds, fish	animal abilities: flying, swimming, etc.	spirit journey	*yadgan*
wild animals, birds, insects	devel. process: egg to bird, etc.	identity despite metamorphosis	*yadgan*
fox, pheasant, snake	specific abilities	immortality of individuals	*kianchi*
womb	maturation of foetus	fem. fertility and child growth	*otoshi*
bones	biological structure	patrilineal structure	*barishi*

[a] The order in the final column represents the main practitioners of ritual first.

sized in ritual, but the list must be read with caution. The form of the table does not represent my view of 'how Daurs thought'. It is provided only as an aid for readers in a complex ethnographic situation. No Daur has ever described to me a single diagram–like Daur cosmology. There were many other natural processes recognized culturally which are not included here. Also, although it is shown below that the category of animate wild creatures (wild animals, birds, fishes, etc.) was used in ritual to exemplify more than one causal process, the list does not indicate other cases of this kind; for example, trees were also used as examples of several quite different processes. Finally and emphatically, it should not be concluded that the list represents the totality of 'shamanism', since the list does not include the large number of explanations of human misfortunes, diseases, and psychological problems, which were the main concern of the *yadgan* shaman.

This list shows, on the one hand, a broad association between large, inanimate objects and the religious activities led by *bagchi* and old men, and, on the other, a relation between animate beings and biological processes associated with various kinds of shaman. This is more surprising than it might seem at first, because as noted above Daurs often claimed that all things in the world, including the sky, rivers, or stones, had their own energy or genius, and these were frequently envisaged as being like humans. Yet these spirits (in the sense of the genius of a natural object) of inanimate things were never embodied by Daur shamans. They were the object of sacrifice and prayer, while it was the spirits of animate beings that were called up and embodied by shamans in their performances. Things in the world that were ambiguous in relation to the animate–inanimate divide, such as rivers, which move but have no life, or trees, which are alive but have no self-generated movement, were the object of other distinctive rituals which were performed neither by shamanic specialists nor by old men, but by women and by the whole community, respectively.

Natural categories selected out in religious contexts were not always as simple as the above outline suggests. Lying behind the interpretation I am giving is the deep philosophical–psychological issue of whether natural categories are discovered or made, or whether, behind this question, we need to see the issue as a dichotomy. I cannot discuss the vast literature on this subject here, but it will be clear by now that the position I am taking is that a combination of these views is possible. We do construct our conceptual systems and they do not spring on their own from the natural world. But our necessary role as agents in the investigation of nature does not preclude an equally determinant role for nature, particularly for the most widespread and fundamental distinctions which are 'phenomenally salient' and appear conspicuous to ordinary people (Hull 1992: 43). In any given place, however, people pick up and elaborate on these in their own way.

How is this done? For ordinary people living their lives, entities and processes in the world are not the object of thinking in the abstract. In fact, occasions of context-less contemplation are so rare as to be virtually non-existent, and this is one reason why anthropologists, though they ignore the results of psychological research at their peril, nevertheless have something quite different to explain. People in any culture have interests in the processes or the objects they think about. This is true even if no particular activity is in hand. Ellen's detailed and perceptive monograph, *The Cultural Relations of Classification*, has shown (1993: 168–71) that a commonly held zoological classification system may include cosmographic knowledge. Within a cultural community a variety of different interests, both pragmatic and symbolic, influence the differentiation of animal categories in specific contexts (1993: 158–60). Ellen nevertheless reaches the conclusion that there is a broad general correspondence between the overall structure of local 'folk' zoological classifications and actual species diversity (the number and objective distinctiveness of biological species), groupings of species, and their relative frequency in that geographical region. Thus, for example, restricted faunas naturally limit ethnozoological inventories (1993: 158). However, a large literature reviewed by Ellen (1993: 216–29) suggests that, when we have to deal with particular examples of given cultures, 'taxonomies' are artefacts of tidy-minded scholars; the cognitive and linguistic constructs employed by native people in classifying are heterogeneous and combined in various ways, and 'categories may be expressed in different ways on different occasions in different places' (1993: 228). This suggests that it may be a mistake to look for a coherent 'taxonomy' in any given folk culture, since, quite apart from the domain-specific presumptions pertaining to different ontological categories, a heterogeneous range of other criteria is also applied strategically. For these reasons, though nature may constrain categorizations, the classes different peoples use are not always the same.

This also implies that the local categories themselves cannot be easily separated into practical and basic as opposed to religious or metaphorical, as Bloch (1989 [1977]) suggested in an early work. In the Mongolian cultural region, natural categories, particularly at more inclusive levels (cf. Ellen 1993: 154–5), are based on a variety of criteria, some of them to do with human practical activity, some perceptual (e.g. on the basis of colour), some selecting out particular behaviour of animals, and others grouping together creatures by a characteristic intention attributed to them. Even one categorization can be based on the combination of several distinguishing criteria. Let us take for example the practically important division of Mongolian domestic livestock into 'hot-nosed' (*haluun hoshootoi*), horses and sheep; and 'cold-nosed' (*huiten hoshootoi*), cattle, camels, and goats. These categories seem to be based on a combination of perceived behaviour (whether the given animals bunch together and preserve body-heat in cold weather or not), attributes of their meat (whether the meat provides 'heat' to human consumers or not), and more intangible symbolic qualities (*haluun* ('hot') is also used to mean 'close' of kin, and *huiten* ('cold') to mean distant or unfriendly). The 'hot'/'cold' distinction is used as a rationale in practical herding (flock composition, winter penning, etc.) and also in ritual (e.g. which categories are correct for a given sacrifice). The 'hot-nosed'/'cold-nosed' categories are not distinguished by Mongol herdsmen from other natural categories, such as species, sex, and age classes of livestock.[92] There is nothing irrational about such folk life-form categories, and they are no more, or less, likely to be culturally emphasized in ritual contexts than Mongolian classifications that correspond with Linnaean categories. Also, all natural categories are available to speculative projections and symbolism. But that is not really the point. If we leave to one side the question of recognizing 'a taxonomy' in people's naming of the natural world, the question of ontology—what a category like 'hot-nosed ones' is thought to be—still remains. I hope to show in this book that, alongside these complex categories, absolutely basic intuitive ideas about simple natural categories are relevant in religious contexts. Even taken in themselves, i.e. not involved in any metaphorical or symbolic thought, natural categories can be the elements of religious (devout, sacralizing) thinking. In a book about religion the task is to specify in context, and for individual people as well as collective groups, how this happens. Therefore, I do not think it inconsistent with the insights from developmental psychology to align this book with recent anthropological work that has emphasized the ways in which perception and action (Ingold 1993*a*, 1993*b*), spatio-temporal experience (Weiner 1991), and practical economic activity (Bloch 1992*b*) combine with intuitive ontologies to create cultural knowledge that is at the basis of religious attitudes.

If we see religion as consisting not in 'their beliefs which seem to us irrational' but in an attitude which sacralizes, then religious ideas need not contradict everyday life in the world: they may build on ordinary intuitive thought, recasting such ideas in a new intentional light. For example, a Horchin Mongol friend of mine told me the following: his father moved to live in a new place. This was a sandy, stony region, but there was a single tree growing there, with thick green leaves. His father thought, 'That beautiful tree is worthy to be worshipped,' and he moved some large stones the size of a man's head to the foot of the tree and started to worship it. This veneration did not imply anything strange or symbolic about the tree: it did not represent some different idea, have a magical origin, or contain a spirit.[93]

Of course 'shamanism' as a whole does not only consist of such phenomena—there are many elaborate and striking violations of ordinary cognition in it. My point is that it does not necessarily and pervasively involve them, and it is not by them that it should be defined. Some highly important collective representations included in 'shamanism', those evoked in the cults of nature, involve taking causal processes thought to occur in the world, or culturally important physical features of objects, and imaginatively tracing their implications. This may involve symbolism. For example, a tree may be seen either as a static vertical feature of the landscape or as exemplifying processes of growth, flourishing, and decay. Either of these dimensions may be symbolically elaborated in different contexts of interest, creating, for example, the tree as a cosmological ladder, or the tree as a universal source of recurrent social regeneration.

I have already mentioned how different are the straightforward ideas in the elders' invocation quoted above from the counter-intuitive 'unnatural' images in the shaman's song cited in a previous section (1.3). It would not be true to say that elders' invocations of natural objects always were as plain as this, since we also find they used conventional poetic tropes, such as hyperbole (*kürüsü-tü altan delekei deger-e* (on the crusted golden earth)), synecdoche (a given mountain stood for the whole world), personification (*naran eh, saran etseg* (sun mother, moon father)), and the evocation of presumed synchronic processes in the world (see 4.2). However, I think we can say that the poetry of the elders tended to eulogize the actual world in its ideal order, while the poetry of *yadgan*-type shamans disturbed that order, presenting images of hostile, invisible currents that would undermine the solidity of the known world and all social institutions built in its image. Shamanic linguistic figures are images of human-like powers that travel between objects, run over them, and destabilize them. Here cross-categories 'animate' the landscape and render appearances deceptive. A shamanic spirit in Buddhist Mongolia was hailed as follows:

> Running-track kidneys and heads[94]
> Transfer places pine-covered heights
> Overnight stop camel stone
> Resting-place treasury lake
> Running-path dim twilight
> My holy Khan Dayan enduring merciful-one [. . .]
> When [you] come the blue eternal sky lists sideways
> When [you] come the crusted golden world shudders
> [You] come transported by cotton white clouds
> [You] come making the outer ocean swell and swash
> When [you] come the waters of the earth erupt from their banks
> When [you] come surfacing red veins pulsate
> When [you] come minds and hearts are bewildered and obscured
> When [you] come the back of the body twitches
> When [you] come the front of the body convulses
> [You have] imperial shamanic (*bøge*) descent[95]
> [You have] white shamanic (*idugan*) ancestry
> Your realm is that of Asuri Tngri[96]
> [You are] eighteen years old
> My unbridled, red, wandering one
>
>   (Damdinsüren 1959: 127–31)

These lines, dismissing with a few words the equilibrium of the sky and the immovability of the earth, were monstrous claims to Urgunge, who would not hear them without a shudder. We can understand their extravagant destabilizing effect only when we also know that Mongolians in other parts of religious life did pay homage to the unadorned natural existence of things in the world. What the shamanic chants were doing was attacking the very evidentness, the kind of knowledge, that as we shall see supported the images of the imperial state, Buddhism, and old age. The shamans' poetic démarche flouted the measured rhetoric of the elders, just as the shamans' exceptional social status countered that of the 'old men' who emerged from among the ranks of men in general.[97]

A great deal of shamanic poetry consisted of semantic anomalies that blocked conceptual interpretation (the impossibility of the 'bull wild-beast', for example; see 1.3). Rather than being self-evident statements, such images presented the listeners with another type of knowledge, one which referred to a cumulation of magical or occult (*id shidtei*) events in the past. The knowledge about the external world referred to in shamans' songs was thus not fully accessible to ordinary people. Stories circulated about these events, but they varied, and therefore people were not quite sure if their stories were accurate. Nevertheless, there was understood 'to be' a truth, to which the songs referred in their indirect and startling images. This was a truth which implied revelation through shamanic practice.

However, one crucial aspect of the shaman's song was intuitively accessible to everyone. The domain where shamans made use of universal intuitive knowledge was that of human psychology (belief, desire, motivations). Very, very generally, we can observe that the male elders used simple images of external nature in the process of elaborating their own contrived and patriarchal views of social relationships, while shamans employed intuitive understandings of the psychology of human relations at the same time as constructing strange, destabilized visions of a natural world.

This can be seen in the following Darhat Mongol song, where a shamanic spirit, Baglain Udagan, laments the death of her children. To understand this we have to know a little of the story. The spirit was the transformed soul of a female shaman who had lived long ago at Baglai, during which time her son was punished and killed by the lords of Düügerch Wang Banner for stealing horses and cattle. Unlike the previous song, which was addressed to a spirit, this text is the words of the spirit Baglain Shaman herself, sung by a contemporary shaman. The main impression is of the spirit's emotion, which appears as a force of humanity fighting for precedence with the forces of inanimate nature. After Baglain Shaman had seen her son being killed in Düügerch Wang Banner, she returned home. Looking at his empty bed she cried for several days; her crying became a cosmic rainstorm:

> From the inexhaustible source of the great red taiga forest
> From the flood torrent of the Khan taiga
> Flare sparks and flames.
> From the misty black cloud
> Pours down black flood water

and when she at last got up, she heard that the entire Düügerch Wang Banner had been flooded, and foals tied to trees had drowned. She continued her song, giving a reprise of her misfortune:

> My hugely grown body
> Kicked the taiga forest green with juniper
> And I gave birth to my son by luck
> I destined my daughter by cause
> With my reddish yellow duck-coloured body
> I fed and raised them
> I was overburdened and I stumbled

And [they my children] became a weak spot in my heart
A bitterness in my thought
A splinter in my body
It was the Khan's edict
It was the lord's law
That summoned and threatened
That attacked and repressed.
It is said he [my son] truly did the deed
It is said what he remarked is probable.
But they destroyed the body
Of my only son, woe! Giyak! [*the sound of the crane, the harshest curse*]
Blow asunder the hearth-fire of Wang Banner
Dispel the fox-like reek! Giyak! Giyak!
O chilly red mountain cliff
May your crust of earth be detached
May your mountain overhang collapse
O you stone crag, you could not save the life of my only egg.
May you be struck by the blue sky
And become sand and dust
In the peeling wind
May I see you blown away.
People of Wang Banner
I take the oath
I will not let [you] see my wet eyelash
I'll make sure you see
The lake become blood, the maintain cairn [*oboo*] turned to flesh,
The breaking of bones.
O cranes who controlled
The life of my only son
I'll make you pay with your heads one by one. Giyak! Giyak! [. . .]
Oh, dry my heart-breaking tears!
My body has not seen light in darkness
I have used the body born in flesh
I have become wrinkled [bearing] the suffering of living in blood.
I have never known the dots called 'writing'
I have not held in my hand the feathered splinter called 'pen'
[*i.e. I am not a lama, so do not expect me to be nice and make merit and forgive you*]
My two seeds have been expelled into the past
I have lost [them] and I grieve,
This is the cause of my going this way
This is my fate.[98]

(Dulam 1992: 65–7)

It seems to me that this song is immediately understandable as a cry of anguish.
We also understand that force of the spirit's emotion is attacking the stability of
nature, though the precise import of the images of foundering cliffs, beheaded

cranes, and blood lakes remains unclear. To decode these images would require further information on the part of our readers, the kind of information held at least partially by most Darhat Mongolians, and so we shall return to this song later (3.2). Meanwhile, the point here is that shamans' songs combined meta-level, occult, and somewhat obscure imagery with absolute clarity of emotional import.

I cannot argue that the religious systems called 'shamanism' all over the world have this pattern. Just because the cultures of the Mongols seem, on the one hand, to acknowledge fundamental understandings of natural processes and, on the other, explicitly to challenge them in this particular way, it does not follow that this will be the case elsewhere. And, as we shall see, what I have presented so far are two poles of sensibility, which in practice were not always kept distinct. Shamans not only acted to destabilize the forces of nature but also sometimes laid claims to them (see 3.2).

What altered over time, and between various societies, in North Asia was the richness, or poverty, of the symbolic elaborations on the intuitive fundaments and the extent of their 'spread' and hold on the imagination in society. Thus, although Daur and Tungus understandings of the world were very similar, their social preoccupations were not. For example, Daurs emphasized the sphere of the 'mountain-clan', while the Tungus used different images to think about their social groups. Therefore, we would not expect to find the same rituals and religious specialists in these two groups, nor a constant pattern in one society over time. Within the body of ideas called 'shamanism' no single metaphysics or cosmology has ever held sway, as far as I know. There was no unified theory that succeeded in, or even systematically tried to, explain everything; in other words, there was no dominant ideology. In fact, having a dominant ideology may be a much less common state of affairs than anthropologists are wont to asume. In the case of North Asia the reasons may not be fully explainable, but may lie in the loosely coherent political-economy, in the absence in shamanic societies of the social and technical basis for any kind of hegemony. But perhaps there always was a tendency for a particular religious causal–cum–symbolic view to attempt to extend beyond its immediate sphere of operation, to try to explain the way things were more generally. Therefore there was a tension in shamanic societies between alternative, often antagonistic, kinds of reasoning, such as that used by the *bagchi*/old man, and that used by *yadgan* shamans. Social movements or prominent individuals were able to favour one above another. Different kinds of religious practitioners waxed and waned in their fortunes, and new cults arose. If, as Ellen has pointed out (1993: 149), even practical classification systems arise through historical processes, how much more is this true of religious and symbolic ideas concerning nature.

One way to make this clearer is to situate the ritualized speech of religious practitioners by discussing the ideas of ordinary people. Here we shall see a far more heterogeneous range of attitudes than the relatively coherent images presented by elders and shamans. There is a strange difficulty in understanding views which are 'outward'-directed and metaphysical, in which analogies from humanity are used to map the physical external world, but which are also 'inward'-focused, such that human society and persons are thought about symbolically by means of categories in nature. Nevertheless, it is essential that these views be described, since they were the assumed background of more specifically religious activities.

Notes

1. Urgunge was born in 1919 and our conversations took place from 1987–9.
2. Most of the Western literature uses the Mongol form 'Dagur', but I use 'Daur' as this approximates to the pronunciation of Urgunge's people and is less complicated than the form 'Da'wr' preferred by Urgunge. 'Daur' is also used by Namtsarai and Hasartani (1983) and Engkebatu (1984). Alternatives are 'Dagur' and 'Daguur' (referred to in Poppe 1930), 'Dakhur' (Jagchid 1988*a*), Dagor (Vreeland 1954), and 'Dahuru' (Kałuzinski 1969, 1970). In 1982 there were some 94,000 Daurs registered in China, a large increase from the 55,000 registered in 1958 (State Statistical Bureau 1985: 23). The official figure for Daurs living in Inner Mongolia, i.e. excluding those in Xinjiang and elsewhere, was 70,959 in 1990 (*Nei Menggu* 1990: 173). As noted by Schwartz (1984), pre-war figures were much higher. For example, Poppe (1930) surmised that there may have been up to 300,000 Daurs in Manchuria. Similar sharp discrepancies have been found in population estimates for other minorities in China. Reasons for the difference include the haphazard nature of earlier estimates, different classification criteria, war and emigration, and a tendency to register oneself as 'Chinese' in cases of ambiguity.
3. This is the Daur pronunciation. In Chinese the river is called Nenjiang, also known in European writings as the Nonni River.
4. Daurs, particularly of the Hailar region, use *saman*, as well as *yadgan*, for both male and female shamans. Smolyak (1991: 56) points out that variants of the term *sama* were used by Nanai, U'chi, Negidal'tsy, Orochen, Manchus, and many groups of Tungus, and that its meaning lies in the Tungus root *sa* (to know, think, or understand).
5. For the Tungus, see n. 29. The Manchus, the neighbours of the Daurs to the south, were descended from the Jurchen, who had founded the Jin Empire in North China (1115–1234). The Manchus were farmer-hunters and shamanists like the Daurs, but they spoke a different language. In 1644 the Manchus took Peking and established the Qing Dynasty. They rapidly expanded through the whole of China, made treaties with the eastern Mongols, defeated the western Mongols, and until 1911 were rulers of a vast Empire stretching to the Altai Mountains in the West.
6. The Khitan (Qidan) were livestock herders and farmers who conquered north China and eastern Mongolia and established the Liao Dynasty (946–1125). A strong argument for the descent of the Daurs from the ruling clan of the Khitan,

which was called Dahur, is made by Cheng (1987). Other writers hold that the Daurs were a Mongol group within the Khitan confederacy. They also point to the fact that Daurs are mentioned as subjects of the Mongol rulers Jochi Hasar and Horchi in the early 13th century (see Shirokogoroff 1933: 83, 99, 348, 361; *DSHI* 1985; Daur History 1986; Baranov n.d.). However, according to Fei (1980: 160–2), the Daurs should be classified as a different people from the Mongols because of their long history of living separately and their inclusion in the Manchu, as opposed to the Mongol, Banner system. In his view the Daurs only came to identify with Mongols recently, after 1911, when they hoped to strengthen their position in this way. However, some writers have seen a political motive in this separation of the Daurs from the Mongols. Jagchid (1988*a*: 332) writes that the Chinese Communists classified the Daurs separately from the Mongols as part of the policy to break up large and potentially secessionist minorities.

7. Daurs speak a clearly Mongolian language, but with the addition of much Manchu and some Chinese vocabulary.

8. Dagur Ündüsten-ü Tobchi Teüke-iin Naiiragulun Bichihu Duguiilang (1989: 41–59) gives maps of clan territories and chiefdoms. For Russian accounts of the Daurs at this time, see Dmytryshin, Crowther-Vaughan, and Vaughan (1985: 185–277).

9. This is why their earlier homeland, which is still called 'Dauria' on the maps, is without any Daur population today.

10. In the 17th century the military Banners of Daurs had been founded on the basis of clans, and clan headmen were made Banner officials. By the 18th century there were a total of 16 Banners in Butha, 8 to the west of the Naun River and 8 to the east, comprising both Daurs and Solons as members. The Banners recruited on the basis of birth, but as time went on not all males became members. Though all members of Banners were subject to conscription, only some were selected for service in the regular army. The great majority remained as farmers in the reserves and they were called up only for particular campaigns or wars. Urgunge's father was one of these, a member of the All Yellow Banner. Among the Daurs, unlike the case in Mongol Banners, Banner officials were appointed or locally chosen, not hereditary. The clans gradually came to diverge from the Banners. Among the Hailar Daurs there seem to have been powerful Daur families based in clans which were able to promote their members as powerful officials (*ugurda*) in local politics. This tendency was blocked by a Manchu decree in the 1890s, according to which the locally chosen leaders of the Daur Banners were replaced by several less powerful officials called *gusaidaa*, who were appointed by the Manchu regional general and in many cases were not even Daurs (Batubayin 1990; Baranov 1907 and 1911). For relations between Manchu Banners and clans, see Crossley (1987).

11. Although the Daurs returned to Butha in 1742, further Daur troops were soon dispatched to Hulun Buir to live there as farmers and reservists. The term 'Solon' was later used for people of Tungus stock, some of whom in the Hailar region were very Mongolized and may have included some Daurs (Lattimore 1934: 189–90 and notes from O. Mamen photographic archive). These Daurs were influenced by the predominantly Mongol nomadic pastoralist culture of that area and by Buddhism. In 1763 the Manchus sent five hundred Daur troops and their families

to far off Ili in Xinjiang. The descendants of these people live there to this day. In 1894 Daur regiments were used on the northern front at Aihun in the Sino-Japanese war, and in 1900 they took part both in Manchu resistance against the European incursions and in the putting down of Chinese peasant insurgency (the 'Boxer rebellions') against foreigners. During the 18th and 19th centuries, the Daurs of Butha paid an annual tax to the Manchus in furs, a system which was not ended until 1908.

12. Also spelled Butaha, Bu-te-ha, and Butkha.

13. Prince Demchukdonggrub, known as Prince De (Teh), or De Wang, was leader of a confederation of Inner Mongols who sought regional autonomy. The Prince did not succeed in gaining the support of the Mongols of the Mongolian People's Republic, who were backed by the Russians, and unable to benefit from the split between Nationalist and Communist Chinese, he had recourse to Japanese support. But this further alienated the MPR and also many Mongols of Inner Mongolia.

14. Urgunge's father had died while he was away in Japan.

15. Urgunge's wife took no part in our discussions. This was partly because she is not Daur, grew up in Buddhist surroundings, and knows little about shamanism, but also because Urgunge wanted to put over *his* point of view.

16. In these clarified versions the Mongolian is translated, words in square brackets are explanations inserted by myself, underlined words are those originally spoken in Mongolian, . . . represents a hesitation, and [. . .] indicates that some words from the original tape have been omitted.

17. The 'bedrock' nature of Urgunge's memories was reinforced by another aspect of his life, which is that I am by no means the only person with whom he has relived his childhood. In the 1950s he was the informant for a section of Vreeland's book (1954) on Mongolian society, and since then he has written his own autobiographical sketches with the assistance of various English writers. One might assume that because he was remembering a 50-year-old event, he was accessing a 50-year-old memory. But as psychologists have pointed out that can only be concluded if the event has not been recalled in the mean time; if it has, then the incident will at least have been rehearsed, and at worst the subject remembers not the event itself but his or her later reconstruction of it (Baddeley 1982: 53–4). In this case, though a certain layer of memories was certainly reinforced by his previous recall of them, I am convinced that Urgunge was directly thinking about his past during our conversations and the results were far more detailed than his earlier accounts. When I reminded him what Vreeland had written he said that Vreeland had misunderstood some points and he supported this statement by long explanations which seemed to come directly from early memory. But once or twice there would be a point in Vreeland on which I had drawn a blank. On these occasions his reaction was, 'Did I say that? Well, it must be right, because my memory was better in those days.'

18. This memory pattern is to be expected, given Urgunge's life trajectory. Human remembering shows a rapid loss at first, followed by a gradual slow-down to something like a plateau, and if two memory traces are equally strong at a given time, the earlier of the two will be more durable and forgotten less rapidly (Baddeley 1982). The plateau of clear memories Urgunge kept returning to can be seen as this relatively durable part. One important factor in the erosion of memories

is the superimposition over early traces of later, closely similar, events and materials, for example when parents forget what their children were like at age 5 because the images of them at 5½ and 6 have intervened. Because Urgunge's childhood had several distinct phases and because he left the village altogether, never to return, in the 1940s, this factor, known as retroactive interference, is relatively minimal in his case.

19. Bokorchien means literally 'buttocks people', not a name Urgunge was eager to emphasize.

20. The houses described by Urgunge were similar in almost every respect to the houses described by Ides in the 1690s for the Daurs in the region of Qiqihar (Ides and Brand 1967).

21. The Naun Daurs grew cabbages, beans, potatoes, melons, turnips, carrots, and onions in their vegetable gardens. These gardens were the province of women, although men sometimes helped with the hoeing.

22. Urgunge thought this was because women would offend the spirits with their impurity (*hwaski*, see 3.5 and 6.6). *Barkan*s were kept in the storehouse not the main house because it was thought that to witness sexual activity would make them angry.

23. The paintings were made on the order of a shaman by a specialist in the village. The style of many of them was similar to Chinese folk-art (see Plate 23). High ranking spirits were larger than junior ones.

24. The blood was put on by a shaman to make the images come alive (*amitai*). It was chicken blood (Urgunge said that pig's blood would have been 'dirty').

25. The temple was dedicated to Guandi (Kuan Kung), a Chinese military hero and defender of the kingdom against insurgents, whose worship may have begun as early as the 3rd century AD. Guandi was officially deified by the Sung Emperors in the 11th century (Day 1940: 52–4). This cult was promoted by the Ming and again by the Manchu court all over the Empire, but by Urgunge's childhood in the 1920s and 1930s hardly anyone ever went to this temple.

26. Urgunge went to this school from the age of 8, and it was here that he learned Chinese.

27. The east bank was thought of as the left bank, since the orientation of the landscape was to look from the north southwards. There were divisions of the eight Banners (*gwas*) on both the east and the west bank of the Naun. By Urgunge's childhood this system had been officially replaced by the district (*xian*) administration of the Chinese Republic, but the latter was much resented and people tended to think still in terms of the Banners.

28. The main crop was millet, the staple diet of both rich and poor. Other crops grown were buckwheat, barley, oats, wheat, maize, and soya beans. The fields were cultivated mainly by men, using oxen for ploughing. The Naun Daurs kept horses, cattle, pigs, chickens, dogs, and a few donkeys. Sheep, so essential to the Mongol economy, seem to have existed in the area in the 19th century (Palladius 1872: 167), but were no longer kept in Urgunge's time. The Hulun Buir (Hailar) Daurs had a more pastoralist economy than the Naun Daurs, and some of them kept Mongolian-type round felt tents, as well as houses.

29. I have used the now obsolete term 'Tungus' because, though rarely used as a self-appellation, it is found widely in the ethnographic literature of the period the book

describes. 'Tungus' refers to a language group closely related to Manchu and it was also an ethnic category applied to a number of related peoples now called Evenki (Ch. Ewenke), Orochen (Ch. Elunchun), etc. By the 19th century many Tungus of North Manchuria had taken up herding or agriculture under Mongolian and Manchu influence. They were called 'Solon' by the Manchus and were organized into Banners in the same systems as the Daur Banners. Indeed some Daurs served as officers in Solon Banners (Lattimore 1934: 179). However, Daurs considered themselves more civilized than the Tungus (Palladius 1871: 444), and this is reflected in their term Hongkor ('wild') for the group now known as Ewenke. For further information on the contemporary situation, see Jahunen 1990; 1991.

30. In Chinese Buxi, Noho, and Nenjiang, respectively.

31. Money was hardly used in the village; the one shop operated by credit accounts which were normally paid in grains. People went to nearby towns for relatively infrequent purchases such as iron plough-tips, cooking pots, paper (used for windows), cloth, salt, oil, guns, and lead for bullets.

32. Daur farmers who went on the hunt were aided by semi-professional trackers. These were poorer people who knew the forest well, either local Daurs or more usually 'Hongkor' Tungus.

33. According to Batubayin (1990), the Daur tribes (*hala*) used to organize large-scale *battue* hunts in the spring and autumn. The hunt was directed by the *arquinda*, the man who was in charge of military matters in the tribe, usually an official of the Banner. Each clan (*mokon*) within the tribe selected their best hunter as a subordinate *arquinda* to help in the organization. The hunt began in a wide circle and was gradually narrowed until all the animals were driven into a small space. Shooting began on the order of the main *arquinda*. The game was shared equally between each clan, and then between each hunter. Such hunts had died out long before Urgunge's time, but they were earlier widespread in North Asia (see Zhambalova 1991 on the Buryat collective hunt and its relation with war formations).

34. There are some twenty-one of these, of which Urgunge knew the Aula, the Merden, the Deedul, the Suduur, the Denteke, and the Gobol. See full list given in Batubayin (1990: chs. 4 and 5). Many Daur *hala*s, such as the Onon (Ernen), are named after rivers in the Amur drainage region.

35. Both *hala* and *mokon* are Manchu words. According to the *DSHI* and Batubayin (1990), there were other terms for clan-like groupings among the Daur in past times, but these were no longer used in Urgunge's childhood.

36. The Manchu script was used, as there was no writing system for Daur. In the 19th century the updating was the occasion for a solemn rite of offering to the ancestors (Batubayin 1990), but Urgunge never observed such a ritual.

37. The bondsman (*hwatih*) family in Bokorchien had formerly been in private ownership, perhaps captured in war. By Urgunge's time the many sons and grandchildren of this family were considered to belong to the whole village. They had their own farms and could no longer be ordered around. However, they did not have the right to enter Daur houses, nor could they take part in the *oboo* ritual. Daurs would not eat with them or marry with them. They were of Chinese origin and by the

grandchildren's generation were able to intermarry with the other Chinese families in the village.

38. *Mani aili shurkul bish*, meaning that once married off an Onon girl was no longer an Onon.

39. Daur has no word for marriage as such. 'Marriage' was a different thing for men and women and expressed differently in language. A woman did not 'marry' but 'was married off' (*xeelge-*, from the verb to disjoint or cut something off). For a man, 'to marry' was to 'take a bride' (*beri aw-*).

40. An in-coming daughter-in-law worked from morning to night and her deferential relationship to the elders of the household was symbolized by her filling their long-stemmed pipes with tobacco before anyone else got up in the morning. Urgunge said that the verb 'to act as a daughter-in-law' (*berichile-*) brings to mind just this action of pipe-filling, which she also performed for honoured guests and for her father-in-law's corpse for several days after he died.

41. *Boigon* refers to the family as a property-owning unit. On household size, see Vreeland (1954: 196).

42. Urgunge's father was known in the village as Ang-Boshig, Ang being the first syllable of whatever his name was, and Boshig being a Manchu term for a local official.

43. This means literally 'good sitting down'. For men it consisted of bending the left knee fully and the right to a lesser extent, meanwhile lowering the right thumb and fist to the ground and keeping the left hand on the left knee. Women laid their right hand over their left hand on the left knee. The recipient of this honour should reply, so the point was: who did *sain hasso* first to whom.

44. Later his second eldest brother was chosen for this position, which was renamed *nutug-daa* (head of the homeland).

45. If someone from another *mokon* used the hunting or fishing areas, they had to supply part of their catch to the *mokon*, which shared it equally among the member families.

46. In the Hailar district, prominent Daur families also had their own separate *oboo*s. For example, En Ming's family had an *oboo* at the Amban Lake, and he sacrificed a sheep and liquor there during the fifth lunar month (Akiba and Akamatsu 1941: 262).

47. It was not the custom, as among the Chinese, to hold an annual spring ritual of sweeping the graves and making offerings.

48. Exclusion from the *mokon* took place for repeated violence and if the exogamy rules were breached.

49. Pregnant women were excluded because they had caused the death of a potential member of the clan by their own death. Pregnancy was also regarded as a mild state of impurity.

50. The Daurs did not use the Mongol terms *zøb* (right) or *buruu* (wrong). In any case, Urgunge said, these words originally referred to a right or a wrong direction, and only came to have moral connotations with Buddhist influence.

51. See Asad (1994: 14–15) for an illuminating discussion of subjectivity. Asad writes that the basis of the liberal humanist principle of self-constitution is 'consciousness', and that this idea is essential for explaining how the many fragments come to

be construed as parts of a single self-identifying subject. However, 'one does not have to subscribe to a full-blown Freudianism to see that instinctive reaction, the docile body, and the unconscious work, in their different ways, more pervasively and continuously than consciousness does. This is part of the reason why an agent's act is more (and less) than her consciousness of it.' Furthermore, an agent's acts are linked to the projects of other agents in the context of political and economic structures that allow or preclude certain options. This also is not a subjective matter (i.e. founded on consciousness of self). Asad's view, therefore, is that *agent* (the principle of effectivity) and *subject* (the principle of consciousness) do not belong to the same theoretical universe (1994: 15–16). This may be a useful tactical move in the kind of analysis Asad wishes to make, but for the purposes of this book I think it is useful to retain 'subjectivity'. Here I would include not only consciously-held ideas, but also unconscious reactions and the attuning of ideas and actions to the context of repressive and other structures.

52. In this section 'shaman' will mean a *yadgan* shaman.

53. It was taken for granted that a childless Daur man would adopt a son from a close relative.

54. Ohnuki-Tierney (1980: 209) contrasts the 'humble' status of the Sakhalin Ainu shaman with that of a male elder. The latter was both a political and a religious leader, especially in his control of the major cult, that of the bear.

55. Elsewhere in Asia the word *baksy* (*bakshi*, *bakhshi*, etc.) was a term for 'shaman', for example among the Kazakh, Kirghiz, Tadjik, and Uzbek. Bartol'd demonstrated that the Central and North Asian use of '*bakshi*' derives from the Sanskrit *bhikshu* and came into the Persian, Eastern Turkic, and Mongolian languages with the earliest spread of Buddhism (Basilov 1992: 48–9). The term has denoted numerous different concepts through history and in different places. In present-day Mongolian *bagsh* means teacher or guru. According to Namtsarai and Hasartani (1983: 478), Daurs distinguish between *bakshi* (teacher) and *bagchi* (reciter of spells, singer, accompanist).

56. A horse, called *onggon mori*, was offered to Jiyachi and other *barkan* spirits. It was decorated with ribbons tied in its mane. Subsequently, it could be used, but not ridden by women. The custom of consecrating domestic animals is widespread in Inner Asia, but the 'reasons' for it vary. Urgunge said Daurs would consecrate a particularly valuable or loved horse when it was ill, in order to give it protection, just as a child was dedicated to Tengger or Ome Niang-Niang (see 6.3).

57. *Chorkirlaa choangaaj* (*choanga* refers to birdsong, or shaman's singing; *chorkirla-* is to scream or howl (Poppe 1930: 100–1; Lessing *et al.* 1982: 207).

58. Darhat Mongols distinguish between the semi-dissociated state known as *yavgan boolo-* (on foot shamanizing) and the deeper dissociation of *unaatai boolo-* (mounted shamanizing). The former was performed using wooden sticks and the latter with a drum. Ethnographers who have seen *yavgan boolo-* say it is not very different from a normal conscious state (S. Dulam and C. Pegg, oral communication).

59. In Mongolian, people say *orshig-* (to be possessed [by a spirit] (from *orshi-* (to exist or reside))), *ordoslo-* (to act as one possessed by an evil spirit (*ordos*)), or *hürte-* (to receive [a spirit]). It is for similar reasons that Holmberg (1989: 142) writes not of trance but of 'seizure' and not of the shamanic seance but of 'soundings' among the

Nepal Tamangs (the latter term comes from the shamans' characteristic activity, *rhappa* (sound their drums)).

60. The Nishan Shaman is the hero of the best-known shamanic epic of the peoples of Manchuria (see 6.5). The provenance of the version quoted here is not certain, but it probably came from the Daur village of Mehertei near Hailar, and it was collected in the period 1920s–1950s. The text is in Manchu, a language known to many Daurs at the period (Yakhontova 1992: 6).

61. The new shaman was not related to Du Yadgan except that both were Onons (see 5.1).

62. *Oweskeebei*, in Mongol *mør garga-*.

63. In the Altai the *yarlyk*s, a relatively recently emerged type of shaman, were not allowed to hunt (Sagalayev and Oktyabr'skaya 1992: 113). Darhat and Tsaatan shamans of north-west Mongolia were not supposed to hunt (S. Dulam, personal communication). Among the Western Buryats, it was forbidden to ask shamans to carry out hunting rituals, specifically the offering to the spirit giving luck in hunting, Anda Bar. Old men or Buddhist lamas were supposed to do this (Galdanova 1981: 46–8).

64. The solution was for the hunter to make a small human or dog-shaped representation of dried grass, 'settle' the soul or spirit into it, and hang it up at the camp.

65. 'The beginner hunters, immediately after the worship of the master deity of the place, would bow to all the old men and feed them with porridge from their bowls. . . . This had one goal, to receive from them happiness in life and hunting. This the old men willingly gave, because when young they had also received it from old men' (Smolyak 1976: 153–4).

66. Dulam (1992: 57); Galdanova (1987: 92); the spirit power at the sacred rock of Avgai Khad near Ulaanbaatar in Mongolia is also called *yum* (see Humphrey 1993). However, Urgunge said that Daurs did not use the word *yum*, as it would have been considered insulting to spirits and hence dangerous.

67. Recently recorded text from the Darhat Mongols of the Købsgøl region in north-west Mongolia (Dulam 1992).

68. *Zønøk* means senile, decrepit, absent-minded, and generally useless; *hairhan* means literally cherished, sacred, supreme, the one above who bestows to those below. *Hairhan*, however, is widely used as a euphemism, for things that people fear may actually be dangerous.

69. *Ozuur* is the Darhat variant of the Mongolian *yazguur* (root, stem); the Daur term is *hojoor*.

70. Both of these are considered extraordinarily impure and revolting, but no one thinks they would actually cause the death of an ordinary human being.

71. Among the Buryats a late death was also inauspicious. Eighty years was considered the maximum span for a human being, and if someone died after that each year of life was 'at the expense of descendants', or the soul was supposed to become a harmful spirit (Galdanova 1987: 55, 60, 64). However, people hardly ever lived so long. For discussion of the idea of the spirit of a man who lived too long, see Dioszegi (1967).

72. These governments were given only limited backing by the Russians and Mongolians. A second attempt at autonomy was overthrown in 1917 when the

Chinese took the opportunity of the Russian Revolution to re-occupy Hailar (Ikeshiri 1981: 32).

73. The application from the Daurs makes clear that they considered their main means of livelihood to be hunting and pastoralism. With the opening of mountain and forest land at the end of the dynasty, they wrote, wild animals had declined, making it more difficult for the Daurs to fulfil their state duty of paying taxes in furs. The letter continues, 'If the Bannermen are assigned the task of opening so much new land for agriculture, they will be unable to do it, since they are already busy with their official duties.' Therefore Chinese should be encouraged to open the land as lessees and labourers. The resulting tax could be appropriated by the Daurs, and this would be beneficial for strengthening border defences and paying salaries of Bannermen (Ikeshiri [1943] 1982: 91). The Manchus ended the fur tax in 1908. The imperial decree was not carried out for some years because the Butha and Qiqihar regions were occupied by the Russian army in 1904.

74. The Daurs reacted with fury, but the disorganization and apathy of the Manchus at this point was such that years went by during which Daur petitions were ignored. In the end, Daurs were granted secure ownership of the land they occupied and a percentage of the prices paid by Chinese farmers for purchase of 'wasteland'.

75. The village where Urgunge ended up was in fact the home of these Chinese, and the man who took him home was one of his affines living there, though not a member of the gang. A ransom was never paid in the end, though the relative received payment for hire of the boat and a small fee for himself.

76. There were many names in Chinese for different categories of bandits (Jagchid 1988*b*). The most common in Urgunge's region was *hung-hu-tzi* (Red Beards). Urgunge thinks that this term, which was used all along the frontier, must have originally referred to the Russian Cossaks, whose advance into the Amur region had indeed been brutal.

77. According to the *DSHI* (1985: 19), there were two types of rebels in the Morin Dawaa uprising, middle-aged hunters, who led the group, and young students. At its maximum size the group reached 200 people. They fought against local bandits, the government army, and Zhang Zuo-lin. Daur houses were burned and property confiscated in reprisals against the rebels.

78. *Shashin* derives from the Sanskrit *śāsana* and must have come into Mongolian together with Buddhism.

79. *Shüte-* is used by Daurs as a verb, meaning to worship or venerate (Todayeva 1986: 184), but not as an abstract noun (religion).

80. *Lun* is distinct here from *li lun*, which are pronouncements formed into a theory.

81. Conversion in Eastern Mongolia in the 17th century involved repudiating the *onggod* (equivalent to the Daur *onggor*, i.e. shamanic spirits, see 4.1) and physical destruction of shamanic idols. Alongside the acceptance of blessings from lamas, learning of prayers and *dharani* (Mo. and Da. *tarni*) spells, the converted retained the worship of mountain and river spirits. Missionary Buddhism gave particular importance to the cult of fierce (*dogshid*) manifestations of deities, especially Yamantaka. *Dharani* spells were used to 'destroy evil', but also for such functions as protecting and multiplying the livestock, or even getting rid of bilious attacks (Heissig 1992: 112–13). Neyichi Toyin was accused of debasing the profound truths of Buddhism by allowing all kinds of ignorant people to recite the Yamantaka

prayers, as a result of which he was banished in the 1650s, ending his mission among the Eastern Mongols. However, as Heissig (1992: 129) points out, propagating Buddhism by means of tantric divinities and spells was efficacious. Spells (*tarni*) entered Daur 'shamanic' practice, and were used by *bagchi*s and other religious specialists (7.1). They may in fact have been present from much earlier. According to Cheng (1987: 47) the Daurs descend from the Khitan, and many of the Daur religious practices, such as the use of tantric spells, rain-making rituals by *bagchi*s, the worship of the goddess Guan-Yin (see 6.3) and the use of the term *barkan* for both Buddhist and shamanist objects of worship, were continuous from the Khitan period (10th–12th centuries) onwards.

82. Banzarov also notes that there is no native Buryat term for shamanism and that the name 'the black faith' (*har shashin*) arose directly as a contrast with Buddhism, which was called 'the yellow faith' ([1846] 1955: 51).

83. For example, a cousin of his used to have constant bad headaches and his mother thought that this was caused by attack from a spirit. Once when Urgunge came back from Japan he gave the cousin a couple of aspirins. The boy took them and next day said that he had sweated all night from the top of his head to the tips of his toes, but now his headache was gone. As a result of this cure, the boy's headaches were no longer attributed to a spirit. Nevertheless the idea of spirits, and this particular spirit, remained as an explanation for phenomena which were resistant to cures of a medical kind.

84. In view of the limited role of the Daur shaman in all this it might have been preferable to use some other word. But every possibility seemed either equally misleading or awkward ('cosmologism'), or already colonized by other theories ('animism') or practices ('naturism'). Galdanova (1987: 95) struggled with similar problems in writing about Buryat religion. She concludes, 'In my book I have used the terms "shamanism" (*shamanizm*) and "shamanship" (*shamanstvo*). The latter was necessary in order to analyse white and black shamanship, in view of the functionally different significance of white and black shamans. However the cult activities of both of them are based on a totality of concepts that are the same for both white and black shamans. . . . In studying shamanism it is necessary to look at the phenomenon dynamically and broadly, taking in the whole religious-mythological complex, not making artifical divisions within it.'

85. The *DSHI* (1985: 256) mentions a shaman's assistant called *zalie* among the Aihui Daurs. Wu (1989a: 84–5) mentions a diviner called *agachin*. Jagchid (1988b) notes the existence of shaman-like specialists called *chang-bang-tzu* in a mixed Daur–Chinese township, see 7.1. Because none of these were present in his district Urgunge had not heard of them.

86. Human artefacts in this religious framework were considered as 'natural', i.e. as having an autonomous existence, as they were independent of the people who made them. Often they were said to have 'originated in the sky', or it was said that the first people who made them were deities. This idea was especially developed among the Buryats (Mikhailov 1987: 9–22).

87. I am using the term 'natural category' in the sense implied by Daur thinking, i.e. for 'phenomenally salient' entities attributed with innate existence and conspicuous to ordinary people.

88. *Odon tngri-yi urixu takixu sudur orusibai*, a manuscript in the archives of the Orien-

tal Faculty of St Petersburg University, inv. 634, mong. D-162, quoted in Dulam 1989: 20.

89. This is similar to Nelson Goodman's discussion of inductive reasoning (1955) in which he introduces the idea of 'projectability': given a particular experience, certain predicates stand out as the ones that can be projected onto other possible experiences, while other predicates are spontaneously left aside as irrelevant, even though they are equally applicable from a logical point of view. Goodman (1954) writes of 'the riddle of inductive reasoning', referring to the question of why some projections seem more natural than others. He suggests that our intuitions about projectability cannot be supported logically or semantically and therefore he has recourse to the idea of 'entrenchment'—some projections seem right because they have impressive biographies from successful applications in the past. This is to argue that predicates are not taken from raw nature; we never shart from scratch. Worlds, therefore, in Goodman's view, are made, not discovered. Atran (1990) and Boyer (1994), on the other hand, would argue that some predicates seem good for projection because they are imposed by inbuilt, universal cognitive mechanisms. For discussion of this issue, see Hull (1992).

90. This is true even though the formal structures of language are not autonomous from general conceptual organization and social and cultural influences; see below (also Humphrey 1974).

91. Hull (1992: 58–9) points out, from the point of view of evolutionary biology, that while evolution may have built certain cognitive predispositions into us, it would be surprising if these were all universal as Atran (1990) claims. Thus, although Atran may be correct that conceiving biological species hierarchically in terms of discrete kinds may be universal, there are likely to be other domains where cognitive dispositions are distributed less widely among human beings.

92. The 'hot-nosed' and 'cold-nosed' categories are characteristic folk life-form classes. Atran points out (1990: 30–5) that such folk life-forms need not necessarily be based on functional criteria but may derive from conceptions of ecological or other processes. They still nevertheless conform to the idea of hierarchical ranking which Atran and others argue is a universal cognitive principle in the zoological domain (Berlin, Breedlove, and Raven 1966; Atran 1990; Boyer 1994). For critiques of these views, see Toren (1993).

93. However, after it was established as sacred the tree was said to have an *ejin* (genius), and thus was aligned with the general Mongolian opinion about worshipped objects in nature.

94. This may refer to kidney- and head-shaped hills.

95. The kind of shaman mentioned here (*bøge*) is the Halh Mongolian equivalent of the Daur *yadgan* shaman. A Mongolian friend explained that the type of descent mentioned here (*udam*) is seen as biological, while in the next line the ancestry (*ugsaga*) from the female shaman (*idugan*) is social.

96. Asuri Tngri is a warlike vengeful personification of an aspect of the sky (see 3.1).

97. Boyer (1980) has suggested that a similar distinction in types of knowledge revealed at initiation rites in Africa was associated with different styles of rhetoric, and that these styles were linked to the social status of initiates. Metonymic codes were associated with the integration of a marginal group into the tribe, while metaphori-

cal rhetoric was linked to the constitution of a deviant social group (religious associations, secret societies, etc.).

98. Recorded from a shaman called L. Duujii in the administrative centre of Bayanzurh in north-west Mongolia at some time during 1991-2 by the research team led by S. Dulam. Dulam (1992: 63–7) gives the song in Mongolian, together with several stories about the Baglain Udagan spirit.

2

In Daur Landscapes

2.1 Differentiated Realms

Urgunge's fleeting observations about the world around his childhood village of Bokorchien never built up into a coherent picture. This chapter reveals several different kinds of discontinuity in his accounts and those of other Daurs. I briefly discuss this point here. Towards the end of the chapter I describe how the various disengaged domains of nature were, however, linked by one particular discourse, that of 'power' or 'mastery'.

Urgunge described the practical landscape of village, paths, and fields, and at the same time, he would mention the existence of devils (*shurkul*), spirit-masters (*ejid*), and shamanic spirits (*barkan*, *onggor*). This chapter discusses implicit distinctions made between mundanely visible and occult beings, and also points to the contexts in which such distinctions were occluded (for a comparable discussion, see Richards 1994). For the Daurs, as Atkinson (1989: 38) observes about the Wana, 'The vision of the world as divided into ordinary and hidden realms is not an idle cosmology, but a powerfully generative theodicy.'

This chapter also describes another set of unresolved gaps, those between the ontologies of different kinds of entities in the lived-in world. The use of the term *ejin* for all natural energies[1] masked the fact that the main categories used for thinking about the world, such as the sky, mountains, rivers, humans, or animals, were curiously disconnected in Daur discourse, and each was attributed with their own kind of causal realm. The Daurs had no all-explanatory and widely accepted creation myths that might have related the various parts of a cosmology to one another.

It was earlier proposed that in Daur 'shamanism' there was a broad homology between the ontology of natural objects or beings and the distinctive ritualized practices of specialists who had knowledge of them. It must be made clear that both for specialists and for ordinary people everyday assumptions about the objects themselves underdetermined the totality of ideas held about them. But it does not follow from this that the ordinary properties attributed to natural objects did not constrain the imaginative ideas held about them in some ways. Everyday intuitive ideas about, say, 'sky' or 'tree' formed a schematic core, on which other suppositions and flights of fancy could be elaborated. Boyer discusses the psychology of such a situation at length and he points out

(1994: 84–6) that the way such suppositions are constructed varies from domain to domain. Among the indefinitely many suppositions that might be made about, say, the sky, only some are entertained. The sky is not supposed to grow, for example. I remain agnostic about Boyer's argument (1994) that such constraints can be sufficiently well delineated to propose universally applicable conceptual structures for religious concepts. However, I have observed certain more or less distinct fields of speculation for the Daurs, and these I attempt to describe here. I use the expression 'field of speculation' rather than 'constraint' here because the latter might be understood to imply logical limits, whereas what we shall find is that, while Daur speculations about natural categories were certainly not infinite, they did include incompatible ideas. In other words, to the types of discontinuity in Daur cosmologies mentioned above (the mundane distinguished from the occult, and the differences between the basic ontologies of various natural categories) we must add another: namely that one natural category, like the sky, could provide several fields of imaginative speculation and these were inconsistent with one another. I shall suggest that such fields arose from particular interests people had in the category at hand.

I focus here on what ordinary people told me. This differed from ritual discourse in that it neither laid out core assumptions like the elders' invocations, nor purposely attacked such assumptions like the shamans. Laypeople jumbled up the viewpoints held relatively distinct by ritualists and shamans, and they added various practical concerns and magical practices that were not taken up in communal rituals. In ordinary life one was beset by seemingly non-accidental 'accidents', haunted places, souls which slipped away, strange dreams, or deeds which turned out to have angered some natural object, and most of this was regarded as not worth calling to the attention of a shaman or a *bagchi*. Here we shall see that Daur cosmologies as related by individuals were not just a matter of abstract thinking about a world out there, separate from the self, but derived also from direct, personal engagement with objects and processes. Still, people tended to link these experiences to culturally shared ideas. Shared ideas could be quite counter-intuitive, and indeed radically different from everyday explanatory schemes. Nevertheless, as I have mentioned, they were not totally arbitrary (Daurs had just as definite a sense of 'mad explanations' as we do). Cultural ideas, i.e. those having some shared currency for an extended period, were non-randomly related to particular types of causes or reasons (*uchir*) attributed to the domains of the natural world (e.g. there were certain characteristic things the sky 'did', or deer 'did'). Laypeople's talk in everyday life, like Urgunge's with me, often merrily overrode the distinction between visible and occult, and was not too concerned with the constructions found in rituals. Instead people linked their own direct experience to repertoires of cultural ideas, and these maintained certain distinct spheres of explanation pertaining to selected objects and beings in the world. Within these fields of speculation people's particular interests created focal points, gaps, and inconsistencies.

2.1.1 The sky: fate, harmony, and the individual

Though Urgunge would rarely agree that *tengger* is just the physical sky, he would say on other occasions that the sky (using the English word) is just the sky. This suggests that at some perhaps not entirely conscious level he made a distinction between a realist perceptual category of sky and what he usually meant by the Daur word *tengger*, which was susceptible to symbolic elaboration at several levels. Children of course see the sky before they can speak, but we may assume that even what I call the basic intuitive category sky is already culturally formed in some degree.[2] So Urgunge's later involvement with American and British culture may have provided him with some stripped away 'sky' foreign even to his childhood perceptions. In fact, the English 'sky' and even the most everyday sense of *tengger* are different: *tengger* meant *both sky and weather*. *Tengger* was inherently changeable, indeed active, its atmospheric variations constantly having effect on the world. This was an important point for metaphysical elaboration.

Daurs preferred to think of substantive entities, rather than abstract categories. They liked the expression *tengger-gajir* (sky-earth), rather than the abstract *delekei* (cosmos) used by Buddhist Halh Mongolians. The earth was the counterpart of the sky. The Daur word *gajir* meant the ordinary ground we walk on, the earth as a place, and soil as a substance. As a cosmological concept, it was 'the earth' in a reified sense. There was an epistemological gap between *gajir* in this sense and its components (mountains, steppes, bogs, etc.), such that no adding up of the latter gave you the former. Urgunge said that the earth in a metaphysical sense was implicitly female, life-giving, and fertile. In religious contexts *gajir* was mentioned only as the pair of *tengger* and was not the subject of any separate worship.[3]

Urgunge tended to talk of the sky's atmospheric effects as actions, as though they were willed. He said that *tengger* was the whole, measureless, fathomless arch over the earth, that its sound was thunder, and that its actions were clouding over, becoming dark and bright, giving rain, snow, mist, and lightning. On numerous occasions he emphasized to me that *tengger* was timeless. It was not created, nor did it create anything. It was not even 'eternal', because time terms did not apply to it.[4] The religious idea of *tengger*, the entity to which prayers and sacrifices were made, was that it regulated the universe, saw everything that happened, knew everything, and motivated everything (expressions for this were *tenggeri sanaa* (sky's state of mind), or *tengger jiyasan* (sky willed that . . .)). Such expressions existed along with phrases like *tengger burku-* (the sky clouds over), which could be interpreted either in a matter-of-fact way, or as implying a willed closure against humanity.

The following quotation from a traveller among the Buryats gives an indication of how a religious response to *tengger* in Mongolian cultures occurred in
spontaneous interaction with natural events:

I was sitting with an old man at Zhirimskaya late one afternoon, when the clouds were
driving across the western sky. He pointed across the prairie to where, a few miles away,
a great radiant shaft of light came slanting down from the hidden sun, through a rift.
'The white *tengeri* are looking from the sky!' he said. A minute or two later, another rift
opened, flooding our village with rosy radiance. My companion, and every one of the
four or five other Buriats in sight, turned and faced the point in the sky whence the shaft
of light was coming, their lips moving in prayer. A week later a Buriat who was driving
me turned round and suddenly pointed towards another 'door-opening' in the west, just
before sunset. He reined in the horse with a jerk, and prayed. Prayer at such moments
is considered particularly likely to be answered. (Digby 1928: 120–1)[5]

A conversation between two Daur women at Morin Dawaa in 1988 showed
me how a person's unexpected experience was linked up with such cultural
ideas, almost as a necessity of understanding. We see here that ontological
concepts (what *tengger* is) were not separate from episodic information, that is
specific experiences of *tengger*, or occasions when *tengger* was brought forward
as a causal explanation for some event. The older woman, H., had been speaking of *tengger-gajir* as a religious idea, something which was under attack by the
Communist authorities, but this slipped immediately and unconsciously into
her own lived experience.

N. Do you pray to *tengger*?
H. It is said that *tengger-gajir* exists, but who knows how it is? In the past, people used
to say that *tengger* came down. Well, I mean just raining, thundering. But this is true!
I have experienced it myself. It is common knowledge. Yes, it happened to me just
recently. Other people don't believe it, they say I was electrocuted. This happened
just half a month ago. From the outer room I heard the terrible sound, 'Ka'. There
was fire!
N. You didn't get hurt?
H. No. The fire came down to me. I stood up on the heated bed and shouted at once,
'This is a human person in the world!', then I jumped down, and thought, 'Do we
have some milk?' And I took a brush with milk and splashed it. We put out heaven's
fire [*tenggeri gal*] with milk.
N. Nothing burned?
H. At that moment I couldn't see the door of the outer room. The table in the outer
room split in two. I splashed some milk and whispered a spell [*tarni*], 'Fire, go
out . . .', and the fire slowly died down. Some other people saw that big fire coming
out of my house. It was true. Heaven's fire came in through the window and went out
through the door. Some while ago at Temeen Hudju [another village, C.H.] heaven's
fire came down and forty people living there could not put it out. One old man came
there with a can of milk. Young people laughed at him, saying, 'What a fool.' He saw
women and children there, and he said, 'You are no use, I am old enough to put it
out, I know the right way to do it; heaven's fire should be put out with milk.' People

stood and watched, but the fire went out. I was told about this by the old man, and
so that day when it happened to me, I did it in the same way.

The old lady was proud and excited that she had known what to do. The
counteracting of lightning by the sprinkling of milk is a 'custom' in the
Mongolian cultural region (Chingel 1991: 223; Abayeva 1992: 98–9; Dugarov
1991: 161).[6] Custom of course can be fragile. If the old Daur woman had not
met the old man, she would have been at a loss when the lightning struck,
without cultural protection. As we can see, many younger Daurs do not have
the idea of 'heaven's fire', nor do they know the practice of putting it out with
milk. Other people have heard of the idea but have been taught to doubt it. To
state what is perhaps obvious: the members of a society can have the same
language and be exposed to similar cultural messages but differ greatly in what
'shared concepts' mean to them and what creatively they do with them in
situations of danger and anxiety.

Urgunge said, however, that all Daurs in his village shared the idea that
tengger had an immense kindness and goodness which kept the world in balance. Therefore a dangerous cosmic event such as lightning, a terrible snowstorm, or a widespread epidemic was evidence that *tengger* was angry and
people had done something wrong. Misfortunes to individual people, however,
were usually not attributed to *tengger*, but to lesser spirits. *Tengger* guided the
destiny of individual lives, as it did of all beings, in the sense that it regulated
the span and extent of things in relation to one another. Thus a normal death
was simply regarded as *tengger*'s will, whereas accidents and sudden illnesses
might be the result of the activities of other powers.

There could be no representation, such as a drawing or picture, of *tengger*; he
was too great and unimaginable for that. 'He', I once pounced on this word;
'you think of him definitely as "he"?' 'Oh yes,' Urgunge replied, 'Always he. I
thought of him as very old, with a long beard like Rinchen-guai's [a famous
Mongolian scholar], a wrinkled face, red cheeks, and big, bright eyes.' He saw
tengger as the oldest person imaginable, he explained, the epitome of old age,
because everyone knew that it was through living and experiencing that power
was amassed and concentrated. This ancient sage never came down to earth.
However, on other occasions Urgunge said that such a human figure was only
a 'representative' of *tengger*, and usually he would insist that the Daur religious
idea of *tengger* is just the abstract regulatory capacity of the sky, whose conscious mindfulness is too vast and intricate for us to understand.

Everyone has a direct relation with *tengger*, said Urgunge, you pray to him on
your own, with your own words. He is addressed by the familiar form, *chi*.
Maybe you do not even need to use words, since your consciousness is part of
his. Actually, what Urgunge said about this was that each living being has a
'small *tengger*' (*ushken tengger*) in the crown of their head. This is a small sacred
and invisible space which has the same nature as 'great *tengger*' (*shih tengger*)

though it is inside us.[7] For this reason, no animal and certainly no child should ever be beaten on the head, as *tengger* would be hurt and angry. The small *tengger* has a counterpart in the sky, which is a star. Somehow these two parts of *tengger* are in touch with one another. 'When I die, that light of my consciousness goes out, and we used to think that our star will also be extinguished at exactly that moment,' Urgunge said. Boys used to gaze at the night sky and look for the brightest ones, joking, 'That one is mine!' If someone saw a star 'falling down', that is, a shooting star, it would mean some great person had died; but the stars of ordinary people just went out, unnoticed.

If these ideas were shared, as Urgunge assured me, there were others which seem more his own. Let us follow his association of ideas. As a child Urgunge thought, 'Just as my father will look after me, *tengger* will look after me.' (Like his personified image of *tengger*, Urgunge's father was old and wore a long white beard.) Urgunge said he felt very close to and at the same time very distant from the sky. 'As soon as you open your eyes you see *tengger* and feel its presence, but physically it is very far away.' This is what he felt about his father. 'You love him, and at the same time you are scared of him. After all, *xundel dairah*—thunder strikes.' Then he continued:

I went to my cousin's place one day. He was 35 to 40 and his mother was very old, around 75. My cousin was lying ill in bed. But I saw this: his mother took out her old breasts and let him feel them, as if he were a baby. She said, 'You are still my son.' My cousin was long married and had his own children. So what did a Daur think about parents? They are sky and earth. The old mother was not trying to cure her son of his illness, she was comforting him. He put his head on her chest, two hands on her breasts, and she stroked his head. That is loving. And what I am trying to tell you is how much feeling they [the Daurs] could have between the human being and the sky and earth. As a child I really thought this way about my father and mother; when I thought about them, I thought about *tengger* and *gajir*. One protects you, the other comforts you. Now you must be careful because the English word 'love' has no equivalent in Daur. To love is *taala-*, but that is love and desire. You could not say, 'I love [*taala-*] my father', even for your mother you wouldn't say it. For *tengger* there is the word *hundle-*, 'to respect', but this word itself includes love. If you do not love someone, you do not respect them.

On many other occasions Urgunge pursued a different series of ideas about the sky, concerning 'balance'. I once asked him, expecting a quite different answer, what was the significance of *erdem* (knowledge) for Daurs. He replied,

It means knowing how to balance things. Even if someone is stupid, he may be able to balance. For example, he likes to eat meat, but he knows he can't eat it all the time; it must be balanced with other things. Now each person is different, that is why knowledge is difficult to define. What is good for you, may not be good for me. You have to know it from your own point of view. That is your knowledge. If you really understand that you yourself are in some extreme [*huluu*] [i.e. not in balance, C.H.] that means that you know what it is to be balanced, and therefore that you understand what knowledge is. You may know something is askew, but what can you do? The shaman is the one who can put things right for people who have lost balance. In the world, in nature as a whole, this balance is what *tengger* regulates. *Tengger* 'harmonizes',[8] and each person in their own way, along their own path, does the same.

He continued,

Balance [*tengchuu*] is the centre of its surrounding world, and each human being should be like this. Like a light, each one shines in their own degree—not everyone shines 100 watts. Maybe weaker, maybe stronger, but each one must be its own light. People used to say, 'Everyone has their own sky (universe), everyone has their own trail' [*kuu kuu sheree tengerti, kuu kuu sheree murti*]. I came to understand this when I was 25 years old.

Tengger was thus associated with light, time, and harmony, not in an abstract and external way, but intimately related to a sense of self. I shall return later to these thoughts.

Urgunge's view of *tengger* as singular is not the only one described for the Daur. Chinese ethnographies record that heaven is called, in the context of ritual sacrifices, 'father heaven', 'mother heaven', 'ocean princess', and 'judge lord' (Achaa Tengger, Ewee Tengger, Dalai Katu, and Notur Noyon, *DSHI* 1985: 242). According to the Daur writer Odongowa (1991), 'The bright, spacious, unreachable blue sky governs the world,' but the Daurs also 'mysteriously and enigmatically' called it by the four names just mentioned, which it seems were imaginatively evoked by aspects of the cosmos. For example, 'The dark-blue and rippling, soft, beautiful ocean water, vast and boundless, made people think of it as a beautiful girl, called Dalai Katu (Ocean Princess).' These four beings are the 'elements' of heaven, but they are not gods, only 'vast spaces with no shape'. Elsewhere in North Asia the sky appears in ritual invocations as even more multiple.[9] This allows the envisaging of harmful and cruel aspects of the sky. Urgunge, however, said that he had not heard of such a division. He was prepared to admit only that some people may have imagined *tengger* as having nine ethereal layers (other Daurs I spoke to said the same). Urgunge laughed when I suggested that perhaps there was more than one *tengger*: how could I be so illogical? Surely everyone can see there is only one sky. In any case, he insisted, 'The Mongols knew only one *tengger*' (as always when he spoke this way the Mongols were the thirteenth-century people of Chinggis Khan's time), and the Daurs were not contaminated by any later ideas. The original idea was one heaven.

Perhaps it is only to be expected that people would disagree about the nature of the sky, which after all is 'an object' that exists only in human perceptions. But the more we talked, the more I became aware of radical discontinuities in what Daurs said about the sky which could not be explained by individual preferences or interpretations. Daurs *agreed about inconsistent statements* about the sky. I began to see what was at issue in such contradictions one day when we were discussing a supernatural being called *endur*.[10] An *endur* rides on clouds, which made me think it must have something at least to do with *tengger*.

c. What is an *endur*?

u. You did not ask me what *endur* looks like to me.

c. [*referring to an earlier description of another kind of spirit*] Don't tell me it is another one with a long white beard and big eyes.

u. [*somewhat crestfallen*] I don't know . . . yeah . . . all of them are like that . . . I have that kind of image. [*Laughs*] But this is very interesting, how is [*endur*] special? I can give you a very good answer you know.

c. How?

u. How? Have you ever seen an 18–year–old Professor? No. When you become an *endur* you will be in most cases old . . . therefore the definition of the *endur* is like retired, em . . . emer . . . emeritus Professor. This is a very, very perfect description of an *endur*. Because he is old and his merit reaches to that point, he becomes *endur* when he dies.

c. Merit?

u. *Gawiya* [achievement, valour].

c. And what kind of *gawiya* is needed?

u. Saved a few lives. But the important point is, he himself, after becoming an *endur*, cannot control anybody's life. He just has . . . after his retirement, you see, he just has a good time.

c. He cannot come back to this world?

u. He cannot come back. He is just roaming round, going to places for fun. To Liverpool, eh, [*laughs*] no, no, I mean Blackpool [a seaside resort]!

This is about as general as our conversations on the *endur* ever got. One gets a certain picture from it, perhaps even a feel for the essence of Urgunge's idea of the *endur*. We talked again about *endur*s, several times, and new 'facts' were added. They carried bags of water, it seems, and could give rain. I also read about them in Daur legends and noted how the word was used in Daur sentences. All these were clues. But it never became enough to answer an exam question on *endur*s, as it were. About many important areas of this being's existence Urgunge simply said he did not know. The articulation of *endur*s with other supernatural beings remained unclear. I think the shamanic world is like this. Each part belongs to the specialized and limited context of interest given it by a particular speaker (or community of speakers), and these contexts are not compared with one another. The context of interest of the *endur* for Urgunge is: what becomes of meritorious old men when they die? The answer is that they become *endur*s roaming around up there.

For Urgunge *endur*s and the sky (*tengger*) belong in different contexts of human interest. This is despite the fact that there would seem to be an obvious logical relation between *endur*s, which travel on clouds, and *tengger*, as the sky. The sun, moon, stars, and clouds are part of, and belong to, the sky. But to ask, as I tried to do, 'Does the *endur* live in the sky?' is more or less unanswerable. Urgunge gave a blank stare, and then extemporized: *endur*s lived just below the bottom rim of the sky, perhaps. This reply seems to have been pure politeness, since he never otherwise mentioned the sky as having a rim, or the existence of any space between it and the earth. The fact that there are certain questions no one ever asks, because they are irrelevant to the interest we have in X or Y, is true of all religions. It is for just this reason, the restricted context of such religious categories, that the following Christian joke is funny: 'Two old people, recently having died, are just getting adjusted to being in heaven as angels. They look around them and at one another, and one says, "I expected the wings. But the webbed feet come as a surprise."'

Such discontinuities are particularly likely to occur in a religion like 'shamanism', where no one has ever tried to work out how many angels can fit on the head of a pin. There is a further essential difference between the status of *endur* and that of *tengger* (sky): not only is the *endur* a relatively insignificant being, but no one has ever actually seen an *endur*. Urgunge said that he 'knew' people of his father's generation totally believed in them, but the fact is that he himself was uncertain whether they really existed, and he did not care much either way. On the other hand, *tengger* at the very least is simply the sky, which everyone has seen. There is no one who has not experienced its awesome power to give the light, rain, heat, thunder, and lightning.

So it is clear that Daurs differ in their concepts of *tengger*, but just as important is the fact that one person, Urgunge, has at least three ideas. As we might see it these are: (1) the physical sky/weather, (2) 'heaven' attributed with consciousness and a cosmic regulatory function, and (3) the benevolent and ancient celestial sage. Odongowa's explanation of *tengger* as both 'vast spaces' and named human-like beings likewise occludes a distinction between the abstract and the personified. As Obeyesekere observed about South Asian culture (1981: 165 ff.), there is a greater tolerance for mysterious elisions than in the West: the boy who is visited at night by his dead grandmother is regarded by others as especially gifted, not as disturbed. The Daur religious ideas have an amplitude which is unfamiliar to our defining spirit. Urgunge might be amused by *endur*, but he was in earnest about *tengger*. He wanted, almost implored, me to be generous enough to assent to such a cosmic space-consciousness.

2.1.2 Entities and beings on the earth

Entities on earth were divided by the Daurs into the primary ontological categories of the animate and the inanimate. Animate beings were called *amitan*, a word which is derived from *ami* (breath). They were distinguished from the inanimate by the fact that they alone were supposed to have 'souls' (*sumus*). It is notable that there was no term for living beings, i.e. a term which would include plants as well as animals, humans, birds, etc. Plants by themselves were known as *orgamal* (growing things). Urgunge said that he thought nowadays, after the advent of universal education, people would extend the word *amidu* (alive, with breath) to plants, making it do the work of a scientific biological concept of life. But what we have to investigate is the world of his childhood in which this extension did not exist. This question is interesting, because cognitive psychologists have shown that the animate/inanimate distinction is recognized very early by children, while a superordinate concept of 'living beings' develops later, around the age of 9 or 10 (Carey 1985; R. Gelman 1990). The lack of a word for 'life' does not mean that Daurs were stuck at some childish stage of cognition as some authors might argue (e.g. Hallpike 1980). Daurs of course recognized that plants grow, decay, and die. What they did not have was an integrated theory of biological organization encompassing all and only plants and animals (cf. Atran 1987: 36). This would suggest that the 'life' of plants was differently conceived from the 'life' of animals and humans.

Yet the Daurs did also have superordinate concepts.[11] As mentioned earlier, all experienced entities in the world seem to have been attributed with a 'spiritual' dimension. Not just the sky and bodies within it, such as the sun, moon, constellations, and stars, and the earth with its components such as the forest and rivers, but also entities within the forest, such as trees, cliffs, or animals, birds, and fish, were supposed to have invisible energy. This was expressed by a variety of words: power (*kuch*), magical energy (*id*), or grandeur (*suli*). Some Daur ethnographers writing in Chinese have tried to express this idea by saying that everything in nature has a soul (Sain Tanaa 1987), but Urgunge assures me that this is incorrect. What everything had was its own kind of indeterminate energy, which was not a 'thing' or a substance or a soul, and this could be verbally described in various ways. This quality correlated with what a particular entity looked like and its place in the landscape: it was greater for majestic, unusual, or lone objects.[12]

We have already met another way of talking about this invisible energy. This is the idea of the (spirit) master (*ejin*), which focused or personified the particular type of power of that object. It is quite difficult to explain how this idea worked, since it applied at several levels (e.g. among humans, the *ejin* might be the Manchu Emperor and, at the domestic level, the *geri ejin* was the master of the house). What is important is that the idea of masters allowed people to talk about the inner or concealed power of entities in the world and to have human-like intentional relations with them. In this view natural objects 'gave' things to human beings, who were to use them in ways corresponding to the given parameters of nature. So stones should not be thrown in rivers, nor sticks chucked into forests, which would be to reject the things created by the river *ejin* and the forest *ejin* (Ikeshiri [1943] 1982: 66); rather, stones should be piled on mountain cairns to renew and support mountains.

2.1.3 Mountains: the question of invariancy

Urgunge was quite clear that mountains are material, solid, cohesive objects that cannot change or move of their own accord. They are not alive and they have no soul (*sumus*). Basically, the everyday Daur concept of *aul* is just like the English category 'mountain' and the objects we would recognize as mountains they would too.

In most of Mongolia one sees nothing but mountains. Immediately in the foreground there may be a valley with a fringe of tree-topped hills. Beyond that six or eight mountain chains may be visible in the clear air, lying as it were in a semi-circle, one behind the other, tier upon tier, with a great range gleaming in the pale background. I once asked Urgunge, 'If you imagine a mountain, how does it look?' He replied, 'As soon as you say "*aul*", you think of a huge solid shape like this (he made a pyramid shape with his hands starting from the peak). Then you will think of a lot of rocks and trees on that one, and at the top, an *oboo* (a ritual cairn of stones). There are small tracks coming down.' This reply suggests that *aul* (mountain) evokes a prototypical image, something which must be *found* in the landscape.

For Urgunge describing it, the prototypical mountain is huge. It looms over you; it reaches up to *tengger*. In that case it is *suliti* (majestic), and especially if you can see some human shape in it, if you can imagine a head, shoulders, arms, that mountain will have some special power. Such mountains exist in Mongolia, China, and Japan, but Urgunge said that he simply does not feel the same about mountains in England. This is not because English mountains do not have the necessary grandeur, but because 'that attitude is not there'. This suggests that, for him at least, a religious stance towards mountains is part of his psychological internalization of a prevailing cultural context; that is, it is not simply an unmediated and spontaneous reaction to the visual perception of any mountain. Nevertheless, everything he said indicates that it is the physical properties of mountains (in Mongolia) that initiate evocations.

It may well be that worshipped mountains do actually have physical features which make them easier to imagine in a human image than surrounding hills. Certainly it is not the case that any convenient protuberance is chosen: often the worshipped mountain is difficult to get to and not at all easy to climb up. All I can say about this is that after many years of travelling in Inner Asia I have the impression that anyone with similar experience would not be surprised when they discover which one in a range of hills is chosen for worship. There does really seem to be some felicity of shape, or awesomeness, which people respond to.

Mountains are worshipped by communities of men. But it is interesting that reverence for mountains in Mongolia can also be personal. In Halh Mongolia people sometimes have their own sacred mountains.[13] And, on the Tuva–

Mongolia border at one eerie place, rather than a single cairn, I have seen innumerable tiny ones, teetering 'sculptures' of piled-up stones. This was like a forest of *oboo*s, irregularly covering a whole area of mountain, and evidently added to by individuals or small groups from time to time. This suggests that there is a back-and-forth interaction between personal percep- tions of grandeur, cultural representations of 'awesome places', individual acts of reverence, realizations that many other people have found this place awesome, and so forth.

But perhaps this is not all there is to say. Looking again at some ethnographic descriptions it occurred to me that the very relationship between perception and cultural representations may be set out as an issue in the case of the worshipped mountains. The first account comes from that cheerful and recep- tive traveller in Buryat country, Bassett Digby:

It was about a mile up to the top of the holy hill, from which there was a wonderful view. . . . I passed an odd pillar made up of a few rocks placed one on top of another. A few hundred feet on I chanced to look back—and the pillar had assumed the perfect silhouette of a little hunch-backed brown-robed man! The witch-doctors are very clever at making these mysterious figures, entirely of uncarved rocks; subsequently I found several of them, always set up so they would be visible against the sky-line from some track across the steppe. (1928: 162–3)

The second was written by Owen Lattimore in Inner Mongolia in the 1930s:

The Great Cairn or Banner Obo of West Sunit is an example of a site that is just about as auspicious as it can be. As we came towards it from the west—and they say it is the same from any direction—we first saw it from many miles away, looking as though it were on top of a commanding mountain. Then as we went toward it the hill seemed to sink, and for a number of miles we did not see it at all. Then we caught sight of it again, but looking much smaller, instead of larger. Again it fell out of sight and again we saw it—but this time a mere knob. Finally, we came, as it were, into its presence, and could see all of the hill; then we found that it stood isolated in a plain. It was not such a very great hill; though majestic it was not too severe, but by Mongol ideas benign and protecting. (1942: 215)

The third is an account by the Mongolian scholar Rinchen discussing cliff- engravings on sacred mountains:

Some of these images have been created so that they come to life only for a few short moments in the rays of the sun. A quarter of an hour, a few minutes, and the images grow dark again, and again become one with the dark rock. Some of them are visible only in the morning; others only during the day; still others only come to life in the rays of the setting sun. (Rinchen 1962).

These accounts suggest that the selection of a mountain as the (sacred) moun- tain places at issue the relationship between the viewer and the object. This is an interesting question in relation to the psychology of perception. Gibson rejects the idea of the static perceiver who looks at objects like a spectator confronting a picture.

The standard approach to vision begins with the eyes fixed and exposed to a momentary pattern of stimuli. . . . The ecological approach to visual perception works from the opposite end. It begins with the flowing array of the observer who walks from one vista to another, moves around an object of interest, and can approach it for scrutiny, thus extracting the invariants that underlie the changing perspective structures and seeing the connections between hidden and unhidden surfaces. . . . The classical puzzles that arise with this kind of vision are resolved by recognizing that the invariants are weaker and the ambiguities stronger when the point of observation is motionless. (Gibson 1979, quoted in Freeman and Cox 1985: 23)

The Mongols recognize this feature of perception, it seems to me, and they construct the sacred object in such a way that it requires the subject to become conscious of the relativity of perception and to arrive at knowledge by means of bodily movement. To achieve greater knowledge, that is, to perceive what Gibson calls 'the invariants', the viewer must be on the move. The viewer must accept the conditionality of his or her perception at any one point in order to understand the true nature of the object. This forces viewers to recognize their own spatial–temporal subordination in relation to the totality of the mountain (or in Richen's case to the sacred drawings, which are there but cannot usually be seen). In various ways, the Mongols choose the mountain (the rocks, etc.) in such a way as to construct this situation, which emphasizes the qualities all such physical objects actually have, namely, immovability, solidity, and invariance. As we shall see (3.1), circular movement is essential in the ritual cult of mountains. Because the human movement involved in perceiving this invariance happens in time, the mountain's quality of 'being' or 'standing' is also conceived as a process—the process, if you like, of being the same. This is an intense preoccupation in the ideological concepts of social categories which the cult at the *oboo* seeks to reproduce.

It must be admitted that these ethnographic accounts all come from nomadic areas and that Urgunge had nothing to say about the ingenious argument I have just made.[14] He said simply that when there is a majestic (*suliti*) mountain people feel that it has a genius or spirit. *Suli* or *suri* is a quality of might or impressiveness tied to physical–psychic presence. It therefore disappears at death in the case of humans ('Winston Churchill was *suliti*,' said Urgunge, 'and his *suli* died with him. But English people will go on respecting it for generations.'). With mountains this quality is inseparable from the mountain and was there when the mountain first came into existence in the unknown past and therefore it is something which is permanent. The idea of *ejin* ('master') and in Mongolia and Buryatiya also *khan* (pl. *khad*) ('lord') is an anthropomorphized version of this. The idea is not that the spirit-master of a mountain rules over (subjugates) the mountain, but that it exists as the permanent genius of the awesomeness of the mountain.

Mostly people do not imagine these powers as having any separate appearance from that of the mountain, cliff, etc. itself. I was told this by many Daur people. However, Urgunge sometimes visualized mountain spirit-masters as the epitome of long life, old men, with white beards, wrinkled faces, and shining black eyes. Spirit-masters had a limited range of things they did. They simply 'made happen' the things that occurred in the mountain area anyway. Thus berries and other things used by humans found on their slopes were said to be 'given' by them, and flocks of birds or herds of deer were 'sent' by them. If the domestic animals sickened, or the crops were attacked by a plague of insects, that was also said to have been intended by the mountain (or the mountain-spirit).[15] They were also implicated in the 'sending' of rain and other weather conditions, even though logically one would imagine this to be the function of the sky. In all these matters mountains were attributed with one simple emotional oscillation: they were supposed to get 'angry' if people did not pay them respect, and they were 'pleased' at the offerings people gave them. Women were anathema to mountains. Daur women were not supposed to climb to mountain tops and they did not attend *oboo* ceremonies. This, Urgunge said, was because their uncleanness would offend the mountain. The same prohibition applied in many parts of Inner Asia (Abayeva 1992: 86).[16]

2.1.4 The forest: realms of gain and killing

The forest (*hoi shibee*) was the whole boundless wooded wilderness beyond the ploughed fields and pastures. An inclusive spirit patrolled this landscape. Bayin Achaa (literally 'rich father') was master of the forest and controlled its wealth, such as animals, game-birds, and fruits. Bayin Achaa was considered to be the kindest of all nature spirits, the epitome of generosity, such that one would call someone of good character a *bainachaa*. Bayin Achaa was both one and many, existing in each place and throughout the wilderness in general.

Let us think about the forest as a world. Urgunge once casually remarked, 'Wild animals of the forest have two kings [*khan*], the tiger [*tasaga*], and the lion [*arsalang*].'

c. The lion? But you don't have lions in Manchuria.
u. They will be thinking of . . . er . . . what is it in English? Leopard. Leopard is just like lion, is that right?
c. But you don't have leopards either.
u. I mean the panther . . . spotted . . .
c. [*doubtfully*] But . . .
u. *Shuluus* [lynx], we do definitely have.
c. But a *shuluus* is not a leopard. Nor is it a lion!
u. No, that is true. So the conclusion is: in reality the *khan* of animals is the tiger; in imagination the *khan* is also the lion, even if we did not have lions in Mongolia.

6. Bayin Achaa carved from a tree trunk. Morin Dawaa in 1987. Date and photographer unkown. [2.1]

Everybody knows the story of the lion who jumped to catch the moon, then it died, you see. This is definitely the lion. The tiger never did that.

I have introduced this to show that in conversation 'the forest realm' can become a kind of ideal category which almost suggests a trajectory for talk to proceed along, conjuring up kings and lions in it. When talking in this mode, birds and fishes are also said to have their own 'kings'. This creates a quasi-mythical, but authentic world, and I tripped against it in introducing the known reality of the Manchurian forest. This put Urgunge in a false position; it was as if, although he was aware that there are no lions, he was unwilling for our talk not to refer to something real. The forest in certain ways of talking embraces unknown creatures, which reflects the fact that the term *hoi shibee* denotes among other things boundlessness, and of course the actual forest does stretch into the unseen expanse of Siberia.

In practice the categories of matter-of-fact animals, Bayin Achaa, and the 'animal kings' normally arose in different contexts (day-to-day hunting, the idea of 'hunting success', and story-telling, respectively). As Bloch points out ([1977] 1989: 15), there are barriers which usually stop the putting side by side of ideas and concepts emerging within different types of communication. Thus, the logical issue of how Bayin Achaa can 'give' hunters their game, when animals also have a king ruling their lives, and each animal life also has its fate allotted by *tengger*, is not a question to which there is any answer. This shows that the category of 'the forest', which at one level is a single ontological domain, is cross-cut by several contexts of human interest, and that these 'frame the category' in different ways.

Going into the forest, one entered an alien but exciting world which was subject to specific rules. Now people should move silently, stalking (*beichi-*) and watching for prey, as if they themselves were wild creatures. The prey were deceived, it was hoped, by hunters mimicking harmless deer, by roe-deerskin coats worn with the hair outside, boots made of deers' leg skins, and hats made of whole roe deers' heads, with the ears sticking out. If hunting involved deception from the start, the hunters nevertheless had to behave with respect towards animals, having placed themselves in their world. The forest thus was a *moral* arena. For the Daurs, one idea was simply that all entities have their destinies which should be left to take their course. Thus it would be wrong to pick up a stone and violently throw it for no particular reason. However humble an entity may be, it still has a right to exist undisturbed in its own way.[17] One should not take a whip anywhere near the fishing-grounds (just as one should not take a whip into a human dwelling), as this would be a sign of aggressive intent towards fishes. Prominent mountains, large animals, and even fish should be referred to by respectful terms, not the ordinary words for them.[18] Someone who maliciously hurt an animal would certainly be despised. Such violations of ongoing normal processes were said to cause incalculable harm elsewhere: 'If you hit one cow's horn, a thousand cow's horns will reverberate.'[19]

Now it might well be the destiny of a person to be a hunter or fisherman, and anyone was justified in killing a harmful, aggressive beast. But all of these activities should only be carried out to the degree which was necessary for human life. If hunters killed a large, respected animal, such as a bear or a tiger, or fishermen took a particularly big fish, they would 'cry' in strange voices, 'Waaa! Waaa! We are sorry that we have killed you! Waaa!' Urgunge and the other boys of Bokorchien found this grown-up 'crying' for a fish rather funny, perhaps because fishing for them was only a pastime and the professional fishermen were a separate group from outside the village, but he took rather more seriously the lament for hunted animals. Now this 'crying' (*waila-*) was not addressed to the lord of the forest or river, but to the animal itself. In other words, it was not a recognition of the proprietorship of Bayin Achaa, the spirit-lord of the forest, but was a formal acknowledgement of the animal's separate

right to existence and sorrow at its death. There were explicit ideas of retribution to follow if animals were treated wrongly. Urgunge said that if a bear or
tiger were killed and no rites performed, its mate might come at night to the
hunter's camp and kill the horses. Among many Siberian peoples there were
rituals, not involving the forest master, to ensure that the killed animal would
be replaced in the forest (Hamayon 1990: 380–1). For the Daurs there is no
detailed information on this. I know only that for large animals rituals involved
respectful treatment of the *zulde*, the head, windpipe, heart, and lungs, in other
words the organs of breath and life (*ami*). The hunter, Urgunge said, should
always share meat if he met a stranger in the forest, but he should never on any
account give away the *zulde*, which was the hunter's 'luck' (the assurance that
the soul of the killed beast would return in animal form).

It may seem improbable, but I wish to propose here that the whole idea of
Bayin Achaa as giver of game-wealth was a different concern (context of
interest) from that of the hunter's relationship to animals as prey. Both contexts
involved morality. Bayin Achaa's sphere was success from the hunt, and what
he gave had to be shared equally, whoever did the killing. The central moral
idea was that the forest belonged to all Daurs of the Eight Banners who had
come down from the Amur River in ancestral times, and 'in order to preserve
the wealth bestowed on us by the mountain forests we should not fight one
another for it but share it equally, and to break these rules would be to profane
the deeds of the ancestors' (Ikeshiri 1981: 73). But in the context of shamans'
explanations for human death the plea that Bayin Achaa had granted you a lot
of game was not a justification for overmuch killing, and it did not exempt you
from supernatural retribution of the animals. In fact the existential problem of
causing death and pain applied even to one single animal as prey, whereas what
Bayin Achaa granted was a collective object of acquisition, game. In the context
of Bayin Achaa, the hunting spirit, it was nothing but glorious to amass great
heaps of slaughtered animals and birds.

Hamayon (1990: 78) has perceptively described the forest wilderness as a
milieu, as opposed to a site. The name *bayin achaa* (rich father) suggests that
this was seen at one level as a bountiful, giving milieu (see Bird-David 1990).
'That one [Bayin Achaa] is like a money god', Urgunge once said, and this is
apt, since the Daurs had used furs from the hunt to pay taxes to the Manchus,
and in Urgunge's day furs were used to sell and barter for goods with Chinese
traders. But the notion of the bountiful milieu was not salient in all contexts,
and it did not make other ideas about the forest and hunting unthinkable. What
the notion of Bayin Achaa did was to allow desire for gain to be separated from
the more problematic question of taking life. Thus we can see the category of
wild animals as divided into two disconnected spheres, 'game' and 'prey'. This
was a morally ambiguous situation and we shall find that the discontinuity
could not be conveniently forgotten. It was shamanic myth that resurrected the

question of 'prey', and abruptly confronted the rash excess of hunting with the preciousness of a single life (6.5).

2.1.5 Rivers: movement and history

In Urgunge's childhood people were rather scared of large rivers (*mur*).[20] They were more frightened of the Naun River flooding than of winter storms or wildfires. Few people could swim. Urgunge's abiding memory of the Naun is of nearly drowning one day, when despite his mother's having told him not to go near the water, he fell off his horse as it was swimming across the river. He only saved himself by grabbing the horse's tail.

In everyday life rivers (*mur*) were conceptualized in several ways: as economic resources, as a series of natural reaches,[21] and as moving bodies of water. The economic interest in rivers as places for fishing and paths for transporting logs was similar to the interest in mountains as places where game and other riches could be found. Urgunge told me that all large rivers had their own spirit-master (*usun-khan* 'water-lord'), which was invisible and lived in the depths of the water. The *usun-khan* of the Naun was imagined by him yet again as an old man with a long white beard and bright eyes. This spirit was said to be very rich and to 'give' fish to people and preserve them in safety when travelling on the river. Boatmen, fishermen, and loggers made offerings of fish to it. As with the forest and mountains, women were supposed to keep away from fishing-reaches and any contact with fishing equipment. Despite his frightening experience of nearly drowning, Urgunge did not take Usun-Khan very seriously. As a boy he dared to urinate in the river, and he joked, 'Why did they offer fish? Usun-Khan likes fish, not chips.'

Urgunge once tried to explain to me the sense in which the river was a boundary. The term *zak*, he said, was not quite like the English word 'boundary', which he understood as an artificial line drawn across an undifferentiated space. The Daur idea of *zak* was more akin to 'edge', or the end of one space and the beginning of a new different one. Thus 'the other side of the river' was in some way qualitatively different from this side, and we can see this idea emerging in shamanic stories where the river formed a boundary between this world and the world of the dead (see 6.3), or where one of the abilities of the shaman was that he could freeze the river at will so that people could cross it.

The most salient aspect of rivers, however, had to do with their wateriness and flow. Rivers in this sense were roads or ways. The word for river (*mur*) is the same as that for animal tracks, as though, looking from a height, one could in both cases see traces of journeys across the earth. The river's carrying of people implied a passage of time in which power was attained as the current bore them to their destination.[22] Urgunge vividly remembers his own journey down river from the bandit lair to his own home. He also has dim memories of a story about one of his ancestors, Chipaatii, who floated down the river to petition the Manchu Emperor at Mukden.[23] The story concerns historical persons, known from Chinese sources about the seventeenth century (*DSHI* 1985: 13, 19, 31), but it has a mythical quality, which crystallizes into a singular adventure what must actually have been many different migrations of the Daur tribes. Essentially the story tells of the Daurs' submission to the Manchus and their acquisition of military rank in the Manchu Empire. I give this story at some length, because it is a foundational part of Daur history and various points in it (not particularly relevant to the question of rivers) will be referred to later in this book.

A long time ago when the Daurs were living on the northern bank of the Amur River, there was a chief called Baldachi who was a royal son-in-law and the military governor of the area. Chipaatii Old Man also lived there and thus he was a subject of Baldachi. Chipaatii had a very beautiful young wife. Baldachi stole her and made Chipaatii a servant. He cut off Chipaatii's legs at the knees, so the Old Man could only crawl. One day Chipaatii's wife said, 'If this continues he will torture you to death. You had better go away. Go to the Emperor at Mukden and petition against Baldachi.' She secretly made some dried cakes and saddled the horse called Khan Haliu (Otter King). One night when everyone had gone to bed Chipaatii mounted the horse, jumped the three-bar fence, and rode away. Next day, Baldachi tried to chase him, but could not catch up.

Chipaatii Old Man galloped on and on. They were living on an upper tributary of the Amur River which was very far from Mukden. When he arrived at the Upper Naun, his food was already used up. There was nothing to eat. He killed Khan Haliu and made dried horsemeat (this place was later called Khan Haliu). He loaded his meat on a raft of fallen logs and floated off down the river Naun. But the raft was very unstable and wavered from right to left. Chipaatii brought it to the bank, got off and lay on the bank and looked at the sky. There was a bird flying up there, and when it moved its tail it could change direction, and when it moved its wings it could change its flying speed. Chipaatii thought he could make the raft do the same as the bird. He made a wooden tail (rudder) and two flat wings (oars), and then the raft flew down the river very smoothly, and it went just as Chipaatii wanted it to go. Flowing along he reached the Butha area. He had finished his horsemeat. There were people here, so he could ask for food, and he met generous people who gave him provisions. He made porridge and continued on down the river to Mukden.

Arriving at the palace he offered some sable furs and petitioned against Baldachi. But Baldachi was also there, and seeing Chipaatii he was very angry. Kneeling before the Emperor he dared not beat Chipaatii, but he took out his knife and scratched the jade floor of the palace as a threat, yelling 'Chipaatii, Baldachi, to! to! (spitting)'. The Emperor was highly insulted, and said, 'Look, coming here and acting in this unmannerly way, one can see how lawlessly he must be acting up there. He is most arrogant and should be punished.' The Emperor decreed that Baldachi's property should be confiscated and nine generations of his people be killed. Baldachi was executed, but some of his people hid and made their escape. They changed their name to Jingkir. The

Emperor said to Chipaatii, 'You have certainly suffered,' and rewarded him with a first-grade red button of rank with a peacock feather and a hat.[24] Chipaatii put the button in his pocket. When the Emperor asked why he did this, he said, 'On the way so many people helped me, and they are my benefactors,' meaning that he owed them a debt of gratitude and wanted to give the button to them. The Emperor thought for a while and decided that this was certainly a very loyal person. So he decreed that buttons of rank be given to each of the benefactors. Chipaatii then wore his own button and gave a red first-grade button to each of the people where he had stayed the night or taken food. This is the origin of the hereditary ranks of the Daur. (*DSHI* 1985: 31)

Here, the flow of the river southwards with its tributaries parallels the movement of the tribute-bearing tribes towards the Emperor. The passage downstream, during which the image of a bird transforms the raft into a purposeful and functional vehicle, gathers in the clans as benefactors and patrons of the crippled Chipaatii's endeavour, and gives him the strength to succeed in his petition to the Emperor. This action is repaid by the outward distribution of rank and office from the imperial court to the provinces. The river system was thus a map of the Empire considered as a political relationship, from the Daur point of view. It is worth noting here that in a different Daur myth, a journey back up river, against the stream to the outer north, leads to a strange 'other world' belonging to a time long ago (see 3.1).

2.1.6 Trees: singular and communal regeneration

The basic Daur folk category 'tree' (*mood*) was like the European folk category (a large woody plant, but not something which has a botanical definition). A tree was made up of roots (*undes*), the entirety of the roots plus a 'growth-point' just above them (*hojoor*), the stem, and the branches, leaves, and seeds. It did not have a soul.

Trees, like rivers and the forest, were taken up in greatly differing religious and ritual contexts. Meanwhile let us see what Urgunge said about them. Urgunge thought that certain particular trees, if they stood out in the land-scape, or had dense, luxuriant foliage, would have special energy and might have spirit-masters (*ejin*). However, as is the way with singular objects, there happened to be no such trees near Urgunge's village, which was surrounded by scrub and steppe. The only *ejintei mood* he had heard about was miles away in the Xing-an Mountains. He reminded me, though, of the cluster of beautiful pines growing at the village graveyard. The graves were sited there because of the trees, and not the other way around. Urgunge said that graves must be near to evergreen trees, pines or cedars, because these remain green and 'alive' through the long months of winter snow.

Stories (*urgil*) are not to be confused with commonsense knowledge, or with explanations for rituals, but I cite one of them to show how Daurs speculated about the 'alive but inanimate' characteristic of trees.[25]

Daurs believed in shamanism and especially worshipped tree spirits. Pine-trees and birch-trees, when they get very old, become spirits. No one should cut them down at will. No matter who cuts them, blood will come out of the tree and this is unlucky.[26] From some trees, spring-water flows out from their heart. It is said that this spring-water can cure diseases.

When I was a young boy I heard this story about Moodo Yadgan (Tree Shaman). There was a young hunter who was preparing to go to the mountains to hunt. Late in the evening, he was resting under an old elm-tree. When he lay down under the tree, and he was not yet sleeping, the tree started to sway. The hunter thought it was very strange, because there was no wind at all. 'How can the tree shake like this?' he thought. While he was looking, a very small willow next to the elm also started to sway. Soon the willow started to talk:

'Tree Shaman, I asked you to come today. My mother is very ill—can you come to look at her?'

The elm-tree said, 'Today I have a guest in my house. I cannot leave him alone. In this mountain we have a lot of evil spirits. If I went, they would harm my guest.'

The willow swayed a little and said, 'My mother may die while I am waiting. It has been a few days already that she has not drunk water and has not taken food. You tell me what I should do.'

The old elm shook itself and said, 'My old neighbour, no matter how much you beg me, I cannot leave my house.'

'My mother is seriously ill, I'm asking you just once.'

'My old neighbour, in my opinion your mother has a terminal disease. I don't think she will last till tomorrow noon. Even if I go, it will be no use.'

The small willow swayed and said sarcastically, 'Thank-you, Tree Shaman.'

The young hunter sat for a while under the old elm-tree. When he heard no more, he got up courteously and bowed to the Tree Shaman, and said, 'My honorable Tree Shaman, I have heard everything you said. It is all because of me that you did not go to take care of his mother's illness. I am very grateful to you.'

Tree Shaman said, 'This is my duty. You should not be too respectful.'

The hunter said, 'It sounds as though you are a famous shaman in this neighbourhood. Can you tell me what game I'll get on this trip? And whether my family is in good health?'

Tree Shaman started to sway, and predicted, 'This hunting trip you'll get a lot of game. Not far from here there is a whitish willow-tree, which is falling over and will hinder your way. That is the mother of the small willow-tree which came earlier.'

The next day the hunter left Tree Shaman and after a few miles sure enough he saw a whitish tree lying across his path. He went round it. When he returned, he brought back many precious beasts. (Sain Tanaa 1987*b*: 247)

In the prologue tree sap is likened both to blood and to spring-water (i.e. to the inner liquids of both animate and inanimate entities), associating trees with both these domains. In the story itself certain ontological characteristics of plants are honoured while the story as a whole creates a fanciful analogy with human society. The specifically biological processes recognized here are so fundamental that most readers will take them for granted: (1) growth changes are predictable and non-random, and living beings increase, but do not decrease, in size with maturation (the child willow is small); (2) inheritance (the mother tree has produced a child tree); (3) species identity is maintained across generations (the mother and the child are both willows); (4) trees experience disease; (5) the need for sustenance (the diseased mother tree is at death's door because she has taken neither food nor water); (6) trees die. The fantastic elements are of course that trees do not speak, have houses, shamans, and so forth. The direction of these imaginings is anthropomorphic, as with the other landscape objects mentioned above, but it is worth noting, in view of the ritual use of trees to be discussed later, that both males and females occur in this story, and for once Urgunge did not say that he imagined tree spirits as old men (he had no image of tree spirits).

The reproduction of trees was an image for religious ideas of human rebirth. The word *hojoor* (roots and 'growth point' of plants) also meant shamanic ancestor-spirit of a clan. Urgunge said, '*Hojoor* means to me very old, very alive.' In myth the souls of unborn children were kept in nests in the branches of trees. As Sagalayev and Oktyabr'skaya write (1990: 52) about the Altaians, who have similar ideas:

The roots and the crown of trees are not radically opposed: there are possibilities of semantic transformations between them. While both roots and crown are connected with situations of *change*, the stem of the tree is the manifestation of *stability*. It is a symbol of the generation living now and simultaneously a real and symbolic support. (Remember the construction of the winter house of Shor hunters: a growing sacred tree was its central prop.) This capacious symbol underlines again that *reality* appears only within the bounds of the middle world; all the rest are possible worlds. The ambivalence in these basic images allows, without contradiction, the ancestors to be 'accommodated' both above and below, in *nature*. The main supposition is simple: the middle world is the world of people. However, the localization of preceding and following 'conditions' is decided situationally.

In Urgunge's eyes too, 'the tree' symbolized a process of rebirth, to which he related the custom of leaving the corpses of very young children and shamans in the branches of trees so that their souls could be reborn again soon (see 3.2).

As well as the singular tree, the Daurs had the idea of a group of twelve different trees, known as the *duwalang* trees (*DSHI* 1985: 257; Batubayin 1990; Odongowa 1991). Each tree was inhabited by a different bird or animal, some of which were mythical creatures. Urgunge remembered nothing about this, and so our information is scanty.[27] We know that Daur clan-villages maintained plantations, but it is unclear what relation (if any) the *duwalang* trees had to them. It is not even clear that *duwalang* trees existed, since the only description of a ritual addressed specifically to them is in the exalted language of the Holieri spirit (see 6.2). According to Odongowa (1991) their vigour or weakness indicated the health of the community (see 4.4).

Batubayin (1990) gives the *duwalang* trees and their creatures as:

> The great willow with *galierte*
> The poplar with owl
> The broad willow with *shimuku* (bird which sucks sap)
> The wild rose with tree-mouse jumping
> The wild plum with eagle
> The white-stemmed red-branched willow with *genshiha*
> The shrub willow with twenty crows
> The larch with ten *angula*
> The white birch with *somuha*
> The *ders* grass[28] with fifty-five sparrows
> The elm with cuckoo
> The camphor tree with python.

Elsewhere in Inner Asia we also find analogies made between the consociation of people in social groups and the consociation of trees in groves.[29] In the Daur case it is perhaps significant that the *duwalang* trees were deciduous and visibly self-renewing, while the grove of pines at the graveyard guarded the ancestors with a more unchanging appearance. However, the *duwalang* trees were not only representative of the vigour of a community, they were definitely associated with shamanship. Each *yadgan* shaman wore representations of all twelve kinds of tree on his magical costume and made images of them for propitiation at the great consecration ritual of *ominan* (5.8). The *duwalang* trees can be contrasted with the *oboo* (mountain cairn). Both images went beyond the simple idea of 'tree' or 'mountain', and they were, rather, archetypal ideals, or symbolic constructs, which crystallized a certain perspective on these ordinary things. The stones and willow branches of the *oboo* were essentially alike, all contributed by the male members of the clan. The *duwalang* trees and their creatures were heterogeneous. The *duwalang* image suggests a different, shamanic, idea of a human community, one which was composed of complex and disparate beings.

2.1.7 Wild animals: identity, metamorphosis, and intentionality

Urgunge said that all animals, including humans, were *amitan* (literally ones with breath'). *Amitan* in its widest sense included birds (*degi*), but extended somewhat uncertainly to insects, worms, and other creatures not seen to breathe. Among animals, wild and domestic classes were distinguished by terms for prototypical members; thus *aduus* (literally 'horses') was used to refer to domestic animals, while the term *gurees* (deer) was used for wild animals in general. Within these classes each 'species' had its own character (*dur*), which was a combination of appearance and temperament, and was derived from close study of their habits and mental and physical abilities. Physiological reproduction in animals was understood to be achieved by the fertilization of the female by the male through sexual intercourse. The Daurs knew through observation of animal heredity that physical and mental characteristics were inherited from both male and female parents. This conflicted with some ideological notions about the primacy of the male and will be discussed later in connection with humans.

An important feature of Daur thinking about animals was that they had their own ineluctable identity. This pertained to the animal species and was acquired through inheritance. This was crucial tacit knowledge, but so central was it that symbolic thought played on it in many different ways. An example is the story Urgunge told me of the blue wolf.[30]

An ordinary wolf was running along and fell into a deep hole. Down there for some reason its fur turned blue. It managed to extricate itself from the hole, but found it was shunned by other wolves because of its strange colour. Unable to bear its isolation, it retreated to a cave, and started a reign of terror, killing other wolves. The wolf population of the forest was puzzled and terrified. Never before had they been attacked in this way. What was this blue creature? Finally a grizzly old pack leader spoke up, 'If the creature you saw is truly a wolf, it will be compelled to howl at the full moon. We have only to wait until the 15th of the month.'

Sure enough, on the day of the full moon, the beast was seen emerging from its cave and slinking with a wolf-like gait through the bushes to the top of a hill. It put its snout in the air, opened its jaws and the howls of its kind filled the night. The waiting pack sprang forward and killed it. Now they knew that the creature was not a devil but just a FREAK.

This story is about 'wolf character' (*guskee dur*), wolf traits which are essential and will be there whatever superficial changes occur.

The story of the blue wolf was often told by one of the boys in the village. Why did Urgunge remember it? It turns out to have unpleasant associations for him: all the boys used to look round and laugh at him when the story-teller reached the word 'freak'. The reason for this is that Urgunge himself was known as 'wolf' (*guskee*) when he was a boy. Was this more than a joke?

To consider this question we need to know about some supporting religious ideas. Religious ideas about animals were quite different from those concerning inanimate entities. Shirokogoroff calls them hypotheses (1935: 76) and the reader may decide whether such a term is appropriate, remembering that 'shamanism' itself was called *lun* ('sayings'). First, all humans, animals, birds, and fishes were thought individually to have immortal souls (*sumus*), the soul being the enduring locus of identity, sentience, and volition. This idea was seen as being proved by the fact of dreams, in which souls had an existence separate from the body and waking consciousness. Souls could take either animal or human form in successive lives. Second, animals were equal to human beings, because the trajectory of their lives was likewise 'destined' by *tengger*. Third, human spirits could take the appearance of animals, as they could of other human beings. In sum, animacy created a domain in which personhood transcended the limits of purely human existence.[31]

Ordinarily the idea that animals had souls like human souls was held in abeyance, but sometimes people did think about it. This happened when someone's personality and physical demeanour seemed to reveal the character (*dur*) of an animal species. When Urgunge was a baby he used to scream at night, and his distraught mother used to carry him out to the yard so that the rest of the family could sleep. Far from quietening down, he would yell even louder, seemingly at the pale disc of the moon in the sky. His eldest brother said, 'He must have been a wolf in a previous life!', and though Urgunge maintains this was a joke, the name stuck. Sometimes people took such ideas seriously. The idea was that the person had a trace of an animal soul, because though their soul was now human, it had belonged to an animal in an earlier life. The reverse was also true: animals might have been humans in previous lives.

U. If a boy walked very slowly, if he was heavy, a bit stupid, then his father and mother
   would think, 'Well, previously he was a cow.' But suppose you were a farmer and you
   had a cow. It was born very bad-tempered, kicked like hell, gave bad looks at you,
   went its own way. You would say, 'That cow must have been a human being, because
   it has such a bad character.' And you think about it and remember that human being
   by yourself.
C. You would think, 'Maybe that was my great-aunt who died'?
U. Yes. Maybe [*laughs*].

The idea worked both forwards and backwards in time. A Daur woman in Hohhot told me that if a child had a big stomach and ate a lot, it would be said that child was previously a pig. On the other hand, she herself had been told by her mother as a child: if you use too much water, next time you will be born as an ox and have to drink a lot of water.[32] It seems that the social context of such ideas about character was mainly in parent–child relationships; in other words, in a situation in which people would speculate about inheritance and inexplicable or unwelcome features in their children. But sometimes people would think in this way about adults too.[33] It is not clear to what extent these ideas about earlier animal existences were internalized, or whether they were just attributes applied to other people. Probably only the agreeable and honourable idea that one had been a tiger was absorbed for oneself. Urgunge remembered a military general who said he had been a tiger in an earlier life. Urgunge said about himself,

No doubt about it, I was someone before I was Urgunge. Perhaps I was my great-great grandfather. When I was 8 I thought I was a shaman in an earlier life. Now I think, maybe I was a tiger before, because a tiger is brave and ventures everywhere—it does not have accustomed tracks like a wolf or a rabbit. The time we are living in is a repetition of what we had before, but in a different shape. Our soul [*sumus*] never dies, but changes shapes, forms [*zus*]. You should know this: there is no time in shamanism. The past is the present, the present is the future, and the future is the past. We never cared *when* something happened in the past. We didn't mind which came first, we only thought about who was a big shot, who was exceptional. What does the present mean? It means simply: you have form. But in our mind, having no form is the highest of all. Think of *tengger*. And you know that Mongol expression *helber-ügüi Dalai Lam* [literally 'without-shape Ocean Lama']. This means he is above all. And the future is just like the past, going back where you came from. When you die you leave your shape here, you are going to meet your ancestors turning round. It may take a long time or a short time.

We shall return later (7.2) to these views of time. But it is important to understand that the idea of persisting animal souls was not logically developed into a system. It was nothing like as definite as the Buddhist theory of *karma*, whereby an animal rebirth is a punishment for accumulated sins. Perhaps the Daur idea was influenced by (or had common roots with) the Buddhist concept of reincarnation, according to which a spiritual identity persists in a series of lives, despite the manifest physical and personality differences from one in-cumbent to another. However, all Daurs I have talked to on this subject judge it to be basically unknowable and more of a speculation than a belief. In fact no one bothered much about the fate of animals' souls. What concerned people was human personality, and traces of animality were a way of talking about this.

Let us pursue another more religiously salient line of thought about animal identity. Animals, birds, fishes, invertebrates, and insects were thought to be the corporeal vessels of shamanic spirits in their wanderings. This was thought to happen in the present, here and now, not like the speculations about the future and past we have just been discussing. I am not referring here to the fact that shamanic spirits had 'seats' in trees or rocks, just as animals had lairs and humans had dwellings, but about these spirits' metamorphoses as animals. Among the Daurs it was only within the domain of animacy, human and non-human, that shamanic spirits transformed from one mode of being to another.

What is at issue here is the understanding of metamorphosis (the Daurs used the expression *zus hobila-* ('to change appearance') for this, and also simply *bolo-* ('to become')). Were spirits of human origin thought actually to turn into animals? Urgunge said *hobila-* means to change, 'but not completely'. I am inclined to agree with Shirokogoroff (1935: 164–5) that human spirits retained their identity and did not entirely become animals, and therefore that the Daurs (until the recent advent of the *kiant* cult, see below) cannot be said to have worshipped animals as such. This contrasts with the case of the sky or moun-tains which were worshipped in themselves. Animals, on the other hand, were like humans, and should themselves engage in worship. The point is worth making because many ethnographies of North Asia misleadingly suggest, for

example, that 'people X worship the eagle'.[34] The religious concern was with
the spirit, not with the animal or human which was its temporary manifestation. However, the confusion is easy to understand, since the spirits taking over
animals were not imagined separately from them. There were no old men with
long white beards here. Shamanic spirits, *barkan*, *shurkul*, or *onggor*, had the
psychological characteristics and abilities of the animals while they were in
them, or rather while they *appeared as* them, but they also had an intentionality
of their own, derived from the human history that made them spirits. So a deer
with a spirit in it looked and behaved just like an ordinary deer, but some tiny
thing it did might reveal that it had a human (spirit) purpose. If you met a wild
animal, normally it would not even occur to you to wonder if it is a spirit or not.
Animals are just animals. But you might have such an idea if an animal suddenly behaved strangely and at the same time there was something wrong, if
you had some inexplicable illness or bad luck. Then that fox really might not be
what it seemed.

   Now though in principle a spirit could appear as any animal, some species
cropped up as affected in this way much more often than others. Shirokogoroff
had one explanation for this, Urgunge has another. I suggest that this difference represents a historical change in shamanic thinking. In Urgunge's view,
which I see as a later development, an elk, deer, tiger, wolf, bear, fish, hare,
lynx, squirrel, goose, duck, or swallow would rarely turn out to harbour a spirit.
The reason is that these creatures are straightforward and their habits are well
known. Some of them may be dangerous to people, but one knows what to
expect. Now a deer acting in a strangely purposeful way might be a spirit, but
deer almost never do this. Foxes, on the other hand, are of their nature
unpredictable and mysterious, sly and deceitful. 'They are living devils,'
Urgunge said. 'They cause people to be ill, to fall over, to lose balance.' This
shows that in practice he elided the distinction between animals' natures and
the presence of spirits, since he gave the *habitual* behaviour of foxes as an
explanation for the fact that they sometimes turned out to harbour spirits. The
other creatures listed by Urgunge as spirit-ridden were: snake, porcupine (or
hedgehog), *solong* (*mustela sibirica*—somewhat like a weasel), pheasant, and
spider. For each of these he gave an explanation in terms of their tricky and
harmful natures. Snakes and spiders are poisonous, pheasants steal corn, por-
cupines spike people, and so forth.

   The other explanation, Shirokogoroff's (1935: 164–5; 175), for the distribution of spirits among wild animals is simply the widespread and indeed main-
stream idea that spirits make use of those animal abilities which humans do not
have. Spirits 'become' animal after animal in sequence as they seek to gain their
ends. So, among the Tungus, the main animal manifestations of spirits turn out
to be: the tiger and bear for their strength; the hare for its winding tracks which
are difficult to follow; the elk and maral deer for their fighting antlers; the
solong, fox, and sable for their ability to penetrate without being noticed; the

eagle for its relentless attack; several kinds of bird for flying; and the carp for its ability to swim under ice. All of these were also important manifestations for spirits among the Daur, to judge from shamans' invocations. This line of thinking again crystallized out particular qualities (*dur*) of animal species, but it was taken far more seriously than the '*X* was *Y* in a previous birth' idea, since it implied danger to humans: the spirit infused with dynamic human intelligence the entire behaviour of the animal and made use of animal abilities too. Daurs in Urgunge's childhood believed in the existence of spirits and quite often interpreted inexplicable events as signs of their presence—though ordinary people could never be quite sure, since they only ever saw an animal possessed by a spirit in fleeting, omen-like encounters. But, in a double transformation, spirit into animal and animal into shaman, the *yadgan* enacted the emblematic animal qualities in an instantaneously recognizable way. Shamans had their own repertoires, a snuffling here, a characteristic four-footed gait there, a pawing, or an eye movement, which brought the spirit-as-animal vividly to the mind's eye.

So far we have mentioned wild animals made use of by spirits because of their extra-human abilities, and wild animals liable to be possessed by spirits because of their intrinsically harmful natures. I suggest that this latter idea developed in a new direction in the early twentieth century. Rather than being the vessels of human spirit metamorphosis, certain animals were now thought to be able to *turn themselves* into spirits. This may seem to be a trivial difference, but it turns out to be a dramatic one in Daur thinking. The nature of these creatures was such that they were thought to have the supernatural ability to prolong life indefinitely. Certain species, not the largest or most impressive, but the most 'spooky', according to Urgunge, notably the fox, the snake, porcupine, pheasant, spider, and *solong*, could concentrate their powers and thus prolong their lives by ritual breathing exercises (*lien ch'i*). By day the creatures hibernated in caves, but they came out at night and concentrated their mental powers while addressing their breath to the moon. After a thousand years such were-animals became huge and immortal.[35] The exercises could work for good or harm. For 'respectful' behaviour (*dor dasa-*) the creature became a benign spirit, but far more commonly it became an evil one (*shurkul*). Such a spirit retained its animal essence but had the power to transform itself into any other desired form, especially that of beguilingly beautiful or impressive humans. According to Shirokogoroff (1935: 158), who notes the emergence of this idea among the Northern Tungus and Manchus as well as the Daurs, the were-animals became wiser than man and therefore could attain immortality. After one thousand years they became black; after ten thousand they became wiser still and white.

Readers will notice that the were-creatures are the same as Urgunge's list of 'harmful' animals, and certainly the two ideas (that animals are possessed by human spirits and that some animals can turn into were-spirits) are indistinctly tied up together in his mind. Nevertheless, it is clear that the cult of were-animals was a historically new phenomenon, which broke into the complex of 'shamanism' in the decade before Urgunge was born. 'Mafarism' (from *mafa* ('ancestor'), the Manchu term for these animal and certain other new spirits) was first introduced by wandering Chinese Daoist and Buddhist monks, rapidly became popular among the Manchus, and it spread to the Daurs and from them to the Birarchen Tungus in the 1910s (Shirokogoroff 1935: 237).[36] Non-serious attacks by these *mafa* (in Daur *kiant*) spirits could be dealt with by anyone. However, some Daur groups had a special kind of professional sorcerer (*kianchi*) to deal with them (Batubayin 1990). These Daur specialists were highly sought among the Tungus, who rapidly came to copy their techniques and add their own flourishes. What is quite clear is that these sorcerers were different from *yadgan* shamans: they had new, dramatic rituals, could only deal with *mafa* spirits, and did not go into the same kind of trance.

Now for Urgunge, and other Daur commentators, the ideas about immortal spirits of animal origin were simply part of 'shamanism'. It seems that by his time they had become an important component of the ideas knocking around in that compendious category. But the documented fact of their recent emergence forces us to realize that 'shamanism' is disjunct and that its parts have their history. The idea of were-animals is possibly of extremely ancient Daoist origin, but it was only taken up by the native peoples of Manchuria as a distinctive religious practice at a time of extreme social crisis. Just as interesting as the socio-political context of the were-animal cult is its intellectual content. Why should people have suddenly become concerned with the idea of immortal were-animals? Why were ordinary shamans (*yadgan*) incapable of dealing with these spirits? These questions will be discussed in 7.1 and 2.

A summary will suggest more clarity than this material actually has, but nevertheless I give one. Wild animals were normally just wild animals, but there were three ways in which they could be more than that. They might have souls which were reincarnations of previously human souls, a speculative and tentative idea. They might be the temporary manifestations of human spirits (*onggor*, *barkan*, and *shurkul*), the earlier shamanic idea. These two ideas continued, but they were joined by a new theory, that certain uncanny animals could turn themselves into spirits by ritual practices, the idea behind the *mafa* cult. The advent of the *mafa* spirits made this disturbing difference: in earlier days if you saw an animal behaving strangely you might suspect it was really a human spirit. The new *mafa* theory told you, if you see a human being behaving oddly, especially a beautiful or impressive person, he or she might really be a wild and harmful animal.

In all these cases the *distinction* between animals and human beings was recognized by the representation of animals as species, whereas humans were individuals; the *equivalence* of animals and humans was acknowledged by those ideas which represented both as having individual and interchangeable souls (see Ingold 1986: 248; Hamayon 1990: 386). I have indicated here how Daurs employed what seem to be universal concepts of animality, the ideas of essential identity pertaining to species, biological processes, and intentional explanations of animal behaviour, to speculate about human personality and powers. In shamanic and mythological contexts, personhood transcended the distinction between human and animal.

Thus understandings of the human personality were projected outwards, seeking for likenesses in the past, in attributes of birds and animals, anyway 'out there', rather than looking for explanations in personal life-history or family relationships. Perhaps we can relate this to the rigid expectations of family and kin relations, which in everyday life were impossible to question. Urgunge told me that it would have been unthinkable and demeaning for him to query, or even really think about, his relationship with his father or the effect this might have had on his own personality. On the other hand, as we shall see, the shamanic human spirits I have briefly introduced here were concerned with just these questions of human relationships. They could take temporary animal form for some particular purpose, but in themselves shamanic spirits had a genesis in the dark and unspoken parts of individual human lives. Roaming abroad, human spirits disturbed the world, injecting creatures and even objects with feeling and intelligence. A reverse move, engulfing human lives with 'external' feral energies, took place with the advent of the *mafa* cults.

2.1.8 Conclusion

I chose the various subjects described in this section because they seem to have formed the most salient domains in the Daurs' concepts of the world around them. Perhaps each of them could be described as 'landscapes'. Though one occasionally comes across symbolic ideas that seem to have linked different domains, far more characteristic is their absence. The effect of this was the situating of humanity in many versions of the world, as it were slatted over one another, each one elaborated and extended in such a way as to come to different causal understandings of human society and personality. Thus the conventional social divisions described in Section 1.2 were not the only way people were seen to differ from one another. People, individually and collectively, also were likenesses of the world outside. We can see this in the idea of the 'cow-like boy' or the generous person who was a village *bainachaa* in the image of the forest. I think these were not mere metaphors (nor were they axioms deriving from the anthropological mirage of autonomously existing 'culture'). These images of people in the likeness of the 'divisions of the world' could supersede those generated by purely social rules of identity, membership, and succession. For example, the men who went to worship at the *oboo* constituted the group of rock-like solidity envisaged in the likeness of a mountain, and this was more important than genealogical rules of eligibility about who could attend, which were, as we saw, partially forgotten. Similarly, it is arguable that the mixed-sex group which went to make a ritual cultivation of the *duwalang* trees (see 4.4) saw itself in the image of that diverse and fruitful grove, and was constituted by this self-image, at least as much as by some prior social delineation.

A particular way of talking recognized the existence of discrete entities in the world, yet linked them in one universal conflictual arena, and this was the discourse of power. As we have seen, humans, animals, mountains, trees, and so forth were all thought to have their own 'energy', and it was highly important that such powers/energies could be strong or weak, thus engaging in interactive existence. To give an example, it was said that a man with strong spiritual energy (*sul'd*) could kill any number of foxes, even though foxes are dangerous and might well contain devils (*shurkul*).[37] However, it would be unwise for such a man to do this, because though the fox power would not be strong enough to harm him, it might well prevail over the weak vital energy of that man's children. Other examples of this way of thinking were given in 1.2, where it was noted that Urgunge's father's bold spirit was said directly to affect the psychic state of his ailing neighbour, and 1.3, where the Baglain spirit attacked the power of the red cliff. The Daurs' talk of the world in terms of such essentially conflictual powers is not of course the same as the distinctions I have been drawing in this chapter which are based on my understanding of mostly unstated conceptual distinctions made by them. However, such a Daur view, which acknowledged difference and placed unlike beings in a pervasive balancing of powers, is perhaps to be expected in this kind of religion, one which achieved its legitimacy from multifarious intentional experiences rather than from a unified dogma.

2.2 Experience and Language

It has just been suggested that some of the Daurs' religious ideas were 'authenticated by experience' and I must now explain this expression. I shall argue that categories created in language formed religious representations, but that their felt authenticity was guaranteed primarily by non-linguistic and direct modes of experiencing natural phenomena. This seems to me characteristic of 'shamanism' as a type of religion. The ethnographic material to document these assertions will appear throughout this book; here I attempt only to explain my approach.

Bloch (1991: 185) has noted, about a controversial field,

That there is no inevitable connexion between concepts and words is shown by the now well-established fact that concepts can and do exist independently of language. This is made clear in the many examples of conceptual thinking in pre-linguistic children, first presented by Brown (1973). Childen have the concept 'house' before they can say the word. We also have studies which show that the acquisition of lexical semantics by children is very largely a matter of trying to match words to already formed concepts.

Non-linguistic concepts are not learned as minimal and necessary check-lists of features, but as prototypes, on the basis of 'families' of specific instances. Thus, the concept of *house*, for example, is not a series of definitions (it must have a roof, door, walls, etc.) If this were so a house which has lost its roof would not be a house. Rather it is a loosely associated group of 'houselike' features, no one of which is essential, but which are linked by a general idea of what a typical house is (Bloch 1991: 185). If this is correct, Daur children will have apprehended concepts such as 'mountain', 'sky', or 'wolf' in this way, developing largely unconscious suppositions about these objects according to early cognitive principles pertaining to different domains.

The role of linguistic input has been studied by Carolyn Mervis among others. As she points out (1987: 213–14), children's initial categories, such as *duck*, are formed on the basis of similarity of shape and predicted characteristic actions or functions, rather than on the basis of adult naming patterns. They therefore may differ from the adult idea of *duck* by virtue of the child's experience in its own environment from which the initial prototype is formed (Toren 1993). Maybe the child has only ever seen the plastic duck in its bath. As children get older the role of linguistic input increases. Children begin to accept the the authority of 'expert opinion', to understand adult talk of 'origins' (baby duck and mother duck are in the same category even if they look quite different), and then to accept purely linguistic allocations, such as when an item is so abstract that it fits into none of the child's existing categories, or when it is ambiguous and language alone determines whether it should be fitted into one category or another (Mervis 1987: 229–30). The learning of nominal cultural categories can take place only after the occurrence of what some psychologists have called the 'characteristic-to-defining shift'. Gradually, and at different times in different domains, children learn that appearances, or characteristic features, are not enough to establish categories. For natural categories they learn of more specialized theories of the inner nature of entities through education. However, for a nominal category such as 'uncle' this shift occurs through social conventions. 'Uncle' ceases to be that unrelated fellow who is a pal of your dad and brings presents, and older children can correctly identify him as the 2-year-old who is a brother of their mother (Keil 1987: 177). Thus, the role of social and cultural conventions is different for natural-kind terms, as opposed to nominal-kind terms. In the latter, intentional components and the importance of conventions and communication all push the composition of the category towards a definition-like structure. But for natural kinds it seems that there is a persistence of the pre-linguistic basis for categories, since people realize that such things are not modifiable by convention or fiat (Keil,1987: 194).

This would suggest that the idea of 'sky', as a natural phenomenon, would have different characteristics as a concept from *endur* (spirit of meritorious old man), which is a nominal kind. The basic concept of *tengger* would develop earlier, be more based on appearance and functional characteristics, and be less influenced by linguistic intervention. A concept such as Urgunge's *endur*, on the other hand, could not develop without language, and although it might well also be based on intuitive assumptions (in this case mostly about psychology) its use would depend on definitional principles. Terms like *endur*, *barkan* (shamanic spirit), or *mudur* (dragon) will always depend on conventional definitions. Therefore, the existence of family traditions, largely autonomous villages, differential influence from Manchu and Chinese culture, etc. can explain what looks from the outside like the uncertain nature of the assignment by Daurs of these terms. But in any given community of speakers people have a more or less shared idea of what concepts they are talking about.

There would appear to be no problem with this in respect of analysis along the lines suggested by Boyer (1991 n.d.): people have a basic category 'mountain', 'tree', or whatever, which has the ordinary ontological characteristics of an inanimate object, and they can also take up a religious stance which brings into focus a new conception, of 'mountain spirit' (*ejin*), which is founded on certain limited psychological assumptions about how a master (*ejin*) behaves. Now it certainly is interesting that regularities in such psychological assumptions are found in so many different cultures (Boyer 1994). However, I do not believe that this description accounts for how people experience the situation. The evidence suggests that people do not feel they have adopted 'a new stance', which would be for them to acknowledge an overt distinction between religious views and reality. It is language which seems to perform this mystifying unification and it can do this because, in a language like Daur, the terms for ordinary and spiritualized entities are the same. Although there will always be ways for the pragmatics of a linguistic situation to make a differentiation, very often people do not do so. I cannot think of any reason for this except that they do not want to. Thus it was natural for Urgunge to say, in conversation, 'the mountain was angry', and though he could have specified, 'the mountain *ejin* was angry', he almost never spoke that way.

In Daur this mystifying effect of language occurs for living kinds and natural entities differently from kinds like *endur*. *Endur* is rather like 'angel' in English: you may have rather few ideas about what angels are like or where they are to be found, but more or less everyone would agree that they are beings which exist within a religious discourse, that there are religious texts and conventions which define them, and that they are not to be confused with living people, despite the existence of expressions like, 'Oh, she's such an angel!' The mystery of a word like *tengger* is of quite another kind, since a strong basic concept exists, as we have said, without language, and what is at issue is the degree of identity with it of spiritual being/s which people evidently conceive in different ways. It seems that a culture prone to 'animist' thinking will preserve this mystery by keeping available usages which genuinely confuse or elide the 'realist' and the 'spiritual' aspects of the sky. This elision-effect of language can work at various levels, at that of simple vocabulary, of idioms, of conversations, and of genres.

A result of this kind of elision is that it is often extremely difficult to express oneself clearly about Daur religious ideas in English. The terms simply do not exist. Urgunge took a positive pleasure in forcing me to abandon Western categories. In our conversations about *tengger* and Irmu Khan (the lord of the nether world, discussed further in 3.1), he presented me with what appeared to be a logical impossibility: the conflation of place with person.[38] Urgunge could not understand why I had a problem with this. He would say something like, '. . . and the shaman went to Irmu Khan'.

c. Do you mean he went to Irmu Khan's realm, or he went to Irmu Khan himself?
u. What's the difference?
c. Of course there is a difference: one is a place and one is a person. In English we always make this distinction.
u. No, you don't. Students say, 'I went to Cambridge'; that means the place and all the people too. [*Laughs*] You must agree.

Perhaps he was right. Soon Urgunge hit on a neat way of talking in English to represent such, to me still worrying, expressions in Mongolian. He took to calling *tengger* 'upstairs', as in, 'The shaman cannot handle that problem. Only one thing can do it. What is that? Upstairs.' By the same token, Irmu Khan became 'downstairs'. This usage can be seen as characteristic of an important feature of conversations in general. As Tannen notes, conversations work by means of various strategies for interpersonal involvement, and one of these is mutual participation in sense-making by creating idiosyncratic images (1989: 135). Maybe Urgunge would not have continued to use 'upstairs' had I not laughed so appreciatively at this solution to the place/person problem. Of course 'upstairs', with its English connotations of the gentry in their country mansion living above the servants below, is in the abstract quite misleading as a representation of *tengger*. It only worked because of a mutual agreement between Urgunge and myself. But it had the right effect: in the end I became quite accustomed to thinking of *tengger* and Irmu Khan as both places and persons.

A further point can be made concerning the kind of contribution language can make to cosmological concepts. The semantic field of a linguistic term such as *tengger* contributes to the concept of 'sky'. This is particularly clear in languages such as Mongolian, where words are built up from one or more meaningful root morphemes, plus grammatical suffixes. Thus any given word is one of a cluster in the lexicon which employ the same root. Now Daurs in some regions use the word *endur* for the anthropomorphic sky-being Urgunge called *tengger*, but language brings in different associations in the two cases. In the case of *tengger* the root is *teng*, which means equilibrium or equality. The idea has a core in the human physical context, as in the two sides of the body, or a load distributed evenly.[39] *Tengger* is found in a group of Daur words including *tengchuu* (balance), *tenggel* (axle), *tengkee* (vigour, force, strength), and *tengkelig* (robust, vigorous). Anyone using the word would have these associations at some level of consciousness. Lakoff (1987: 82) has described a complex internal structure for 'radial categories' of this kind. By contrast, there is no such cognitive field for the word *endur*. *Endur* came into Daur from Manchu, and has no lexical associations for the Daurs as far as I know.

The question arises whether such lexical clusters and conventions of usage reflect conceptual structures or merely constitute linguistic devices. Of course it is common to find quasi-anthropomorphism created by linguistic means such as metaphor. For example, the English newspaper headline, 'Six Cheat Death in Freak Accident', does not mean that English people really think death is a person who can be cheated (for a discussion of this point, see Keesing 1985). However, we need not conclude that such tropes are simply linguistic devices. As Lakoff (1987: 87–8) points out, radial categories and metaphors which map domains onto other domains are necessarily some part or other of our cognitive apparatus. The mechanisms they employ (central and peripheral members of the category, etc.) are conceptual, and they are present for all adult members of cultures. The formal structures of language itself are not autonomous, but are reflections of general conceptual organization and particular cultural-social environments.

This being said, the work of psychologists and the material presented in this book indicate that a linguistic structure obtained through analysis of some term or expression, conceptual though it may be, cannot be all there is to the concept of a natural, experienced entity or activity. Expressions in language are only parts of concepts. Furthermore, they inject their own linguistically structured sequential element to knowledge. As Bloch (1991: 193–4) pointed out, most knowledge is of the ways things look, sound, feel, smell, and so forth, and is experienced all at once rather than in linear fashion. This means that trying to understand concepts of nature by starting with particular words and their metaphoric or metonymic extensions, as Lakoff does, is likely to be dangerous.

If, on the other hand, our interest is not in concepts of natural entities as such, but in what makes such concepts religiously salient in society, then language must be our key. As I have tried to show here, it is language which effects the elision between 'mysteriously powerful mountain' and 'active mountain spirit' or between 'sky'/'weather' and the 'controller of destinies'. It is language which contributes the echoes of a lexical field, and which even achieves the magic of amalgamating place and person.

Let us now return to the issue I raised at the beginning of this section. What is it that makes people feel such religious concepts are authentic? Sperber's (1990) contrast between 'intuitive beliefs' and 'reflective beliefs' is a good place to begin. 'Intuitive beliefs', he writes, are typically the product of spontaneous and unconscious perceptual and inferential processes. They are the basic concepts of things and people, which are on the whole practical and reliable in ordinary circumstances. 'Reflective beliefs' are thoughts about thoughts, or more accurately, interpretations of representations. To count as 'beliefs' such second-order ideas are related to basic intuitive concepts (though they may also occur as embedded in other reflective beliefs) (1990: 35). This is a valuable insight, since it enables us to attempt to explain the ways in which symbolic and metaphysical ideas are related to basic concepts, by means of different kinds of authenticating contexts. Sperber, perhaps thinking about life in Paris, discusses validation from two contexts, logical reasoning and reliable authorities (such as teachers). However, neither of these seems apposite for most shamanist 'reflective beliefs'.

I suggest instead that the authenticity of many reflective beliefs in 'shamanism' derives from a reflexive move of deliberately re-experiencing the intuitive perceptions, in other words, in consciously enabling the welling-up of evocations—emotional, sensory, and conceptual—by (re-)immersement in special, often ritualized, experience. Since ordinary experiential ideas, for example that a rock is solid or that water flows, are spontaneous and not consciously held, the 'reflective beliefs', which people are conscious of holding, also come to be felt as primary and immediate at these moments. Though Sperber's idiom is radically different from that of anthropologists inspired by phenomenology, and indeed they would seem to be natural enemies, this need not be the case if authentication is understood in phenomenological terms.

Sperber (1990) points out that everyday intuitive beliefs may not be represented, that is held as conscious propositions or images. This view is not inconsistent with that of Merleau-Ponty, for whom 'consciousness' is based on perception by the human subject in the world and initially not necessarily a matter of represented, objectivized images. Consciousness derives from one's sense of oneself in one's body and experience of its movements and activities. 'Consciousness in the first place is not a matter of "I think that", but of "I can"' (1962: 137). Thus Merleau-Ponty writes that our bodies can understand the world without having to make use of the symbolic or objectifying functions. 'Even if subsequently, thought and the perception of space are freed from motility and spatial being, for us to be able to conceive space it is in the first place necessary that we should have been thrust into it by our body, and that it should have provided us with the first model of those transpositions, equivalents and identifications which make space into an objective system' (1962: 142). Sight and movement are specific ways of entering into relationship with objects, which do not cancel out their diversity but link them to one another, guiding them towards the intersensory unit of a 'world'.

It is this experiential certainty, it seems to me, that the Daurs are *returning* to in much of their religious practice.[40] Hence the importance of simple gestures which place the physical self in relation to objects in the world. Certain rituals enjoin these (re)experiences. For example, in the *oboo* ritual one must pick up a hard, cold stone and throw it with a clink among the other stones on the cairn, and one must walk several times round the cairn on the mountain top, perceiving with one's own faculties the idea of centrality from which the surrounding world is viewed. At sacred springs people must feel the wetness and coldness of the water, drink and splash themselves with it. Such religious experience also occurs in less ritualized situations (as we have seen, people become aware of sudden shafts of light and turn to worship the sky). The cultural approval of direct, sensuous experience explains why ordinary people's religious ideas, like the 'genius' of a natural object, are so variable. It explains why Urgunge and all the other Daurs I have met never minded that other people seemed to conceptualize things somewhat differently.

Nevertheless the simple religious acts of (re)experiencing are not devoid of sense, and they can move from a primary to a metaphorical, emotional, or symbolic significance.[41] In 'shamanism' the subject projects himself or herself into an open number of other intentional positions, not just of natural objects but also of animals and other people, which provide meaning in their very contents, such as 'the self as a tiger'. Dreaming, trance, and spirit possession are other such cultural modes which make possible the realization of the openness of the body-image to the world. The movements or cries, the style of an action or speech or song, are 'consecratory gestures which draw affective vectors and discover emotional sources' (Merleau-Ponty 1962: 146). Urgunge's explanation of *tengger-gajir* seems to me an example of this kind of discovery, if we remember his spontaneous and almost musical composing of diverse experiences (bringing together the sky, the earth, father and mother in his memory of his aunt offering her breasts to his sick cousin). Shamanship was far more complex than worship of the mountains or sky, since its primary object of knowledge was the human heart-mind. As we have seen (2.1), the understanding of humanity was often refracted through enactments of animals and birds, or brought to mind by symbols that attempted to cross-cut domains.[42] It was the shaman's incomparably difficult task at each seance to turn these evocations into the felt experience of the audience.

Other ways of authenticating reflective beliefs, especially by accepting the word of some social authority, were of course also present in Daur life. There were elders who dominated lineage groups, *bagchi* ritualists who had charge of prayers, also shamans who taught novices. In this sense a recognized and senior clan shaman like Du Yadgan can be ranked alongside the other representative of social authority. He gave authority to his interpretations of the world by the same elaborate code of hierarchized relations of respect as the elders, as well as by his inspiration. We can therefore envisage an inchoate 'shamanism' at odds with shamans, a disturbing inflow from the religious space allowed to *anyone's* experience. I shall suggest later (7.1) that while constant (repeated) sources of experience in society may have sustained some shamans' traditions, historically new experiences subverted them and may have been the dynamic origin of new shamanic practices.

What this also implies is that even in so-called 'shamanic societies' personal, direct sacralized experience was not inevitable but had to be achieved: it had to be rediscovered within the authoritative conventions of the family, the clan, the military Banner, and even occasionally the shaman. This forces us to rethink earlier European perceptions of 'shamanism', which still linger today. In the early romantic views of Herder the noble primitives of Tartary, North America, or Thrace lived in worlds which were all of a piece, which were effortlessly 'shamanic' through and through.

Their [the shamans'] songs are the archives of their people, the treasure of their knowledge and religion, their theogony and cosmogonies of the deeds of their fore-fathers and of the events of their history, reproduction of their heart, image of their domestic life in joy and sorrow, at their bridal bed and grave. (1777, quoted in Flaherty 1992: 142)

This was to envision 'them' as having in their spontaneous entirety the Orphic 'doxologies of ancient sacred symbols' that European cultures had lost and could only rediscover again through poetry and performed song. But as this book shows, 'they' (the Daurs) were no different from us in this respect. Shamanic 're-experiences' were hard won, and had to be achieved amid other conflicting, mocking, and authoritative views, and among other easier genres. Some cultures cut off such possibilities, others open up only a few, and yet others, like the Naun Daurs, made available rather many; but in any case the shamanic opening up of the self to experience was something which was very often achieved through suffering in the mind and body. Participating in shamans' performances was only one of the ways it was achieved, and maybe the most difficult. In the shamanic performance, the combination of highly complex imagery with authentic emotion, the sha-man's art of revelation could fail to come about (see 5.7; Atkinson 1989: 230–52).

This section has suggested that vivid intentional re-experience, opening oneself to evocations, can give legitimation to religious beliefs, along with (and often at odds with) reasoning and relying on social authorities. Now abstract reasoning is not something most people associate with shamanism. Still, it was there, and I explore one important example in the next section.

Notes

1. Urgunge said that this generalizing term *ejin* was much less widely used among Daurs than among other Mongolians.

2. Carey (1991) notes that children only gradually distinguish air from 'nothing', or understand the difference between an object and a continuous substance. Her research on concepts of air, materiality, and 'taking up space' suggest that children's concepts of the sky as a physical entity are likely to change between the ages of 4 and 10. However, her view that a radical conceptual shift is involved is invalidated to my mind by her assumption that adults have scientific understanding of these categories. It seems more probable that most adults, like children, do not think of air as a material.

3. Other cultures in Inner Asia have given far greater prominence than the Daurs to the earth (Humphrey 1994*b*). Among the 14th-century Mongols, 'the earth' was personified as a female deity, Etugen. For discussion of the various linguistic forms and meanings of '*etugen*', and the relation between this term and *udagan* (female shaman), see the notes to Banzarov (1995) and Dulam (1989). Urgunge saw a connection between *etugen* and the Daur respectful term for 'old woman' (*eteuw*).

4. Hence Urgunge disapproved of the Halh Mongol expression '*mongke tngri*' (eternal sky).

5. Among West Mongols in Uvs Aimag, on the other hand, a sudden shaft of sunlight is thought to bring bad luck, for example if it strikes a herd, and there is a ritual 'to close heaven's door' (*oktorguin üüd haana*) (Dulam 1989: 176).

6. When lightning strikes in the first month of summer an abbreviated version of the Halh Mongol custom is that the household head dresses in his best clothes, takes bowls with yoghurt and milk, and circumambulates the tent making libations to the sky, earth, and tent, with the spell, 'Disaster go away! Summer come here!' (*Zudaa tsaash n', zunaa naash n'*) (Chingel 1991: 223). This is not just a story but is actually done among both Mongols and Buryats. A Western Buryat told Dugarov that when lightning struck his house in the 1930s, after he had made the milk libation, the household and neighbour did a ritual round dance (*yookhor*). The idea of this is to return the lightning to the sky (Dugarov 1991: 161). Urgunge said, 'To a Mongol there is nothing more terrifying than lightning. If lightning strikes, Daurs think that *tengger* is punishing someone. If it hits a tree, that tree definitely will become something to be worshipped. It will be changed for ever.'

7. The 'small *tengger*' is not the same as the soul.

8. Urgunge used the Mongolian words *evlüüle-* and *nairuula-*; the first is a causative from the stem *ev-* 'peace' 'harmony', and the second means 'to blend'—it is also used of editing a book.

9. Buryats are said to have imagined 99 southern, 55 western, and 77 northern *tengris*, alongside an idea of a single Blue Eternal Sky (Mikhailov 1987: 12–13). Many different enumerations and characterizations of skies appear in the literature. Eastern and northern skies were said to be cruel and to be in conflict with western and southern skies. The same kind of divisions applied to the earth. Among early 20th-century Halh Mongols, there was the idea of 77 or 88 earth-masters (*etüged-ün ejed*) (Vladimirtsov 1927).

10. *Enduri* is a Manchu term meaning 'deity'; Urgunge used it only in the sense outlined above, but it will be seen later in this book that other Daurs used it in other ways.

11. Educated Daurs were aware of the Chinese system of *feng-shui*, which attributes natural objects with energies and good and bad consequences for human beings. It was not used in Urgunge's village. *Feng-shui* is a system that co-ordinates many different influences (wind, water flow, rock contours, etc.) on a given spot. Daur ideas about natural energies, by contrast, focused on separate exemplars, 'the mountain', 'the river', etc. and did not relate the entities in a landscape.

12. Sometimes words such as 'heaven' (*tengger*), 'spirit' (*onggong*), or 'shaman' (*yadgan*) were also used attributively for these special objects, with the meaning sacred', for example, *onggong delbur* was the sacred mane of a horse, which should never be cut (Poppe 1930: 88).

13. This is a mountain with *oboo* with which there remains an emotional tie, even if the person no longer lives in the vicinity. The mountain's pardon is begged for having moved away, and its protection sought for new endeavours. In times of trouble a special visit is made to the mountain.

14. The Daurs do not make cliff-engravings, which are, however, widespread in Buryatia, Mongolia, Tuva, and the Altai.

15. Urgunge said that there was a certain mountain near his village (not the one with the *oboo*), which had the capacity to stop forest fires. How did he know? Because he remembers there was a raging forest fire and people he knew prayed to the mountain and the fire miraculously stopped. After this a small shrine was set up at the foot of the hill, in the form of a little wooden box on stilts for offerings.

16. The counterpart of mountains in Inner Asian landscapes were caves, which no reader will be surprised to hear were associated with cults of female fertility (Humphrey 1995). There were no caves (*nugu*) in Urgunge's childhood surroundings. He thinks of them as repositories for unpleasant creatures like giant poisonous spiders, snakes, and a huge fish-like creature called *awurag*. However, the sexual and reproductive connotations of caves are apparent in the Daur stories of Gashina Cave. This seems to have been a legendary place. According to one story, great treasure was hidden in the cave. Some thirteen miles away from the cave to the south there was a huge screen of pines which was its cover. *Tengger* and the monster Manggee competed to take over the cave. Whoever could shoot an arrow through the cover into the cave would win it. Needless to say *Tengger* won, while Manggee's arrow fell short and he was chased away to the shore of the Western Sea. After this human beings started to multiply (Sain Tanaa 1987*b*: 287). It seems that caves were perhaps the subject of cults among the Daurs in some areas (Schwarz 1984: 163), but Urgunge did not know about them.

17. Alternatively, this particular injunction would be explained by saying that such an abrupt action might disturb a peaceful spirit, which would be angered and attack you.

18. Examples are: tiger *auli koko* (mountain cat) rather than *tasaga*; bear *sardai ku* (aged man) or *eterken* (old man) rather than *baabgai*; fish *awurag* (huge reptile) rather than *jaus*.

19. *Nek hukury heuryn tarkaas myangan hukury heuryn sherkirbei.*

20. Small rivers, 'like the Cam in Cambridge', were called *hwarga*, not *mur*.

21. Along their length rivers were divided up by the character of the place (reaches between high cliffs, places with sandy banks, a sudden dog-leg, etc.), and in some parts of Mongolia, rivers change names along their course by this principle. Although these stretches of river did not necessarily coincide with clan-village fishing-reaches, they were thought to influence the well-being of nearby inhabitants. Urgunge said, 'At one place our Naun river flows straight, from north to south, for three miles without a bend. The villages in that area were so successful, they produced ten famous generals. Everyone said it was related to the straight-flowing of the river.'

22. There are numerous Daur stories in which a person or thing is thrown into the river, only for it to reach some distant place, magically transformed.

23. Chipaatii was one of Urgunge's distant lateral ancestors in the Onon clan. He was the great-grandson of Emugai, the 'first ancestor' of the Naun Daurs. In the 1630s the Daurs, it is said, were divided into two tribal coalitions. One, headed by Bombogor, occupied the huge area of the Shila and Ergune Rivers; the other, headed by Baldachi, lived to the east of the Jinchili River and along the northern bank of the Amur River. On the 27th of the 5th lunar month in 1634 Baldachi made his momentous submission to the Manchus, travelling to Mukden with forty-four followers and presenting 1,818 sable skins to the Emperor. Baldachi took a Manchu princess as wife, thus becoming a royal son-in-law, and he became military leader of the Daur region (*DSHI* 1985: 13). Chipaatii was one of Baldachi's subjects.

24. Graded precious stones, which were worn on the tip of pointed hats adorned with peacock feathers, were the signs of the ranks of officials in the Manchu Empire.

25. This was recorded in Urgunge's district of Morin Dawaa in the 1970s.

26. Buryats call cedars and pines 'eternal trees' (*münkhe modon*) and they think that to fell one of these would be to cut short one's own life and that of one's descendants (Galdanova 1987: 31).

27. I have been unable to trace the meaning of *duwalang*. A Daur man told me that a similar word, *duwagalang*, means 'birdsong', so it is possible that *duwalang* refers to the combined image of a tree with a creature living in it. The lists of *duwalang* trees differ slightly in various accounts.

28. *Achnatherum splendens*, which grows in dense thickets and is an indicator of underground water. It has not been possible to translate all of the names of the *duwalang* creatures.

29. 'The majority of older people among the Hakass,' write Sagalayev and Oktyabr'skaya (1990: 54), 'say they belong, besides their clans, to some other kind of community of people, symbolized by one or other species of tree.' One old woman said, 'Our tree-community (*shula*) is larch. The Russians are birch. If when you are asleep you see a larch tree fall, that means one of your kin will die. . . . The tree community means strong life' (1990: 55).

30. Though Urgunge spoke as though this was a story invented among the boys of the village, it is similar to stories about a blue wolf found in other parts of Asia, even in the Subhashita. However, the point of these other stories is different from Urgunge's.

31. For discussion of literature on this idea in circumpolar cultures, see Ingold (1986: 243–56).

32. This woman told me that parents would be counted fortunate (i.e. having a good destiny) if their child had had a good previous existence, but if the child had been an animal it might well have been treated badly by the parents in that earlier existence and therefore they, as its present parents, owed it a debt. The child would behave badly in this life as a way of taking back the debt.

33. Often animal names (i.e. designating behaviour traits) would be used as epithets and insults. Rather than use abstract expressions of a general moral kind, such as 'that's cruel!', people would say, '*Shi shogoo!*' or '*Mog*' ('You falcon!' or 'Snake!'). These typical qualities are highly abstracted, so a tiger soul just represents bravery, an eagle remorseless fierceness, a chicken just distracted greed, a bear power and acquisitiveness, a cow just slow clumsiness, and so on. Note, however, that the characteristics attributed to animals are mainly psychological.

34. Shirokogoroff (1935: 164–5) is scathing about the 'primitive mentality' theories which lie behind such writings. The Tungus recognized certain mental faculties belonging to animals and also the superior abilities of animals in physical power, sharpness of sight, keenness of smell, etc., but all Tungus believed in their own mental superiority.

35. I use the expression 'were-animal' in line with Endicott, who notes a similar idea, distinct from possession, among the rural Malays (1979: 139–40).

36. Urgunge did not know the term *mafa*, though Shirokogoroff says it was used by Daurs in the 1910s. No other ethnography on the Daurs mentions the term. I use it here only to distinguish these spirits from others in this text.

37. Mongols use the expression *tsog sul'd* (spark spirit) for this vital energy. Another term, in a more Buddhist idiom, is *hii mori* (wind horse); see 5.8.

38. Academic writers on this topic have thought it necessary to come down on one side or the other. The Daur ethnographer Mendüsürüng, talking in Mongolian, told me that Irmu Khan is definitely a place, the nether world. This is despite the fact that the literal translation of 'Irmu Khan' is 'Lord Irmu'. The same elision occurs with certain other categories, such as *awurag*, which Urgunge said meant both the cave and the being (huge, horrible, snake-like) in the cave.

39. Hangin (1989: 532) gives an evenly distributed load as the root meaning of *teng*. The suffix *-ri* (the written form of *tengger* is *tngri*) indicates a noun designating a place or result of an action (Poppe 1964: 49).

40. Why do I write here of a return rather than a simple experience? It is a return because the deliberate putting oneself in the way of consciously realizing experience is not the same as everyday purposeful activity, and it is the grounds for (but not the same as) the worked-out reflective beliefs which people may hold, things like a belief in spirits. I am not trying to explain what the beliefs are (their content), but to identify one of the most important ways in which people hold them.

41. It is consistent with this continuity with intuitive thinking that Daur symbolism tends to be 'analogical' or iconic. As Barth proposes for the Baktaman (1975: 189), in such symbolizing practice, 'natural species enter individually into large ritual contexts, each of them separate, more or less dense symbols, carrying an aura of connotation.' These symbols do not form a structure (like 'totemism'), which would permit isomorphic comparisons to be made with other structures, such as relations between social groups. Nor do their values derive from arbitrary sign systems. Instead, Daur symbols start with perception of close similarities, or evo-

cations and connotations which extend outwards. The mountain, for example, initially symbolizes solidity and perpetuity (as well as many other things in various contexts). Such is the general absence of systematic and widely understood arbitrary signification that one Daur prophetic poem which does have this form ('black velvet' stands for earth, 'loosen the bridle' stands for taking off earrings in mourning, etc.) is always cited as an example of a mysterious utterance that has to be explained (*DSHI* 1985: 280–1).

42. Significantly, objects and creatures that symbolically linked domains morally held distinct were associated with shamanship, though not in a consistent or universally recognized way. Examples are the bat and the flying squirrel ('animals' and 'flying creatures') both of which were said by some Mongols to have been shamans (Potanin 1881–3, IV: 169; Jahunen 1989: 186). The deer's antlers that grew to the sky (worn on the shaman's hat), the *duwalang* grove, the rope which pulls a waterbucket up a hill (*Daur Folktales* 1984: 60), and the *toroo* tree of death–rebirth are further examples. The fact that these symbols were only partially acknowledged is indicative of the uncertain power of shamanship itself.

3

Space and Time Beyond the Village

3.1 A Tripartite Cosmos or an 'Other World'?

One often meets in the literature the idea that the peoples of North Asia think in terms of a tripartite cosmos, consisting of an upper world (the sky), a middle world (the earth), and an underworld. However, listening to Urgunge and other Daurs talking I found they mentioned this structure only in a particular context, as destinations for souls after death and, less often, as sources for souls yet to be born. Such talk might go along the lines that souls of good people go to the sky and bad souls go to the underworld, and then of course there was our own visible world. So that makes three. But there was also Irmu Khan, which Urgunge described as a holding-place for souls while their fate is being decided. Did that make four? Urgunge prevaricated on this point. And then perhaps we should consider the nine layers (*yesen davhar*) in the sky and the fact that Irmu Khan in some accounts contains the 'hells' (*tam*) of the underworld. Thinking about all this one cannot avoid the conclusion that the tripartite cosmos was one particular rationalization, one 'result' of pondering existence after death, which often turned out in some other way.

We find that the tripartite cosmos appeared mainly in certain language genres, in explanatory stories (*urgil*). Thus it was not primarily a 'world-view' in the sense of a static visualist model from a time-free standpoint (see Classen 1991) but arose in particular narratives. That these did not pretend to be all-encompassing master narratives is shown by the fact that the tripartite cosmos was not employed as an idea either in the cults of natural objects or in shamanic performance. Even in rituals of death (3.2 and 5.2), it was far from the only representation around.

Thus although the tripartite cosmos idea has been welcomed by ethnographers,[1] who tend to grasp any rationalization like a branch in a swirling river, talking to Daurs, whose religion was without books or church institutions to stabilize such ideas, it seems a fragile structure. Still, as such metaphysical reasonings were not only part of Daur culture but can be found all over Inner Asia, let us briefly look at them.

In Daur stories there is an elaborate nether world, identified with the realm of Irmu Khan,[2] imagined as having many layers (or 'compartments' or 'prisons'). Irmu Khan had walls and gatehouses, huge guard-dogs, soldiers, palaces, yards, and offices. It was shady down there, lit by a dim, yellowish light. Irmu Khan was imagined as a warrior-king and he bore weapons of every description.

Urgunge said that he 'was rigorous and just; he was like *tengger*'s registrar-general'. He had a book in which were written the dates of everyone's birth and death. The derivation of the name Irmu Khan from the word for 'male' (*Ir*, see note 2 above), and the image of his world as a militarized and bureaucratic state, suggest that the idea of the tripartite cosmos was closely related to a vision of the self as subject within the patriarchal polity.

A Daur woman I spoke with in Hohhot[3] luridly described what her mother had told her about how people sat out their time with Irmu Khan enduring punishments for the crimes they committed on earth, but she was laughing as she talked, as one might when talking of a fairy-tale world.[4] Urgunge was also uncommitted to a punitive Irmu Khan, but for a different reason. He said that too much emphasis on tortures and prisons was part of moralistic Buddhist 'cause–effect' thinking and therefore 'not authentic'. He said Irmu Khan was simply a kind of general clearing-house before people took up their rightful places among the honourable and anonymous ranks of ancestors somewhere in the sky.[5] The souls of people who had commited crimes or suicide became spirits and went elsewhere, to another place 'beyond the mountains'.

Even in stories shamans could not embody Irmu Khan; rather they specialized in outwitting and bargaining with him. Only *yadgan* shamans had to do with Irmu Khan. One of their most heroic tasks was the rescuing of souls stolen from living people by vengeful spirits. These souls were taken to Irmu Khan, who might, however, agree to let them out again. Venturing down there, shamans could bargain with Irmu Khan for a definite number of years' life for the soul they had rescued. The classic story of this kind, known among the Manchus, Daurs, and Tungus, is Nishan Shaman's epic journey to Irmu Khan to rescue the soul of a rich boy (see 6.5). Now the Daurs had actual shamanic rituals for rescuing souls, and in these the mythology of the Irmu Khan underworld might be drawn upon in shamans' songs for dramatic effect. But the operative notion was that of a night journey (*dolbor*), see Section 5.7.

In other stories a nether world is approached by entering a deep cave, by falling down a well, by penetrating to the source of a winding river, being sucked through a whirlpool, or by travelling to the ends of the earth and crossing a river on a raft rowed by a lame boatman. By these same tunnels and paths evil spirits could steal someone's soul while they were sleeping and carry it away to the unknown placeless realms of their existence. Here we begin to get a sense that the journey takes place in a horizontal plane.

In the 1920s Poppe recorded an interesting Daur story of this kind:

During the Yuan Dynasty [13th–14th centuries] there was a man. This man one day went to a river, sat in a boat, and when he went a little upriver on both sides there appeared very beautiful trees. He was greatly surprised and as he went further it got even better. He thought, 'Let's get to the source of this river,' and thought and went further and the trees on either side became smaller. When he went a little further he saw a great mountain. When he got close to the mountain he saw a little opening. He was greatly surprised and when he got close to the cave he saw it was exceedingly dark inside. He decided to enter, left his boat, and went in. It was very narrow and dark. Then he went a bit further and it became wider and lighter. Then he went on and it shone and became very, very bright. Hearing people's voices, [the noise of] ploughing fields, the [barking of] dogs, and [squealing of] pigs, he was greatly amazed. When he looked at the fields they were like the fields of this world (*delkeye*). When he approached the people ploughing they were terribly frightened and fled to their houses. When he went into a house and enquired, they asked him, 'Where did you come from?' 'As for me, I came out at the time of the Yuan Dynasty; how did you get here?' he replied, and they said, 'As for us, several thousand years have passed since the time an old man of ours came to this place! From that time, we do not know what is happening in the world (*jalan*).' They said, 'Tell us what is becoming of our world, tell us something good.' When the man told them about life in the Yuan Dynasty, none of them could understand anything and they said, 'We do not understand present existence (*baidal*)! We ask you, when you go back to earth (*gajir*) do not tell anyone about us! Since we left the world several thousand years have passed!' They took the man back to the opening. The man came out of the hole, got in his boat, and returned to earth. Then when he told a lord (*ejin*) about it, that lord said he would send [a] [the] man back, but that man fell ill, although he knew the road (*terguul*) well, and that man became nothing [died], and no one could go there again. (Poppe 1930: 49–50)

This story contrasts our earth with some other place exactly like it but somehow magically refracted in both space and time. I suggest that the construction here—two worlds mutually ignorant of one another—is what shamans really operate with in their rituals. They, alone among living human beings, can find 'the way'. The operative idea is not tripartite but dual, defined by the different shamanic way of knowing the other world. Shamans could travel in regions seen only to them, in an altered state of consciousness, and they could find out what was going on there by means of special shamanic dreams (*soolong*).

This opens up the possibility that some Daurs conceived of 'the other world' not as some separate place, but as the unseen aspect of this world, that is, not as existing on any plane, but omnipresent. Alternatively, as we have seen, people imagined another world as existing somewhere below or far away, being the place of the origins and endings of lives, tied to humanity. These two ideas, the closely present but unseen, and the distant goal-cum-source, coexisted side by side, creating a multidimensional sense of the unknown. A similar cross-cutting of concepts of the limits of the world seems common in 'shamanism' elsewhere, and what Severi (1987: 75, 77) has eloquently written of the Cuna applies also to the Daur:

The result is a world full of danger, where enigmatic 'fractures' in visible reality give hostile force a hiding place. . . . One of the basic functions of Cuna shamanism [is] to represent, in a symbolism only partially dependent on mythology, the ambiguous and anxiogenic dimension of the unknown. In terms of Cuna cosmology, this dimension is described as an unknown, yet possible space, a *terra incognita*, in which traditional thought represents the foreign, the new and the incomprehensible.

There is no name in Daur for the unknown place (or places) where spirits dwell, and there could be none. We may see it as a confused space, constructed between experience-near projections, the unknown of the things and people right beside us now, and imaginative and mythological narratives which are fanciful and unreal, and perhaps for this reason have a wide currency among many different North Asia cultures and are truly close in the subjective sense to nobody.

What are we to make, then, of Eliade's influential book *Shamanism: An Archaic Technique of Ecstasy*, which proposed that shamanism is defined by ecstatic ascent to the sky? One is left wondering, what is this ascent to? Eliade explains the fact that among most North Asian peoples such an ascent is *not practised* by a theory that the original religious ideology, based on faith in a celestial Supreme Being, died out with the onslaught through history of numerous new spirits, lesser deities, and goddesses. The ascent to the celestial Supreme Being nevertheless survived in the archaic, but now deteriorated, symbolism of shamanic practice ([1951] 1964: 505). This theory raises many extraordinarily complex issues, especially if we look not just at one ethnic group but at North Asia as a whole. Furthermore, the history of these ideas probably can never be adequately reconstructed, though scholars from Russia have made interesting attempts to do so (Dugarov 1991; Potapov 1991).

In the case of the Daurs, *yadgan* shamans 'went to Irmu Khan', but they did not, as Urgunge repeatedly emphasized, 'go to *tengger*'. This does not mean there was no symbolism of ascent to the sky, but whatever there was was fragmented in Urgunge's day and he himself was hardly conscious of it. However, since this question will come up later (6.3) I outline some of the issues involved.

One misleading aspect of Eliade's theory is that it suggests that the celestial target of the shaman's travels was the sky. On the contrary, closer reading of the ethnography of Inner Asia reveals that the sky (even in reified form) coexisted with another celestial world in which gods resided. Not even the most deluded shaman would attempt to 'ascend' to something which was an abstract regulatory energy. It might in theory make sense to travel to *tengger* as an anthropomorphized receiver of sacrifices, but the Daurs did not hold this idea (and indeed there seems something redundant about combining sacrifice as a mode of interaction with *tengger* and a shamanic journey, see 4.3). In those places in Inner Asia where the shaman's ascent existed (e.g. among some Altaians and the Yakuts), the ascent was in fact not to the sky, but through the sky to a range of spirits or 'animate' creator-deities. The celestial world was thus the equivalent on high of the mythic field of action which was the nether world of Irmu Khan below.

Among the peoples of the Altai and Tuva there were narratives of a world in, or beyond, the sky, having mountains, trees, rivers, rocky passes, tracks, white and black sandy places, herds, grasslands, numerous human inhabitants, and cloudy realms stacked on top of one another. This was a 'super-earthly world' (*cher ada*) (Potapov 1991: 140–1). In this world people were said to be just like those of our own, except that they tied their belts under their armpits, not at their waists. Such spirits were not of the sky, rather they were in the sky, as we may speak of an airplane being in the sky. Probably influenced by Orthodox Christian missionary teaching, people said these spirits were creator-gods.[6] The point of the shaman's journey to these deities was to lead the soul of the horse offered in propitiation by people to the god. This task involved number-less obstacles and difficulties, such as the white sandy place where the horse strayed away and was nearly lost. It is important to realize that in the Altaic cultures the celestial creator-gods were found alongside a separate, differently named, idea of the reified sky (or skies) (*tängri*). The cult of *tängri* disappeared in many places by the 1930s, but the Altaian Kachins, Beltirs, and Sagai kept it up by means of a sacramental sacrifice conducted on the summit of a holy mountain. In this shamans played no part and altered states of consciousness were not involved. Women and girls were forbidden to attend. The Abakan Kachins took the exclusion of females so seriously that even mares and ewes were banished from the site (Potapov 1991: 264–7).

Thus the shaman's journey through the airy realms to a celestial god was not a matter of worship of the sky. It was a cosmic oscillation whereby the shamanic adventure was swung from a horizontal to a vertical sequence. It was the light, bright counterpart of the shaman's dark, downward expeditions to Erlig-khan (Irmu Khan). Among Buryats and Yakuts in the early twentieth century these two rituals were conducted by different shamans ('white' and 'black').[7] Although each ritual was in itself dualistic, involving this world and another, without reference to a tripartite cosmology, most communities of Yakuts, Altaians, and Buryats at this period had rituals of both types, held at different times. Nevertheless, we need to be careful about assuming, in structuralist vein, that 'white shamanship' at all times implied the existence of 'black shamanship', and vice versa. Indigenous writers on 'shamanism' in both Buryatia and the Sakha-Yakut republic have stressed that sky-oriented rituals, with or without the participation of shamans, have a different history from black shamanship (Dugarov 1991; Alekseyev 1993). Recent (1990s) religious activity among the Evens, for example, has re-created only the former.

Moving geographically closer to the Daurs, we find the vocabulary changes. Among the Tungus of South Siberia and Manchuria, shamanic rituals con-structed the idea of 'day' and 'night' roads (Shirokogoroff 1935: 149). The Daur shamanic imagination dwelt above all on the night. In Tungusic dialects the night road was called *dolbor* (the word also used by Daurs). Now the night road was often said to take the shaman to the realms of Irmu Khan, but even so the journey was not conclusively underground. There were intimations that a single sense of otherness collapsed the dark and light. One Daur woman even told me that the shaman on his return by the *dolbor* way might say he had come back from or through the sky (*tenggerees irlee*), though the world she described was dark and harsh.

All this indicates a verticalization of shamanic practice among Buryats, Yakuts, and Altaians, in contrast to the mainly horizontal visions of Daurs and Tungus. The totality of Buryat, etc., shamanic ritual added up, through the idea of the 'two sides', the white and the black, to a tripartite version of the cosmos; that is, it retained the idea of two directions or sources with which humanity, located in the middle, had to engage. Among the Daurs, on the other hand, the tripartite vision was undercut by the fact that people operated with two much more distinct practices within religious activities as a whole, *bagchis* addressing themselves to a vertical dimension of the sky by sacrifice and prayer, and *yadgans* engaging with horizontal or more ambiguously 'downward' journeys. Furthermore, quite disjunct from either of these spheres, I was to learn that the Daurs had a cult of a capricious female Womb Goddess in the sky, Tengger Niang-Niang (6.3), and this was conducted by another specialist, the *otoshi*.

Such heterogeneity seems intrinsic not only to 'shamanism', but to religious life in East Asia in general. Chinese culture of course accommodates several traditions, Confucianism, Daoism, Buddhism, and other 'folk religious' practices in various combinations. In the case of peoples like the Daurs and Buryats the disjunct traditions were not permanent presences but had their own histories of emergence and decline, and furthermore they were not always harmonious but could involve people in numbing psychological quandaries (5.4). The idea of a unifying tripartite universe was not strong enough to stand as a structure against the turbulent appearance of 'other' powers attributed to different parts of the universe.

Why should we be interested in whether the cosmos was conceived in a dualist or tripartite way? One feature of the dualist vision is that it removed the possibility of spatialized differentiation based on ethical human action. With a tripartite cosmos the upper world could be 'good' and the lower world 'bad', and they could easily be thought of in terms of rewards and punishments for actions on this earth. But this particular kind of moralizing was an impossibility with a dual cosmos. Since life in this world could neither be seen as totally good or totally bad, an 'other world', one which mirrored our own, was not envisaged in judgemental terms. Among Daurs ethical ideas such as the meritorious ancestor (*endur*) or the punishments in Irmu Khan for being rude to one's parents were to a great extent confined to parental instruction and 'model' stories. They were relatively trivial in comparison with the harsher, more austere, and bolder understanding of warring powers which derived from shamanic practice (6.1–4).

The possibility of slipping between dualist and tripartite cosmologies also did strange things to time. The 'other world' of the Yuan Dynasty story was both past and contemporary. It may be remembered that Urgunge said, 'There is no time in shamanism.' He was referring here to the idea that the souls of the dead went to 'another world', which thus had the aura of the past about it, but nevertheless it was from this same other world that the souls of the unborn were to emerge in the future. The ritual *toroo* tree was the symbol of this mystic death–regeneration, the tree whose spreading roots mirrored its spreading branches (see 2.1). The *toroo* appeared at shamans' mortuary sites (3.2), at the great clan renewal ceremony *ominan*, which was also the public initiation of a new shaman (5.8), and at the ritual of the Womb Goddess (6.3).

In these rituals the sky itself was brought to mind. Here and there across North Asia we find the remnants of a general, community-based euphoric and hypnotic dance to the sky and sun, in which men and women worked themselves up to a state of hyperaesthesia, feeling they transcended this world. There are survivals and recent revivals of this archaic dance through the 'gateway of the world', which evoke the turning of cosmic cycles in time. Among Evens the dance was performed without the participation of shamans (Dugarov 1991: 57; Alekseyev 1993: 25–34),[8] and among Buryats it seems to have been part of 'white' shamanship, recently also done without shamans (Dugarov 1991: 57). Yet among the Daurs a *yadgan* shaman took part (see 5.8).

Eliade ([1951] 1964: 200) recognized the difference between these dances to the sky and the Altaian shaman's ritual of upwards travel to a god. He called the latter a 'laboriously mimed ascent', making use of the technique the shaman acquired in other seances, notably at his own initiation. When a shaman made the journey in an altered state of consciousness, he was not 'possessed' by the deity to whom he was travelling, which clearly would make no sense. In fact he was not possessed at all, but gathering his helper spirits in the drum, he gradually rose to the celestial regions while climbing a tree, and at the same time was said to be symbolically mounted on the sacrificed horse (and when it got tired, on a powerful flying goose spirit). Now things did not happen in quite this way among the Daurs; there was no concept of deities in heaven to which shamans could ascend. However, in one ritual, the great periodic *ominan*, we find the elements of symbolic ascent by a shaman, a communal dance, and the ritual tree-ladder (see 5.8). Eliade's view was that the Altaian shaman was usurping an ecstatic ascent originally done by the people in general. We shall never know what was originally done, but it does seem important that in some places and times shamans led the people and gave themselves greater cosmic/geographic pretensions than in others; it is to this subject that I now turn. We have seen that the tripartite cosmos idea only occasionally surfaced among the Daurs. It was pushed aside by the dualist field of action of this world, this sky-earth, *tengger-gajir*, with its unseen powers. In this battleground too, as I hope to show, shamanship took over more of religious life in some regions of Inner Asia than elsewhere.

3.2 Death Vitalizes the Inanimate

Scholarly traditions of seeing 'shamanism' as a fragile remnant, always the passive object of other developments, have deflected attention away from its expansive possibilities. The most crucial of these in Inner Asia was an invasion of the landscape, the enlivening of static objects with the human sensibilities of spirits. The landscape, as I use the word, is not a blank background to human affairs, nor is it simply a cognitive ordering of space. It is the result of a land having been used in certain practical and value-laden ways, in our case the Daurs' rough-and-ready farming, herding, and hunting. The lives of shamans created their own occult power points in this dwelt-in world, and they were related in a complex way to the energies of natural objects like mountains and rivers. To discuss this it will again be useful to make comparisons with other regions of Inner Asia. I do this because I wish to avoid suggesting that the Daur pattern was somehow inevitable, that it arose from a 'natural' interaction with the world. There were similar ideas in the various 'shamanisms' of Inner Asia, but it is necessary to be clear about the fact that they were combined in different ways and also differed in their appeal to people and their importance in society.

Shamanic practice invites us to see a landscape like a map of events in shamans' lives, marking especially their deaths, which were simultaneously the beginnings of other shamans' existence. Unlike the instantaneously recognizable *oboo* cairns which marked places of nature worship, many shamanic mortuary sites were hidden from outsiders and visually unpretentious (see Plate 7). In fact, a passer-by would not notice them unless someone in the know pointed them out. The paths between mortuary sites designated remembered migrations of ancestral shamans (Humphrey 1995). The idea that the landscape is iconic of human history has often been expressed by anthropologists, among them Weiner (1991), Ingold (1993 n.d.), and Rosaldo (1980), and the latter makes an observation about the Ilongot which could equally apply to the Daur and other North Asian peoples, 'The Ilongot sense of history [is] conceived as movement through space in which (and this is the usual analogy drawn) people walk along a trail and stop at a sequence of named resting-places' (1980: 5). Urgunge laughed when I mentioned this quotation to him and pointed out that Mongols would normally ride. Be this as it may, all these journeys, trails, and stopping-places were only events in lives which led up to death, and in the

7. Mirror, bead, and human bones at a shaman's grave in Huuchin Barga, near Hailar. The characters read *Tien Xia Tai Ping* (Great Peace under Heaven). People are afraid to approach the site and the objects had lain untouched in the sandy steppe for many years. Photo: 1993, Hürelbaatar. [3.2]

Daur view it was significant deaths which, paradoxically, inserted conscious-ness into the inanimate world.

In North Asia, very broadly speaking, as the great empires of the steppes have waxed and waned in history, there has been a corresponding fluctuation of the influence of shamans. Once a centralized state was established, great sacri-fices organized by clans and other polities, of which the present *oboo* cults are a continuation, increased in importance. Shamans, who were spirit-masters, were pushed aside, remaining socially significant only in the periphery (Humphrey 1994*b*). Often the state ceremonies took on a Buddhist form, Buddhism having repeatedly become the state-promoted religion in the Khitan, Jurchen, Mongol, and Manchu Empires. Shamanic resistance to Buddhist missionaries in the periphery is well documented, especially for Buryatia during the late nineteenth century (Gerasimova 1970; Abayeva 1986). It is among the peoples who happened to be on the fringes of empires at this time, when ethnographers began to study them, that we discover descriptions of the flourishing of shamanship, a rococo luxuriance of spirits, myriad types of shaman, ritualist and curer, and shamanic rituals which touched almost every aspect of life. The various tribes of the Altai Mountains, Tuva and Buryatia, located on the borders between the Tsarist and Manchu Empires, are cases in point. I mention this because the invasive potential of shamanship in these regions has been the cause of misunderstanding of 'shamanism' in general. It has been assumed that the Buryat (or the Altaian) forms *are* 'classic shamanism' (Potapov 1991), whereas in fact the ethnography only describes a particular and extended state of shamanic practices at a given historical time (late nineteenth and early twentieth centuries). Looking at the same peoples at a different date, or at the people located deep inside the great Empires, like Urgunge's Daurs, would show different patterns.

Here I discuss the native idea that death transforms the souls of certain people into spirits, which are thereby freed from physical human bodies and able to reside in other objects in nature. I shall describe how this encountered the idea discussed earlier, that natural objects have energies and powers of their own, and I show how in some places the two struggled for supremacy and in others merged in an uneasy linkage. The different patterns are significant not only as sensibilities, but also because they implied competing kinds of claim over land.

Among early twentieth-century Buryats we find that 'master-spirits' of the land (*ezhid*), instead of being conceived on Daur lines as identical distant white-haired old men, had quite different characteristics. They were male and female, young and old, named, often called ancestors, had experienced birth, suffering, and death, came out of their tree, water, or mountain habitations to ride or fly around, wore clothes of particular colours, took on various animal and bird forms, talked to people through shamans, and often interfered in human life. They had relationships with one another, and in the landscape they had their 'seats', 'running places', and sites of notable mishaps and adventures. Above all they had personalities, feelings, and motives.

Now very often the expressions used by Buryats conflate such lively spirits with objects in the landscape; for example people say they 'worship the pine-tree' (*narhanda mürge-*). However, recent ethnography makes clear that such trees are the sites of human deaths. The master-spirits are not spirits *of* the tree, rock, or hill, but souls-turned-spirits located *in* them (Galdanova 1987: 31). The difference from the Daur stories is that such sayings are not about trees so much as about a real human event. Noteworthy ancestors, virtually always shamans, were in fact buried in trees. The entire corpse,[9] or, after a second funeral just the bones, was placed inside a hollowed-out tree trunk and the bark carefully replaced so the tree could continue to grow.[10] The soul-turned spirit in the tree then became the master-spirit (*ejin*) of that place.[11] Unlike the *oboo* cult, which could be carried out at any suitably impressive mountain and could be transferred to another mountain if a group moved away, the shaman-ancestor cult was tied to *unique* places, just as each shaman was unique in a way that clan elders were not.[12]

However, although all shamans' deaths everywhere in North Asia resulted in the emergence of spirits, these spirits were not always seen as masters of the land. The Naun Daurs were highly parsimonious in this respect. Urgunge mentioned only one place he thought might have been a shaman necropolis, a grove of trees on a hill on the way from the millet fields. Not only were the villagers unsure that this was a shaman's grave, but even if it had been they would have avoided it rather than carry out any worship there.

I remember my older brother telling me about what happened one day when he was coming home from the fields at dusk in his cart. He was hurrying because it was getting dark, and he took a new route. As he passed the grove he suddenly froze with fear because he heard a bell. it must have been a shaman's grave. Just a distant tinkle. But none of us ever went near there after that.

Omachi (1949: 24) and Mergendi (1987) confirm that Naun Daur shamans were laid to rest in the branches of trees or the tops of mountains at distant quiet places 'where the barking of dogs cannot be heard' and that these sites were soon forgotten. The souls/spirits of shamans floated free from the land and its powers.

However, among Darhat and Barga Mongols, Hailar Daurs, Buryats, and many other Siberian peoples, shaman mortuary sites are found everywhere and are remembered for generations. This perhaps correlates with genealogical memory in general, which went back among Naun Daurs for only three to five generations, but among Buryats sustained immense backward vistas of ten to twenty-five generations (Baldayer 1961; Humphrey 1983: 389–90). One could advance several reasons for this difference. Among Buryats many practical decisions depended on clan ancestry, such as land rights, political position, and complex marital relationships, but among Daurs the Banners had many of these functions. The shamanist Western Buryats were conquered by the Russians and gradually forced out of their best lands from the seventeenth century onwards.[13] By the late nineteenth century a decline in population had also set in, and this was often seen as due to lack of attention paid to ancestors and land-spirits. With the increasing powerlessness and fragmentation of their patri-clans Western Buryats laid ever greater emphasis on magical, shamanic, and female ties to land (Humphrey 1979). Their political leaders were glad to strengthen their powers by themselves becoming shamans, something unthinkable among Naun Daurs in recent centuries. There was an almost neurotic refusal to let go of ties between people and unique places.[14] The Buryat landscape thus had to find room for large numbers of remembered ordinary ancestors, as well as shamans, and indeed, when a clan lived in a place for a long time the nearby hills accommodated whole groups of them.[15] Even in Buddhist Buryat regions like Selenga every local section of a clan worshipped both at several *oboos*, where rituals were conducted by lamas, and also at several shamanic burial sites (Abayeva 1986: 76–85).[16] The hills, rivers, and trees were seeded with ancestral spirits, awake and threatening, thus turning the whole landscape from the venerable to the prophetic.

The Daurs of Hailar were more prone to such ideas than Urgunge's people. Perhaps this was because Manchu-Chinese state structures were weaker and clan groups stronger in this frontier area. In the early twentieth century, sovereignty over Hailar swung between China, Russia, and Mongolia, but the real powers were local aristocratic clan sections. In the region of Hulun Buir, of which Hailar was the capital, the many different ethnic groups were in competition for territory. Whatever the reasons, all the people of this area (Bargas, Buryats, Daurs, Evenks) remembered shamans' graves.

Among Hailar Daurs a special *oboo*[17] and the shaman's grave were constructed right next to one another, but even so there are hints that the two ideas, the 'energies' of natural objects themselves and such objects as the vessels for the souls of deceased shamans, were kept separate. The shaman had to have a double 'burial'. The dead shaman's body, wrapped in a cloth, was laid at any place he or she had decreed, usually on top of a high hill. Shamans approaching death would 'examine their dreams (*soolong*)' to discover where this place should be. The corpse was placed on a scaffold on the hill-top and this was called *shand* or *shandon*. To the north, some 30–40 metres away, people piled up stones in a cairn, and this was called the *shandoni oboo* (Omachi 1949: 24). After some time, when the flesh had disappeared from the bones, or after the corpse had been burned by wild fire, a member of the family or clan went to collect the bones for the second burial.[18] The bones were now put in a wooden container inside a white cloth sack. Stones were piled up around it, and a pupil shaman of the dead man established a nearby tree as the *tooroo* (ritual tree). This complex, the tree-plus-cairn (*shand*) with its nearby *oboo*, was a sepulchre for the *hojoor barkad*, the spirits of the shamanic ancestral line (*DSHI* 1985: 258; Mendüsürüng 1983: 272).

Only shamans, and certainly not Buddhist lamas, could control these spirits. Every three years the next shaman from this line should visit the site, circumambulate it (*shand erge-*), and pay his respects to the 'ancestor'. A Daur from Hailar told me that on these occasions a few people would come to ask the shaman to call down the spirit and make prophecies. They would bring a sheep to kill as an offering. 'Don't make us suffer! Please be kind to us!' the people would beg the spirit. 'Tell us what will happen. We are all innocent!' Mendüsürüng, a Daur scholar from Hailar, sang me a song which the shaman used to sing at the *shand*,

> When two dragons [*mudur*] are struggling,
> When the blue grass and willow-leaf vegetable is flourishing,[19]
> *Oboo shand* renewal, what is this?
> Go round [them], build [them] up, make an offering.
> The time is when the willow-leaf vegetable is flourishing.

Mendüsürüng told me he thought the two struggling dragons referred to conflict between the shaman's spirit and that of the local territory (in Hailar

land spirits were known in Mongolian as dragons (*luus*)).[20] Among the Høvsgøl
Darhat Mongols a fusion between the shamanic and locality spirits seems to
have been ritually averted, since the shaman's second burial was called 'separating [the bones] from the land spirits' (*gazar-un ejed-ece salgahu*) (B. Rinchen
1962: 254). However, despite this, both Hailar Daur and Darhat made claims
that their spirits 'were' mountains.

Shaman ancestor spirits proclaimed geographical and even cosmic powers in
those areas where shamans were socially powerful. Shamans' songs referred
obliquely to titanic struggles between shamanic spirits in their cosmic manifestations and the energies of other mountains and cliffs in the landscape. As
an example let us return to the song of the Darhat Mongol spirit, Baglain
Udagan (see 1.5), bearing in mind that the reason I reintroduce this contemporary material is to draw some contrasts with the Naun Daurs.[21] Here we
return to the background knowledge held by ordinary people which enables
them to understand (to some extent) the strange images of shamans' songs.
The Baglai spirit sings through the shaman about giving birth to her son and
daughter:

> My hugely grown body
> Kicked the taiga forest green with juniper

Now this, according to local people, refers to a magical vast bodily extension,
such that the spirit's head is pillowed on one forest while her legs kick another
forest. A story is told about this.

When the high lama Jalhanz Hutagt Damdinbazar was on his way to Hüree,[22] he saw a
huge rainbow stretching from the Agaar mountain range in the north to the Øgløg range
in the south. He told his disciples and followers to stop his sedan carriage and said,
mysteriously. 'Hoo, now we must offer milk to this married woman.' The lamas
sprinkled milk and the rainbow immediately disappeared. What was this rainbow? The
Agaar mountain's spirit, Baglain Udagan, had sworn to insult and pollute a Halh
Mongol Living Buddha by making him pass under her crotch. So the transformed body
(*huvilbar biye*) of the mountain stood on the back range of Agaar and stretched its other
foot to the front range of Øglog and was looking shading its eyes with one hand. The
Jalhanz Hutagt knew this, offered milk, and dispelled it. (Dulam 1992: 76).

Here we see that Darhats understand the spirit to have taken the form of a
rainbow and also to be the 'transformed body' of a mountain. Now this is a
really existing mountain in the vicinity, of which Baglain Udagan is the master-
spirit, and its name, Agaar, means 'Airy'. The mountain spirit's existence in
these ethereal forms is combined, later in the song, with insistence that it also
has a human physical life (her reddish-yellow body, flesh, wrinkles). All of this,
the denial of geophysical solidity, the magical ability to take other forms, the
fleshly body, the 'luck' and 'fortune' of giving birth, are challenges to the
patriarchal cult of mountains and the Buddhist repudiation of physical birth.

The shaman rages against secular and Buddhist powers together. So the mountain which is the emblem of the hated Wang Banner prince (who, it may be remembered, had put Baglain Udagan's son to death) is attacked by the shamanic line of spirits. Thus, the Baglain spirit rails against the 'chill-air red cliff' and conjures its crust of earth away, and we later learn that this very conquered cliff is the same as the 'red cliff of Hundas [place-name]', where Baglai Shaman's son, also a shaman, became an eagle and used to perch (Dulam 1992: 77).

'Chill-air red cliff' and 'Airy Mountain' were shamanic ways of talking about the landscape which overturned ordinary ontological expectations and laid claims to occult powers over the vicinity. I have suggested a historical argument why shamans in some areas made these claims, while in others, as among Urgunge's Daurs, they did not. But perhaps such an explanation is insufficient, and we should think also of the cognitive effect of shamanic images. It is a fact that particular images which deny ordinary assumptions in quite specific ways crop up again and again in Inner Asia, across thousands of miles and over centuries. Heissig (1992: 99–104) cites a Chahar text of the early seventeenth century in which a shaman dies and is interred on a red cliff, and, as the people worship, the cliff is surrounded in cloud and fog, a magic sign; the dead shaman's soul then allies itself in friendship with the spirit-masters of the place (*gazar-un ejid nibdag shibdag*) and becomes the protecting genius of the red cliff. Perhaps some ideas are more attractive or salient than others and can spread, last, or re-occur for this reason (Sperber 1985*b*, 1990). For Daurs of Hailar the idea that spirits of the animate shamanic type invade the landscape is compelling, and it pushes into the background the idea of the intrinsic energies of inanimate things. This may explain the otherwise somewhat confusing statement of a Hailar Daur woman to me:

The Daurs do not think that there is a soul (*sunesu*) in all things. They think that only those beings which are alive (*ami gool-tai*) have souls. If people see mountains, water, and trees as having souls this is because some shamanic master soul (*ezelegchi*) has been put in, and because of this people say they have souls, but this is not really a soul of the mountain, water, or tree. Daur shamans never worship land spirits (*gazar-un ezed*), they only worship their own dead shamans' spirits. But this said, the dead shaman spirits are immediately made to reside where the land spirits live and become assimilated with them.

Whatever the reason for these ideas, the result is a landscape linked by a skein of interrelated points of shamanic power. For example, there is one small district near Hailar, Hargant Sum in Huuchin Barga Banner, where even today around thirty shaman's mortuary sites (*shand*) are recognized in a population of some one thousand people. These are frightening and dangerous places, best approached only by other shamans (see Plate 7).

The land itself at such places, though hardly externally marked at all, is a medium for the transmission of shamanic power. One of the best-known

Hailar Daur shamans earlier this century was Pingguo Yadgan, who went one day,

with his grandfather when he was 17 years old to a *shand* in Huuchin Barga to pay his respects. On the way back they realized that they had left the silver offering cup behind. Pingguo went back alone to fetch the cup, but because he was in a hurry he did not bow to the shaman's grave again. He just took the cup and turned his horse to gallop back. Normally the horse was very quiet, but it suddenly threw Pingguo to the ground. Pingguo's back and shoulder were dislocated and he went out of his head. The grand-father waited, and when he went back to look he found his grandson lying completely mad, yelling and yelling. He had to be taken back by ox-cart. His back and shoulder soon recovered, but the madness did not go away. No shaman could cure it. Pingguo used to go round the village with a small knife, cutting his own belly and tongue. People were scared and hid their knives from him. Sometimes he was normal, but sometimes he was very bad. He said that unless they let him become a shaman he would be a danger to everyone. In the end he took La Saman as his teachers of shamanic rituals, and at the age of 18 he went through the *ominan* ritual under La Saman and became a regular shaman. (Omachi 1949: 27)

This discussion has enabled us to see a significant difference between Naun and Hailar Daurs. In Naun Daur society at the time of Urgunge's youth the male-focused religious cult held shamans in check locally. It is for this reason, I think, that the symbolic human vitalization of the inanimate world did not get very far in their cosmology. As we have seen, in Urgunge's village the grove where a shaman was rumoured to have been buried was a place of muted significance, and no rites were held there. A crucial tie between the shaman's existence and that of the lived-in landscape was absent. So perhaps it is not an accident that Du Yadgan, the shaman Urgunge remembered from his child-hood, was absolutely unconcerned with (perhaps debarred from) the public political life of society, whereas we shall see that in the Hailar region there was a shaman, Huangge, who was intimately connected with secular power, even though she was a woman. Furthermore, one of the greatest *oboos* of Hailar district, attended by all manner of princes, dignitaries, and foreigners, was said to have a female shaman's grave beneath it—and this was despite the fact that no women or shamans were allowed to attend *oboo* rituals there (see Plate 10). In Urgunge's region of Butha, on the other hand, the landscape had its own energies, and the spirits of shamans were powerful in other ways. As I describe in 6.2, they were manifested pervasively, in creatures, sounds, insects, or parts of people, and their mobility and dispersal was oriented not to local claims but to the Empire itself, centred in Beijing.

3.3 An Interlude: A Literary Traveller's Tale

How far away was Hailar from Urgunge's Butha district? We can have no idea of distance until we know about the means of travel and the difficulties of the road. Perhaps the idea of the hunting falcon was so seductive because of its effortless speed, and the shaman's magical journey the more so.

The Daurs had narratives of fantastic and cosmic shamanic journeys (6.5). But the people sitting and telling stories in the dark winter nights knew many other kinds of journey too. There was a very popular genre of travel odes, which were realistic accounts told in the first person, though using a lofty style.[23] Real journeys were fascinating to the Daurs, and we need to know how they were represented, and what kinds of oral-literary devices were used to make them understandable. The story I shall describe here concerns a journey over the mountains to sell carts at the Gangjuur Monastery fair in the Hailar region in the sixth year of Kuang-hsu (1880).[24] Here we come to understand the distance between Butha and Hailar as travelled by the most ordinary means, the lumbering horse-cart. Urgunge as a child knew about these cart-selling expeditions, which were still a regular part of the local economy.[25] Composed in rhymed couplets,[26] the ode (*utsun*) starts with a low-key preamble:

> There is nothing much to do sitting in the steppes
> but compose odes to spend the time.
> While rivers and mountains stand still,
> years and months circle on.
> Under the light of the August moon
> let us enjoy reciting odes
> while free from official duties.

8. Butha Daur cart-sellers' shelter at the fair at Gangjuur Monastery, with supports for cart roofs in the foreground. Photo: 1931, O. Mamen. [3.3]

Setting out from the village to sell carts, the caravan suffered at the foot of Ombochi Mountain for lack of water. Along the Arun some wheel-rims broke, and by verse seven we hear that there were round stones which were hard going, and verse eight concerns flat oval stones which were sharp and looked like lice. After some time the caravan arrived at Tulder Mountain which reached to the sky. Who could have chosen this road, the author wonders. Which generation of ancestors could be responsible? The carters barely made it up three slopes, and reaching the top they found an *oboo*. The caravan men prayed here for profits on the trip:

> We said our prayers to ourselves.
> I wondered whether [the spirit] understood.

After descending the mountain and plodding over numerous marshes, the caravan arrived at the Bogatu horse-relay station, then crossed the swift current of the Yaali River. Here they came across a terrifying waterfall, pouring down water from a hundred mountains, and knee-high rocks were slotted over one another like the bronze mirrors on a shaman's costume. The carts went haltingly forwards like scared camels and some of them broke down. The sounds of crying and shouting echoed in the mountains and cliffs. Angrily taking it out on their horses the carters dragged themselves to the top of another mountain. On the summit they found a red-roofed building. They had to ask what this tastefully constructed place was. The Lao-ye Miao, they were told.[27] The author wondered, 'Can this mountain really be where spirits [*endur*] reside?' A thin fog descended, and struggling forwards they came to a shadowy thick forest where there was a fence made of twigs. Nearby was a spring of cold pure water, which the author drank with both hands. His thoughts were as clear as the water. The next verses describe more stones, then a long stretch of bog and red-coloured mud; lurching through this was like the action of *twaalen* [a shaman's swaying when driving out spirits]. They pressed on right through the night and the author says that he stupidly lost his shoes. After many such mishaps at last they crossed the Baga Mountain range, and before them found a steppe, so full of sheep that they looked like flocks of geese. Here the carters suffered from lack of water. But from far away they could see the city of Hailar, where their goal was situated, the Gangjuur Monastery.

It took them some time to cross a dry steppe and then a rich grassland area, but at length they reached the monastery. Here in the bustle they saw tall Mongols who were wearing marten-fur hats. The author comments:

> They don't know how to use the furs
> but it would be a pity to waste [furs by not selling them to the Mongols].

He noticed girls wearing all kinds of dresses and young men who appreciated them, touching the hands and legs of the girls. People were doing business everywhere. The lamas all seemed to have girl-friends. The author then comments,

> A thousand strange-looking Buddhas,
> Golden gods of a thousand kinds
> Looked like handsome human bodies,
> But can they imitate a real human being?

The lamas sitting on their identical cushions, he continued, looked like little upright hills, and the sound of a thousand of them reading scriptures was like the croaking of frogs. The Da Lama was sitting at the centre and grandly ordering the service. They were all making 'ong, ong' sounds which we could not understand. They made 'kung, kung' sounds which were not understandable either, and then as we were looking at them they began to sound like wild geese. The temple music, however, the cartmen enjoyed and that was something to touch the heart. They observed many other things too: the young lamas running round with tea-pots but managing not to spill a drop, the graceful Manchu inscription over the door, the pregnant women who came in kowtowing with each step (but taking a terribly long time mumbling with their mouths at each Buddha), the people who came to 'call back souls' who lit lamps in golden cups, and the strange deities depicted trampling on devils. The whole thing was impossible to describe. Here the author permits himself a brief moral thought:

> *Tengger* existing from ancient times
> Created countless things,
> But when we sit and think about it
> That multitude is not all the same.
> The roads of men's destinies
> Are not equally good.

Then they are on the way home again. The weather became cold at the foot of the Xing-an Range, dark blue clouds began to gather, and snow started to fall. Miserably wet and cold, they struggled on, and the author soon concludes with this couplet:

> Having toughened our very being,
> Barely reached home, we!

The point of this account is not to introduce fantasy but to represent reality, with our (Naun Daur) eyes. The tale establishes the horizons of our own shamanist valley, the wandering tracks in the mountainous forest, and the further horizon of the Buddhist other world of Hailar. The narrative structure and devices, even the tone, are not dissimilar to European travellers' accounts of Mongolian monasteries. Facticity is established: the place-names are given, the author lost his shoes, he was not sure if the mountain spirit understood him.

Strange things over there (huge flocks of sheep, the lamas) are likened to humdrum things back home (geese, frog-noises). Fun is made of the Buddhist lamas, whose exoticism and hypocrisy is correspondingly emphasized. As with all the travellers' accounts we know so well, the author makes sure his audience realizes how terribly difficult and uncomfortable the journey was. Perhaps two things can be said about this. First, there is nothing naïve about this account, which like most travellers' tales subtly serves to reinforce a sense of superiority while representing the marvels of elsewhere. Secondly, the world in general may think of shamanism as primitive and peripheral, but it is quite clear that this is not the view from within. Instead, the author has a firm sense of his place and his values when he questions, can all those golden Buddhas imitate a real human being?

Notes

1. Shirokogoroff (1935: 125) complains of the same tendency of ethnographers to latch on to folklore and mistake it for conceptions people really hold, and even worse, to conflate European rationalizations with those of the indigenous people (1935: 54). This tendency is evident in ethnographic descriptions of ideas about the soul as well as the construction of the universe.
2. Also, Ilmu-khan, Yalaa-khan, or Erlig-khan. The Mongol equivalent is Erlig Khan. *Er'/Ir* is the Mongol and Daur word for 'male' or 'man', while *-lig* is a noun-forming suffix indicating 'having the properties of'. Thus Dulam (1989: 182–3) interprets Erlig-Khan as the incarnation of maleness.
3. Hohhot is the capital city of Inner Mongolia and many Daurs live there.
4. For example, if you look at your parents or elders in a hostile way you will have stakes driven into your eyes in Irmu Khan; if you say hostile words, your tongue will be torn out; if you raise your hand, your limbs will be systematically broken or torn off.
5. A Hailar Daur said, 'If a young person died and they did good things then their soul goes down to Yalaa-khan but it will be reborn: the soul searches the world and enters a woman's belly and becomes human again. Old people over 50, provided they have grandchildren, go to Yalaa-khan and then soon become *endur*s, and then they are never born again.'
6. The Altaian deity Ul'gen, for example, not only created the world and people, but in at least one ethnic group was said to have been a historical personage, Chinggis Khan (Potapov 1991: 250). Ul'gen has wives and numerous children and is essentially concerned with human offspring and health, the fertility of flocks and abundance of harvests. However, such are the variations in the images of this deity among the numerous tribes of the Altai region that Potapov concludes it to be essentially a female earth-deity (*Ul'gen-eke* ('Ul'gen-mother')) known among Mongol groups, later taken up by the Altaians, and transferred by them to the sky (1991: 251–2). Such an idea seems largely speculation, but it is significant that Ul'gen-type deities are not found in early and medieval sources, and

Potapov's other theory, that the concept emerged or was at least strengthened under the influence of Christian missionaries, seems more probable (1991: 140: 245–6).

7. In the Altai the same shaman might conduct both, but the downward ritual was done at night, while the celestial one was done only in day time in summer. The shaman wore different clothes for the two rituals, wearing his shaman's costume only for the night journey (Potapov 1991: 273). To my mind Galdanova (1987: 81–7) has provided the best account of the diverse and fragmentary information on 'white' and 'back' shamans, which makes clear that the distinction was analogous to the difference between the *bagchi* and the *yadgan* among the Daurs. West Buryat white shamans conducted large communal sacrifices. In the 19th and early 20th centuries clan elders, men of great old age, were often called white shamans, though they could also be called by other names, for example *hada tahigsha* (conductor of offerings to cliffs) (1987: 83). White shamans often performed without drums or the special shaman's costume (1987: 85). Black shamans were not allowed to take part in the clan rituals of the white shamans, nor were married-in women coming from other clans. The black shaman differed from the white in that his (her) spirit ability (*utha*) came from outside, by the female line, whereas the white shaman was always identified with the patrilineal clan (1987: 84). However, it is important to take notice of the fact that white shamans *were* held to be shamans (*böö*). According to some accounts (Khangalov 1958: 153), they too were 'chosen by the spirits' and used altered states of consciousness.

8. For example, among the Evens in far northern Siberia, the people see themselves as riding reindeer and then crane in a journey to 'meet the sun' in an annual ritual which began and ended with circular dancing (Alekseyev 1993: 25–34). Such rituals could involve ritual specialists ('white shamans') but not those of the 'black' category, more akin to the Daur *yadgan*.

9. This was done in Barguzin in Buryatia: Bair Gomboev, personal communication.

10. A ritual for worship of one such site in Alar is described by Ksenofontov (1992: 138–46). The shaman ancestor in this case had died three hundred years ago and all signs of the burial had long since disappeared. Therefore people did not know exactly which tree it was that contained his bones. The worship was addressed to all growing trees at the site, including birches, even though the shaman's remains were said to have been placed in a pine-tree.

11. It should be noted that the term *ejin* (pl. *ejid*) itself does not denote any particular kind of spirit. Some of the Buryat *ejid* are not derived from ancestors, for example, those of the sun, moon, etc. Shirokogoroff (1935: 126 *et seq.*) notes this word is used for a wide variety of spirits also among the Tungus. Although they always existed in some definite place or object, Buryat *ezhid* could also 'rule' abstractions and activities, such as ploughing, fighting, administration, musical sounds, metal-work, shamanic abilities, learning, arts, games, weddings, family accord, and numerous diseases (Mikhailov 1976: 302–13).

12. The ongoing history of shamans' deaths was the model, by reference to which non-ancestral deaths also pervaded the landscape. In each case there was a reason why the person's soul became a spirit. The village of Fofanovo on the shore of Lake Baikal at the mouth of the Selenga River has as its *ejin* the spirit of a retired Russian major, Yefim Pavlovich Sedykh, and this cult started when there was an epidemic

of the plague in the region. A nearby village had as its *ejin* a Russian ambassador who died in 1641 (Mikhailov 1979: 141).

13. Earlier, in 1702, the Khori Buryat clan chiefs had organized a collective delegation to the Tsar to establish their rights to specific lands in Trans-Baikaliya and they took a young woman shaman, Abzha Udagan, with them. She was received by the Tsar, Petr I, as an equal with the head of the delegation, Badan Turakin (Chimitdorzhiev 1991: 30–3).

14. The Western Buryats, if they migrated to another region, which many thousands of them were forced to do by Russian colonial settlements, would return with great trouble and expense to invoke the spirit of a particular place even many generations later.

15. Examples are the *Tarsain ahanad* (the elders of the village of Tarsa) and the Ardain Arban (the Ardai ten) (Manzhigeyev 1978: 18, 70).

16. The term *oboo* in such regions was polyfunctional and used for (a) any ritual conical construction of stones or branches, (b) hills sacred in themselves, (c) sites of ancestor worship (both shamans and other people who turned into spirits (Abayeva 1986: 74). Buddhist lamas took over the clan *oboo*s and those erected for worship of mountains, but they actively campaigned against the worship of shamans' graves (Abayeva 1992: 74–5).

17. This was different from the *oboo*s constructed by clans, Banners, or villages.

18. According to Omachi the person collecting the bones was accompanied by a shaman, the next in the shamanic line (1949: 24).

19. Mongols and Daurs call the first emerald green grass of spring 'blue', and I have translated *kumbil*, a type of salix, as 'willow-leaf vegetable'. *Kumbil* is a sign of spring. It is used by Daurs to make a soup.

20. Urgunge agreed with this idea, though two struggling dragons are elsewhere said to refer to the advent of rain.

21. The Darhat material is contemporary (collected in 1991–2); therefore I use the present tense here.

22. Hüree is the present-day city of Ulaanbaatar.

23. Examples of this genre are the story of the soldier who had been to serve in distant parts of China, the ballad of the official sent to guard the northern frontier with Siberia (Poppe 1930: 21–5), or the account of the official inspection tour of the River Ergune (Engkebatu 1985: 37–48). Some of these have been written down.

24. The author of 'Ode on a Journey to Gangjuur Monastery to Sell Carts' was Mamegchi of the Ne clan of Haalchin village in the Butha region. He gives the date of his journey as 1880. It is not clear if the ode was first oral and then written down or whether the original was written. Daur was normally written in the Manchu alphabet at the end of the 19th century, but the published version is in Daur (in the Latin script) with a Mongolian translation (Odonggow-a (ed.) 1987: 309–37).

25. The Naun River Daurs, being farmers and living close to forests, were local experts in cart-building. Hailar, on the other hand, is situated in a wide steppe and most of the population were nomadic pastoralists. The Daurs living over there were farmers too, but living far from any woodland they relied on the Naun Daurs to provide carts.

26. By 'rhymed couplets' I refer to the standard Mongolian technique of linking two lines by rhyming the first words. This is called (in Halh) *tolgoi xolbogdo-* (to link the heads) and it is used in many different genres, oral as well as written.
27. This was a Chinese Guan-gung Temple, according to Urgunge.

4

Male and Female Traditions in Ritual

4.1 Ritualization and its Absence

The traveller's tale shows how even a deliberately prosaic representation of reality has its subtleties and its point of view. Its facticity is not transparent but constructed. Ritualization introduces other kinds of construction that can intensify the particular interpretations of reality of social groups and individuals. Just as 'reading a book' evokes a different visualization of the places and characters from 'seeing a film', the particular compositions of rituals make possible their own otherworldly and enchanted ways of putting ideas together. But although 'shamanism' does not exist anywhere without ritualization, we should beware of thinking that rituals are all there are to it. It is interesting to think about which parts of religious life are not ritualized and why this should be so.

Urgunge, however, would interrupt here. The sequential description followed in this book—concepts of natural objects, thoughts about them, and rituals addressed to them—is my idea, not his. He said he did not understand the word 'ritual'. He had of course heard English people using the word, but for him it was like a tag attached here and there, one of the useless preoccupations of academics (and pressing me to explain it, he was delighted to discover that anthropologists do not have a very clear understanding of ritual either). For him, things I called rituals were what had to be done to achieve some aim. Perhaps this attitude can be explained by the fact that 'shamanism', Urgunge's primary experience of religion, was rather little ritualized.

Rituals in North Asia are made up of action elements, which are combined variously on different occasions. These juxtapositions cross-cut any division which might be made between shamanic and non-shamanic practices. Thus a non-shamanic ritual, such as the Daur offering to Bayin Achaa, contained actions which were also used in shamanic performances. But the elements were brought together into different groupings and could be given different meanings in these two situations, and this also explains why many of these ritual elements were also compatible with quite different ideologies, such as Buddhism.

What were these elements? Amongst them were: aspersion (the throwing upwards and outwards of liquids, scattered into many drops); libation (pouring out liquids); fumigation by smoke; lighting small butter lamps; daubing with blood and other liquids; piling up stones; sending scented smoke; making offerings of cooked meat, tea, money, matches, and milk products; eating sacralized food; bowing and obeisances; circumambulation and circular dances; 'beckoning'; constructing a 'vessel', 'path', 'antenna', or 'obstruction' for invisible energies; tying scraps of cloth, ribbons, and hairs to sacred objects; setting up ritual (cut) trees; making scapegoats through which evil energies can be expelled; 'directing' the head and inner organs of an animal killed in propitiation; whistling, weeping, prayers, invocations, and the uttering of various shouts or calls which repelled or summoned supernatural powers. This is by no means a definitive list and it is meant only to convey the idea that there was a repertoire of ritual acts, which were often even called by the same names (or local variants) over thousands of miles in North Asia.

Rituals may be the major social occasions on which ideology is publicly proclaimed, but I do not agree with those anthropologists who suggest that ritual in itself is inherently ideological (e.g. Bloch [1985] 1989). It is necessary to have ideas in order to *give* meaning to liturgical (i.e. strongly ritualized) action, as such action is in principle separated from the usual intentionality which allows meaning to be inferred in everyday life (Humphrey and Laidlaw 1994). The ideas used to interpret ritualized actions may be ideological, i.e. representing the interests of a dominant social group, or they may equally well be idiosyncratic, heterodox, or tentative. They may even be absent. People can perform rituals with no idea about what they mean. There may also be rituals that seem 'deliberately' to construct gaps, empty even of those marked actions to which meaning might be attributed, leaving spaces for sensory experience. Daur worship of the sky was multivalent in this respect: it could take more, less, and non-ideological forms, and worship could also vary, independently, in the extent to which it was ritualized (in the sense of having established and repeated ritual procedures). This being said, the prism of ritual could refract a very specifically coloured view of the world, for example in the *oboo* sacrifices.

For the individual it is quite possible to hold ideological theories about the world without ritualizing them (and Urgunge is a case in point: he is a 'shamanist' in England where there are no shamans and no shamanic rituals). More generally, while the social establishment of ideology may well require there to be 'a systematic and furious assault on non-ideological cognition' (Bloch [1985] 1989: 129), a fragmented social organization may find such an assault difficult to sustain.

The actions comprising shamanic performances were much more variable than the sky or mountain rituals, and this is what one would expect with a practice concerned with managing the unpredictable (Hamayon 1990: 729–44). Shamanic performances included rather few sequences of named, pre-established, actions that 'had to be done', like other rituals. It is true that the actions of calling down a spirit, the entry of that spirit into the shaman, and the speech of the spirit, were marked in various conventional ways and can be described as ritualized (Siikala 1978). But all this took place among multifarious other components of the performance. These were mostly like ordinary everyday action in the sense that they could be changed easily to accomplish a goal. For example, one method of exorcism could be substituted by another 'better' one, or a technique of impressing and shocking people could be changed for another more sensational one (for examples see 5.7).

Urgunge's incurious attitude to ritual made me see that it is important to draw attention to religious activities that existed in its hinterland, in particular to actions that were undertaken by people on their own. Here I distinguish (*a*) lone rituals, (*b*) tacit rituals that were often not given propositional meanings in language, and (*c*) religious ideas and actions that were perhaps symbolic but were not actualized in ritual at all. I give some examples here.

Among the Daurs long periods spent by oneself, hunting, herding, logging, hoeing, and journeying, often meant that ritual worship, appeasement, and entreaty were done on one's own. A flick of alcohol in the air, a stone placed on a cairn, a horse's hair tied to a branch, leaning one's forehead against a rock, such actions could perhaps be seen as 'rituals' (or fragments of them), in the sense that they were elements in a culturally prescribed repertoire of ways of behaving, outside everyday activity and without an obvious 'point'. However, we must be careful here with the idea of cultural prescription. As Ingold (1992*b*: 453–4) notes regarding language,

We are inclined to think of use as founded on convention, when, in reality, convention can only be established and held in place through use. Thus to understand how words can acquire meaning we have to place them back in that original current of sociality, into the specific contexts of activities and relations in which they are used and to which they contribute.

The implication here is that use sometimes does not sustain convention, but changes it, and to explain this we must place the ritual action again in the 'current of sociality'. An example of this is 'kowtowing' which acquired a particular political weight during Urgunge's youth. The Chinese *kou-tou* and Mongolian *mørgø-* denote knocking one's forehead against something, and in the past this was the ground. Such deep prostrations came to be identified with submission to the previous 'feudal' state, the Manchu Dynasty, and particularly among nationalist Chinese became incompatible with the upstanding 'self' of the twentieth century. Daurs had kowtowed to *tengger* and to their parents at the New Year, and also to the *oboo*. By Urgunge's adulthood the Chinese would laugh scornfully at Mongols or Daurs for such an extravagant gesture, and therefore, even on their own, people altered the gesture of worship (*mørgø-*), now touching their foreheads to something more or less at head height.

Ingold (1992*b*: 451–2), following Langer (1942) and one might add Merleau-Ponty ([1945] 1962), has written that gestures are not representational but

'presentational', 'they do not *have* meaning, but *are* meaning, standing for
nothing other than themselves.' Ritualization, however, makes meaning (in the
sense of the point of the action) uncertain—the difference, say, between tying
your horse's rein to a tree and tying a scrap of coloured cloth to a tree. Rather
than looking for propositional or intentional 'meaning' in such actions, and
puzzling over whether they are to be counted as rituals or not, it is more salient
to think about the sensations 'presented' by the action. Religiously motivated
actions may involve touching some object (for example, the tree) or refer
to some external entity, but, 'the very existence of "things" is modeled on his
[the human being's] own inward expectation of strains, directions and limitations of his felt actions' (Langer 1972: 48). Urgunge said that when he returned
miraculously from the bandits his parents did not hold any ritual of thanksgiv-
ing. His mother went aside to 'pray' (*jalbira-*) by herself. When I asked about
this, he said *jalbira-* here did not refer to words, but to a gesture. His mother
put her two hands, with closed fists, on her breasts and bowed her head and
upper body in the direction of the north-west. This gesture was at once her
sensation of her physical self and her submission to bodily intimation of the
direction of *tengger*. At the same time, this action referred to other occasions of
'praying'.

Thus, though these sensations may be sought far away from other people, to
the extent this is done through rituals there always is some link with rituals
performed in communal contexts. As Atkinson writes, discussing Wana people
who go out to the forest to seek for secret magic 'on their own', 'I began to see
how much of the secret knowledge consisted of condensed allusions to the
public dimensions of healing ritual' (1989: 53). A Daur passing an *oboo* cairn on
his own and placing a stone there in some sense performs an echo of 'the *oboo*
ritual'. But at the same time, it seems to me important that the communal
ceremony has in the background the numberless occasions of lone and silent
enactments of this simple gesture.

Let us now turn to a different point. Contrary to the impression given
by some anthropologists, the absence of ritual does not mean you are any the
less religious.[1] On the contrary, as I understood from Urgunge, spontaneous
unmediated directness was most often sought for worship and awareness of
tengger, the most important of Daur religious ideas. The 'small sky' in one's
head was felt to be a part of the great sky overhead, and consciousness of this
alone was sufficient for realization of worship. In times of anxiety, foreboding,
or grief such a felt act of linking with the Sky was one's first recourse (not that
Urgunge was solemn about this—he called it a hot-line).

Why should the Daurs have preserved so much of religious life apart from
communal ritual? It was not that they were suspicious of ritual itself, as happens
in so many 'protestant' world religions (Humphrey and Laidlaw 1994: 36–42).
I had no hint from Urgunge that activities I would call ritual were regarded
as anything other than a worthy and suitable way that humans could act to

influence unseen powers, energies, and destinies. But perhaps keeping the possibility of religious experience apart from ritual had to do with the feeling that the energies of everything in the world were always and pervasively 'there', and present for everyone all the time. In this situation it is significant that communal rituals addressed to nature were quite limited socially. Virtually all of them were rituals either for men, or for women.

In most of these men's and women's rituals freshly butchered and cooked meat was offered and it is appropriate here to say a few words about 'shamanism' and sacrifice. The literature on North Asian shamanism generally calls any ritual in which an animal is killed 'a sacrifice'. However, it is useful to make a distinction between sacrifice and propitiation, as models to explain broad tendencies in Daur rituals of this kind. By 'sacrifice' I refer to the mystical giving-up of the life of the animal in return for a transcendental energy, which infused the social group with *keshi* (blessing, good fortune, luck). 'Propitiation', on the other hand, exchanged the animal's flesh for a variety of definite returns, such as the spirit agreeing to stay away or remove a disease. Daurs used different verbs for these two modes.[2] Celebrants ate most of the meat in either case, but Urgunge said (laughingly, because he now thinks this naïve) that in the type of ritual I call sacrifice this meat was considered still delicious, since the deity had taken only the life-force of the animal, whereas in propitiation the meat was tasteless, as the deity had consumed the essence of the meat itself, its vapour (*uur*). I see the rite at the *oboo* cairn as an example of the sacrifical model and the offerings made to various shamanic spirits (*barkan*) as typical propitiations. However, my distinction refers to the aim or mode of the ritual, rather than its addressee, so the Sky for example was given both sacrifices and propitiations.

Shamans did not carry out sacrifices and we can now see the logic of why this was so. Sacrifice was an intervention in the processes of the world, and the indeterminate blessing it brought was essentially simply the good fortune that the cyclical current of harmonic world processes should be maintained. It was the social group, represented by the *bagchi* or the 'old man', which made itself an actor in the drama of renewal by sacrifice. When benign renewal was disrupted, as with floods, wild fires, epidemics, plagues of locusts, absence of game, and so forth, the sky, mountains, or forest were also offered *ad hoc* propitiations. In Inner Asia as a whole shamans might, or might not, intervene in such situations, depending on whether their spirits, which were of human origin, had become land-masters and therefore potential causes of the disaster. In Urgunge's region natural calamities were not explained by shamanic spirits, because such spirits were not masters of the land (3.2). This is why both sacrifices and propitiations addressed to natural objects were carried out by the *bagchi*, who represented humanity itself as a constituent part of nature.

The rites of renewal of nature were carried out by both men and women, but separately and using different imagery. The *bagchi* served them both, using prayer and sacrifice. But despite this common idiom, the separation of the rituals suggests that in its address to the natural world humanity was considered as having two 'natures', that of men and that of women. We shall see later that this idea was challenged by shamanic practice. Meanwhile I briefly describe some major Daur rituals addressed to the natural world, followed by a discussion.

4.2 Single-Sex Rituals

*Rituals of men: New Year worship of the Sky (*tengger taki-*).*[3] The only regular offering to the Sky was on the eve of the lunar New Year (*anee*). This was a happy occasion, when the Seven Stars[4] and all of the spirits (*barkan*) of a household were also remembered. On New Year's Eve a small table was placed in the yard, on which were placed nine bowls of water and sticks of incense (*küj*).[5] Urgunge remembers a huge bonfire being lit just outside the courtyard.[6] The idea was that the smoke should rise to heaven. This fire should produce such heat that it would melt the icicles on the whiskers of the dragon (*mudur*) in the sky, as Urgunge's father used to say.[7] There were firecrackers and people would dance all night. Unlike the blood and meat 'fed' to the *barkan* spirits in the storehouse, the Sky was honoured with fire (*gal*), smoke (*honi*), and plain water (*os*). Urgunge said,

Tengger, humans, fire, and water, those were the elements. If we think about it, there is the vast arch of the sky, and the sun and the moon, like *tengger*'s eyes. If we look, the sun is fire, the moon is water. In fifty years' time, all of humanity will realize that clean air and pure water are the most important things in this world.[8]

The family was vulnerable at this time and closed in on itself. The family's protective spirits were said to have gone up to heaven in the great fire's smoke to receive blessing. All cracks on windows and doors were patched up. It was forbidden to call someone by name inside the house if you were outside. It was even inadvisable to look in a mirror in case an evil spirit 'came in' and made you lose your mind (see also 5.7). The worshippers stood by the table and individually bowed to the ground (*kou-tou*) before *tengger*. The head man of the family officiated and the shaman did not come. Women had to stay in the background, and if they bowed to *tengger* this was done as hierarchically lower members of the patriarchal family.

Since the purpose of the ritual had to do with the turning of the year, giving thanks for protection during the past year and requesting blessing for the coming one, the timing of incense-burning and kowtowing to *tengger* was very important. According to Li *et al.* (1955: 491), there was an elaborate series of dates over the New Year and during the waxing of the moon in the succeeding months when incense should be burned. Urgunge also linked time, in this case the life-span, with space when thinking about sacrifice to the Sky:

Inside the house there was a piece of cattle *hals*, a thin, transparent skin. It was a bag, something like a stomach membrane, and it was nailed up high on the wall in the main room. This represents your sacrifice to *tengger*. That was why it was put in the north-west corner [*hwaimar*]. If you are in trouble, you pray to *tengger* in that direction. Why the north-west? We always thought that the sun went down in the north-west, not the west. It rose in the south-east, and that is why the door faces always a little southwards from the east. Therefore the north-west was important, as man's destiny [Chinese *guishee*]. It was your coming death, just as your life follows the path of the sun.

*Sacrifices at sacred cairns (*oboo taki-*).* The ritual at the sacred cairn was the occasion to sacrifice not just to the mountain spirit but many other forces of nature, including *tengger*, Bayin Achaa, and neighbouring hills, cliffs, and rivers. The *bagchi* listed these places and their qualities. Rituals were conducted regularly in spring and autumn.[9] People prayed for human prosperity, for male descendants, for timely rain, wind, and warmth, for the elimination of calamities, storms, and cattle diseases, for abundance of the five cereal crops, the flourishing of domestic livestock, and the banishing of ticks and crop-eating insects.

Urgunge's village *oboo* was on top of a hill in the middle of the grain fields, which were some miles from the village. All the men of the village would go up the mountain for a sacrifice. No adult women could be present, as it was thought that they were unclean (*hwaski*). The shaman could attend only as an ordinary clan member, not as a shaman. The men would take a sacrificial cow or pig with them, buckets of water, pick up stones to put on the cairn, and carry fresh green willow branches which were stuck into the top of the cairn. They circled the cairn three times and tied coloured cloths to the branches. The sacrificial items were provided by the richer families. The animal was slaughtered, correctly butchered, a fire made, and the meat cooked. The bones were not burned, but left at the site. Incense was burned, bowls of alcohol and blood thrown to the cairn. The meat was then laid out piece by piece in the shape of the animal in a big container and placed to the front of the cairn (the south).[10] The participating men stood in order of genealogical seniority and an officiant, either a clan elder or the *bagchi*, would pronounce the prayers. In rhymed speech he asked the mountain spirit to 'come down', to deign to grant the people's requests and accept the offering. The participants splashed water all over the cairn and one another, and then they again circumambulated the site three times in the direction of the sun. Finally they had a big feast. The cooked meat was thought to be blessed by the mountain spirit and by heaven. Giving the deity food to eat was not the important meaning given to the rite; rather the meat was offered as a sign of reverence, and, one might say, as a material medium for the blessing (*keshi*) which was received in return.[11] The splashed water was said to signify the rain which the clan desired. Finally, the head, skin, and hooves of the sacrifical animal were hung on a tall pole facing the sky in a south-pointing direction, and left to the ravages of the weather.

Each of the eight Banners of Butha also had its own larger *oboo*, as did the central office of government (*yamen*). Throughout Inner Mongolia such grand *oboo*s were patronized by military, Buddhist, and civil authorities (see Plate 10). Whole regiments would attend, herds of cattle were driven up the mountain for sacrifice, and the prayers were said by the generals themselves. The construction of the *oboo* became an elaborate complex.[12] Most famous *oboo*s, like the ones in Hailar at Gangjuur Monastery and the Hot Springs (Haluun Arshan) were permanent, but the Daurs also selected lucky sites and made new *oboo*s every year (Akiba and Akamatsu 1941: 259). These large rituals were always followed by the 'manly sports' of archery, wrestling, field-hockey, and horse-racing.

Discussion. Urgunge was remarkably silent about the *oboo* ritual, which he thought of simply as 'something that had to be done'. However, meanings which may have been attributed to it emerge if we consider the present-day collective sacrifice to the sky (*tenggri takih joson*) among the Horchin Mongols, who live to the south-west of the Daurs.

The Horchins 'sacrifice to *tenggri* at hill-tops and hillocks, piling up trees or stones as a sign, every year in spring and autumn' (Manzang 1991: 73). The officiant is not the ordinary shaman (*boo*) but a specialist for this ritual, called *hondon*, who is the collector-in of blessings (*huriyachi*). The Horchins imagine ninety-nine *tenggri*s at different parts of the sky, and though the Skies vary the basic order for worshipping them is always the same. It consists of (*a*) a ritualized statement that the day chosen is the correct one for the main Sky being sacrificed to (this is done by correlating the directional position of the *tenggri* with the movements of constellations); (*b*) a song saying that the patron of the sacrifice is making a libation of alcohol and a sandalwood incense-offering in true belief; (*c*) a calling down of all of the ninety-nine *tenggri*s in groups, e.g.

> 'O riding on a blue cloud,
> Following a lucky cloud,
> Coming across airy space,
> Twenty-five *tenggri*s, come down!'

(*d*) a ritual called *shuus zaana* (to point out the juice), consisting of 'calculating' the live animal's surface parts, praising them, and then showing them to the sky; (*e*) the killing of the animal; (*f*) collecting in the blessings; and finally (*g*) giving out the shares of sacred meat (1991: 77).

While the parts are being 'pointed out', the sheep or goat, which must be physically perfect, should stand still and be sprinkled with alcohol while a drum is beaten. When the meat has been cooked, it is put in a closed pot and placed on a table. The *julde* (heart, windpipe, lungs) is put separately at the highest place of all. Then the patron, the person who provided the animal for the sacrifice, kneels while the *hondon* 'calls in' the blessings. The *hondon* now takes the *julde* in both hands and makes the patron of the sacrifice eat it. Just as he makes to bite it, the *hondon* moves it back and forwards, pulling it and pushing it in his mouth, and everyone makes jokes at the kneeling patron's expense. The patron of the sacrifice at last manages to bite the *ug* (root, stump, trunk) of the *julde*, severing it and eating a piece. At the very end of the ritual everyone tastes the liquor and the meat, says some auspicious words, and then they disperse.

One compelling interpretation of such rituals can be deduced: the living, juicy, perfect parts of the animal are given to the sky or mountain spirit. The *julde*, which signifies animate life, is ritually transformed, blessed, and made 'eternal', and the communal eating of those same parts injects blessed 'life' to the clan (see Bloch 1992*a*). Note that the *ug*, the part of the innards the patron should eat, is called by a word which is used in all Mongolian languages to mean patrilineal origin and descent. Daurs and Mongols often pair this word with *yazguur* (Daur *hojoor*) 'ancestry'. Both words, *ug* and *yazguur*, refer not only to human descent but also to plant growth, to that spot from which roots grow downwards and the stem grows upwards.[13] Although Urgunge could not say which part of the *julde* (breathing organs) was called the *ug*, the situation seems clear enough: the patron ingests that part identified with patrilineal origin and growth and which is now sacralized by the spirit.

A related interpretation seems possible here too: as with the scattering of water at the Daur *oboo*, the Horchin manipulations with this organ in the patron's mouth may well symbolize the male part in procreation. Male fertility is commonly associated with *oboo*s. The Mongols and Daurs put the skulls of favourite horses on *oboo*s; when the skull is that of a stallion people take their mares to the spot to ensure it will bear young (Chabros 1992*a*: 77). Elsewhere in Mongolia it is very often children who are taunted with the chosen bit of *julde* meat and, amid general laughter, they fight to snatch and bite it (Chabros 1992*a*: 96). Chabros sees this struggle as part of the ritual (children are normally respectful and quiet in the presence of elders) and as the creation of energy by a necessary degree of violence. Indeed, one could liken this to the forceful 'manly games' which take place at the end of the ritual.

All over Mongolia the last section of this type of ritual is called *dalalga*.[14] This term denotes both the gesture of beckoning, a circular waving of the arms which draws in the blessing, and the sacralized meat in the pot to be shared by all those present. *Dalalga* involves the transfer of blessings, usually through an arrow, into the contents of a sacred container. It can occur on its own, simply to draw down blessings to a family, but more commonly it is added to a host of

9. Men circumambulating the sacred cairn at Banchir Bogd's *oboo* near Hailar. Photo: 1931, O. Mamen. [4.2]

10. A man with a long pigtail (left) bows to Buddhist lamas at the *oboo* ritual of Bayin Hoshuu near Hailar. Photo: June 1931, O. Mamen. [4.2]

other ritual actions: for example, sacrifice to the sky, the *oboo* ceremony, calling
in the migratory birds in spring, sacrifice to the fire-deity, calling in the blessing
of the camels, beckoning the blessings of a bride back to her kin when she leaves
on marriage, or those of a son when he leaves for war (Chabros 1992*a*). Although Daurs did not have some of these rituals and only used the *dalalga* for
the fire offering (see 4.4) and the bride (Batubayin 1990: 169), we can see echoes
of the ritual elements of *dalalga* in Daur mountain and sky sacrifices, especially
the concern with verticality, the idea of the sacred container, and the sharing of
blessings.

The ritual of the *oboo* seems to be related to a sacramental tie between men
and their land. The celebrants were those who, by a sacrificial exchange,
acquired the blessing of the mountain spirit to make use of the land for the
reproduction of life. At the same time the *oboo* games were actions in time
which propelled the good future into existence. Kabzinska-Stawarz, who has
made a study of Halh Mongolian 'manly games', found many symbolic acts
supporting these assertions (1991: 87). For example, the wrestlers rubbed earth
on their hands to gain strength from it and touched the earth before and after
the fight. The winner touched milk foods (*tsagaan idee*) to his forehead and then
threw them towards the spectators, the *oboo*, the mountains, and the sky,
'sharing the victory' with them and other young wrestlers, and the whole
population were said to gain strength from this (1991: 89). When an archer hit
the target, the spectators shouted a long-drawn cry, 'Uuhai!'. This call reached
the *oboo*, the sky and mountain spirits, making them rejoice. If the locality spirit
was asleep it would wake him up, resulting in rain and abundance (1991: 104–
6). The archery competitions, horse races, and games of field-hockey organized
by the Daur clan 'to maintain the physical vigour of young men' (Batubayin
1990) probably involved similar ideas[15] (see Plate 11).

The ideological aspect of the *oboo* ritual and the associated games can be seen
in the fact that the renewal, the vigour, and the blessings came only to male-
defined groups—the patrilineal clan, the military Banner, the administrative
unit, etc.[16] In other words, we see here the ritual activation of what Bloch
([1977] 1989: 13) calls 'social structure'. 'Social structure,' he notes, 'far from
being society, turns out to be a system of classification of human beings linked
to other ritual cognitive systems, such as the ritual notion of time.' Real human
sexual reproduction was excluded from this idea of renewal, the banning of
Daur women being explained explicitly by their *hwaski* (pollution from sex,
menstruation, and childbirth). It was men and boys alone, who, by each placing
stones and willow saplings, and splashing water over the *oboo* and one another,
symbolically put themselves in the position of the object to be 'fructified' by
rain from the Sky.

Even today outsiders, like anthropologists or guests, are kept out of the heart
of this ritual which is the sharing of the sacralized meat (Sneath 1991: 150–9).
This exclusivity is not because there is a feeling that the blessings were scarce.

11. The winning horse at a race in the 'manly games' after the ceremony at Bayin Hoshuu *oboo* near Hailar. Photo: June 1931, O. Mamen. [4.2]

Rather, this is an ideological *definition* of the particular social grouping engaged in the compact with ongoing nature. In the past this pointedly excluded women and shamans.[17] The permanence and solidity of the mountain was an analogy for the 'eternal' clan (Urgunge refused point blank the idea that any *mokon* or even *hala* had ever split), and the 'renewal' of the mountain by adding stones to the cairn paralleled the renewal of the clan by new male births. The circumambulation of the cairn not only enabled perception of its fixity but effected a symbolic binding-in of all the branches and flags brought to the mountain by the men and boys. And of course it was from this ideological viewpoint that all the spirits of replenishing Nature were imagined as deathless old men.

Propitiatory rituals in the all-male idiom used many of the same ritual actions, but were more explicitly concerned with the exchange, that is with the items given and the benefits to accrue. Preoccupation shifted to the value of the proffered animal itself, which was eulogized with elaborate hyperbole. In propitiation 'giving' and 'receiving' took place strategically, in awareness of other jealous actors in the metaphysical world.

Occasional offering to the sky (tengger taki-). I describe this rite because it has many features of the propitiation mode and indicates some important points of

contrast with the sacrifice to heaven. It took place if serious trouble threatened
a family. The ritual was done in strict privacy, but for different reasons from
those mentioned above for the New Year ceremony. According to the *DSHI*
(1985: 242–3), the family locked the big gate to the yard, or if they did not have
a gate they closed up the entrance with a rope net. A pair of boots was nailed to
the gate, or alternatively a man was posted on the roof with a bow and arrows.
Inside the house, they hung up a sheet to screen off the ritual area. The *bagchi*
would officiate. He pronounced a prayer as an ox or pig stood in the yard ready
for killing, and he scattered grains over it. The animal was given water to drink,
and its nose and ears dipped in milk. Mergendi (1987: 304–5) writes that a table
was put out in the yard, with a cooking-pot between it and the house, and next
to it was erected a tall tree with a bunch of grasses tied to its top. After the
animal was killed and skinned, small pieces of meat cut from the seven aper-
tures and the four hooves were put into the bowl of millet on the table. The
head, neck, heart, windpipe and lungs (*julde*) were cooked in the pot in the yard
and then placed on the table while the rest of the meat was taken indoors for
boiling. The cooking was done by men, and consisted only of meat and water,
unlike usual dishes, which had salt, onions, etc. added. The *bagchi* then invited
tengger to come down and partake:

Heavenly father, listen to our prayers,
Heavenly mother, understand all we say,
Heavenly princess sitting on the upper seat,
Please listen with your magical ears,
Heavenly lord sitting on the corner seat
Please observe with your snow-bright eyes.
Not because we have no reasons to seek your protection,
Not because we have no disasters to beg for your help;
Scrupulously we carry out the promises of the ancient day long past,
Now we offer the animal to you that you need.
Let us report our offering to you,
The pig is served by our own hand as follows:
It has ears like winnowing-fans,
It has eyes like blackberries,
It has black velvety short hair,
Its fat is like human fat,
It has a mouth like a ploughshare,
It has a ribbon-like tail,
It has fork-like hooves.
We have cut the life-vein of the animal,
We have opened up its internal organs.
We have reported about the killing to the gate spirit[18]
We have used the slaughtering-knife,
We have cut the tendons of its four limbs,
We took out the diaphragm,
We smeared the fresh blood on our spear,

We have put the important skeleton on the two sides of the offering table,
We have laid down the buttocks, shoulders, and shoulder-blades before your eyes.[19]

There followed an account of the family sufferings to be relieved. After everyone had eaten a small piece, the *julde* with the skin was hung on a long pole and the eleven small bits of meat were put in a cup attached to the tufted tree. These poles were then moved next to the gate and stuck in the ground so that the animal head and skin pointed upwards to the sky.[20] Then, having kowtowed to Jiyachi, the spirit of domestic livestock, everyone went inside and the master of the house continued praying and kowtowing before a table in the north-west corner on which the rest of the meat had been placed. After feasting on the meat, the people 'saw the spirits returning to Heaven'; the family then opened the gate.

The secrecy of this ritual was explained by Daurs not in terms of narrowing down the benefits to the family, but to hide it from Jiyachi, who would be jealous of the offering of livestock to heaven (Mergendi 1987: 304; *DSHI* 1985: 242).[21] An analogous idea seems to lie behind the boots on the gate and the man with bow and arrows on the roof, this time in relation to human neighbours: a woman told me that the first Daurs to propitiate *tengger* had stolen an ox for the offering, and to hide its footprints they made it wear human boots. The boots later became a sign that no one should enter because the ritual was in progress. These notions suggest that propitiating *tengger* was seen as an illicit procedure in relation to regular, communal worship of the Sky.

In propitiation the animal killed was understood as an object of value, strategically given. An extraordinarily large part of the invocation to the Sky was devoted to extolling the virtues of the pig, immediately followed by a description of the family's suffering to be relieved. In the propitiation model the meat was not transformed and blessed, but becomes the tasteless left-overs of the deity. With sacrifice, on the other hand, the medium of contact with the sacred was not conceived as an economic value (it could be fire, plain water, or grains in various enactments of *dalalga*). Crucially, the blessing in sacrifice was a normal or inevitable outcome produced by the rite, without the need for persuasion or bargaining with the deity. Blessing came to people as a result of the beneficent putting-in-motion of the way things are in the world, and therefore it was not necessarily enjoined that the powers in nature be seen as anything other than that. Propitiation, on the other hand, specified a responsive, jealous, human-like recipient, a being who noticed the cost of the offering and had to be persuaded to give something in return. This is why the speech to the Sky in the propitiatory mode specified anthropomorphic forms of *tengger* (i.e. father, mother, princess, lord), just as the prayer to Jiyachi specified him as the cook from Mongolia (see also 5.8).

Although Daur *yadgan* shamans did not make propitiations to the Sky, they did to other spirits and we can see that the propitiatory mode suggested the existence of human-like recipients in the world. We have seen how the Daurs and other peoples in Inner Asia veered between conceiving the world in more realistic and more anthropomorphized ways. The existence of the shaman was the corollary of the psychologizing, animating imagination, and this enjoined that a different, more calculating rationale be attributed to what were on the surface very similar acts of ritual killing of an animal. Such bargaining was an important part of shamanship (Hamayon 1990), but in my view did not constitute its 'essential structure', since it had many other ways of acting upon the occult world besides.

In the sacrificial rites, by contrast, shamans were kept out. These rites enjoined a view of humanity itself as 'natural', of men as different from women, of social processes 'being like', or paralleling, those of nature. The ethnographic literature about the Daurs, as if echoing this ideology, hardly mentions women's involvement in ritual. However, there were rituals for women alone, and although Urgunge did not know much about them, let us look at what materials we have.

Rituals involving women: sacrifice to the women's oboo *(*oboo taki-*).* The women of Urgunge's village had their own *oboo*, located on a ridge near the vegetable gardens which were right beside the homesteads.[22] The stated aim was to bring rain to the gardens, which were worked by women. This *oboo* was worshipped once a year. No males were allowed to take part, except young children and the *bagchi* who organized the ritual. The women took branches of trees and stones to place on the cairn, and a slaughtered chicken, or cooked chicken-meat, porridge, and dairy products to offer.[23] In Urgunge's village the women also took pails of water, while Batubayin says that the ritual was conducted in flooded land beside the river. Like the men, the women doused one another, to much laughter. This ritual was called *wudamla-* ('making *wudam*'—*wudam* is heredity, origin) (Batubayin 1990).

Propitiation rituals for the river. When the river was seen as an abundance of flowing water, rather than as a milieu for productive activities (fishing, log rafting), a female set of relations came into play. Urgunge remembers that it was women, not men, who made offerings to the Naun River at times of drought. This was an important ritual. Men, apart from the *bagchi*, were forbidden to attend. A headwoman gathered all the women of the village and they went on a trip which Urgunge knew as *duud gara-*, to go out on the *duud*, the distance of a pheasant's flight.[24] They went to a place on the river bank, if possible a flooded area where a flourishing tree was growing. The women took chickens and other food to offer; the *bagchi* helped them by killing the birds and chanting requests for rain while the women kowtowed. They had a feast at which the meat was shared. The women alone then went down to the river with buckets or bowls and splashed one another.[25] The chicken skins, feathers, head, and feet were left hanging on a tripod of posts by the bank. The authors of the *DSHI* (1985: 256) just hint at naughty goings-on: 'Those in the prime of life would splash each other until they were wet all over, and when they had really enjoyed themselves they would go home. This offering by Daur women to the river is not just a religious occasion, but also an opportunity for them to gather and engage in splashing and other activities.'

This ethnography implies that women's rituals were parallel and equivalent to the andro-centric rites of renewal, involving perhaps an ideology of 'women reproducing women'. Here, however, the idioms were different, involving mobility (the flow of the river, the flight of the pheasant), as opposed to the static ranks of mountains. This interpretation is supported by the evidence of women's ritual dances.

Women's ritual dances. Daur women had dances called *lurgel*[26] which were watched and admired by men. From one *lurgel*, however, men were totally excluded. This was the dance for Yao-li Gu-gu, which was performed each year at the New Year festival by all the unmarried girls and married wives of the village. *Yao-li* is a Chinese word for a large wicker rice-ladle with holes in it; *gu-gu* means aunt (father's sister). Urgunge used to watch secretly. He said that if you wet your finger and rubbed the paper window you could make a little hole to see through.

This is what he saw. The women took a pole and tied the rice-ladle to the top of it. They put the Yao-li Gu-gu pole in the middle of the room and danced round it. Three or four women held on to it with their right hands, making it go up and down. 'Someone told me,' Urgunge said, 'that the Yao-li Gu-gu will tell them if they will have children. It will fall over and point to those women who are to have children. When they dance madly like this the Yao-li's spirit (*onggor*) comes into the ladle, and they say Yao-li Gu-gu will dance all by herself!' An account given by a Daur woman ethnographer gives more detail (Sain Tanaa 1987a: 66–7). People say there was an old couple in the village who had a beautiful daughter, very skilled at dancing. She was their pride and joy and everyone loved her. She used to dance at the New Year, when people should eat dumplings. But the entire village only had two ladles. One day the daughter ran from the east to the western part of the village to fetch a ladle, but just as she was getting home, she tripped on a frozen cow-pat, and she died right on the spot. Everyone was very sad, particularly the other girls when they danced the *lurgel* at the New Year. They missed her so much they imagined she was dancing with them as before. But she was dead, and they broke off their dancing in an unhappy mood. Then they carved the wicker ladle, made legs for it, painted its face, put on beautiful clothes, and put on ornaments and hair-decorations. They took Yao-li (ladle) to the cowshed to call back the spirit, crying 'Yao-li Gu-gu, come back and dance *lurgel* with us!' Then they went back to the house and started to dance and sing. They got up on the heated bed and danced faster and faster, jumping merrily, and now they were expecting the Yao-li's spirit to come down. Yao-li swayed to the west and the east, lurching here and there, and in the end its legs were broken. Then the women said, 'Yao-li has come down . . .'. Holding one another in couples, two by two, they twirled, singing in a loud clear voice, '*Akenbei*' ('Success!'), and hearing this gave a pleasant sensation to the whole village on this festival day.[27] While the women dance with one another and with Yao-li Gu-gu, the old men tell the story of the death of the spirit to the young men.

Discussion of single-sex rituals. It is notable that the sexes were separated at these rituals, each performing equivalent rites on their own. In principle rituals are subject to various indigenous interpretations, and anthropological interpretations will therefore differ from them. A useful explanation from my point of view is that these single-sex rituals were symbolic inducements for internal regeneration of each gender. This is to suggest that the *oboo* rituals can be seen not just as the symbolic reproduction of the patrilineal clan, but in terms of a more abstract idea of 'replication', the reproduction of like by like, separately within each gender (see Strathern 1988: 182–5). The ritual created a framed context for the performance of relations; in the men's ritual these subsumed 'femaleness' within the manifestation of maleness, and in the women's ritual the reverse was the case. The relations which men had with women and women with men were bleached out. As will be discussed further in 4.4, this allowed for 'replication' and at the same time it made the two ritual processes parallel, though not symbolically identical, to one another. The 'male' form was centred. It took place at the *oboo* cairn, which all through Mongolia represented the focal point at which vertical appeals were made to the sky. The major 'female' ritual, by the river, by contrast, was uncentred and horizontal.

The name of the riverside ritual, 'pheasant's flight', was an image of starting and stopping and starting up again. In my interpretation, this was an analogy for the men's view of the movement of women in society, as they passed between clans. The rite included both in-coming wives, and sisters or daughters who were shortly destined to leave. This means that at least three clans were involved: the one from which the mothers came, the clan of the husbands to which they were now attached, and the clans to which the daughters and sisters were to go. The outward movement of women was counteracted by a *dalalga* ritual held at the time of a wedding by the bride's father in his own home (Chabros 1992*a*: 56–60). This was intended, according to some accounts, to call back the 'blessing' (*buyan kesig*) of the bride, which we may interpret as calling back some essence of the girl who was physically just leaving. However, it is interesting that the Torguud Mongols said the ritual was for calling a *new* 'blessing', to replace that of the lost girl. This, as Chabros (1992*a*: 60) remarks, may well have referred to the power to perpetuate life of the in-coming daughters-in-law who could now be sought by using the wealth acquired from outgoing daughters' bride-price. If so, the *dalalga* for the bride would represent a means of encouraging the linked movements of women on which the clan depended, while maintaining the boundaries that separated this clan from others.

However, perhaps there was another view from inside the Daur women's ritual. The flooded site, the source of water, and the experience of wetness all belonged to the river. Rivers in Mongolia virtually all have female names. Joining all women together, the rite itself in fact ignored clan boundaries, and separating women from men, seemed to take energy from the 'female' current itself, that is from the idea of the river as indissolubly unified and yet moving. We have intimations of women's viewpoints, which were not restricted to mimicking those of men (as at the women's *oboo*) but could also construct specifically female contexts of fertility. The annual Yao-li Gu-gu rite substituted the power of a dead girl's spirit for the male partner. It made the female energy of abandoned dancing the medium for a magical conception, and at the same time, in breaking the ladle, periodically destroyed the external instrument of procreation.

These single-sex rituals were not only concerned with 'replication' of men and women but with the compelling of natural events, and perhaps we can understand this by looking at the concepts of time that were implicitly involved. Although the 'calling-in' section of ritual in one sense was just what it claimed to be (beckoning-in the blessings), in another sense statements and chants associated with such rituals suggest that while this action was performed people supposed that something else happened in nature at the same time; notably the advent of rain. I suggest that this construction occurred both in the beckoning rites and the games that followed them.

Mongolian games were not at all a matter of leisure and the whiling away of time. Up to the mid-twentieth century they were a sacred duty, according to Kabzinska-Stawarz (1991). Games aimed to accomplish something, simply by the enactment of the necessary movements and gestures. To give an example, a favourite Mongol game, much beloved by Urgunge in his youth, is played with animal ankle-bones (small squarish bones) and one variant of this is simply to thow three or four bones in the air and catch them before they can fall to the ground with a continuous vertical movement of both hands. Now the ankle-bone games called 'mare milking' (*güü saa-*) and 'cow milking' (*ünee saa-*) were intended to bring an increase in dairy products and wealth. They were played only by boys. Kabzinska-Stawarz (1991: 21) writes (about Halh Mongolia),

An apparent line which the astralagus bones drew in the air was compared by my informants to a stream of milk or a white rope, while the bones were compared to female udders 'milked' by players. In order to make this symbolic milking more credible and magical, players assumed poses characteristic for people milking particular kinds of females. Therefore a player who 'milked a cow' placed his left knee on the ground leaving the right one raised, while the player who 'milked a mare' did the opposite. The one who 'milked sheep' sat on his heels, spreading his legs wide and bending his knees, while the person who 'milked female camels' placed his right leg bent at the knee on the knee of his left leg which was stretched out and upon which the weight of his body rested.

The ankle-bone players put themselves in the intentional position of milkers and performed an action which was meant to induce the real thing to happen at the same time.

The 'manly' games at the *oboo* were similar, in that they accomplished one thing with the aim thereby of bringing about some other analogous event(s) in the world. The games established winners and losers (see Plate 11), that is, magnificent winners and defeated losers, a tilt of balance which one can imagine like the first upswing which sets in motion a huge wheel. To explain what is meant by this I refer to a paper by Alfred Gell (1974). Gell puts forward the idea that many rituals work by constructing relations of synchronicity in the world. What this means is that the coincidence of some event *A* with another event *B* is constructed by the agent, but not simply as a chance, rather as the impulse of an invisible, pre-arranged occult articulation of the world. Gell's example is a Halh Mongolian one, the rite of the 'calling of the birds' (*shubuuny dalalga*) in spring. Just as the first migratory birds are seen to fly over, the elders beckon them to appear in their thousands, while referring in the chants to mares dropping their foals, another event that is imminent with the coming of spring and which indeed is the primary interest of the people conducting the ritual. The two events are constructed as synchronistically tied together. The 'calling of the birds' will bring about the mares' giving birth to their foals. In effect, the presumption of such synchronistic relations permits the manipulation of transcendent contingencies which lie outside normal possibilities for action. Gell writes (1974: 25), 'My suggestion is that having grasped the world as an articulated whole of synchronistically related events, external contingency comes to be perceived as symmetrical with the synthesizing activity of the mind, by a kind of mirror effect.' I am entirely in agreement with this, with the proviso that the principle of synchronicity may be more patchily applied than is suggested above, and that it cannot be the only kind of reasoning that is operative. The Daurs linked social intentional action at regular rituals with events which were generally seasonal but which might or might not happen: the growth of healthy plants in spring, the migration of wild animals, the rainy season (midsummer), or plagues of insects. However, they did not apply this kind of thinking to other, irregular aspects of the unknown, like the diseases and misfortunes brought by spirits. If I am right that synchronistic thinking was at the heart of the regular *oboo* rituals, then the idea of the mountain spirit's awareness, or that he 'sends' rain or deer to people, was just one way of talking about the gap of the unknown separating the human action from hoped-for events in nature.

In this light let us consider the beckoning gesture again. At one level this circular waving of both arms might be interpreted as a direct 'beckoning-in' of the blessings from the sky, mountains, etc. But the gesture itself is not in fact towards the human subject; rather it is in front of and parallel to the body, describing a circle in a rounded sweep. If we think now of the events imminent in the natural world when the *oboo* rituals happen in spring and autumn, and if the idea of synchronistic thinking is accepted, then the gesture can also be seen as a 'turning' which will propel the desired regularities of the world (the increase in herds, the growth of crops, the summer rains, and so forth).[28] By the successful ingestion of blessing, by renewing the ranks of men and women, by establishing the glorious 'manly' winners, the ritual accomplishes one 'natural' event in order to set in train the others. It is absolutely central to this understanding that the *oboo* ritual, and all traditional games, had to take place at the appropriate times in the year and this is why the dates for the rituals were always a matter of concern. In Mongolia, so inevitable was the connection between the game and ensuing events that watching the games was sometimes a form of divination. The old men watching would remark of some physical feat, 'This shows the year will be good' (Kabzinska-Stawarz 1991: 65).

Though guests are welcome at the feasts and games, they do not take part in the exclusive sacred rites at the core of the *oboo* ceremony, and this applies of course to myself. A Mongolian colleague was, however, allowed against some protests to make a video film at his own homeland *oboo*.[29] The rite, it was specified, had to happen at dawn. As the sun rose, numberless horsemen appeared from across the shadowy plain, trotting up the slope to the cairn, which suddenly shone yellow in a gleam of light. Pressing together, hooves clattering and bridles clinking, the horsemen went round and round the cairn. Later, as men dismounted and squatted in a densely packed and crowded circle, drinking, tossing bowls of alcohol in the air, and drinking again, an elder hoarsely shouted the chant. A forest of arms now rose from the shadows and circled slowly in the air, and amid a general masculine growling, voices rose and fell, calling 'Hurui! Hurui!' ('gather, gather'). My curiosity, looking at such an intensely male scene, was analogous in a way to Urgunge's, as he peered through the hole in the paper window at the women dancing madly inside the house. For each of us our own constructs of gender were standpoints for our interests and our ignorance. But the equivalence implied by my image is really only a trick. Not only are English and Mongolian gender ideas disparate and jarring, but in Urgunge's case he was recalling a completed memory distanced by his subsequent life, a matter of amused nostalgia, whereas I was looking at the video as a part of 'research', and seeing it only made me want to find out more.

4.3 To Manchuria

There came a point in my conversations with Urgunge when we both sensed that a phase of our explorations was drawing to a close. Questions occurred to me, but increasingly I could predict what he would reply and I even felt I knew what kinds of things he would have forgotten. Great lacunae, those areas of Daur life he could hardly have known about as a boy and young man—primarily concerning women—had become evident to me as the separation of male and female lives took shape in his accounts. It was not just that he described a historic past, a time seemingly gone for ever, but the space Urgunge created for me to know the Daurs began to seem cramped. The pictures of everyday life that hung between us, the images we by now so confidently shared in conversation, began to seem more and more unreal. There were sketches of Daur houses in my notebooks, but what would it feel like to be in one? I began to feel that I could not possibly write this book without having seen the place, without at least having sniffed the air.

I had worked in the Soviet collective-farm villages of north-eastern and southern Buryatia, and among the nomadic pastoralists of central and northern Mongolia. This had made me aware of some common features in Mongol cultures, which, impressionistic though they must seem, are nevertheless hidden in all anthropological work: the deep appreciation of nature, the respect for elders, the concentration of so much meaning in small things (a kind of knot, a way of cutting a horse's mane), a certain combination of independence and 'instinctive' acceptance of authority, but also of many differences, such as the Halh practicality and openness and the Buryats' cautiousness and more nuanced sense of genealogy and history. So it was the pressure of such accumulated intuitions, together with my recognition of the partiality and insufficiency of this knowledge, that made me feel I had to discover more about the place of the Daurs in the immense, interpenetrating mosaic of Inner Asian culture.

It was difficult to broach the topic of going to Manchuria. Urgunge had not been back to China and he maintained no contact with his surviving relatives. He would not talk about them. Furthermore, as he rightly assured me, the Naun region was closed to foreigners. Nevertheless, I felt I must make the journey, inconsequential though it must be in comparison with his own journey to the West, and even though I knew that it would be an intrusion on the world created by his memories. 'Go then,' he said, 'I want this to be a good book. It's up to you.'

In the summer of 1987 I went to Beijing, where I had arranged to meet Soyol, a Chahar Mongolian teacher of English, who would be my guide and interpreter of Chinese. With Soyol I went by train to Hohhot, the capital of the Inner Mongolia Autonomous Region, which included, many hundreds of miles away to the far north-east, the west bank of the Naun and the village Horli, to which Urgunge's family had moved after the Japanese invasion. Hohhot was Soyol's native town and through her I met many Daurs, teachers, students, housewives, and people in various urban occupations. No one was sure how I could get permission to go to Molidawa (Morin Dawaa), which I discovered is the present name of Urgunge's district. Police as well as state and academic permission would be necessary. In the end, the President of the Inner Mongolia Teachers' University kindly gave me a letter of recommendation to the authorities in Hailar, which had become the prefectural capital with jurisdiction over Morin Dawaa. Some kind of further security authorization—to this day I am not sure how this was done—was arranged through a high-up contact of Soyol's. Hailar, I discovered, is a town set in the most wonderful steppe, an endless expanse of rich green, the grasses interspersed with wild irises and sweet-smelling herbs. At its heart, surrounded by large modern Chinese buildings, are low Russian log-houses, grey with age. Here the dusty cheerful streets bustled with sellers of pine-cones, bilberries, red currants, and some orange-coloured berries unknown to me. The place had an improvised, frontier feel to it. Mongols, Evenks, Bargas, Buryats, and Daurs, all were there, and, though I was not yet at Morin Dawaa, I had the feeling I was getting close.

At the hotel two officials came to see me. My documents were insufficient, they explained. I would need not only the University letter, but also documents from the government and the military authorities, and two of these I had not got. The officials looked negative. There was some desultory talk. Horli had been renamed Tengke Shyan, they said.[30] It seemed to me they laughed unkindly when Soyol said I knew my destination as Bokorchien ('buttocks-place'). Soyol talked to them in Chinese, and then turned away in silence. In desperation I mentioned Urgunge, and that I was writing a book with him. Immediately the officials exchanged looks; they got up and left the room. Soyol gave me a level stare and said, 'Sometimes I think you really are a fool.' We waited gloomily in the hotel room. Soyol said she was now going to leave me, in order to find her young son who was staying with relatives at a village near Hailar, but she would arrange for an acquaintance of hers to go with me to Morin Dawaa, should I get the permission. Hours passed. The only possible hope, Soyol said, was that one of the two officials was a Daur. Suddenly officials came pouring into the room: they were giving me permission to go, they said.

Everyone sat on the beds and lit cigarettes. How old was Urgunge? When did he go to England? Whom did he marry? Has he got children? They said they would send an Evenk woman, Delger, with me to Morin Dawaa as a security guide. She did not speak English, but she knew Mongolian and Daur well. I spent a few days in Hailar, meeting some Daurs and talking about shamanism, and then Delger and I set out on the two-day train journey to Qiqihar, on the way to Morin Dawaa.

Qiqihar is a large and industrial city, entirely Chinese in atmosphere. We soon left and went by car to the town of Morin Dawaa, which is the centre of the district of the same name and is located by the Naun, some miles to the south of Tengke Shyan. The drive took all day. Cheerfully I scanned the view. It was flat, prosperous land. Fields of wheat, maize, and tobacco were interspersed with grassy swamps; figures in blue were bent working in the fields; lorries and horse-drawn carts passed us on the road, which was lined with well-grown planted trees. The villages of mud-covered houses were surrounded by vegetable gardens, and each yard was a fruitful tangle of sunflowers, drying chillies and mushrooms, and stacks of tobacco. Children played among the geese, chickens, pigs, dogs, and cows. This was passing pleasantly by and I was thinking that it looked like a vision of pre-industrial France, when I became aware of a growing unease. Hadn't Urgunge told me this was Mongolia? Where was the steppe? Where was the forest? Where were the mountains, for God's sake? I scanned the horizon—surely they would begin soon. The road was smooth. Not even forest was visible. We passed through a village where a stone turtle bore on its back a plinth engraved in Manchu in honour of a famous general (see Plate 12). The trees by this memorial had been cut down and the place looked neglected, but at least this was something Urgunge had told me about. We swept round a bend, and suddenly there was the confluence of the Naun with the Nomyn Gol, two huge, gleaming blue rivers, flowing swiftly and smoothly southwards. The rivers were the same azure blue as the sky. The gently rising fields went almost to the bank, and a similar flat greenness could be seen on the distant far side. I realized that I had arrived, and that the real power in this landscape was the river, not mountains at all.

Delger and I stayed for a week or two at Morin Dawaa, which is a small country town. From here, and from the other towns and villages, the rivers cannot be seen. Social life is constructed some distance away, almost as if people are turning their back to the rivers, perhaps analogous to the non-recognition by the clans of the flow of women passing between them. The people said there were no shamans here these days, though there were some in other villages. I talked with many people, especially women, and made recordings.[31] They said that the granddaughter of one of Urgunge's older brothers was living at Tengke (Horli), a woman of about 40. Someone warned me not to take photographs. A Frenchman was rumoured to have travelled here; he had taken photographs of people, and then an old man had died. Now no one would want to have their photograph taken by a foreigner. I began to feel nervous about meeting Urgunge's relatives and asked Gerel, the innkeeper, if she would find out whether I should not stay away. 'No, you should go,' was the reply, 'everyone is expecting you to go.'

We set out for Horli a few days later by car, along a road running parallel to the river. It rained heavily and a thin mist came down. The country got rougher, with thickets of scrub, and less frequent fields. Hazelnut bushes tangled in the mud. Some boys came by riding bareback on horses, soaked to

12. Memorial gravestone
(*beye chuluu*—body stone) for
a Daur general of the Qing
period similar to the one
Urgunge remembers in his
village. Photo: Morin Dawaa,
August 1987, C. Humphrey.
[4.3]

the skin, driving a herd of cows. Now there were some gentle hills, and a mare
and some foals came out from behind a mound and disappeared again into the
mist. All this felt more familiar, but it was dark when we arrived. Next morning
was grey and bleak, but I got up at first light to walk around. I was no longer
surprised by anything. A sea of thickly growing tall maize and tobacco met my
eyes, and within it there could just be seen the thatched roofs of widely
scattered houses. Muddy paths wound between the dense stands of foliage. In
their fenced yards each house seemed separate and private. Far in the distance
were low green hills. When I told Urgunge about this scene on my return to
Cambridge, hinting that the impression he had given me was rather different,
and what about all that tobacco, he said dismissively, 'Yes, we used to grow that
kind of stuff.'

In the next few days we visited several houses, which were detail by detail as
Urgunge had described them. I was not taken immediately to Urgunge's relatives. One day we went to a particularly old house. It had a brick floor, a lattice
door carved in dark wood, and in the main room were three high brick heated

platforms (*hanj*) edged with shiny wood. A photo of Mao was pinned over the door and a wooden box hung high on the north-west wall. I knew this must contain a painting of Niang-Niang Goddess (it did, as I was told later). Seated on the *hanj* there presided a dignified old lady, quietly smoking her long pipe. All of the people in my entourage, which included rough-hewn farmers and Party officials, bent low in *sain hasso* before her; one man who rushed in late and forgot was sharply told by an official to mind his manners. The old lady was suspicious of me; she knew nothing about religion. Then somehow it emerged that she had been at village school with Urgunge, she remembered him, he used to tease her, and gradually conversation became easier. A roomful of people listened to my halting attempt to mix a few Daur words with Mongolian. But soon they could take it no longer, and a fervent conversation broke out about the old times. Stories and recollections tumbled from our hostess, she spoke fast and strongly, there was this famous shaman and that amazing incident, and voices in the room questioned her, starting arguments of their own all at once. I tried vainly to follow. Tape-recording this cacophony was impossible. Delger was too occupied in her own heated discussion to translate.[32] This was my frustrating but also deeply touching experience in several families.

One day I was told that Urgunge's relatives had invited me over. As we wound our way through the fields I remembered the tragedies that lay between these people and far distant Urgunge in England. We came to a high wooden fence, a gate, the usual yard with its carts and slumbering black pigs. Inside was a modest house, with paper windows, not glass. A woman came out, and I almost cried out because she looked so like Urgunge. Children appeared hesitantly behind her. When we went inside we talked a little. They asked me about Urgunge, and I also tried to remember everything about them to tell him. There was a sad feeling of emotions fastened down and things left unsaid. As I got up to go, Urgunge's cousin asked me to wait because she wanted to give him a present. She reappeared with a package wrapped in newspaper, containing folded tobacco leaves, dried mushrooms, and some dark, strong-smelling herb. This I took back to England and gave to Urgunge. He hardly looked at it, but that is the Mongol way with gifts, which pass silently between people, being both essential and taken for granted. This visit made me realize that I could not, and should not, try to penetrate behind Urgunge's own memories. His relatives were worn down with hardship, and I could represent only a danger to them. Urgunge himself had too much bitterness even to focus his thoughts on present-day Daur life in China. I felt I had no right to probe further, and that I should accept his memories as they were.

On the other hand, the journey suggested new directions to me, and I reflected that I had learned many things from the women of Morin Dawaa. They had given me a different perspective with which to understand 'sha-

13. A Daur woman sitting on the heated bed of her house at Horli (Tengke), Morin Dawaa district. Photo: August 1987, C. Humphrey. [4.3]

14. A Daur house at Horli (Tengke), Morin Dawaa district. The roof is made of woven twig thatch, and a ground-level chimney stands at the far end to let out smoke from the stove. Photo: August 1987, C. Humphrey. [4.3]

manism'. And their excitement about shamanic incidents had impressed on me the enormously strong emotional impact of such moments, affecting the direction of people's lives. I also felt reassured, because everything that Urgunge had told me now rang true (not that it was identical to what other Daurs said, but I could now more clearly see where it came from, its place and its import). '*Mini deu* [younger sister], you didn't quite trust me,' he remarked when I got back, and I had to admit he was right.

On this journey I made another discovery. Earlier (Section 1.4) I mentioned Merse, the Daur communist revolutionary from Hailar. He had a sister, I was now told, who was a famous shaman. Her name was Huangge. Back in Cambridge I looked again at my notes and discovered that Huangge was the shaman whom the anthropologist Ethel John Lindgren[33] had met and photographed in the early 1930s. Then I found that Huangge also appeared in the writings of Poppe (1930) and Mendüsürüng (1983), though without any mention of her politician brother. Merse had disappeared without trace in the early 1930s. At one of our last meetings in the early 1980s Lindgren had been pointedly silent on this subject, implying that such subjects were too dangerous to pursue. I resolved nevertheless to find out more about this brother and sister. Perhaps the conjunction in one family of shaman and revolutionary would prove unexpectedly illuminating.

15. Confluence of the Nomin and Naun Rivers. Photo: August 1987, C. Humphrey. [4.3]

4.4 Inside the Female Gender

One afternoon in Horli an old woman was telling a long story to a roomful of
people. I was recording this and only half-listening when someone asked, 'And
was that an *endur*?' The story-teller replied, 'The so-called *endur* is a fairy girl
gone to heaven' (*tengger deer yawuu dagini uin*). I pricked up my ears and
noticed that her beings in heaven were always female *dagini*.[34] When I got back
to England, since I remembered Urgunge's statement that heaven was peopled
by old men with beards, I played this part of the tape to him, and he calmly said,
'Well, the old lady always says *dagini* instead of *endur*. To me *endur* is always a
man, but to her it is a *dagini*. It's all based on who is talking.' I was disconcerted
by Urgunge's attitude. He neither knew, nor cared, what women thought.
When I tried to get out of him what 'the Daurs' thought, he just smiled, and
later he said, 'You won't get anywhere by pressing me.' Only much later did I
come to see that his assumption that there would be different viewpoints was
not an annoying personal egotism but intrinsic to his understanding of shamanism (see Chapters 7 and 8).

In Manchuria I had noticed the confident bearing of Daur women and the
many responsible positions they held. Without thinking much about it I had
taken this to be an effect of universal education and other policies under
Communist rule, but Soyol put me right. Daur women are quite exceptional,
she said, compared with women in virtually any of the Inner Mongolian
groups. But as far as I could make out Daur women had been subject to the
same patriarchal restrictions as elsewhere. 'No question,' said Urgunge. 'It is
because of shamanism.' And what did that mean? This section begins an answer
which will be taken up again in 6.5 and 6.6.

The starting-point of Daur patriarchal ideas about gender in Urgunge's time
was that each sex had a discrete and separated identity. The sexes had to
approach one another across a divide in order to have sexual relations, create
children, sustain economic life. Marilyn Strathern has pointed out the implication of this way of thinking about gender (as opposed to the idea that differentiation between men and women is not known in advance of their interaction
and is in fact constituted by it).

The discrete identity of men and women (there is no ambiguity about sexual ascription)
is the basis for the transactions between them: the one is not axiomatically encompassed
by the other. In such a context, where the transactional entities are by their prior
nature already differentiated, their transactional engagement has to be forced. (1988:
124)

Strathern suggests that such a schema creates anxiety about the productive
combination of men and women. In the Daur case the unmediated combining
together of men and women in sexuality and its result (childbirth) certainly
created anxiety, and their marriage process can be seen as a means of control-

ling such fears, by mediation (the use of go-betweens, exogamy, etc.) and rules
of clan membership (which maintained the notional separation of the partners).
The same-sex rituals were part of this way of constructing gender, but now I
became aware that they were an ideological contrivance, in that another strand
in Daur thinking posited each gender as internally differentiated and composed
of interactive parts, as will shortly be shown.

A text recorded by Poppe from a Hailar Daur man in 1927 shows the
close connection between gender and the ascription of specific productive
practices:

Daur people from ancient times have lived by agriculture. They keep livestock, and
they also like to go hunting. At home the women do sewing, prepare food, milk cows,
tend the vegetable plot, and collect berries. As for the men, they cultivate their fields,
go out hunting, herd the horses, learn reading and writing, and carry out military
service. As for the daughters, they stay at home, learning to sew fine embroidery, to
make dresses and clothes, and they go to the vegetable plot and collect berries. They
make flower-beds and plant flowers. Now as for the old women, they plait ropes, spin
threads, and manage the daughters-in-law. As for the old men, they decide about
everything, are in charge of life in general, and give orders to their sons and juniors.
(1930: 55–6)

This way of talking about men and women shows them as different, but instead
of taking up the biological distinction it stresses instead practical activities (see
Collier and Yanagisako 1987: 1–50), and rather than insisting on female subordination posits all activities as useful contributions. It is also noticeable that the
rank distinction between older and younger is as salient here as the difference
between sexes.

However, in everything that pertained to male values, and especially the
religious life of the clan, all Daur women were subject to restrictions. I reca-
pitulate here a list of such restrictions based on statements by Daur men.
Women could not own property such as land or houses. They were not supposed to go near horses, nor to ride. They should not go to the fishing-grounds,
which would drive the fish away, nor should they go hunting, nor touch any
hunting implements. They should not trade or travel on their own. Women
should not climb on the roof of the house. For one month after giving birth
women should not leave the yard for fear of defiling the Door Spirit, nor should
they approach a well. No visitors were to be received during the birth period.
Women were not allowed to squat facing the fire, nor look into the fire in the
family stove. They should not go near the family or village graveyards and
certainly not pass the head of the grave. It was forbidden for women to climb
the hill where the *oboo* was situated. They were not allowed to touch a shaman's
garments or instruments, whether the shaman was male or female. Except for
very old and respected women they were not supposed to go into the section of
the storehouse where the family's spirit images (*barkan*) were kept. They were

debarred from active participation in the sacrifices to *tengger*, *oboo*, Jiyachi, the hearth-fire, Bayin Achaa, and the clan ancestor spirits (*hojoor*). They were, however, allowed to take part in the rituals of shamanic renewal, the *undaan* (*ominan*), New Year purification rites, and *jirden*.[35] One is led to wonder what power women had that they should be externalized in this way.

Urgunge explained all these restrictions by women's pollution (*hwaski*), stemming from menstruation, sexual activity, and childbirth. But even from the list above, which is certainly incomplete, we can infer that what women were essentially debarred from was the capacity for independent production and the means towards such production (horses, guns, nets, freedom of movement, etc.). At one level, this was a division of production, into direct appropriation, by fishing and hunting, and processing of the game, which was done by women. At another, the restrictions imply an idea of the reproduction of wealth and society by religious means, by the cult of ancestors, the *oboo*, and shamanic protection, from which women were also debarred. However, neither in everyday life nor in religious thinking can this schema be taken at face value. The totalistic-seeming vision was subverted in many ways, which will emerge only gradually through succeeding chapters in this book.

When I was in Morin Dawaa I began to get indications that ideas of males could include femaleness. Urgunge had told me about the fire spirit, the male guardian of the hearth. However, I gradually became aware of inner femaleness within this very focal point of male ideology. All over North Asia the domestic fire is regarded as the symbol of continuity of the patriarchal–patrilineal family.[36] The actual fire was kept alight if at all possible, and to say, 'May your hearth-fire be extinguished' was the worst of curses. However, despite the androcentric notion of the family and the invocation during fire rituals of other deities in the male ideology,[37] an essential spirit of the fire was female. Among the Horchin this was a young unmarried girl (*hüühen*), among the Manchu it was an old woman.[38] People in the Naun region told me that there were two fire spirits, though Urgunge had conflated them into one. There was the male spirit represented by a Chinese paper print, called Jooh Barkan, which lived in the stove and was easily offended by sex. The other was Gali Barkan ('fire spirit'). It was this latter spirit which was widely associated in North Manchuria with an 'old woman', and which was nevertheless the sign of the continuity of the patriarchal family.[39] My Horchin friend told me his family too kept a Chinese paper print, a host of figures being crowded on it including servants; but that was just an image: the 'real' fire spirit was female. The Ordos Mongols made a special seat for the fire spirit consisting of an iron ring which was attached in turn month by month to the four (north, south, east, west) legs of the trivet standing over the fire (Neklyudor 1992/3: 311). This suggests the idea of an all-inclusive deity, taking over both space and time from a point of centrality.

The image of centricity could be unequivocally female, as can be seen from the following Halh Mongol verse from a *dalalga* invocation (Dulam 1989: 39):

Køkø mønggün tngri-yin dogogur	Under the blue eternal sky
Kørüsü altan delekei deger-e	Over the golden crusted world
Kødüleküi olan monggol ulus anu	The mobile numerous Mongol People
Kødülesü ügei jayagatu gal eke-degen	To their motionless destined fire mother[40]
Ebcigü ba tosu, ariki-bar takimui	With breast-meat, fat and spirits make sacrifice.

On New Year's eve, Horli Daurs said, Gali Barkan went up to *tengger* in the flames and smoke of the great fire (4.2). The stove-god was also renewed. As he/she was a chatterbox, some gluey porridge was pasted over the mouth on the picture to prevent the spirit from telling the family's secrets on high.[41] Then the whole thing was burned. A newly acquired picture was installed in the New Year. At the same time, each family gave Gali Barkan a special *dalalga* beckoning ritual. In Hailar either the *bagchi* or a Buddhist lama could officiate at this; in Butha it was the male head of the family (when I asked whether the shaman was ever invited, I was told, 'Shamans do not take part in *dalalg*-type things, they have their own faith').

The blessings of femaleness were thus sought at the domestic heart of patriarchy and by the ritual means (*dalalga*) used in male cults. It is significant that the hearth-fire was also the agent of purification of any object tainted by *hwaski*. Thus by implication the Daur-Manchu 'old women' of the fire were not only identified with the very symbol of perpetuity of the patrilineal family but were also the agents of removal of pollution deriving from younger women. This is something which was hinted at in a conversation in Morin Dawaa (see below).

Gender among the Daurs was thus a more complex and less coherent matter than it seemed initially. This can be seen in two related ways. First, attribution with ideal 'full' female gender was not a lifelong state. Men too were not inevitably and permanently assigned to the male gender, since by becoming a shaman (*yadgan*) one entered a quasi-androgynous state (see 5.1). If real men and women entered the state of full gender identity only for a period, another challenge to the simple totalistic view came from a different direction. In fact, in Daur religious life an unambiguous inter-mapping of sex with gender categories was really only sustained in certain 'ideological' ways of talking, the stating of pollution rules, etc. If we look more closely at some of the single-sex rituals, the monolithic depiction of 'male' and 'female' begins to fall apart. As suggested earlier, internal complexities within gender categories are evident. Rather rather than look again at the male-only *oboo* ceremonies, where it may be remembered that the biting of the *ug* and the establishing of winners/losers in games set up differentiation among males, let us take up the women's dances again.

Most *lurgel* dances were performed by women, amongst themselves, for men. The dances were accompanied by songs. On these occasions 'women' made themselves audible and visible for men, who were spectators. The musical form was normally a dialogue, while dances were done by women in pairs, the one 'opposed' to the other. Both songs and dances imitated animals and birds and familiar economic activities. Thus a musical dialogue might go:

> *Katar!* What is flying away with this sound?
> *Kangar!* What goes with this sound?
> With *katar* a pheasant is flapping its wings,
> With *kangar* an eagle is on the hunt.
>
> What is fleeing, jumping in a hurry?
> What is following immediately behind?
> A frightened rabbit is fleeing,
> A hound is chasing behind.

> (*DSHI* 1985: 282)

Lurgel dancing, usually accompanied with song, was done in pairs. It started with a mild melody, and the steps followed the rhythm. The steps became faster and wilder with the music. Finally, each dancer placed one hand on her waist and reached out the other to the partner, each twisting and jabbing their hands in turn so it looked like fighting. At this moment, a third party could join the 'weaker' dancer and confront the 'stronger'. They danced as long as they liked, and when they stopped another pair took over. The words and movements were imitations of animals and birds, and also activities such as carrying water or milking. All these everyday actions were made funny and dramatic and interactional, so 'looking in a mirror and combing your hair' was another dance (with yourself and your reflection).

This shows, with the utmost simplicity, women representing themselves as 'double' in the images of processes in the world. Both men and women were present at these dances, but 'women' is no longer a singular, passive category. Inside the gender they interact and 'fight', in the abstract sense that things in the world 'conflict'. So they present to the audience not just the eagle, the bird of prey, but the pheasant, the hunted bird too, not just the chaff but the wind, not just the flour rustling but also the swishing sieve.

This provides a context in which to investigate the idea that *hwaski* could be acted upon among women themselves. But why should they want to do this? Let us reconsider what *hwaski* is.[42] It was noted earlier that objects polluted by *hwaski* could be purified by being waved over the hearth-fire. This applied also to people who had been made impure, especially someone coming back from a long journey. He, occasionally she, was supposed to go in a circle 'sunwise' around the hearth, or wave his hat in a circle over the fire, or light a taper and circle the flame three times round under his hat. This would get rid of the dangerous supernatural influences which might cling to the traveller from the journey. Such defiling influences were not necessarily *hwaski* alone, but they were supposed to include it because in strange places people do not know what they are supposed to avoid. From this we can see that menstrual/birth pollu- tion was not *sui generis* but was part of wider ideas about pollution related to the outside or alien. The idea that the innermost secretions of women were akin to the amorphous impurity of the outermost world problematizes the apparently simple physical derivation of *hwaski* from women.

Urgunge said, '*Hwaski* is dirty, but it can save your life.' He said that when you are very scared by thunder and lightning, if you can find 'dirty things' and put them on your head, the lightning will not strike. Women could use their underclothes to ward off attacks by devils (*shurkul*), by waving them in the air when passing some dangerous spot at night. This would work most powerfully if the clothes were stained with menstrual blood. In a story told me by a Daur woman, a boy determined to attack a demon in the 'other world'. 'I will go on one condition,' he said. 'I need to have some women's menstrual underclothes.' The boy put them on, buckled on his sword and set off. This clearly shows that the clothes were a 'female' weapon, equivalent to the 'male' sword. Each of these items represented its own kind of abstract power and was both feared and celebrated.[43] It was described earlier (in 2.2 and 3.2) how milk was used to counter the celestial disturbances of lightning and the shaman's rainbow. We see now that menstrual-cum-birth blood in a negative sense, and milk in a positive sense, were gendered and powerful objectifications of women's capacities to reproduce and nurture that could be appropriated by men. That ostensibly female body-secretions could become attributes of men (the Buddhist lama with milk, the boy-hero with menstrual pants) destabilizes the notion of personal gender as a fixed essence given by nature.

This opens out the idea of *hwaski* to a wide set of contexts where it could compete with other powers, and rather than seeing it as a 'biological given' inherent in all women we can see it as an objectified notion, a product of generative activity (sex), which, perhaps because it was not that other intensely desired product, the child, had a negative force. The detachability of *hwaski* was something on which women could work for themselves. The relation between seniority and juniority among women could be put to work to produce ritually a new balance in the world. A conversation in Morin Dawaa again revealed to me that *tengger*, the sky, was in women's eyes not so purely male as Urgunge had proposed, and that this female element was part of an interaction among women to purify the dangerous power of *hwaski*. This purification was part of a sacrificial exchange which set up a relation between women and the sky which was radically different from any we have encountered so far.

Readers may well have forgotten this, but Urgunge described, on the western wall of the house, along from the cow's membrane representing the blessings-bag of *tengger*, a Chinese coloured print representing the goddess Tengger Niang-Niang (see Plate 23). To Urgunge the goddess was 'women's business',

Chinese in origin, and nothing to do with *tengger* the sky. I began to see that other people may have constructed this differently when Mendüsürüng told me that the ritual of consecrating a sickly child to a higher power, which Urgunge said was a dedication to *tengger*, was to Ome Barkan ('womb spirit'), one of the main manifestations of Tengger Niang-Niang (see Mendüsürüng 1983).

Though no one could describe it as crystal clear, the following conversation implies that for women Niang-Niang was integrated with ideas of *tengger*. I have added Urgunge's comments when we played the tape-recording in Cambridge. Note that Daur does not distinguish between male and female pronouns, which in any case are usually omitted. Thus the shaman mentioned could have been female, but I write 'he' since the great majority of shamans were men. Urgunge could not understand the presence of a shaman at this ritual, which is basically a sacrifice, and he said he thought the shaman was probably acting here simply as a diviner, to locate the presence of *hwaski*.

OLD WOMAN. The sacrifice to *tengger* is the same as the sacrifice to Niang-Niang.
[U. She means Niang-Niang is beside *tengger*, high on the wall.]
C. What do you sacrifice?
MAN. When you sacrifice, you close the fence and gate and don't let anyone in.
NARAN [*a middle-aged woman*]. You sacrifice to *tengger* and Niang-Niang together, all at once.
OLD WOMAN. You put all the meat in one container, on the right side for *tengger* and on the left side for Niang-Niang. We give the *julde* of a chicken for Niang-Niang, and the pig's shoulder, a rib, and a blood sausage for *tengger*. You invite *tengger* to take the meat in exchange [*soli-*]. And you make seven bowls of oatmeal porridge [*laali*]. You make it thick, and press up the edges, pour in melted butter, and make cotton twisted wicks, and light them. You wave seven sticks of incense in a circle and put them in. This is called *tengger tualbe*.
[U. Now we must use our super-brain to understand this. This really means 'stabilizing heaven'. *Tualbe* has the same root as the Mongol word *tulga* [the four-legged trivet which holds up the cooking-pot].][44]
OLD WOMAN. We stir each bowl in a circle seven times. This is women's work, a matter for women like me. We pray that women should be made clean. And the young wives [*beri benesul*] call out, '*Gan jing Gegeen* [Clean Bright-one], come down! We have become dirty [*laibar*], now make us clean. We have sinned [*nogul boljee*].[45] Make us clean.'
[U. What a lot of Chinese and Mongol words they use! This must be a special kind of dirt, they are not using the ordinary word for dirt, *bajar*. *Nogul* [sin] is just a Buddhist word. *Laibar* must mean bloody dirt.]
NARAN. What exactly is *laibar bolson* [became dirty]?
GUOLIANG [*another old woman*]. The young wives did not look after their pots and pans well. They became dirty [*laibar*]. Because of this we conduct the 'supporting heaven' ritual.

NARAN. Aren't you saying bad things about the young women?

GUOLIANG. Well, the wives and young women were not too clean [Ch. *gan jing*]. But it is not insulting them, it is just a fact. Dirty is dirty, clean is always clean. You must distinguish between living clean and living dirty.

OLD LADY. When the lamps are lit, the shaman takes his whip and calls down his helper spirits [*onggor*]. Then he goes into the other room [kitchen], holding the ritual drumstick [*gisuur*], and he investigates, singing out if it is clean or dirty. He says, 'There are old clothes here.'

[U. That must be women's dirty underclothes.]

GUOLIANG. He sang the refrain, '*Yo go gui yee!*' And the young wives prayed, 'We have not been clean, our pots and pans became dirty; now after sacrificing, we shall polish them! Now forgive us for the dirt!'

OLD WOMAN. He comes back, sits on a special chair, and holds the short ritual fan [*delbur*]. Then the shaman calls down the helper-spirits again.

C. What does he say?

NARAN. We cannot say what he said: only he knows what he said. We cannot repeat it.

Unfortunately the conversation now took another turn, but if my intuitions are correct, this ritual involves old women calling on *tengger* and Niang-Niang to cleanse the impurities of young women and such a making-clean is somehow stabilizing of heaven, just as the trivet holds up and supports the cooking-pot, which contains the food offered to heaven.

What is the import of the idea that to clean the pots is to support the sky? The Daurs, like other Mongols, liken in riddles the large domed cooking-pot to an inverted version of the arch of the sky. This creates a homology which explains why, of all the female items that might be used ritually, it is cooking-pots that represent what is to be purified. But we can go further than this. The significance of the ritual, I think, lies in the fact that it refers to an 'absence', and not just any absence but an acknowledged and fundamental one. The Daurs, again like other Mongols, have a saying which recounts the three absences ('non-existences') of the world:

The sky has no support (lit. 'trivet')	*Tenggerde tualga uwei*
The ocean has no lid	*Daleed daiba uwei*
The mountain has no belt (sash)	*Aulda bes uwei*

Consider the first and third of these lines. It is these very absences, it seems to me, that the most important rituals symbolically negate, by symbolically creating the cosmic objects otherwise acknowledged not to exist. The men circumambulating the *oboo* cairn accomplished the binding of the mountain, like the binding of a sash. With their seven bowls with lamps, incense sticks, and uprising smoke, the women create the absent trivet support for heaven.

If the women's ritual reiterates the identification between young women, sexuality and pollution, it nevertheless refuses to hide this as a shameful thing, but projects it outwards to cosmic dimensions. Pollution is removed by this ritual, which locates the agency of purification not with men but with older women. Most important, all the women by this ritual action place themselves in a different relation to the sky than men. Their orientation is to provide support, rather than just to receive.[46] So, rather than seeing the exclusion of women from the mountain cult, and their subordinate role in sacrifices to the sky, as 'repression' (i.e. in effect taking the patriarchal point of view), there is a basis for thinking that from their viewpoint women had no need of those rituals.

Shamans fantastically elaborated the internal differentiation within sexual categories, as will be discussed in Chapters 4 and 5, and in effect gender was shattered by them into meaninglessness. So let us turn to one way in which the shamanic imagination challenged the socially dominant idea of men and women coming together dangerously for reproduction. This is the curious legend (or was it a real ritual?) of the *duwalang* trees, mentioned in 2.1 above. It may be recalled that single-sex rituals took place for men at the top of a mountain, while women celebrated on the river bank. The *duwalang* trees were similarly situated, as two groves, one at the top of a mountain and one on the river bank. This apparent reference to 'male' and 'female' was overridden. It was from amongst the branches of these trees that Womb Spirit (*ome barkan*) fetched the 'eggs' which became human embryos. Sexual reproduction is here replaced by a notion of self-seeding.

The only source to elaborate on the *duwalang* trees is by a woman Daur ethnographer, Odongowa (1991), and this, together with the silence of male writers and Urgunge's ignorance, suggests that the cult may have been promoted by women. Odongowa's narrative is ethnography which is so *engagé* as to be virtually part of its subject-matter. I quote it in full, since apart from the argument about gender, it is right that our readers should experience its immediacy. However, it is impossible to say who is narrating, or with what kind of voice. But did this ritual really happen? Is it a myth? Is it the rendering of a shamanic song? We do not know, but the narrative demonstrates an asexual plant-focused imagery of human reproduction which is different from those so far discussed.

Shamans have twelve *Duwalang* which are twelve pieces [embroideries? C.H.] representing twelve trees. According to the words of the Holieri ancestor spirit, there were twelve *Duwalang* trees, which were divided into six trees growing on the river bank and six trees on the mountain top. The aim of the ritual was to take care of the growth of each *Duwalang* tree. If a tree grew densely, human beings would be healthy; on the other hand, if a tree was withered, humankind would meet all kinds of hardships. During the offering to the trees people should earth up the trees and water them and restore their life and then people would get well and hardship would be removed. Therefore it can be said that the *Duwalang* was the life-tree existing between the shamanic spirits and human beings. For the offering of sacrifices to the trees on the river bank, the people would walk a long way through the grassland. Before starting the journey, they would tidy up everything, and they loaded things such as the Holieri's spirit's two-dragon tent-shrine, cooking-pot, bowls, gourd ladles, and pots on domesticated deer. And they started on the journey, panting deeply. They went through temple gates, villages, streets with halls; they saw soldiers gathering together and shouted at them. The momentum was very powerful. They went through sandy beaches and deserts, and they boldly stepped through flood lands. Just as they were about to take a rest, they suddenly saw the *Duwalang* poplar and prickly-pear trees. They inspected these trees and there was nothing wrong with them, so they went further. Here some of the trees were aged and the top branches were broken. Some of the trees were facing the midday sun to bloom and some were falling towards the direction of the rising-sun and were on the point of withering up. So the people harnessed black and white spotted oxen to carts and brought in dark, rich top-soil, cart after cart, one hundred and eight carts-loads in all. Soon they had piled the earth round the roots of the trees, and they stamped it down until it became as hard as the frame-wood of a Mongol yurt and as strong as the Daur's house. They poured fresh animal blood onto the roots of the life-trees, they watered them with fresh blood. After this treatment, the trees grew densely, their branches were like pieces of jade, they were healthy, the golden leaves looked alive, and each leaf showed living energy. The leaves in the shade were green, the leaves on the sunny side were fresh. The six life-trees flourished. The birds came here in a group, they flew away in a flock. In this way, the people relieved the burdens and fetters of the *Duwalang* trees and their own hardships were also removed. Each time the people journeyed to the *Duwalang* trees, marching along the way, they sang the same song, about the origin of the road which Holieri spirit went through. Going to the high mountain *Duwalang* trees, one travelled through the heavenly world and across the human river. One sat on a square raft, rowed by a lame man, who ferried the souls of the dead. The condition of the high mountain *Duwalang* trees was similar to the six river-bank trees. These twelve life-trees consisted of: poplar, prickly pear, white birch, willow, pine, camphor, and others (Odongowa 1991).

Instead of the divided and hierarchized relations which were characteristic of the single-sex rituals, the image presented here is communal and egalitarian. Nor are the actors here involved in an exchange. They engage in ritualized husbandry or nurture which, because they themselves are isomorphic with the trees, is at the same time cultivation of themselves. Thus the community/grove is reproduced without any coming together of opposites. It is significant, though, that the manifestations of life/liveliness in the *Duwalang* trees, though not mentioned in this particular passage, are not replicated but substituted forms, i.e. they are not more trees but small animals and birds (see 2.1 and further discussion in 6.2).

What I have tried to indicate in this section is how women appear not only as the object of classification and social restrictions but just as importantly as the subjects of knowledge. Looking at gender from outside, as an anthropologist, I showed that unlike attributions of sex, people through their lives moved into cultural gender classes, rather than being permanently and inevitably in them. It was then explained how the female gender was constituted by women and demonstrated to men, as incorporating internal and interactive agencies related to conflictual processes in the world. Each gender, it seems, could in this way incorporate abstract attributes associated with the other. Thus, even from the men's point of view, the 'male' deitiy presiding over the household fire was in some way a mask for a pure and universal vision of women. Again, there was a sky-oriented ritual in which old women became the agents of the restoration of cosmic stability by acting on the pollution of young women. In such rituals even ostensibly self-evident gender attributes, like menstrual blood and milk, were objectified as the products of interactions, and this detachability made it possible for there to be rituals, myths, and even practical actions in which gendered pollution was used by either sex like a weapon or negated like a cauterized infection. Finally, such gendered, if internally complex, images were contrasted with the shamanic asexual myth or ritual of the *Duwalang* trees, which, in a different idiom of health and growth, renewed the people as a whole. It will be shown how the *Duwalang* trees were an essential part of the iconography of Ome Niang-Niang, the womb spirit, and that this constituted a separate field for women's power, which was both destructive and cosmically empowering.

Notes

1. I am indebted to Vinai Srivastava for the clear formulation of this point in relation to the religion of Raika pastoralists in Rajasthan.
2. The verb *taki-* was used by Daurs for respectful, worshipping rituals like sacrifices, while *tayi-* was used for offerings with a bargaining element. *Tayi-* also meant to spoil, as of a child. A similar word used for offerings to spirits was *huura-*, meaning to placate, also used in relation to demanding children. It is possible that both of these words are related to *takim* (the hollow behind the knee-joint) and to a range of words suggesting bending of the knee. The noun *tayilga* (*tayilag*) may have a different etymology. It was not used by the Naun Daurs, but was employed in the Hailar region, and widely elsewhere in Inner Asia, for the very largest, communal sacrifices.
3. Other rituals only involving men were offerings by hunters of fresh blood and cooked meat to Bayin Achaa in the forest, and offerings by fishermen of fish to river spirits. These were relatively simple, *ad hoc* affairs.
4. *Doloon Hod* (Ursa Major), also known by Daurs as the 'seven old men' (Jagchid 1988*b*: 327). Seven lamps were lit for this constellation.
5. Another table was set to the east of the house and here were burned seven sticks of incense, one for each star in the Pleiades constellation. Offering a pleasant smell to the deity by incense was differentiated from fumigation by *swaikh* (a kind of artemisia) which was burned in other rituals as a purificatory agent (see Hamayon 1977).
6. It was kept going for about a month. Among Horchins this fire was called *tengeriin*

oboo. A mound was made of packed snow, covered by earth, and then the fire was built on top of *hargana*, a tough bushy plant that gives off sparks when lit (Hürelbaatar, personal communication).

7. In nearby Jirim, Horchin Mongols say that all the spirits go up to Heaven at this time, and the huge fire is to warm them as they come back to earth frozen from their journey in space.

8. Other Daurs told me, 'The idea was, may we be lively like flames, may we be pure like water.'

9. Such regular rituals seem to have been the rule among Daurs (Batubayin 1990; Ikeshiri [1943] 1982), but Urgunge only remembers irregular rites, when a drought threatened.

10. Urgunge recalls that there were different rules for the butchering (*mojila-*, from the term *moj* (branch of a tree)) of the various domestic animals, but he remembers in detail only the eight pieces of a chicken sacrifice. The parts had higher and lower status and were designated for people in various genealogical categories.

11. The Daur term *keshi* is related to the Mongolian *keshig*, which means grace, blessing, luck, or fortune bestowed from above to below. *Keshig* also means 'one's turn' (one's place, time, or opportunity in a scheduled or alternating order) (Lessing *et al.* 1982: 460).

12. The *oboo* at the Gangjuur Monastery was described as follows: 'I saw a big round-shaped *oboo*, and its circuit was 62 steps. There was an octagonal paling on top, into which many willow branches had been packed. In the centre was erected a red pole and many prayer-flags (*hii mori*) were flying. At the top of the pole was a golden globe, called *ganzir*, with five-coloured cloths hanging from it. There were another eight small *oboos* erected to the east and west of the main *oboo*. Thus there were seventeen altogether. There were many small prayer-flags attached to a rope tied to big poles at the far eastern and western *oboos*' (Akiba and Akamatsu 1941: 256).

13. On the repeated analogies made between plants and animals from Aristotle to medieval times, and the locating of a 'heart' of plants at this spot, see Atran (1990: 224–6).

14. Lit. Mongolian *dalalga*, usually pronounced *dallaga*.

15. Horse-racing was less common among the Naun Daurs than in Mongolia, but wrestling was widely practised. Polo (*boiko*) was a kind of field-hockey, played without horses. There were two teams of approximately equal size and goals (*anag*) as in hockey. The game was often played at night, when the wooden ball would be hollowed out and filled with a burning substance so that it glowed and threw out sparks. Games would go on for hours. According to Urgunge they were rough and exciting, and boys were often injured, especially during the night games. For an interesting discussion of a comparable Mongolian game called *tsagaan mod* (white wood), which evidently had magical functions in relation to fertility, see Kabzinska-Stawarz (1991: 63–8).

16. Omachi (1982: 192) mentions worship of clan ancestors at the *oboo* among Hailar Daurs, though Urgunge said this did not happen in Butha.

17. In some *oboo* rituals revived in Inner Mongolia after the Cultural Revolution women are allowed to attend. However, there are still many *oboos* from which women are excluded, and in Mongolia the exclusion of women is general.

18. In Batubayin (1990) this is: 'We have requested the honoured Spirit of the Gate, To meet you Lords and show the way to the sacrifice.' Urgunge did not remember the gate spirit, which seems to have been relatively unimportant and was perhaps an idea taken from the Chinese.

19. Mergendi (1987: 310). This text was translated by Urgunge from Chinese. A very similar text appears in *DSHI* (1985: 243–5).

20. The structure of four poles supporting the offering was called *delkin*, and it was also used for propitiation of *barkan* spirits. Possibly *delkin* is related to the Mongol word *delekei*, meaning 'universe'. According to Jagchid (1988b: 331), a *delkin* might be used for disposal of a child's corpse rather than a tree.

21. The pole structure was covered by a quilt, meant to hide it from Jiyachi (Batubayin 1990).

22. I have not heard of the existence of women's *oboos* elsewhere in the Mongolian region.

23. According to Urgunge, women were frightened to kill animals (in fact, they were not allowed to). He also said that a fire could be dangerous during a drought, and as women would not be able to handle this, they offered prepared food.

24. The *duud* is the length a pheasant can first fly in one breath before it is exhausted, a mile or less; subsequent flights were shorter. The *duud*, according to Urgunge, represents the 'power' of the pheasant. Women were often compared with pheasants in poetry because of these birds' bright plumage, and their habit of bending over to eat, like women bending to work in the fields.

25. According to Batubayin (1990), this symbolized falling rain.

26. Urgunge remembers this term as a verb, *gurgeu-*.

27. A more accurate translation of *akenbei* would be '[our] thought has been realized.'

28. Chabros (1992a: 150) also sees the *dalalga* gesture as expressing the circularity of the relationship with the ancestors, 'which is the precondition for life itself'.

29. Video made by B. Telenged of *oboo* ritual at Hovd Sum, Uvs Aimak, Mongolia, summer 1993.

30. Tengke Shyan is the name of a district, to which several village populations were moved. The former 'Bokorchien' is now an entirely Chinese village on the other side of the Naun.

31. I spoke in Mongolian, which was more or less understandable to most people. However, I could only understand the simplest of replies in Daur and relied on Delger or another Mongol-speaking woman from Morin Dawaa, Naran, to translate.

32. Delger had her own reasons for being interested in my research. On the way back, as Delger and I were approaching Qiqihar, where we were to part, she said her own father was active in shamanic matters. I was surprised, because this after all was the girl sent to watch over me. 'Well,' she said, 'people said he was a shaman.' Delger hardly knew him, because she had been sent to the countryside in the Cultural Revolution. 'I did know my grandmother,' she added. She had done farming work and she had missed years of school. Later she had been sent to the Party School.

33. Ethel John Lindgren, a Swedish-American, worked as an anthropologist in Mongolia in the 1920s and later in Manchuria. Most of her research was on the Tungus reindeer-herders living to the north of Hailar. Unfortunately, she published little. She became a lecturer at Cambridge University.

34. From Sanskrit *dakini,* female spirits prominent in Buddhist trantras; in Mongolian epics, etc. they are young and beautiful and live in heaven.

35. *Jirden* was an annual ritual, on a relatively small scale, at which the *yadgan* invited all spirits and made a blood offering to them (Batubayin 1990; *DSHI* 1985: 264).

36. Domestic fire (*gal, gali*) was distinguished from wild-fire, which was called *tuimer* and regarded as a punishment sent by spirits of the land.

37. This included Chinggis Khan among the Mongols, the masters of mountains, and the 'Seven Old Men' (referring to the seven stars in the constellation of the Great Bear; Daurs called it Dualo Hod and made offerings of seven lamps to it when a child fell ill).

38. The Buryats (Banzarov [1846] 1955: 72–6 and Galdanova 1987: 24) and the Birarchen Tungus (Shirokogoroff 1935: 126–9) also had the idea of a female fire spirit.

39. Haslund (1949: 125) mentions a fire divinity called 'fire king' or 'youngest brother' and seven maidens in the fire. This information is from Inner Mongolia; however Haslund also mentions an exotic and dramatic ritual for the Holy Fire Maiden from the Altai (1949: 132–8).

40. *Eke* means 'mother', also 'origin', 'source'; *eke* is sometimes used for women in general.

41. This was also a Chinese fancy, but Urgunge and other Mongols assure me that they feel the idea to be Mongol.

42. Urgunge told me that menstrual cloths had to be buried in secret to the north of the house and underclothes washed and hung dry in some secluded place. Ordinary blood from a known source was not *hwaski*. If a woman cut her finger and spotted her clothes that would not be *hwaski*. Now it was also the case that the menstrual blood of young girls who had not yet had sexual relations was not *hwaski*. On the other hand, if an older woman had stopped menstruating but was still involved in sexual activity she would continue to be *hwaski*. It seems therefore that it was both age and sexual activity, the conjunction of men and women for reproduction, which 'caused' *hwaski*. In fact both men's and women's sexual fluids were regarded as *hwaski,* but semen to a lesser extent, and it did not have any of the magical power attributed to menstrual/birth blood. The sexual act was regarded as deeply shameful and so were all the endearments and caresses which pointed in that direction. The genitals of both men and women were both secret and sacred. Urgunge said that it was because the spirits would be offended by seeing sexual activities that his parents kept their spirit boxes and representations outside the house in the grainstore. He said that the fact that *tengger* and Niang-Niang were inside the house showed their greatness—they were above taking petty-minded offence.

43. Urgunge reported that he had heard that a Mongolian commander in the 1930s would test soldiers suspected of being spies by making them pass under a rope on which women's dirty underclothes were hung. If they were telling the truth they would be strong and pure enough to withstand this, but if they were telling lies the pollution would get to them and cause illness.

44. This interpretation is supported by Engkebatu's Daur–Mongol dictionary (1984: 257). The Mongol *tulg-a* is an iron support or trivet, on which the cooking-pot is placed. Figuratively, it means 'support', and the verb from it means 'to press against, touch, reach, charge with, or confront' (Lessing 1982: 840).

45. There was a spirit called Nogul Barkan, which was the revengeful spirit of an illegitimate child.
46. There is evidence that the sky might *need* support from women in the ethnography of North China. Birrell (1993: 71–2) cites a myth in which the primeval goddness Nü Kua mends the foundering sky by setting up four poles. Tao and Mu (1989: 177) describe a ritual in Shanxi province commemorating this event: women of every household bake flat pies and put them on top of their roofs, and they call this 'mending the sky'.

5

Shamans and Shamanship

5.1 *The* Yadgan *Shaman and the* Onggor, Hojoor, *and* Barkan *Spirits*

Despite all the complexities of gender just described, we have a strong sense of the separateness of men's and women's lives. Shamans created a way to merge them again. Whether they were male or female, *yadgan*s' identity came from spirits and these represented human predicaments in a way that deliberately overrode gender. I propose to show this using the example of a woman *yadgan*, Huangge. While I was in China I discovered that Huangge was not only the sister of the revolutionary Merse, but was herself a brilliant and famous woman, and I resolved to search for whatever information I could find about her.

My conversations in Manchuria gave me a new understanding of shamans when I realized that people rarely talked about them as a category. They were remembered as individuals. Mendüsürüng,[1] who had grown up in the Hailar district, remembered Pingguo Saman, Huangge Saman, Lam Saman, and Jaban Saman.[2] As he talked, Mendüsürüng constantly broke into song. He was overcome by the melodies, one like a lullaby, another like a romantic entreaty, and a third confident and happy. These were the signature-tunes of individual shamans. They were the musical refrains (*iroo*) from longer chants (*gisaar*). It seems that many of them had been melodies from popular folk-songs, and that a shaman would gather tunes from the people and transform them into his or her own song by replacing the words and inserting the tune into a longer chant. Conversely, in the communist period shamans' *iroo* were turned into folk songs. Urgunge too used to sing me the refrain of Du Yadgan's night journey (*dolbor*). I realized that each shaman left aural traces, which were the most spontaneous memories of them. Mendüsürüng once wrote, 'The sound of the shaman's voice can take away your heart *setgel-iig buliyana*' (1983: 255).

Omachi (1949: 18) gives a table showing the clans and spirits of four shamans active in the 1930s–1940s in the Daur Hailar population living in the two districts of Nantun and Mehertei (see Table 5.1). In fact there were more shamans and people than noted here, but the table is still a useful guide to names and places that will be mentioned again in these pages.[3] Before returning to these *yadgan*s, I first summarize the actions undertaken by shamans, since the reader should have a general idea of this, especially as it will not be possible to describe all of the types of performance in detail. Certain rituals were calendrical: the *yadgan* protected the clan by propitiating the spirits at regular

TABLE 5.1.

Clan	Sub-clan village	Population (households)		Shaman	*Hojoor* spirit
		Nantun	Mehertei		
Aula (Ao)[a]	Denteke	30	10	Pingguo (M)	Bo-hor-de
Aula (Ao)	Kurichien	3	0	Jaban (M)	I-e
Gobol (Guo)	Manna	40	15	Huangge (F)	Red Spirit[b]
Merden (Meng)	Alagchien	20	0	—[c]	—
Onon (E)	Bosogchien	5	0	Lam (M)	Leg[d]

[a] Chinese rendering of clan name in brackets.
[b] *Ulaan Barkan.*
[c] There was an Alagchien shaman, Fu Leng-chen, who died ten years before Omachi's visit in the early 1940s and no successor had appeared.
[d] *Duwe-chien kuli* (leg of the Duwe people) also known as Doglon Kuli (lame leg); see Chipaatii story in 2.1 and also 6.2.

ominan rituals, and by purifying himself, his costume, and the populace at an annual rite held shortly after the New Year. Otherwise all performances were incidental. The shaman divined the causes of unexplained illnesses and misfortunes; divined the whereabouts of lost animals; explained dreams: 'enlivened' the spirit-placings people kept at home; invoked and bargained with spirits; conducted rituals of sacrificial payment to spirits; magically expelled or calmed spirits attacking people; exorcized spirits through substitute objects; retrieved human souls stolen by spirits; placed children under the protection of *tengger* or a spirit called Ome Niang-Niang; invoked and propitiated the souls of dead shamans at the *shandan* burial site; and finally he or she might consecrate live animals to certain spirits. Daur shamans were invited above all to cure mental illness and depression, but a *yadgan* was also sometimes called in to restore 'balance' in social life, for example if a family could not live in peace, if someone died without allocating his property, or to negotiate with bandits and other outsiders.

This list does not, however, enlighten us about the ontology of shamans, what shamans were thought to be. This chapter works towards discovering such an ontology and will show why shamans were remembered as being so different from one another. Earlier it was suggested that certain rituals, notably the *oboo* festivities and the *lurgel* dances, constituted the male and female genders as internally divisible in such a way as to enable their own, separate self-reproduction. To recall the terms suggested by Strathern (1988), the single-sex creativity of the *oboo* and *lurgel* enactments was one of 'replication' (like creates like). Later in the book I shall be exploring another, shamanic way of understanding reproduction, and shall look again at death, which in Daur explanations was both an end and a beginning (5.2), and at birth, which replaced something unformed with a new kind of being (5.8 and 6.3). In Strathern's terms this shamanic reproduction was more like a process of 'substitution' ('relations are made visible in a form other than themselves' Strathern 1988: 182). The shamanic death–rebirth was symbolic and separate from the physical death and burial of ordinary people, in which shamans took no part. We may paraphrase the Daur idea as the creation of something which was inherited and yet different. The images were those of biological transformations: in death, the physical shedding of dead matter, in birth the transformation of seed into plant, egg into bird, or chrysalis into insect. These were metaphors for changes in the status of human feeling-thought (*sanaa*) and the soul (*sumus*). Gender as a preoccupation fell away. Although I think that it may be possible to suggest an association between 'female' processes and birth and 'male' processes and death, I do not wish to imply that such links were essential. It is not that whether a life was male or female did not matter, but that within the shamanic context human life was seen primarily in its psychological dimension, as a matter of desires, threats, and memories, and here non-gender-specific images were used to represent change. The symbolic idea of the human journey (*ayan* or *ayin*) was used to express the concept of a cumulation of metamorphoses in which a certain identity-relation was retained.

The distinctive feature of a shaman was that he or she was master (*ejin*) of a complex spirit, called *onggor*. Shamanic spirits in general were called *barkan*, a respectful term with the same origin as the Mongol word *burhan* (Buddha, god). However, Daur *barkan* could not be less like the Buddha, as we shall see. The *onggor* was a particular kind of *barkan* consisting of the soul-spoor (*sumusi mor*—'track of the soul') of previous and now dead shamans. It was when this entered a young person, becoming identified with their soul, that he or she had to become a shaman.[4]

Usually what happened was that a young man (read 'or woman' in the following passage) became inexplicably and incurably mentally ill, 'running along the top of fences, or cutting himself with a knife', as Mendüsürüng described to me.[5] The worried relatives would ask a shaman to divine the cause. If it was discovered that a dead shaman's soul had entered the ill man, then there was no way out but to take steps to become a shaman. Sometimes the family did not believe the prophesy and did nothing. But then the sick youth would have a sudden relapse (*ergen huviraga*—'turn', as of meat turning rotten) and if he died the neighbours would talk about this as a 'blocked death' (*bitgüriin* or *bitüü ükel*) and attribute it to his not having become a shaman (Mendüsürüng 1983: 257). Sometimes people remained in the state of being a potential shaman all their lives. They were known as *butur* (something like an insect hidden in the silk-worm's cocoon and waiting to emerge).[6] The afflicted young man apprenticed himself to some older shaman, as Pingguo Saman did to Lam Saman (3.2). These two chose some distant spot on the bank of the river or in the willow woods, where they practised melodizing (*ayalgulal*) and the skills (*arga*) of calling (*uriya-*), inviting (*jala-*), and directing (*jara-*) the *onggor* spirit. This training went on for at least a winter and a spring, and sometimes for two or three years. When the young shaman first lost consciousness during a dance to invite the *onggor*, it was considered that he had begun to master the spirit.

When the teacher judged that the young shaman was learning well, he requested the clanspeople to prepare the magical gown, a long and expensive undertaking. Then the young *yadgan* would be inducted at the great triennial ritual called *ominan*, at which the pupil followed his teacher in every step of the performance. The young shaman was then an authorized *yadgan*, but not yet qualified to wear a shaman's crown; she or he wore a red cloth covering the head. More training took place over the next three years, until the next *ominan* was held. After this the shaman could wear a crown and was considered fully qualified.

Let us now turn to Huangge Yadgan.[7] I was able to trace the wayward path of Huangge's *onggor* from an account given in Poppe (1930: 12–13), who describes how he met a man who also claimed to have been possessed by this *onggor*. Now this man did not call himself a *yadgan* but a *barishi*, a bone-setter, and we can infer from this that he was probably unable to master the *onggor* spirit. He said that he had once, in a trance, written down the whole history of the *onggor* in the Daur language, but had subsequently forgotten it. The following is what he remembered. The story is recounted in full here, since it explains not only how an *onggor* was inherited but also gives an example of what an *onggor* was.

Once upon a time on the Nomyn River near Qiqihar there were some clans occupied in brigandage. Among these people were an old man and woman, who had no children. One day, the lonely couple asked heaven for a child and Hormos Tengger sent them Otoshi Ugin[8] as a daughter. She was born when the couple were over 50 years old. The girl grew up and looked after her aged parents, sowing peas and feeding the old couple with them. But being completely without brothers, sisters, or friends, she often used to cry. Her tears fell on the peas, which as a result took on their blotchy colour. When she was 15 her parents died. Her kinsmen and acquaintances could not be bothered to conduct a funeral and as a result the old couple remained unburied. There was even talk of selling the girl. From grief, and everything she had suffered, she went out of her mind and ran away. A spirit entered her. Anguished by the uncaring behaviour of the people who had not buried her parents, she began to hate humankind. On her journey she met a young man suitor, but she despised him, and filled with vengeance, she killed him. After this she destroyed two villages.

She met a lama, who appeared at a place called Altan Hangai. He tried to compete with her over whose magic strength was stronger, but he was defeated, and became her follower. This lama was called Ganchi Lam.[9]

Then she came across someone called Orchin Dog,[10] one side of whose body was paralysed. When she cured him, he too became her follower. These three persons, Otoshi Ugin, Ganchi Lam, and Orchin Dog, have the common name Guarwan

Ayin; *Ayin* is also the name given to the representations of spirits made of felt or paper.

After this Otoshi Ugin wanted to go to heaven, but *tengger* was angry with her for destroying two villages. He instructed her to stay on earth to do good and atone for the harm she had done. Now she has her existence at Barga [i.e. the Hailar region, C.H.], where this *onggor* does only good.

This *onggor* was called Guarwan Ayin, which can be translated as 'Three Journeys'. *Ayin* (or *aysan*, Mo. *ay-a*) also means 'song/melody', and Mongols tell me that this is because you sing while you are on the move. Soldiers sing on the march. Singing gives courage but it can also awaken and lure in spirits. Urgunge said that hunters would always sing (*jandaa-*) on their way to the forest and on their return. However, they had to stop when passing graves, and it is significant that singing, apart from that of the shaman, was not allowed anywhere near the village. Even the Farmers' love-songs died on their lips as they approached home from the fields. Songs, journeys, and shamanic spirits were thus linked, and kept apart from the static, 'punctual' world of the village with its graveyard.

Poppe (1930: 13–14) then describes the shamans who bore the 'Three Journeys' *onggor* after the Daurs moved to Hailar (Barga). The first shamaness in Barga was Immen.[11] She was born from a couple who were the bondsmen of the grandfather of Poppe's informant (this grandfather, Banchan, was a very energetic, unsuperstitious person, who did not believe much in shamans). Immen became a shaman as follows: when she was 13 she was berry-picking in the forest with the daughters of the house. She saw something and fell down unconscious. When she came to, she could remember nothing. Banchan was annoyed with her, so he fumigated her with the smoke of dog's dung, and for this she punished him and he fell ill. Seven years afterwards she destroyed him and he died. Besides this, Immen attacked many other people. Her *onggor* was the Guarwan Ayin, and when she died her soul joined it. The *onggor* then went to a certain Fukan, who became a shaman. Fukan was the cousin of the informant. He was one of the most famous shamans in all Barga, and died when the informant was 12. After Fukan's death he (Fukan) too became part of the *onggor*. Now illness and death appeared in the informant's family. The *onggor* however went to another cousin, Huangge (Poppe 1930: 8–14). Mendüsürüng told me that Huangge's *onggor* contained some other characters, including a shaman who was a wrestler. Significantly, he knew these people by their mortuary sites (*shand*) rather than their names. 'All these places were in her *onggor*,' he said.

Poppe (1930: 14) adds that the last in a series of *onggor* spirits was known as the *borchoohor*, and this was held to be the strongest. *Borchoohor* means 'brown-spotted' and refers to a bird, which was a form taken by the last, most powerful, *onggor* spirit in the line. So Immen was *borchoohor* to Fukan, and Fukan was *borchoohor* to Huangge. *Yadgan* shamans wore two padded cloth *borchoohor* birds on the shoulders of their gowns.

How are we to understand all this? The *onggor* started with a tragic human event, which was the cause of an emotion, in this case revenge, motivating subsequent attacks on people. The *onggor* then set out on a journey, assimilating to itself other people (the defeated lama, the paralysed man, and the rejected suitor), and demonstrating its power in the following fashion: the repulse of men, the subjection of Buddhism, the cure of paralysis. In Poppe's account there is a break between the mythical first episode, which took place near Qiqihar in the Nomyn–Naun region and which explained the content of the *onggor* called the 'Three Journeys', and the second historical episode in Barga which concerned real shamans. The *onggor* moved to the Barga–Hailar area, first afflicting Immen in a forest, and it then traced the inheritance pattern of shamans, passing from Immen Yadgan to Fukan Yadgan, and then to Huangge. As it moved from shaman to shaman it assimilated these people to its complex make-up.[12]

This example shows that an *onggor* moved freely between the sexes, between the social classes (Immen was a girl of bondsman origin, while Huangge came from a distinguished family), and between people of different religions. Indeed, the incorporation of new different forms, substituting one mode of being for another, was crucial to the idea of the *onggor*, and this contrasts, of course, with the similarity of people so important in the patrilineal genealogical way of thinking. I have given these details of Huangge's *onggor* because they show why each shaman's spirit constitution had to be unlike that of any other current shaman, since their *onggor*s had separate histories.

Huangge was the most revered of all Daur shamans of her time, and her range of powers was by no means limited to her *onggor*. The *onggor* was a series of spirits whose clan affiliation could be various, or even unmarked. All types of shamans had *onggor*. However, the most powerful spirits were ancestral clan spirits (*hojoor*, root or stem). *Hojoor* were sometimes numbered among the *onggor*, but were distinct from them if the ancestor in question was not a shaman. Since *hojoor* belonged to patrilineal clans, the relation of a woman shaman like Huangge to her *hojoor* was a complex matter, as can be imagined. I ask my readers to bear with me as I give an initial outline of the situation here, leaving clarification of the social issues to later (6.1).

Huangge was born in 1888 in the Gobol clan into an aristocratic family which was described as 'not only the number one among the Daurs of Hulun Buir but among all the Mongols in general' (Omachi 1949: 25). She died in 1973.[13] Now Huangge married into the Aul clan, but she took her *hojoor* spirit from her father's clan. Huangge became a shaman only after her marriage. In 1917 she fell ill with a heavy bout of dysentery-like illness. She had only just recovered when she began to have mental problems. Sometimes she would be clear as normal, but then unexpectedly she would see all kinds of different small animals invading her house and she became confused. She was ill in this way for the next five years. They asked a *yadgan* to cure her, but he said that she herself should become a *yadgan*. Eventually she promised to become a shaman and so recovered. In 1920 she took Fu Leng-chen, who was the shaman of the Alagchien section of the Merden clan, as a teacher, and following his guidance became a shaman (*DSHI* 1985: 258). It is not known when in this sequence of events Huangge acquired her *hojoor* spirit.

The word *hojoor* was used in ordinary conversation to mean male clan ancestors in general.[14] Most ancestors were soon forgotten, but a *hojoor yadgan* was a shaman who communicated with a non-shaman clan ancestor who had become a spirit (*hojoor barkan*). Like the *onggor* the *hojoor* spirit seems to have been imagined as a singular entity encompassing plurality. Here we need note only that *hojoor* were often aggressive and did not confine their attacks only to male members of their own clan. In particular they followed (*daga-*) women leaving a clan to get married, so brides would take along images of their *hojoor* in order to be able to propitiate them in case they started wreaking havoc in the husband's clan. Such in-coming spirits were called *naajil ajin* (mother's family's spirit). Huangge may have brought in her paternal clan's *hojoor* in this way, or acquired it separately, but whatever the case this *hojoor*, of the Manna section of the Gobol clan, was known as Ulaan Barkan (red spirit) and Huangge was often called after it, Ulaan Saman. The story told is as follows:

It started with a man of the Manna clan just as the Manchus were rising to power [the 17th century, C.H.]. He refused to fight on the Manchu side and was taken prisoner and jailed. His parents grieved for him at home. But using magic, and taking off his clothes, he escaped from the prison. He died in the mountains on the way home. The soul of the dead man became a *togel* bird [a red-poll, C.H.], which winged its way to his old home in Butha, and flying in at the window landed on the western edge of the platform bed. He told his father and mother what had happened, comforted them, and announced that he would now be an ancestral spirit [*hojoor barkan*]. (*DSHI* 1985: 258; Omachi 1949: 19)

Even this short legend indicates that *hojoor barkan* spirits were very far from straightforward patrilineal predecessors. They could take the form of wild animals, fish, or even artefacts, and frequently they were women (see 6.2).

So we see that a clan shaman had as part of his or her make-up at least two spirits, the *onggor* and the *hojoor*, each of which was internally differentiated and represented a complex series of events. The shaman-teacher added knowledge of further spirits, and it is significant that in all the examples I know of the teacher came from a different clan from the young shaman. This feature must have helped spread and consolidate shamanic ideas. Both shamans and ordinary families made images of *onggor*s and *hojoor*s, ready for propitiation.[15]

One further piece of the puzzle must be mentioned in order to explain a shaman's full range of abilities.[16] We have seen that young shamans had to have at least one spirit under their control (the *onggor*), and this was necessary because only in union with the *onggor* could a shaman discover, deal with, and subdue other spirits (though it must be said that the expression 'helper spirit' often found in the literature seems a peculiarly anodyne term for the Daur *onggor*). Through their careers shamans gradually learned to master new spirits, but there was always a number which were outside a given shaman's competence. These untamed 'wild' spirits were unattached to any clan and were known by Daurs simply as *barkan*, and sometimes as 'external' *barkan* if they happened to be spirits of Chinese or other origin. They also had names, placings, and histories. The Daurs knew some thirty-five of them according to Li *et al.* (1955). These spirits grew more numerous with the end of the Manchu Dynasty and shamans with widespread powers were urgently needed to cope with them.

Finally, besides the *barkan* spirits there were large numbers of un–differentiated demons (*shurkul*), which roamed around and caused harm. No pictures or other placings were made of *shurkul*. These nameless demons could be suppressed, exorcized, or banished by *yadgan* shamans, but also by many other specialist practitioners. They were not normally considered serious enough to merit a performance involving the invocation of the *onggor*. Even ordinary people could get rid of them if they happened to know some magic (*ilbi*) or a spell or two (*tarni*).

It was the serious and individually named *barkan* spirits which were the main concern of the shaman. To avoid confusion let me divide *barkan* spirits into three categories: those which initially attacked the shaman and subsequently provided his or her own power (*onggor*), those which were held to be 'ancestors' of clans (*hojoor*), and the large, heterogeneous category of those remaining (which I shall henceforth call simply *barkan*). It is important to understand that all these spirits could attack people and one another. What this means is that a shamanic performance was above all a trial of strength, or a battle.

A 'spirit' was in effect a psychological-intentional scenario (or rather a cumulative series of scenarios) initially activated by the hatred or desire for vengeance of wronged and afflicted people. Now if it was an *onggor* which was diagnosed as attacking the patient, all the shaman needed to do was to manifest the *onggor* and induce it to remove itself. However, if a *hojoor* spirit or a *barkan* spirit was divined as causing the trouble, then the *onggor* was first invoked and used as a weapon (or a series of weapons) against the *hojoor* or *barkan*. In effect, this was to counterpose the 'power' of one scenario against that of another, socially and psychologically a quite extraordinarily complex matter (see 6.1).

However, it should be added that there were ways of talking among ordinary people that quite by-passed any delicate psychological issues involved. In everyday talk, spirits were often brutal forces, and they slugged it out against other powers in the world:

This event happened at the end of the Manchu Dynasty around 1911. There was a wrestler called De-Buku from Urekuwe village. He did not believe in the power of *yadgans* and couldn't care less about demons. One day he got drunk and out of mischief defecated and pissed in a cave near the village where some demons lived. When he got home his feet became very painful. He was furious. He hobbled back to the cave and put his sore feet inside, roaring, 'You demon bitches, come out and let's have a showdown! If you don't come out, I'll seal the mouth of your cave!' Instantaneously his feet stopped hurting. De-Buku's uncle was a shaman. They lived together and the uncle heard the wrestler boasting about his victory. One evening, as De-Buku was returning home a big pig attacked him. But a strong man like him had no reason to fear a single pig! De-Buku thought, 'Aha, a windfall!' and he started to grab the pig, but it turned out to be preternaturally strong, and his strength began to fail. In the end he even had to pull a stake out of the wooden fence to defend himself and save his life. The pig disappeared into the darkness. De-Buku went home and found his uncle sitting there smiling. 'How was it? Did you win?' the uncle asked. Only then did the wrestler realize that the pig was his uncle's *onggor*. After that he believed deeply in the power of shamans. (Omachi 1949: 26)

Here we see the *onggor* depicted as crude power, deployed 'physically' to take down the pride of human strength a peg or two. Spirits were not 'higher' than human beings, just different. Urgunge said, 'If you ask me whether *barkan*s were higher than human beings that's almost like asking if a horse is higher than a cow, or a cow higher than a horse; they are just entirely different.' Nevertheless, spirits derived from humans. Another time, Urgunge said to me, 'You know, I cannot remember any female *onggor*s. Why? Because women have weak bodies. And the character of women is weak. They have no will power, so they would be no good as *onggor*s.'[17] Now this must be almost deliberately selective memory at work—as we have seen that there certainly were female *onggor*s—but it shows one way that men conceived of shamanship. Shamans were involved not just in reacting to unseen powers in the world but in forcing them to bend to shamanic will. The wild *barkan*s were waiting to be tamed. Urgunge continued, '*Barkan*s, . . . they are *barkan*s only because no shaman has yet conquered them. In my family, if I had been a shaman, that Koton Barkan (spirit of the military barracks) would have been turned into an *onggor* long ago.'

There are many ways of talking about shamans, and if we turn to the gentler descriptions of Mendüsürüng or Odongowa (or Urgunge himself in a different mood), the Daur shaman appeared truly as the 'wounded healer'. She had to suffer from the spirit and be incapacitated by it before she could become a shaman. Internalizing the *onggor* spirit was what made someone a shaman, and therefore 'learning' the spirits and how to control their coming and going was a process of learning about oneself (oneself as a shaman). In this way 'oneself' as a shaman was very different from the ordinary social person, who was imprisoned in a given gender, in the hierarchy of patriarchal society, and the particularity of place.

This section has shown several characteristics of shamanic thinking which require further investigation: first, the *onggor* was a cumulation of distinct individuals who were nevertheless a unity, spoken of in the singular. I explore this idea in 6.2. Secondly, there was the crucial role of accident. Remember the various people Otoshi Ugin happened to meet on her way, Immen who 'saw something' when out picking berries, or the wrestler who got drunk and relieved himself—all fortuitous moments that nevertheless were the instants of spirit metamorphosis. The accidents happened on 'journeys', space-time that involved movement and transformation. Now this very idea of the chance encounter was also represented as a spirit. Daurs told me that many people kept an image called *Ayin Barkan* (Journey Spirit) or *Oluur Barkan* (Found-thing Spirit) and that this was quite separate from the Three Journeys *onggor* of the Manna clan. The Journey Spirit came about if something gave you a terrible shock while you were travelling in the wilderness, or if you happened on an old spirit image someone else had thrown away, or accidentally tripped on something belonging to an unseen being. If you then began to feel depressed or some bad luck happened, it was imperative to take the object, whatever it was, ask the shaman to enliven it (*amiluula-*) and then pay it respects. The Journey Spirit was recognition of the power not just of unfortunate events in the past, like other spirits, but of accident itself, i.e. the idea that 'accidents' must happen. And thirdly, we have seen that the shamanic idea of spirits involved transformation and the possibility of flight. It is not that this was ever spelled out. There are only mythic incidents or snatches of songs to go on; but these seem to imply an understanding that we have yet to grasp, perhaps an idea of escape related to 'necessary' predicaments and fated accidents, a flight or metamorphosis which implicitly posed the question 'flight from what?' Here is one of Huangge's songs of her *onggor*—opaque indeed, but such songs were what everyone remembered.

> Roe deer! Roe deer!
> Zhe ru! Zhe ru!
> Roe deer's eye, roe deer's ear,
> Zhe ru! Zhe ru!
> Fly! Fly! Fly wing to wing!
> Circle, birds in the air,
> Sing, you hawks!
> De ye ku.
>
> (Odongowa 1991 n.d.: 11)

The *onggor in principle* was an idea that leapt beyond species, gender, social rank, and the confinement of place. It was a generalization of the human condition, in the sense that its singularity appeared in a cumulation of readily understandable emotions (jealousy, revenge, rage). The emotions were generated by predicaments that were spoken of as though they were unique real events but can also be seen as archetypal scenarios. Thus there was a shift, from the reparations and discriminations of everyday life to the spirit-scenario, and this was marked by specific departures from commonsense thinking. This move, which for ordinary people was often seen as an 'accident', was the initiating moment of the shamanic journey (*Ayin*). The all-important idea of spirit power was therefore related to the overturning of the principle of the everyday and to the making archetypal of particularities. But such a generalizing power would have been groundless and meaningless in the shaman's attempts to help clients without the continuous feeding of it with things to transform, namely the rich life of the incidents and emotions of ordinary people. Nevertheless, what the shaman did was to manifest these fundamental and understandable emotions through the eyes of *other* people, people who were dead and had become spirits. This otherness was represented, I think, by the strange and non-intuitive images of the physical world portrayed by spirits, who would not see the world as we see it. This may seem rather an abrupt and confusing summary so I shall return to these ideas in 6.1, when I discuss the social and psychological relations set up by shamans' performances. Meanwhile it is time to look more closely at the process of metamorphosis of human life to spirit existence, that is, at the process of death.

5.2 The Coffin and the Tree

Shamans' death rituals differed from those of the clanspeople. The difference reveals two perspectives on human trajectories of life through death and beyond, and though they were attributed to 'the shaman' and 'the clansman' they were available as hypotheses which anyone could apply in thinking about the relation between humanity and the world.

In several respects Daur thinking is well accounted for by Bloch's theories about death. Bloch (1993) has argued that death in many societies is seen as a process, not an instant of extinction, and that the nature of this process is to be explained by the conception of the person as composed of several elements which separate from one another at different stages. He further suggests that in societies with a lineal kinship system, whether patrilineal or matrilineal, there is a dual system for dealing with death. The lineage system is concerned with the terrestrial survival of the lineage as a social group (often symbolized by the hardness of bones), and death rituals serve to renew social lives in lineages; that is, the elements of the person clanspeople share with other clanspeople are reproduced. However, a different religious system is called into play when the person is considered as a unique individual. In this case, world religions such as Islam or Buddhism, which often coexist with lineage systems, concern themselves with the aspect of death which is the disappearance of the individual. In an essentially asocial rite the deceased individual is faced towards God, and this at the same time purifies the part of the person which is to return reincarnated as a member of the social group. Bloch (1993: 16) notes that dual funerary practices are not restricted to regions where clans coexist with world religions, and so his theory invites us to consider the role of shamanic practice as the individuating, purifying, asocial part.

In many ways this analysis is very illuminating with regard to Inner Asia. However, I do not think it correct to contrast, as Bloch does, the social with the individual. I shall argue that for Daurs the social, in the case of both clans and shamanic practice, incorporated the idea of the individual. What we have to deal with is a contrast between the social as a regularity or an abstraction, and the social as irregular, unpredictable relationships. In the former case, human life was seen as an appropriate span of physical existence, whereas in the latter, the shamanic view, it was a matter of variable 'spiritual' energy constantly threatened by the energies of others. The shamanic view of society was to see a movement between a self opened out in limitless, branching, emotional involvements and a self at rest at 'home', whereas in the clan view people proceeded through life, not without individuality, but subjected to the norms of the lifespan and appropriate times for the occurrence of life changes.

When ordinary people died after a full life the funeral was in the hands of the *mokon* (local lineage) and shamans were not supposed to take part.[18] Urgunge remembers that people in his day used to anticipate their death. It was thought that 50 years was quite old for a human, and 60 was a complete life. A young person's death was *gomdoltoi* (with grief) but Urgunge said that the death of an old person was not regarded as a traumatic event. Daurs said, 'When a man approaches death, his words have power. When a bird approaches death, its song has sadness,' and 'Death does nothing but change the shape of things.' Death was the destined occasion for metamorphosis into an ancestor.[19]

Many years before death approached old men made their own coffins (*avs*). Urgunge's father discussed with other old men which wood to choose, what shoes and clothes he would wear, and what decorations he would paint inside and outside the coffin. Coffins were rather large and roomy and shaped like tall houses with pitched roofs (see Plate 16). For several years Urgunge's father's coffin was kept in a storage barn, not far from the wooden boxes which held the representations of *barkan* spirits.[20]

When a man died, the body was laid out in the house on the floor with the head facing north. The body was washed, shaved, and the nails cut, and new clothes, including a hat and belt, were put on. The face was covered with a white cloth. An animal was killed and cooked meat and other foods laid by the head. The daughter-in-law laid a filled pipe by the mouth of the corpse and lit it from time to time. Paper money was burnt. Meanwhile women were sewing mourning clothes of white cloth. Relatives began to arrive, all of them, men, women, and children, making deeper bows (*sain hasso*) to the corpse than they would ever have done to the man alive. Urgunge said, 'When you die, your status goes up.' As they came and sat by the corpse, all the relatives had to cry (*waila-*) with a special keening noise, like singing. (People said that it was because singing reminded them of mourning that it was not allowed in the village. If a child even hummed to itself, the mother would stop it, saying, 'I'm still alive!') The visiting relatives, especially those from the mother's side, were treated with the utmost respect, seated on the heated bed while the family sat on the floor. They were accompanied everywhere, offered food, drink, tobacco, their horses and carts taken care of, and all this was partly for them, but partly also to show respect to their own dead ancestors. And the visitors also had to behave with the utmost quietness and propriety, following custom to the letter. If they did not do this, they would be severely criticized, and thought 'not even human'.

A window was opened to allow the soul of the dead to depart. This was said to happen naturally and inevitably, without any ritual intervention. During this time, the souls of children were called back under the eaves in case they be tempted innocently to follow. However, even with its soul departed there was the possibility for a short time that the corpse might 'come alive', particularly while the body was still not buried; in winter, a corpse might have to be kept for months before the ground unfroze to permit burial. An enlived corpse was known as *bong*. Urgunge said that they were feared, but also thought rather pitiful and funny. The *bong* was not a wandering soul, because souls were disembodied entities. Rather, they were bodies briefly made to come alive without souls (*sumus*). We can see here the belief in a 'life force' (in the North Asian literature this force is sometimes described as another kind of soul, Shirokogoroff 1935: 134–5). One woman at Molidawa told me that the life force (*ami*—breath) should come out of the body via the arm-pits, but if for some reason it did not, because the body had been incorrectly buried, then the ghost would hang around. 'Oh, there are many *bong* around here,' she said.[21] In Urgunge's view, such a ghost did not really do any harm, but it was very frightening. When he went to America and lived for a time in New Haven, he saw a hoarding there, 'The Dead Shall Rise Again!', and he wondered how Americans could acclaim such a horrible idea.

While the corpse was lying at home a saddled horse (*hwailag*) was tethered outside in the yard. A thin rope was attached from the corpse, near the head, to the animal.[22] Urgunge thought this string was a 'rein', though he was not sure, and that the horse was the soul's mount on its journey to the other world. The horse should be elderly and a castrated male, one of the deceased's much-used animals. The horse was killed and its heart, liver, lungs, and spleen removed, cooked, and placed beside the coffin. The rest of the meat was eaten. The word *hwailag* was sometimes used as a curse, but within the family it also had an intimate, joking feel, partly because the animal was an old favourite, and Urgunge said that he was sometimes shouted at by his aunts, 'You *hwailag*!'

Inside the coffin were now placed the things which might be useful to the soul in its further existence: a small cooking-pot, a knife, chop-sticks, a plate, cup, salt, tea, tobacco, paper money, and so forth.[23] The particular beloved objects of the dead person were always included, his or her pipe, tobacco-pouch, flint and steel, and any other small objects to which the person had been attached. Some Daurs added a small model boat, for crossing the river separating this world from the next. All these things, including the dead person's clothing, were ritually 'destroyed' by slashing at them with a knife. Paper money was burnt in large amounts. An inscription was placed at the head, saying this was such a person, of such a clan, from such a place. Urgunge's father had painted a sun, moon, and seven stars inside his coffin lid, his heavenly destination. The coffin was nailed shut. It was, as Urgunge said, the dead man's universe. Over this coffin a respected elder would give a eulogy, describing the deceased's life, clan, illnesses, date of death, and the amount of money and animals sacrificed at his death.

The coffin was taken out by ox-cart at an auspicious hour and buried deeply at the graveyard in the designated place. Both men and women accompanied it, walking in order of genealogical seniority. Offerings, lamps, and some of the cooked meat of the *hwailag* were placed at the grave, and more paper money was burnt. The dead person's clothes were also burnt. Amid general weeping, and with dishevelled hair, the mourners made a three-times circumambulation of the grave. The mourners returned home for a solemn feast, and during the main mourning period of three months they wore special clothes (*sinig*); did not wash, put on new cloths, or remove lice; refrained from sex, cutting hair, laughter, shouting, quarrelling, and singing.[24] For three years, at each New Year festival (*anee*), people would lay offerings by the empty bed of the deceased person and then say prayers. A Daur funeral was the most solemn and resplendent of occasions, and poor families would go into heavy debt to pay for it.

The Daur funeral can be seen as what had to be done with the accumulated aspects of the person. Individuality was recognized by gathering particular objects (the favourite horse, the much-used small belongings) and they were linked to the corpse and then concentrated together by being placed in the coffin. The breaking of the objects separated their physical aspect from their notional aspect, which allowed the latter to proceed with the soul to the other world. All social and individual attributes of the person were focused in the coffin, which at the same time became a microcosm, notionally 'expanding' to become a world.

Adults who died young, however, were another matter, because they had unfinished business on this earth. Especially if they died without children everyone would know their souls would be bitter and unsatisfied. The body was often burned, rather than buried.[25] A *hwailag* horse was not provided in such cases, nor did anyone use the euphemism he or she 'became a *barkan*', and this was because it was feared that the person might indeed turn into a harmful spirit (*shurkul*). Such spirits were not located distantly in another world, but were active in this one. Shirokogoroff (1935: 136) has written with regard to *shurkul* that this was not so much a class of spirits as a 'bad word', a term of abuse, an epithet used to denigrate spirits and also people. Urgunge said, 'It's true, if someone came home late at night, fighting drunk, you would call him *shurkul*. If a woman let herself go, became all dirty, slept around, shouted, kept her hair all wild, she would be called *shurkul*. But *shurkul* are really spirits and they cause a lot of harm.'

Perhaps we can think of *shurkul* as images of unfinished, banished lives.[26] They had no names. They appeared at night. They could take the form of small animals and come into seemingly harmless objects, like combs, knives, or pots. They could enter people's bodies and 'possess' their minds, but more commonly they penetrated only to suck blood, kick and bite from inside, causing pain but not mental disturbance. They were afraid of the sun, and afraid of women's menstrual cloths. They had fires, but these were abnormal, bluish fires far out in the steppes, lit in the skulls of dead animals. They often tried to lure people out to their wild haunts. Urgunge said that if you were travelling in the countryside at night, you would feel secure if you were with a shaman, because his *onggor*s were always stronger than any *shurkul*. *Shurkul* attacked only in their own clans and they preserved some features of the dead social person: if he or she was afraid of something, the spirit would be too; if he or she had greatly respected someone, the *shurkul* would leave that person alone and take it out on someone else.

So far we have seen that an ordinary death implied a gathering in of the signs of sociality and individuality and then their projection outwards, away from human society, into ancestral anonymity in the cosmos. With a tragic early death, on the other hand, the soul did not proceed away, but instead returned to attack people, and this was perhaps the reasoning behind the name for such deaths *bitüü ükel* (blocked-off death). Another way of putting this is to say that different kinds of deaths created specific types of supernatural being. Death after a full and appropriate life would result in quite a different being from a premature, vengeance-creating death. The most important idea here was the completeness of a life. By contrast, uncompleted or over-extended lives were the sphere of shamanic activity.

Any living being's life-span was determined by destiny (*jiya*) which came from Heaven. When talking about this, people said, 'Destiny is just like this, destiny is your share' (*Jiya immer yum aa, jiya huv yum aa*), meaning nothing can be done about it. In Morin Dawaa I met a woman whose five sons had all died, leaving her with three daughters. She said simply, 'In my life it was my destiny not to have sons. So my sons died.' Remember also the reaction of

Urgunge's mother when the bandits took him away (1.4). The destined life-span was assimilated subjectively. The idea of the 'full life' was integral to the patrilineal ideology, which replaced a complete life with an endless succession of other complete lives.

The most incomplete life was that of a baby dying before incorporation into clan society. Around the age of 5 there was a hair-cutting rite for Daur boys, at which they were given presents by kin and welcomed into the paternal group.[27] Urgunge thought it was impossible for a baby to have a funeral. 'Suppose a young child dies, there is no such thing as a funeral. You just wrap up the body and put it in a tree, and that is it. A funeral is just for an old person'[28] (see Plate 17). Now this did not indicate that a baby was not involved in social life. The idea of putting a baby's corpse in a tree was so that it should be closer to *tengger* and therefore available for its soul to turn around (*erge-*) and search for a woman's womb in which to return. There was a similar idea about the shaman's 'burial'. The Naun Daurs placed the shaman's corpse in the branches of a tree in the wilderness, or on top of a mountain, together with his mirror and drum, and the aim here also was that the soul should quickly reappear in the world.[29] No one should cry for a dead shaman. Before he died a shaman should desig-nate another (divined in a dream) to officiate at his funeral and expedite his transformation into an *onggor*. 'It was high and lonesome,' Urgunge said, 'but that was because the shaman had an exceptional position in society, like an Emperor or Queen.' In the case of an ordinary person who died at a respectable age with male descendants, the soul peacefully left the body and made its way to the ranks of ancestors in the other world. From this journey it was not expected to return. But the tree-burials of the baby and the shaman show that there was another idea of society too. This society was not bounded by death but went beyond it and incorporated it as a point of metamorphosis, enabling the soul to return more or less at random and certainly outside the membership of the clan.

Shamanic thought disregarded the life-span and dwelt on actual, irregular times, the definite amounts of time people really lived. This was to acknowl-edge that at any particular time in the present one's destiny could not be known. Shamanic thinking raised the possibility of taking decisions on one's destiny and creating it by one's actions, always in the fearful knowledge that one might be wrong. After all, it could always be the case that some event happening now was *not* one's destiny, and it was the point of having shamans that they could find this out. Such decisive moments could radically change one's life. This view existed alongside the fatalist, passive view of destiny and often superseded it. Shamanic thinking insisted that one should act to accom-plish one's destiny, constantly being aware, from one's own inner promptings and from signs noticed in the world, that one might have to change direction, and that there might be difficult things one had to do.

Tochingga Yadgan, whose story now follows, is an example of this.

16. A coffin waits outside a Daur house near Hailar. Photo: 1931, O. Mamen. [5.2]

17. Tree 'burial' of a baby, the body in a bark container, Mergen region in the Naun valley. Photo: 1927–9, Stötzner. [5.2]

Tochingga was a *hojoor yadgan* of the Manna section of the Gobol clan, as Huangge was after him. Like her he was empowered by the Red Spirit. The events of Tochingga's 'death' happened in the 1890s, a sufficiently distant time, it seems, for the account to appear in mythic form by the time it was recorded in the 1950s. I was told this story by a very old woman in Morin Dawaa, but she was constantly interrupted and lost the thread. So the version given below is that recorded in the *DSHI* (1985: 261–2).

Tochingga Yadgan's younger sister fell very ill in her husband's home. Though they asked many shamans to cure her, none could do so. They asked Tochingga too, but he kept on refusing, because he had bad relations with Yikedai Yadgan of the other village, a bondsman village, and he was afraid that if he cured his sister, Yikedai would kill him secretly. But his mother was very worried and reproved him: 'Your sister is ill; you must cure her.' He had no option and set off. As he was about to leave, Tochingga said, 'My power will definitely decrease.' He took a man with him as an assistant, each of them riding a horse. They loaded up the shaman's clothes and set off for the sister's house. On the way, the heart-protecting mirror jumped out of its bag onto the ground and rolled away to the north-west. They both chased after it, but did not capture it. Tochingga said, 'The loss of that bronze will further decrease my power.' When he reached his sister's house he did not do a spirit dance, but simply made a hurried propitiation of the spirits with livestock. Even so, his sister's health improved. Two or three days after reaching home, he felt unwell and said to his family, 'I am being killed by Yikedai, and will die today. Wait until I am dead and then dress my corpse in my magic clothes, strap it up with the drum and drumstick onto an oxcart, and take it out to a wild place where you can no longer hear the barking of dogs. Then unhitch the ox and tie it to the cartwheel, then return home and wait for me three days and three nights. If by that time I have not revived then you must think I have passed on. But in case I manage to revive, you must tie a *shuanna* rope from the house door to the main gate, and hang my old clothes on it. In front of the door you must burn a censer of *gangga* grass, and everything will be all right.'
    After he died his family did as he said: they dressed him in his magic clothes, put the corpse on an oxcart, drove him to Hargana Zalaga, unhitched the ox, tied it to the wheel, and then went home. They waited, and on the morning of the third day, as it was growing light, they heard far away the sound of a drum, which got nearer and nearer. They prepared things as they had been told. They opened the door and saw the dead man in front of the oxcart, dancing as he approached the house. As he passed in front of Denteke village all the people thought that the dead shaman of the Manna clan had already become a spirit. He arrived at his family's gate, and following along the *shuanna* rope danced three more times, casting off the magic costume and putting on the old clothes set out for him. He came into the house and said, 'I exchanged my body for that of a crow. If you go out and look at Hargana Zalaga you will find the carcass of a crow there.' After this he took some incense and going to the bank of the Imen River, burnt it there; then he leapt into the river. When the incense had burnt half way down, there came floating down the river a dead carp, more than five feet long. Then he jumped out of the river and said, 'The stains on my body I have transferred to that great carp; now I shall live until I am seventy.' Indeed, he lived to be seventy years old.

Tochingga's double death almost too neatly reverses the death process of the ordinary clansman. Instead of gathering up the recognized parts of a life, closing them in a coffin, and removing them from home to another world, the shaman's death involved separating aspects of the person, dispersing them in nature, and returning from the wilderness to home. Rather than the completed life-span and the abstract genealogical structure of the graveyard, Tochingga's death involved specific, irregular times and spaces. His route home reversed the funerary journey by ox–cart, whose trundling outwards was replaced by dancing inwards. Propelled by the dancing, he entered the interior space of the house by means of a *shuanna* rope. This rope occurred in many shamanic performances and denoted a symbolic 'road'.[30] The spirit road here was mapped on to real distances known to the community, such as the route between Hargana Zalaga and the home village, or the distance between the gate and the house door. Similarly, the story refers always to specific times (dawn on the third day, the time it took for half the incense-stick to burn, the 70 years of his life).

I am reminded in this story of James Weiner's perceptive discussion of the Heideggerian appreciation of the temporality of human 'being' in the context of Foi culture. He contrasts those 'inauthentic' acts (of Foi men) striving to bring temporal continuity to a halt, impelled by reference to a contrived and artificially transcendent moral authority, with what Heidegger calls being–towards–death, the authentic, concernful being which encompasses its own finality as an integral part of its temporality, which is the concern of Foi women (1991: 117–18). However, on reflection it becomes clear that this contrast does not apply to the Daurs. For a start, there was no such politically correct division in terms of gender, since both men and women had their own cults of timeless perpetuation at their *oboo* rituals, and shamanic practice was a joint or androgynous venture. The death practices described here suggest that both the clan-based and the shamanic imaginations involved authentic understandings of being–towards–death, and that they both also constructed unreal, time–defying scenarios. The clansman's anticipation of mortality was seen in his construction of his coffin long before death and in his carefully considered choice of its contents; the shaman's was evident in his intimations of weakness and death as he was obliged to take part in a contest of powers. Where the two differed most was in their representations of society and the individual's place in it. Practices at death made clear that there were two different trajectories, crystallized by the difference between the deeply buried house-like coffin and the airy tree in the wilderness. This was a distinction between enclosure and dispersal as arenas for human action. It was this openness/dispersal which was distinctive of shamanic practice. Tochingga's death did not 'take place' but was spread out in the landscape, as it were, and it involved both incorporation of external harm and extrusion of rejected aspects of himself. Although Tochingga's death did not happen in domestic space it cannot possibly be seen as asocial. The trial of strength in which he died and revived was one between affines and different social ranks (both of these being social categories excluded from the clan).

Urgunge remembered a woman who was the mother-in-law of one of his family's servants. Her husband had died during the winter. Because the village was snow-bound the body had to be put in the storehouse to wait for spring when it could be buried. One night this woman had to fetch some flour from a high shelf in the storehouse, and in the dark, she tumbled from a ladder and fell onto the rigid, frozen corpse of her husband. She fainted with horror and never recovered. Her mental malady was *beleng*, an uncontrollable affliction (see 5.5). Shamans were also struck by madness (*koodoo*) after terrible events, but a shaman recovered because he 'controlled' multifarious spirits (tragic scenarios), whereas the old woman's contact with death affected her mind for the rest of her life. We can see now why shamans were respected as courageous, brave people. Society's respect and belief were absolutely essential to shamans, not only in sustaining their performances (5.7) but also in mythologizing their lives. This is what attached shamans to their skeins of previous incarnations as *onggor*s, and it meant too that the events in their present lives were often retold like echoes of the earlier *onggor* adventures.[31] The people also sustained shamans in another way, by creating their armour, and it is to this subject that I now turn.

5.3 Elegant Armour and Ancient Trouvailles

A shaman's costume was an independently existing object, separated from its makers and even from its owner, having its own magical power. For Daurs it had the historic resonances of conscious tradition, like a priest's vestments or a top hat and tails in England. But unlike either of these, the symbolism of the shaman's costume was an active meta-statement, referring not just to the past but to an acknowledgement of 'the past' as objectivized, a source of power. Making such a costume for their shaman the people placed him or her in a world-conquering time-machine.

A woman from Hailar described to me the elegant (*gangang*) and artistic (*uralig*) costume of her grandfather who was a shaman. It was rich with silk embroideries, especially the lower part of the back, where there were multiple layers of streamers depicting birds, animals, and trees. She said the costume was made by her mother and aunts, who got the shaman to help by looking after their children while they sewed. 'What is the function of embroidery?' she asked rhetorically. 'The first woman in the world, when her sons were ill, wanted to protect their lives, so she made an embroidery, just one line of flowers. That is how embroidery originated. If you believe and have real faith, then spirit (*barkan*) will give you the shaman's costume and the embroideries;

it will give the lines and flowers and patterns one after another so people know how to make them.'

Chaussonnet (1988: 208–26) discusses the contribution made by women as seamstresses to the luck of hunters in North-East Asian and Alaskan cultures. Animal skin, transformed into a second skin for humans by the work of seamstresses, still retained its animal identity and thus signified a hunter–animal symbiosis. Chaussonnet writes (1988: 212 and 225–6):

The seamstress helped reconcile humans and animals, not only by indirectly participating in hunting but also by reinforcing the transformational relationship between them in the clothing that she made. . . . Transvestism in the shaman's garments represented his or her position between the male and female worlds. The shaman's position between the human and spiritual worlds was symbolized by the use of contrasting black and red, or dark and light. The passage between gender identities and other passages throughout the lives and death of Siberian people were marked on clothing with the same care that the Alaskan Eskimo represented the transformational relationship with the animal world.

The Daur shaman's costume was made by both women and men, the gown with its embroideries being created by women, while the drum and drumstick were made by men. The metallic or hard additions, pendants, shells, mirrors, bells, metal parts of the helmet, were purchased (see below). The gown was the same, whether the shaman was a man or a woman.

For Urgunge the main aim of the shaman's costume was to be impressive and gain attention. It certainly was this, but its many parts also had relatively clear symbolic meanings. There are numerous descriptions of Daur shaman gowns (Poppe 1930; Lindgren 1935*a*; Haslund-Christensen 1944; Mergendi 1981; Mendüsürüng 1983; *DSHI* 1985; Batubayin 1990; Odongowa 1991), and all agree on the main components, their names and, more or less, on their symbolic significance, which suggests that the costume was one relatively stable aspect of the shamanic complex. What did it add up to? To start with, if the costume was a symbolic statement about 'the shaman', what did it say about gender?

Bernard Saladin d'Anglure (1986), following Czaplicka (1914), has proposed that among the Inuit gender categories were not binary but ternary, with shaman as a third sex. This was both an ontological construction, linking the asexual foetus to the shamanic capacity to change sex, and also a sociological one, related to the presence in Inuit society of significant numbers of transvestites and *sipiniit* (people considered to have changed sex on birth). With regard to Inner Asian peoples, this idea of a mediatory gender category has much to be said for it, since it was crucial that the shaman's consciousness could become one with the minds of both men and women. As we have seen, the Daur *onggor*, whose presence defined the shaman, always included both male and female elements, and the shaman-to-be was categorized in the asexual form of the *butur* (chrysalis). However, if we can agree that the idea of the shaman created a third androgynous gender, it is not the case that a third gender was all there was to it. The shaman's consciousness amalgamated with that of birds and animals too, and was sensitive to the presence of all invisible energies in the wind and waters and hills. If we look at the Daur shaman's costume as a symbolic construction, mediatory gender representations were much less prominent than politico-military symbols, in particular the ideas of protective-offensive weaponry, armour, and the citadel. The anthropology of shamanism has ignored these aspects, with the result that its own political effect has been the elevating of individual, sexual, and mystical motives at the expense of social and historical issues. These socio-political symbols were physically attached to objects representing time, space, and all kinds of beings in the world. This established the shaman as an alternative agent in power relations, and placed him or her in direct relation to other powers in society, notably the chief or war-leader.

In the following description for the sake of consistency I give only one interpretation, that of Odongowa (1991 n.d.: 4–7), which has the merit that the author takes a partisan view.[32] The main gown (*sumaski*) was made of the leather of an elk (*handgai*) or male maral deer (*buga*) and was carefully tanned and softened. The sleeves, chest, and skirt were cut tightly, which made the costume elegant, but difficult to dance in. Two bunches of leather thongs ending in tassels were sewn to the arm-pits and they were clutched by the shaman when dancing to make the costume jangle.[33] These plaited thongs were said to be the roads (cart-tracks *terguul*) by which the spirits entered. One Hailar Daur called them 'snakes' (Lindgren 1935a: 372). On the front and back of the costume were sewn numerous small bronze mirrors (*toli*), like overlapping plates or scales, and these were said to represent fish and snake scales, armour, or an impregnable city wall[34] (see Plates 7, 18, 20, 21). There were eight large bronze mirrors on the front (the eight city gates) and several large mirrors on the back, one of which was huge, and was intended to protect the shaman from attack. In front there was one further medium-sized mirror, called *neker-toli*, which was the heart-protecting mirror. The mirrors reported to the shaman on the unseen happenings in the world. 'When the master was attacking demons who had stolen official documents from the state treasury,' writes Odongowa, 'the mirror was the first to take action: it rolled all the way to the grave where the demons had hidden the documents and thus showed the way.' The shaman openly and proudly praised his mirror, singing,

> '[You, mirror] have shaken the universe and space,
> [You] are a good and free spirit of mine,
> [You] have protected my life and health,
> [You] are my golden Neker Mirror!'

> (1991 n.d.: 5)

Below the mirrors were rows of bells (*hwangart*), numbering in total 60 or more; these symbolized the wooden outer city wall. The eight copper buttons down the front of the gown represented the eight gates of two cities. On top of the main gown the shaman wore a yoke or short jacket which was sewn with numerous cowries and one or more wild boar's incisors. The shells were called 'tooth-shells' and also represented the days of the year. Attached to the sleeves and skirt were twelve black straps symbolizing the four limbs and eight bone-joints of the human body.

The shaman's costume had an elaborate rear (*halbangha*) in three lapped layers (see Plate 18). Over the lower back there was sewn a large black pad, on which were embroidered the sun, the moon, a pine-tree, a crane, flowers, a mountain, a river, and a large deer, raising its head towards the sky. This was called 'space' and represents the idea that a shaman freely wanders in the huge, wide heavens and earth. Under the black pad there were twelve long black

18. Back of Huangge's costume, showing ritual scarves (*hadag*) knotted to the pronged crown, large bronze back mirror, embroidered cosmic scene over the buttocks, and two layers of embroidered tails. Photo: 1931, O. Mamen. [5.3]

straps or streamers, embroidered with flowers and grasses in the upper part and
twelve trees below them. According to Batubayin (1990) these represented the
twelve months of the year.[35] Above these were a further twelve shorter
streamers embroidered with the *duwalang* trees together with their birds and
animals (see 2.1). Odongowa writes of this: these *duwalang* trees were grown in
the best richest soil, fertilized by the blood of livestock; they became spirits
of the *yadgan*, and it can be said that they also became the spirits of all
humankind. All twenty-four streamers together represented the tail of a flying
pheasant.

The hat or crown was a black cloth skull-cap surmounted by a metal plate, to
which were fixed six 'towering' metal deer-antlers.[36] Five multicoloured silk
scarves attached to the antlers were the rainbow, the road the shaman followed
in his journeys. In front of the hat there was often a fringe which hung over the
eyes, and above it a glittering glass mirror, which frightened demons by reflect-
ing and shining light at them. Between the antlers was a metal bird, a cuckoo
according to Odongowa, who goes to some length to explain its meaning.[37] The
cuckoo was the main form taken by the shaman's soul. It was said by Daurs that
the cuckoo could only hear birds' voices but not see them. Some Daurs also
held that the cuckoo was a spirit-bird because its nest looked like a coffin in
which it hid a glossy egg, though no one had ever seen this. But in fact,
Odongowa continues, the cuckoo does not build a nest but lays eggs in other
birds' nests, letting them hatch the eggs for her. So when the baby cuckoo
emerged from its shell the Daurs thought this was a great mystery. The teacher
shaman had to first of all instruct a young shaman how to mimic the cuckoo,
'leading him to walk into the world', because the first spirit a shaman summoned would be a cuckoo (his *onggor*). Models of a male and a female cuckoo
also perched on the shoulders of the shaman's gown. These (*borchoohor*) were
the shaman's emissaries (see also 5.1).

The shaman had a large round one-sided drum (*kuntur*) covered in goat-skin
and a birch drumstick (*gisur*) faced with antelope skin.[38] 'The shaman's singing
inspires the people's hearts, and at the same time he beats his drum hard and
turns it so that its mighty sound scares away and oppresses the evil spirits,'
writes Odongowa, and she adds that in the old days the drum was two-sided
and hollow in the middle. The shaman could sit in that kind of drum and fly
around in space, and use it to escape from any entrapment (1991 n.d.: 6). In this
way Odongowa suggests the primarily aural presence of the shaman, taking
form as sounds (the cuckoo's call, the boom of the drum) in the air. Thus one
strange effect of the costume, although it was clothing, was to dissolve the
human physical body presence of the shaman.

Odongowa (1991 n.d.: 7) then tells us in an extended hyperbole how she feels
about the *sumaski* as a whole:

The Daur shamans from ancient times wore the costume to represent the world and
humankind, being an elegant gown, a hat with towering deer-antlers, under the guid-

ance of the powerful cuckoo bird, with beautiful brown-spotted bird envoys, and steel mirrors forcefully smashing through; with the ding-ding sounds of the copper bells, [he/she] used the shoulders to rise up slowly in the universe, thundrously shaking heaven by beating the mighty drum; like a flying bird spreading its twenty-four tail-feathers, singing joyfully in a loud voice, turning around flying to dance, singing the beautiful melody, [the shaman] will be the intermediary between humankind and the spirits. In the beautiful world which [he/she] has created, the shaman will sing sincerely for the people, guiding [them] to the spiritual place from where to get understanding.

Many people spoke to me of the seductiveness of shamans, and the mesmerizing lightness with which they danced, though weighed down with heavy bronze mirrors.

One cannot but be struck by the density of symbolism concentrated in the shaman costume, in which almost every component was given more than one propositional meaning and other evocations which reached out to many themes in Daur religious life. The costume notably fused the symbols of the antlered stag and the bird. This combination is very ancient, the motif of the stag with bird-headed antler-tines first appearing in South Siberia, Mongolia, and the Ordos in the fifth century BC (Jacobson 1984: 113). Tracing the development of this early conceptual order in metal plaques found at gravesites, Jacobson notes the enormous elaboration of the tines which became translated into the branches of a tree by the third century BC. Somewhat later the fusion of antlers and trees was discarded and the tree, *qua* tree, appeared as the primary motif.[39] Jacobson documents the disappearance of the stag with bird-headed antler tines by the time human images appeared regularly in the Scytho-Siberian regions. 'The tree as center, the stag as indicator of that center; and the archaic sacrifice as sign of vital transformation: these essential congruencies were severely eroded by the fourth-third centuries, weakened by a concern with human heroes and military power. They survived only in late Mithraic and then Christian traditions, or—more clearly—in the beliefs of several Siberian peoples' (1984: 129). Among these peoples we must count the Daur, who had a myth in which the boy hero ascended to *tengger* by climbing the antler-tines of a stag. As the boy climbed back down again, the deer asked him, 'When will my antlers fall off?' 'They will fall off now,' said the boy as he stepped off the lowest antler on to earth, and as he said this the deer's horns, which had reached the sky and the sun, made a terrible noise like huge trees crashing down, but they did not fall on the boy (Sain Tanaa 1987: 173).

Perhaps more pertinent is the fact that shamans' costumes in Inner Mongolia and South Siberia incorporated these very bronze plaques, that is the animal-style plaques found at ancient gravesites, or metal items made in imitation of them. Haslund-Christensen, who noticed large numbers of these plaques on shamans' costumes in the Chahar region, surmises that they were brought from northern Mongolia, the Hailar region, and South Siberia by tribes migrating southwards in the last four hundred years (Haslund-Christensen 1944). Buryats thought of the plaques, also daggers, flint and metal arrow-heads, coins and other ancient objects discovered by chance, as having been flung down by *tenggeri* as thunderbolts and consequently full of power (Baldaev 1961: 206–18).[40] In the case of Daurs, similar objects were called, curiously, 'heavenly hair' (*tenggeri us*) and were said to have been thunderbolts launched by the sky to kill spider-spirits. Jaban Saman had three of them, a copper arrowhead, a bronze human figurine, and some cultured pearls, all of which he said were 'heavenly hair' although they were clearly man-made (Omachi 1949: 27).[41] The other most powerful objects of a shaman's costume, the bronze mirrors, which were both rare and valuable, were recognized by Daurs as having had a very long history in Asia.[42] Finally, the cowrie-shells, a Daur woman in Hohhot told me, were 'the money of ancient peoples'.

Thus the shaman's costume was not a mere collection. It was a construction which was a conscious appropriation of powers. It proposed its own space (the back-pad), time (the twelve year straps, the days of the year shells), roads (the cart-track straps and the rainbow streamers), and vehicle (the drum); it incorporated the idea of renewal (the antlers which are shed and grow again) and mysterious metamorphosis–birth (the cuckoo-chick which emerged in the nest of a different species). It also established the shaman as a socio–political arena, the armed citadel.

Particularly significant is the appropriation of foreign treasures and ancient-ness. Like 'classical' pediments on post-modernist buildings, the shaman's plaques, arrowheads, etc. were a *comment* on time, since the ancient objects were fixed to a gown representing years and months. They substituted their own meanings for the long-lost functions of these objects, as we see from the fact that the cowrie-shells, which were known to have been used as money long ago, now symbolically represented both 'days' and 'teeth'. Similarly, the huge shamanic mirrors (*toli*) were no longer really mirrors to look in (see 5.6). Thus the shaman's gown cannot be seen as a primitive thing, handed down and unselfconsciously copied. In fact, the creation of elegance, of an androgynous glamour, seems to have been a strong element. Processes common in the creation of art, in a tradition that was consciously a tradition, seem to have been at work here. Important ideas, like the representations of the human limbs, were made almost invisible (just more plain straps among the many other straps), whereas the cowries, the bells, and the embroideries were artfully displayed in elaborate patterns. Perhaps the shaman's gown had what Steadman (1979) calls a skeuomorphic character. Skeuomorphs are transformations of previously practical features into decorative ones, like the patterns of stone strips applied in diagonal lattices that imitate the structure of timber frames in English churches of the Norman period, or the origin of the classical Greek stone pediment in the wooden gable end. As Steadman (1979: 119) writes:

It is not just that timber forms are copied in stone, but that structural forms themselves are used decoratively or symbolically, applied to the surface, and not in fact performing the supporting functions to which they refer. The pilaster, for example, which imitates the structural form of a free-standing column, has itself no structural role; nor, often, does the pediment over the window or door which the pilaster 'supports'.

The shaman's costume seems to have something of this character of a very long-lasting, yet endlessly reworked and self-referential tradition. It would require a great deal more research than I have been able to do to reconstruct the earlier forms, but the bird's tail that has become the beautifully embroidered *duwalang* trees, the bones turned into dangling straps, the drum that is no longer a closed-in vessel for travel, and the mirrors that were either colossally expanded or very small, all suggest changes in the direction of artistic effect. And if one may be permitted to talk of function these days, we could say these objects would appear to have lost their functions, were it not that 'vestiges' can carry a very potent function, precisely related to their aesthetic attractiveness.

The shaman's costume was magically beautiful, all Daurs agreed. The use of archaeological finds also declared, this is something very, very old. Now the ancient finds were also said to be 'sky's hair', thunderbolts, an image of destructive power. It is to this aspect of the shamanic implements, their power in history, that I now turn.

5.4 Shamanic Implements Menace the Future

The question of what happened to a costume when a shaman died was a matter of urgency, since the artefacts comprising it would exact terrible revenge if they were not controlled and cared for. But the sense of doom projected forwards in time by unattended implements was not simply a matter for the next generation to deal with. Shamans' weapons were in constant interaction with the other dangerous unseen powers which they had been designed to confront. An experience related by the Danish explorer-ethnographer Haslund-Christensen (1944) makes this very clear. The events happened in the 1930s in Chahar in central Inner Mongolia and they illustrate the conflict between shamanic power and Buddhism. We can place this in relation to Urgunge's life. When he came south to Chahar to join Prince De, Urgunge never dared reveal the shamanic beliefs of his northern childhood. Not only would the Prince have thought he was 'primitive', but, as the following story shows, amid all the momentous political events of the 1930s–1940s in Inner Mongolia this religious conflict was still something that was deeply felt in people's lives. Haslund-Christensen romanticizes the story for his European readers (but then, as we have seen from Odongowa, dramatic embellishments are common in native accounts of shamanic matters too). There certainly seems to have been some disingenuous-

ness all round in these events, but its very obviousness makes the substance of
his report believable.

In the summer of 1938 Haslund-Christensen was working at Tsagaan Küre,
an abandoned Lama temple on the border between the Chahar and Sunit
Banners (1944: 12–15). He was determined somehow to obtain a shaman's
costume. Through his somewhat unscrupulous assistant he met Purup, the
hero of the story, whose family were Bargas who had migrated south from the
Hailar region.[43] Purup was the son of a famous shaman who had died in 1908.
He was the only surviving member of a family which had produced shamans for
eight generations, but he himself had neither the ability nor the inclination to
carry on the tradition. When he married in 1931 he was an ordinary desert
nomad, who simply was guardian of his father's shamanic implements until
such time as the spirits would call a new shaman to reactivate them. But from
the day that his young bride, who was a Buddhist, moved into his camp
disasters had visited the family: his cows and mares had abandoned their young,
sickness decimated his herds, and in the end he could only produce enough felt
to cover the one small black-felt tent where he kept the shaman's costume and
implements. When his wife moved her red Buddhist altar into the same tent as
the black shamanist altar, disasters closed in on them even more. Despite all the
oil lamps lit at her altar, and the meat and alcohol sacrificed at his, two babies
were stillborn. When the wife was due to give birth again, she was so hysteri-
cally unhappy her parents had to be sent for. They pitched their tent nearby
and insisted that the baby should be born there. Here a lovely boy was born, but
at a couple of years old he crawled into the black tent where he had seen his
father disappear so often. At the moment he crossed the threshold he fell to the
ground, one eye staring fixedly at the black altar to the west and the other at the
Buddhist idols to the north, and from that day he was to remain cross-eyed.
Poverty, misery, and despair now reigned in the little camp, and the young wife
was expecting a child yet again.

It was pitch dark when Haslund arrived and was put up in the tent of the
parents-in-law. Next day he visited the dismal Purup, who was mending a
saddle in the black tent. Behind him were the shamanic implements, a drum, a
black chest with the costume inside, two horse-headed iron sticks,[44] remains of
meat offerings, and two macabre masks, one made of leather and the other of
copper, both with big lumps of meat in their wide open mouths.[45] (see Plate 20).
The unhappy couple explained that each time one of them offered up sacrifices
to his or her gods it angered the other, and this struggle between the two powers
could not end until one of them was driven away from the tent. They asked
Haslund in uncertain voices what they should do.

Haslund told them that the same evening Purup should keep vigil alone by
the altar of his ancestors. At midnight he was to carry all the implements out
into the desert, where he was to put them at a place two hundred paces to the
north-east of the tent, and he was then to remain in the tent during the night

with the door and smoke-hole closed. At sunrise he should visit the spot and if he found that the costume and implements had disappeared, this would be a sign that the spirits had fled to the north-east where they belonged and that they would never again visit his tent. Then the couple should bow to the Buddhist altar and in future make offerings to it alone. As a further contribution to placating these gods, Haslund was willing to offer four dollars on the red altar.

When he travelled in the region a month later, Haslund heard that all had happened as he had predicted: the black altar had disappeared, and the fact that soon afterwards the wife gave birth to a healthy boy was taken as proof that the angry spirits had indeed settled down away to the north-east. The shaman's costume and implements are now in the ethnographic museum in Copenhagen.

From this, which recalls accounts centuries earlier of warring between shamanic and Buddhist powers in this region (Heissig 1992: 61–136), we can see how the presence of objects which irreducibly represented a shamanic way of thinking exerted a continuing influence, which was endlessly 'confirmed' by the sad misfortunes of the young couple. The story shows how historically conflicting ideologies were not so much thought out and explained by people, as *felt* by them—experienced as uncontrollable forces within their lives. In the next example the Cultural Revolution takes the place of Buddhism. The history was told to me by a Daur woman from Hailar. This tragic recollection shows again how 'shamanism' can be a psychological burden which contains its own force of perpetuation. The memory was so painful that the woman avoided referring to herself and her father wherever possible. To make the story understandable I have had to insert pronouns, and readers should understand that 'the old man' was the narrator's grandfather, a shaman.

In my clan there was an old man and he had sons and a grandson.[46] When he was dying, the old man said, 'I do not want to pass on my powers to younger generations.' I was young and could not understand why he did not want it. My uncles went after him every day, begging him to teach them something. They all wanted to be *yadgan*s. But he said, 'I'll make none of you shamans.' I was puzzled by this, so one day I approached grandfather and asked him why, and he said, 'Shamans are above ordinary human life, above people's tongues, above people's eyes. But piercing into one's eyes, into one's life, there are people who talk good of you and people who talk bad of you. If you have abilities people will praise you, and if you haven't, people will curse you [*haraa-*]. The *yadgan* has to call down his *onggor*'s power and then people will bow, but if you cannot do it, then they will pierce your life. I will not have such a kind of *yadgan* in my clan [*mokon*]. Now my life is ending I will fold my *jawa* [shaman's costume] and with leather thongs it will be tied up.'

So he did what he said, folded and bound up the *jawa*, with seven ties. This way seven knots and that way four knots, backwards seven and forwards four, and he said a spell [*tarni*] and put it in a box.[47] This [*jawa*] is sacred and must be put in a high place like the edge of a cliff or on a mountain. When the old man died he was placed in a sitting posture, and his body was put in a very high place. You see, when a lama dies his body is put on the ground, but when a shaman dies the body is put up in a tree, which is called 'celestial burial' [Chinese *tien zang*], and this means consecrating the body to the world of heaven, and also means ascending to heaven. And in this way, the clan's *yadgan* was finished, the line was ended. My grandfather said, 'If I pass on my ability to the next generation I will only become a nail in the eye of other people and meat in the mouths of other people.'

We often moved house. We moved several times. We moved to Fularji. In front of Fularji there was a big tree. That was a most significant geomantic [*feng-shui*] place. When my grandfather was dying, he said, 'Place my body in that tree.' So we did that. And you know the *jawa*, he also instructed us where to put it: on the roof of the granary. We made a special board platform up there and that's where we put the box with the *jawa*. Then we moved house again. But during the Cultural Revolution you know there were people looting and plundering, especially religious things, and we were afraid the *jawa* would be taken away. That would have been against our custom. So one of his sons went back and buried the *jawa*, in violation of the old man's will. We were very superstitious in those days. And what happened? Many of my grandfather's descendants committed suicide. Some of my grandfather's sons and his granddaughter killed themselves. The one who wanted to be a *yadgan*, the one who buried the *jawa*—oh, there was only a small pool of water, and when we came back from the town we found he was dead, with his face in the water. On his way back from Fularji he was thirsty and drank the water, and as soon as he drank it he was dizzy, fainted, fell and died. The people said this was caused by the violation of the old man's will, burying the *jawa*. People say it was a terrible portent for the next generation.

People brought up in a shamanist ambience may thus not so much consciously rationalize as live out in their own experiences an irreconcilability between 'shamanism' and other historical movements, feeling the pain of this conflict even while at some level they decry 'shamanism' as superstition. The woman recounting this memory was overcome with sadness. The 'he' who was found dead in a pool of water was her own father, as I found out later. But the words she actually used described the final tragedy without mentioning herself at all. She was telling me what she felt, but leaving a gap for herself. One might say that this was simply Mongolian-Daur linguistic style, and it is true that people avoid the word 'I' so as not to seem proud or self-centred. But then, why should this be so? I cannot pretend to answer this question adequately, but an important element of a reply must concern the conceptualization of the self, which, as we shall see, seems to envisage a fragile openness that makes the 'armour' discussed in the last two sections more understandable.

5.5 *Bodily and Psychic Energies*

The shamanic spirits that attacked people caused what Europeans would see as many *different* kinds of harm, accidents, miscarriages, depression, madness, cattle epidemics, loss of a dear person, destruction of one's crops, and so forth. All were encompassed in the Daur word *joblong* (suffering). The import of this for the shaman's practice needs further consideration. One implication is that the shaman's curing was not exclusively a practice of the physical body (Kuriyama 1994).[48] Many medical systems make the study of illness and the study of the body virtually inseparable: the roots of sickness are sought within the patient. But Daur shaman's healing was not a science of the body, since the spirits might have attacked in some other way. The task was to correct (*jasa-*) the situation by severing the oppression (*dara-*) of the spirits. Spirits attacked people, not bodies alone. In this section I address the Daur ideas of the human being, and suggest that it was constituted as a fragile and changing unity of parts, and that bodily entities had psychic as much as physical qualities. This is to challenge the mind/body (soul/body) dualism of much writing on shamanism, and also to propose the idea of the human being as a relational field, a place where other people's thoughts-feelings may enter. In a discussion of spirit-possession I further investigate the idea that bodies were not only the objects of discourse but, as the physical sites of disturbances, were the inchoate sources of people's wonderings about relationships.

Daur thinking around the idea of *sumus* (soul) deserves more discussion than it has received up to now. (I use the word 'soul' despite its Christian origins mainly because it is less clumsy than a more neutral phrase, such as 'metaphysical aspect of the self'.) I do not intend to go into the question of the number of souls a person was supposed to have, since no Daur I met had a clear idea on this subject.[49] From numerous, labyrinthine conversations it emerged that the word *sumus* could refer to an immortal consciousness that after death would become an ancestor, or to a consciousness that was normally extinguished in sleep (but could leave the body in dreams), or to an entity that separated from the body at death, 'changed appearance', and returned to the world in some other form. There were also ideas of a life-energy (*ami* (breath)) and an inherent might (*sul'd* or *suli*) both of which were different from the *sumus*, according to Urgunge. Although the literature on shamanism has called any or all of these 'souls' (see discussion in Shirokogoroff 1935: 134–8), Urgunge said that living creatures have only one soul (*sumus*), and furthermore that it made no sense to talk of this in relation to someone who was alive and healthy. One talked of *sumus* when people were suffering, dreaming, at death's door, or indeed dead. *Sumus* was thus an overarching concept that implied a human existence both in and beyond the confines of the body. What physical/psychological condition did the loss of one's soul correspond to? What was the relation between this and spirit possession? In order to answer these questions I shall begin by considering the body and disease in general, and then go on to discuss what existence was like with a soul gone away or damaged.

The heart (*jurke*) was the centre (*gol*) of being and the fount of 'thought-feeling' (*sanaa*). Urgunge said that 'disposition-mood' (*setgel*) and mental ability (*okaan*) came from the heart too, which was also the place of suffering, depression, and disappointment. There was an idea that the more forceful a person was the larger the hole in the heart, the inner 'air' (*kein*), which gave vision and foresight.[50] The notion was that this gap allowed thinking with penetration (*sanaa newtreu*). The head, on the other hand, was the location of the senses, hearing, seeing, smelling, and tasting, and the Daurs thought of the brain (*ogh*) as just another organ with no clear function.[51] Courage was the most important function of the heart. *Jurketei* (with heart) meant brave, and it was *sanaa* (thought-feeling) which told people how to behave. Educated people might have the word *okaan* in their vocabulary, which was like the English 'intelligence', but ordinary people attributed all intention to *sanaa*, located firmly in the heart.

Nevertheless, the head (*heke*) was respected as the highest part of the human body. It represented the sacred in the body. As mentioned earlier, living people were said to have a 'small heaven' in the very top of their heads, connected with, or part of, the great *tengger* above. The eyes were said metaphorically to represent the sun and the moon. Anything to do with the head was vulnerable to pollution and violence (a hat, for example, should always be kept at a high place and should never be stepped over). This sacredness of the head we can see as linked by language to the head's symbolic position in relation to the rest of the body, i.e. representing 'height' and associations with height, like the tops of mountains and trees (Lakoff and Johnson 1980). It was an abstract, non-individual sacredness, but at the same time it was one source of the sense of self, an individual's link with the universal principle of harmony which was *tengger*. This was quite different from the supernatural quality of the soul (*sumus*), which was human and social.

The parts of the physical body had separate 'energies', with psychological attributes, not unlike the 'âmes innombrables' held to be located in each limb, organ, and joint of the body by societies in Indonesia (Lévi-Strauss 1977: 11). It was not that each part symbolized some other different attribute, but that the entities themselves embodied that person's actual physical state in relation to ideal biological qualities. Long arms, for instance, demonstrated a person's physical-mental power. A straight nose embodied integrity, which was linked with steady, calm breathing and healthy lungs. The mouth showed a person's lack of worry and their satisfaction with life, whether they had enough food to eat, and it was associated with the condition of the stomach. When the teeth became old and yellow one knew that the bones were becoming weak. The ear-lobes should be full of blood and supple, showing a parallel flexibility in the sinews. Hair which was not black and springy indicated that a person's blood was thin (*singgen*), a condition which applied both to the very young and the very old. Weak, dilute blood was associated with a general absence of ability (*chadal*). Both men and women had these bodily energies, but it was thought that women were physically and mentally weaker. People said, *ugiin biye jurke jowlon* (a girl's body and heart are soft), which also implied kindness. The most telling of all, for both men and women, were the eyes.

The eyes (*nid*) showed the state of the heart and soul and should be big, black, and glittering. Beauty lay in women's eyes. If someone had grey-blue eyes, which was rarely found among the Daur, this was strange and sinister. Urgunge's father had blue eyes, and this was one reason for his fearsomeness to his son. In black shiny eyes a tiny human reflection could be seen. This figure was called *haniaka* (friend older brother). Little girls used to make cut-out human figures from paper, which were also called *haniaka*. They would line them up, make dresses for them, and even sleep with them. Not only were there many stories in which the little girls' *haniaka* came to life (see below), but in fact people were afraid that this might really happen.[52] Urgunge said the phrase *nidni haniaka* (eye friend) was used in expressions of love. To say, 'I will protect you as my *haniaka*,' meant, 'You are in my eyes; through my eyes you go to my heart.'

Not to see was to be stupid, as in expressions like '*Wantaa!*' ('You're sleeping!', i.e. 'You fool!'). Conversely, to see was to have power. People used to say that if you stared at the eyes of a wolf or a bear they would never attack you. The fringe on the shaman's hat was not to prevent him seeing, but to protect his eyes from the vision of others and as an indication he was seeing another world. In a Daur story a childless man made a human figure of mud, and he looked at it, and it came alive (Daur Hel' Bitegy 1957: 6). The eyes had a kind of directional force, 'like spotlights', Urgunge said. So when an animal was killed in propitiation to a *barkan*, the eyes would be taken out and offered separately, but only when the whereabouts of that spirit was known. The eyes were laid pointing in that direction. Furthermore, the eyes had to be uncooked, that is, still recognizable as eyes. The embodiment of directionality, the eyes 'took' the animal's soul to its destination.

Life was a temporary union of different parts, which could easily be disordered or unbalanced. In all this there was no clear separation of the physical from the mental, or of the mental from the emotional. Because it was common to have to try several different remedies for an illness it makes no sense for us to attempt to tie particular spirit-causes to defined symptoms (and it seems bodily symptoms of illness were not clearly delineated by ordinary people).[53] Certain psychic/physical processes were considered properly the charge of specialists other than the *yadgan* shaman: fertility and child-health were the province of the *otoshi*, bone-setting was the domain of the *barishi*, and birth itself was taken care of by the *bariyachi*. These specialists had their own knowledge (see 6.3, 4, and 7.1). However, even in the case of problems in these areas the *yadgan* might also be invited, because it was never certain that his spirits (the spirits he was best able to approach) had not caused the misfortune.

Urgunge mentioned the case of his cousin's wife. She was badly mentally disturbed (*koodoo*) and shamanizing and numerous expensive propitiations had failed to cure her. Everyone knew the immediate reason for her madness: her daughter, when a young girl, had gone swimming in the Naun and had tragically drowned. It was from that time that her mother had gone mad. Why had this happened? The well-known spirits had proved non-responisve. The cause was probably one of the unmastered spirits. Taussig (1987: 463; 465) rightly complains that Evans-Pritchard's well-known analysis of this kind of situation, his neat explanation 'sorcery explains coincidence', 'prevents us from appreciating the extent to which coincidence and sorcery pose questions concerning one's life's environment, opening out the world as much as closing in'. In the case of the woman who lost her mind, people continued to ponder the tragedy even though a causal theory was available and the situation was considered hopeless. Was the daughter pulled under the water by the river spirit, and the mother just went mad? Had both mother and daughter been attacked by a demon (*shurkul*), which caused the daughter to drown and made the mother mad? Or was it that the daughter herself, having drowned and lost her future, became a *shurkul*, who came back to haunt and cause the madness of her poor mother? This incident was never explained.

With regard to that wide mass of sufferings which were the province of the *yadgan* shaman there were always numerous possibilities. They were not really separate for the Daurs initially, but might become so in the very process of the shaman trying them out. A spirit could enter and attack a physical part of the body; a person could lose their soul; a spirit could cause an 'accident' to happen; and a person might both lose their soul and have a spirit possess them at the same time. It is significant that no one mentioned to me the possibility of conflict between an incoming spirit and soul (this happened mainly 'in' a shaman, whose soul also *was* a spirit, *onggor*). The ordinary person's soul, it seems, was imagined rather as passive, as giving way to spirits. Thus the phenomenon we call spirit possession was called by Daurs *sumus darsen* (soul oppressed).

Loss of the soul. Loss of the soul did not imply immediate physical death, but a state of vacancy or psychological numbness. Usually loss of the soul happened only to babies and young children. Soul-loss was also manifest in listlessness or recurrent illness, and it was thought that unless something was done the child might die. Adults, on the other hand, had stronger 'energy' (*kuch*), which kept their souls firmly attached, and their souls could wander during sleep without causing problems. Adults' souls were not 'lost' (*gee'u-*), but, and this was very rare, stolen by spirits and taken elsewhere. This is the subject of the *dolbor* journey discussed in 5.7.

One has the impression that the baby only just held together as an entity. The slightest fright, a dog barking, or a shadow moving at night, could cause a baby to lose its soul.[54] It hardly needs saying that children were regarded as the greatest blessing, given all possible love and protection, and kept in close physical proximity. Once out of the cradle they slept with their parents, the youngest child in her mother's arms. Children were breast-fed until 3 or 4.

Nevertheless, it seems that a baby's soul so frequently disappeared that searching for it (*sumus eri-*) and calling it back (*sumus dauda-*) were regular parental tasks. In its simplest form calling back the soul would consist of dressing the baby in bright clothes, holding it in one's arms, and calling, 'Hoo-yee, come back! Come back to your mummy, come back to your daddy, eat your food. Don't go by *onggor*, don't go by *daaga*,[55] come back home.' If this did not work, there was a magical attempt. It had to take place at night, even if the soul had escaped by day, because, 'The soul is the dark side of the world.' A bowl filled with water was put down at the place in the yard where it was thought the child had been frightened. In the house the mother held the child, slowly rubbing its head with a circular clockwise motion, and then she carefully retraced in reverse the steps of the child when it was frightened. Reaching the bowl, the mother dropped some unmarked pieces of paper into it, saying, 'You have come back now.' The rubbing was intended to create heat in the child, an action which was also one of the shaman's gestures.[56] The bowl represented the child's body and the paper its soul. This most modest of magical acts reminded Urgunge of his favourite expression for the universe, *sab-shim* (*sab* 'container', *shim* 'juice', 'sap', 'essence'). 'I like this idea best in the whole of Mongol vocabulary,' he said.

If magic failed, the family would consider calling a shaman. The idea now was to call back the soul and place it and the child under the protection of the spirit called Ome Barkan (womb spirit).[57] Several people described to me a child's consecration to Ome, in each case rather differently. Common features were that special bright clothes, toys, and something representing the child, like a ball of his hair, were tied up in red and yellow cloths and put in a bag which was also tied;[58] the soul was called into the bag, and it, together with a bronze mirror (*toli*), was attached to the picture of the Ome *barkan*, which was kept in a box. The shaman called out any disease spirits remaining in the child, and then he danced round the child, beating his drum softly and singing in a gentle voice a song like a lullaby. This same mirror was given the child to wear around the neck at the New Year greetings to a shaman (5.8) and whenever a shaman came to perform.[59] After three years the mirror was given back to the shaman, with great offerings, obeisances, and thanks. Here it seems that per-haps the child's soul was not with him for some time and only gradually returned to the body. During this time both the bag with the soul and the child were guarded by mirrors. It would be wrong to read anything too clear into this rite: no one said to me that even after the soul is called back the child neverthe-less lives for years with its soul separately in a bag, and I know that I could have got no clear answer on this point. People simply told me what they did. What does emerge is the importance of closure for sacred things (the tied-up bag, the Ome box), and the 'openness' of young children, which made them such a tender attractive target. In clothing, we may contrast the male (*büstei* 'with belt') whose sash was bound tightly round and round his body, with the female (*büsgüi* 'without belt') and the shaman, whose dress in different ways was more open.

More generally, these practices suggest the idea of life as having many components, all of which were attributes. Rather than thinking of life simply as the means of physical-conscious existence, it was seen as a number of qualities, which pertained to *amitan* (those with breath) but could also be *taken away*, just as happiness or fortune could be given or taken away (see L'vova *et al.* 1989: 132).

It was in dreaming that an adult's soul could leave the body (this was true of animals as well as human beings). If someone sighed during their sleep, this was a sign that their soul might be crossing the boundary of the mouth and starting to roam. A sigh was different from a breath. Urgunge once said, 'You know the most interesting place in Cambridge to me? It is the Bridge of Sighs. Why? Those mouths [arches] sighing, I am thinking of souls floating out, you see.'

When a soul left in a dream (*zeuwde*), it could enter the world of the dead and meet the ancestors. Urgunge remembers one of his brothers saying that he once woke up suddenly, just in time to put out a fire in the house. How did this happen? An ancestor in his dream had just told him there would be a fire. Many events in dreams were considered to be omens. Very often these were related negatively to the event foretold. For example, if you dreamed of cutting off your hair, this would mean that one of your parents would die soon, it being understood that hair was not cut during the period of mourning. These dream interpretations were to some extent standardized. People could cite lists of 'meanings'.[60] Often a dream was not clear and people would lie in bed in the mornings discussing the dreams they had had. However, nothing was ever done to avert a catastrophe, even if it was more or less agreed that a dream boded ill. Only if something was later identified as the predicted event would people even remember the dream (Humphrey 1977). There were also dreams which were reckoned to be individual and non-prophetic.[61] However, Nanai shamans constantly interrupted their descriptions of spirit journeys to ask the patient about his or her dreams. 'Did you dream you were in a dark village and didn't know where to go?' 'Yes' 'I am going through that dark village,' the shaman would say. 'Did you dream you were on the sea and ice was floating?' 'I did.' 'That is the road I am following, the ice has stopped . . . ,' said the shaman (Smolyak 1991: 190). Urgunge dimly remembers such questioning also among the Daurs.

Although the dreamer experienced his or her body present in the dream, Urgunge said, nevertheless the idea was that the soul had gone away from the body. This left the body in a vulnerable condition, in which spirit possession could more easily occur. Some nightmares (Mong. *har darsen* (black oppression)) were interpreted as the intrusion of an unspecific spirit.[62] As ordinary people's dreaming thus wavered between soul loss, spirit possession, and some indeterminate private fantasy, it was almost never straightforward, but elliptical or opaque. This was because people were not sure they had the ability correctly to understand dreams, or perhaps because dreaming for them was a condition of being undone and separated out. Both of these conditions were overcome by the *yadgan*, who could deliberately dream a special dream (*soolong*) which would reveal the truth. The *soolong* dream was the main method of divination before any shamanic seance, and by it the shaman could tell people which spirit was active, where it was in the universe, and on which day to make propitiation.[63] Dream-knowledge was the kind of knowledge shamans had that ordinary people did not. It was almost a commodity. Shamans frequently refused to dream for people, until begged respectfully many times and given presents (Mendüsürüng 1983: 258).

Spirit possession and beleng. 'Spirit possession', which might seem only to imply an interior condition, involved recognized exteriorizing behaviour. A fairly defined set of actions was recognized as spirit possession of the soul, and these were the same as the initial illness of the shaman-to-be: unprovoked weeping and laughter, hiding in a dark place, climbing on top of things, shouting and singing, speaking in foreign languages, and especially 'running away into the forest'. Shirokogoroff writes, 'The person may run comparatively far and remain in a "wild state", sitting among rocks. It happens commonly that they climb up a tree, or thrust themselves between the near-standing trees or branches of a tree, assuring themselves and other people that they cannot liberate themselves' (1935: 254–5). Spirit possession was relatively infrequent and it happened to both men and women; if it was recurrent the sufferer generally became a *yadgan* or some other occult specialist as a way of counteracting the attacks with one's own spirit power.

When your soul was oppressed your consciousness was taken over by the spirit, that is, by actions that might be taking place somewhere else or at another time. A Daur woman at Horli told me the following (I am not sure if this was thought to be a real incident or a magic story):

A young man went out hunting with his two uncles. He had wonderful luck on the hunt and killed a beautiful deer. The uncles were outraged when he did not share out the meat equally and they killed him. They set off for home, intending to pretend their nephew had met with an accident. Meanwhile the wife was cooking at home. There was a sound 'kangar, kangar' in the crockery. 'That's funny,' she thought. Then she was terribly scared. She started to cry. They asked the old man next door what was going on. '*Sumus darsen* [soul oppressed],' he said. They covered her face and eyes with a black cloth. She started to talk, 'I was hunting in the forest with my two uncles and I followed them, and then I saw a beautiful deer . . . ,' [she recounted the whole story in the consciousness of her husband, C.H.]. So when the two uncles got back everyone knew what had really happened and they were punished for their deed.

In persistent possession people launched away from themselves. They literally ran away, or mentally participated in distant events, or experienced other people's experiences, and they often spoke the words or sang the songs of spirits, not their own words (and these were sometimes in foreign languages because the spirit themselves were held to be foreign).[64] In spirit possession the mountains, rocks, and trees were not objects of worship, but rough, cold objects in the wilderness and the 'other world'. The afflicted person ran to them, hid in them, merged with them. A Daur *yadgan* called Jin Hai Agvan[65] suffered from spirit possession from the age of 16. He was exhausted and confused. He suddenly took all his clothes off and, naked, plunged himself in the river, even though there was snow on the ground.

Soul oppression always involved suffering, but it was not disapproved of. On the contrary, the afflicted one would be the focus of attention and concern, and efforts were made to expel the spirits as quickly as possible. This contrasts with the mental condition known as *beleng*, which was ridiculed, and the difference is enlightening. *Beleng* was not thought to be caused by spirits and was more or less incurable. *Beleng* also involved externality, since its main characteristic was that, given a particular stimulus, the affected person imitated its movements, actions, or words. The *belengchi* was easily startled, would shout obscenities and sexual words (coprolalia), and had phobic reactions. Aberle (1952: 292–3) mentions some examples: a Halh Mongolian lama who tipped over a skin container of fermented milk wanted desperately to right it, but instead had an irresistible impulse to imitate the sound of the milk running out until it was all gone; or a nun, who swayed to and fro for a long time, imitating the swaying of a weed with a tuft of camel's hair caught in it, unable to stop until someone came along and removed the tuft of hair. A Daur man who screamed and shouted obscenities when someone startled him was said to 'act *beleng*', but another man with a snake phobia and a fright reaction even to the word 'snake' was said to be 'made startled' rather than *beleng*.

Urgunge remembers a midwife, his neighbour, who had this trouble. She responded to negative commands with helpless imitation. She could be made to run, bow repeatedly, or drop objects by being ordered not to drop them. She was very easily startled and then would shout. The boys teased her terribly. One would squat down in the street and shout, 'I'm having a baby!' Another would shout at the midwife, 'Don't you deliver it, I will!', and she would immediately rush over and start groping around the boy's genitals, and only later realize what she was doing. Such tricks were played often, though she would beg her tormenters to desist. This was the same woman mentioned in section 5.2; *beleng* started after she got the terrible shock of falling on her husband's frozen corpse.

Shirokogoroff (1935: 249–52) interprets *beleng* as a psychological reaction within the realm of normality (it was so regarded by the Tungus). It had a hypnotic element whereby the subject involuntarily submitted to the person producing the stimulus, and it also had an important social aspect, since people were amused or offended by the strange repetitive acts of the subject, and the strict rules of social deportment were exactly what the *beleng* violated. Aberle (1952: 296–7) sees *beleng* as a defence against the fear of being overwhelmed, manifest either in imitation (identification with the aggressor), destruction of the stimulus, flight, or in the case of coprolalia, a shout which drove back the unconscious fear but at the same time allowed it a partial, involuntary, and 'meaningless' expression in the very choice of words. He relates *beleng* to ambivalence over submissive behaviour. There was an unconscious connection between this submission and a dreaded and desired passive sexual experience, akin to being attacked.

Beleng seems to have been an experience of a loss of selfhood, notably the ability independently to control one's own actions. Afflicted people were timid, passive, and ashamed in daily life. But they were still seen as 'normal'. Perhaps we can say that they had only strayed too far in the general human condition of relationality, which was so emphasized in Daur thought. Now unlikely as it may seem, there is a striking parallel between *beleng* and the state attributed to the revived corpse, the *bong*, which was a being without a soul and without volition (5.2). This analogy with the ghost can tell us about what it was that people were so afraid of losing. Here is a Daur story on this subject:

There were two sisters playing with paper people [*haniaka*]. A cloudy day came. The younger sister kept talking about ghosts, 'The *bong* is like this, the *bong* is like that.' The older one said,

'Don't talk like that; I'm afraid they'll come.'

'What is there to be afraid of in ghosts? It's just a word. Don't worry. Tonight when we get home we'll confuse them.'

'Oh, don't! How can you confuse them?'

'Calm down. You'll find out.'

Evening came and they stopped the game. Once home they made preparations. They took a birch-bark bag and an iron box. Then they put down two basins on the floor. Over there they put a basin full of oil, and in front of themselves they put a basin full of water. The birch-bark bag they put some distance away. Now they put their heads in the basin of water and started to wash their hair. So they were washing, and it came. The *bong* looked and the girl was washing her head in the water. This way and that he hovered. The *bong* put his head in the other basin imitating them, but there was oil in his basin. Speechless and silent he copied them. The girl now finished washing her hair and took the iron box and put it in the water to wash it. The *bong* took the birch-bark bag and put it in his bowl. The girl put the box on her head. The *bong* took the bag and put it on his head. Now his oily head burst into flames. He ran out, and as he ran, he asked her:

'What is your name?'

'Myself,' she replied.

As he ran away the *bong* screamed in his misery, 'Myself! Myself! Myself!' Lots of *bong*s came and asked:

'What's the matter? Who has been treating you so badly?'

'Myself! Myself!'

'What kind of talk is that?', and so they killed him.

(Engkebatu 1985: 182–7)

What was it that made *beleng* (and the poor deluded *bong*) so different for the Daurs from the behaviour that was identified with spirit possession? Maybe the difference lies in the perceived pointlessness of *beleng*, which was a result of the understanding that *beleng* was not, and never could be, a matter of interaction with the world but only a helpless imitation of its surface. Everyone was fragile, open to attack, but *beleng* was a mechanical reaction: possession, on the other hand, was an inclusion or a joining up. Both were relational social states, and it is significant that, unlike soul loss, children were never, and very aged people only rarely, affected by spirit possession and *beleng*. Both afflictions were incoherent and disconnected from the will of the sufferer. But in the case of spirit possession of the soul, some pattern greater and more mysterious than any individual pain was making its tortured appearance. 'Spirits' themselves were consciousness of complex amalgams of tragedy and accident, and they were experienced in a way that was both inside and outside oneself.

Taussig (1987: 462–3) sees a relational articulation between experience (sensory impressions) and the aprioris of knowledge as intrinsic to 'shamanism':

To this fundamental break with models of knowledge and of knowledge-making that assume the thinker alone with his or her thoughts, or of thought alone with itself, the healer–patient relational model also differs in that included in the 'sense-data' of raw experience are not merely sensory impressions of light and sound and so forth, but also sensory impressions of social relations in all their moody ambiguity of trust and doubt and all the multiplicity of becoming and decaying. By excluding the sensateness of human interrelatedness, the 'knowledge' with which traditional Western philosophy from Plato to Kant is concerned cuts itself off from the type of sensory experience and power-riddled knowledge—implicit social knowledge—on which so much of human affairs and intellection rests. Sorcery and (so-called) shamanism, on the hand, present modes of always locally built experience and image-formation in which such social knowledge is constitutive.

Daur spirit possession, which was defined by intersubjectivity, could not be simple, because the *identity* of the being(s) present in the self was arrived at through the intervention of another mind, that of the shaman. The situation thus represented in extreme form the paradox of understanding other people in general, which is that we can only know them through subjectivity (normally our own) and we are not sure that we know *them*. At the same time, in the idea that spirits were transmuted beings, no longer individual persons but exemplars of tragedies belonging in some way to the whole local community, 'possession' put the subject in the position of being open to the recapitulatory experience of historical mysteries which transcended personal existence.

This is why the sufferer from spirit possession was the object of such intense interest and concern. The weeping, the running away, the inchoate cries were physically felt, but they were totally unclear indications of what was going on. It required a shaman's dream for a sudden ray to illuminate the hitherto dim and tangled relations of the victim's life with others. Neglected moments of anger or hurt would be picked out as significant, relating the sufferer to some great spirit theme. But then, at the very moment when people (or the subject herself) made these connections, it would also be clear that they might be wrong. As long as the spirit possession was not 'solved', one might follow an Ariadne's thread of interpretations linking the sufferer's experiences to past misfortunes of other people, and it might be a mistaken path. But, even so, even if the identity of the 'causative' spirit never became known, the possessed person was a potential source of revelation, about the forbidden, the disconnected, or the forgotten. People intuitively understood the emotions and the relations which gave rise to them. Thus the shaman's discovery of the identity and nature of the spirit was a discovery for *everyone*, because it consisted in redefining what initially was presented as a personal flight away from society into a re-engagement with the phenomenal condition of sociality everyone was born with.

People also constantly happened across spirits in moments that fell short of possession. A presence felt at night, or a clammy touch, was frightening, and at the same time it could be a dread reminder of an act of cruelty buried in the past, some neglected person who might have become a spirit. At such moments the 'body' itself was sensitive to spirit presence. It was no more discrete and closed than was the soul (think of the *haniaka* in the eye and the questions of reflection, projection, and creation this raises). Having said this I hope it is clear that a relationship of the soul with the body parts, and with other energies such as breath, air, and human might, was never clearly articulated in general, because there was no general theory, only contingent conjunctions articulated at particular times. The possibility of identifying parts of the body with qualities of personality and emotions meant that at uncanny moments people had many different sensors to register physically the effects of hidden social currents, even if this was not consciously done.

5.6 *The Mirror and What can be Seen in it*

Urgunge said that the shaman's mirror (*toli*) was more important than his drum. However, it is not as obvious why this should be so. It does not seem to be the case that Daur shamans looked into their mirrors like a crystal ball to see the future.[66] We cannot even assume that what was seen in the mirror was oneself. What is the image that was found there? And why should it have made the mirror so powerful?

Let us first see what powers were attributed to the shaman's mirror. It could purify water; it could flash and frighten away spirits; 'press down' (*dara-*) on and gather up in itself spirit manifestations (diseases and sufferings); contain a soul or replace a soul; act as a symbolic wall or armour against spirits;[67] and Urgunge had a memory that the shaman might take off his 'back mirror', spin it, and see which way it fell; smooth side upwards meant the patient would recover. Physically, a shaman's mirror is a heavy, round bronze object, polished on one side and usually with some signs and a metal loop on the other. The smooth side is slightly convex and the reverse a little indented. Among the representations on the back one may find the twelve animals of the time cycle, or Buddhist symbols such as the *ølzii* 'eternal knot', or Chinese characters. Two shamans' mirrors described by Lindgren had the Chinese characters (see Plate 7) for, 'May your five sons succeed in the examination for graduates' (1935*a*: 372). Some mirrors are plain on the reverse, and it seems that the signs on the back were not regarded by Daurs as much more than decorations. In point of fact not much can be seen in the mirror, because even the smooth side is not very shiny.

Ordinary glass mirrors were called by the Manchu word *belku*. Urgunge thought of *toli* as primarily religious objects, not really meant for looking into, but he said that historically they had of course been used as mirrors, and the Halh Mongols (always his touchstone of authenticity) still used them 'for beauty'. But the capacity of shiny surfaces to reflect images was never straight-forward. If you looked in someone's black eyes you were absorbed into them as their minuscule friend, *haniaka*. The following story plays with the questions: what is reflected by different kinds of mirror surfaces? Is it me? What am I like?

There was an old man and an old woman. They had a son and a daughter-in-law. The son was away doing state duty. The daughter-in-law looked at her reflection in the water-butt and coiled up her hair. Then she went into the house. Mother said:

'Ai! Your hair's all twisted!'

'Ai! Mother, how can I manage to see my own head?'

'Get someone who is going into town to bring you a mirror,' the mother advised.[68] The daughter-in-law said to the returning father, 'Father, if you go into town please get me a mirror.'

The father went to town, but no matter where he looked there was no trace of a mirror, and but in the market there was a cracked bottle. 'This can be a mirror,' he said and bought it. Daughter-in-law put this mirror of hers in a box. When she got up in the morning she coiled up her hair, picked up the mirror, and when she took a look, her father and mother-in-law were to be seen. In the evening her man came back. When she picked up her mirror to do her hair the image of her husband shone out.

'What are you looking at?'

'I'm looking at the mirror.'

'That's not a mirror. Let me go to town and take it back.' He went to town and got her a mirror and gave it to her. She got up early and looked as usual in the water-butt but could not see to do her hair. Then she took her mirror and looked and there was a very beautiful person. She cried [with amazement]. Mother-in-law jumped up; she saw her daughter-in-law was crying. She took the mirror and she could see a person who was completely white.

'Look at that! Where did such an aged person come from?' Hearing this, her husband got up and looked round the house, but [seeing nothing] sat down again. Then he asked, 'What are you looking at?'

'The mirror that your son brought is what I am looking at.' The father-in-law peered at the mirror.

'Look at that! The reflection you have been looking at is a man with a beard and moustache!' (Hasartani 1983: 610–11).

So you cannot see yourself properly in the water-butt, and the rounded glass of the bottle just reflects everyone else. The mirror shows the truth, as it were, but no one in this idiotic family can recognize themselves.

Perhaps the story points to something else. What you see in the mirror is yourself and not-yourself. It is a depersonalized, two-dimensional, image which you do not spontaneously know, but have to recognize. Maybe the mirror does not reflect ordinary reality: the mother-in-law sees a girl crying with her own eyes, but when she looks in the mirror a stranger, a white-haired old lady, has appeared. The idea that one sees 'something else' in the mirror was expressed in the prohibition on looking at one's reflection at the New Year in case that allowed evil spirits to enter the house. The mirror thus seems to show the 'other world,' and it drives its translucent surface through the notion of 'I', producing before our eyes a self which one may not recognize.

The shaman's *toli* was thus worn facing outwards and it attracted images. Urgunge said to me, 'As a shaman, the more mirrors you have, the more you become wise, majestic, and intelligent. And glamorous. Because you acquire all kinds of things through your mirrors—natural things, the sun, moon and stars, all are absorbed into your body. The whole cosmos, and you feel wise and powerful.' It is not difficult to see why another meaning of the Mongol word *toli* is dictionary or lexicon.

At the same time the shaman's mirror was said to deflect harm by aggressively flashing light. The blinding of spirits was the purpose of the small mirror on the shaman's cap. A similar idea was expressed in another usage of the term *toli*. In the sense of 'deflector' it was used of the small round piece of metal where the blades of the plough-share met; the earth divided and was pushed away at this point. The capacity of the mirror both to gather in and deflect at the same time was of course not contradictory, Urgunge said. 'Think about sunglasses: they receive the good rays and keep out the bad ones.' A demon in one Daur story was discovered buried in a coffin wearing sunglasses (*DSHI* 1985: 260).

However, if we return to the fact that the original function of a mirror was to reflect an image, perhaps especially of oneself, the Daur understandings of the self can be seen better if we contrast them with the radically different ideas developed in the Western, especially Christian, tradition. Stephen Bann points to the shift in interpretation of the Narcissus myth that occurred with the emergence of Christian theology. The myth with its theme of self-reflection, as Narcissus falls in love with his own image in the pool, was earlier part of a Platonic metaphysics, where the ideal was envisaged as being outside the self; Narcissus himself was depicted as self-deceived, which led inexorably to his hopeless passion, his tragic death and metamorphosis into a flower. It was the later Christian emphasis that transformed the Narcissus myth to an internal dialogue of the soul with itself, and transformed his desperate self-communion into a means for self-knowledge and self-mastery (Bann 1989: 105–19). We find in the shamanic ideas something quite different, where the mirror never reflected your own simple physical image but the whole world of things 'out there'. Yet the mirror, as we have seen (5.5), was also quite clearly an external container of the soul.[69] A man in Holdi told me a story of a conflict between a lama and a shaman in which the lama managed to harm the shaman's mirror, upon which the shaman died and a blue light appeared glowing from the mirror. The shaman's soul thus not only has an existence outside the body, but being in the mirror seems open to an infinity of metamorphoses. So perhaps the mirror was an instrument not only of containment and absorption but also for breaking out of the world into another state which reflected the hitherto unseen truth. If classical and Christian Western thought has dwelled on the deception, distorted perspective, and self-absorption implied by the self gazing into the pool, the shamanic idea was to elaborate the attraction and deflection of occult images in the mirror, allowing the self yet another projection into the 'other world' which surrounds us.

The shamanic visions described in Chapter 5 have shown us the decomposition of gender certainties, a divisible and externalizable 'self', a humanity subject to the penetration of illness, to death and metamorphosis, and a present consciousness which was always under threat from the working-out of past tragedies in the present and future. Yet as I proposed earlier it was the integrity of the sense of self which was able to give authenticity to religious experiences.

It seems that 'shamanism' constantly fragmented and then reintegrated the unity of the self. People's visions of externality were real, in the sense that they were the understandings of real psychological processes, and it was the shaman's task to catch them and control them, to re-create a unity and a balance (*tengchuu*).

5.7 The 'Night Road' and Shamanic Performances

Dolbor[70] was the shaman's night journey to fetch a soul from the other world. It was done very rarely, when a patient seemed to be hovering between life and death. Said to be the most dangerous of the shaman's journeys, *dolbor* led in the dark through realms where the shaman's life was also threatened. *Dolbor* was performed as a ritual with set episodes, but it could be followed by other magical actions to extinguish or get rid of spirits diagnosed as attacking the patient's body.[71] These curative treatments were hardly ritualized and were very varied according to individual shamans' abilities. This magic was also performed on its own and by other people 'with power' (*idtei*, *kuchtei*) apart from the shaman. In this section I make a distinction between shamanic performances like *dolbor* and the less ritualized magical acts. Both required the suspension of ordinary beliefs about the world (the workings of gravity, biology, 'what one sees with one's own eyes', etc.), but in different ways. *Dolbor* involved a 'commitment', the tacit acknowledgement of all participants that they were taking part in a ritual in which their actions counted as specific ritual episodes (see Humphrey and Laidlaw 1994). This was hardly the case with magic treatments, where the patient was brought cold face to face with whatever surprising acts the shaman could conjure, and the effects were immediate and sensational.

The suspension of disbelief of shamanship, if we take this whole bundle of activities together, was different from the exorcism practised in Buddhist societies such as Sri Lanka. There, 'illusion' was a native category. To be fooled, to treat the illusory as reality, was to be subordinated and subjected to the control of the trickster, but to see the reality behind the illusion, to be the unmasker, was to exercise dominance and superiority. 'The Buddha holds primacy in the Sinhalese cosmological order because he saw through all illusion and unveiled the tricks which were performed against him' (Kapferer 1983: 112). In Daur 'shamanism' there was no such hierarchy of knowledge. *Tengger*, though superordinate, did not unmask the 'illusory'. Rather, it was assumed that there was a universe-wide confrontation of powers, which people understood in their own ways, and a shaman's trickery consisted not in pretending there was some supernatural power when there was none, but in claiming to control a given energy when he or she could not, or in wrongly presenting X as having power when it was not there that power lay. In fact, a shaman's weakness was of more concern than trickery. Shamanic performances were not 'symbolic' reflections or representations of social relations. In a real sense they constituted these relations and became in this way an arena of power (see also

6.1). However, of all the people taking part in a performance the shaman was the only one to act both as himself/herself and as another (the spirit), and in this for the shaman to act with inspiration (*hii bisirel*) the people's support by their belief (*süsüg bisirel*)[72] was essential. Daurs often told me, 'It is impossible to become a shaman by your own wish,' and this is perhaps another way of saying that communities created their shamans in the processes of spirit possession and performance (see also Atkinson 1989: 292). So, to summarize, the fringe presence of Buddhism in Daur life had not succeeded in implanting an idea of the illusory nature of being, and shamans and people together enacted the confrontation of forces whose existence was assumed. But the nature of the engagement was different in rituals like *dolbor* and in more magical performances, as we shall see. Here I give two different kinds of account, one written by a doggedly observant Japanese describing a magical treatment embedded in a somewhat perfunctory shaman's seance, and the second an account of *dolbor* by the Daur scholar Mendüsürüng.

On 1 September 1935 a Japanese scholar who had been feeling unwell for several days went to visit Pingguo Yadgan in the village of Nantun near Hailar.

He examined my aching belly and leg and then prayed, holding his hands together in front. Then he started telling his beads and questioning me.

'Is there belief like shamanism in Japan?'

'There is no such belief,' I answered.

'Your illness is not serious. It will get better, so you don't need treatment.'

'But I want to be treated, because it hurts all the time.'

'You have no disease.'

'The pain is real, so I want to entrust myself to you.'

'Well then, have a brick of tea blessed, boil it and apply it to the top of your head, then you will be all right.' Having said this, the shaman reluctantly got up, held a brick of tea wrapped in paper in front of him and said, 'Hai.' He moved his right hand up and down beside his chin, though not touching his face. He kept shaking his head and reciting a chant and then gave me the tea. I asked him how to take the blessed tea, and he said:

'Put it in seven bowls of water and boil it till three bowls are left. Then put some white linen in the tea and wrap your painful leg in it. Throw the tea grounds away in a pure place which the feet of men do not touch.' This was apparently the shaman's simplest method of curing and it was clear from his appearance that he was trying to avoid me and didn't like the fact I was a stranger. Although I understood his feeling, I pretended not to see it, and I politely went on asking him to give more treatment. He said,

'If you do not have a dream, the rite cannot be done. If you dream tonight then I'll do it for you. If you truly believe, then you'll certainly dream. You can come tomorrow. If you happen to bring a little *arhi* [alcohol] you don't have to bring anything else. Japanese *arhi*, Chinese *arhi*, anything will do.'

The next day, accompanied by a colleague, I went there with five packs of incense, three mooncakes and a bottle of strong *arhi*. The shaman said, 'A shaman doesn't treat people like a doctor or lama by taking their pulse. He treats sickness by the power of the *onggor*. And I know that if I put on my shaman's dress I might do anything without realising it. Then you'll run away.'

'Whatever happens I won't run away.'

'If I stab you with a knife, it won't leave any wound.'

After some further parleying, in which it is clear that Pingguo was highly unwilling to proceed, the shaman at length called for his assistants, placed the offered cakes, etc. on the heated bed, and burned incense in a fire-shovel to purify them. His assistants dressed him in the heavy gown.

Then he took his drum and beat it several times, facing the door first, and then the four directions. Continuing to beat his drum he started his invocation and the assistant accompanied him. Meanwhile the fire-shovel with incense burning on it was placed in the doorway; they say this is to purify the way and invite the *onggor* into the body of the shaman. He was sitting on a chair in the middle of his tent, swaying from side to side, and reciting something, 'De-ke-re, yesu, yesu,' and he and the assistant repeated it together about ten times. Then he stopped, held the drum in his arm-pit, his body swaying and his legs trembling, and took on an unnatural appearance. He got up and took four steps forward and four back, beating the drum and singing, bent forwards. The assistants waited behind. Ceaselessly reciting the refrain, he turned round five times clockwise, closed his eyes, took five steps forwards, and then very quickly danced five times clockwise and three times anti-clockwise, moving savagely so the mirrors clanged and all the bells rang. Then he beat the drum softly three times, made three clockwise turns, and suddenly fell down facing the door. Two assistants held him up from behind and another held the shovel with the incense by the door. The *onggor* entered the shaman at that moment. His appearance went quite strange. He and the assistant recited the refrain forty-five times. One of the assistants went into the kitchen. The shaman now stood up, beating his drum and whistling. He recited the refrain, walked up and down by the door, and suddenly beat the drum with all his strength. The leather strap at his side was shaking. His assistant appeared from the kitchen with a red-hot knife-like flat-iron which he had been heating up. Suddenly the shaman signalled to me, 'Unbutton your shirt and show your stomach' (the place which was painful). Straightway I did as I was told and the shaman blew sparks from the flat-iron. It was frightening when he put out his tongue and licked the red-hot iron. Jumping and leaping with a terrifying aspect, he next pointed the red-hot iron at my stomach and made sudden poking motions, thrusting at me. At this point some other people there were scared and ran out of the door, leaving only two of us, myself and the Embassy man who had come with me. The shaman lunged at me with the iron twice more, and frankly it was unimaginably frightening, a horribly shocking experience. Only afterwards, when the fire-part of the shamanising was over, did the shaman turn round beating his drum three times and wake up.[73]

Urgunge never saw anything quite like the above, and we can understand this, because Du Yadgan had his own methods, different from Pingguo's.[74] It is significant that Pingguo's treatments often involved knives, as it may be remembered that his 'madness' was manifest by his knife-attacks in the village (3.2). This part of his magic was not an abstract recipe, like the blessing of the tea, but a more controlled acting-out of the personal psychotic condition experienced when he was first possessed by the *onggor*.[75] Du Yadgan's curing was much calmer. He rubbed the drum on his own chest and heart-mirror and then used it to fan empowered air over the patient; he blew sacred water from his mouth onto the patient;[76] he stroked the patient's bare wet body with the *toli*.[77] All of these actions were called *dara-* 'to press down, suppress [the invasive spirit]'. Urgunge does not remember the shaman being in 'trance' for these cures. Despite what Pingguo Yadgan said to the Japanese scholar, shamanic magic treatments did not always require calling in the *onggor* spirits and did not always involve mentally dissociated states.[78] What was essential to the magical cures in Urgunge's account was their direct, sensational nature: the feeling of wetness and the shock of the cold metal on one's skin.

In contrast to this, Mendüsürüng's memory of *dolbor* consists almost entirely of the shaman's songs. Daur shamans' chants or songs were dialogical and intentionally directed, that is they were always a response, an invocation, an order, and so forth, in relation to some other subject in the performance. However, they were not dialogues. Spirits, even if they were considered to be ancestors, were not interrogated by the people present (an exception to this was the questioning of recently dead shaman-spirits at the *shandan* burial site, 3.2). This differentiates North Asian shamanship from that of South Asia, where people engage in intimate, informal conversations with their dead relatives through the shaman as a medium (Obeyesekere 1977; Vitebsky 1993). The idea of *barkan* and *onggor* spirits assimilated even recently deceased people to a relatively small number of communal and distanced examples of human predicaments.

To start now with Mendüsürüng's account of the ritual of the night road: if someone was extremely ill, virtually at death's door, the family would beg the shaman to 'watch his dream'. The shaman's dream would indicate that a *dolbor* must be done and which kind of *dolbor* it should be. In the performance described, the shaman set out just before sunset on the chosen day and killed a goat in propitiation to the south of the village. Four small willow-trees (*delkin*) were set up at the spot and the goat's head, hide, liver, heart, and lungs were hung up on them. After this he went to the north-west of the village and made a propitiation of a two-year-old calf to the *dolbor* cult.[79] They cooked the meat of the calf, and having offered it, everyone ate the remainder.[80]

After this everyone went to the shaman's house where he put on his costume with the help of his assistant (*bagchi*). A smoking censer was placed near the door. The shaman warmed his drum at the fire, and began to invoke his *onggor*s from the eight directions. Touching his drum to his forehead many times, he gave people to understand that he was shamanizing with deep thought (*gung* *bodoltoi*), whistled[81] and danced. On the dance, Odongowa (1991 n.d.: 12) writes:

The shaman's dance was called *he-kai-ku* and it was a very serious, sacred action for which there were fixed times and movements. Rules governed each kind of step and the number which should be taken under which conditions. Nowadays, some people write that shamans beat drums and danced in a disorderly way, that shamans were irresponsible and frivolous. Some people even say they would like to learn to do shamanic dances for fun. But that would be like trying to draw a picture of a tiger when you only know a cat.

Inviting his *onggor*s to aid him on the journey the shaman sang as follows, and three or four assistants led the audience in repeating the refrain:

SHAMAN. Deng deeni kuu yuu [*refrain*]
  Deng deeni kuu yuu
  Deng deeni kuu
PEOPLE. Deng deeni kuu yuu
  Deng deeni kuu yuu
  Deng deeni kuu
SHAMAN. When you (patient) searched for me,
PEOPLE. [*refrain*]
SHAMAN. Whenever I thought of dear baby you,
PEOPLE. [*refrain—henceforth this should be read as repeated after each line*]
SHAMAN. There was no way but I had to walk to you
  When there is a heavy (difficult) aim
  When there is deep faith in the task
  Although over 60 years old
  Although over 70 years old
  I have always been embodying my *borchoohor* ['brown spotted' *onggor*].
  Let us try to make [it—the disease?] completely white
  Let us try to make [it] pure [*arigun*] white.
  On the mysterious meaning of what [I] have seen
  Let [me] tell the deep-penetrating meaning of what has become known.
  I have got Gesui Lama to confirm it
  Lama Laiching has verified it.[82]
  I have my hunting camp in the ruling [lit. governor '*amban*'] pine-tree
  I have my quarters in the huge [lit. 'camel'] pine-tree
  I have transformation in the lightning-filled sky
  I have my hunting-camp in the thundering sky.

Having invited his *onggor*s like this, the shaman made a fumigation of *gangga*[83] near the threshold and now all the lamps were extinguished. The house was in complete darkness. The shaman beat the drum as loudly as possible, jumped, and started dancing, going backwards nine steps, turning round and going forward nine steps, turning round and going backwards nine steps; then chanting in a loud voice, turning, turning on the spot, he went back to the door, and suddenly stopped; tottering backwards he pulled hard on the leather thongs attached under his armpits,[84] and he was about to fall down when the assistants who had been carefully following caught him from behind, and as he was falling towards the north-west gently lowered him to the floor face downwards. It is at this point that the *onggors* entered. The shaman's soul, now joining with the *onggor*, set off on his *dolbor* journey. Suddenly all the noise of drum beats, rattling, chanting, clashing of bronze mirrors and ringing of bells, stopped. There was total silence and you could hear your own heart beating. No one was permitted to move or speak. The people sat transfixed in the darkness and the shaman's body lay inert.

'For how long?' I asked. 'The time it takes to light the stove and boil the tea,' replied Mendüsürüng (a time varying from ten to twenty minutes). At last in the expectant darkness a single bell from all the thirty-six bells was heard to ring, and this was a sign that the shaman's soul was coming back. (Urgunge remembers the shaman shivering convulsively, snorting like a horse, and spitting, all of which showed he was back in his body again.) He weakly sat up and in a low, clear voice, as though wearied by his arduous journey, began his report:

SHAMAN. Dolborai, dolbon juu [*sung refrain*]
    Dolborai, dolbon juu
PEOPLE. Dolborai, dolbon juu,
    Dolborai, dolbon juu
SHAMAN. In the empty space of the black steppe,
PEOPLE. Dolborai, dolbon juu
    Dolborai, dolbon juu [*henceforth repeated after each line*]
SHAMAN. There are two sparse, north-side forests,[85]
    Your blue ash-coloured goat
    I tied up by a long halter from its neck,
    Your black ash-coloured goat
    I have tethered to the *haragana* bush.[86]
    When I was approaching Irmun Khan[87]
    There was a many coloured palace
    With seventy storied *dayimen*[?]
    With eight storied *ninggil* [pole for large tent]
    With doors of precious stones
    With a multicoloured stone threshold
    With white stone windows
    With flint stone pillars.
    Huge Hasar Basar guard dogs[88]
    Were lying right across the threshold.
    [Someone] over 50 years old
    With his beard in five plaits,
    Over 60 years old

With his beard in six plaits,
Over 70 years old
With his beard in seven plaits,
Over 80 years old
With his beard in eight plaits,
This kind of powerful male person
Opening his door came out.
Holding a sword he terrified
Holding a spear he threatened
Holding tongs he lunged
Holding an axe he intimidated
Holding a dagger he thrust
Holding a meat-knife he attacked
Roaring like a tiger
Snarling like a lion.
Our two lives [*ami nasu*, i.e. the patient's and his own]
I only just managed to rescue.
I loaded on my back mirror
Your chronic diseases and sufferings,
I loaded on my front mirror
Your illness and suffering.

Now the shaman sang the refrain melodiously and gently, and gradually he finished.

What strikes one about this is the clarity and expectedness of this text. In the first part the shaman tells of his parent-like sympathy for the patient and makes sure everyone understands what pains he himself has been to, despite his advanced age. He says he will explain the deep meanings and furthermore that he has the legitimation of weighty religious figures behind him ('Useless!' said Urgunge, 'Shamans should never be deferential'). In the second part, the shaman relates his encounter with Irmu Khan, describing him in the standard terms found in epics and other genres. Unusually for a Mongolian text, the subjects and objects of sentences are made clear. The whole thing tells people what they already know, or is so much what might be expected that it seems almost redundant. So far it is difficult to understand how the *dolbor* ritual could have been as powerful as everyone said it was.

What actually happened was that the *dolbor* songs were buried in noise, or rather, they emerged out of noise. The shaman's assistants had loud ringing cymbals (*chaan*) and with the drumming and clattering of the mirrors they made a cacophony which convinced Urgunge he did not understand the words of the shaman. But amid this din, song and regulated dance was a thread of order to subjugate disorder. It is for this reason that I introduced Odongowa's defence of the rules of the dance, and even the Japanese account insists on the repetitive presence of the chanted refrain and the numbered steps. Evidently ritualized order gave power to the dance, so the shaman could become like a tiger as opposed to the disorder of the frivolous and weakly cat. Note that it is Daurs who insist on this idea, not the anthropologist. This ordering of sound and movement, in which everyone present had to participate by singing the refrains, was inherent in the ritualization of the performance.

Taussig (1987: 389–90) may have been right to accuse Lévi-Strauss ([1949] 1967) of *creating* order in his celebrated analysis of Cuna Indian shaman's healing song ('the very analysis of the magic of the shaman was no less magical than its subject matter'). But he is wide of the mark when he derides anthropologists' cosmology of the ritual leader, mystical flight, the harmonics of heroism and order as 'fascist fascination' (1987: 443). The fascination, at any rate, was shared by the participants in these rituals. In a Latin American context such images may be completely misplaced, but in North Asia we have to recognize a shamanic practice that used these images to demonstrate the power of order, for the very reason that it engaged with chaos and accident. Now sometimes shamans embodied a series of spirits, very fast, a few minutes each: a bear, a lame person, a badger; an inexperienced shaman might fail to control these spirits fully and blunder round the room, knocking things over and bumping into people. He or she would give the impression of being more 'tranced out' than an experienced shaman, not being practised at attaining the mental state and soul energy required to dominate the spirit. But this would arouse criticism. So it is not that there was no disorder in the Daur historical predicament, nor that disorder was not wildly acted out in other parts of religious life (see 6.6). But the *yadgan*'s ritual performance, if it was at all successful, was not where disorder reigned.

The refrains, which had to be repeated by competent assistants leading the whole audience, were essential to raise the shaman's soul energy.[89] The shaman's body channels were opened by means of the smoke of a sacred plant (*swaih*) to enable soul energy to travel out and spirit energy to come in.[90] Rhythmic sounds, melody, and vibration inspired the soul energy, enabling the shaman to sing ever more loudly, dance with vigour and liveliness, and carry the heavy human sufferings loaded on mirror or drum. A shaman's physical weakness was overcome not by wild improvisation but by constant repetition of the plain rhythmic patterns, the beloved tunes of the refrains (*iro*) sung by the assistant. The more fluid, trembling, or improvisatory notes of the shaman were supported by the overlapping voice of the assistant, who sang—sometimes almost shouted—accented and highly rhythmic short themes. Because the voices were interwoven there was no point during the song when there was an absence of sound. The overlapping of the voices also meant that there were three rhythms to attend to: that of each shaman on their own and the combined music of both.[91]

The sense of the words as we have seen was uncomplicated. However, and it is as difficult to convey this in words as adequately to describe a brilliant actor's performance, in many performances the shaman *became* other spirit beings, calling, admonishing, dismissing the spirits in people (this felt as though you yourself, sitting there, were being attacked). Everything was in the tone, sometimes sung in a harsh, piercing cracked voice, virtually shrieked out, sometimes melodically, and sometimes in a soft beguiling voice. Shamans whispered the name of spirits when they did not want the audience to hear. The words of songs like the *dolbor* one fail to convey their effect, and musical notation is equally inadequate. Manchu shamans introduced 'lively notes', notes without fixed pitch,[92] which 'made the music miraculous and alive', as one shaman said. Like the free nature of the soul energy, the characteristic of lively notes was unfixed tonal movement (Li Lisha, personal communication, 1994). Manchu shamans, and Mongolian musicians too, linked the vibratory sound quality of their singing with unsettled sounds in nature, such as the noise of river water or wind blowing over mountains.[93] Thus the order in powerful shamanic rituals, which was made up of expected, repetitive words and movements, was infused with a poetic play with order, a reaching beyond created order that found correspondences in nature. This was only possible as an effect of the shaman's mastery: the ability, for example, to sing true notes, which everyone recognized and yet which were enlivened by occasional warbling quavers suggesting something beyond.

The quality of Pingguo Shaman's performance with the red-hot flat-iron seems very different. The shaman was clearly unwilling to engage in a seance and call his *onggors* for someone who was uncommitted to shamanic beliefs, could not understand Daur, and would not recognize the ritual 'elements'. In the end the performance had to rely for its effectiveness on fright and magic. Pingguo seems to have been highly successful in panicking his Japanese visitors.

Now the *dolbor* night journey ritual as described by Mendüsürüng differed from the seances where shamans devoted most of the performance to assuming the identity of their *onggors* (for example in the lament of the Baglain Udagan spirit (1.5)). In the *dolbor* ritual the shaman only briefly took on the identity of the *onggor* ('I have my hunting-camp in the ruling pine-tree, etc.') and most of the time spoke as a shaman, describing what he or she did or saw. What are the implications of such differences? There were many different variants of shamanic seances, and performances often combined various modes, but it is possible to delineate three major tendencies, present across North Asia, and here Siikala's work is helpful.

Siikala (1987, 1992) has analysed Siberian shaman's rituals in terms of 'elements' consisting of songs or chants. These elements, such as 'call addressed to the spirit-helper', 'description of the shaman's journey', 'description of a point in the topography of the underworld', she calls motifemes. They are like compartments that can be filled by various motifs, i.e. contents (1992: 41). Siikala made an exhaustive study of shamanic ritual among many peoples (1987) and on this basis she identifies some twelve of these motifemes. In any given performance larger or smaller numbers of the elements could occur, in more or less any order. Noting this, Siikala (1992) compares the performances of two Chukchi shamans at the turn of the century both of whom were trying in turn to get their spirits to quell a snowstorm. One shaman performance consisted of a number of motifemes presenting his journey to another world in the person of the spirit-helpers, while the other used a more limited set of motifemes to call his spirits in to his everyday body, where they were manifest by 'tricks and ventriloquism'. The interesting thing about this is that the two types of performance created different relations between the shaman and the audience. In the first shaman's ritual, the audience's attention had to be engaged by the consciousness of weird spirits in the other world, the whole series being the shaman's 'journey'. In the latter, the shaman, having introduced the spirits into his body, *himself* made a 'journey' which he described ('I saw . . .'); the spirits were no longer of significance as the shaman recounted his adventures. This shaman thus maintained a direct interaction with the audience, akin to that of a story-teller. The song categories central to his performance were therefore different from those of the first shaman, and they were looser and less ritualized (Siikala 1992: 53–4).

Clearly the Daur night journey described here was closer to the second than the first type of shamanizing. Now Siikala interestingly relates this audience-close type of performance to changed social relations among the Chukchi at the beginning of the century. The shaman using 'ventriloquism and tricks' was in constant contact with the audience, able in his own person to observe their reactions and respond to them. He was in a much lighter trance than the first shaman, who had to attain a definitely altered consciousness to reveal and display the spirits' lives. Siikala (1992: 55) suggests that 'an established and close band of supporters', such as that provided by clan society, was necessary to maintain the audience–shaman relation in this first type, a point also made by Lévi-Strauss ([1949] 1967). But socio-economic changes at the beginning of the century had placed the Chukchi communities in ferment, disrupting clans and the intense common memory of ancestral spirits they promoted. 'The status of each individual Chukchi shaman was directly dependent on the favour of the audience, and the ventriloquist seance technique provided an easier route to favour than the classical journey type.'

If this was the case, how much easier was a third tendency in shamanship, represented by Pingguo Yadgan and his frightening lunges with knives and the red-hot flat-iron. Even the most silver-tongued description of the threats of Irmu Khan must have been less compelling than actually having a red-hot pointed iron thrust at one's belly. But what was most significant here was that no beliefs, no shared knowledge of arcane spirits, not even knowledge of the widespread tales of Irmu Khan, was necessary to make such performances effective. We can see now why Pingguo's seance for the Japanese had to be of this type if it was to work. Later in this book I shall take up this point again, when discussing Daur shamanship in the disturbed social world of early twentieth-century Manchuria (7.1 and 7.2).

It is interesting to compare the attentiveness at shamanic performances with that at the *oboo* rituals. At the sacrifices at the cairn, Urgunge said, one could easily switch off, and participate though mentally miles away. Young boys could play or run around. In the end what was important was that the ritual happened and the people received the blessing. The shamanic performance, on the other hand, required one's undivided attention, which was constantly excited by the shaman's movements, sounds, and dramatic appeals. So spellbound was the audience that the shaman could sustain rapt interest in the *dolbor* performance when nothing happened for well over ten minutes. In this case children at the performance were not day-dreaming. On the other hand, they might collapse in hysterical laughter, which was perhaps an over-reaction with extra imaginative input (as when Urgunge and his friends were overcome with their joke, 'Du Yadgan's grinding well!'). Urgunge when talking about the *oboo* ritual was, if anything, bored, but he often returned to the fascination of *dolbor*, the sense of danger, and the mystery of how a single bell could ring. Was this the extraordinary physical control of the shaman, gently to shake one bell among all the dozens of metal objects on his costume, or was it really something occult? To tell the truth he joked about the night journey too. He used to say, 'I'm going on *dolbor* now,' meaning he was going down the three stories of winding eighteenth-century staircases and corridors into the basement of King's College where the lavatories lie.

5.8 Ominan, Remembering the Spirits

The shamanic tradition at any given place would have lapsed had it not been deliberately maintained and transmitted. Once every three years the clan-village would hold a lengthy ritual at which all the spirits were invited to descend in turn. The *ominan*[94] (*undaan* in Urgunge's dialect) was the greatest of the shamanic rituals and one of the few in which all villagers participated communally.[95] It combined the public initiation of a young shaman, propitiation of all spirits, renewal of the strength of the home shaman, and an intense evocation of clan solidarity. The *ominan* took place in the 'beautiful, blooming season of full summer' (Mendüsürüng 1983: 271) and it was accompanied by feasting, games, and wrestling. Not only was it a shamanic equivalent of the communal sky/mountain cult, it was also a 'meta-ritual' containing an overarching summation of *yadgan* shamanship as a whole. Although *ominan* was a joyful occasion, the anxiety that lay behind it was that some spirit power might be inadvertently missed out or forgotten.

The issue of forgetting involves questions raised by Barth (1987) and by Whitehouse (1992). Barth shows that Baktaman sacred knowledge is sur-

rounded by secrecy and taboo, and that religious understanding is produced in
ways which are a response to the constant dangers of forgetting. The long time
gaps between performances of initiations, as many as ten years, and the veils of
mysterious secrecy and lack of discussion, place heavy demands on memory.
Whitehouse interestingly compares the Baktaman initiations with the rituals of
the kivung religion, which are continuous, standardized, and frequently performed, and run no risk of memory failure. Whitehouse argues that the complex, logically coherent, and speech-based rituals of the kivung religion would
simply be impossible to reproduce at intervals of ten years. On the other
hand,

The [Baktaman] tradition is insulated from the dangers of memory failure in two major
respects. On the one hand, the separateness of metaphors implies that modification or
elimination of any particular symbolic process, whether due to memory failure or to
some other specific cause, does not substantially undermine continuity in the religious
tradition as a whole. This would not be true of a logically integrated structure, where
interference in any one sector of the religion can have profound consequences for the
entire system. On the other hand, the bombardment of the various senses and the
cultivation of pictorial and emotionally charged associations, which occur in Baktaman
ritual, may be regarded as powerful mnemonic devices, greatly reducing the risk of
forgetting and thus of the unconscious or unintended introduction of innovations in
subsequent performances. (1992: 8)

Daur shamanic forms of understanding are in some ways similar to the
Baktaman, especially in the disparateness of the parts and the emphasis on
sensuous experience. Whitehouse's insight is to see that the forms taken by
religious rituals are related to the cognitive demands made by memory. His
argument applies equally to a situation where demands are made not only by
memory but also by innovation. In all North Asian 'shamanism' there was a
sporadic generation of new spirits, arising from the death of shamans and from
extraordinary external events, new manifestations and sensibilities. At the same
time, as we have seen, there was the constant, menacing presence of spirits from
the past, whose neglect was definitely regarded as the main reason for their
taking vengeance on people today. The Daurs dealt with a certain type of
incremental innovation by incorporating new spirits in the compound categories of *onggor* and *barkan*. This was a constant process. (However, I have
argued that radically new manifestations were not incorporated in this way but
became the focus of separate cults, with their own specialists, rituals, and
concerns (see 7.1 and 2), and this contributed to the disparate, segmented
character of 'shamanism' as a whole.)
    Simultaneously with the process of incremental change I shall suggest that
there were other features of the *ominan* which made it a repository of genuinely
ancient practices (or rather, of these re-enacted). Spatial, artefactual, and
bodily representations are often more durable than the ideas attached to them

(Connerton 1989). If some elements of the ritual, by chance or design, happen to be actions or objects which over a period of three years (or any regular and relatively frequent performance) would be difficult *not* to reproduce in more or less the same form, the conditions for retention of archaic forms are there. In the Daur *ominan* one of the main spirits was Abagaldai, represented by a mask made of copper (see Plate 20). Although no one had anything much to say about it, if your aim was not to forget, then obviously such a durable object as the Abagaldai mask would continue to appear. More generally, the experiential basis of shamanic practice provided its own kind of continuity, through the use of extremely simple and memorable spatial forms and bodily gestures around which people's individual evocations floated and differed (a comparable point is made by Whitehouse 1992: 13–14). A circular dance round a focal object, for example, was not readily changed, nor was the action of binding together, even if the instrument of binding—thong, rope, etc.—might change. These actions were recognized by Daurs to be ancient and therefore generally a good thing, even if their urgent aim was not to preserve them so much as to 'refresh' the spirits, which were retained mainly in oral forms of memory. Thus, if an explicit concern with not forgetting in an oral culture could incorporate a gradual, largely unacknowledged, change in certain discursive contents, it could also endlessly renew deeply archaic forms of gesture, spatial constructs, and artefacts.

The date for the *ominan* ritual was carefully selected, and the people of the *mokon*, neighbouring sub-clans having no shaman of their own, and any other non-clan clients[96] of the shaman gathered beforehand with their offering items.[97] Two *yadgan* shamans were required, a home shaman and one invited from outside. The outside shaman was categorically senior.[98] If a young candidate was ready to begin his life as a shaman, the two would be the teacher or 'great' shaman (*Da yadgan*) and this new home shaman (*shine yadgan*). Teacher   —A shamans were normally from different clans from their pupils. Urgunge said that the idea behind inviting an outside shaman was like the European doctor seeking professional advice from another doctor when ill: you need an external review to make sure that all is well. From an anthropological point of view, we can see that this ritual, which also gave prominent place to spirits of the affinal (mother's brother) clan, must have served to integrate various local traditions to some degree.

The site for the ritual was at the shaman's house, or at an open place where people erected a tent-like awning supported by a cartwheel raised on several cart shafts. Inside this structure, or just inside the door of the house, two leafy birch trees freshly cut from the forest were set up. Between them, like a ladder, were tied three horizontal plum branches, with the images of the *hojoor* spirit of the host clan, the *hojoor* of the mother's family (Najil Barkan),[99] and the Abagaldai mask hung on them. A large piece of fat was stuffed in Abagaldai's mouth. The two trees were called *geri tooroo* ('house sacred tree').[100] Outside, about 20 metres to the south-east, was erected another tree called *beed tooroo* ('outer sacred tree'). On this tree were hung images of the Jiyachi and Keiden spirits. The trees had to be fresh and 'alive', but none of them had their roots buried in the ground; rather they were supported by stakes hammered in the gound. The stakes were called the 'gold and silver gate'. Between the *geri tooroo* and the *beed tooroo* there was a red cotton rope (*shuanna*), which was said to be the road of the spirits. An iron ring was hung on this rope. The trees were said to lead the shaman's spirit to the outer universe. People laid their offerings at the foot of the trees and tied ritual scarves and multicoloured ribbons to the rope. 'Everything was festive and beautiful,' Urgunge said.

The senior shaman danced (*tooroo tol-* (erecting the sacred trees)) round the trees, and then, in two sessions a day, he began to invoke the spirits, one by one. Urgunge remembers all sorts of animal and human spirits, some of which were more or less jokes. If a young candidate shaman was involved, the teacher sat by the *beed tooroo*, called down the spirit and sent it down the rope in the iron ring to the junior shaman who was seated by the *geri tooroo*. The new shaman had to bring himself to trance and correctly remember the spirit's characteristics, whereabouts, refrain, etc., all of which was rather like an examination. The idea was that the tree would act as an antenna or lure for the spirits, which would arrive at the outer tree and then go and sit on the inner trees. Indeed, Urgunge said that the name for the whole ritual in his village, *undaan*, was derived from the verb *ende-* 'to coax'. It was the specific task of the older outside shaman to see that the clan *yadgan* was keeping up smooth relations with spirits, especially with his own *onggor*.

As each spirit was invoked the master *yadgan*, who was the visiting shaman, led the younger host shaman in a dance round the trees. The latter followed copying step by step, while the assistants, the *bagchis*, beat drums and sang the refrains. When a spirit came to the host *yadgan*, he fell to the ground trembling, and lay there while the drums and refrains continued. At last he was gathered up by the assistants and seated. The spirit spoke through the *yadgan*, telling people about its history. The people now came forward holding bowls of alcohol or milk and they told the spirit how much esteem they had for it and how they would now redeem promises for propitiations made earlier.[101] They pleaded with the spirit not to cause diseases and troubles. The spirit spoke again in a singing voice, pointing out what it had done for people, recalling mistakes made by the shaman, and how to get rid of further sufferings. Then it was time for the spirit to leave, and both shamans performed a farewell dance. Each spirit was given an offering.

Towards the end of the *ominan*,[102] there was a ritual called *kuree* ('circle' or 'surround'). All the clan members, men, girls and children, were bunched together under the awning and the two shamans bound them with a leather thong (*sor*) going round and round twelve times.[103] Menstruating women, in-married wives, and pregnant women were excluded from the circle, as this part of the ritual was specifically for clan members in a state of purity. Each *yadgan* held one end of the belt and pulled until the people were squashed together. Then the belt was measured. If it was longer than it had been three years ago this was a sign of the flourishing and increase of the clan. This was done three times. The rope was then plaited in three strands and one by one people ducked under it to get out and this was said to guard against illness (Mergendi 1981: 309; *DSHI* 1985: 263). Mendüsürüng does not mention this literal-minded gauge of population, but he notes the binding together. He writes (1983: 271) that the people had a 3-year-old calf with them inside the belt, and together they tumbled it over, squashed it down and killed it. In the mêlée the people's diseases and troubles were transferred to the calf.[104]

Proceeding from the *kuree* ritual the shamans went to the outer tree and danced round it three times. Then nine large birch-bark bowls (*tanggula*) filled with milk were set out on a white felt between the trees and offered to the sky, the earth, the *oboo* spirit, and the masters of mountains and rivers. Now, everyone, the shamans, assistants, and people danced in a circle round the outside *tooroo* tree, leaping round and upwards towards the sun. 'That dance was the unity of the clan,' Urgunge said. It expressed the people's happiness, and it gave power to the shaman, exhorting him and encouraging him. People shouted a long-drawn cry, 'Oh-oo-oo-oo!' to raise the shamans' soul energy. Then, in Mergendi's account (Urgunge does not remember this) both shamans lay down on the ground and were rolled over and over between the *tooro* trees three times by their assistants. This symbolized raising a three-storied pagoda to the spirits (*DSHI* 1985: 262).

The last night of the *ominan* was devoted to 'blood drinking'. In the dark all lamps were extinguished. A calf which had been tied to the outside tree was now killed and its blood drained into a bowl, where it was mixed with milk.[105] The shaman called his spirit (according to Batubayin an eagle, according to *DSHI* a cuckoo) and all those present shrieked in a bird's voice, 'Kar! Kar!', working the shaman up to the coming of the bird spirit. When the young shaman heard these squawks, people showed him the bowl of blood and milk. With bird cries he threw himself on it, desiring to drink the blood, but the master shaman would not let him. The new shaman chased the teacher, he was shown the blood again, and it was snatched away, all of which was repeated three times. At last the shaman was allowed to drink the blood and milk, and with this people said that they had satisfied the spirit's thirst and the shaman had renewed his whole organism.[106] The shaman also took pure blood in his mouth and blew it over images of spirits hung on the trees, the nine Yisile (lizards),[107] three Mangaldor,[108] and the twelve Duwalang (tree-dwelling creatures, see 2.1). Finally, the *tooroo* trees were taken out of the village and planted, the young shaman gave gifts to the visiting shaman, and the *ominan* came to an end.

Urgunge explained,

The *tooroo* tree means height, from its roots to its topmost leaves; it represents reaching to *tengger*. The dance around the tree is an ancient Mongolian custom—you remember in the *Secret History* how they danced till they made a channel in the earth around the tree?[109] Of course in our case it was not really a dance; in English you would have to say jumping. The shamans and people were jumping around the tree with happiness. Now why was that? The *undaan* is like a great party for your *onggor*s: you invite them and they come to the tree, and they put their marks on the leaves. You know when there is a British wedding the names of all the guests are written down? It was like that, leaving their marks on the leaves, saying, 'I was present.' And the blood—that is what *the spirits* like to eat.

No Daurs ever drank blood or raw milk, he said; both had to be cooked and processed into foods, and he found the very idea of eating this mixture disgusting.

Hamayon (1990 and 1992: 134–7) has interpreted similar Siberian rituals as a great dualistic exchange between humanity and the spirits of nature. The shaman fed the spirits with sacrificial blood as a subsititute for the human blood they would otherwise devour, and in return the spirits allowed humans to take wild animals in the hunt, the essential source of human sustenance. This does make anthropological sense, particularly of the part of the ritual where bird and animal versions of spirits were involved. However, it must be said that no Daur ever gave me an interpretation mentioning hunting, and there were large tracts of the ritual, involving specifically human ancestral spirits, symbolic ascent, dancing, and so forth, which seemed to represent concerns quite other than an exchange with nature.

Ominan had no logical structure of speak of, apart from the incremental adding on of further spirits until everyone was exhausted. Descriptions of the ritual differ in whether it ended with the general dance round the tree, the blood-feeding, or the encircling, and indeed each of these elements is dropped in one or another ethnographic account. Inclusive, vivid, and shapeless as it was, the *ominan* was like a pool in which ancient practices rose like branches to the surface. This book is not the place for a lengthy exposition on this point, but the next few pages will show what led me to make this suggestion.

The ritual moved backwards and forwards between the outer tree and the two home trees. Let us start with the spirits on the 'home trees'. Alongside the *hojoor* of the host clan and the mother's clan, there was hung the copper mask of Abagaldai (see Plate 20). 'Abagaldai' is a name meaning 'with [the power of] *abaga*' (senior uncles in the patrilineage). The ferocious Abagaldai mask was considered the vessel of a *barkan* spirit rather than an item of apparel, and it was worn by a shaman only once every three years at the *ominan*. Mendüsürüng told me,

Abagaldai is the main *barkan* of the ritual and they put most of the offerings before him. The aim of Abagaldai is to chase devils. He is the most hero-like of the spirits, he can pursue anything. They polish his mask up for the ritual, and it is so awesome [*surtei*]

that as soon as he comes all those evils things are frightened. Abagaldai is shaped like a male face and it has 'four beards' [*dorvon saxaltai* (head hair, eyebrows, and a beard)] of bear's fur.

According to *DSHI* (1985: 256), Abagaldai was the spirit of a black bear, 'always in control' of the shaman's *onggor*. Apart from Mendüsürüng, the Daurs I met knew almost nothing about Abagaldai.

However, the Abagaldai spirit was also found among the various Evenk and Buryat groups of Transbaikal and Manchuria (Dioszegi 1967: 189–96). From legends of the Buryats, we learn that Abagaldai was nothing other than the downside of the clan male. In one story he was married to a shamaness, Heterhen, who was called away to conduct a ritual, during which time Abagaldai was so eager for a smoke he abandoned their baby son in search for tobacco and the boy fell in the river and drowned. In another, he was a handsome and famous young warrior, married to Heterhen, daughter of the Khan of Korea. However, Abagaldai began an affair with his wife's sister, who was married to his own patron, Bubei Khan. Out of grief Heterhen cut off Abagaldai's head and threw it in the river Angara. The river spirit was naturally angry and visited illness on fifteen families. The people had to agree to raise Abagaldai's head and make it a spirit. The head came alive and flew to Heterhen, begging for tobacco and alcohol, and she agreed to give them if the spirit would drive evil spirits away (Dioszegi 1967: 190). Speaking through the shaman, Abagaldai Spirit gave himself some bear-like attributes: hibernating in the forest, he was wakened by the ringing sound of the shaman's dancing and came 'with slow steps'. In Daur myths the bear stole human women and took them off to the forest (Humphrey 1994*a*). The impression that Abagaldai represented the bad, antisocial, blackbear-like aspect of the clan elder is strengthened by the fact that it was mostly female shamans who maintained this spirit (Dioszegi 1967: 190). Among the Hailar Daurs, Huangge Yadgan (a woman) kept Abagaldai and it was one of her most powerful attributes, but Pingguo, Jaban, and Lam did not have it.

Thus at the 'home' tree the Daurs put two ancestor *hojoor* spirits (dubiously protective, as we have seen) and the antisocial Abagaldai. Let us now look at the 'outer' tree, where they hung Jiyachi and Keiden. Jiyachi was the spirit of domestic livestock, known also among the Mongols, Buryats, and various Tungus groups. Hailar Daurs represented the spirit in the form of a cloth placing, with human shapes made of horsehair (*hyalgas*) sewn to it (see Plate 19). It was daubed (*milaa-*) with the first food and drink of meals and the first milk each spring. Soaked and encrusted with fat and hanging by the stove, this image became black and strong-smelling. In spring, tufts of calves' hair were attached to it.[110] Considered basically benign, Jiyachi both caused and removed cattle epidemics (4.2), was particularly partial to horses, and also gave people good fortune, descendants, luck in hunting, and wealth. The Daur shamanic

19. Representation of Jiyachi
barkan, made of felt, with two
figures representing the
spirits made of horse-hair and
beads. Hailar region. Photo:
1931, O. Mamen. [5.8]

story of Jiyachi is that he was a Mongol cook slaving in a Buddhist monastery.
When he heard about the prosperous herds of the Daurs he decided to escape
from the temple, but on the way he was struck by lightning and became a spirit.
His invocation goes:

> Had his birth origin in the inner land
> Among the thousands of Mongols
> Was a cook to thousands of lamas
> Searched for the Daur Solon,
> On his way met a small cloud
> Struck by five lightning flashes
> Split to pieces by nine lightning flashes
> Cracked the elm trees
> Broke the fruit trees.
> When he got to the village and the ørkøø[111]
> [He] became the 'one who gives fortune' [Jiyachi].[112]
> On the west side a double-dragon altar was set up
> There was a double-dragon throne.
> With nine young boys dancing

Nine young girls dancing
[We] make offerings to the deity Jiyachi.
(Wu 1989a: 174–6)

At Urgunge's house there was a small box hung on the outer wall of the house high on the north-western corner. This contained the Jiyachi image, and, he thinks, some small wooden carvings of horses and cattle.

Keiden was altogether a more mysterious spirit.[113] Mendüsürüng told me it was made of air (*kei*), that its meaning was 'empty', 'with the power of air'.[114] Other snatches of information are that Keiden was the middle part of a complex *hojoor* spirit, its upper part being called *kenger dailale borchoohor* (breast *dailale* brown-spotted birds) and its lower part called *hojoor dolbor* (ancestral night road) (*DSHI* 1985: 251). Keiden was also a particularly vicious part of the complex Bogole Barkan, driving people mad; it was represented as a human and a bird, as nine humans, and thirty sky dragons (*DSHI* 1985: 253).[115] In Daur *kei* (*kein*) also means wind, and from ancient times in East Asia wind has been imagined as the bringer of disease, change, and disorder (Kuriyama 1994; see also 6.3 for the imagery of tornados, gusts, and whirlwinds in Daur shamanic poetry). Thus, taken together, it looks as though the spirits on the outer sacred tree, Keiden and Jiyachi, represented concern with anger emanating from the sky and from distant, ancestral Mongolia, and this was envisaged in the symbols of dangerous unseen contact from the upper airy cosmos: lightning, long roads, shattered trees, dragons, and rapacious birds.

In sum, we can deduce that Jiyachi belonged 'horizontally' to distant parts of this geographical world and Keiden 'vertically' to the wild cosmos, while the 'home' spirits represented the clan ancestor, the affinal clan ancestor, and the bear-uncle Abagaldai. These and all the other spirits were fed, through the shaman, the anti-food of raw blood and milk. This whole shamanic cosmology was counterposed to the idea of the harmonic universe regulated by the Sky whose blessings were obtained through *oboo* and sky sacrifices. It was an alternative, perhaps even a rival version. This is seen, for one, in the prominence of Jiyachi in the shaman's cosmology. Not only was Jiyachi's jealousy the reason why the sacrifice to *tengger* had to be closed off and hidden (4.2), but Jiyachi 'the fortune giver' was himself an alternative to the fate-fortune given by the Sky. The *yadgan* made Jiyachi and Abagaldai (antithesis of the good clansman) into his or her main spirits. Elements of this alternative cosmology were certainly of long-standing: Tungus shamans' copper masks were first collected by Russian investigators in the early eighteenth century (Dioszegi 1967: 171–2) and a livestock protecting spirit called Jol-Jayagachi (Fortune Fate-giver) appears to have been already traditional among Halh Mongols in the mid-sixteenth century (Banzarov 1955: 79).

It is impossible not to notice in this great *ominan* ritual the insistent presence of the two sexes (the spirits with male and female roads, the nine young boys

20. Huangge Shaman in her tent, with Abagaldai mask behind her. The mask's mouth is filled with fat and the head is covered with a silk offering-scarf (*hadag*). This tent was used for Huangge's *ominan* ritual; normally she lived in a house. Photo: 1931, O. Mamen. [5.8]

and nine young girls) and the allusions to conflictual sexual relations. Abagaldai was not an abstract male clan-member, as in the *oboo* rituals, but let down his wife, abandoned his son, engaged in sex with his clan patron's wife, and took the form of the woman-stealing bear. Even the process of inheritance of the Abagaldai mask seemed to have involved transgression of the strict sexual code of the clan. Mendüsürüng told me that Huangge had had to make her own Abagaldai mask. This was because her shaman predecessors, who should have handed it down to her, had been overly indulgent to wives and mistresses ('a disturbance of the social order') and the shamanic spirit had 'branched out' and got lost down these female lines.[116]

The ritual moved from the intense human complexity represented at the 'home' tree to the great communal dance round the 'outer tree'. Perhaps we can interpret the dance as a journey into the 'outer' cosmos for the renewal of soul energy, something like the Eliadean celestial ascent.[117] A *tooroo* tree was part of the shaman's mortuary complex, the place of the death–rebirth of the shamanic spirit (3.2). The 'airy' nature of both Keiden and Jiyachi on the outer tree, the fact that the pegs supporting the trees were called a 'gateway' as in other Siberian dances to the Sky (Alekseyev 1993: 28), and that the trees were said to lead to the outer universe, all suggest some such idea. This joyful, energizing encounter was for all people, not just shamans, and not just the male members of the clan. Though the *kuree* encircling rite was limited to clan members, the jumping dance round the trees was performed by both men and women.

A circular dance of both sexes occurred sporadically among the Western and Khori Buryats, Yakuts, Evenks, and several peoples of the Altai and Tuva. But it would be wrong to suggest this implies a common single idea. What is found in Central and North East Asia is the irregular occurrence here and there, over

21. *Tooroo* trees, shamans and assistant at an *ominalen* ritual of Orochen (Tungus), Mergen region in the Naun valley. Photo: 1927–9, O. Stötzner. [5.8]

vast distances, of sacred actions which had an existence not only on the surface of religious life. They appeared as part of the repertoire of shamans' and the clan elders' sacred performances. But somewhere, one is tempted to say, deeper than this, they were also present among the people as one of the fundamental ways of constructing occult movement, along with the stopping, receiving, sending, encircling, and propelling of soul-spirit motion. These 'ways of doing things' were often latent, i.e. not practised for long periods, but ready for use in the invention of 'new' cults. As noted earlier (3.1), in recent revivals of Siberian shamanism it is specifically these communal dances to the sky that have reappeared (Alekseyev 1993: 25–34).

Let me give a brief impression of the parallels that appear at distances thousands of miles apart in North Asia. The round dance (*yookhor*) among the Buryats was clearly a symbolic ascent. The Yakuts had a similar communal ecstatic dance. Performed by 'sons and daughters' or 'nine boys and nine girls', these were long drawn out rituals of increasing fervour, which whirled their participants up to the sky. At the Khori Buryat festival of inviting all spirits and introduction of a new shaman (*shanar*), the dancers made in this way a spiral road for him and 'danced him up to the sky' (Poppe 1940: 25–34). After an electric storm, the Western Buryats in the 1920s–1930s would make aspersions of milk and circumambulate the stricken house, and then they had a round dance lasting several days to propel the 'thunder arrow' (lightning) back up to the sky (Dugarov 1991: 162; 171–7). In the Even ritual of 'meeting the sun' held at the New Year, having made an offering of milk, men and women moved across a fire which was lit in the 'sky gateway' between two trees linked by a sacred rope. Ascending to the sky as reindeer (turning into cranes on the way), they were blessed by the sun and returned to earth at the encampment, after which a circular dance was held. This round dance imitated the mating dance of cranes, geese, and swans (Alekseyev 1993: 25–34). What we see here is similarity of form and practice, not identical meanings.

However, some interpretations given to these rites are relevant to the Daur *ominan*. At the Eastern Buryat celebration for a new shaman, 'mother' and 'father' trees (*tuuruu*) were erected at the ends of lines of numerous other trees in rows, and between them a rope was strung, which was the road of the shaman and the spirits. The shaman climbed the 'mother' *tuuruu* tree and took three eggs from three nests with his mouth, ate them, calling like a cuckoo, and this was said to be his birth (Dugarov 1991: 54). As far away as the Yenisei, some thousand miles from the Daurs, the Tungus said that between day and night there stands a tree called *tuuruu* with nine nests in it, each one higher than the other, and in these nests the souls of shamans are hatched (Dugarov 1991: 55). This is like an echo of the Daur idea that the young shaman's spirit was the egg of a cuckoo, hatched out from a coffin-like nest that was *not its own* (see 5.3). Perhaps we are entitled to see in the *ominan* the symbolic metamorphosis of previous shamans' souls into the initiated or renewed soul of the host shaman.

But no Daur ever said this to me, and in the ritual as described crucial links in this line of reasoning are absent. The *ominan tooroo* trees did not contain 'nests' and seem to have figured mainly as perches for rapacious birds. Furthermore, the Daur shamans did not climb the *tooroo* trees, as happened among the Buryats ('the ascent to the sky'). Such absences in relation to cults elsewhere could be taken to imply either that the Daurs had forgotten the shaman's ascent to the sky, which would be Eliade's line, or that the *yadgan* tradition turned its back on it. In either case, the Daur shamans' distinctive action symbolizing the 'raising of a pagoda to the spirits'—rolling on the ground, not climbing trees— is curiously earthbound. In my view the hesitant Daur appropriation of the symbolism of ascent was the result of the fact that the images of spirits invented by *yadgan* shamans were composed in a primarily horizontal, geographic vocabulary (e.g. Jiyachi, see also 3.1 and 3.2), and this may be because the imagery of sky and air was taken up by another shamanic tradition, that of the *otoshi*, which will shortly be described, see 6.3.

The Daur *ominan* seems to have been altogether more complex than a simple exchange with animal spirits of the wild, or communal ascent for the encounter with heaven. Both these elements were present in it, but the abiding impression is that the ritual in fact represented a shamanic view specifying the menacing complexity of such movements. It thus existed in contradistinction to the relative simplicity of the single-sex rituals, such as the offering to the forest-spirit Bayin Achaa, the *oboo* rites, or the women's water game by the river. Incorporating the destructiveness of human relationships, its own version of fate-fortune, and the danger of the flying blood-drinking spirits, the ritual nevertheless temporarily overcame all this by manifesting the power of shamans to master all spirits.

Something more should be said about the large number of ritual and mythic parallels through North Asia, always slightly different from one another, always with somewhat different local interpretations, but elusively similar. For the great majority of these 'common phenomena' any clear process of recent diffusion is out of the question: most of these peoples have had no direct contact with one another, the geographical spread is not uniform, and does not follow historical river or trade routes. It might seem easy to explain, by diffusion, why the Bargas living near Hailar had a story of a shaman, Lo-Tu, whose adventures were almost exactly the same as those earlier described (3.2) for the Daur shaman Tochingga and his predecessor Gahucha.[118] But it is more problematic to use such an explanation for the Darhat legend of talking trees (Rinchen 1962), which closely parallels the Daur story of Moodu Yadgan (3.1). The Darhats really live very far away from the Daurs and I have not heard of contact between them. Anyone interested in this topic might be driven back to the reconstruction of early common 'origins', such as the Turkic people called 'Kurykan', who inhabited the Baikal region in the ninth–tenth centuries before the rise of the Mongols, who moved north to become part of the ancestors of the

Yakuts, and who engraved nine dancing boys and nine dancing girls on the cliffs. However, such hypothetical common ancestors do not provide a good explanation in many cases. For example, in 1917 or thereabouts, the Altai Oirots started a new messianic religion called Ak-Sang which was expressly aimed to be different from shamanism, Buddhism, or Orthodox Christianity. Now the characteristic religious sites they set up, when observed in the 1930s, were like variants on the lay-out of the Daur *ominan*. They constructed an enclosure with four posts before which was laid a white felt mat with bowls of milk and a short distance away were erected two trees. Ribbons and ritual scarves were tied to threads between the posts and the trees. The cult priests started by circling the two trees and then they moved in to circumambulate the enclosure, followed by all the people circling many times (Danilin 1932). That this was called *kure*, like the encircling of the Daur *ominan*, seems at first not so surprising, as this is a Mongol word and Mongols live between the Daurs and the Altai. But it is rather like saying that France lies between the Shetland Islands and Tunisia—the Daurs are separated from the Altai by thousands of miles, different languages, numerous peoples, and the massive presence in the centre for the last few hundred years of Buddhism. The ritual constructions of the Ak-Sang movement were consciously a matter of striking a new ritual pattern different from previous practices. So this rite cannot be seen as faithful constancy to a continuous tradition stretching back to an ancient 'origin', but was evidence of something far more fitful, and perhaps in any given place only kept alive by traces of physical practices whose symbolic meaning had been forgotten.

So having started by saying that the *ominan* was aimed at not forgetting, I leave it with the idea that, behind consciously trying to remember and allowing innovation, there were perhaps some 'ways of doing things' which imposed themselves surreptitiously and inadvertently. There is no reason to suppose that this was some hidden monolithic structure, waiting to be exposed and analysed by the anthropologist. The surface of shamanism was disjunct and fractured (the Daurs did *not* consciously make the connections). The 'archaic' actions of the *ominan* were fragmented too, and the only reason for saying they 'lay behind' is somehow to express the idea that, drawing on some unconscious reservoir of possible ritual actions, people may have again and again brought to the surface closely similar actualizations.

Notes

1. Mendüsürüng is a now a professor at the Inner Mongolia Normal University in Hohhot. He was brought up in Hailar, where his mother was much involved in shamanist activities.
2. The terms *saman* and *yadgan* were used interchangeably in the Hailar region.

3. The table leaves out Daurs belonging to other clans than the four mentioned here and the Daurs living in Hailar town. The villages were not far from one another and merged into a common settlement area known as Emel Ail. Mendüsürüng estimates there were 200 Daur families, over 1,000 population, living in the area in the mid-1930s.

4. Lewis (1989) proposes an ideal model of shamanic initiation, which moves from involuntary possession through the domestication of spirits to controlled and voluntary trance. This model seems in principle correct and it certainly applies in the case of Buryats (Humphrey 1971–2).

5. *Hii solija-* is the Mongol expression for this illness used by Mendüsürüng; *hii* is 'life force' and *solija-* means to be mentally unstable or mad. According to Urgunge, the term *hii* is of Buddhist origin and was not used in this sense in his region, where *hii* (*kei*) meant wind; see also 5.8.

6. A *butur* sometimes became a socially recognized shaman, but even if this did not happen he or she was recognized as having the ability to handle simple problems caused by the spirits. Some *butur* were said to be more capable than full shamans. Their practice was called *buturbei* (to act as *butur*). They did not have shamanic robes and could not embody the *onggor* spirits (Omachi 1949: 25).

7. The term *yadgan* originates with the word for female shaman used widely among Mongol-Turkic peoples in North Asia, *udagan*, as distinct from the terms for male shaman which differs from place to place. *Udagan*, or variants thereof, was used by Halh Mongols, Buryats, Bargas, and Yakuts for female shaman, and this term was also borrowed by several groups of Tungus (Shirokogoroff 1935: 270). The term for a male shaman in Buryat and Halh Mongol is *boo* (written form *boge*); in the Altai and Tuva the term is *kam*.

8. The etymology of *Otoshi Ugin* derives from the Mongol words *otachi* (doctor) and *okin* (daughter, girl). See 6.3.

9. This name means Lone Lama.

10. This name means Twisting Shaman according to Poppe (1930: 76), who says *dog* is an archaic word for shaman. However, *doglon* means 'lame'.

11. Poppe (1930: 13) notes that Immen is the *ejin* [spirit] of Emel Bogto (South Sacred Hill), an example of the 'vitalization of the landscape' with the spirits of dead shamans in the Hailar area (see 3.2).

12. Readers may find it somewhat confusing that Otoshi Ugin is mentioned in a spirit complex that belongs to *yadgan* (or *saman*) shamans, rather than to *otoshi* shamans. This does not imply an overlap of the *yadgan* and *otoshi* categories. A shaman's *onggor* line could have all sorts of people and animals in it, including various kinds of shamans, like Otoshi Ugin. In shamanic practice the activities of *yadgan* and *otoshi* were kept separate. Jaban, it seems was both a *yadgan* and an *otoshi*, having inherited both kinds of *onggor*. He acted now in the one role and now in the other, but never in both at once (Omachi 1949: 202–3).

13. I was also told she died in 1966.

14. Urgunge said that only after four or five generations would a dead person become a *hojoor*, i.e. when the individual personality was forgotten. The reappearance of a dead soul among the living, on the other hand, took place in close generations, when some feature of the remembered ancestor was recognized in the baby. Once a *hojoor*, an ancestor would not be reborn among the living. There are some minor

differences between the account given in this section and that in Vreeland ([1954] 1962). Urgunge says that there are some misunderstandings in Vreeland's account of *hojoor* due to Urgunge's poor knowledge of English at the time.

15. Ordinary families all kept images of the *hojoor*, but otherwise only of those spirits that had attacked them. Omachi (1949: 21) mentions that Hailar Daurs kept three to five images in each family, but I also heard of households with up to forty. According to Omachi, a shaman's relatives and clients would make an *onggor* image immediately after the death of the shaman.

16. Pingguo, reckoned a highly competent shaman, mastered the following spirits: (1) his Aul clan *hojoor*, (2) the wider *hojoor* known as Da Barkan (see 6.2), (3) Doka Barkan (gate spirit), (4) Aulai Barkan (mountain spirit, a fox), (5) Sum Barkan (temple spirit, also a fox), and (6) Niang-Niang Barkan (Omachi 1949: 22).

17. Urgunge remembered the following *onggor*s belonging to Du Yadgan: Dau-darsan (noise-making, i.e. thunder), Doglon (lame), Krel (mottled face), Aduuchin (horse-herdsman), Sohor (blind), and Gwarban Sum (Three Arrows). All of the people referred to by these names had died unnatural or violent deaths.

18 However, shamans had to conduct the funeral if the death was likely to result in the emergence of a spirit. Such cases were when someone was struck by lightning, a still birth, or when someone died from *oni eul*, an acute illness thought to be characterized by the growth of black hair inside the abdominal cavity. In the last case a shaman had to 'draw out the water' at the funeral, otherwise the disease would stay in the deceased's family for generations (Omachi 1949: 26).

19. People did not use the word *uke-* (to die), but the euphemism *barkan bolson* (became a spirit) or *tengger awaad yawsan* (tengger took went).

20. I have little information about women's funerals. They seem to have been similar to those for men, but less elaborate. Women, Urgunge said, were more frightened of death than men, and therefore could not face making their coffins in advance.

21. Urgunge said that the corpses of *bong* were dug up and burnt in order to make a final end to these ghost-zombies.

22. Poorer families used a cow (*hun-shu*). The meat was cooked and eaten. It was tough and not at all tasty, according to Urgunge, because the family would only use an animal at the end of its life.

23. The paper money was to pay one's way, perhaps pay bribes, on one's way to the world of the dead.

24. Mourning clothes were worn for your father for three months, father's young brother one month, older first cousins one week. For non-clan members no special mourning was worn, except for the mother's brother, who was mourned for three months.

25. The following kinds of death required the body to be burned, according to Li *et al.* (1955: 479): women dying in childbirth; a person who died in a far-off place; a rotten and unrecognizable body; a person dying of epidemic disease; a sudden, unexplained death.

26. Urgunge imagined *shurkul* as having red eyes, long teeth, very long straight hair, yellow skin, dirty clothes with holes, and thin, bony hands.

27. This rite is found among all Mongol groups. In Urgunge's village it was known as *gejihe handaa-* (pigtail cut) and all the older male kinsmen cut a lock of hair. It was not done for girls.

28. According to Li *et al.* (1955: 469), the child's body was placed in a specially woven willow-basket and placed in a tree at the foot of a mountain, or on a specially erected wooden stand. This was called 'air-burial'.
29. See 3.2 for description of Hailar Daur shaman's funeral. In Butha the place of disposal of the corpse in a tree was secret. After three years the corpse was removed from its coffin, wrapped in a mat, and buried in the forest in a peaceful place. There was strong belief that the shaman would be reincarnated after this second funeral. The shaman's costume was not left with the body, but this was mainly because it was expensive to make and required rare objects, and therefore was handed on from generation to generation (Omachi 1949: 24).
30. In exorcism rituals a rope 'road' is sometimes used to lead the spirit off, but it can be omitted and instead the shaman embarks on a real trek out to the wilderness, bearing the effigy away (Heissig 1992: 157–68).
31. The shaman before Tochingga in the line of *hojoor yadgan*s of the Manna clan was Gahucha, who started life as a slave and horse-herder. After he became a shaman Gahucha had an extremely powerful mirror, which rolled by itself here and there. As this mirror protected the shaman's heart, it was dangerous for him to lose it. We see echoes of this in Tochingga's story. Gahucha's mirror was said to have been passed on to later shamans of the Manna clan, and one of them, not wishing it to roll away, weakened its efficacy by wrapping it in women's underpants. It is said that this mirror is even today worn on the costume of Worgaibu, the most recent *hojoor yadgan* of the Manna (*DSHI* 1985: 261).
32. I cite from an unpublished manuscript (1991 n.d.) of a paper later published by Odongowa (1991), which I have not seen.
33. Batubayin writes that these thongs were called *asalong*. While the shaman was becoming entranced and the spirits were entering him, he would hold tight to the *asalong*, then releasing the thongs he would take up his drum and sing the words of the spirits.
34. According to Odongowa, there were 20 on each side; Lindgren mentioned 30 on each side; and Batubayin also mentions a total of 60 or 72 small mirrors.
35. Lindgren says that the Hailar Daur shaman's costumes she saw had the animals of the twelve-year cycle embroidered on these straps (1935a: 374–5).
36. Haslund-Christensen (1944: 18), discussing the antlers on the hat of a Solon shaman from the Hailar region in the 1930s, says that new tines appear as the shaman gains victories over hostile forces. The new points 'break through' in the fifth month, at the same time as the grass starts to grow in the steppe.
37. Some people, including Urgunge, say that this bird is a falcon or other bird of prey. Some say the falcon can turn into a cuckoo. It is generally agreed that the two birds on the shoulders of the gown are cuckoos.
38. Daur shaman drums are round and about 0.7 m in diameter. The skin is stretched over a frame made of willow or elm and tied at the back of the drum by leather thongs attached to an iron ring in the middle. This iron ring is the handle.
39. 'A similar visual disintegration of antlers into trees is indicated by the Mongolian or Ordos plaques, showing horse-like creatures savaged by wolves, tigers and bears. On all the plaques from that region, the reference both to antlers and to trees has become weak, incoherent: sprouting from the head of the savaged

animal, the antlers wander carelessly into a bordering function, reminiscent only of tendrils' (Jacobson 1984: 125).

40. Their date and place of finding were carefully remembered and rituals to them were conducted by shamans to bring rain, healthy children and livestock. The objects were kept by the families which found them in hollows made in wooden posts erected to hold them. They were also worn by shamans (Baldaev 1961: 206–18).

41. If a child's hair was tied up in a knot, people said there would be no danger of their being hit by a thunderbolt. Perhaps what lies behind this strange idea is that hair, like the thunderbolt, was thought of as a power-conductor (see Nishan Shaman legend, 6.5). People finding 'heavenly hair' should take it immediately to a shaman, as otherwise trouble might ensue. Women were particularly vulnerable from these objects and their bodies would be covered by ulcers if they touched one (Omachi 1949: 27).

42. The production of bronze mirrors in South Siberia dates from the second millennium BC. These mirrors pre-date, it seems, the earliest finds in China (7th century BC), although Chinese mirrors of later periods were widely traded across Inner Asia. Buryats of the early 20th century used Chinese mirrors in shamanic ritual and also made their own (Mikhailov 1980: 190).

43. The Bargas are Mongols with close affinities to the Buryats.

44. Horse-headed sticks were used by Barga, Darhat, and Buryat shamans as mounts for journeys to the other world.

45. The copper mask was almost certainly that of Abagaldai, which was widespread in the Hailar region in this period and was also used by Daur shamans, see 5.8.

46. Note the omission of all women, including herself, from this first sentence.

47. Haslund-Christensen (1944: 8–9) notes that an old shaman living near Hailar locked up the spirits of his costume with 'two primitive Russian padlocks' before he died, fearing that there was no shaman to inherit the costume and therefore no one would be able to control the spirits.

48. Kuriyama (1994: 25–7) discusses the historical change in early Chinese medical practice from the Shang, when causes of illness were sought in ancestral dissatisfaction, to the Han, when healing became a science of the body. While Han healers recognized the destructive power of external pathogens like winds, they nevertheless maintained that they could only harm individual bodies with predisposing weaknesses, and this necessitated the study of the pulse, the organs, acupuncture sites, and so forth.

49. Sain Tanaa (1987a: 293) mentions Daur ideas of three souls, the 'everlasting soul', the temporary soul which lasts only as long as the body is alive, and the 'rebirth soul', which is recycled by Ome Goddess. According to Shirokogoroff (1935: 52), the Birarchen Tungus, who are culturally closest to the Daur of all Tungus groups, have an idea of three souls: (1) the soul given by Omisma, called *omi*, and which goes after death into animals, (2) the soul which has no place, and (3) the soul which goes to the ancestors. He describes similar ideas for other North Manchurian peoples and also mentions that many people think of these souls not as separate but as aspects of one soul.

50. This idea may be related to the concept, common in Buddhist Mongolia, of *hii* (written Mongol *kei*), which means both air/wind and also psychic vitality of

fortune (see 6.8). However, the Manchus also imagined the heart as having holes, an idea Shirokogoroff (1935: 135) suggests they took from the Chinese.

51. If someone was knocked out by the blow to the head, it would be thought nevertheless that it was her heart that had been damaged, making her lose consciousness.

52. Odongowa told me that it was forbidden to paint faces, and especially eyes, on the *haniaka* as this would make it more likely they might come to life. Children were instructed to talk only indirectly when playing with *haniaka* ('She went in the house') and never directly ('Go in the house'). It was feared that by speaking directly the child's life-breath (*amin uur*) would enter the doll and enliven it. For the same reason *haniaka* were not used for long. They were burned every year or two and new ones made.

53. The main categories of illness (*ewur*) and suffering (*joblong*) remembered by Urgunge were: *jadag*—a long-term, non-contagious disease with weakness and pains in the abdomen and genital area, mainly a problem for women; *haluuntai*—'with heat', fever; *lenge*—eye-disease, with pus and redness; *ilga*—or *huar*—'flower', small-pox, chicken-pox, and measles (there were differentiating terms for these which Urgunge does not remember), recognized to be contagious; *darch waina*—'to get cold', shivering and colds; *muu ewur*—'bad illness', heart attacks or stroke; *galzuu*—rabies, frenzy; *beleng*—phobic reactions, echolalia, echopraxia, coprolalia ('Arctic hysteria'); *soliyara-* (or *demireke-*)—to be mentally unbalanced; *koodoo*—psychotic madness; *teneg*—weak-minded, simple; *sanaa dwatar ewurtei*—'to be ill in the heart-mind', depression; *sumus darsen*—'soul oppressed', spirit possession; *sumus gee*—'soul lost'. Apart from these a large group of illnesses with vomiting, pains, and weakness was known simply as *dwatar muu bolson*—'became bad inside'.

54. The expression used was *sumus gee-*, where *gee-* means to lose inadvertently, to discover something has gone, whereas *alda-* is to lose consciously, to let go. *Gee-* was used if you looked in your pocket and found money had gone, whereas *alda-* would be used for money lost in gambling.

55. Unclear what this word means, possibly Mongol *daaga*, 2-year-old colt.

56. The soul left and returned through an infant's fontanelle, but for adults people talked about the mouth or the armpits as points of entry to the body.

57. Some such rite was performed for Urgunge when he was about 5, and he is convinced that he was placed under the protection of *tengger* (*tenggert tushi-*), but he can remember little about it except that a shaman was called and a sacrifice made. It is possible that he was mistaken and that the consecration was to Ome, whose other name is Tengger Niang-Niang. My reason for thinking this is that shamans were not normally involved in any rituals to do with *tengger*.

58. In the version described by Mendüsürüng, they put in a human figure, beautiful children's clothes, small birch containers, five animals cut from birch-bark, and a sheepbone gnawed clean, all tied up with a ritual scarf (*hadag*) (1983: 259).

59. In Urgunge's case he wore a bell not a mirror. His name was changed, which was a common way of deceiving the spirits.

60. For example: if a hunter dreams about a horse, it means he will be lucky; if you dream you are wearing white (mourning clothes), you will become rich; if you dream of eating a lot of food, you will become ill; laughter and drinking were also

bad omens. Dreams of a river, ocean, sun, moon, stars, dragon, snake, or a famous person were good omens.

61. Urgunge as a boy used to dream of flying high in the air, swooping over the earth, coming down to look more closely, and riding up into the clouds at will. He attached no significance to this.

62. Generally, Urgunge attributed dreaming of any kind to a person's low physical condition. After any vivid dream people would experience a feeling of malaise and weakness.

63. Other methods of divination were (1) by means of scrutiny of the cracks on a roasted animal shoulder-bone; (2) study of the colour of the shoulder-blades of animals and the breastbones of birds; (3) scrutiny of the ashes of burnt paper; (4) pouring water in a bowl and observing whether chopsticks would stand vertical or how they moved; (5) putting an egg on a horizontally placed mirror (Batubayin 1990). ·

64. It was common to know several languages among the peoples of Northern Manchuria. However, Shirokogoroff documents cases where people possessed by spirits were able to talk in tongues they did not know in everyday life (1935: 256–7).

65. Jin Hai Agvan was a cavalry soldier aged 42 in 1935 when the author met him in his barracks at Bugutu in East Xing-an Province. He became a shaman when he was 19, but had since given up (Akiba and Akamatsu 1941: 59).

66. Mikhailov (1980: 189), however, writes that Buryats used the mirror for divination by looking in it, striking it, or casting it to see which way up it faced. Shamans' mirrors were said to have been thrown to earth by smiths in the sky.

67. Batubayin (1990) mentions a 'purifying body ritual' done by the *yadgan* at the beginning of the first month of each lunar New Year. He puts his breast mirror and some coloured stones in a big pot of clean water and then makes a fire and boils the water. The water is then considered to be *arshan* (sacred water), and it is splashed over the shaman's body with a kitchen brush, then over those of the clan members present. The aim of the ritual may be to give protection rather than purification. An analogous ritual done for children, *uhan budlyaa*, is mentioned by Manzhigeyev (1978: 77) among the Buryats, in which the shaman says, 'May the black stones be your door, may the brown stones be your wall, That you may not cry or be ill, That you may grow quickly.'

68. The story is published in Daur and Mongolian and uses *belku* and *toli* for 'mirror' in the respective languages.

69. See 5.5. In Tungus-Manchurian languages the mirror is called *panaptu*, which Dioszegi's etymological analysis shows definitely to mean 'soul holder' (197: 366–70).

70. This word is found in Tungus, meaning 'night road' of a spirit (Shirokogoroff 1935: 154). Urgunge said Daurs knew it to be a foreign word. For him *dolbor* meant a way, going from south-east to north-west in a downwards direction.

71. Magic was known by a variety of terms, e.g. *domog* (used for magical actions as well as stories) *ilbi* or *howus* (practices involving instruments), *tarni* (magic using spells).

72. *Hii bisirel* is literally 'air faith', or 'mental faith'; this and *süsüg bisirel* (devotion faith) are Mongol expressions used by Mendüsürüng and Urgunge rejected them

as too 'religious' and influenced by Buddhist vocabulary. He agreed that people had to participate in the performance with their heart-minds, but said there was no real word for this among the Naun Daurs, perhaps only at a pinch *itge-* used as a verb in the sense of 'to accept'.

73. After this the shaman agreed to be photographed outside. Then he returned to the tent, beat his drum, danced and recited the *tarni* in a low voice, and finally held his drum over the incense and took off his dress.

74. Urgunge remembers that in most cases of illness the shaman would first chat with the patient and his or her family, maybe feel the pulse or look at the tongue. He sometimes knew immediately which *barkan* required a propitiation, otherwise he would ask the family to wait until he had dreamed. Sometimes a shaman would say he still did not know, but usually he would state which sacrifice (chicken, pig, cow, etc.) would be required, when it should be offered, and to which spirit. The shaman never explained anything to the patient, never said, 'It might be this spirit, or it might be that.' In fact, he often did not even reveal the name of the spirit but simply called the one in question at the time of the sacrifice. If the patient was a young woman the shaman would hardly look at her. Du Yadgan had been practising in Urgunge's village for thirty years. He knew exactly how much each family could afford, which *barkan* images they kept at home and which were likely to attack them.

75. In Mendüsürüng's description (1983: 269) the shaman took off his boots and put melted butter on the soles of his feet. He now stepped on a red-hot iron plough-share, and flames flared up. This frightened the spirit and amazed all the people, because there was no scorching or burns on his feet. According to Li *et al.* (1955) this was called 'putting on red shoes'. Other actions of this type were 'climbing the ladder' (the shaman walked on a series of knife-blades set cross-ways like a ladder); 'wearing the red sash' (the shaman donned a red-hot iron chain round his waist); or 'entering the lake' (the shaman walked on a path of red-hot cinders). Just attempts to impress naïve audiences in some outsiders' narratives, these were dangerous tests of a shaman's fortitude and abilities as recounted by the people themselves. A Manchu initiate had to steel herself or himself to such acts in order to become a shaman, and then was able to use them in curing (Lisha Li, personal communication).

76. 'Pure water' according to Urgunge was just plain water; other authors (Batubayin 1990; *DHSI* 1984) mention putting the bronze mirror in the water with stones and heating this up to make 'pure water'.

77. This was often part of a more extended exorcism ritual. Urgunge said that the attacking spirit was gathered into the mirror (not into the shaman himself), and the shaman might then transfer it to a human-shaped straw image called *beemee*. A chicken would be killed, fresh blood applied to the mouth of the straw image and then the *beemee* was taken outside and burned (see also Heissig 1992: 157–68).

78. Lindgren stoutly remarks, 'Certainly, what knowledge I had of abnormal psychology before engaging in fieldwork was a great help to me. It prevents one, for instance, from thinking that a person who appears to be temporarily unconscious is necessarily in a 'trance', as shamans are always said to be; I have never seen a shaman who was more than slightly dissociated' (1935c: 176). Of course, the

impressive presence of Lindgren herself, over six-foot tall and with a personality to match, might have kept some shamans more alert than they might otherwise have been.

79. *Dolbor Sitügen*. The Mongol word *situgen* can mean religious worship, place or object of worship, cult or shrine. Mendüsürüng told me that *dolbor* is a place, not a spirit, but his use of terms was unclear. See discussion of Irmu Khan as both place and person, 2.2.

80. Urgunge said that propitiations were not made for the *dolbor* rituals in Butha. Batubayin (1990) gives further details and his own interpretations of such rites. The ritual called *betlebe* was both an offering to the *barkan*s and an action to drive away those spirits causing harm (not clear if they were the same spirits). The shaman first prayed to the spirits to help him cure the patient. The animals were killed, the flesh cut joint by joint, and the meat boiled. Meanwhile a long rope (*zele*) was tied to three willows in the yard. The meat was put at the end of the rope. The *yadgan* made a short second prayer and some meat was thrown over the rope (i.e. offered to the invited *barkan*). All the people present, including the shaman and the patient, then ate the meat. When they had finished two hawk-shaped straw-braided birds, whose beaks had been soaked in the blood of the killed animals, were thrown over the rope (i.e. sent to report to the spirits about the sacrificial offering). The *yadgan* shot three arrows over the rope (i.e. he expelled the spirits). Finally, he picked up the three posts and threw them to a place as far away as possible (i.e. cutting off all relations between the human and spirit worlds).

81. Whistling was a call to the *onggor*s. It was strictly forbidden outside a ritual context.

82. Gesui Lama probably refers to the *geskui*, the superintendent of a temple. A *laiching* was a type of magician common among sedentary Tumed Mongols (Heissig [1944] 1992: 2–3) and was not in fact a lama, but a layman or woman. However *laiching*s used much Buddhist symbolism. They exercised their power through prayer and magic spells. Daurs seem to have seen Lama Laiching as a kind of shamanic spirit (6.2).

83. Wild thyme (*Thymus serpyllum*), widely used in North Asia as a purifying agent.

84. These thongs were the 'roads' by which the spirits entered the shaman's body, 5.3.

85. This could refer to two single trees; in any case they were growing on the north side of the mountain. Generally in Mongolia, since the prevailing winds and rains come from the north, trees do grow on the northern sides of hills, while southern slopes are bare.

86. A desert-scrub bush, *Caragana arborescens*, indicating a sacrifice to the south.

87. A different pronunciation of Urgunge's Irmu Khan, lord of the nether world.

88. These are common Mongol names for guard dogs.

89. Talking to Daurs I found this idea expressed by the Mongol idea of *hii* (air-energy); Urgunge talked about the brightness of the light of the star of a person's soul.

90. 'Manchus believe that the hot smoke entering the body can make the inner air energy rise up to help the shaman experience the ecstatic journey' (Li Lisha, personal communication).

91. This description is based on recordings of Daur shamans' invocations to Niang-Niang and other spirits. It was decided not to include a transcription of the songs here in western musical notation, as this would give a misleading impression of the sounds and rhythms.

92. These notes were performed sometimes slightly higher, sometimes slightly lower than the normal pitch, or they moved continually up and down.

93. Carole Pegg (personal communication, based on information from Western Mongolia). Mongolian and Buryat musicians are also adept in creating splintered sound, producing the overtones of notes and attending to the dying of these sounds at different times in given acoustic situations. These many-layered sounds, flying above a basic drone, are said to make manifest the various simultaneous realities introduced by the shaman (Karatygina 1989: 95–6).

94. Also *omna*, *umna* (Engkebatu 1984: 39, 46), or *ominalen*, cf. Tungus *umnaa* (Shirkogoroff 1935: 352).

95. The other major communal, though smaller scale, ritual was held annually by each shaman in their own home shortly after the lunar New Year (*oni ugtahu tahilga*). Thus in Hailar Jaban Yadgan held his ceremony on the 8th of the first month, Huangge on the 13th, Pingguo on the 18th, etc. The shaman invited and called down his or her *onggor*, offered it tea, then sprinkled all those present with sacred, purifying water (*arshan*), and finally saw off the *onggor* (Omachi 1949: 23, 26; Batubayin 1990). (See also n. 67.)

96. These people were called *nimgart* (Poppe 1930: 10). Up to two hundred people would attend an *ominan*, according to Mendüsürüng.

97. People brought cattle, sheep, goats, pigs, alcohol, incense, ritual scarves, and money as offerings. The scarves were tied to the trees. Most of the offerings were piled in front of Abagaldai.

98. Thus when Du Yadgan was getting old the shaman he invited was younger than him, but was still called the Da Yadgan ('great shaman').

99. Possibly the mother's family of the host shaman, otherwise unclear.

100. Also called *bodi tooroo* (? *bodi* 'real', 'material'). According to Mendüsürüng, there was only one home tree and it was an oak (*chars mod*).

101. At an ordinary curing ritual people would promise to make a sacrifice to the spirit but did not actually do so unless the illness was cleared up. Such promises were redeemed at the *ominan* ritual.

102. On the third day according to some respondents, on the seventh according to others.

103. The belt was made from a whole ox-skin cut in a single unbroken strip.

104. In poor villages a sheep or goat was used. The meat of the calf was later eaten. Urgunge's village did not have an exorcism in the *ominan*.

105. According to Batubayin (1990), the blood was sometimes that of a swan rather than a calf.

106. Alternatively, according to Batubayin (1990), the two shamans dance round, beating their drums and calling with a cuckoo's call, and the people echo with cuckoo's cries. The spirits are said to take the form of these birds. At the climax of the shouting the lamps are lit again and the master shaman dips his fingers into a bowl of blood mixed with cow's milk, alcohol, nine pieces of incense, and nine pieces of cow lung and smears this on the mouths of the spirit images, including

the twelve *duwalang*s. Mendüsürüng told me the shaman gulped down the blood, and people would say, 'Just drink a little! You must not drink so much!'

107. Cf. Shirokogoroff (1935: 152) *isole* (lizard).

108. Possibly the same as Manggee, hairy, human-shaped monsters.

109. 'Qutula was raised up as qahan (Khaan) and they danced round the Saqlaqar (many-leaved) Tree of Qorqonaq until they (wore) tracks up to their chests, until they made dust up to their knees.' Paragraph 57 of the 13th-century chronicle, known as the *Secret History of the Mongols* (Onon 1990: 13).

110. These were the *keshi* (blessing) of the calves. When Daurs and other Mongols sold cattle or horses they used to keep a bunch of hairs of the animals (*malyn keshi*) to retain their 'luck'.

111. The ancient ditch and rampart, sometimes called 'Chinggis Khan's wall', built across north Mongolia and Manchuria.

112. *Jiya* (fortune, fate), *-chi* (suffix 'the one who').

113. Urgunge did not remember Keiden.

114. On a different occasion, Mendüsürüng said that some people also made Jiyachi 'of air', i.e. this spirit was a non-physical presence to them, without a material vessel.

115. Shirokogoroff (1935: 154–5) describes the clan Kaidun of the Birarchen Tungus as a spirit originating in the mountains and composed of three parts. One was the night road (*dolbor orgu okto*), which was considered to be 'male' and consisted of five men, five birds, two dragons, and two trees; another was the day road and was 'female', comprising four women, four birds, two dragons, and two trees. The third consisted of nine females and nine males. The Tungus said Kaidun was a 'free, independent spirit' and that its night road was responsible for mental disturbances. A man could become very sick if he was travelling and met a manifestation of this spirit, such as a tree struck by lightning. The shaman contacting this spirit went journeying as an owl, and its manifestations, apart from the humans and birds already mentioned, were: owl, tiger, leopard, crane, and boa-constrictor (Shirokogoroff 1935: 165–7).

116. As against this, Omachi (1982: 36) writes that Huangge used the Abagaldai mask handed down from Gahucha Yadgan, who lived 150 years ago.

117. See 3.1. For a useful critique of Eliade's ideas and their elaboration by de Heusch (1981), see Lewis (1989).

118. Lo-Tu died at the hands of an enemy shaman and was reincarnated again, dancing into the village along a rope like Tochingga, and dug up a corpse wearing sunglasses and reading a book, like Gahucha (Kormazova 1929: 39–40).

6

Shamans in Society and History

6.1 Shamans and Human Relationships

In the great ritual just described, shamans danced between the home trees, with their images of ancestral disasters, and the outer tree, bearing its spirits of double-edged fortune and maleficent void. Nothing in this shamanic universe was a single indivisible unit, and nothing was simple or devoid of threat. Such a universe arose, I suggest, from the shaman's real-life practice, which was deeply implicated in the psychology of a *knot* of relationships. Although the individuals calling on the shaman's services were different on each occasion, the shaman's performance involved a necessary cast of intertwined roles. One can go further and say that shamans' practice created its own social relations. Elucidating this can help us understand one of Urgunge's most puzzling statements, his insistence that shamanism was about power, but Daur public life was without conflict.

Let us start with the shaman. One day I was telling Urgunge what I had heard about Huangge Yadgan (whom he had never met), how she was of short stature, was married to . . . , and suddenly he said, 'A husband was not enough. Undoubtedly she must have had a lover.' I hasten to say that Urgunge had no known grounds for this assertion, but this was his assumption about shamans: notionally they were not so much socially transgressive as attractive, sexually magnetic, active in drawing people to themselves. A shaman was a relational being, who needed other people to give him or her energy and support. We have seen how this worked in relation to the shaman's spirits and now it is time to think about the clients, neighbours, and villagers, the other participants in the performance of which the shaman was the centre.

The immediate aim of a performance was to discover the cause and nature of the suffering of some victim of spirit attack, but leading up to this was a skein of interrelated acts and the shaman's diagnosis also implied some subsequent acts. Therefore the shamanic nexus of relations has to be understood as dynamic, and, as I shall argue, endless. The ancestral (*hojoor*) and other spirits were images relating to particular events, but they can also be seen as discursive interpretation of archetypal, and therefore repeatable, relationships. The first relation was one occurring in the past between an Aggressor and a Victim in which the Victim was ravaged and became a spirit. We now move to the present, because the Victim-spirit's vengeance was wreaked not on the initial Aggressor, but on the Sufferer, the person whose illness motivated the shamanic performance. This involved not only the Shaman, as diviner, mediator, and interpreter, but also the *onggor*, which engaged in Counter-attack. Finally, the shamanic performance necessitated a Redressor, usually someone from the patient's family. The Redressor promised to assuage the hurt to the Victim by cosseting its spirit and making propitiations in the future, if the attack on the Sufferer was lifted (see Fig. 6.1).

It might seem that vengeance would be taken on the one who did the harm, in other words that the Aggressor and Sufferer would be the same person; but this was usually not the case. There are several 'reasons' for this. The initial hurt to someone who became a *barkan* spirit almost always happened in the distant and mythicized past, whereas the vengeance was taken on someone living now who just happened to be the innocent sufferer. Secondly, the initial hurt was often caused by the way things are in society, such as the structure of male dominance, social neglect, or war, and therefore the Aggressor in these cases was a general category such as 'our ancestors' or 'powerful officials'. Thirdly, as Urgunge explained to me, 'If in life you were afraid of someone, in death you would be too,' meaning that the initial victim, a young woman spirit for example, would not always dare to take revenge on a powerful man. This was the case even if it had been just such a man who had tormented her and caused her to die and become a vengeful spirit. Finally, even if in principle there was a certain specialization in revenge–attacks, most spirits were in fact composite (for example the 'Three Journeys' spirit in 5.1) and therefore caused many kinds of harm to a wide range of people. All we need to remember here is that although the Aggressor harmed the Victim-spirit, the Victim-spirit would then haunt a different Sufferer (or an unbounded set of Sufferers). This not only created a possibly endless cycle, but it rendered the initial injustice relevant to all the potential 'innocent' victims of a revenge attack, revealing this situation of hurt to be a matter of a more general intersubjectivity.

Only the involvement of a further crucial person, the Redressor, could halt

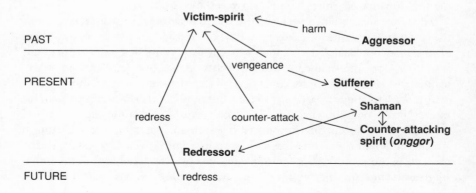

the vengeance by atoning for the wrong. Now it might be imagined that it was the present Sufferer who would redress the hurt to the Victim, for example by making a propitiation, thus freeing themselves from the haunting spirit. However, this seems to have hardly ever happened. Rather, another person was involved, this being someone who cared for the patient and was therefore willing to make an offering (or anything else demanded) on their behalf. The Sufferer from vengeance was essentially passive, except that suffering itself evoked the love of the Redressor. There could be nothing worse, Urgunge said, than being left to bear the haunting of a spirit unaided. Indeed this was virtually unimaginable. The loving relative had to bear the cost of redressing the ancient wrong, however ruinously expensive were the propitiations demanded by the Victim-spirit.

The shaman was focal in this nexus as the one who revealed the hidden causes and mediated between the actors: he or she found out which spirit harmed the Sufferer, what hurt had been done by the Aggressor, if this was not already known, and what redress was required. A shaman's first action against some outside *shurkul* or *barkan* was to call on his *onggor*, the Counter-attacking spirit. A contest between the *onggor* and a *barkan* involved one complexity in battle against another, two theatres of mythic wrongs, which resonated and echoed with the actual human drama of the patient and his or her family. Through this drama people could see that the love and support of the family was absolutely necessary, because almost always it was abandonment or careless cruelty which had caused a dead person to become a vengeful spirit.

This suggests another dimension of the involvement of the Redressor. The Redressor had to be someone who *could* make amends with an offering; that is, normally he was a property-owning elder, prominent in society, and we can see that in effect he was often the representative in the present of the same kind of social person as the Aggressor, the initial perpetrator of the harm in the past (though people were only subliminally aware of this). However, because full redress was only promised at the performance and not always given straightaway, a gap was open for the repetition of the whole scenario. Normally a small propitiation, perhaps a chicken, was made during the performance itself, and some larger offering was to follow if there was the slightest sign of improvement in the Sufferer's condition. But many promises to the spirits remained unfulfilled (it may be remembered that at the *ominan* people redeemed or again promised to redeem earlier undertakings). This meant that there was always the anxiety of not having done enough, the danger that vengeance might again be taken.

Now we can see why the propitiatory offerings appeared so prominently in the shaman's chant (see example in 6.3). They were not just incidental or bargaining points with spirits, but had a dual meaning. They were the tangible representation of the love of those drawn into the web of relationships by their concern for the patient. At the same time, as one woman said to me, 'It does not matter so much what you give, but blood must flow.' The demons and spirits fed on blood and meat-vapour. The shaman had to persuade the spirit to accept the blood and soul of the animal as a substitute for the blood and soul of the patient.[1] In this way the offering outwards to the spirit of the sacrificial blood crossed the inwards trajectory of the spirit attacking the patient. The two bloods had to be 'separated', and by this means the shaman re-established balance (*tengchuu*).

The relationship-constellations I have described involved individual people, but we can see that essential actors, denoted here by capital letters, also represented social categories and acknowledged human predicaments. Indeed, this is what distinguished the *barkan* as a cause of present misfortune, from the more abstract ideas of synchronicity, the sky's anger, etc. in the case of the cosmic and natural misfortunes, or the more haphazard, asocial situations attributed to demons or fox spirits (see 7.1). To illustrate the deeply social nature of *barkan*-caused affliction I give two examples here.

An old woman at Horli told me the following about the ancestral *hojoor* of this clan-village, a spirit which was invoked by a female shaman (quite possibly herself[2]).

I will tell you about the Horlichien clan *hojoor*. A long time ago there was a young woman of the Horlichien family betrothed to a Merden man. But before she was married she became pregnant and her seven Onon uncles were angry. She just hit her knees and flew away. The old woman said, 'She has become a spirit. How could she do that? Catch her,' and she sent many men after her. But they couldn't catch her. She flew on, and then she met an old man and she begged him, 'Please hide me in your store-room, if they catch me they'll treat me so badly.' The old man did so. When the pursuers arrived, the old man said, 'No, she hasn't been here.' After a while she came out, but she was still being chased. She hid in the mountains. There was a small river between great mountain cliffs. They were coming closer. She ran further. At last she cut off her little fingers and put them in her beauty case. She reached the cliff and had no other way than to throw herself into the river, and she drowned. The little fingers of the girl became a bird and flew out of the beauty case. This is the Horlichien *hojoor* and she also became *hojoor* of the Merden people.

This spirit attacked the Horlichien people. The initial relationship in question was between the unmarried girls and the old men and women of the clan, and the subsequent relational structure became: we (unspecified Sufferers today) are attacked by the spirit because our clan ancestors (Aggressor) drove the daughter to her death (Victim-spirit), and she will go on wreaking vengeance unless she can be appeased by propitiations from the current senior clan-members (Redressors).

Note that both the Onons and the Merdens placated this girl spirit as an 'ancestor' (*hojoor*), although she could not have been an ancestor for either of them. The *DSHI* (1985: 250) provides a text which gives us a sense of how this spirit inhabited a whole landscape. The spirit was addressed as follows:

> From our ancient ancestors we have been sacrificing to you as a spirit.
> Speaking about where it came from
> The reasons have come from times long past
> Connected with the lands of the Bordered Yellow Banner.
> In Horli and Kaiko villages are the answers.
> [She] was hiding in the cliffs of Yisir
> Climbed high to the top of Gwaile rocks.
> In deep water there is a haft
> In the green water there is a lock and chain
> In the clear deep water there is a sitting-place.
> [Her soul] transformed from the comb-box
> [It] became a spirit emerging from the red cover of the vanity-case
> Flew out as a red coloured house-sparrow
> Jumped and played with the carp
> Became the companion of the silver Crucian carp
> Lived in the rocky mountains of Arhachien
> Wandered round the cliffs of Nirgi.
> [It] made a connection with the seven Merden clans
> Spreading to the nine Mushi branches of the maternal ancestors
> Became the Dobuchien clan's female deity
> Commander of ten lineages
> The origin of twenty families
> Her soul became an *onggor*.

The meaning of some of this remains unclear, but the sense is conveyed that the spirit was all about, in the water, in the cliffs, in the small birds, in the fishes, in the ancestors. All the places mentioned were local sites. But unlike the genii of the landscape discussed in 2.1 this spirit was not about these objects, which were merely its temporary haunting sites, but rather it represented a distinct socio-psychological nexus of concerns, that is, the impossible shame for the Onons of giving away a bride who was pregnant, the loss for the Merdens who did not save her, and the plight of the girl herself (whose self-mutilation was necessary for her to become a spirit).

The old lady at Horli told me about the origin of another spirit, the *hojoor* of Kaliertü village.[3] I introduce this to show that the burden of ongoing spirit punishment concerned not only interpersonal relations but also wider ethnic and religious ones.

There was a lama, Rinchin, who impressed our Daurs quite a lot. He used to read scriptures when the senior people invited him. But younger people were cruel to him. One day he mounted his horse. People asked him what he was going to do, and he replied, 'You needn't look for me, ever.' He rode towards the hill. The old people didn't want him to go. They thought, he had been a lama for so many years, how could they let him go in silence? They said, 'Go and find him quickly', and dispatched eight people on horseback to persuade him to come back. When they arrived they found the lama had died while sitting and reading the scriptures. They didn't want to leave him that way, so they took a lot of grass, piled it up and burnt him. This burning transformed his soul into Kaliertü's *hojoor*.

Sain Tanaa (1987*a*: 68–9) writes about this *hojoor*:

A widow lived in Kaliertü village and she had a bondsman to do odd jobs around the house. One day in the vegetable field, on a clear sunny day, a black cloud suddenly appeared, with thunder and lightning. It hovered over the widow, turning nine times round her, and then went away. She was terrified, but unharmed. Three years later she had a son. The baby was covered with boils all over its body, and furthermore as soon as he was born he could walk and talk. 'Is it a human or a devil?' people wondered. They decided to kill him, took some grass and firewood to the mountains, piled it up, and burnt him alive. Just as the child stopped breathing a column of black smoke came out and soon it turned to white steam, reaching to the sky. Soon some Tibetan lamas were on their way, looking for the reincarnation of a famous Gegeen. 'How come he could be born in such a remote mountainous place?' they thought. Riding their donkeys, they came to Kaliertü, where the boy had just been burned.[4] 'There is bad *feng-shui* here.'[5] When they found out what had happened, they were angry and stamped the ground, saying, 'You are very bad people. The Gegeen Lama was born in your place. He intended to protect you, but you have burned him to death. Your luck has run out.' When the old woman and the bondsman died the Kaliertü people made a shrine for this spirit, which they called Black Spirit (*hara barkan*), consisting of a painting of three people, the widow, the son at her breast, and the bondsman. They offer an ox and a cow every year, burn incense and kow-tow, begging the spirit not to attack them and to make them prosperous and give them children.

The ancestors ill-treated a widow and her son. Furthermore, they subjected the high representative of Buddhism to a horrible death. It is true that the story gives the ancestors several excuses—the child was covered in boils and very peculiar, it was born long after the mysterious thunderstorm, and the implication is that everyone would imagine it to have been the illegitimate son of the bondsman (Urgunge said, 'Of course she was having an affair with the bondsman, but no one would say so openly'). Nevertheless, a deed was done, and arbitrarily, inexorably, it turned out to have been wrong and dangerous. The people of Kaliertü suffered as a result, and knew they had to make continuous expensive sacrifices to redress the harm.

In this *barkan* not only kinship relations were at issue. Gleaming through the domestic tangle of the widow, the bondsman, the son, and the villagers is the sense of a historic act having been performed. After all, the Naun Daurs did reject Buddhism and went on rejecting it. The existence of the Black Spirit implies the fearful realization that people might have to suffer for this independence.[6] The burning of a corpse, as we have seen (5.2), was the treatment for external and polluted deaths; here it was given to the representative of the politically powerful religion of Buddhism.

These examples of the Onon, Merden, and Aul clan *hojoor*s show that shamans' spirits denoted individuals as exemplars of social categories, for example as exemplars of Buddhism or a given clan. Now the shaman normally belonged to the same clan as the Sufferer on whose behalf the performance was held. However, it must be admitted that this already complex situation became more complicated when the shaman was a woman. A woman was considered a member of her husband's clan, but on the other hand her origin was in her father's clan. Let us investigate this situation by returning to Huangge.

Huangge was socially unusual for a shaman: she was a woman when virtually all *yadgans* were men, and she came from an aristocratic family when most shamans were from poor families. People told me she could not read or write, but she was brave (*zorig-toi*) and wise. Her father used to discuss all important matters with her. She was good at housework, loved Peking opera and the Mongolian horsehair fiddle, and enjoyed playing mah-jong. She married a rich and cultivated official from the Denteke section of the Aul clan.[7] She did not give birth, but adopted one or two children. Though she was a quiet person in everyday life and it is said that her voice was not as good as that of Pingguo Yadgan, she was considered extremely powerful and held in high respect. People told me that this of course was not just a matter of her personality but because of her spirits. Though she married into the Aul clan and her shaman teacher was from the Merden clan, Hunagge's *hojoor* was that of her father's clan, the Gobol (see Fig. 6.2).

It may be remembered that when they married many women used to bring with them a placing for their father's clan spirit (5.1) This *naajil ayin* (spirit of the mother's father's clan or wife's father's clan) was kept separately from the husband's spirit placings.[8] If the wife fell ill this was said to be caused by the *naajil ayin* and therefore nothing to do with the husband or his clan. It was the wife's responsibility to keep the spirit in a good mood and make sure that it did not attack anyone in the husband's clan. The *naajil* images were thrown in a river or a field when a woman died. It was thought that after her death her children would no longer be vulnerable, since they belonged unequivocally to the husband's clan and were subject to his ancestor spirits. However, the wives (in effect all women) were liable to attacks from the *naajil ayin* throughout their lives, and according to Omachi (1949: 21) the husband's clan shamans washed their hands of all responsibility for their plight (see Tochingga story in 5.2 for an example of this).[9]

Now Huangge's *hojoor*, the red bird, must have been a *naajil ajin* for all the clans which had received Manna Gobol women as wives. Since the Manna was the most numerous clan in the Hailar region, this meant in effect that Huangge

was in demand not only in her (father's) clan but to protect women in every
other clan too.[10]

We can now see some structural reasons why Huangge rose to such prominence. As far as I know she was the only female *yadgan* to master a clan *hojoor*
in the Hailar district, and her aristocratic birth may have had something to do
with this. We can say, following Fortes (1953), that as a woman she was able to
master the spirit in 'complementary filiation' (*naajil barkan*) in relation to her
husband's clan. However, her situation was not without its conflicts. I was
assured very firmly by Aul people (Huangge's husband's clan) that Huangge
was 'ours'. However, she was by birth a Gobol, and this meant that from the
Aul point of view she was not their *clan* shaman.[11] She thus practised alongside
a separate line of *hojoor yadgan*s in her husband's clan, the redoubtable knife-
wielding Pingguo being the last of them (see 3.2).[12]

Now people told me that Pingguo and Huangge were friendly on the surface.
They sometimes danced together at the *ominan* with synchronized gestures,
like a chorus-line of two. In many ways their services must have been complementary, and certainly their *hojoor*s were very different from one another.

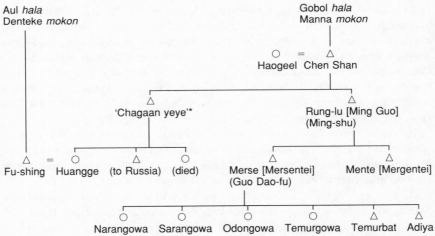

Fig. 6.2. The family of Huangge and Merse according to Odongowa. Around 1917, in
Rung-lu's absence, the family was subject to a terrible attack by Russian Cossacks. Both
Huangge's and Merse's mothers were killed, along with about ten children of the
extended family. For this reason Huangge and Merse were brought up together by their
grandmother, Haogeel. Huangge was very close to Merse's family and spent much time
with them even after she was married. Names used at home given in square brackets;
Chinese names in round brackets.

* *Chagaan yeye* means 'white grandad' and his given name is not known by Odongowa or Adiya (see 1.2).
Haogeel's name is only remembered by Odongowa because it was similar to the word for the colour pink,
haigee, for which she recalls having to substitute the term *chaivagar*, 'whitish' (on name taboos and substi-
tutions, see Humphrey 1978).

Huangge's Manna Gobol *hojoor* originated from a soldier who refused to fight for the Manchus (5.1); Pingguo's Denteke Aul *hojoor* was a young girl who was struck by lightning (Omachi 1949: 19–20). However, Huangge usually invited another shaman, a Solon from Butha, to dance with her, and Mendüsürüng hinted that she and Pingguo were rivals for prestige. Numerous stories show that affinal clans were typically on bad terms and that shamans fought one another to establish precedence.[13] Odongowa told me that Huangge's husband's relatives despised her shamanic powers and sought to represent her in public as 'just our daughter-in-law', i.e. a subjected person whose task was to work hard, bear sons, and keep quiet (Humphrey 1978). Despite these insults, Huangge became a beloved saviour for the people of many clans.

At the beginning of this section I suggested that shamanic practice set up knots of relationships. This was not quite just a metaphor. In the Hailar district the clients of a shaman would knot sacred scarves (*hadag*) or streamers of silk to the shaman's headdress or the costume (see Plate 18). The more senior and successful a shaman, the greater the number of streamers (*DSHI* 1985: 265). Pingguo, like other shamans, used to hold an annual purification rite for his clients on the 18th day of the first month. The entire clan would come to his house, tie scarves to his two 'journeying-sticks', and be splashed with purified water. A recent paper by Purev (1993) explains how significant knots were for Darhat shamans. They represented the relations between the shaman and the people around him so we should look more closely at their meaning. Among the Darhat Mongols and among the Daurs such streamers and cloth strips were called 'snakes' (*mog*).[14]

Purev (1993: 86–7) explains that a real snake was considered either a good or a bad omen, depending on a host of conditions such as its colour, direction of movement, or the time of the encounter. The snake-models, called *manjig*, were similarly labile in meaning, since they were tied on after a performance as a sign of what had happened and this could be 'good' (strengthening the life-energy of a child) or 'bad' (a black snake denoted 'fighting evil with evil'). They were knotted to the shaman's garment in groups, one set being permanently attached and the other added to from time to time. The permanent set represented the shaman's ties to the spirits. The latter group of *manjig*s was added to every time the shaman performed to save someone's life. It was subdivided into right, middle, and left clusters of *manjig*s, for services for clanspeople, for members of the shaman's family, and for outsiders, respectively. Further *manjig*s were added by other people, such as the teacher shaman or the shaman's parents, and on occasions such as when the drum was mended, when a child was born to the shaman, when an animal was slaughtered in propitiation and when the shaman was given livestock by grateful clients. The knots themselves were significant. Not only were there different knots for gifts of sheep, goats, cattle, and horses, but the number of twists in the knots showed the age and sex of the animal.

The knots had one major principle: those for the shaman's children and close relatives were firmly tied (many of them were in the permanent group), while those for the shaman had to come undone easily. This was because the shaman had to be free to obey the spirits and travel to another world. To quote a Darhat shaman (Purev 1993: 91): a shaman is the spirits' coachman and must stay if the word is 'stay!' and go if the command is 'go!' A spirit can call the coachman any time, which renders him dead, so the 'knots of the shaman's life' had to untie quickly. We can understand this as follows: the 'snakes' represented the various attachments people had to their shaman, which were like lifelines to them. But to save other people's lives the shaman had to be able to 'die', and this implied symbolically unloosing the knots which bound him to the world. He 'rode away', now attached only to the harness of the spirits. When he returned he was bound again by yet further ties, the *manjig*s of the gifts of the grateful survivors. Thus the shaman came to be a knot of knots, representing all the performances of a lifetime. For example, the shaman C. Khorol had 92 knots in her permanent set, and in her added-to set she had 114 knots to the right, 65 to the left, and 5 in the middle. These represented thirty-five years of shamanizing from 1925 to 1960, during which she had performed 93 times; received gifts of 23 sheep from her teacher, parents, and relatives; received 48 sheep and 15 horses from clients; offered goats six times to evil spirits; patched her drum six times and 'renewed' it twice (Purev 1993: 87–92).

Motivating the tangle of relationships were love and support, on the one hand, and the understood but unspoken forces of neglect, hurt, and anger on the other. The latter especially gave dynamic movement to what I started by representing as a static diagram. Michael Taussig (1987: 393) has described for people of the Putumayo the analogous force of envy as a 'constantly charged scanner' of implicit social knowledge:

Quite often in the Putumayo, listening to people in a healer's home talking about life and problems, I get the feeling that the sensitivity to envy is as ever-present and as necessary as the air we breathe. This sensitivity is not merely a foundation of what we might call shamanic discourse, organizing a sense of the real and of personhood; it can also be thought of as a sort of sixth-sense or antenna of what I call 'implicit social knowledge' slipping in and out of consciousness as a constantly charged scanner of the obtuse as well as the obvious features of social relatedness. Acquired through practices rather than through conscious learning, like one's native tongue, implicit social knowledge can be thought of as one of the dominant faculties of what it takes to be a social being.

The Daur sensitivity was less to envy than to hard-hearted neglect and its corollary, revenge, which moved inescapably through social life, from past hurts through the present and into the future. The cure of a patient by a shaman was thus never simply a cure but more like a drama-in-history, a revival of 'memories' which spread their tentacles into the present, giving the hue of ancient emotions to the present suffering. As Taussig writes, 'Envy is not so much the cause of sorcery and misfortune as it is the immanent discursive force for raking over the coals of events in search of the sense (and senselessness) of their sociability' (1987: 394). The shaman provided the public explanation. He could rearrange the jagged parts, sending back the spirit, 'tuning' (*nairuula-*) the multiplicity of twisted human relations, but everyone knew that this was only a brief respite, as the past had its momentum, caused by the endless activity, the blundering and the cruelties of the people in the past.

Shifting the causes for misfortune to the mythicized past had one notable effect. It meant that human relations at the present could be envisaged as harmonious, as if they really corresponded to the clan ideal. The relations of aggression were with the spirits.[15] Urgunge said, 'No one quarrelled in Daur [i.e. in his childhood]. You don't want to believe it, but you have a Western point of view. They dared not quarrel. Everyone knew their own limits [*kemee*], they followed the pattern [*keb*]. You could not show your anger; you clenched your teeth; you bore it. If someone acted beyond his limit [*ter kuu kemgui aashilaj baina*] that was very, very bad.' It was not that Urgunge thought humans are by nature good or moral, as we shall see, but anger was repressed and cast backwards to archetypal scenes. Only very old men could show their power [*kuchi ujiile*] by harsh words or action. For everyone else, there could be nothing more shameful than even a small sign of repressed anger, such as audibly gnashing one's teeth.

The power attributed to the spirit, I think, was thus related to the religious disempowering of the principle of everyday life, and to the generalization of the particularities and discontinuities of real anger. But in the actual practice of shamans the notion of spirits required also that this separation be overcome. The spirit would have been a groundless idea were it not repeatedly fed with real predicaments and complexities. The shaman was the medium by which this was done, and therefore she had to be tied with the people's knots—just as the knots had to be untie-able for the shaman to reach the existence-in-death of the spirit. Hence the strange, repeated, reversals of complexity this section has revealed: from one point of view the harmony of village life contrasted with the multifarious angers of the spirits, but if we look at how this situation was generated we can see that the *onggor* was imprisoned by its being a spirit. The *onggor* in the end was one thing, which could only be added to, and the source of the adding was ordinary life, with its terrible diverse accidents. But assimilation to the *onggor* meant another simplification. . . . All of this endless transformation back and forth was done without ideology, without there even being an explanation that it was going on, Rather it was done through practice, through the 'journey', the extended journey of death and the momentary journey of the shaman's performance.

6.2 Holieri, the Shattered Ancestor

Urgunge was looking forward to meeting his ancestors. Once he said,

They will recognize me. Many, many people are waiting for me. I see so many black heads. Sometimes I wonder whether there are white men's heads among them, and I don't know, but I think they are all black. My very ancient ancestors I can't see clearly, even though they are all my relatives. Five hundred years ago people must have been different from us. I always thought they were much bigger than I am, and physically more powerful. After all, could present-day men draw an ancient Mongol bow? I would like to meet my grandfather. He drank a lot, I heard. They also told me about his wonderful horse—it could jump such a high fence. And I want to meet my four sisters who died. I wonder if they will still tease me and call me *hwailag* [funeral horse]?

Behind this image of welcoming ancestors lay frightening glimpses of ancestral spirits, only recalled when some trouble threatened. The greatest of these was Holieri, the *hojoor* ancestor of virtually all Daur clans (Omachi 1949: 22; *DSHI* 1985: 283).[16] What I wish to convey in this section is not so much the multiplicity of the constituents of such spirits, which has already been described (5.1), but the nature of their agency in the representation of Daur history. Shamans used the discursive form of the song to reproduce their own idiosyncratic histories that were quite different from the genealogies and narratives of the elders. Although they might use the same idioms, such as ancestry and imperial power, shamans suffused these ideas with subversive content, thus creating a distinctive sense of identity for the people. Holieri presented, through shamanic performance, a landscape of the Daurs' place in imperial domination, their escape from it, and the reconstitution of supremacy in another, wilder form. Holieri relieved the madness and suffering it had itself caused. At the same time enacting its drama had, it seems, a creative, regenerative purpose.

The *onggor* and *hojoor* spirits described earlier were locally situated, without reference to the theme of universal balance, or the 'vertical' resonance of the subjective microcosm with the Sky, which so preoccupied Urgunge (2.1). With the *ominan* celebration of *yadgan* power we saw how the shamanic imagination engaged fitfully with those unifying modes of cosmology. Now with the Holieri spirit we are confronted by the shamanic engagement with the enactment of imperial power, as mediator between heaven and earth.

Here we can begin to address the fact that shamanic spirits arose and held sway within history. Holieri Barkan, Naun Daurs said, was given to them by the Tungus (Orochen) at some time in the very distant past. The Hailar Daurs took it up in the mid-nineteenth century (*DSHI* 1985: 244). Meanwhile, worship of a very similar and even earlier spirit of the Naun Daurs, Bogule Barkan, was only begun by the Hailar people in the 1890s, though this cult was later forbidden (*DSHI* 1985: 252).[17] From this information, limited as it is, it can be seen that spirit worship arose, changed and spread, and that along with the official disapproval of shamanizing in general, which intensified during the 1930s–1940s (Shirokogoroff 1935: 391; Heissig 1992: 198–214), certain spirit cults were considered sufficiently rebellious to be condemned specifically. This section describes the Holieri spirit as remembered by people in the 1950s–1970s, a period when shamanship was altogether forbidden. Since Urgunge had only the dimmest of memories of Holieri, I begin with his understanding of a spirit he took to be very similar, City Spirit (*Kotong Barkan*).[18]

With the decline of the Manchu Dynasty new 'outside' spirits began to appear among the Daur. Two of them were City Spirit and Barracks Spirit (*Kuarang Barkan*). They soon spread to every group and Urgunge remembers Kotong Barkan as the most important of the spirits his family kept for worship. They attacked adult men in the family, causing depression and bad luck. 'He must have been a big-shot ancestor,' said Urgunge. 'He went to Beijing in the army as a great general and was killed.' Kuarang Barkan was also said to have originated from a fox. My first interpretation was that the Daurs began to identify troubles in their villages with the negative feelings they now had about serving in city barracks for the weak and failing Manchu Dynasty. This spirit was not about the eternal fear of going to war, being wounded, and dying far from home, expressed in soldiers' ballads. Rather, in the lethargy and opium-soaked paranoia of soldiers in the early twentieth-century Manchu army (Crossley 1990) this spirit represented Daur apprehensions of the psychological trouble experienced by men who had served with, or identified with, the army.

Urgunge had a completely different interpretation. 'This spirit is to do with the Daurs' warrior tradition. We produced so many generals. This spirit shows our bravery.' When I asked, 'But why does the spirit harm brave men then?', Urgunge replied, 'Do you understand what is needed to be a leader? To be a leader you must have a rosary in your right hand,' and here he imitated a benignly mumbling lama at prayer. 'And in your left hand you must have a sharp knife. Fssst! If someone is no good, you must be able to chop him off!' Here he demonstrated a violent beheading. 'A *barkan* always has a cruel side. You cannot expect all good—that is a different religion.'

The disorder and darkness of our ancestral nature flowered in Holieri Barkan, which was widely considered to be a *hojoor*. *Hojoor* (ancestry, base, stem) was also an everyday word and I now look briefly at how it was used by Daurs in a significant political negotiation earlier this century. Three times between 1912 and 1930 the region of Hulun Buir (Barga), of which Hailar was the capital, became the location of brief independent governments. Lattimore observed, 'By virtue of their energy, capability and inherited tradition of official service, the Daghors have always tended to monopolize high official appointments in Barga. At the present time they dominate the tribal affairs of the whole region. . . . The leaders of all political parties are Daghor' (1934: 167–8). These nationalist and revolutionary developments will be discussed further in 7.3, but here I remind our readers that the idea of detaching the region from China to join up with Mongolia was a recurrent project. In 1912 Daurs from the Naun valley led by Myangbuu (Ch. Ming Bao), sent petitions to the new Outer Mongolian autonomous government, asking to be accepted as subjects in the greater Mongolian state. Myangbuu's letter uses the Mongolian ancestry of the Daurs (Mong. *izaguur*, Da. *hojoor*) as his claim to inclusion.[19]

Petition presented by Myangbuu and other high officials of Har Mørøn [Amur River] region desiring to submit to the Bogt Khaant [Holy Imperial] Mongol Nation.

My ancestor was the Crown Prince [*huangtaij*] of the Shuan-di Emperor of the Yuan Dynasty,[20] who retreated from the Ming army, and taking his body-guards came out of Yin-chang city and crossed over the Amur River and settled there. Because our people were from their origin [*ug*] engaged in hunting, we were called the 'hunter people' [*gørøøchin ard*]. Our tribal name was changed to Daguur. By origin [*izaguur*] my ancestors were camped at t⌐ ₋ river Onon and because of this we are named Onon.[21]

In the first year of the reign of Kevt Yos [1909] I myself and two hunters were chosen from the three cities[22] and we became provincial interpreter officials. We protected our higher and lower people in [legal] decisions, but the Chinese officials always exploited our people. Even though I, Myangbuu, was angry inside, there was nothing I could do but endure it, and the political situation changed dramatically and we have been suffering severely from the Chinese people. Because of this, I, Myangbuu, joined with Great Hailar and established a lawful army [*zurmyn tsereg*], and hereby I have informed the three cities that [I] would like to give our ancestral homeland [*ug nutag*] to the Holy Enlightened One [the Bogd Gegeen, theocratic ruler of Mongolia] and have him rule us.

As the matter is known to the Chinese officials, it is impossible not to take action, and because of this I shall come to have audience with you and present you with a petition. If possible, please bestow favour on me by accepting my people of the three cities and in doing this please accept the civil revolution of the Amur region; in order to repay your ten thousand favours we shall serve you far into the future as horses and dogs. Our regional administration is now in the hands of the Chinese, and the only reason for our petition is to obtain ruling power, a petition which we respectfully present and also beg the favour of your high-ranking officials.

The second year of the reign of Elevated by All [1912].

(*Mongolyn* 1982: 268–9)

In this document the words *ug* (root, base, origin, cause) and *izaguur* (stem, foundation, genesis, descent) are keys to Myangbuu's argument, being used to tie the Naun Daurs to Mongol Imperial ancestry, a homeland in Mongolia (the Onon River), and a non-Chinese occupation (hunting). Generally the word *hojoor* (*izaguur*) was used to refer to the ranks of undifferentiated patrilineal ancestors. Both *ug* and *hojoor* meant the base of a growing stem, and they were among a group of plant-related words including *undes* (roots) used as metaphors for ancestry. An old lady from Horli village said to me, '*Hojoor bol gyabyn ontsgoi gene*' ('The *hojoor* is the most important point of a genealogy they say').[23]

Myangbuu's letter shows that ancestry (*hojoor*) was also seen as a principle of attachment to the state, and thus also of a shift of loyalty from one polity to another. The Manchu–Mongolian understanding of the state was quite different from the European and was in some ways like the 'galactic polity' described by Tambiah (1985: 252–86) for south-east Asia. Rather than constructing sovereignty as an irreducible unity, enclosed by a single territorial boundary excluding that which was outside, and thus defining the independent polity by virtue of its recognition by other states similarly constructed on principles of unity and exclusion, the Manchu state operated through the successful encompassment of other centres of power. The emperor's task was the summation of the powers of other rulers within his own kingship. This sovereignty was enacted in Manchu Qing ceremonial practice of the obeisance audience (kowtow (*koutou*)), and Hevia (1994: 186) has argued that it 'manifested the generative powers of a superior to initiate, and the capacities of inferiors, through their actions, to bring to completion the sequence of events set in train by the emperor'. In Hevia's analysis the completing capacity of an inferior was crucial in the formation of such relationships, especially since 'the superior–inferior relation thus produced corresponds with the relationship fashioned in the Sacrifice to Heaven, where the emperor performs the "full *koutou*" acting as the inferior to a superior heaven' (1994: 186). During the Qing Dynasty the Daurs formed part of the inner ring of Manchu Banners, as opposed to the outer Mongolian Halh Banners. However, the peripheral geographical position of Hailar meant that it could as easily attach itself to the new expanding polity centred in Mongolia. I suggest that Myangbuu, as self-made leader of a small polity, sought inclusion in the proposed pan-Mongol state in this sense.

In point of fact, Myangbuu's use of the language of ancestry as legitimation for incorporation was archaic for 1912. The Mongol Bogd Khaan himself employed a Buddhist idiom, combined with a new rhetoric of autonomous governance. Be this as it may, the Holieri ancestry is a claim, and the Holieri shamanic performance can be seen as a rebellious drama within the general conception of inclusive sovereignty. Already anachronistic by Urgunge's childhood, the Holieri spirit performance brought into focus the hierarchical relations of the imperial court and transformed them to its own purposes. The spirit created a specifically shamanic understanding of Daur history, and perhaps this is why it lingered on in the imagination beyond the political institutions that gave rise to it.

Early in this century Holieri Barkan was the most generally recognized and most powerful of all Daur spirits. It was called *Da Barkan* ('great spirit').[24] Its placing consisted of a wooden box, with two doors or a curtain in front,

containing a series of carved objects, representing tens of spirit-parts (see Plate
22). The box was opened only at rituals to propitiate the spirit. Women were
not allowed to see it. People in Horli told me that it could also be made very
simply: one took a bit of wood in the shape of a human, broke it, and worshipped the parts. We shall see why both of these images, the multiform and the
broken, represent Holieri. The following is a story about this spirit recorded in
Morin Dawaa in the 1950s (*DSHI* 1985: 244–6):

In the great mountains of Tibet there was a huge rock. One day this rock was split
asunder by lightning, and from inside the rock there came an antelope. It went straight
to Shenyang [Mukden], where it began to harass the people.[25] The Manchu government
had it seized, placed in a bag of cow leather, and flung into the river. The strange
creature drifted down the river until it met the floor dragon, when the bag burst on the
dragon's horn. The antelope pushed its way out of the bag, gained the bank and once
more began to harass the people. The Manchu court again had it seized, again placed it
in a bag, and loading it onto the back of a horse, sent it off. The horse followed its nose
northwards to the Amur River, where it was captured by a tribe of wild Orochen.[26]
They thought there must be something very nice in the bag and opened it. The antelope
leapt out and began to wander in the nearby woods. Every time rain came or lightning
struck, it took refuge among that tribe of people. One time many people were killed, but
the deer escaped by sheer luck. The lightning chased it very hard and it escaped to
Butha. Where the Nomin River meets the Naun, near Eileer and Bitai villages, an
Evenk farmer was ploughing. When the antelope ran up by the farmer there was a great
crash of thunder and lightning and the antelope was smashed into ninety-nine pieces.
Since then the antelope's spirit and that of the farmer and all the animals struck by
lightning joined forces for haunting. This *barkan* was first recognised by the Orochen
and then by the Qing court.

People in Morin Dawaa told me that Holieri Barkan 'happened without people
being aware of it', that it came out of the Amur River, that it was ageless and
came about when Tengger-Gajir was formed.[27] The spirit was wild, but unlike
a real deer, was intrinsically harmful. The wild deer ancestor here was not a
peaceable subject of the state, but tried constantly to escape from it, using the
natural flow of rivers and the undirected wandering of a horse. Shattered by
lightning, the ancestor joined with the farmer and other living creatures to
harass the living, unifying the present way of life, farming, with hunting in a
universal vision. It was as though the wild part of what we are superseded all
others, forcing them to join the destructive chase, such that, in the end, even
the epitome of order and hierarchical society, the Manchu Court, had to
acknowledge its power. The following was the shaman's invocation to Holieri
barkan:[28]

> At the pole of the earth is the home of the spirits.
> Before Niang-Niang Goddess was discovered
> The sacred seat was established at the end of the earth
> By the Ji Shilka River

Appearing in the waves at the source of the Ergune River
By the cliff at the spur of Shenchile Mountain
At the source of the Shenge spring;
[He] makes his home in the cave of Souchi Mountain
With pines and cypresses as the walls
A flagpole of Korean ('red') pine,
Bedding made of fragrant shrub leaves
[He] has ninety-nine yurts.
Struck by lightning nine times
Those hit are smashed to pieces
And become the Half ones—Cut-off ones [Koletardi-Kaletardi].
Those hit are broken up
And became the Black ones—Frozen ones, [Kalani-Kachani].
Wherever they began to grow in power
Their origin land is the Amur River.
Following down the Jingchile River
Bringing the *birji* [clans] together[29]
Gathering all the different kinds of living creatures
Aiming at the Southern Sea as their destination;
An island in the sea was prepared as their home.
Going to the birthplace of the Dalai Lama
Raiding the city of Beijing
Occupying the seat of orthodoxy,
A loud voice singing in the palace
A piece of jade, a precious stone on the heated bed
This is the resting place of the real pearl, the master pearl.
Gaining strength from there and moving on
Crossing all borders and provinces
[It] again reached the Solon and Daur.
Worshipped in this house
Stood on the north-western wall
Given a three-seated shrine
It has a plough as its seat,
It is hidden in the plough mirror[30]
The *dalaile* is in its original place.[31]
With offerings to the two dragons
With a precious seat of the two dragons
With all kinds of satins, damasks and silks
Silk offering-scarves of all colours
Sitting in a robe of Mongolian grass
Wrapped in costly satins
Trampling the clean satin.
Laquered and decorated with figures
There are carved statues
Cut out of Korean pine
Fashioned from poplar [namely]
Hunchback and Swayback ones (Bukogaier-Takagaier)

Half and Cut-off ones (Koletardi-Kaletardi)
Black and Frozen ones (Kalani-Kachani)
The ones with no eyes (Semorken-Kentele)
Babukai-Batulu[32]
Baolodi-Bukuo.
Where the rivers all flow together
Where they flow down is a dug-out canoe
Tossing here and there against the waves.
The Orochen people in the dense forest
Kill the boar and are skilful hunters [but]
[These are] the tracks they cannot find
The footprints they do not see
The gold-coloured tortoise
The silver-coloured frog
A buzzing angry wasp
A spider crawling back and forth
Wriggling lizards and snakes
The sound of a shaken bell
A cuckoo calling loudly
A leopard growling
A huge and fearless wild boar . . .

Of all shamanic spirits it is Holieri who most clearly fuses the song with the idea of journey. Its home was at the pole of the earth which was somehow at the same time located at a series of real rivers, tributaries of the Amur (i.e. the homeland of the Daurs before the seventeenth-century move to the Naun). It is not clear how this was related to the secluded and pleasant encampment with the pine flagpole, but the shattering of this place by lightning produced the vengeful onward movement of the spirit. The song established a riverine landscape (as opposed to the mountain-centred landscape of the *oboo* rituals). The spirit travelled by river, collecting clansmen and animals as it went, and then penetrated to the heart of the state, exulting in the honour accorded it.[33] Effortlessly crossing all boundaries it spread outwards again, reaching the Solon and Daur, where it fetched up in the plough mirror, but it was also unattainably everywhere—even the Orochen master hunters could not track it down. Thus its trace (*mor*) criss-crossed the world, from the pole to the capital city, and every kind of living creature was vulnerable to it.[34] It should also be pointed out that lightning was the manifestation of the anger of heaven. But what did it mean to say that this creature, appearing from the end of the earth, an animal and half-Tungus (Solon, Orochen, and Evenk are all names for Tungus groups) was 'our ancestor'?

    To answer this question we must look at the full contents of the 'seats' of Holieri ancestors, that is, the material forms taken by the spirit (see Plate 22). In one example the first fifteen items were carved from willow wood and the last two were made from cloth.[35] They comprised: (1) nine Manggee spirits, (2) a

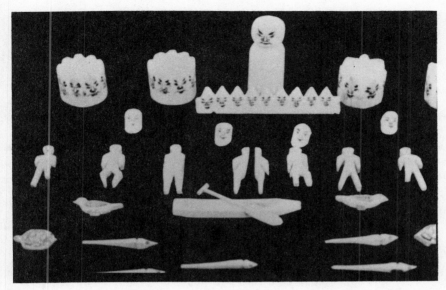

22. A version of the Holieri *barkan*, also called Hwaimar *barkan* (deity of the respected section of the house). Carved in wood. It comprises according to its owner, from top to bottom: nameless spirit; four round nine-headed *manggee* (monsters); a horizontal nine-headed *manggee*; four small head-only *manggee*; seven damaged people (lame, *doglong*; crippled, *pachel*; armless; half-people, *koltegin*; hunchback; another cripple; another lame person); two birds (*degi*); a boat with paddle; two turtles (*kabile*); and several fish. The owner said that the *barkan* should include Keiden, see 5.8, and some tigers. Photo: Morin Dawaa 1987, C. Humphrey. [6.2]

nine-headed Manggee, (3) nine human skulls, (4) a bent-backwards human with two spirits, (5) a hunchback person with two spirits, (6) black-frozen person with two spirits, (7) two halves of a person struck by lightning, (8) a single leg, from the buttock to the sole of the foot, (9) two golden turtles, (10) two silver frogs, (11) two people with no eyes, (12) a notched wooden stick for keeping records, with one spirit, (13) two cuckoos, (14) wooden livestock pens, made of nine wooden stakes each with its own spirit, (15) a hunting gun, with one spirit, (16) two dragons, one strong and one stubborn, (17) nine dancing boys and nine dancing girls (*DSHI* 1985: 246; Wu 1989*a*: 154–8). This great complex thus included humans, animals, birds, aquatic creatures, artefacts, and mythic beings—in other words, this was a comprehensive vision which went beyond the specific social tragedies of lesser ancestor spirits to create a world in which each category of knowledge was made occult and presented a possible danger.

Chesnov's observations on the dragon are relevant here.[36] In the Chinese tradition the dragon was not a simple mythic animal but a creature of maximal differentiation: it had the head of a camel, the neck of a snake, the claws of an eagle, the scales of a carp, the belly of a mollusc, the paws of a tiger, the ears of a cow, the horns of a deer, and the eyes of a demon. Chesnov (1986: 60–1) writes:

In Siberian societies animals or plants with some anomaly are attributed with super-natural qualities, giving life. Such animals give success, and the plants or objects are used as amulets. At the basis of all these ideas is the attempt to express, through the *singular*, i.e. the departure from the norm, the *maximally universal*—the principle of life itself. The image, externally consisting of functionally and 'genetically' different parts, represents the principle of the universality of life and its unity. . . . The cutting up of the carcass of a wild animal gives at the same time the possibility of creative (productive) articulation of its parts. (emphasis added)

Chesnov is suggesting here that the very diversity and divisibility of the dragon is, like the dismembered carcass reassembled at a sacrifice, an allusion to the universality of supernatural life and to the ritual means whereby to create it. It seems to me that the conception of Holieri was similar to this idea. Self-identity was not located inside a unique bounded 'we' but shattered outwards to embrace all forms including the broken, the imperfect, and the humble. We can see how such an image of ancestry was 'life-creating' if we remember the relational concept of the soul, if we recognize the Daur idea that identity-agency could be found in all things, and the shamanic idea that the breaking of the everyday material form set free the existence of the spirit. The dynamic process of Holieri ancestor, shattering apart, assembling together, and then fanning out invisibly into the creatures and sounds of the world, was absolutely different from the idea of the mountain *oboo*, which was a static point, binding together its similar components.

In its inclusive claims Holieri did not allude to the sky, nor to fire or mountains, the 'vertical' loci of the patriarchal cults. It specified its home as a cave, its protective walls as trees, and its way as rivers, all of which were ideas engaged with primarily in shamanic performance contexts. Nevertheless, it is evident that this spirit was a powerful actor in a world conceived as a political domain, and that it was destructive as well as creative. Kapferer's observation (1983: 127) about demons in Sri Lanka is relevant here. 'Demons, as conceived by exorcists, are dispersed, divided and fragmented by the power of the hierarchy and structure. They are scattered to all points of the compass. It is when demons are no longer subordinated in hierarchy that the demonic can assemble in its greatest power, and in its assemblage fragment, rather than be fragmented.' To get further in understanding the political and economic import of such ideas among the Daurs we need to look at the drama of performance itself. Here my information comes from Mendüsürüng (1983: 271–2) writing about the Hailar region, where Holieri was called Great Spirit, *Da Barkan*.

Many years ago the worship of this spirit was carried out by the Orochen people, and later for some reason the number of worshippers spread to the Hailar Daurs. I have heard many times that the Daurs living near the Amur River also worshipped it.

The sacrifices to this *barkan* were too heavy a burden. When the Orochen and Daurs were living on the Amur they never offered small livestock but only bulls, stallions and rams. Economically it was very hard to bear, and when they could not stand it any more, they threw the Great Spirit into the huge river.

The spirit-image floated on the current, but when it got to the Imen River near Hailar it went no further. The Aul clan people saw it and gathered together. They thought gold, silver and precious stones might be in the box. They took hooks and went to the Imen River and hooked out that box, but when they took just one look they discovered that inside were beautiful dragon robes of silk and satin, smeared [*milaa-* ('libated')] with blood.

The people loathed it extremely, bundled the whole thing back in the box, and pushed it into the river. But when it was pushed into the water, it would not float onwards. It turned round, they say. On this matter superstitious rumours spread like clouds and fog.

Just at this time, some men and women of the Aul clan fell ill and became crazy and deranged. A shaman was brought to diagnose, and it is said that he prophesied: 'Immediately bring back that floating god. If you do not make a sacrifice when you bring it back, the people's illness will not clear up.'

Then the people of the clan again hooked the spirit out of the river Imen and took it to the village where they made it their sacred religious object [*sitügen*] and sacrificed to it. The Aul clan Daurs went on sacrificing bulls, stallions and rams to Da Barkan for a long time. Then, when this began to be thought inexpedient and ruinous for the economy, they gradually began to use two-year old colts, two-year old calves and one-year old foals instead.

The entire population greatly worshipped the *barkan* and were greatly scared of it. During the sacrifice to Great Spirit, the shaman said, 'You must point out the most beautiful clothes of the ill person and bring them, and his favourite objects must be named, because devils [*ada chitgur*] have come into them, and you should offer them to the *barkan*.' According to the shaman's order the people took these items and offered them to the god.[37] 'Not only this,' the shaman said, 'but you must not wear clothes embroidered with dragons and flowers, nor should decorated silks and satins be used, no matter whether they are men's or women's. If you have these things you should offer them to the *barkan*. Also, during the New Year festival and weddings, the best part of the most delicious foods should be sacrificed to Great Spirit first of all.' The families of that clan kept good this instruction for generations and handed it down.

To this account it can be added that the spirit's song in the Hailar region was largely in the Orochen language and was difficult to understand, that nine boys (*noon*) and nine girls (*uyin*) were involved in dancing and making offerings, and that Da Barkan had its own ritualist (*bagchi*) who helped the shaman in the very complex and expensive performance (Omachi 1949: 27). Odongowa demonstrated the dance to me as a kind of bouncing or leaping, and she said it was called *mudur zasa* (literally 'to put right the dragon'), which can be interpreted as a joyful dance of thankfulness for the life-creating aspect of Holieri ancestry.

Urgunge's interpretation was that the Da Barkan performance was a kind of subversive mimicry of the Manchu state ritual. Specifically he referred to the reception by the emperor of subjects and envoys who would perform the *koutou* and bear tribute, in response to which the emperor would make bestowals to the guests. Now, as mentioned earlier, this ritual, carried out in sumptuous splendour, was an interaction, a nuanced negotiation of imperial power. Hevia has argued (1994: 193–4) that the reception of tribute, comprising the most precious things of the domain commanded by the inferior, implied imperial recognition of the specific attributes of the subject domain. This acknowledgement was completed by the bestowals in return from the emperor.

The shaman instructed people to render not only their oxen and horses but also their ceremonial silk clothing to the spirit. How should we understand this? The Daur worshippers constructed an 'imperial' glory, but it was that of the spirit, not of the Manchu state. Raiding the city of Beijing and singing in the palace, the spirit vaunted its high-handed masterfulness. Reaching Daur lands, the spirit itself was wrapped in dragon robes, seated on a dragon throne, and given offerings. But the trampling on clean satins and the robe of Mongolian grass turned the elegant relations of the court on their head. Zito (1994: 115) has described how the dragon robes of the Manchu emperor were covered with cosmic signs, with mountains represented jutting into a cloud-filled sky where dragons fly. 'When the robe was worn and the head emerged above the clouds on the collar, the observer was presented with a mobile microcosm of the . . . universe.' The emperor's exercise of encompassing and hierarchizing contrasting categories, which Zito calls 'centering', was done through creating interfaces which were charged with significance. The dragon robes were one such boundary domain, a site of emergent significance, coextensive with the skin. As we saw with the shaman's costume too, in the case of the Manchu emperor 'the "centering" action of the self through the body paradoxically takes place at its edges, on its surfaces and through its senses, which act as gates to the outside' (Zito 1994: 117). The construction of the body as an interfacing membrane depended for its power on interaction with others, the regard of acknowledgement. Holieri's song alluded to all this but insisted on another reality, since the body inside the robes was that of an animal or half-people, and the robes themselves were trampled.

We should not be surprised that spirit performances like those for Holieri were forbidden by the state, since Manchu imperial ritual was not 'symbolic', i.e. referring to another reality, but was in fact the enactment of power relations (Hevia 1994; Zito 1994). It is important, furthermore, that the subject participants in the court ritual also wore dragon robes, thus pointing, in the continuity between the emperor's clothing and that of his entourage, to the emperor as exemplar (of filial piety, of human perfection before heaven). Daurs were participants in state ritual both in Beijing and in regional centres.[38] Thus the Daur shaman's injunction that people must not keep their silks and satins was a direct call to transfer loyalty to the spirit. At the same time the silks and satins became tribute to the spirit—tribute already referred to in the heavy burden of providing horses and cattle for the propitiation.[39] Several authors have shown how the peoples of North Asia in the early twentieth century allowed the inflation of spirit demands for propitiations to reach intolerable levels, and how this resulted often in the abandonment of these spirits, together with terrible anxiety about the consequences of doing so (Shirokogoroff 1935: 389–90; Mikhailov 1987: 176; Kosokov 1930: 70).[40]

Yet all this was not really an outright rejection of hierarchy and the imperial idea. People like the Daurs, peripheral 'tribes' in great empires at the beginning of this century, may have nevertheless kept some deep awareness of earlier times when they themselves were at the centre of imperial domains (Humphrey 1994*b*). The remote ancestors of Daurs may have been the ruling clan of the Khitan Liao dynasty. It is interesting that the Daur writer Batubayin (1990) looked for a 'real' ancestor as the origin of Holieri, and found one in a martial hero, Kuler (i.e. Holier), who led his people to the north after the Liao Dynasty was overthrown. However, if contemplation of the deep past suggested such heroic images to Batubayin, the content of Holieri as enacted in this century surely also showed a sense of betrayal by history. Perhaps the representations of 'loyal subject' peoples in great empires have been too little studied. The Holieri spirit, simultaneously spurning the Manchus and usurping their imperial prerogatives, seems to have proclaimed the inevitability of there being a tyrannical power and the necessity of subjecting oneself to it. The people tried to get rid of the spirit too. Mendüsürüng's account shows that in the end there was recognition of the relation between the economic burdens of providing for the spirit and the lifting and falling of the sufferings caused by it. But the Holieri spirit went further than mimicry of the state. In the shamanic vision, escape from the Manchus constructed something different, a spiritual battle of force against force in a wider, and at the same time more intimate, realm than that of the historical state. To understand this it is once again necessary to look again at the idea of ancestry.

Shirokogoroff (1935: 145–6) makes a categorical distinction in the concept of ancestry between the Tungus cultures and the Manchus. Among the various Tungus groups ancestors might plague the living because their souls were unable to reach the 'other world', or they became demons (*hutu*) of a collective type, or pitiful irritating ghosts, but they did not become named, worshipped deities of the Holieri type. The idea of *hojoor* was absent among the Tungus, it seems, and though they had many complex spirits these were not thought of as ancestors. Among the urban Manchus, on the other hand, real male forebears became worshipped spirits, were given 'placings' and their names written on the secret lists of clan spirits. These lists gave prominence to the names of great historical heroes, such as Nurhaci, while the myriad mythic spirits, such as 'Heaven's Children', 'Golden Buddha', or 'White Pheasant' were no more than stereotyped images without much significance.[41]

Thus the metropolitan Manchus 'reduced' the ancestors operative in their rituals to the patrilineal genealogy studded with real historical personages. This is explainable, not just from the influence of Chinese ancestor worship, but also by the imperial necessities of standardizing the rituals of a people holding on to a tenuous hierarchical status as rulers of a vast cosmopolitan empire (Fu 1993: 244; Humphrey 1994*a*). The Daurs adopted a position between that of the Tungus and the Manchus. On the one hand, like the Tungus, they made almost nothing, in shamanic practice, of their own real patrilineal ancestors and they reached for a lateral, inclusive, and metamorphic idea of what an ancestor might be, but on the other, like Manchus, they framed history in terms of ancestry.

Who were the 'ancestors' Daurs honoured? The answer is a litany of the misfortunate and the hunted: a neglected young wife (Merden clan *hojoor*), a young man who refused to fight in the Imperial army (Manna clan *hojoor*), a harshly-treated servant girl (in Huangge's *onggor*), two brothers lost in the mountains and killed by lightning (Onon clan *hojoor*), the illegitimate son of a bondsman or rejected lama (Kaliertü village *hojoor*), a mother forgotten by her sons (Merden Eteuw *hojoor*), a Chinese girl bondswoman (Merden Eteuw *hojoor*), a widow who commited adultery (Wushi Barkan), a girl who became pregnant before marriage, and women killed in war (Shi Ewoche and Wuhiken Ewoche). It must be significant that the Daurs, living in the very region set aside by the Manchus as their hunting-grounds, imagined their greatest ancestor as a pursued deer.

Shamanic thought thus systematically negated the patriarchal version of smoothly succeeding ancestral generations. It encompassed all people and indeed all natural phenomena as ancestral, and the Holieri performance evoked this diversity to replace the state as a statement of identity. Yet these spirit cults were not mere 'imaginings' but the refracted recall of events believed to have happened. Even Urgunge, the arch-sceptic, was convinced of the historical nature of the riverine journey of his Onon ancestor Chipaatii to obtain recognition from the emperor at Mukden. Pain was part of this reality and at the same time it was frightening and a source of power. Readers may remember that the journey was made after Chipaatii's legs had been cut off (2.1). Severed legs appeared not only in Holieri but also in the Onon clan *hojoor* spirit (5.1), and Urgunge remembers Du Yadgan enacting the 'lameness' of his ancestor-spirit. The idea of 'broken' forebears could be reduced to the most laconic sign: as the woman said to me, just take an ordinary stick and break it, and that represents Holieri, the most powerful ancestor.

Among the carved images in the Holieri shrine-box were several not yet mentioned. The most numerous single type was the 'Manggee' and 'Nine-headed Manggee'. *Manggee*, as briefly mentioned earlier, were frequently encountered in Daur stories: they were hairy monsters who lived in the wild and appeared at night to rob and pillage and eat people's flesh. At one point in our conversations I conceived the idea that Manggee might be a metaphorical way of talking about bandits. I was encouraged in this idea by a Daur scholar, Nima, who said that Manggee stories in Inner Mongolia were told on particular occasions, when men and livestock were attacked by robbers on the way to a new camp, or 'when life became intolerable'. The telling of the monster story itself had magical powers, and the story-tellers acted wildly, violently breaking their way into the house and onto the heated bed, shaking the house wall, using a knife as the bridge of their fiddles, bringing a pack-saddle to sit on on the bed, and acting so roughly it made the children cry. Nima said that this kind of action was necessary to subdue the monsters. I put the idea that *Manggee* were supernatural bandits to Urgunge. But he replied,

In my view the word *manggee* has two meanings. *Manggee* means monster, but *manggee* also means the one with ability. The Daurs say, '*Ter ku shih manggee*' ('that is a very capable man'). The idea that *manggee* must be a bandit is completely wrong. It can be anybody. Now why are you looking so puzzled? I'll explain it to you this way. Once I said a very clever thing to Brian Moser and he called me a devil. He actually said to me, 'You're a devil!' What does that expression mean to the mind of the English? Is it good or bad? Of course it means that clever man and devil are the same idea. I have told you this before. Look at me, no, look properly at me—you think Urgunge is a nice guy? At the same time, I am not good, I can easily make you cry. *Manggee* is that part of human nature.

I have repeated this point of Urgunge's because it took me a long time to see its implications. The images that make up the spirit seem as though they are defined explicitly as 'not us'; that is, they look like everything that is outside or excluded from Daur male-defined society. But this is not so, Urgunge was saying: on the contrary they *are us*, in the punished-aggressive part of our nature.

There is, however, one last twist to our account of this most complex of spirits. The people of the Aul clan were terrified and disgusted to find the clothes in the box spattered with blood. I asked Urgunge why the blood in the floating box was so horrifying, and he replied, 'Oh, because you don't know what kind of blood it is.' He thought for a while and continued, 'These clothes must have been ritually anointed with blood.' He reminded me that in Mongolian culture, when anything is used for the first time, a yurt, or clothes or a gun, it is anointed (*milaa-*) with various liquids, including blood. So when people first wore their specially made new festive clothes at the Daur New Year celebrations, they bit their thumbs when putting them on, otherwise they would not be considered properly initiated. The blooding of something with one's own blood was to make it one's own, and the hatefulness of the box of clothes was that the blood was unknown and foreign. But the Da Barkan would not go away; inescapably it was the ancestor, and thus we ourselves, the descendants of the ancestor, were worshipping this thing which was contaminated by (our) foreign blood. There was nothing we could do about this. Alienness came to us with the flowing down of the river. We threw it back in the river, but still it circled round.

Of course, unstated in all of this, absolutely not mentioned in this entire elaborate construction of Holieri ancestry, were the real physical ancestors who were foreign and yet give birth to the clanspeople amid polluting blood. The next three sections discuss women in the shamanic cults of the Daurs.

6.3 Ome Niang-Niang, Womb Goddess in the Sky

So far this book has been concerned mainly with understandings of the world in the *yadgan* shaman's perspective. But there was another whole area of 'shamanism', the *otoshi* shaman's cult of Ome Barkan, also known as Sky Niang-Niang, which was practised almost entirely by women. Ome Barkan was concerned with procreation. This cult was not only universal among the Daurs, but similar ideas were found widely across Inner Asia, from the Altai in the west to the Lower Amur in the east. Interestingly they seem not to have been present in Halh Mongolia or in Ordos, regions where Mongolian state traditions and Buddhism were strongest. I shall suggest that the Ome cult proposed an understanding of the origin of life that was antithetical to the reified 'reproduction' of society that went on at *oboo* ceremonies. It was also different from the *yadgan*'s cults, which, as was shown in 5.8, only hesitantly concerned themselves with 'birth' at the *ominan* and were really more concerned with the struggles of adult lives.

The Ome Niang-Niang cults created the most celestial images of all, but Eliade ignores them, mentioning only 'reductions' of earlier beliefs in a Supreme Being of the Sky whom he assumes to have been male ([1951] 1964: 505). Other standard works, on which the secondary anthropological literature has been based, have also failed to give these cults their due.[42] Perhaps it would not be worth mentioning this omission were it not that it matches the partial view taken of 'shamanism' by some native people (like Urgunge in a certain frame of mind). The Daur woman writer Odongowa, on the other hand, produces a different perspective in which the cult of Ome is central.

In some ways the Niang-Niang cults in Inner Mongolia might seem to fit Lewis's ideas (1971: 88) concerning possession as an oblique protest strategy by women against their exclusion from full social and political participation. Lewis's model of 'peripheral possession' depicts women (and deprived men) as marginal to society and therefore more likely to be subject to compensatory neurotic and hysterical attacks than upstanding men. In Inner Mongolia the

Ome cults were to some extent marginalized by being called 'Chinese' and by according the *otoshi* less prestige than the *yadgan*. However, the Ome Niang-Niang cult was extremely powerful and was not simply a matter of involuntary possession but involved full shamanic manipulation of spirits. In any case, I do not believe that the sociological aspects of shamanic cults can explain them. These cults were concerned with bringing children into the world and ensuring their health, i.e. with a particular interpretation of life and a particular cosmology, and in this they took their place among alternative views. It seems that their sexual aspects were particularly abhorrent to Buddhism as interpreted in Inner Asia and were long ago destroyed in its heartlands, though lamas' struggles against them went on in places like Buryatia (Humphrey 1995).

What made the Ome Niang-Niang tradition so powerful, I suggest, was not only that it transcended sexually confining rules, pollution concepts, and patriarchal pressures, but that it also created an image of startling antinomy. Ome Niang-Niang combined the images of fertility and healthy nurture with their opposite, internally diseased children and death (the diseases were of the infectious *huar*, smallpox, type[43]). Furthermore, Ome Niang-Niang was said to reign in the sky, a 'fact' only reluctantly recognized by Daurs like Urgunge who preferred a different cosmological vision.

In Urgunge's region the cult of Ome Niang-Niang was invariably in the hands of the *otoshi*, who was always a woman. *Yadgan*s did not take part in the Niang-Niang cults. Indeed, Ikeshiri writes that were a *yadgan* to invoke these spirits the patient would get worse and die (1943: 60).[44] In Hailar the outlines were less clear, since not all *otoshi*s were women, just as not all *yadgan*s were men. Furthermore, it was possible for a practitioner to be both a *yadgan* and an *otoshi* at the same time, though in such a case the two traditions were kept separate.[45] Even if in Hailar Niang-Niang was sometimes invoked by a male shaman, it must be right to see these as a separate and female-oriented set of visions. But rather than giving us women's view only of women, they composed women's view of being human.

Thus the spirits cultivated in the *yadgan* and *otoshi* traditions were different visions of the human condition, which were associated predominantly with male and female shamans, respectively. Hamayon (1984) has asked, 'Is there a typically female exercise of shamanism in patrilinear societies such as the Buryat?' Her answer is that there was not. Because men and women had different social positions, becoming a shaman for a woman brought prestige and was more socially liberating than was the case for a man. However, for both men and women shamanic practice involved crossing boundaries and acquiring characteristics associated with the other sex. In this, we can say that the *otoshi* tradition was similar to that of the *yadgan*. The difference lay in the imagery of the spirits, which created contrasting fields of causality. The *yadgan*'s spirits were imagined in the terrestrial landscape of rivers, forests, hills, towns, and political institutions. His spirits were the 'reasons' (roots, causes, origins) for the constitution of society, both in its overt patriarchal form and its repressed and dominated aspects. Niang-Niang was envisaged above all in the sky, with images of airy turbulence, and this was the realm within which 'explanations' were given for physical human existence, the emergence of life, health, and infectious disease.

However, in the construction of the idea of 'shaman' the *otoshi* was in many ways similar to the *yadgan*. She was not attached to a clan, so in one village there could be several *otoshi*s and in another none. The *otoshi* could be married and have children. Like the *yadgan*, she was not buried in an ordinary grave-yard but was given a 'wind-burial' in a tree (Mergendi 1987: 306). The rite of public acknowledgement of a new *otoshi* was conducted by a senior *otoshi* at the house of the new shaman.[46] The *otoshi* 'inherited' an *onggor*, and again this was neither by patrilineal nor matrilineal descent but 'by will of the spirits'. In a reversal of the situation with *yadgan*s, whose *onggor*s were largely female, the *otoshi*'s *onggor* was usually male. Mendüsürüng told me this was an old man with a face pitted by smallpox. The *otoshi* could, it seems, also pretend to mastery of other spirits, as well as Niang-Niang. A woman in Horli remembered one *otoshi* as claiming the power of the banished Rinchen Lama spirit (see 6.1):

Horli's ancestry [*hojoor*] is from Lama Rinchen who was put into fire and became a spirit. He used to have a drum, and the *otoshi* held this drum in her hands, and around her neck were three sashes, one red, one green and one yellow. She wore a red and yellow skirt. She had a shaman's staff.[47] Her crown was carved like a flying bird (*guarad*). She put this on top of her cap, and at the back there were three tassels, green, yellow, and in the middle, red, crossing at the shoulders and hanging very long. The cap had something that looked like ears.[48]

Possibly *otoshi*s were sometimes rivals of *yadgan* shamans for influence over common clan spirits.

The particular division of labour between shamans I am describing here, it should be pointed out, was not the same all over Inner Asia. All ethnic groups had various kinds of shamans, and all had a range of spirits providing 'explanations' for aspects of life, but the link between a shaman of the *otoshi* type with the cult of female sky-spirits may have been specific to the Daurs (see n. 44 above). The sources are not clear on this point. What is important is that there were distinct cults of female fertility spirits, the keepers of the souls of unborn children, which were both extremely old (Potapov 1991: 37–9)[49] and very widespread in Inner Asia (Smolyak 1991: 124–8);[50] these spirits had their own iconography and rituals, and usually their own shamans specializing in their cult.[51]

Among the Daurs the *otoshi*'s competence was firmly based in the cult of a number of goddess-like *barkan*s, all entitled Niang-Niang. Urgunge remem-

bers all of them as just one spirit, Tengger Niang-Niang. Other Daurs
mentioned just one Niang-Niang too, but there were also a series of separate
Niang-Niangs with differentiating first names. The category of Niang-Niang
was more definitely subdivided than, for example Holieri, since the various
spirits dignified by the Niang-Niang title had their own names, histories, and
representations.

The name or title 'Niang-Niang' (Ch. 'mother-goddess'[52]) was almost certainly of Chinese origin, since cults of goddesses by this name were widespread
throughout China. Wu (1989*a*: 174–5) says that the Daurs substituted Niang-
Niang for two earlier *barkan* spirits called Shih Ewoche and Wuchiken Ewoche
('great mother' and 'small mother').[53] These were both names of diseases as well
as names of spirits.[54] It is not clear when, or why the name Niang-Niang was
introduced. However, though the name and the picture of the Daur 'goddesses'
(for want of a better term) may have been Chinese, there seems little else that
was Chinese about them. Perhaps the use of the Chinese title 'Niang-Niang' for
various Daur spirits may be quite old, the term being used essentially to mark
these spirits as feminine and 'alien'. This is in contrast to other Daur spirits,
where gender was systematically called into question.

Niang-Niang was the most highly respected of all Daur spirits, according to
Ikeshiri ([1943] 1982: 60), though Urgunge gave a short laugh when I mentioned this statement. In the wider East Asian context, Niang-Niang cults were
indeed highly popular, so let us briefly look at the Chinese and Tungus cults
which bore the same name. Cults of Niang-Niang goddesses were known all
over China (Sangren 1983) but were particularly fervently celebrated in Manchuria (Liu 1972). The Chinese cults have been described as basically Daoist,
with elements of 'nature-worship', Buddhism, and Christianity. The Niang-
Niang category in China included Hou-Tu, goddess of the earth, Xi Wang Mu,
queen mother of the West, and Guan Yin, the goddess of mercy, whose
worship is documented from ancient Han times. These cults had three major
concerns: (*a*) luck, riches, and longevity; (*b*) fertility; and (*c*) healing of diseases
(Liu 1972). Early this century the Chinese in Manchuria worshipped at least
four major Niang-Niang goddesses, together with numerous minor ones, each
of which had a particular function (guaranteeing birth, increasing the number
of births, delivering children safely, making the mother's milk flow, maintaining good eyesight, curing measles, smallpox, and so forth). In late Manchu
times there were 270–80 Niang-Niang temples in Manchuria, some of them
dating back at least to the seventeenth century. The annual celebration at a
large temple (1920s–1940s) would attract two or three hundred thousand devo-
tees, both men and women. They were by far the most popular festivals in the
region. Apart from offerings of incense, dumplings, fruit, etc. the cult activities
consisted of magical-propitiatory activities, such as receiving the goddess's
blessing on a doll, which was then taken home, and returned to the temple only
if a child was born. The festival involved a great market and fair, and this was

the only occasion in the year when women would leave home to have a good time. Whole families would go together (Liu 1972).

The Tungus N'ang-N'ang was very different. No temples or festivals were involved, and rituals took place at home. N'ang-N'ang was a complex *barkan* spirit associated with the sky, and there was in fact a term for 'sky' in several Tungus dialects and in Manchu which was phonetically similar to the Chinese title (T. *n'angn'a-n'angn'a*; Manchu *n'ayn'a*). It is probable that the sky-oriented cult existed from early times and was only recently identified for prestige reasons with the Chinese Niang-Niang goddess (Shirokogoroff 1935: 157). There were both male and female spirits in the complex, the latter comprising seventy-two manifestations which were identified with various diseases. Among the spirits under N'ang-N'ang was the dangerous Bushku (blood spirit, see 6.4) and a male group which was associated with foxes (see 6.6).

The Daur Niang-Niang cult was domestic, and in that sense similar to the Tungus (according to Urgunge, Daur women never went to Chinese temples or fairs). The spirit was worshipped at home, its vessel being a box with a purchased picture in the Chinese style inside (see Plate 23), or a home-made cloth figure with a white face in embroidered clothes. All families with children kept her image and she was often made the patroness of ailing children whose souls were entrusted to her. A woman from Hailar told me,

We never called her Niang-Niang but only Ome Barkan.[55] In her box we put her picture and a ball of rolled up first hair of the baby, all tied in red and yellow cloth,[56] and we made a tiny model of a cradle [*daadag*] from birch-bark and put it in too. A skilled seamstress would put in her best embroidery. This box was hung from a small tree which was put up in the south-eastern corner of the room.[57]

Odongowa (1991 n.d.: 8) adds:

In order to show that a child is born to the world through a mother's body they attached an inflated sheep-gut to Ome's white bag. During a sacrifice for Ome the Daurs took out all the items from the bag and hung them on a rope; in this way the shaman could represent [these aspects of] the spirit. Some people added to the bag cloth models of the twelve Duwalang animals or birds, together with eggs, chicks and the young of various creatures.

A Daur household might thus have had two sacred bags, the cow-stomach membrane containing the blessing from Heaven (4.2) and the sheep's gut representing human birth from the womb. However, these fleshly containers were each items in different assemblages, and although each set of ritual items referred to the Sky, the cosmologies involved were ritually separated. Thus the sacrifice to the Sky did not refer to Tengger Niang-Niang, while the women's 'supporting Heaven' ritual (see 4.2) was carried out using an idiom of purifica-

23. Ome Niang-Niang of the Sky surrounded with children, painted in colour on paper in Chinese style. This picture is kept by the door. Photo: Morin Dawaa, 1987, C. Humphrey. [6.3]

tion which, as we shall see, was characteristic of the sky goddess cults and not of the worship of Heaven as such.

What then was the iconography of the sky goddess? The woman from Hailar continued:

That box was one thing for summoning the soul. Then there was another way. A family would take some millet seeds [*ner budaa*] and sow them in water in a bowl. You covered the bowl with cloth and put it by Ome Barkan. Then you would come back and take a look, and you found the soul had left a footmark. I was so surprised! If you looked carefully you could see the seeds had changed shape and had some spots.

The theme of plant growth occurs also in Daur versions of the famous Nishan Shaman epic. The shaman-heroine made her journey to the nether world where she met Ome, who showed her around. As they walked about, the shaman asked, 'Why is that tree of yours so green and blooming?' Ome replied: 'It is the sign of the flourishing of the children of the human world.' 'And why is that tree so withered?' 'That tree is the sign of infertility, because those people, without cause or reason, burned the grass which was meant for cattle and horses' (Sain Tanaa 1987*b*: 98–9). Here the symbolism of the regenerating tree, which was muted at the *ominan*, was brought to the fore. If the *ominan* developed the idea of trees as perches or attractions for birds (carnivorous, attacking birds), the tree in the cult of Ome evoked a range of different images—the flourishing of leaves, the morphology of seed growth, and trees as places for nest-like containers for soul-eggs. Some Daurs told me that Ome's tree in the 'other world' was the site of metamorphosis where the souls of the dead were held in nests before turning round to re-enter the world of the living.[58] But why so many different trees? What was the relation between the *duwalang* trees, the *tooroo* mortuary tree of shamans, the trees stuck in the *oboo*, and Ome's tree? 'Shamanism' created such possible identities or fractures, but never directly answered such relational questions.

Ome Barkan (Niang-Niang), though considered to be 'good', could bitterly disappoint people. In this case she like other *barkans* could be jettisoned, and this is really to make the point that a relation with any shamanic spirit was a personal matter. It was like a dangerous friendship. I was given the strong impression that people would first approach this spirit themselves, using their own improvised words and prayers, only later inviting a shaman. If this failed, people could call on a different Niang-Niang spirit, on the suggestion of the shaman, and this practice may explain to some extent the very large number and overlapping character of these spirits. But abandoning a spirit was never done lightly. The same woman continued,

Ome Barkan was invited by my mother to make her children well and peaceful. But later the children died. Mother got very angry, 'What's the use of praying to you?' My mother's sons died. My three brothers, one was 6 years old, another was 4, another 2, they died of smallpox. My mother cried, 'You took my children one by one, so why should I pray to you?' and she stopped making sacrifices. But my mother became mentally ill from this (*soliyara-*). That was long ago, when I was only 5 or 6. My mother went mad and stopped offering, and then we moved to a different place.[59]

Despite their feminine title the Niang-Niang spirits could never be wholly 'female', because like other spirits of the Daurs they started with tragedies and consisted of whole 'journeys' or adventures in which other beings were absorbed on the way. Let me cite the example of *wenchin wushin* Niang-Niang. This spirit consisted of: three women thrown into a river to die, another female spirit, one male bone-setter, a lame red plough-ox, a sacrificial sheep tied to the 'Journey Sacred Tree' (*ayin tooroo*), nine snakes, and also the cave and forest inhabited by the fox spirit (*DSHI* 1985: 254). However, though the Niang-Niang spirits shared this syntactical complexity with other spirits, they constituted a different tradition in the sense that their agency in the world was always connected with specifically female processes of reproduction and nurture.

Ome was by far the most important of the Niang-Niang spirits. In the mythic vision Ome Ewe ('womb mother') was an old woman with snow white hair. She had a nine-storied pagoda sited among nine white felt tents, and in the court-yard were gold and silver pine trees, with male and female phoenix birds guarding the gate. Nine hot springs dashed out their water and from their source eggs appeared. Ome took the eggs from the springs and carried them on her back and held them in her bosom. She had such large and long breasts that she could 'throw her breast over her shoulder to feed the baby on her back, she could pull the breast through under her arm to feed the baby at her front'. There were many, many babies at her pavilion, playing with roe-deer ankle bones inlaid with gold and silver. When the babies grew a little Ome would spank their buttocks and say, 'Go' [to the human world and be born] (Odongowa 1991 n.d.: 7–8).[60] This mythical landscape of generative life was the 'other world' created by women, a bright equivalent of the dark, bureaucratized world of Irmu Khan's nether world (see 3.1). Males were notably absent.

I wish to convey here both the specificity of the iconography of this other world (springs, trees, eggs, birds), and the light-hearted tone in which it was described by Odongowa. Other simultaneously existing myths of the origin of human life were similarly good humoured. Readers may feel that such myths are the sort of item which should come right at the beginning of a book. But in the case of the Daurs this would not be right, since the generally held idea (before modern education) was that human beings, like everything else, had always been there. Therefore most tales of human origin were not really foundational and were often almost incidental, the chimera of 'human origin' being a good point on which to hang a moral. These origin stories were extraordinarily different from one another, as one might predict given the disjunctive nature of Daur cosmology. A woman in Hohhot told me (speaking in Mongolian),

H. I asked my mother how one person is lame, why someone has a crippled arm, why someone else has no eyes, and she replied, 'Why, if you rub your arm, does black stuff come out of your skin? Because human beings were first made of mud.'

C. How were they made of mud?

H. *Endur barkan* made them out of earth. There they were. Suddenly there was pouring rain, uhaa! Teeming rain. One by one the mud people were brought into the house; some had lost their legs, some their hands: they just broke off coming into the house. Ha. Ha. Because they were earth turned to soft mud, you see. So what is the point in washing every day if we are made of mud?

[Here she recollected she was talking to a foreigner and added a few things about how good it is to wash every day.]

C. How did the people come alive?

H. *Endur* made them alive. In hardening them out in the house he made them alive.[61] First they were dry and they had no life. Then the rain fell, so he brought them in, and then he dried them out and they became alive. Of course some of them had no legs and things.[62]

My respondent clearly kept this story in her fairy-tale compartment, but she was quite serious when she later talked about Ome Barkan. Evidently individual people found a personal relevance in different parts of the compendium of Daur 'beliefs' and they chose the genre which best expressed their own relation to the object of concern. So for this woman the broken mud people were just a tale, but as we have seen Holieri Barkan presented dramatically and poetically what was essentially the same vision of humanity, as maimed and damaged, passive subject to the fatal onslaughts of lightning and rain from the Sky. A similar shift in register, between the light-hearted and the desperately serious, occurred in the Ome cult. The people I talked to would smile at the mention of Ome's tremendous breasts, but her protection of real young children was another matter. In the crises for which her help was invoked there was a different, but equally terrible, vision of the human state. Here people were whole, but they were contaminated.

The shaman's songs for Ome Barkan were built on ambivalence. This was not only a matter of content (the one who gives us children is also the one who harms and infects them) but also appeared in the pragmatics of the shaman's singing, which had to draw in the patient, the redressor, the spirit, and the shaman's relation with them. The song had somehow both to represent disease (as subjectively felt) and be the shaman's 'objective' power to remove it. All of this resulted in a constant textual switching, of mood and stance, coming back again and again to particular motifs, perhaps in response to minute signs from the patient or the audience. Because the Ome chants were agents in this interrelational way they did not 'tell a story' or have a structure of their own.

Three invocations to Ome Niang-Niang are among the few shamans' song to be published in the Daur language, rather than in Mongolian or Chinese (Engkebatu 1985: 387–414). In written form they appear as 'lines' of three words, with the first and third words rhymed by the device of 'connecting of the heads', and a series of lines is linked by a common grammatical structure, such as a series of imperative verbs. This creates a cantering rhythm which leads on from line to line, occasionally being broken by the emphatic inter-polation of a four-word line. The ideas thus occur in 'blocks', and these blocks are repeated here and there, creating the mosaic-like switching mentioned above.

In the first shaman's invocation from the Horli region, the spirit was ad-dressed as follows. I have denoted by [R] lines which are repeated here and there in the song.[63]

> Though our prayers are simple,
> Our promises without prestige,
> In this our existence, [R]
> There is a child's torment, as you know. [R]
> [This] is a child's disease.
> [While we] suffer till senile old age,
> Who will harmonize the cause?
> From where has the suffering been aimed [at us]?
> From where has the craving [to attack] infected [us]? [R]
> Arisen in the family's house, [R]
> Staying on the western wall.
> The sacred great worshipped-one,
> Growing, swelling for ten thousand years.
> Ruling for a thousand years,
> Ome Wushi Beautiful Niang-Niang.
> I [shaman] shall rule Niang-Niang spirit.
> I will promise favour to you [R]
> I will search for peace for you [R]
> I will beg compassion for you [R]
> Connecting across your void.

(Engkebatu 1985: 387)

Ome Wushi Barkan was a compound spirit consisting of several people. I should explain the story: a widow committed adultery and bore a bastard. To protect her good name she killed the child. The baby's soul met fox and weasel spirits and greatly increased in spirit power. The picture (*nuwargan*) of the spirit consists of the child, its natural parents, the midwife who delivered it, and her husband (*DSHI* 1985: 253; Batubayin 1990; people in Hohhot and Horli). However, none of this was mentioned in the chant. The spirit was alternately begged and ordered to remove the disease, which was at the same time part of her own nature. Flattery, inducements, reasonable arguments—all were brought to bear. The spirit was firmly identified with a female role (cook and hearth-keeper).[64]

> Having alighted, thinking kindly,
> Having descended, thinking warmly,
> Do away with the things which have become raw!
> Cleanse the 'golden flower' [smallpox] [R]
> Banish the 'precious flower'
> O one with a 'noble flower' nature,
> O one with a 'lotus flower' seat,
> O *endur* worshipped by Solons,
> Cook and hearth-keeper.
> In this our existence
> Here—is a child's suffering.
> If this is truly your doing
> Relieve the sufferings you intended! [R]
> Unbind the pain you have brought! [R]
> Tear off your hot fever!
> Wake [him/her] from shivering cold!
> Stop your going and coming!
> Turn round from your penetration and flee!
> Clear the 'flu-like illness! [R]
> Collect up your typhoid-like infection! [R]
> Go away together with the sufferings! [R]
> [Our] aim is friendly accord,
> [You] tender, harmonizing living-being,
> [We] offer you the body of a living being,
> A huge yellow chicken,
> [We] lay before you its whole body,
> Offering you the breasts
> Laid out on the table below.
> If you become good tempered again
> [This] will fit your goal.
> Count the shares,
> Take them with good humour, [R]
> And when you find your own path,
> When you accomplish your intention,
> Release what you have taken!
> Forget your grudge against us!
> Restrain your treachery!
> Flay it without leaving a core!

(Engkebatu 1985: 387–400)

The shaman then recounted how she would set out on her journey, 'returning Ome Niang-Niang to the sky'. I have placed inverted commas here because it seems in the nature of such texts to be deeply unclear whether the shaman transitively 'returned' the spirit or whether she 'joined with' the spirit and took part in a double journey. I had asked Urgunge, 'Who is travelling on the crooked road?' and he replied, 'We don't know. There are no subjects in the sentences, so it is impossible to say.' I later came to see that my question was inappropriate. A Western rationality which requires, and therefore always searches for, the individual subject, sovereign of discrete actions, does not make sense here. This mystery was deliberate and central, since the shaman, the patient, and all the people present took part in the experiences of the spirit chanted and at the same time were observers of it. A subject indicator is present in one or two Eliadean lines, 'Putting on my bird skin I flew away', but elsewhere the reader should remember the absence of a grammatical subject, though this is almost impossible to render in intelligible English.

> Worshipping and speaking to soothe [you]
> [I] pacify and turn you back.
> I have promised my tribespeople to go
> On the Si-Mu Niang-Niang connection[65]
> On the Wang-Mu Niang-Niang track
> The blocked and crooked up road.
> The path which has changed direction [R]
> The column of the rising sun
> The pillar of the setting sun
> Beginning at the southern sea.
> [I have?] archive records at the sea island
> Genealogy at the four oceans.
> A sitting place at the *leker* sea.
> [I] have transformed the southern sea.
> Putting on my bird skin I have flown away
> Putting on my feather gown I have leapt out.
> [The one] with origin in the high sky [R]
> Has harmonized heaven to earth. [R]
> When [?you] strive towards the black earth
> [You] join up with the numberless clanspeople.
> [Your] source is the diseases of the year [R]
> [Your] origin the diseases of the season [R]
> The road which changed as it went out [R]
> Will transform in the red sacred vessel. [R][66]

The 'road' (Daur *mor* (track, spoor), or *wajin* (trail)) is a means of transformation and certainly not a simple way from A to B. Ome's road was a wandering circuit, going to the sky, or coming from it.[67] If this was 'ecstatic celestial flight' it was a nightmarish journey. Let us take up the second invocation.

> The origin starts and then twists,
> The fallen and crooked road,
> The source of the diseases of this time,

> The metamorphosis of the diseases of the year,
> The road which changed as soon as [?we] set out,
> The night wandering trail,
> The blocked off road,
> The narrow sunken path,
> Struggling from the wild steppe root-origin,
> Succeeding by the pure open steppe,
> The night disturbed wandering road,
> A breath of air hovered.
>
> (Engkebatu 1985: 405–6)

This theme of the difficult journey sung as the suffering patient lies before the shaman recalls Lévi-Strauss's well-known paper ([1949] 1967) in which the argument is made that the journey symbolically maps the pains of the woman in childbirth. The Daur shaman certainly implies that the track and the illnesses are transformed (*hobilsen*) and somehow related to one another. But I do not think that the Daur shamanic journey has quite the one-by-one analogical relation with a sequence of physical experiences proposed by Lévi-Strauss. The chant must involve switches of stance by the shaman. Having equivocally flown with the spirit down the twisting track, the shaman offers chickens, constructing them as as living substance (*bod*)[68] whose blood is equivalent to the blood of the patient, but ultimately to be separated from it.

> The chickens flap in the *koorin* (?)
> Flying chickens are nine living bodies,
> The chickens will fly by nines,
> We are offering living substance,
> Ascending by threes like arrows,
> Take them in the high mountain gorges!
> Separate the *dergen* (?) from the body!
> Gather up the living body! [R]
> Collect up the blood body! [R]
> Evaporate the bodies' bloods! [R]
> Keep the patient awake until [he/she] recovers,
> Go and fly over the spleen,
> And now when [you] have found [your] way,
> Now [you] have attained [your] aims,
> Having found the blood, separate [from it], [R]
> Having found the body, free [yourself], [R]
> Blow to the winds what you have placed there!
>
> (Engkebatu 1985: 404)

The separation of bloods is the cure. If this does not happen and the patient dies, the spirit is still attached to the body and must be made to return to the sky at a special burial ritual (Ikeshiri 1943: 61).[69] On the other hand, the chant evokes a widening and refiguring of suffering in an experience which culminates in metaphysical splendour. Severi (1987: 82) writes perceptively of a similar ceaseless interpenetration of different levels in Cuna shamanism:

To pronounce the healing chants—in Cuna terms, 'to follow the path'—is to use the word to explore the way leading to the many invisible replicas of the world, while creating a model for the experiential crisis that suffering always represents. The key-words in the Indians' commentary on the chants now acquire a deeper meaning: to 'travel' means to attempt to understand the world's modifications, perceived through a model of physical pain, or the anguish that accompanies the delirium.

I have tried to show that the 'invisible replicas' of the world were the poems created for different spirits. Both Holieri's and Ome's chants involved 'other' subjective position, in a way that was different from the simple first-person descriptions we found in the Dolbor ritual (5.7). In the second text Ome's journey started on earth, from inside the grave, and reached into cosmic realms, from where she was to separate the bloods and 'return the soul'. The invoking of the grave introduces another theme, the idea of the creation of life from the closet of death. Ome was exhausted, and now we can see that the term 'model' used by Severi should not be seen as an image (of something else) but as the form taken by the tiredness embodied physically by the shaman, in turns the exhaustion of a traveller, of a spirit chased by a shaman, or perhaps that of a mother giving birth:

> [I] with a source beginning at the previous earth
> With a link attached to the original earth
> With a base-camp in the stone on the road,
> [I] made countless somersaults,
> Twisting around without settling,
> [I] burst out from the dark-blue sorrow [grave],
> [I] was loosed from the burial sorrow [grave].
> Transformed by a whirlwind gust,
> On the changing path by which [I] set out,
> With a yellow pillar link,
> Red fire metamorphosis,
> Transformed by a tornado,
> [I] have a hollow in high heaven,
> [I] have an enclosure in blue heaven,
> And spreading out to the world,
> Striving towards the black earth
> [I] join up with the diseases of the time,
> Turning into the sickness of the year.
> Travelling along the road which changes as it goes,
> Getting there by the village road,
> Crawling along the state highway.
> Looking on both sides, [I] became tired out,
> Suffered till [I] became feeble-minded.

Your [the spirit's] fissure became known.[70]
When you softened without delay
The turning season you longed for in your mind
Set on fire ten thousand stars,
Glittering, dazzling thousand stars.
. . . .
Return the great soul!
Clean [it] in the bright sun rays!
Turn [it] round in the purifying heat of the sun!

(Engkebatu 1985: 101–3)[71]

This is not the conclusion of the chant, and indeed it is impossible to see any narrative, dramatic, or even practical order in what the shaman sings. The shaman chants about the patient gaping on his bed, and the spirit pressing on his spleen. There follow many lines about the yellow chickens; then suffering and disease; then the winding road again. In the shaman's chant the Ome Niang-Niang spirit is no longer a single image as in the myth. She becomes rearranged items, seemingly haphazard moments in time, fragments of movements; and the patient, the offered chickens, the blood, the fevers, the 'flowers', the road also become part of a kaleidoscopic composition. Through all this, in the movements back and forth, there is an insistence on transformation and purification,[72] which must refer at some level to the purification of death pollution and its replacement by pure young life. The airy winds and the drying sun are the agents of this cleansing:

At the right moment I fanned [the patient] with my fan,
I have revived [her] with the wind of the sky,
I have cleansed [her] with the western wind,
Every speck of dust blown and blasted away.

(Engkebatu 1985: 414)

These images identify Ome Niang-Niang with the sky. The images of fire and purifying heat remind us also of the female spirit of the hearth-fire (4.4). But winds were also the bearers of disease (5.8). In the end this cult tells us: just bringing souls back into the world is not enough. Foetuses, babies (and patients) are liable to be infected. Born from women's bodies, their vital reality is blood, and they must be strengthened, protected, and purified to live. The 'cause' which turns dead souls into children also enables or prevents their healthy survival. Of course, this idea may seem obvious, but it has to be read in relation to all the other suppositions of Daur culture, in particular the bone symbolism of patriarchy and the transparent directness of vertical contact with *tengger*. Both Holieri and Ome transformed the usual conventions of the symbolic landscape; with Holieri the rivers, at one level 'female' counterparts of 'male' mountains, became the pathways of madness-causing, yet vital and powerful ancestors; with Ome Niang-Niang the sky was no longer just the

supreme 'father' and 'khan'. It turned into a place of cavities and winds,
the source of a 'female' occult fomentation which no sky imagined as a
timeless sovereign (Mongolian *møngke erketü tngri* (Heissig 1980: 48)) could
control.

Otoshi and *yadgan* shamans used gendered images, and yet violated their
exclusivity, and they did this in order to create specific all-human visions
particular to their own types of practice. We are reminded of Strathern's
warning (1988) not to assume that women speak only from the gender identity
of women. In this case, the *otoshi*'s vision of the overcoming of infection by the
wholeness of healthy child growth did answer to a concern of women, but I
have tried to show that it was not reducible to this concern, just as the *yadgan*'s
enactment of broken ancestors re-combined for vitality and power was not
merely a male interest. Both types of shaman spread imaginative images outwards to the world, undercutting its usual non-shamanic symbolic associations,
and thereby they created refracted spaces for dramas concerning their particular understandings of human strength and folly.

6.4 The Hidden 'Way of Blood' and the Shaman's Sympathy

In the *ominan* ritual a 'disgusting' mixture of blood, milk, and cow's lung was
fed to voracious bird spirits. All blood was frightening and electrifying, as
Urgunge said. Just the sight of blood aroused emotion. Unknown blood and
women's menstrual or birth blood (*hwaski*) was not just polluted but caused
illness. Can we say that *hwaski* blood had to maintain its danger and difference
in order to serve as the darkness against which safety and purity were defined?
Taussig (187: 220) would disagree:

> The wildness here at stake tears through the tired dichotomies of good and evil, order
> and chaos, the sanctity of order, and so forth. It does *not* mediate these oppositions.
> Instead it comes down on the side of chaos and its healing creativity is inseparable from
> that taking of sides. Club in hand, battered by hail and tempest with lightning flashing
> the return of the dead, these creatures of the wild not only bear the burden of society's
> antiself, they also absorb with their wet shaggy coats the best that binary opposition can
> deliver—order and chaos, civilised and barbarian, Christian and pagan, and emerge on
> the side of the grotesque and destructive.

Wildness, Taussig is saying, destroys signification itself, disrupting the conventions upon which meaning and the shaping function of the image rests. Our
situation is subtly different. Daur trance shamans were also partisan, but they
took the side of the suffering victim caught in the grinding pressures of social
order. This was not an abandonment of signification, a prising open of the unity
between signifier and signified, but on the contrary it was to create meaning in
the voids neglected in the institutions of the day, that is, to force these spaces

upon the attention, demonstrating them by signification, and insisting 'They are here, in this patient and in me myself.' Sympathy was the 'action' of the Daur shaman, even with the most disgusting and dangerous diseases of all.

There was a spirit about whom all Daurs were silent, which was mentioned only by the doctor Shirokogoroff. This was Bushku, a spirit which harmed not by a sudden illness, but by permanent spreading disease. It was said to be more powerful than ordinary spirits, harming by seeping from person to person, from tribe to tribe. The Birarchen Tungus associated this spirit with Daurs, but it was known also among the Manchus who considered it to be impervious to shamanic control (Shirokogoroff 1935: 159, 387). Bushku, known by Tungus as 'sister' (1935: 130) attacked little by little, 'eating' the infected person, destroying their blood and sinews. These paths of internal bodily articulation were known as the 'blood road'. Bushku could not live outside human beings. It would settle in a young man or woman, who, if not resistant enough, would make a human-shaped placing of wood wrapped in cloths soaked in menstrual or childbirth blood and regularly serve it with fresh *hwaski* blood. The spirit might then leave this victim intact for a time, spreading to other people living with the spirit-keeper, attacking other spirits, and continuing through generations (1935: 159). The peoples of Manchuria and the Amur region had different ideas about whether this spirit could be mastered. Shirokogoroff (1935: 160) writes that blood diseases, syphilis, leprosy, and tuberculosis, which often affected several generations, were thought its manifestations, and that Daur shamans were said to be able to manage it, while Manchus could not. Bushku was generally agreed to be one of the Niang-Niang group of spirits (1935: 159–60).

Women's movement between clans was also known as the 'road of blood' (Shirokogoroff 1935: 177). The road emerged from women in the in-coming group, went through one's own family, and was passed on by the daughter into her husband's group. This matrilineal flow, Shirokogoroff implies, was the line of seeping and long-lasting infection taken by the Bushku spirit (1935: 177). Its pervasiveness was more threatening than the idea of the Najil spirit, which was the *hojoor* of the wife/mother's patrilineage and ceased to have effect after she died.[73]

The shaman mastering Bushku spirit situated herself in the female 'road of blood'. She took sides, as Taussig insists, but not to express a dissipating anti-order. She glorified and made manifest what was hidden, conjuring up the bloods, singing about what was never normally talked about. In this way she identified with the matriline, and indeed she established this as a counter order. No shamans, as shamans, belonged to either a patriline or a matriline, since their 'ancestry' was the haphazard gathering of men and women which comprised their *onggor* spirit. Therefore the shaman's identification and self-positioning was a positive act of sympathy, an attentiveness to a fissure which lay within public social construction.

The shaman who mastered Bushku was frightening to people of other clans and ethnic groups, who could not trust her ability to master it (Shirokogoroff 1935: 159). But both the spirit and the shaman had a certain doubtful honour at home, dubious because they were both powerful and 'bad'. Here the shaman was not so much an even-handed mediator as the one who was bold to take this step into pollution. She discovered and elevated the hidden tracks, unfurling them to view. Rather than objectifying and problematizing the patient, she incorporated the patient's suffering in herself, and then exposed their joint pain to the excoriating vision objectified in the spirit. A shaman's song was more intimate than a love-song, Urgunge told me. The shaman's sympathy was more dependable than the fallible love of the family. Mendüsürüng used to sing with feeling:[74]

> Because of thinking of you [patient] I had no way but to come,
> Because of you, my darling, I had to walk [to you],

and this sympathy was drawn out by a mutual feeling from the patient, his faith:

> Because that courageous faith of yours is thick,
> My incense and lamps are powerful.[75]

I have no Daur shaman's song of Bushku, but the shaman's understanding of his own sympathy shines through the poetic tropes of a song from the Mongol Kuriye Banner to the south.[76]

> To grow everywhere
> Is the fate [*ziyaga*] of the willow-tree.
> To cry before everyone
> Is my special wretched fate.
> When the mountain flower withers
> Does it still have pure fresh colours?
> When someone has been seized by pitiless illness
> Is his appearance still fresh?
> When the water-lily withers
> Does not the sun-flower also fade away?
> He who has never been ill
> Does he know the agony of sickness?
> The rich man who has never been reduced to destitution
> Does he know the pain of poverty?
> He who has never been lonely
> Does he know the pain of the mad outcast?
> But this body of mine
> Knows the sadness of the forsaken man!

In my eighteenth year I fell violently ill
And learned to know pain of disease.
At the age of nineteen years
When my father died,
I came to know the sorrow of the orphan.
. . . .
Neither to the old nor to the young
Is any respect (*kündülbüri*) given.
Someone touched by illness
Do they keep their lively appearance?
And whether aged or young
Can they find love (*hair-a*) [even] in their own household?

(Heissig 1992: 67–8)

Thus the *otoshi*'s sympathy was not derived from a religious theory but was the presentation of intuitively understandable emotions, projected to the audience across the prism of ritualized language and gesture. What was special about the shaman was that these intuitions had been magnified and empowered by the crucial first experience of oppression (*dara-*) by the *onggor*'s tragedies, by knowing both what was in herself and what was beyond herself but part of her society's relational awareness.[77] The shaman's taking sides, her empathy, was absolutely crucial, since this was the only way to reveal what no one else would even speak about, and to fasten this to the objectified visions of spirits in the landscape. Without the agency of the shaman's sympathy the saving visions would have remained out of reach, and there would only have been dull and blank suffering. The shaman was like the sounding-board of the world, and it was by the shaman's enveloping songs that the patient was drawn into awareness of the spirit-consciousness out in the sky or elsewhere. The shaman's social memory engaged with the social imagination of the audience. Yet a shaman's vision would in the end falter and fail if it did not resonate with deep, perhaps unconscious, currents of human feeling, the 'courageous faith' referred to by the shaman; yet faith was always prone to countervailing mockery. It is difficult to find a better expression for this mutuality than to say that the shamanic visions needed *keeping alive*, and this of course is to fall into the same idiom as that used by the shamans themselves (not that it is absent from European modes of thought either). Though they tapped psychological knowledge accessible to anyone, the emotions producing 'sympathy' were thus also part of the politics of everyday life (cf. Appadurai 1990: 110).

The shaman's power, as we have seen, seemed to lie in the transformation of widespread and sporadic real misfortunes into the mythicized emotions of particular, yet constantly added to, spirits, belonging to an unseen reality. This transformation, realized by the shaman, was different from the notion of transcendence, in that the process did not prescribe any qualitative hierarchy between existence in ordinary society and existence in 'beyond-society'. Inside 'shamanism' the spirits were conceived as reactive to humans in ways that intensified, but did not transcend, ordinary human emotions. However, now it is time to take a step outside this equality which was so essential to shamanship, and so different from religions like Buddhism. The next section shows that, in the wider context of socio–political life, the Daurs did also have a reflexive understanding of the place in society of shamanic practice and belief as a whole, and that this involved an ambiguous victory against conventional morality. It was central to this narrative that the shaman–hero was a woman.

6.5 The Isan Shaman and Cultural Reflexivity

All over north and east Manchuria there was a popular epic story about a young woman shaman, Nishan (Da.: Isan),[78] who successfully rescued the soul of a rich boy hunter from the underworld. This was a story *about* a shaman; it was not part of shamanic practice and should not be read as telling us directly about beliefs or rituals. The Nishan Shaman ditched social conventions. She wanted only to accomplish her aim. The interest of the story lies in what it indicates about how the peoples of Manchuria judged the shaman's endeavour. The Daur stories have notably a more triumphant ending than a well-known Manchu version (Volkova 1961), and this shows again that even compliant subjects of the Empire saw shamanship in a different light from those who were unequivocally committed to the imperial vision.

The Isan story was basically a morality tale. This was a literary genre which was essentially foreign to the Daurs, who associated moralizing with Buddhism and Confucianism. Nevertheless, such tales seem to have been popular among Daurs, just as, for example, American Westerns are beloved in England and France. The Daurs' own stories about shamans were not moralistic (see the Tochingga story in 5.2). But in telling the story of Isan the Daurs were also giving their own version of the famous Manchu story of Nishan, and in doing this they rejigged several crucial moral crisis-points.[79] In my view this was not a naïve substitution but a sophisticated manœuvre, since the Daurs were quite well aware of the different Manchu solutions to these key points. In other words, the Daur Isan story was an exercise in cultural reflexivity. The teller and listeners were no longer just the 'bearers' of a shamanic tradition. Through the prism of a foreign literary work, which was in itself a judgement on shamanism, the Daurs presented their values in contradistinction to the Manchus and their reflection on 'shamanism', as opposed simply to living it.

Nishan (Isan) was in effect *the* tale about shamanism in the region; no other compared with it in popularity or cultural salience across the boundaries of language differences, localities, and ethnic distinctions. Now in this story the archetypal shaman (*yadgan*) was not a virile and respectable man, as most *yadgan*s actually were in Urgunge's time, but a young woman of anomalous social position, i.e. what shamans in some sense were symbolically.[80] Also, in the longer versions of the tale Ome Niang-Niang appeared in yet another guise: she was now a denizen of Irmu Khan's nether world, handing out children it is true, but only to those who deserved them. Ome became the main arbiter of moral action, and this points to the creation of a female axis (victorious female shaman, exact moral judge, and female life-giving spirit) as the symbolic pivot of shamanship in society. The major male axis, by contrast, consisted of a series of men who acted rashly, immorally, or ineffectually (the rich young man who commited the fatal act as a result of which his soul was taken, the mother's brother's ghost who stole the soul, the shaman's dead husband who remained unrescued, and so forth). Thus although shamanic practice when seen from inside was non-gendered, when viewed from outside, in its relation to patriarchy and the Imperial government, it was manifested in female guise.

I give here a short version of the story told me by a woman in Morin Dawaa. The tale mostly speaks for itself, and I forbear from giving an extended commentary, mainly because this would only be to repeat points made in the excellent studies of the Manchu version by Nowak and Durrant (1977) and Durrant (1979). I have added some comments based on Daur versions published by Engkebatu (1985) and Sain Tanaa (1987*b*).

Nishang Shaman is a Mongol story and Nishang was a Mongol shaman. We Daurs always say, Isan Shaman [*yadgan*].[81] Isan was living by a river, at Isan Gol, and she was called after that place. Oh, this was an ancient thing! There was a widow and she had given her son in marriage to Isan Shaman. So when he was killed, not only was the mother-in-law already a widow, but Isan became a widow too.

The Isan shaman's story happened this way. In the direction of the rising of the sun there was a rich man called Barlo Bayin. The rich old man's son was called Heregdei Pyanggi, and he was a scholar and a gentleman. He was a hunter, and every time he went out he killed a lot of animals. He killed a female deer [*suwa*]. Then all the beasts went to the empire of death [*ukel gurun*] to raise a lawsuit against him. 'He is killing us all,' they said. After this, one day when Heregdei was hunting in the mountains, the Khan of the empire of death pounced on him, whipped out his guts, took away his soul and he died.[82] He was the young son of Barlo Bayin, who was very old. What could the old father do? He cried.

The moral point here is that Heregdei killed too many animals, and specifically a single female deer. This gives us two reasons why his soul was taken. Hamayon (1984: 15) writes: 'The images which understand the hunt as a deceit emerge in a type of society that no longer lives by hunting, and considers this activity as non-productive, subversive and uncontrollable. Vehicle of the nostalgia for a life of hunting illusiorally seen as a life of independence, or, as feeble and isolated . . . these images represent, for the disinherited, the marginal and the excluded, an escape from the established order'. Such a vision may have been characteristic of recent Manchu reflections on hunting (the Manchus being considerably more urbanized and sinified than the Daurs). In the Manchu version of Nishan, the young man was no longer integrated in a world where the animals matter, since he simply went hunting and died 'according to his fate' (Nowak and Durrent 1977: 42). The Daur version, on the other hand, added something new: the boy specifically killed a female deer. The life of even a single animal was important. Furthermore, Daurs had the idea that the female deer might be a spirit which could make infertile women pregnant. For this reason hunters paid special respects to female deer if they killed them, and some women kept images of such deer and made them offerings (Batubayin 1990: 189).

Then someone said to Barlo Bayin, 'Isan Shaman is living by the river. Ask her to come over and she will fetch out the life [*ami gargana*] and revive your son. She will be able to bring back his soul.'

Barlo Bayin mounted his horse and rode to Isan Shaman's house. He crossed the river and asked people where her house was. Someone said, 'It is that one over there by the river,' and [Barlo] rode over, dismounted, tied his horse to the gate-post, and entered. Isan Shaman was washing clothes in the kitchen. He asked, 'Where is the shaman?' She said, 'You have made a mistake. Isan Shaman's house is on the sun-setting side.' He thought this was strange, since people had told him this was the house. Leading his horse, he went to the other house on the western side, but the people there said, 'No, no, that was Isan's house over there.' So he went back, tied up his horse, and entered. Seeing Isan Shaman's mother-in-law, he kneeled before her. The old lady said, 'It's not me! The one you want is in the side scullery, my daughter-in-law.' When he looked, she was just a 17–18-year-old girl. He got to his feet and went over to kneel to her. But when he bowed deeply before her, she ignored him! Then later on she asked, 'Why did you come?' He described everything that had happened to his son, and explained why he needed her help.

'I'll call down my *onggor*s and see' [*bi onggoroo bulgaj uziye*], she said. 'If I can do it, I'll go. If I can't do it, I won't go.' So she called down her *onggor*s, and she decided to go. After she had sent away her *onggor*s, she went to her mother-in-law and asked, 'Should I go?' and the mother-in-law said, 'Go!' Isan loaded up her gown and drum on a cart and went to Barlo's place, and when she arrived she saw the son lying dead. Then she said, 'There is no one here who can sing the refrain [*iro daga-*]. Who are we going to get to follow the refrains? In the southern direction there is a man called Narati Anggu ('Sunny Anggu'); you had better call him. Otherwise I can't do it.' So they sent two servants to call Narati Anggu, and the servants went over to this house and told him that Isan Shaman had invited him. So he came. The old man Barlo went out to meet him at the gate, invited him in, and they all sat down.[83]

Soon Isan summoned her *onggor*s. She danced the dance of shamans [*heke-u*], she turned round and round, she poured water,[84] went round and round again, and then she herself died [*ugsen*].

And after dying she went far away and came to a small river [*hwarag*] There was no one on this side, but on the other side there was a lame man with a dug-out canoe. She called, 'Lame Old Man! [*Doglon Lau-ye*] Lame Old Man! Come here. If you ferry me across I'll give you a *pomon*.'[85] 'That's too little.' So she said 'I'll add one more *pomon*.'

'Even two is too little.' 'I'll add one more and give you three.' Then Lame old Man came over to her side and rowed her across. She went onwards.

She arrived at Irmu Khan's barracks. She looked, and saw the boy (Heregdei) playing with Irmu Khan's son. But there was a wall and no one could get inside. So she summoned her Guarad bird.[86] He was flying above, swooping around. Guarad was flying covering the sun. Guarad was a crane. Isan said to Guarad, 'Can you, or can you not, load that boy on your back? Can you snatch him? It's up to you. You know whether you can do it or not.' The bird said, 'Now look, he is playing with Irmu Khan's son. How can I do it?' And Isan said, 'You can do it!' The two were playing. The bird flew in with his wing-feathers half-folded, snatched the boy, put him under his wing, and handed him over to Isan.

Isan tucked him under her arm and set off. On her way she met her husband [*ergun*], dead. He begged her to revive him. She said, 'How can I save you after such a long time has passed? It is too late.' She did not do anything for him and instead she stamped on her husband's face and mouth, and went on her way.

In another Daur version (Sain Tanaa 1987*b*: 96), the husband says, 'You frivolous and shameless woman, you can save a person's life, so why not save mine? Were all those years we spent together for nothing?' Isan [Nizang] replies, 'Dear husband, listen carefully, you have been dead for so long, your flesh went rotten long ago, your sinews have broken; you will come back at the appointed time, but how can I revive you now? Please let me pass.' The husband was even more angry and ground his teeth making 'kaba, kaba' sounds, and said, 'You flighty woman, after my death you failed to take care of family matters and you travel around everywhere, and meanwhile I have been waiting for you.' The Isan got angry, and pointing out that she was after all looking after his mother, sang:

> You take a look at me now, heidü heidü,
> [You] forgot my loving kindness, heidü, heidü,
> You want to kill me, heidü, heidü.
> [I'll] throw you into Feng-du city, heidü, heidü,
> And make sure you never revive again, heidü, heidü.

> Without a husband [I'll] live happily, hailu, hailu,
> Without a husband [I'll] live without restraint, hailu, hailu,
> I can travel around everywhere, hailu, hailu,
> And appreciate the beautiful scenery, hailu, hailu.

My respondent continued:

Isan went to the place for registration of longevity of life. A person there says how long people can live. Isan begged, 'Give him [the boy] a long life.' 'No, no, we can only give 47 years old.' She complained, 'But that is only a son's age. How can you give so little?' After a long argument they agreed on eighty-seven years. And after getting the grant for 87 years, she picked up the boy, put him under her arm, and went on. Then she met Ome, who told her all the punishments of the hells. I'm forgetting the story now.

Interestingly, the part this woman forgot concerned the parables, which listed immoral deeds resulting in punishment from Ome after death. These were, according to Sain Tanaa's version (1987*b*: 97–9): burning grass meant for oxen and horses; adultery of husbands and wives; cheating when weighing goods for trade; rolling stones and logs in such a disorderly way as to hurt Bayin Achaa; robbing travellers; women seeking pleasures behind their husbands' backs; men being cruel to their first wives and having affairs; washing one's filth in pure water and polluting it; women living in a dirty and unfrugal way.

Anyway, soon they arrived at Lame Old Man's place. And then they arrived home. The father Barlo Bayin was so happy. He loaded Isan's cart with as much as she could take of good things. She became very famous. But she had got herself involved in a crime [*uil iskeesen*].

At this point the Daur versions differ significantly from the Manchu. In the latter, Nishan becomes a reformed character, stops her love-affair with Nari Fyanggo (Da.: Narati Anggu), and begins to live in an upright and proper manner. Despite this she is punished by the Emperor for the unforgivable crime of not bringing back her own husband. 'As she got rid of her husband, let us get rid of her shamanic implements,' he decreed, and she was killed (Nowak and Durrant 1977: 88–90). The Daurs, on the other hand, avoided ending the story this way. My story-teller continued:

I am not quite sure how this happened, but the Manchu Emperor [*ejin khaan*] asked her to cure his wife. Isan Shaman came to save her and went on *dolbor* [i.e. to the nether world] to fetch the soul. But the whole thing went on too long; she stayed down there too long. The Emperor waited and waited. 'Why doesn't she come?' He thought she was cheating and he was angry, so he threw her into the bottom of nine hells [*tam*]. He did not wait till she got back. By decree of the Emperor they dug the ground and buried her, at the bottom of the earth. She was chained by chains. But she left behind a small black bottle [*longh*] and said, 'After my death some famous shamans will come out of the bottle, many famous *yadgan*s will appear.'

Another woman said at this point:

Isan Shaman had nine *onggor*s. That's why other shamans were jealous of her. They thought she would become owner [*ejin*] of so many places. So they oppressed her and killed her.

Someone else added:

It's said that the chains which bound her when she was put in the earth are still there. They emerge from the ground somewhere near Hailar. So when people go to that district each person tugs at the chains. Link by link the chains are coming out. They are piled up. We don't know if it is true or not, but they say that when the last link is pulled out Isan's *onggor* will come with it. A senior person said, 'Leave those useless chains alone.' But that was another shaman, who was afraid of Isan coming back. Those chains are made of silver and are extremely strong. They are attached to her heart and she has them like a hobble round her ankles.

Then a man asked,

'How long ago did all this happen?' The story-teller replied, 'My father was at that place when he was 58, and I am nearly that now. Count it up for yourself.'

In all variants of this story the Nishan (Isan) Shaman is arrogant and demanding, daring and brave. She violates the following social rules: (1) family seniority (she has more power than her mother-in-law); (2) sexual propriety (she is having an affair with Narati Anggu); (3) being respectful and truthful to a senior aristocrat; (4) the obligation to bear children (Isan is always specified to be childless); and above all (5) marital loyalty (she refuses to rescue her husband). I asked Urgunge what he thought of the story, and he said,

Are you asking my present brain or my childhood brain? In those days I would have said she should be punished. After all, she had a boyfriend, though no Daur story will ever say it directly. But today I think that this was the story of a young girl married to a much older man. She was left a widow. He died long ago. What the heck—why save him? She was a shaman, she was independent, she was the centre of her own world. This is a story of opposites. She *saves* (the boy) and she *does not save* (her husband). She *chooses*. This is far too extreme for the old-fashioned oriental mind, so you will only find this story among shamanists.

The ending of the story is crucial, because in it shamanic practice is judged in its place in the social world. In the 1913 Manchu version (Volkova 1961), Nishan Shaman was tried by the Board of Justice, justly punished, and never reappeared. The Emperor here was said to be the Tai-tsung Emperor (r. 1626–43) (Nowak and Durrant 1977: 89–90), and the whole thing happened in the historic past, when the Manchu Empire was in its early days and the Daurs were just coming under its sway. However, we have to look at the tale in relation to the values prevailing at the time it was told, the early twentieth century. For this period the punishment ending is not surprising, since the Manchu government had in fact repressed Manchu 'wild shamanism' during the nineteenth century and strictly regularized the ritualized clan (*p'ogun*) variant. In the early twentieth century local authorities were unable to enforce the ban completely, but in places they were able to insist that official permission be obtained for each performance (Shirokogoroff 1935: 391).

However, none of the Daur variants end with Isan's defeat. In Engkebatu's (1985) Daur version, Isan was opposed not by the Emperor but by the even more powerful patriarchal powers of Tengger and Irmu Khan, to whom the aggrieved husband's soul had appealed. The King of Heaven and the King of Hell got together and both agreed that Isan must be put down. This was not in fact because she failed to save her husband. The mighty Khans agreed that he had died of natural causes and was far too long dead anyway. What disturbed them was the idea that such a forceful shaman could rescue everyone from death and if no one ever died there would be no place left for people to fit into the world. So the High Sky [*deed tengger*] threw Isan into a bottomless well. But Isan tore off her hair and it spread over the ground. She cried, 'Let as many *yadgan* arise as there are hairs!' and that is why we have shamans in later generations.

The conversation which took place after the story-teller had finished was highly important. The whole text was taken up and given an orientation to the listeners sitting in the room with me. This can be seen from the speculations about the chains near Hailar and the question, 'How long ago did all this happen?' What this did was to establish this story as a 'magical' communication *addressed to us*, and in this way the Isan text came to have (at least) two modes of existence, as a social comment on shamans, and as a 'sacred message' of which the teller was only the bearer. Although space prevents me from developing this theme here Losev is perceptive in his comment, 'Plot-based texts and their fragments in the form of imperative taboos, prescriptions, or popular beliefs constitute . . . a world of "concepts", the source of which is not the "worldview" *per se*, but the realm of oral communication' (Takho-Godi 1989: 78; see also Novik 1984). The Isan story could thus be a part of 'shamanism' as a generator of ideas and values, even though it was not directly a practice upon the world like shamans' songs and rituals.

It is interesting that Urgunge hardly remembered the Isan Shaman story and it formed no part of his picture of 'shamanism'. Yet Isan (Yisen) was important in the account given by the woman writer Odongowa (1991 n.d.). Of course what people put forward as narrative explanations of their religion does not necessarily account for all they know in other ways. But the differing contents of oral explanations do indicate the range of concerns (and absences) that are

TABLE 6.1.

Odongowa	Mendüsürüng	Urgunge
Tengger seen in image of a family	Origin of shamanism	*Tengger* in image of old man/regulator
Shaman's garment	Shaman's garment	Shaman's curing
Ome as source of life	Ome as protector of young children	*Tengger* as protector of young children
Isan Shaman	*Dolbor* journey	*Dolbor* journey
duwalang trees	Holieri (Da Barkan)	Mountain cults
Shaman's songs and dances	Curing/exorcism ritual	Onon clan *hojoor*
	Ominan	*Ominan*
	Shaman's grave	Bayin Achaa

possible conscious interpretations of 'shamanism'. Therefore I think it is useful
to compare the pattern of elements provided by Urgunge (who told me about
almost everything, but I am referring here to the topics that interested him
spontaneously and to which he returned again and again) with those of
Odongowa and Mendüsürüng (see Table 6.1).[87] This allows us to see, within
the complete range which I have tried to present in this book, some varying
patterns actually held by individuals, each of which were valid interpretations
of what 'shamanism' was (i.e. was for them). Perhaps we should not place too
much weight on these differences, but it does seem possible to discern here a
'male view' of shamanism (Urgunge and Mendüsürüng) which was substantially different from a 'female view'. The presence of Isan Shaman, whom
Odongowa describes as though she had really existed, is a critical marker of the
latter.

Notes

1. It was sometimes said that the animal's soul would be 'used' (*jara-*) by the spirit,
   and after serving its duty (*alba*) would be reborn on earth.
2. This woman knew so much and talked so passionately about shamanism that I had
   the impression she might have been a shaman earlier in her life.
3. Kaliertü village near Horli is the village of Urgunge's mother's clan, the Aula.
4. Urgunge said that anyone riding a donkey would be considered both foreign and a
   figure of fun by the Daurs.
5. *Feng-shui*: the Chinese system of geomancy.
6. In the North Asian context, where the colour yellow is identified with Buddhism
   and black with shamanism, this name means simply 'shamanic spirit.'
7. Her husband worked as an official for the administration (*yamen*) in Hailar and
   knew both Chinese and Manchu languages.
8. Urgunge remembers one such incoming spirit, kept by an aunt, which was called
   halay. The placing was made of leather, with four or five human figures of metal
   attached to it. This *halay* came from the Merden clan. Urgunge thought most
   women kept such images, but he was not sure because these external spirits were
   resented by the Onons and therefore women hid them. They were only brought out
   occasionally for offerings.
9. However, it cannot have been the case that clan shamans always refused to treat the
   in-coming wives, since Urgunge remembers Du-Yadgan performing treatments
   for wives of the Onons.
10. According to Mendüsürüng and Odongowa there was another shaman in the
    Manna Gobol clan, Origi Bøø, who had main charge of the Ulaan Barkan *hojoor*
    spirit for members of that clan. However, Huangge seems to have acted for the
    married-out women of the Gobol clan.
11. A clan shaman was known as *mokoni yadgan* or *mokoni saman*. Because Origi Bøø
    held this status in the Manna Gobol clan, Huangge, who was married out from the

clan, had the status of *gadyn zamyn yadgan* (outside road shaman) according to Odonogowa.

12. Pingguo was born in 1904 and he was still alive in the 1950s.

13. For example in the story called 'The half-sided girl' (*DSHI* 1985: 112) a brother refuses to help his sister who was half-eaten by a spirit, and the sister's son later took revenge on him. In the story called 'Harimi Yadgan' (Sain Tanaa 1987: 51) a shaman mother's brother fights with the sister's son's wife, who turned out to be a small spirit called *yabaga*. The *yabaga* killed the mother's brother and as a result the mother refused to have her in the house any longer.

14. Lindgren (1935*a*: 372). Buryats (Czaplicka 1914: 222) and Tungus (Shirokogoroff 1935: 289) also called these cloths 'snakes'. However, Urgunge said that they were called *dalbaga* (flag) and that it would be impossible to hang snakes on the shaman's costume because people hated snakes.

15. Daurs did not explain misfortune by reference to people now alive ('witchcraft', 'the evil eye', etc.).

16. The name Holieri perhaps comes from *holee-* (to stir, mix up); another interpretation is that it relates to the Mongol word *solioro-* (to go mad) (s alternates with h in some Mongolian dialects). Omachi (1949: 22) and *DSHI* (1985: 283). Holieri Barkan was called by different names in different places, such as Malo Barkan in the Aihui region (Shirokogoroff 1935: 151–2) and Da Barkan in the Hailar area (Manduertu 1991: 94). Mendüsürüng, however, told me that Holieri and Da Barkan were different spirits.

17. Bogule Barkan, also called Olon Barkan ('many spirit'), seems to have been similar in many ways. Its twenty-four forms or 'seats' were: judge, blacksmith, Laichin Lama, southern *yadgan ominan* ritual, northern *yadgan ominan* ritual, fisherman, hunter, merchant, three coffins, fox spirit, *bong* ghost, infant, *tooroo* tree, crow, cuckoo, male and female deer, lizard, Mountain Fox spirit, Niang-Niang spirit (*one*), Niang-Niang spirits (nine), earthworm, dog, and snake. Apart from this it contained auxiliary *keiden*, dragon, and other spirits (*DSHI* 1985: 252–3).

18. Urgunge said he thought City Spirit was the same as Holieri, i.e. the name used for Holieri in his family. However, this seems doubtful, as other sources mention the existence of City Spirit in parallel with Holieri.

19. This is the full text of the letter; my explanations in square brackets.

20. The Mongol Empire, founded by Chinggis Khan in 1206, adopted the dynastic name of Yüan in 1273. It ruled China till 1368, when it was ousted by the Chinese Ming Dynasty.

21. The Onon River flows through north-east Mongolia and is one of the historical sites associated with Chinggis Khan.

22. Urgunge says this must refer to Mergen, Buxi, and Noho, all towns on the Naun.

23. *Hojoor* can also mean 'real reason' or 'cause'. For example, a man in Morin Dawaa describing the cure of a boy by Chinese medicine, said to me, 'And then we had to find out the real cause [*hojoor*],' meaning the real (presumably spirit-caused) reason for the boy's illness.

24. Also called *Hwaimar Barkan* ('North-west Spirit', i.e. spirit of the honoured north-western part of the house, or *Wussel Barkan* (*wusse* (to grow, mature))).

25. Shenyang, whose Manchu name was Mukden, was the city where Chipaatii had

submitted to the Manchu Emperor (see 2.1). It was the place chosen for the capital of the last 'puppet' Manchu Dynasty, set up with Japanese backing in the 1930s.

26. Both Orochen and Evenk are Tungus groups.

27. A woman from Horli said, 'One day a person got a plough-share (*anggis*). He thought, "Why not use it to plough the land?" And so he did. The next day he was struck down by lightning. He was about to die and people called the shaman. The shaman said, "Why do you use that to plough the land? That plough-share is Holieri Barkan."'

28. This also was collected in the *DSHI* in Morin Dawaa in the 1950s. Three versions of the text are published in the literature, all in Chinese translations, and very possibly all three are based on the same Daur text.

29. *Birji* is an archaic term for a clan.

30. This is the round piece of shiny metal at the front of the plough where the earth divides.

31. The meaning of *dalaile* is unknown.

32. The meaning of this and the following line is not clear.

33. Urgunge said that the Daurs would probably have identified the Dalai Lama with the 'seat of orthodoxy' in Beijing.

34. The road taken by Holieri was the same as the road to the *duwalang* life trees, according to Odongowa (1991: 10).

35. For discussion of the forms and substances of such vessels and traces of spirits among Buryats, see Humphrey (1973 n.d.).

36. Holieri was called Malo by some northern Daurs and by the Tungus, and it is significant that while dragons appeared within many spirit-complexes, the Dragon Spirit itself was said by Tungus to be Malo (Shirokogoroff 1935: 168).

37. The clothing was not only seen as an offering. Mendüsürüng later told me that when someone fell ill, they would put their finest dress in a box and that would become the placing of Da Barkan in that family.

38. Not only were there high-ranking Daur military and administrative personnel but one of the wives of Puyi, the last Manchu Emperor, was a Daur, Wan-lung of the Gobol clan, daughter of General Zhang-sun.

39. This was a high-handed reversal of the centuries-old transfer between China and the nomads, whereby silk had always come 'down' as a bestowal from Beijing.

40. For example, the Buryat scholar Zhamtsarano noted that the Kudinsk Buryats in 1905 had 4,000 sheep and several hundred horses driven from Mongolia, all to be used for communal shamanic religious offerings. The animals were paid for by rich people, including the local shaman. Individual families could be ruined by the cost of offerings if someone in the family suffered a lengthy illness (cited in Mikhailov 1987: 173–6).

41. This observation of Shirokogoroff's does not apply to the 'wild shamanism' of the Manchus, but to the domestic, military, and court-based cults. The former, which is still active in remote parts of Manchuria, is far more like the Daur variant (Lisha Li, personal communication). See also Fu (1993: 245–7).

42. For example Banzarov (1955), Shirokogoroff (1935), and Heissig (1980). The cults are, however, described in lesser known works, such as Manzang (1991), Potapov

(1991), Smolyak (1991), L'vova, Oktyabr'skaya, Sagalayev, and Usmanova (1989), and Chabros (1992*a*).

43. See Ch. 5 n. 54.

44. But Pingguo Yadgan was said to master Niang-Niang (Omachi 1949: 22). More generally it was common for the *bagchi* to assist the *otoshi*. Chabros (1992b: 60) mentions that among the Jarud and Naiman Mongols in Inner Mongolia a 'white shaman' or a *laiching* conducted a ritual of offering and praise of Niang-Niang at a summer ritual held at a special tree or an *oboo* dedicated to the goddess. In this Buddhicized region Niang-Niang was envisaged as an old woman, the female counterpart of the White Old Man. The configuration of cults of female spirits seems to have varied widely in Inner Mongolia, and several people told me that Ome and Niang-Niang were different from one another. However, the shamanic texts to be discussed in this section represent 'Ome Niang-Niang' as one spirit.

45. Omachi (1982: 202–3) mentions that Jaban Yadgan of the Hailar district also became an *otoshi*. This happened when there was an outbreak of smallpox in Jaban's clan, and a child was possessed by the spirit of an ancestor who had been an *otoshi* (he was called *ye-ye*, 'grandfather' in Chinese]. The 'grandfather' speaking through the child said that a picture of Niang-Niang should be drawn and worshipped, together with his own portrait. This 'grandfather' became the *onggor* of Jaban when he was acting as *otoshi*. Jaban kept his two practices separate. As an *otoshi* Jaban treated sick children by offering to Niang-Niang and the *otoshi* ancestor, and as a *yadgan* he conducted the cult of the clan *hojoor*.

46. An old woman at Horli told me that the female shaman's ceremony of public recognition took place as follows: 'The older shaman sat in the middle of the *kang*, with a desk before her, on which was placed a teapot and some cups. The young shaman sat by her side. She put on her costume, with 12 tassels, 58 bells on the shoulders and 108 *yogosana* (?) on the cap. The senior woman asked the *onggor* to come down. Senior people in the family threw the *hotoli* (?) in the air, and as it came down, they asked, "Who is my ancestor? Why do you want this woman to be a shaman?" For this occasion one *tooroo* tree had been erected outside the door and another in the courtyard. They tied a sheep to the latter, and many people gathered there. People tied many colourful silk scarves and cloths to the outside *tooroo*. The senior shaman then danced outside and the young shaman in the inner room. The senior shaman had a drum which she beat, and she was followed by an assistant who beat in time with cymbals. This went on for many days. People came from all the neighbouring villages to watch, all bringing scarves (*hadag*) to tie. When the *onggor* came down the senior shaman hit her forehead once. If there was no response, she hit herself three times, and then the *onggor* would answer.'

47. Among the Daur, Buryat, and Darhat Mongols a shaman's staff (*taig*) seems to have been an alternative to a drum; like the drum it was often seen as a magical vehicle for movement. Buryats had 'horse', 'snake', and 'human' staves, used for various kinds of journeys, as signs of mastery, and as weapons to punish offenders (Mikhailov 1987: 107–8).

48. The *otoshi* wore a skirt (*wualarsi* ('sole of foot' or 'skin')) and a distinctive colourful hat. Sometimes the *otoshi* did not use a drum but a special fan (*deribule*) made of

colourful silk strips (Batubayin 1990). Urgunge remembers the *otoshi* in his village as having prayer-beads.

49. Potapov (1991: 274, 285) writes that Umay was mentioned in runic inscriptions of the 6th–9th century Turkic peoples of the Altai. In one inscription Umay was credited, along with Tengri and a deity called Iyer-sub, with granting victory in war. Later medieval Turkic documents do not mention Umay as a deity, but give the word *umay* as meaning 'placenta' and 'womb' (1991: 285).

50. The cult of Umay or May ('womb', 'child's soul', 'goddess') reappeared by the 19th–20th centuries among all the Altaian peoples (Potapov 1991: 285–97). The peoples of the Lower Amur had a similar cult of Maydya Mama (Smolyak 1991: 119–27). Om'i (Um'i, Omosi Mama) was a similar spirit among the Tungus and Manchus (Shirokogoroff 1935: 128). There were also echoes of the idea of celestial fertility spirits among the Buryats (Galdanova 1987: 42–3), but these ideas were less prominent among the Halh Mongols.

51. The Ul'chi of the Amur told Smolyak that only certain shamans would specialize in the rituals of preserving unborn, foetal, and children's souls (1991: 118). According to Shirokogoroff (1935: 128), ordinary shamans would have nothing to do with the cult of Omosi Mama (or the Chinese version, Niang-Niang) among the Manchus, and we therefore must suppose the cult was undertaken by other ritual specialists.

52. Liu Mau-tsai (1972) gives the Chinese meaning of Niang-Niang as follows: Niang-Niang means 'mother' and 'girl', and the term also evokes the idea of 'mother of the state'. Evidently, in the Sung period Niang-Niang was used to designate one's own mother, and the Emperor used to call his mother by this term.

53. Shirokogoroff (1935: 130) mentions that the Birarchen Tungus renamed a spirit called Julaski Buga ('southern sky') N'ang-N'ang under Manchu influence. Prayers to Julaski ask the spirit to remove infectious diseases and purify people with cold spring water (1935: 228–9).

54. The groups of smallpox, measles, etc. diseases, according to Ikeshiri, were divided into two kinds: *ukur-ewoche* (lit. cattle mother) and *shilter* (grit). The former disease was divided euphemistically into *shih jargalang* (great happiness) and *wuchiken jargalang* (small happiness). It was said that only shamans could distinguish between these diseases. Ikeshiri mentions exorcism as part of the ritual for the *ukur-ewoche* diseases: a cake-box was filled with sand and a tiny flag stuck in it, and the whole was covered with white paper. After the spirit had been induced into the flag, the box was carried from the patient's bedside 100 paces away and then thrown out (1943: 60). Daurs put up a sign outside the door when someone had one of these diseases. Visitors were not supposed to enter. This suggests some idea of infectiousness; however, if a stranger did enter, this was supposed to cause harm to the patient, not to the visitor (Ikeshiri 1943: 61).

55. Other people too said that 'Niang-Niang' was only a Chinese label, and that the spirit was Eme ('woman', speaking in Mongolian) or Ome ('womb' in Daur).

56. Galdanova (1987: 43, 52) writing about Buryats notes that a lock of the child's hair was called 'womb hair' and should be left intact at hair-cutting. This hair was sacred and said to contain life energy and blessing (*heshig*).

57. Mendüsürüng told me that the breast-bone (*ovchuu*) of the sheep offered should be included in this bag. This bone should be gnawed clean by an old man, so clean that

not even the membrane next to the bone should remain. He had no explanation for this.

58. Among the Xing-an Tungus, the Om'i/Umisma spirit was said to have a tepee and a tree on which the souls of not-yet-born children were sitting in the form of birds (Shirokogoroff 1935: 128). In the Manchu version of the Nishan story, Omosi-Mama, 'who causes the leaves to unfurl and the roots to spread properly', receives dead souls and gives them back to the world (Nowak and Durrant 1977: 75, 78).

59. This sad episode must have happened in the early 1950s. The woman added that the family's home town was liberated around this time. She was sent to school, and after she got a new education these 'old things' receded into the past.

60. The babies would yell at this, 'Wa, wa', and this was a sign that they were born. The blue patch on the baby's buttocks was the hand-print of Ome (Odongowa 1991 n.d.: 7). The blue patch refers to the 'Mongolian spot', an area of dark skin genetically inherited by certain North-East Asian peoples.

61. *Gertee hataaj amitai bolgasan.*

62. This story is similar to one told by Sain Tanaa, where the creator is not *endur* but 'grandmother' (mother's mother—*taitai*), who mixed the mud with her own feathers in order to make people. These mud-feather people were both sister and brother, and wife and husband (Sain Tanaa 1987*a*: 269). The feathers have echoes in another myth of origin, widespread throughout North Asia and also known by the Daurs, in which the first people derived from the union of human male hunters and heavenly swans who come down to bathe in a lake. The brothers stole their feather clothing, thereby condemning them to stay on earth as their wives (Sain Tanaa 1987*a*: 288).

63. This is a translation of the beginning of the first of three invocations to Ome Barkan collected in 1980–1 in Morin Dawaa district and published by Engkebatu in 1985. The text is published in Daur and Mongolian. The three invocations are similar to one another and some of the same 'blocks' are present in all three, but small differences in these and whole new sections indicate that shamans' songs were not set pieces. The punctuation is that given in the published text.

64. This may also refer to the female fire spirit (see 4.4).

65. Si-Mu Niang-Niang: Western Mother. Si-Mu (Xi-mu) was a popular figure in Chinese mythology, popularly known also as Wang-Mu (Imperial Mother). Si-Mu was half animal and half human, and in Daoist cults in central China was seen as an immortal. She was in charge of all the disasters in the world and protected people like a 'mother'. She was believed to live at Kun Lun mountain, which lies to the south of the west sea.

66. The red sacred vessel (*hulaan keiden*) refers to the shrine built for the spirit which is transformed (*hubila-*) when the spirit enters it. This text continues with a further 27 lines describing the magnificence of the shrine and instructing the spirit to take the offerings and to 'Go by the proper path for coming, Go, flying by the two chickens.' The ending is a repetition of various previous lines, such as 'Collect up your illnesses,' etc.

67. Tungus, Manchu, Ul'chi, and Nanai shamanic practice created large numbers of roads ('night', 'day', 'upstream', 'downstream', 'male' and 'female', etc.) and these tracks belonged to individual shamans who mastered the spirits involved. In the

Lower Amur also these roads were circuits, going round and coming back to the same place (Smolyak 1991: 137). Among the Tungus whole complex spirits were not identified with particular 'roads' and parts of them could take alternative routes (Shirokogoroff 1935: 149–50).

68. This may refer to the Mongolian expression for large livestock such as cattle and horses (*bod*) as opposed to small livestock like sheep and goats (*bog*).

69. If someone died of measles or smallpox the family invited a shaman to clean the body, wrap it, and place it in a coffin. This coffin was then taken to a high place, such as the top of a mountain or the branches of a tree. On a mountain-top a construction of three wooden posts held up the coffin. This was left for 100 days to allow the smallpox spirit to return to heaven, and no one could on any account approach the spot, even if the coffin was destroyed by a storm and the body fell out. The body was buried after 100 days (Ikeshiri 1943: 61).

70. Daur *Tabi taan tanisen*. Urgunge thought this meant, 'I [shaman] got to know your weak spot.'

71. Daur *Hutaan nardin hortsilga*. Here *hutaan* refers to the act of scorching or purifying by fire.

72. The Daur text uses various terms for this, *giree*, *bolgushe*, *alligu*, all of which are translated in the Mongolian by the term *arilhu-* (cleanse, purify).

73. The Daurs had a highly approved marriage system, called *torsen jalgana-* (linking the birth-kin). This joined the children of two male second cross-cousins, resulting in a repetition of earlier marriage links every third or fourth generation. As a result, foreign in-marrying women were not so very foreign at all, and given that there were only four large *mokon* in the mid-Naun region (and the same in Hailar) and that most marriages were local, it meant that everyone was ultimately related to everyone else. A possible reason for this marriage preference may have been to limit the power of the Bushku spirit brought in by women on marriage, by ensuring that this female 'blood road' ultimately went in a circle, that is by denying it and regularly swamping it with 'patrilineal blood'. For an analysis of the marriage system, see Vreeland ([1954] 1962: 237 *et seq.*). Urgunge, who supplied Vreeland with this information, says that *torsen jalgana* was bilateral.

74. The following lines were not sung for Bushku, which Mendüsürüng said he had never heard of, but for Niang-Niang.

75. *Zorig süjig zuzaan chini, huj zul xündet* (in a Daur shaman's song sung to me by Mendüsürüng).

76. This was a chant of Jangcha Shaman, a male Tumed Mongol of Juugachin Ail in Kuriye Banner. The chant was dictated and written down by Mongols in December 1942. The Mongol text is given in Heissig ([1944] 1992: 1–50).

77. 'At the heart of shamanism there still lies a kernel of psychological realpolitik. Shamanic initiations are designed to tackle a genuine psychological and ontological dilemma. "How shall I know the way of all things?" wrote Lao Tzu, "—by what is inside me." But what is inside me? Only what I have experienced for myself: and that in principle cannot be all there is. No matter how effective the natural strategies that human beings have for extending their personal experience . . . there are bound to be areas of experience that individuals have no access to. Shamanic initiations, especially the dream journey, provide, as it were, a crash course in

personal experience: a thousand years of human living rolled into a day' (N. Humphrey 1986: 130).

78. Known as Nishan in Manchu, and Yisan, Isan or Isen in Daur.

79. This point applies even if the Nishan story originated among the Mongol-speaking people of Manchuria rather than among the Manchus. By the early 20th century the Manchus had developed numerous elaborate versions of the tale (Stary 1990) and some of these were certainly known to the Daurs.

80. Note, however, that among the Manchus the majority of shamans were, and still are, women.

81. Volkova (1961) agrees that Nishan was a place-name rather than a personal name; however, see Yakhontova (1992: 130). *Isan* means 'nine', a lucky number.

82. In longer Daur versions (Sain Tanaa 1987*b*: 75), the boy's soul is stolen by Mongoldai Nagchu (Mongol Mother's Brother) on the orders of Irmu Khan.

83. In another version, almost certainly Daur (Yakhontova 1992: 108–9), Nishan greeted Nari Fyanggo (Narati Anggu) 'with a smiling face' and teased him, 'If you can't beat the drums and cymbals in time I'll hit you eighty times with my drumstick. If you can't beat them loudly, I'll hit you forty times.' Nari said with a smile, 'Why does the elevated Nishan Shaman have to explain so much?', and both of them entered the house laughing.

84. Urgunge thinks this water must have been poured on the corpse to purify it.

85. *Pomon*: unclear.

86. Guarad, bird deriving from Indian mythology (Garuda). Possibly this bird was Isan's *onggor*.

87. These lists are taken from the contents of Odongowa (1991) and Mendüsürüng's article (1983) 'A Study of Dagur Shamanism'.

7

'Shamanism' in Twentieth-Century History

7.1 Archaism and the Dispersed Character of 'Shamanism'

By now readers may be wondering about the almost perversely archaic content of the shamanic materials I have presented. Here were people in the 1920s and 1930s of this century, within reliable reportage-range of great revolutions and new ideologies. Cars, planes, radios, and telephones were not totally unheard of. Many people knew several languages. Daurs had taken part in wider regional struggles for autonomy from 1912 onwards, and later their leaders were involved in modern schemes to reorganize society along with the Chinese, Japanese, and Mongolians. Yet absolutely none of this appeared overtly in shamanic discourse. Daur 'shamanism', and perhaps that of all North Asian native peoples, appears in this respect quite unlike that described for Latin America, which seems to have been reactive, absorbative, and frantically hyper-aware of colonial powers and technology. Taussig argues that it was in a sense formed from reactions to White fears of the 'primitive' (see Taussig 1987; Severi 1987, 1988). How can this difference be explained?

This book makes the case that North Asian 'shamanism' was segmented or dispersed as a phenomenon. The ideas and practices of the various parts were associated with different kinds of knowledge and specialists having particular abilities (*chidal*) in these spheres. This will be shown by extending the discussion to the specialists called *bagchi*, *bariyachi*, *barishi*, and *kiyanchi*. In this section I wish to make the following argument: given the dispersed character of 'shamanism', no single part of which encompassed the totality of human exigencies, people faced with unexpected and unintelligible forces in the world could not but react by creating another 'segment'. This pieced together a new kind of knowledge-base and it had its own specialists and different rituals. The other, earlier traditions may have adapted a little (5.8) but basically they were left with their inveterate methods, dealing with the core of what they had always dealt with, and now weakened in their pretensions to wider explanations. Thus they had every reason to reinforce whatever was most fundamental about their practices, that is, their own kinds of psychological awareness. The Daurs I spoke to saw the *yadgan* and the *otoshi* as 'real' shamans and as having greater prestige and power than the other specialists. However, it was among these others, in particular the *kiyanchi*, that important reactions to new events were created in the 1910s–1920s. I deal with the *chiyanchi* and 'mafa' cults in the next section, and here discuss the series of traditional specialists who were faced with modernity.

The idea of a dispersed series reminds us of the important point made by Barth (1987) concerning social organization and the possible kinds of coherence and patterning to be found in different cosmological traditions. Earlier descriptions in this book showed how disjunctions in cosmological thought were created by 'contexts of interest' attached to domains of knowledge. These contexts acted to delimit the range of information people needed or wanted to have in particular circumstances. My argument was made on cognitive grounds, such as the different conceptual principles needed to understand static objects in a landscape from those needed to understand human relationships. Barth makes the point that such disjunctions can also be created by social and cultural organization. It is mistaken, he argues (1987: 77), to search for the general 'integration' of a culture on the basis of logical analysis and abstraction, looking for 'a generally valid basic structure of premises which orders the cultural materials in question'. It is equally wrong to assume that the pattern which obtains in an individual's world-view is of the same kind and exhaustive of that which might obtain in the culture of the group. This is because culture is 'distributive', to use a term borrowed from Schwartz (1978).

> The distribution of the items of knowledge and ideas on the interacting parties in a population is a major feature of the organization of that body of knowledge and ideas; it is not only a matter of social structure but simultaneously a matter of cultural structure. It is self-evident that a particular pattern of social organization will produce and reproduce a particular pattern of distribution of knowledge and skills. Equally, a certain distribution of these cultural elements between persons motivates their interactions and exchanges, and thus animates a particular social organization and infuses it with its constitutive qualities. (Barth 1987: 77)

Among the Daurs the clan-village organization, economies oriented to local subsistence, and rigid age and gender distinctions must have contributed to the organization of religious knowledge into 'spirits' known to certain groups and not to others and to differing women's and men's perspectives on cosmology.

However, the existence of *yadgan*s, *otoshi*s, *barishi*s, etc. was a different matter, since every community reproduced such distinctions between specialists. This was true not only among Daurs but widely all over Inner Asia.[1] Everywhere, the native explanation for this, with which I agree, was that these specialists had their own kinds of knowledge. These people were thought to have natural (see 1.5) super-human abilities, inherited from ancestors and not acquired by teaching. Sagalayev and Oktyabr'skaya write about the Turkic peoples of the Altai (1990: 99), 'What is significant is that these numerous sacralised persons always exist alongside the shaman, as his necessary context, setting off and sharpening appreciation of the shaman's gift, but at the same time having an independent significance.'

During Urgunge's youth the Daurs gave precedence to the *yadgan* over other specialists, and in this respect the *yadgan* could be called 'the shaman' along the lines of the quotation above. But in earlier periods of Inner Asian history other types of shaman had social priority (Humphrey 1994*b*). The Mongolian writer Rinchen, himself a believer in shamanic power, wrote (1977: 149–50): 'The words "shaman" and "shamanism", so familiar to western writers, were completely unknown to the Mongols and to their shamans and Buddhist monks, who wrote so many epistles against them. Rather than think in terms of a unitary word "shaman", capriciously and superficially adapted to their purposes by European scholars, we should look at the root meanings of the Mongol terms.' These are built up in such a way that their morphology reveals their inner meaning. There were four kinds of religious practitioner, *bøge*, *udagan*, *zigarin*, and *abiy-a*. The term *udagan* (the Daur *yadgan*) is made up of a root *ud-*, from the Turkic *ut* (fire), followed by *a* (vowel regularly added between consonants and without meaning), followed by *-ga-*, a suffix meaning 'the one who does something', followed by *-n*, a suffix meaning a person or a thing. *Ud* + *a* + *ga* + *n* therefore means 'a person who produces fire'. By the same kind of analysis Rinchen concluded that *bøge* means 'someone who acts to intuit unknown things', *zigarin* means 'a person who unconsciously experiences another (spiritual) being's act of drawing attention to a phenomenon', and *abiy-a* is 'the one who obtains magical sounds'. The difference between the Mongol *bøge* and the *zigarin* was that the former used intuitive abilities, while the *zigarin* (pronounced *jaarin*) was a more priest-like figure who was the medium by which spirits, gods, etc. made their wishes known (Rinchen 1977: 150–2). The *zigarin* was known as the 'great shaman' in the medieval period (Dalai 1959: 21–2).[2]

Clearly a word can come to be given different connotations from those embedded in its morphology. In fact there is nothing the Mongols like better than chewing over the obscure 'original' meanings of the roots and suffixes. The Daur term *yadgan* certainly has no connotations of making fire these days. Nevertheless, what Rinchen's observations show is that quite different concepts were involved from the start in the construction of the terms for these various specialists. Now it might historically and socially come to be the case that actual practitioners all did more or less the same thing (as priests, vicars, curates, chaplains, etc. all have more or less the same function). The case I am making here is that among the Daurs and other North Asian peoples distinctions in expertise were preserved between specialists.

We saw that the *otoshi*, rather than the *yadgan*, had charge of female fertility and foetal/child development. However, there was another specialist in the actual delivery of the child. This was the *bariyachi* (midwife, 'one who takes hold'), who had a kind of knowledge that was both physical and occult. All men were excluded during childbirth. The midwife manipulated the baby as it was born, tied the umbilical cord with a wild animal's vein, cut it using scissors, and washed the child in salty water. The mother lay on dirty cloths. At the time of the birth a bunch of grass was hung at the door (Jagchid 1988*b*: 331) a cart axle was erected in front of the house as a sign (Ikeshiri [1943] 1982: 54). Visitors were not allowed to enter unless they had stepped over a fire for purification. The mother was considered polluted for a month, during which time she was not allowed to go beyond the gate of the yard.

Giving birth was encased in ritual, and symbolically it was akin to death. The Daur rituals echoed those found elsewhere in Inner Asia, which more clearly placed the act of giving birth in the 'wild'. The mother was given an animal skin or grass to lie on, sometimes a separate skin tent to give birth in, and the pole (tree) before the door was called *turuu*, like symbolic mortuary tree of the shaman. Dolgans said that leaning on this tree, the mother's soul arose again after the birth of the child and returned to life (L'vova *et al.* 1989: 149).[3] The midwife was thus entrusted with a vital symbolic task alongside the physical one of ensuring safe delivery; she had to ensure a safe transfer from the state of wildness and death into the world of social life. The Daur midwife did this by praying to Ome Niang-Niang and using spells (*tarni*), but mainly by invoking another spirit, Auli Barkan (mountain spirit). Auli Barkan, despite its name, was not the spirit of a mountain, but was a dangerous fox which lived in mountainous country. The *bariyachi*s were very proud of their mastery of this spirit, according to Batubayin (1990: 124). Calling down the fox spirit, the midwife was taken over by it like a shaman, and it guided her every step of the way during the delivery. After the birth she presumably had to return the fox to the wild, just as she brought the mother and child back to this world, though my sources are silent on this point.

In Urgunge's village one of the midwives was subject to *beleng* attacks (5.5), and all of them had low prestige and tended to come from poor or bondsmen families. He said, 'All midwives were a little bit *koodoo* [crazy].' Everyone was a little afraid of them, not as personalities, but because they dealt with blood and evil powers. Their special spiritual ability (*onggor*) was associated with the *hwaski* (polluted) nature of their task, and was inherited in the female line. The Fox Spirit, as will be described further in the next section, was considered to be a creature of maleficent, unclean wildness, and its main evil effect was to cause madness.

Though their names were similar, the bone-setter (*barishi* ('the one who holds')) was very different from the *bariyachi*. Bone-setters were always male and were said to inherit their *onggor*s in the paternal line.[4] There was one bone-setter in Urgunge's village, who used trance and also 'blew spells' (*tarni*) to cure his patients. 'He knew all the tiniest bones of one's foot, or the cavities in one's wrist,' Urgunge said, 'Like X-rays over here.' This was not knowledge anyone could acquire. Urgunge said that the *barishi*'s spirit was an unclear matter, but

324   '*Shamanism' in Twentieth-Century History*

people thought that, whatever it was, it must have been responsible for giving understanding of bones, since the bone-setter's son, aged only 13, seemed to have perfect knowledge although he could not possibly have had much experience. This was physical understanding, known by touch, and it also had symbolic connotations. Given the symbolic link between bone (*yas*) and patrilineage, it is significant that the inheritance of the *barishi*'s ability was passed down from father to son. Although the *barishi* was not regarded as a representative of the clan, could work for anyone and travel around, this male, lineal aspect of bone-setter ability was recognized. Among the Horchin Mongols of Jirim, it was said that the Imperial clan of Chingghis Khan, the Borjigid, could include bone-setters, though never trance shamans.[5] In Jirim all bone-setters were Borjigid and all were related to one another. It was said that the first bone-setter received his dream from a snake, and thereby got a snake's power.[6] Perhaps it was the paradox of the fluid bonelessness of the intricately bony snake that made it apt as the inspiration of the *barishi*s.

Daur bone-setters seem to have had more diffuse pretensions than other specialists and a wider range of techniques. They could take charge of the ritual sacrifice to Heaven if no *bagchi* was available (*DSHI* 1985: 242), but they also, falsely it is implied, laid claims to being inspired by the Niang-Niang goddess and the fox spirit (Batubayin 1990; *DSHI* 1985: 267). They could deal with boils, sores, back pain, and skin diseases as well as fractures and dislocations. They used cauterization with hot iron, spitting chewed incense, and blowing hot air or sparks on affected parts. They had many spells (*tarni*) at their disposal, and they also kept prayer-beads, one hundred and eight in number, consisting of one precious crystal and animal bones. This list of techniques, together with the hazy ideas about the bone-setters' *onggor*s, suggest that they were called in before a shaman was approached, for a wide range of ailments. It was a more serious and dangerous matter to call a shaman.

To know was to understand and have power over the object known. The Mongol and Daur verb *mede-* means both to know, recognize, or discover and to manage or rule (Todayeva 1986: 154). The very fact that knowledge implied a power relationship with the object known, which had its own energies, was a reason for the conservatism of shamanic traditions and the maintenance of distinctions between them. Shamans in particular were wary of mastering new spirits, because they had to be absolutely certain they could succeed. 'If a shaman cannot "master" a spirit and introduces it into himself, he may be "mastered" himself by the spirit, i.e. he would become "crazy", might "lose his mind", etc. It is very unlikely that a young, little-experienced shaman would try such an introduction' (Shirokogoroff 1935: 322). Shamans *as shamans* did not address hunting and fishing spirit-masters, because the correct mode of interaction with them was prayers not the shamanic manifestation of disturbing spirits. And *yadgan*-type shamans did not figure in child delivery, since, although spirits were involved here, these particular spirits were beyond the shaman's control (6.3 and Shirokogoroff 1935: 322). Similarly, midwives and bone-setters were unable to invoke the major spirits of the *yadgan*s.

The idea of there being separate and different spirits thus preserved the separation of specialists. However, this did not mean they could not collaborate with one another, each performing part of a ritual or cure using their own expertise. So the *otoshi* might help the midwife, especially if the mother got a fever at the time of birth, and the bone-setter would collaborate with the *bagchi*. The basis of the specializations was the idea that nature could only be truly understood by certain people with particular abilities. When the Daurs conceived human nature in primarily reproductive terms they constructed two major physical-symbolic domains, that of 'bones', which were known by the *barishi*, and female birth-giving, which was known by the *bariyachi*. The two processes of reproduction, through men and through women, were also comprehended in wider cosmological and religious ways, through analogies with processes and qualities in the natural world. When the reproduction of clans was seen as consonant with images of mountains, rocks, and rain, the *bagchi* was the specialist involved; when female life-giving and infant disease were understood through images of trees and winds, it was the *otoshi* who had charge. However, these specializations were not immutable, since they depended on understandings of the world which might change. As Hull has written (1992: 42), 'Distinctions that we now take to be fundamental later generations may dismiss as irrelevant and artificial. Perhaps nature has one and only one structure, but in our attempts to discover that structure we keep on changing our minds.'

Before discussing a momentous change of this kind in Daur thinking, I should explain that doubts about the methods used by specialists could alter their relative positions in the economy of knowledge-power. The danger increasingly felt to be involved in shamanizing paradoxically threatened shamanship itself while raising the status of the *bagchi*. The distinctive abilities of the *bagchi* were discussed in 1.3 and 4.2. His main sphere of operation was the sacrifice to heaven, and the mountain, rain-giving, and river ceremonies undertaken by each sex separately. Crucially, the *bagchi* was not considered to be able to master an *onggor* and therefore was unable to perceive the spirit world through its eyes.[7] Praying (*jalbira-*) was regarded as less powerful than trance shamanic knowledge by Naun Daurs, but on the other hand, the *bagchi* was thought to be better at it than a *yadgan*. Now Shirokogoroff (1935: 386, 398) notes that among Tungus groups praying came to have greater prestige in the 1910s. This was partly due to Russian Christian missionary influence in some regions. But more important was the disturbance of hitherto relatively closed communities as a result of war, migration, and banditry and the emergence of new spirits. Alien shamans roamed abroad. The Tungus especially mistrusted Daur shamans, if only because they were suspected of bringing the Bushku spirit (6.4) with them. The Birarchen Tungus would oppose the foreign shaman masters of these spirits on the grounds that they might just as easily use the spirits for harm as for protection.

Owing to this, among the Birarchen the use of prayers instead of shamanizing is becoming more and more common. If the prayers are effective—and they may be so in all cases when suggestion may help and naturally when the prayers are granted—they can quite successfully compete with shamanism. (1935: 389; see also Howell 1994 on the contrast between prayer and shamanic invocations)

The construction of trance shamanism was such that whatever the shaman did, he or she inevitably disturbed the spirits and brought them close. Prayers, on the other hand, were used at a distance, and could even be used in an attempt to send the spirits away altogether.

This longing to be rid of spirits reveals an increased sense of threat, the feeling that the balance of benign and injurious effects of spirits had tilted conclusively towards harm. The paradox was this: the experience of new pervasive misfortunes and pestilence was constructed by 'shamanism' as being the result of the activity of new spirits, almost always from outside. It would be best to get rid of them completely, but how was this to be done? Shamans were the main counters to spirits, but on the other hand, they brought them in by their very activity and frequently failed to master them at all. Prayer was an alternative recourse. For example, after the Birarchen Tungus began to live in 'crowded' villages with strangers, rather than out in the forests, they began to experience illnesses which were attributed to a new spirit, Ainy Burhan. There were seventy-two manifestations of Ainy Burhan, cough, neck pain, ear trouble, headache, fever, vomiting, hallucinations, weakness, loss of consciousness, small problems with the eyes, etc. The intervention of a shaman, it was said, would result in immediate death (Shirokogoroff 1935: 156). Now clearly many, if not all, of these illnesses would have been thought curable by shamans before the advent of the new theory of Ainy Burhan. But this new spirit was said not to be pacified by shamanizing, only by prayer. This method came into conflict with the older theory of how best to deal with spirits and 'the competence of shamanism' was decreased (Shirokogoroff 1935: 390).

There is one Daur document, written in 1936 by one Urgungbu, a *bagchi* from Butha, which gives an insight into the thinking of people opposed to shamanizing.[8] Written after the invasion of the Japanese, the paper shows that modernizing ideas were beginning to penetrate by this time and some people felt a self-consciousness about shamanic rituals making the Daurs a 'laughing stock'. Urgungbu recommended building a hospital, employing doctors, and providing education in hygiene; but at the same time he did not reject the sacred and occult nature of the world. I cite this document at length, since it gives a remarkable insight into the thinking of someone who doubted shamans while still remaining within the wider sphere of Daur religion which Urgunge would certainly call 'shamanism'.

We Daur Mongols are located in the remote frontiers and have not been educated. We have illnesses, and we do not know how to cure them. We rely only on the shaman's dance. We have been deceived by all kinds of shamans' theories, and we have been slaughtering cows and killing pigs, which bankrupts families and even makes them die out. If one asks how can spirits make people ill, the answer is that it depends on the rise and fall of the person's fate (luck), which gives a chance for spirits to attack. I, Urgungbu, have many times seen the dancing of the shaman for Niang-Niang in the morning and Fox Spirit in the evening, but in the end there is often no result. The shaman just says, 'It's the will of Heaven'. It's said that the shaman dances on the life and on the luck [of the patient].

    . . . There are many ways to worship, but how can we say that making offerings to evil spirits is the rightful way? . . . Now I do not call shamans criminals, because I was also a person who would ask the shamans to help me. I became a *bagchi* to pray for the lives of others, so I should know what I am talking about. I have no quarrel with shamans. Even if I said one hundred things against shamans they would hardly hit the target, and I would just be asking for spitting and curses. I simply state the facts. Every time they make offerings to evils, our people suffer spiritually and financially. They lose the result of their work, they kill their livestock, go into debt, and carry out unreasonable rituals, usually for nothing. They may trust in the spirits, but everything is not clear. As human beings, we still lack something, namely the knowledge we do not have. The people entrust their fate to Heaven, and the Mongols would think this way as well, but when the people give offerings to spirits they lose their senses and never wake up. They give up their livestock. If it works, they can never thank the shaman enough and they even ask him to demand more!

    This is our situation: (1) we are controlled by our common customs which we cannot repudiate; (2) we are lost in superstitions, which we have to obey; (3) there are negative and positive things, both good and bad fortune in the world, which cannot be predicted. How can we get rid of the bad?

    To save a person from calamity is a good deed and will be called a good deed in the next world. A person who masters the skills to save the people is a good person. But even if a shaman can do this, there is corruption in the practice. For example, a patient who recovers may become superstitious; or, a shaman who cures may think himself like a god; or, in order to repay the costs of the offering, a patient who is cured will have to work hard, even though this is an avoidable thing for him . . . People blame doctors when they are unskilful. But because they cannot see the devices used by shamans, all the blame is shifted onto the spirits, and this is why shamans are never blamed.

In the next section, Urgungbu discusses the nature of the human body and the psychological theory of shamanship. Along the way, he contrasts the Daurs with the good example of the Russians (he has a slightly shaky knowledge of their history). All through he gives most space to the ideas he ostensibly disagrees with, and in the end one cannot help feeling he had not managed to extricate himself from them.

I have been told that medical doctors consider the human body as a physical thing which requires material medicine to cure it. However, shamans treat the body's life as both negative and positive, and thus they seek help from spirits which can be neither seen nor smelled. I cannot say which is the best way, but is it not better to walk on a concrete road than to walk on air?

If there are good results, we should follow them. For example, in ancient times the Slavs [Russians] worshipped wooden images and their faith was even beyond that of the Mongols. But they started worshipping the Jesuits and forbidding sexual rituals, and now we never hear of any of them getting well because of devil spirits. The rise of the Slav country has nothing to do with that. But among us there are people who insist that if there is positive, there also must be negative. If there are people there must be demons. Therefore, if a person gets ill, it must be caused by a demon. If the disease was caused by a demon, how can it be cured by a medicine? Therefore, they conclude, we do not need to ask for help from other people: when a person lives in the world, their own heart is the centre. When we have made up our heart-minds, even a hundred evils cannot attack us. Thus, if we become ill because a spirit has attacked us, it is we who are harming ourselves; if a man thinks himself to be a spirit, a spirit will never come [to him] to ask for punishment.

Urgungbu ends by contrasting his position with that of a 'narrow-minded' atheist called Yuan Zhan, who criticized a demon, and as a result became ill and could not recover. Indeed, it is implied that Yuan Zhang himself became a spirit:

Yuan Zhan caused trouble after his death. I am not an atheist. I have a wider analysis and therefore I am different from him. I love my people and advise them faithfully. I only talk of the cheating of shamans and the changing times. We should do away with ill-mannered rituals and endless expenses, which are not good for the people and make us a laughing-stock. If a man is ill we should take care of hygiene, find out the causes and suit the remedy to the cause. If we help the good ones, if we make sexual desire a calamity, if we renew the good ones and punish the bad ones, this is the old principle of the relationship of darkness and lightness. I act as I think, and the evils within my own heart will not be able to bring harm to me.

Urgungbu the *bagchi* rejected the extravagance of shamanship, but he hesitated to deny the existence of spirits, and he certainly retained a religious view of the world. If this was an enlightened view of the 1930s, let us go back now to an earlier period, when *yadgan* shamanship was challenged by the advent of the wild cults of the were-animals. This will show how, despite a shift in emphasis in the *yadgan*'s range of spirits, his type of causal explanation, in terms of the psychology of human relations, nevertheless lost ground to a movement which had other premisses.

7.2 Were-Animals and Modernity

The snake, fox, and pheasant. The specialists may have reacted in their own ways to the crisis of modernity in Manchuria, but they were unable to create a new vision of the uncontrollable and essentially foreign forces now felt to be abroad. The response instead was the outbreak of cults of were-animals (*kiant*), notably the snake, fox, and pheasant. Harmlessly bucolic though these creatures may sound to us, as *kiant* they were considered to be evil and Urgunge called them devils (*shurkul*). The cults began to take hold among the Tungus in the 1910s and seemed to have reached the Daurs just before (Shirokogoroff 1935: 235). These cults had their own practitioners, whom the Daurs called *kianchi*.

The were-animals, it may be remembered, were those creatures which trained themselves by magical breathing exercises to achieve longevity, that is, to supersede the conditions of 'life' and become immortal (2.1). After ten thousand years of training they were able to change appearance into human beings. Now, a powerful, invincible animality invaded human society. The essential technique, the breathing exercises, were associated by Urgunge with Chinese ritualized martial arts, which he said became a glamorous if foreign idea as the military prowess of the Banners turned into a fading memory. When the Banners were disbanded as army units after 1911 over two thousand men in Butha lost their positions and their income (Ikeshiri 1943: 30). Disinherited, reduced to mere farmers, and finding much of their land alienated to the Chinese, many Daurs found the rumours of alien power-techniques all too compelling. The were-creatures were said to acquire skills or science (*erdem*) along with their transformation. The animals most often mentioned were: fox (*huneg*), yellow weasel (Mustela sibirica *soolgi*), python (*mog*), spider, and pheasant (*gurguul*), and I also heard of hedgehog, racoon, dog, hare, and badger. Urgunge's statements, backed by Li *et al.* (1955), indicate that the cult did not become strong in the enclave of Morin Dawaa, but flourished along the railways and in the regions of Qiqihar, Hailar, and far northern Manchuria, which were more urbanized and exposed to Chinese and Russian incomers.

The concept of were-animals was a new one for the Daurs and will be discussed further below. However, some of the were-animals, especially the snake and fox, coincided with animals which had always been symbolically marked out in Mongol cultures. Thus for these animals there was a mixture of old and new ideas, and it was these two creatures which the existing practitioners incorporated in their repertoires. The fox in particular came to have a double role, as a new and 'external' (non-ancestral) shamanic spirit, Auli Barkan, maintained by shamans like Huangge and some midwives, and as the main protagonist in the different and antagonistic cult of the *kianchi*.

To give an idea about how people talked about were-animals I cite a passage from my field notes. In Morin Dawaa I had asked an old woman:

c. Can a human being become an *endur*?

Instead of replying along the lines I had anticipated, with the *endur* as the meritorious ancestor described by Urgunge, the old lady used the term *endur* simply as 'occult being' and launched into the following reply:

G. No, the opposite. We understand that an *endur* becomes a human being. A wild beast or a monster [*manggee*] can become an *endur*. Then it changes [*hubila-*] into a person. Oh yes, there are eight spirits [Ch. *baxian*] flying over the ocean. That is shown in a movie too. When their magic power [Ch. *fa-shu*] gets to a supreme point after many, many years, their knowledge becomes plentiful [*medeh n'walan*] and they become wild beast spirits [*heer gurees endur*]. They know everything and become skilled [*erdemtei bolno*] and can change into absolutely anything [Mo. *yu ch hulbilj chadna*], even humans, that's what they say.

N. [*a younger woman*]. Gradually, gradually formed, the snake becomes an *endur*. Breathing towards the moon, hoo, hoo, when it breathes its spells [*tarni*], it becomes a Great Snake [*dartu mog*]. When it exhales, spirit-vapour comes out [*aur hiin garbe*] and everything is blown away as by a gale. When it inhales, all kinds of things are sucked into its windpipe, drawn into its body, even whole chickens. This is how the snake inhales . . . hooh . . .

G. A Daur became mad [*kodo*] by the snake. There was a bride who came to an Ongur family . . .

N. Was she frightened by it?

G. No, no, she was it. When she waved her arm it was boneless [*yasgui*], when she moved her leg it was boneless, and then she laid down her head and body, she was that crazy, and when she disappeared she was flying over the mountains, shuur, shuur . . . uurr, and someone tried to catch her with the best ambling horse, whipped it repeatedly, and couldn't keep up with her! That Daur family had piled up firewood, adding to it generation after generation. It became as big as a mountain, that firewood, bigger and bigger, and that is where the snake made its nest [*huri*], and one day the gigantic snake came out, kur! kur! So when the bride came to this family she became ill with the snake-power. She ran away. The people chased after her. But they couldn't catch her.

Madness, loss of memory, disorientation, and loss of physical control were the main harms caused by these animal spirits. The most important of them was undoubtedly the fox. The Daur fascination with the fox goes back long before the emergence of the were-animal cult in the 1910s and 1920s, and therefore I shall briefly describe these earlier ideas. What is striking about the fox is that it symbolized both the wild and 'external', and femininity, which was 'internal' (human) but rejected.

It was remarked earlier (6.3) that the Daurs have several quite different origin myths. One of these was that they were descended from the union of a hunter with a female fox.

In ancient times there was a Daur man who wore clothes made of bark-cloth and was roaming around the the wild. One day he came across a small house where a white-haired old man was living with his beautiful daughter. The old man cooked a meal for him and gave him his daughter as wife. In fact, the old man and the girl were foxes. The couple produced many children and their descendants gradually became the Daurs. Therefore Daur people treat foxes like ancestors and respect them. (Li *et al.* 1955: 491; also Baranov 1907: 58)

'This is complete nonsense,' said Urgunge. 'We hated foxes.' However, let us persevere with the respect-for-foxes line. Another story posited the aged spirit-fox as the wild helper of the Daur people at a time of political crisis.

When the Manchu general Nurhachi attacked the Daur people in 1642, the Daur people were starving, and their leader Bombur (Bombogor) went to Outer Mongolia to seek aid. One day, on his way, he saw a white fox sleeping. He thought to himself, 'I have heard that if a fox has black hair it means the fox is 1,000 years old, and if it has white hair it means it is 10,000 years old. This fox's hair is white and therefore it must have high moral attainments.' He said to the fox, 'If you can help our people to have provisions for three years I shall ask our people to worship you as an ancestor spirit generation after generation.' When he got to Mongolia, the people there did not help him, and there was nothing he could do but go home. But for the next three years the Daurs had enough provisions. When the provisions were exhausted they submitted to the Qing (Manchu) Dynasty. Since Bombur had promised to venerate the fox, that is what the Daur people do. (Li *et al.* 1955: 491–2)

The fox here reminds us of the accidentally-found sacred object which was made into a worshipped spirit in the shamanic tradition (5.1). Indeed, Mendüsürüng told me that in his opinion the Journey Spirit (*ayin barkan*) or Found Spirit (*oluur barkan*) discovered in the wilderness was a foxy-type of creature.[9]

In the Qiqihar, Morin Dawaa, and Hailar areas Daurs kept small wooden shrines in their outhouses for a fox spirit, known as Auli Barkan ('mountain spirit', see also 7.1). Its image was made of a picture with a fox body and a human head. Urgunge remembers that some of the *barkan*s in his father's storehouse had drawings of foxes beneath them and that wisps of grass were put into these boxes for the fox to lie on. People in Morin Dawaa told me that a family would keep either this fox spirit or the weasel spirit, which would be offered cakes, alcohol, and cooked meat on the eve of the New Year.[10] A large number of ills were attributed to these spirits. Auli Barkan was extremely fussy and would insist on propitiations of, say, a black pig with two white legs of a certain age and sex. Women were strictly forbidden to enter the storehouse where this *barkan* was kept. Batubayin (1990) mentions that families with hunters and loggers would usually keep it, because the fox inhabits the mountain forest, which also explains the name of the spirit. In Qiqihar region the spirit also protected against burglary, since it enabled the owner to foresee marauding attacks in his dreams (Li *et al.* 1955: 491). Everyone agreed that the Auli Barkan caused people to go mad.

For Urgunge foxes were sly, clever, unpredictable, and associated with the smell of human sweat, especially the repellent odour of European women. On the other hand, if a fox turned into anything, it would be into a sexually attractive woman. This is a Chinese idea of ancient vintage:

> When a fox-spirit becomes old, in an abandoned tomb,
> It transforms into a woman with an engaging look,
> His fur becomes her chignon, his muzzle her powdered face,
> His long tail turns into a dress, crimson and trailing . . .

(Bo Juyi, cited in Mathieu 1985)

I heard of several encounters with fox spirits, not always women, and I cite one example, just to suggest the flavour of this 'now you see it, now you don't' kind of phenomenon. This was told to me by a Daur man from Hailar in 1988.

My brother knew a workman who went out hunting to the south of Hailar. He was looking out for game when he noticed a man sitting up on a hill, squatting as though defecating, outlined against the sky. The hunter shot at him and his hat flew off. He shot again—it was a fox that was hit. The hunter went home. Later he was out driving in the steppe. There was a *mood* [i.e. a telegraph pole]. There was no one around, and for no reason he just drove into it and was killed.

Many things remain deeply unclear about the worship of fox spirits. Why, if women were forbidden even to see the images of spirits, did the midwife take such a pride in being able to bring Auli Barkan to her aid? Why did the bone-setter also claim Auli Barkan power? Why were foxes said to be components in the Barracks Spirit, the City Spirit, the Widow Spirit (*wushi barkan*), Bogole Spirit, Temple Spirit (*sum barkan*), and Vegetable Garden Spirit (*kerizhe barkan*)? Finally, Batubayin (1990) says that Auli Barkan did not appear among the Daurs until the beginning of this century and was said to be the *Husan Taiye* fox spirit of Chinese legend. But some Daur people told me that Auli Barkan, though definitely a foreign spirit, was different from *Husan Taiye*.[11]

I do not propose to try to unravel all the layers of meaning attached to foxes, but suggest only that ideas about fox spirits were a dense symbolic area on which the cult of were-animals was superimposed. The association between foxes and the external wilderness—suggested by all of the materials above— was conceived as benign in the context of the origin and early history of the Daurs, but became menacing and inexplicable in more recent contexts. Even the image of the wife-giving clan, seen as foxes in the story above, became grist to the mill of the new cults—the evil were-animals were known as *euke* (oldest male affine), suggesting that this previously distant relationship had acquired a new bitterness. Standing for a multitude of external powers, the were-fox was invulnerable. In its mountain roaming-ground, Mendüsürüng told me, it was the one animal a Daur hunter could not kill. In the bandit-ravaged villages, with their rumours of approaching great powers at war, the image of the malevolent, invulnerable, and penetrating fox acquired an extraordinary and multiple salience, and this was the reason, I suggest, why several different kinds of specialist practitioner tried to include it in their repertoire.

Like the fox and snake, the pheasant had occurred in shamanic imagery
before the advent of the were-animal cult. As mentioned earlier (4.2) women
were likened to pheasants, and the shaman's costume was said to have a
pheasant tail. Why did they come to have a new prominence? One simple
explanation is that the Chinese have pheasant spirits, and the Daurs may
have taken on this idea without thinking much more about it.[12] I think a
more probable explanation lies in the fact that pheasants can perceive low-
frequency sounds not heard by humans. Pheasants use the shock-waves produced at about 14 Hz by wing-beats, which are inaudible to us, for a variety of
functions, such as warning off males, attracting females, and advertising the
position of the male in his territory. These facts were known to hunters of
Mongolia. Pheasants have a sensitivity to loud, low-frequency sounds such
as distant thunder, earthquakes, or gunfire, and they react with alarm calls
in winter and crowing calls in summer (Yamomoto 1971; Ridley 1983).[13]
During the First World War the shrieking of pheasants told people in England
of the start of bombardments in France. It is very possible therefore that in
Inner Asia too, when people became aware of a new insecurity, pheasants'
calls were interpreted as warnings of thunder—the anger of *tengger*—or of war.
Perhaps indeed pheasants were seen as harbingers of doom, or even as invoking
it.

Ultimately a new cult was necessary because a new relationship between
people and spirits was being created. The new images of the origin of spirits
were no longer embedded in socially-meaningful acts of human cruelty or
neglect, and therefore they could not set up the social and psychological echoes
of present relations described in 5.1.[14] Foxes, snakes, and pheasants were
animals, and they were also without history. They just happened. 'If a spirit
fox ran alongside, you were done for,' said Urgunge, 'That could transform
someone into an evil spirit.' It is true that shamanic spirits were also often
said to have originated by accident, and in the case of Holieri was also said to
have started with an animal (a deer). But shamanic spirits were always
incorporated in human relational and historical scenarios and they all had their
annals. This was not so with the were-spirits. It was presumed they had
performed magical exercises, but nothing else was known or said about them.
The very basis for shamanic treatment, a dense interaction of human relationships, was gone.

Kiant *cults among the Daurs*. The hypotheses on which the cult was based were:
(*a*) there are new spirits around which cannot be mastered by shamans and
which are responsible for troubles formerly cured by shamans, (*b*) there are
better, non-shamanic, methods of neutralizing spirits and even making them
benevolent to human beings, and (*c*) other ethnic groups closer to modern
developments will have better methods than we do (Shirokogoroff 1935: 233).
As soon as these ideas gained ground ordinary people searched for new

methods and new sorcerers, copying those of other ethnic groups or inviting their practitioners to perform. Thus the Birarchen and Kumarchen Tungus mainly copied the Daurs, but they also knew about Manchu techniques and even those of wandering Chinese specialists. Some people resisted the foreign cultists because of the danger they brought with them, and often a neutral building like a Chinese shop was hired for the performance. However, once misfortunes had been identified with were-animals, there was nothing to be done but invite the strangers to deal with them (Shirokogoroff 1935: 235, 387).

What were the cult practices among Daurs? People invited the *kianchi* when they were hit by disasters, illness, had lost their livestock, or needed guidance about some decision. The *kianchi* was any ordinary person struck by a were-animal, and he (most were men) had no special dress, no drum, did not call *onggor*s, and did not use altered states of consciousness. The *kianchi* got a *bagchi* to help, and both went to the house of the troubled family. Many other people came to watch. Everything took place at night. A table was set up in the main room with a plate and many bottles of alcohol on it. All lamps were extinguished and the people in the packed house were instructed to close their eyes. The door was firmly closed. As the seance started the *kianchi* and the *bagchi* tried to get into the house but were stopped by several robust young men inside, who stood against the door, which was also tied by rope. Suddenly there was a piercing whistle from the *kianchi* outside in the yard. Yelling and screaming, the *kianchi* and *bagchi* burst into the room, despite the best efforts of the young men pulling hard on the rope. Once inside they acted as animals, 'producing sounds of anger and desperation, making noises of bitter entreatment, filling the room with terror and mystery' (Batubayin 1990). According to Mendüsürüng, the noises were 'not human, ka, ka, ka, like stuttering chickens'. No one could understand.[15] Suddenly they stopped yelling and there was a dead silence in the room.

Now it was time for the people to see what answers the spirit would give. Mendüsürüng told me that, in the total darkness, an old person would ask, 'Can we stroke you?' and the spirit would reply, 'Don't make me tremble (*bitgii naiguulah*). You must stroke downwards, not upwards' (i.e. not against the lie of the fur). The old people dared to do this, but young people were afraid. They stroked the fox's spine (*daram*). And the person who stroked found it was very soft. That was no animal fur: it was so soft you could hardly feel it.

Mendüsürüng continued, 'Then people would ask whether to send their sick daughter to a doctor, and when they should move to the riverbank. He would tell them, "Move on the fourteenth," and my family would move on the fourteenth. All this happened long ago, before I was born.'

A Mongolian friend present at this conversation was puzzled. He asked, 'Whose body did they stroke?'

'The body of the *kianchi*.'

'But the spirit can't be seen. Were they stroking an empty place?'

And Mendüsürüng replied, 'It was completely dark, there were no lamps. It was a frightening thing. Was a fox fur there? We don't know.' Mendüsürüng said that cats and foxes have the kind of fur which should not be stroked the wrong way. The cat's fur produced shocks (? static electricity) and if a cat jumped over a corpse it would galvanize the dead and make a zombie (*bong*). This was an image of the inhuman, mindless energy emphasized in the *kiant* cults.

In Omachi's description (1982: 204–5), the *kiant* was a 1,000-year-old pheasant, and when it burst into the darkened house it flung itself across the room from one side to the other. The audience had to be quiet and keep their eyes tightly shut. If someone opened their eyes, it was said the *kiant* would fling grit in them. Once a man had tried to trick the *kiant* by catching hold of it and people said his stretched out hand was instantaneously turned into a hairy paw. The *kiant* screamed at him: 'You tried to cheat me! Your heart is not settled and you have no power to tie me!'

Shirokogoroff was present at several were-animal (*mafa*) performances conducted by Daurs among the Birarchen Tungus. His descriptions tally closely with the above: the darkness, the door closed with a rope and held by the strongest young men, the noisy rough behaviour of the spirit whirling into the room (it made the young men fall over and shout; it glugged down the alcohol, and yelled in Russian, '*Vodka dai! Vodka dai!*'—'Give vodka!'). The spirit seemed to wrestle with the *mafa* in the dark. Then acupuncture was performed using a red hot needle. There were jugglers' tricks, and borrowed fragments of exorcisms by means of rifles, chopsticks, coins, etc. All performances involved using several languages, Daur, Mongol, Manchu, a local Tungus dialect, Chinese, and even a little Russian, to speak with foreign spirits (1935: 235–7). We cannot doubt that Mafarism, as Shirokogoroff called it, was a means of dealing with the disorienting impact of powers from outside.

The political background to the spread of these cults was the end of the inclusivist state of the Manchus. The northern peoples who had had a secure and privileged position in the Empire were now cast into a lawless and threatening arena. The social background was the breakdown of clan society in the vicinity of cities and along the railways, where new administrations, armed invasion and later the influx of Japanese agents, Russian refugees, traders, builders, and so forth, had caused widespread dislocation as well as new economic opportunities.

Mendüsürüng insisted that the *kianchi*'s activities were different from and in opposition to shamans (see also Shirokogoroff 1935: 235). Shamans and the other traditional practitioners were clan-protectors, or, like the *otoshi*, acted as protectors in counter-point to the patriarchal clan. They had farms and families in the villages. The people who spread the were-animal cults, on the other hand, were 'half-medicine men, half-sorcerers', wandering professionals, living off their performances. People in native society who took up this profession tended to be cynical, rootless, greedy, and clever, widely travelled and knowing several languages, and were disapproved of by ordinary villagers as flouters of custom. Shirokogoroff gives an example of someone attracted to the *mafa* cults: he was a Birarchen Tungus, physically strong, a headman, well-travelled and speaking several languages. However he had offended the local Tungus because he refused to go hunting, made his living by trading and carting for strangers, and seemed somehow dishonest (Shirokogoroff 1935: 238). In the *mafa* cult those requesting help were no longer inevitably dependent on the practitioner attached by common *hojoor* ancestry. They were a free-floating clientele who chose this particular technique. Mostly they were people who already doubted the shaman's power.

I was very persistently asked by many of them [Tungus] about the effectiveness of Manchu *mafari*; they frequently confided in me their suspicions as to deceptions generally practised by the *mafa*s. On the other hand, the same people wanted to believe in mafarism and they repudiated shamanism. (Shirokogoroff 1935: 238)

Sometimes people went along for no other reason than to test out the performer by lighting a match in the darkness. The *mafa* seance brought with it a new kind of violence, incoherence, and bare-faced trickery. It was very unlike a shaman's performance: there were no controlled dances, no beautiful costumes, no beloved songs, no familiar addresses to 'ancestors', and the *mafa*s did not 'bring the audience or themselves to the state of passionate contact with the spirits' (Shirokogoroff 1935: 235). Shamans were in principle understandable to their audiences and employed assistants to explain any moments of incoherence (see 7.1 n. 3). The *kianchi*s preferred sensation, babble, foreign languages. The people who actively promoted these cults and invited the *mafa*s were already in conflict with local traditions. Yet, who better to deal with the disturbing effects of the half-known modern world?

Shamans did not let all this happen entirely without reaction. True, among the secluded Naun Daurs it was mostly other traditional practitioners, the bone-setters and midwives, who attempted to absorb the new fox manifestations into their practice. Clan shamans, like old Du Yadgan of Urgunge's village, continued with the archaic ancestral spirits. But Huangge (see 5.1, 6.1) took on the new 'external' spirit *sumu barkan* (Temple Spirit), which she amalgamated with her existing 'Three Journeys' *onggor*. Temple Spirit was a fox which claimed an ancient origin amid mountain-cliffs, 'becoming black over a thousand years, becoming white over ten thousand years, maintaining a connection with the Lamaist temple altar' (Poppe 1930: 27–8). This spirit included twelve small white animals and some horrible little three-legged and one-legged black creatures (Batubayin (1990) and *DSHI* (1985: 256)). Huangge hallucinated that she was beset by these. In Morin Dawaa also people told me they felt invaded by these creatures, which could penetrate even the best-built house. There was no story attached to *sumu barkan*. It had no history.

It could be managed in the old way by Huangge only by squeezing it in alongside the well-known 'Three Journeys' *onggor* spirit and attaching it to a temple. This was essentially a domestication of the wild and claim of authority over the *kiant*. Perhaps it was insufficient. The marauding penetration of harm was far more dramatically captured by the bursting in of the incomprehensible *kianchi*.

Evidence suggests that the modern world, which was manifest in northern Manchuria above all by the invasive railways with their accompanying armies, was felt by many to be a hopelessly invincible power. In remote areas in the 1920s even motorcars frightened Mongols into fleeing their camps (Ma 1949: 186). Hardly any Daurs worked on the new railroads, but some of them lived in settlements near the tracks. Jagchid (1988*b*: 324) mentions that Daurs had recourse to yet another type of shaman at these places, the *ghiamun*, who were mostly Chinese. These were known as soldiers of Wu San-kuei (a seventeenth-century Chinese general who had gone over to fight for the Manchus but later set himself up independently of them in South China, though he was ultimately defeated).[16] Little is known about this cult, but there is evidence elsewhere of opposition to the railway engines themselves. Haslund had lived for a week in the mid-1920s with the Solon Ba Shaman at Mehertei, which was a partly Daur village south of Hailar. On his return in 1936 Haslund found the old shaman dead, and tells the story as follows:

As his only son had been killed by a Japanese car, he decided on a last attempt to stop the development which was destroying his world. He thought that he would be able to achieve this by fighting one of the Japanese locomotives that had begun to push their way through the wilderness which had been a quiet refuge for him and the spirits. He prepared for the fight for many days, assisted by his fellow tribesmen. The blood from many sacrificial animals coloured the snow, night after night the forest echoed with the beating of the drums and the piercing cries for help to the assistant spirits, and when Ba Shaman finally went off to his fight he was possessed as in the great days of his youth. But as the days and weeks passed without Ba Shaman returning and as the Japanese steam-engines continued to rush through the wilderness of the Solons, his people understood that the old spirits had had to give up in the face of a new stronger power. (Haslund 1944: 7–8).[17]

It seems unlikely to me and to Urgunge that a shaman would have attempted to battle with something without psychological attributes like a steam-engine— 'unless he was mad', as Urgunge put it. But one never knows. Possibly this was suicide. In either case, it was hopeless opposition to the very emblem of early twentieth-century progress.

However, it would be a mistake in my view to see 'shamanism' only through images of defeat. Even in remote northern Manchuria echoes of modernist ideas reached across the land-mass of Eurasia. As the Communist revolution was being accomplished in Russia, in Beijing Chinese nationalists and revolutionaries were seeking new images and ideologies of a non-Imperial political order. From both west and east, word of such ideas reached the Daurs. Outer Mongolia established a revolutionary government in 1921, and by the late 1920s the Daur socialist Merse had spent long periods in Beijing and had also visited Moscow and Western Europe. The Chinese Nationalist government banned shamanism, divination, geomancy, and 'superstitious practices' in general in 1928–30 in a plan to establish a rational, modern, and scientific society. As Duara (1991) has shown, the slogans against superstition were not just indications of new values. They were used in a power struggle in which the state and advocates of modernity sought to expand their power. 'Each episode of intervention in the name of modernization also involved a restructuring of power in local society, ending up, more often than not, with a significant expansion of the power of the state' (1991: 81). The revolutionary Mongolian government established strict new controls, particularly at its frontiers, where incomers were rigorously examined for their ideological reliability and inspected to make sure they were not spies. All this, in decades of incessant war, gave impetus to a lurching sea-change in political identities, which was well expressed by the Russian Futurist Rozanova. 'The war did its business with us,' she wrote, 'it tore away the pieces of the past from us—it shortened one thing, it lengthened another, and, changing the world to a new speed, it gave a malignant background to our lives, against which everything seemed tragic or insignificant' (Yablonskaya 1990: 97).

In the far distant steppes and forests the shamanic peoples responded, creating cultural manifestations in their own ways. The metropolitan modernist projects stressed disjunction and contradiction, the separation of construction from feeling, of representation from human psychology. The images were of the mechanical in the body and the alienating-exhilarating effects of self-transformative striving whereby the materiality of modern life took over. In cubist painting, abstract hard shapes, cogs, and newsprint merged with and refracted the human body, and at the same time Picasso and Stravinsky made the delineaments of 'raw' African images or the 'primitive' rhythms of Russian peasant dances emblems of power. I think that the brute images of the were-animal cult can be better understood in this light. They too had a fascinating power, acknowledged by the frightened and curious responses to them of audiences. Of course the Daur images were created within their own culture, and drew upon ideas of noxious, death-defying animality rather than the mechanical artefacts as in Europe, but they represented some common features of early twentieth-century sensibility. There was a similar estrangement from inward-looking familiar explanations, a rejection of humanist, ancestral readability, and a new openness to alien powers. The purposeful construction of the invincibility of modernity in the notion of the were-animals revealed the seemingly human, modern person to be a feral, inhuman creature with no understandable connection between appearance and inner being. The new cults were not patient-centred. They drew upon wider feelings of uncertainty and troubledness. Unlike the shamans there was no question of empathy on the part of the *kianchi*. In these cults the human personality and personal relations were displaced from their position of centrality in religious practice.

The idea of achieved immortality is extremely old in China, but it was foreign to the Daurs. In my view, it came to represent a new understanding of time. In earlier shamanist thought, objects and beings were thought to have their fated span of existence, to be replaced by others in an endless process of cosmic reproduction. 'For a shamanist,' Urgunge said, 'A man has a man's lifetime, a tiger has a tiger's lifetime. In shamanism everything has its timespan, like a car-tyre. What is the life of a car-tyre? You have them, then you must get some more.' There was no end, no beginning, and no concept of change except that of replacement. But the were-animals represented something different, a linear view of purposeful metamorphosis, culminating in the acquisition of skills and invincibility. Paradoxically, 'immortality' in this perspective repre- sented an acceptance of the finality of death. Death was no longer the moment of a beginning, but was to be avoided and put off at all costs. In remote Inner Asia the new significance of this ancient vision was not attached to an ideology of a coming world-mastering society to put in the place of individual decease. Instead, masterful asocial traits were abroad, making their appearance in people's craziness and anxieties.

Maybe it seems far-fetched to represent the Daur *kianchi*s as agents in a far- flung modernist reaction, and it is certainly possible to look in a more orthodox way at the cults' historical antecedents. They seem to have been an appropria- tion of an older popular form of religiosity of the Chinese and Manchus. Thus in the 1880s, James, of Her Majesty's Bombay Civil Service, had been amused to observe possession by fox, stoat, snake, hare, and rat spirits when he travelled in southern Manchuria. He was amazed at the magnificence of the Temple of the Fox at Mukden (Shenyang) and by the fact that it bore the same legend over the door as Christian churches in China, 'Ask and you shall receive' (James 1888: 190–2). In Beijing there was also a flourishing cult, long-established in the 1940s, of foxes, weasels, hedgehogs, hares, and snakes (Li 1948). The creatures achieved immortality by asceticism, which was difficult for them and necessitated retiring to mountain fastnesses to practise their exercises. The 'bad' ones relapsed, absorbed evil vigour during sexual intercourse, and then could not refrain from attacking people (Li 1948: 3–5). Established among Muslims and lower-class workers, the cult was regarded by respectable Chinese as heterodox and 'inferior'—its sacred animals were said to flee from officials and the Imperial Palace environs even while they secretly inhabited the statues of more dignified gods (Li 1948: 21–3).[18] The 'shamans' in this cult were said to belong to animal families and only appear physically to be humans. They attempted to absorb their clients and turn them into members of the animal families—the hedgehog family, the weasel family, etc. Suddenly the spirits would flee, forsaking the city for their native mountains, but again they would reappear and new spirits would also arise (Li 1948: 74–8). It seems likely that it was this evanescent, self-renewing, essentially urban cult that the northern peoples chose to imitate, but in doing so, in taking power from elsewhere, they were unconsciously following a pattern of popular religiosity which was spreading over all China at this time.

It is at least arguable that it was the Chinese Boxer rebellions of the 1890s that first thrust the modern world in the faces of the farmers and hunters of the remote north. The were-animal cults were in many respects quite unlike the Boxer sects, but the differences are instructive. The Boxers were martial arts societies formed among the rural poor in Central and Northern China. They agitated against everything new that seemed to make their lives more abject: the unemployment caused by imports, modern systems of transport, and above all against foreigners and missionaries. Their attacks on missionaries were an excuse for the foreign powers to intervene. Those in favour of the Boxers (mainly Manchus) then gained power at the court, and the Qing Empire officially declared war on the Western nations—with disastrous results including the invasion of all northern Manchuria by the Russians. The Daurs did not join the Boxers, but those living on the northern Russian bank of the Amur were driven south, many losing their lives (Shirokogoroff 1993: 100).

Now the Boxers themselves consisted of numerous cult-like societies, which used spirit-possession, healing, chanting spells, and burning incense alongside the martial arts in their meetings. Moral purity and asceticism were proclaimed. There were millenarian announcements. The spirits which possessed the Boxers were heroes from popular operas, novels, and storytellers' tales. What these possessions crucially conferred was invulnerability, so that swords and bullets could not harm the initiates. Violently loyalist and xenophobic, the Boxers attacked foreign shops, installations, and mission posts, singing:

> Rip up the railroad tracks!
> Pull down the telegraph lines!
> Quickly! Hurry up! Smash them—
> The boats and steamship combines.
>
> (Esherick 1987: 300)

The martial arts societies were not the only evidence of widespread alienation in north China. There were numerous other sects, some of very long-standing (Naquin 1985: 255–91). Sects, martial societies, and popular rebellion fed off one another, though they had different patterns of leadership. The Spirit Boxers sect arose seemingly from nowhere, spread extremely rapidly, and then disappeared from the historical scene (Esherick 1987: 221). This Esherick attributes in part to the fact that possession could come upon anyone, making him leader for a time, to be followed by other cells as other men were possessed. 'The possession ritual's capacity to give anyone the identity of a god gave the Spirit Boxers the capacity to make anyone a leader' (Esherick 1987: 240). When the rebellion's epicentre moved to the Beijing area and southern Manchuria, the ambivalent attitude of the Manchu conservatives to the Boxers was probably shared by Daurs. But shortly afterwards, some of the same features, of lightning spread from region to region, self-elected cult leaders, borrowed fragments of ideas and rituals, and the themes of ascetic subordination of the body and immortality, applied to their own cult of the were-animals.

However, the north Manchurian were-animal cults were not millenarian, nor were they militant. The cult did not enjoin that people themselves do spirit-exercises and acquire strength. They did not pretend to that ability. Instead, as we have seen, the most scary animals were attributed with power (*kuch*), and their brutal invasion of the house was accepted by the people sitting cowering in the dark. The point of the cult was perhaps that the spirit was placated. It was given alcohol; it was softened; it was stroked. Violence was not turned outwards. The image of the ageless and invincible creature was invented, only to wreak havoc in the households of the community, where the stroking of the fur seems to have been as much exploratory as anything else.

Perhaps the submissiveness of the audience in the were-animal cults can be related to the Daurs' new perception of political loss and of themselves as peoples at a lower stage of civilization than the Chinese. It is significant that by the 1930s the were-animals were called by Daurs, in Chinese, *hu xian* 'the barbarians' (Ikeshiri [1943] 1982: 59).[19] During the Qing Empire, people like the Daurs had themselves been called 'barbarian' by the Chinese, but they could deny the label, at least to themselves, by virtue of their close association with the ruling Manchus. With the advent of the Chinese Republic, this was no longer possible, and the idea of 'barbarian' acquired a new dimension. It had referred to the 'raw' peoples of the outer periphery (peoples who had, however, repeatedly conquered the Chinese). Now the civilizational connotations of the term were compounded by new ideas of social evolution from Russia and Western Europe. Here is a mild example of the Chinese attitude:

The Mongols are the forebears of the Oriental people, but the Chinese are the representatives of Oriental culture. That the Chinese and the Mongols have a common genealogy is proved beyond doubt by considering their features and skeletal framework. . . . But the survival of any people is derived from their culture. Chinese culture is superior to that of the Mongols and is the foundation on which the Chinese state has been erected. Hence, from now on the Chinese should exert every effort to confer their culture upon the Mongols, who should strive to receive it, so that we may revive our common ancestry.[20]

The Daurs now had no shield from Chinese contempt for their culture, but at the same time, by invoking the 'barbarian' spirits they could at least fling the label back and fix it on something outside themselves.

The dispersed structure of 'shamanism' meant that there were always other identities to provide a point of vantage. The *kiant* cult never took over all of religious life. It did not achieve predominance, nor did it eliminate the other shamans. Thus, different as it was from shamanic practice, Urgunge always maintained that it was 'part of shamanism' and I think he saw it as rather an inferior part. I was puzzled by the motivation of the were-animal spirits, and once I asked him:

C. If no one harmed the fox, why was the fox spirit so hurtful to human beings? What was in it for him?
U. What good English! I remember La-Bagsh [Owen Lattimore] once used that phrase, 'What's in it for me?' Well, no problem, I can tell you. Somehow, the fox wanted to be a human being, but he was unable to do it. He worked very hard, but still he became no more than a 1,000-year-old fox. Therefore he was unsatisfied. Just one inch short . . . he changed shape, he knew everything. But he was not a human being, his brain was still foxy-loxy. Jealous. He was jealous of human beings.[21]

From the shamanic perspective human relations were always most valued and humanity central, though humanity was not seen as dominating the world. From this point of view, Urgunge used to robustly dismiss the values of the West.

The spirits weren't really greedy for food. We gave them meat, but that wasn't really what they wanted. Now you listen to this. What does 'a poor man' mean to you? The British people assume a poor guy is one who hasn't got money, no house. But we Mongols think, 'Oh poor guy, hasn't got parents, a wife and children.' This is very important.

If you think now,—what a beautiful society it was, very simple, very honest, very decent. And that shows one thing, why they never allowed singing in the village. Suppose you have a room, father and mother living there with children, and suddenly I want to sing. My father would have been shocked almost to death. Hey! What's going on here? That's because singing was luring . . . luring lust. So you must understand, only the shaman was allowed to sing. He sang to protect us and turn back the desiring ones. But over here, of course, you have your theme-song, 'Diamonds are a girl's best frie-e-nd.' And where does that get you?

Urgunge had tremendous confidence, given perhaps by the supremacy of humanity in his vision of shamanism, and also by the multiplicity of viewpoints which required the individual to choose their own way. 'Human nature means everyone wants to be good, to be the best. Then you have to decide what is the best, what the best means.' This meant distinguishing between the individual and the collective. 'The Chinese think they are the centre of the world, but the neighbouring peoples, the Mongols, the Tibetans, they don't buy that idea at all. Not at all. So what about us? Did the Daurs think they were the centre of the world? Individually yes, every one of them may have thought that way. But collectively they may not have thought that at all. If you think that way collectively, it is not good.'

I have traced a somewhat circuitous route, by drawing out Urgunge's attitudes, to show that the *kiant* cult could well have dramatized one widespread apprehension of political and cultural vulnerability, but this did not mean that individual people were therefore downcast. Other shamanic ideas cross-cut these and buoyed people up.

The *kianchi* cults made no use of overt ideology, mythology, or indeed any devices explaining the spirits themselves. It was this blank ferocity and the associated mutual suspicion of performer and audience, together with the almost abject role taken by the households, that must be contrasted with shamanic practices. Indeed, by comparison, the shaman's performances seem havens of confidence, culture, and sophistication. I do not mean to imply by this that the were-animal cults were found in some de-cultured, proletarian area of society separate from the rest. The *kiant* and *mafa* cults were an attempt to respond to the conditions of life experienced by everyone. Nevertheless, it is true that the traditional shamans, who continued to flourish after the advent of the new cults, were familiar figures in the upper echelons of Daur society. Here we shall return to Huangge, who grew up in one of the most progressive and well-educated families of all the Daurs.

7.3 The Shaman and the Revolutionary

Huangge Shaman, born in 1900, was brought up in the same large family as her first cousin Merse, who was born in 1894 (see Plates 24 and 25, and family chart in 6.1).[22] They lived in Mehertei, the village from which Ba-Shaman fought the steam-engines some thirty years later.[23] Huangge became the most famous shaman in the Barga region. Merse was one of the leading revolutionary thinkers and activists of his time in the whole of Inner Mongolia. The conventional view would be that these two lives and outlooks must have been utterly opposed and separate. However, this was not the case, and it is arguable that shamanist attitudes lay behind both kinds of active participation in the world.

What kind of man was Merse? Let us first look at his family, which was distinguished, wealthy, well-educated, and accustomed to producing leaders. His mother's brother, Duke Tsend of the Aul clan, was both an international statesman and a scholar.[24] Tsend's son, Merse's cousin Erdentei, was also a well-known scholar. Merse's father, Rung-lu, was Deputy Governor of the Solon Left Wing Banner and then became an official in the Hulun Buir Futudung Gungshu. Later he was active in the 'Daurian Government'.[25] This was the short-lived attempt by the Buryat Semenov to establish a separate 'Asian' state in Dauria, just over the Russian border from Hailar in south-eastern Siberia in 1918–19.[26] Semenov's army fought against the Bolsheviks, but he refused to accept the authority of the Russian White forces and maintained close links with the Japanese, who were then trying to increase their influence in this part of Asia. The Daurian Government included in its motley assemblage the fanatical Baron Ungern-Shternberg, who was shortly to strike out on his own and invade Mongolia, and a Buddhist lama, the Neisse Gegeen, who, it was hoped, would attract Mongols to the cause. A significant part of the Daurian army was based over the frontier in Hailar itself, where the eight hundred ferocious Harchin Mongol cavalry of Fushengge were quartered. Manchu restorationists, Japanese interests, Czech troops as well as the Red and White armies were all involved. As the local administration of Hailar was largely in the hands of Daurs, the leading families could hardly avoid involvement in the complex politics of the time. What is clear is that from his childhood Merse must have been familiar with Asian politics in the widest sense; he must have known about Mongolian history, about the clash of right- and left-wing ideologies, and about the repeated attempts to establish some form of political autonomy in the Hailar region. Merse's family had moved beyond local politics to operate on the world stage. Merse's own family was attacked by Cossacks in a tragic incident (see 6.1).

Merse seems to have had definite modernizing principles virtually from childhood. He was only 14 when he startled his father by stipulating ten rules of frugality in running the household and locality, including the elimination of superstition. He used to read aloud at gatherings of the *mokon* (clan) and thereby gained the approval of the elders. When he arrived home from school in Qiqihar in 1914 he had cut off his pig-tail, the sign of loyalty to the Manchus (though restorationist currents were still strong at this period). Then he presented his father with instructions for managing his estate and set about lending family livestock to the poor without charge. Rung-lu doubtless found this behaviour unbearable and Merse was punished. Making this a turning-point in his life, Merse left home to study at the Russian Language Institute in the Foreign Affairs Department in Beijing (Engkebatu and Erkembayar 1987*a*). On hearing that the Mongolian rebel Bavuujav (Babujab) had attacked Hailar he returned and soon persuaded his father to let him open a school there.[27] He personally travelled to remote places to recruit the best teachers and collect money from local rich people, and he arranged a modern curriculum and brought in girl pupils, the first in the region. However, soon the school had to be closed because of an outbreak of plague in Hailar, in which Merse's own grandfather and younger brother died. He went back to Mehertei village in 1919 and founded another school there, promoting a new way of life for the Daur and Tungus peoples. One of the teachers was a young Buryat woman from the USSR, whom Merse invited to teach Russian and tell the students

24. Huangge's family, close-up. The old man with moustaches is the grandfather. Merse stands in front of him with belt and cap. The little girl with head-dress seated beside her grandfather, Chen Shan, is Huangge. Photo: date unknown, photographer unknown. [7.3]

25. Huangge's household posing before the gate of their house near Hailar. From left: 1st: unknown; 2nd: Huangge's father, Chagaan yeye; 3rd: Merse's father, Rung-lu; 4th: Huangge's teacher shaman, Fu Leng-chen. White Russian officers unknown; date and photographer unknown. [7.3]

about the Bolshevik revolution, science and technology, hygiene, and the back-wardness of feudal and superstitious views.[28] In 1918 Merse founded the Hulun Buir Youth Party. When the plague had subsided in 1920, Merse returned to Hailar. He established yet another school there, invented a writing system for the Daur language using the Latin alphabet, set up a co-operative for marketing the livestock products of the herding people, and began a project for improving the breeds of sheep, cattle, and horses of the region. But Merse was soon driven away from Hailar by the warlord Wu Junsheng, who rightly suspected him of 'turning the place red'.[29] Merse went to Beijing, then to Mongolia and Moscow.[30] On his way back he composed an ode to Lake Baikal.

After his return to China Merse became the General Secretary of the Inner Mongolian People's Revolutionary Party. The Party was modelled on the revolutionary party which had taken power in Mongolia with Soviet backing, but in Inner Mongolia political conditions were complex and the IMPRP had to negotiate a position among the competing forces of the Chinese nationalists, communists, and warlords (see Atwood 1992). The IMPRP, with its army, decided to back Feng Yu-xiang, a powerful warlord with progressive inclina-tions. However, Feng was defeated by Zhang Zuo-lin, then in control of Manchuria and northern Inner Mongolia. Merse and his Party retreated south to Baotou, and Feng fled to Mongolia. In 1926, forced ever westwards, Merse ended up in the desert province of Alasha, where he incited the herdsmen to rebel against their princes. This venture was a disaster. Merse was already on bad terms with his fellow-leaders of the IMPRP. He now became disillusioned and left for Mongolia. While in Mongolia he came under increasing Commu-nist influence and, if he had not been already, he now became tied to the Comintern. From his base in Ulaanbaatar he reorganized the Hulun Buir Youth Party, drew on support from Inner Mongolians in Russia and Mongolia, and prepared to take Hailar. In 1928 he moved into Huuchin Barga and rallied herdsmen to join the insurrection. The young Lama Reincarnation of the Gangjuur Monastery (the goal of the cart-sellers' journey, 3.3) was persuaded to back the movement. The coup was at first successful. But promised help from Russia never materialized, and Merse's small army was soon defeated by forces supporting the regional warlord, Zhang Xue-liang. Peace negotiations were held at the Gangjuur Monastery. Merse was imprisoned for a time, but he soon accepted a position as adviser to Zhang Xue-liang in return for a promise that the general would reform administration and education in Hailar (Engkebatu and Erkembayar 1987*a*). In 1927 Merse had set up a school for Mongols at Shenyang. He now returned there and made it a training ground for nationalist and revolutionary ideas.

It was around this time, 1930, that Merse met De Wang, Urgunge's prince, leader of the Mongolian movement for autonomy in Chahar (see 1.2). 'Why was the Outer Mongolian independence movement successful?' he asked the Prince rhetorically. 'It is because the sacred Reincarnation, the Bogd Gegeen, became the central belief for the Mongols, unifying their will and concentrating their strength, while we Inner Mongolians exist only in discord' (Lu 1980: 8). He advised the Prince to invite the Panchen Lama to become such a rallying point for Inner Mongolia. This the Prince hurriedly did, building two magnificent temples for the great Lama. He was afraid, according to Lu, that otherwise Merse himself would bring in the Panchen first, thus moving the centre of gravity of the independence movement away from Chahar to Hailar (Lu 1980: 9). However, Merse made no move to invite the Panchen to Hailar.

In fact, Merse disappeared in mysterious circumstances soon after this. By the time the Japanese invaded Manchuria in 1931, he had been dismissed from his position as head of the school at Shenyang and was under daily threat to his life as a known revolutionary. He went straight to Beijing to discuss a common policy with other Mongolian leaders, and then to Hailar.[31] He may have hoped to organize resistance there, while being pursued by the Japanese, who almost certainly wanted him to turn to their side. Whatever his plans were, they failed. One day Merse set off alone to the Soviet consulate in Manzhouli, saying he would be back soon, but he never returned (Enkebatu and Erkembayar 1987*a*). It has recently become known that Merse was arrested by the Russians as a Japanese spy.[32]

Merse was a revolutionary, but he was above all a man who wanted independence and a better life for the Mongols. He argued for the Mongol identity of the Daurs. He wrote probably the most outspoken attacks on Chinese policy ever printed in Chinese by a Mongol (Lattimore 1934: 132). He was equally scathing about Russian hypocrisy, denouncing its 'benevolence' to Mongolia which only masked repression (Kuo Tao-fu 1930: 754–62). Mongolia was useful to him as a base for activities, but in the end he did not agree with government or Party policy there. His speeches, songs, and anthems used the Daur metaphors we have come to know so well in this book. 'After his meetings he came down from the platform and went among the young people, telling them, "You are like trees when they are luxuriant. The whole tree's growth depends on the shoots. The responsibility for rejuvenating the nationality depends entirely on you."' His anthem composed for the Revolutionary Party listed each of the 'scattered', 'declining', and 'pitiful' peoples of Inner Mongolia and hailed their resurgence, which was marked by each having its flag planted on a green mountain-top (Enkebatu and Erkembayar 1987*a*).

'The Mongols thought Merse was an arrogant guy, you know,' said Urgunge.[33]

But he managed power as it should be managed. In the great Mongolian families they always distributed different kinds of power: one son became the prince, one a lama, a third another big-shot. This is what Merse did. He wanted political power and he let his sister have religious power as a shaman. In Hailar there was one great political leader, Merse, and one great shaman, Huangge. In the Naun valley we had neither big leaders nor great shamans, and the reason for that is that we were in a backwater, and the reason for that is that our road led nowhere, neither to Russia nor China, and we did not even have a railway at that time.

Urgunge pointed to a very important, and ancient, political principle, known by the Halh Mongols as *arag bilig* (means and wisdom), the support of religion by the ruler, and legitimation of the ruler by religion. The idea of introducing famous Buddhist figures had occurred sooner or later to many of the Mongolian leaders of his period (for example, the role of the Neisse Gegeen in the Daurian Government, that of the young Gangjuur Monastery Gegeen in the attempted coup in 1929 in Hailar, and the reported conversation with Prince De in 1930). But Merse was not a Buddhist. We must look for more subtle relations with his own Daur 'shamanism', in which *arag bilig* as an overt principle was unknown.

It turns out that Merse, along with all his other activities, was a *bagchi*. Furthermore, unusually, he had an *onggor* spirit. He did not have a special shamanic costume (*jawa*) and did not shamanize (deliberately induce an altered state of consciousness), but when the *onggor* came upon him he was transported and in this state was unable to teach the pupils at his school in Shenyang. He could foretell the future. He also used incantations (*tarni*) and was able to cure people with them.[34] His son told me: 'Merse could speak beautifully and calm people. He helped women during hard labour-pains.[35] He helped miserable people to laugh and be happy. They say this among the people.' Merse and Huangge were very close to one another.[36] After he became a revolutionary Merse stopped making sacrifices himself, but he never renounced his *onggor* or quarrelled with shamanic beliefs. After Merse's death, his son Adiya became the beloved 'protected child' (*umiesen kuu*) of Huangge and wore a bell she had given him.[37] Just as this book was going to press, I discovered that Odongowa, the author so often quoted in this book, is Merse's daughter.

Huangge remained greatly respected in Merse's family during the many long years after her brother's disappearance. They said she was powerful (*erketei*) from her spirits, which took the form of a wolf and a fox, and they loved her for her wisdom and kindness. She was dignified and self-restrained. For example, Huangge did not drink alcohol; on her becoming a shaman shortly after her marriage, her parents advised her that as a shaman she should now give up such things. When Huangge died in 1973 the official disapproval of shamanism was such that it was not possible to build her a *shand* (shaman's mortuary cairn). She was buried according to her own prescription: to protect against spirits she held a model bow and arrow (*num sum*) in each hand, and two were also placed at her feet.

The *shand* had been crucial in the relations between shamans and political powers (see also 3.2). Merse's son said to me, 'I don't really know, but I think the Daurs' *oboo* was really a *shand*. At the Mongol *oboo*s they invited Buddhist lamas to conduct the rituals, but this did not happen with the Daurs. We did not invite lamas. Huangge invoked her ancestral spirits at the Züün Bogd (Eastern Sacred) Shand.'

The significance of this is that the ritual cairns called *oboo* (but which in this case may 'really' have been shamanic mortuary sites) were the places where political leaders made their appearance in religious life. It was here that they invoked the blessings of the sky, mountains, and land spirits on behalf of the whole community for the coming season. In the Hailar region the *oboo* was asked not so much for an abstract blessing as for a practical one: abundant rain, good green pastures, more horses, and healthy herds (Akiba and Akamatsu 1941: 262).[38] Throughout the Hailar region, there were *oboo*s for each village and Banner. There were also *oboo*s for the *zuo-ling* (a military rank under the Manchus) and for certain influential families (Akiba and Akamatsu 1941: 262). At large public *oboo*s people looked for further occult power than the genius of the place itself. A man from Ordos said to me, 'We see an *oboo* and know it must be here for a reason, so what interests us is what lies hidden beneath it.'[39] Thus even in Buddhist regions there was the idea that an *oboo* was constructed over some other mysterious power. If the many Daur *oboo*s were located at shamans' mortuary sites, what this meant in effect was a pervasive spread of shamanic influence into the religious sphere of the patriarchal elders. In Hailar even some non-Daur *oboo*s worshipped by Buddhist lamas were subject to this process: the famous *oboo* (see Plates 10 and 11) was said to be sited over the grave of a female shaman.

Revolutionary or not, Merse worshipped at the Gobol *oboo* on the southern hill at Mehertei. In the entire Mongolian region everyone goes to *oboo* festivals, and they are still the major public rituals at which the entire populace will appear. The local leadership turns up in force at their *oboo*, lined up in order of rank. Today even Chinese Communist Party officials take the seats of honour, notwithstanding the fact that the religious ceremonies mean nothing to them, and this is because the *oboo* festivals are the most joyous celebrations of public life. Indeed, it would be considered an insult for a prominent person not to attend. Secular leaders are *seen to be leaders* at the *oboo*. They give the orations and their offices provide the funds for general feasting, and this is a major source of their popular legitimacy.[40] Merse must have appeared at *oboo* festivals whenever he returned to Hailar. As a *bagchi* he may have chanted the prayers. Though he used the written word to campaign among intellectuals, he needed wider acclaim too, if only for the recruitment of Party members and soldiers. Besides this, he must have benefited from the fact that his sister was a renowned shaman. *Oboo* rituals, if they are sited on shamanic graves, make absolutely no reference to this fact. Nevertheless, people know about it. On analogy with other Mongolian leaders of his period, Merse would only have gained from the idea that, along with his modern activism, he also had access to dark and strange powers.[41] The conclusion must be that the regional authority of Daur rulers was significantly legitimized by shamanic power.

It was proposed earlier (1.5) that the cosmologies of *bagchi*s and *yadgan*s were antithetical, in the sense that the elders drew upon the plain natural features of mountains as models for an ideological view of society, while *yadgan*s attacked such landscapes, insisting on the real diversity and awkwardness of social relations. These two perspectives were kept separate in the Naun valley, but it appears they overlapped in Hailar (3.2). Now we see that a brother and sister could represent these different cosmologies, and at the same time, in their own relatedness, could personify their overlapping. Both of them made some moves in the direction of the other. Thus, Merse was unusual among *bagchi*s in having an *onggor*, even if he did not control it. Huangge's fox spirit meanwhile proclaimed its attachment to the Buddhist temple and acknowledged the mastership of mountains (Poppe 1930: 28):

> The lone hill is my surprise
> The southern hill is my master
> My brown-spotted [bird] spirit
> Descend now in your true body!

For a shaman to provide a source of power, it was necessary for shamanism itself to maintain authority among the people. To some extent Merse himself may have contributed to the tradition. It is inconceivable that he, as head of such an influential family, could have simply allowed his sister to become a shaman. He must have supported the venture, which, it will be remembered, was validated at the large public ritual of the *ominan* (5.8). In fact, Merse's son told me, 'He made Huangge a shaman.'

However, the influence of 'shamanism' must have rested on more than the support of one leader. The theme of this book suggests that the different parts of 'shamanism' would have different fates in history. In fact the practices of bone-setters and midwives have been eroded by modern medicine, and the *kiant* cults died down with the ending of banditry and the fear of external invasion.[42] The perseverance of the clan was crucial to the continuation of the *yadgan*'s cults of ancestral *hojoor* spirits. Now after 1911 the clan gradually lost ground as a vital element in Daur social life. The images of collective ancestral spirits, which had provided interpretations of history and geographical movements and ethnic identity, became less important (Manduertu 1991: 95). Nevertheless, the reorganization of population by the Japanese and the supplanting of the clan by other social groups (the multi-ethnic village, the workplace) did not end the *yadgan*'s practice, just as it did not eliminate the cults of the sky, the mountains, and springs. It changed the social basis for these activities. By the 1940s most of the *oboo* festivals in Hailar were based on territorial-administrative groupings rather than clans and they were attended by all local residents irrespective of ethnicity (Akiba and Akamatsu 1941: 256–62).

It is only to be expected that the content of the *yadgan*'s repertoire would change correspondingly. Thus accounts of Huangge hardly mention her Red Spirit clan *hojoor*, but dwell rather on the Temple Spirit of fox origin (Poppe 1930; Odongowa 1991 n.d.). More general descriptions of Daur beliefs in Hailar in the 1940s mention Niang-Niang, the fox spirit, and fire spirit as having more importance than the ancestral spirit (Akiba and Akamatsu 1941: 294).[43]

Such gradual changes in the repertoire did not, however, alter the essential cognitive basis of the *yadgan*'s practice. This was still founded on intuitive understanding of human psychology, the relation between belief and desire, and relational emotions. Thus the idea of the *onggor*, which was a succession of human dramas, continued to be the crux of the *yadgan*'s identity. The *onggor* was itself an idea of a dynamic process, since each shaman added new persons to it. In Huangge's case the 'Three Journeys' *onggor* (see 5.1) was supplemented by the spirit of her predecessor Fukan, and by the fox of the Temple Spirit. This enlarged her personal geography of spirit-haunted places and allowed the explanation of new sufferings, such as infectious diseases (*huar*) coming from the city of Qiqihar. It is worth noting that in her invocation of her *onggor* Huangge referred not only to the Manna clan but also to the far larger regions of Barga Mongolia and Hulun Buir as the place where her spirits flourished (Poppe 1940: 28–30). The idea of the *onggor* could thus expand to the socio-political dimensions relevant to the shaman's clientele. But the emotional traces of earlier shamans were not lost, and they were revived each year at that shaman's *shand*. Merse's son 'remembered' above all Huangge's predecessor, Fukan (see 5.1), even though this shaman must have died before he was born: 'Fukan was kind and he tried to help poor people. He never accepted gifts like meat or silk. If the patient was destitute Fukan would provide his own items for propitiation. That is the warm-hearted person he was.' It is most important, when considering these emotional memories, that we should not ignore the dual existence of the shaman, who lived in everyday society as well as becoming one with the spirits. The fact that shamans were survived by their children and grandchildren, who had intimate knowledge of their personalities, contributed also to these memories, because people searched descendants for signs inherited from their ancestors. All these were factors in the strange reversibility of the *onggor*: thus the spirit of Fukan both took the cosmic form of an otter, which was 'fed' fish, *and* it was the close, kindly relative who helped the poor.

It was dense networks of relations which ensured the continued relevance of the *yadgan* tradition. Close-knit communities would always have sufferings and tragedies that were best explained by the familiar and incremental *onggor*. In this chapter, in one family of the Gobol clan we have discovered both the shaman (*yadgan*) and the 'old man' (*bagchi*). In neither case did their life-courses arise from nothing, since the source for both Huangge's and Merse's occupations arose from networks of predecessors and kin who provided the preconditions for their achievements. Both of them were remarkable people, and I think that this remarkableness may have been inspired by the shamanist culture. It enabled two quite different careers to be sustained in close proximity and evidently with mutual respect. Now shamanic practice was essentially subversive of patriarchal authority, and Merse, we should not forget, was a rebellious person. He challenged patriarchy from his earliest years, but he was forced, in order to amass power himself, to compromise with local structures and even to work for the war-lord Zhang Xue-liang. He thus became, possibly uniquely, a revolutionary *bagchi*.

The image of the *shand-oboo* demonstrates a sense in which shamanic energies were thought to 'lie below' others. The character of shamanic power, its propensity for turning itself inside-out, transforming the mundane and close suddenly into the distant, strange, and powerful, must have emboldened this brother and sister and given them far vision. Merse was arrested when he was only in his thirties, but Huangge must have had extraordinary resilience to continue as a shaman during the decades of repression and persecution.

Notes

1. None of the shamanic peoples of Manchuria had fewer than four types of practitioner and many had several more (Wu 1989*b*: 263–9). For a discussion of 'three forms of expertise' among the Wana, see Atkinson 1989: 277–8.
2. Both Daur and Tungus *yadgan*s had an assistant called *jaare* (*DSHI* 1985: 267; Batubayin 1990; Shirokogoroff 1935: 329). He followed the refrains, continued drumming while the shaman was 'away' (i.e. was insensible in trance), helped find out what were the spirit's desires, and explained unclear words to the audience.
3. For a description of these rituals among Yakuts and Altaians, see L'vova *et al.* (1989: 148–59).
4. Mendüsürüng told me that the *barishi* of his village had an *onggor* which was the transformed soul of a warrior who went to war, was killed and began to haunt people. The shaman declared that a new *barkan* had appeared, and it should be placated by making offerings to its picture. This *barishi onggor* was depicted as an old man with a beard, long gown, a waistcoat, and a hat with an official button.
5. A. Hürelbaatar, personal communication. This was traced to the spiritual defeat of a famous aristocratic shaman, Prince Hobogtai, by the Buddhist missionary Neyichi Toyin in the 17th century, after which time the nobility had no shamans of their own (Heissig 1992: 209). It is interesting that Hobogtai was known as the spiritual descendant of Køkøchü Teb Tenggeri, the 'shaman' who was a rival of Chingghis Khan and defeated by him (Heissig 1992: 209; see Humphrey 1994*b*).
6. A. Hürelbaatar, personal communication.
7. For an exception to this, see 7.3. In his assistant role, the *bagchi* could explain to the

audience the spirit's words sung by the shaman (Batubayin 1990), and this sense of his role was quite similar to the notion of the priest-like *zigarin* of the early Mongols (see above).

8. This short book was written in Manchu and Chinese while Urgungbu was head of the Internal Affairs Section of Butha Banner of the East Xing-an Province under Japanese occupation. Urgungbu gave a copy to his friend Akamatsu, who published sections of it in his own book in Japanese (Akiba and Akamatsu 1941: 277–88). I have not seen the original and the quotations here were translated from Japanese by Urgunge. It seems from the text as though Urgungbu had given up being a *bagchi* by the time his book was written.

9. *Ayan jin yawdaj baigaad olson barkad hüneg-manag takisan yum shu.*

10. The fox was known as Shih Shar (Great Yellow) and the weasel was called Bag Shar (Small Yellow).

11. See also Jagchid (1988*b*: 326) who notes a similarity between the Daur fox and weasel spirits and those of the Chinese. *DSHI* (1985: 254) confirms the recent date of the appearance of Auli Barkan. For Japanese fox spirits see Blacker [1975]1986: 51–68.

12. A. Hürelbaatar, personal communication.

13. A variety of birds such as Long-tailed pheasants (*Syrmaticus* spp.), Gallopheasants (*Lophura* spp.), Capercailie (*Tetrao urogallus*), as well as some species of grouse (Tetraoniae) and guans (*Penelope* spp.) use infra-sound. These observations are therefore likely to apply to whatever species of pheasant was the focus of the were-creature cult.

14. This is not contradicted by the story of the hunter who shot at a squatting man, since the point of the story was not the cruelty of hunters to animals but the inviolability of the man/fox.

15. However, Mendüsürüng thought that if a shaman had been there he would have understood the meaning of the noises.

16. These were held to be third-class shamans by the Daurs (Jagchid 1988*b*: 324). No sources apart from Jagchid mention the *ghiamun*.

17. As Ba Shaman died in a spot designated a Japanese military zone, the Solons had been unable to retreive his body for burial. Haslund got permission to visit the forbidden area. He found Ba Shaman's body at the foot of a railway embankment, took back the body to Mehertei, and himself obtained the shamanic gown and equipment; it is now in the Nationalmuseet ethnographic collection in Copenhagen.

18. Daur fox spirits were also said to avoid official buildings (*DSHI* 1985: 254).

19. Ikeshiri mentions specifically that the *hu* is that for 'barbarian', not 'fox'.

20. This quotation is from a foreword to Ma Ho T'ien's account of his journey to Mongolia in the 1920s (Ma 1949: 202).

21. Urgunge said this was why the animal spirits were said to shade their eyes with their paws. They were coming out of the dark, looking into the light, and at the same time they were imitating the human being they wanted to become.

22. Siblings and agnatic first cousins are considered so close that the latter are normally called 'sister' and 'brother'. Though Huangge was born after Merse she was known as his 'older sister' because her father was older than his.

23. Or Moersi, also Moerse. He also used the names Guo Junhuang and Guo Moxi. He is best known under the Chinese name he took at the age of 20, Guo Dao-fu (Kuo Tao-fu). The Guo is the first syllable of his clan name, Guobol (Gobol).

24. Tsend Gung (in Chinese Zheng-guo-gong Chengde) had been a major figure in the 1911 Hulun Buir autonomous movement. Later, as representative of the Hulun Buir region, he became Deputy Foreign Minister in the Mongolian government. It was in Mongolia that he received his title of Gung ('duke')—the Daurs did not have titles of their own. Alongside his career in international politics, he was the first translator of the *Secret History of the Mongols* into modern Mongolian (Engkebatu 1987: 153).

25. Rung-lu (Chinese Ronglu) accompanied Lingsheng to the governmental conference in Dauria in 1919 (Enkebatu and Erkembayar 1987*b*: 186).

26. Semenov was more than half Russian in parentage, but he emphasized his Buryat identity. According to Yusefovich (1993: 38–41), Semenov had little ideology beyond a desire for local military power, but his lieutenant Ungern was obsessed with the idea of establishing a purist, pan-Mongolian state to counter and overturn degenerate European culture. Semenov had strong links with the Japanese, who were hoping to increase their influence in this part of mainland Asia.

27. The Naun Daur Ming Bao, whose letter to the Mongols was cited in 5.2, became a staff-officer in Bavuujav's army. Bavuujav was killed in 1916. The remnants of Bavuujav's army, under Sebujingge, were dispersed and became bandits, according to Urgunge.

28. By 1925 five women students from the school had learnt enough Russian to be sent to Ulan-Ude in Buryatia for further study. They made their way across the border disguised as herdswomen.

29. Merse encouraged over fifty young Daurs, Mongols, Evenks, and Bargas from the region to go to Mongolia or the USSR to study revolutionary principles. These people later became the mainstay in Merse's 1928 insurrection.

30. Merse attended the Mongolian and Tibetan Institute in Beijing, which was the most important centre for Inner Mongolian intellectuals to meet one another. Merse made several trips to Mongolia. His knowledge of Russian gave him a role in many international negotiations.

31. Owen Lattimore met Merse in Beijing at this point and noted his nervousness and his secrecy about his activities. Lattimore's subsequent account (1990: 27–8) of Merse's death is incorrect; the true story did not become known until after Lattimore had written his memoirs.

32. Merse's son, now living in Hohhot, has a document from the Russian KGB dated 1989, stating that Merse was arrested in Manzhouli, accused of fomenting nationalism and armed uprisings in collaboration with the Japanese. He was sentenced to death in 1934, but the sentence was commuted to ten years in a labour camp. It is not known if Merse survived this sentence.

33. As an example Urgunge recalled the following story about Merse. 'He arrived late at an important meeting in Beijing. This was in the 1920s. The other Mongols teased him, but he put them down by saying, "I just started out this morning" [i.e. he came by plane, almost unheard of in those days].'

34. Two methods were used. One cure for flu involved putting the sacred plant juniper in a bowl of cow's milk, then saying the incantation and making a libation of the

milk. The other technique was to say an incantation over a block of tea, which would then have medicinal properties when drunk.

35. This was one of Merse's ritual services as *bagchi*, i.e. calming and praying, rather than assisting in the birth itself, which was done by a midwife.

36. Merse did not, however, act as *bagchi* assistant to Huangge. She had another *bagchi*, a distant relative from the Gobol clan.

37. All of the information about Merse's activity as a *bagchi* was given me by his son, Adiya. Adiya was born in 1931, after Merse's disappearance, and he never met his father. An *umiesen kuu* was a boy or girl of the village who was made the protected child of a shaman, literally an 'wombed child' from *ume* 'womb' or Womb Goddess, see 6.3. The child was given a bell hung on a blue silk ribbon. The bell was worn to guard against spirit attack when going on a journey or when riding a horse.

38. For example, the 'wind-horse' flags attached to the *oboo* were interpreted not as signs of spiritual vitality in the usual Buddhist idiom, but as directly related to horses. 'They painted horses on the *hii mori* flags because this signified the safety of the horse herds' (Akiba and Akamatsu 1941: 262).

39. Often, in other parts of Inner Mongolia, sacred objects were first buried at a place before an *oboo* was constructed there. I have heard of a sacred bowl being buried at one site in the Hulun Buir region. Liang (1983: 50–3) reports the burial of Mongol *gers* (round felt tents) in deep pits beneath *oboo*s in the Ordos area. Lamas would enter the tent and pray for three days before the entrance to the pit was sealed off and the *oboo* consecrated. This custom suggests that the earth beneath an *oboo* had to be domesticated and purified, possibly from shamanic spirit power.

40. Thus it has been a pattern throughout this century, with an interlude in the 1950s–mid-1980s when the festivals were forbidden, for Mongolian leaders to rely on communal religion. There have been regional differences. In Hailar, while aware of the role of religion and prepared to take advantage of it, secular leaders did not subordinate themselves to religious figures. This was different from the situation in Halh Mongolia, where the highest Buddhist lama, the Jebtsundamba Hutagt, was also head of state from 1911–21, and from the position in the Ordos region of Inner Mongolia, where lamas became political and even military leaders in the 1930s–1950s and consequently came into conflict with the local princes (Atwood 1992).

41. On the hold gained over Mongols by the military leaders Dambijantsan and Ungern-Shternberg in the 1910s by virtue of their supposed possession of terrible occult powers; see Yusefovich (1993).

42. By the 1950s the *kiant* cults were thought of as 'old' and were virtually defunct. However, the fascination with the idea of self-transformation through spiritual breathing exercises has revived with the great popularity of Chinese *qigong* (air-energy) in recent years. *Qigong* is widely practised by all ethnic groups in Inner Mongolia, especially in the cities. It is interesting that, as in the old *kiant* cults, animals and birds are expressive media in some forms of *qigong*, though the movements of animal-like energy are now experienced as liberating, not frightening and oppressive. Ots (1994: 130) describes how the *qigong* craze surged and diminished with each phase of political repression in China in the 1980s.

43. These observations may have been superficial and influenced by the fact that the

reporters were Japanese, but such as they are they suggest that Daurs had abandoned *kiant* cults and were looking instead to warrior-deities. Akiba and Akamatsu (1941: 294) also report worship of the Chinese war-god Guandi and Chingghis Khan by Daurs. For an account of the Guandi myth as a framework of identification between the state and the peasant, see Duara (1988).

8

Urgunge's Way

8.1 Some Concluding Remarks

'Shamanism' as a whole conglomerate of beliefs and practices was not only about the knowledge we have, but about the various kinds of knowledge we ordinary people do not quite have. This knowing was not, however, thought of as supernatural. It was knowledge of what was there to be known, but only certain individuals were gifted to know it or discover it, and they did so in different ways. For this reason 'shamanism' could encompass and deepen ordinary knowledge of nature (including human nature), thus revealing what made the ordinary marvellous.

This being said, there were great differences between the various knowledge traditions of trance shamans and other practitioners, and these depended on how knowledge itself was constituted and sustained, for example by lifelong social experience (elders), or by physical touch (bone-setters). The altered state of consciousness of *yadgan* shamans was another means to knowledge. The poetry of shamans' songs reveals this to have been understanding of an emotionally candid reality, for which the conscious subject was not the standard patriarchally defined person but all imaginable kinds of individual selves. The self was not conceived as being alone, and the shaman's practice aimed to reconstitute and make effective this very consociality for the sufferer. The notion of consociality that shamans brought into play extended beyond death to previous sufferers and beyond the boundaries of humanity to the consciousnesses of other living beings such as animals and birds.

The replication of like by like in the patriarchal ideology was confronted with cumulations of distinctive, unique, and anomalous beings (complex 'spirits'), which substituted unlike for unlike, and thereby constituted a different sense of wild creativity, linked to an idea of maximal universality (6.2). The standard ideas of age, seniority, and gender were thus taken apart and rendered powerless in the shaman's practice, even while they continued as organizing principles in other domains of society and ritual. The power given to acute emotion in the *yadgan* shaman's practice had the effect of destabilizing and overturning all external verities. It did this by insisting that the relevant knowledge was 'psychological' knowledge and that to have knowledge (*medel*) was also to control the object known. Consequently, the fount of this 'knowledge-power' being not just the mind but the 'heart-mind' (5.5), emotions, even ancient

emotions of people long dead, would colour the landscape, as the shaman
mother's anguish made the solid world crumble all around (1.5).

Spirits had to be remembered, because they were held to cause present
sufferings which mirrored their own. Thus, although shamanic practice differed from place to place, and between *yadgan* shamans and other types of
shamans, there were institutions which served to maintain and transmit
shamanic knowledge in distinctive traditions. The most notable of these was
the *yadgan*'s *ominan* ritual (5.8), the festival of remembering all the spirits,
where external shamans from other clans or ethnic groups were given a super-
visory role.

This book aims to go beyond earlier studies of shamanism which have
focused on definitional problems and social organization, such as Firth's (1959:
129–48) useful and well-known distinction between spirit possession,
mediumship, and shamanism. The aim here has been to delineate how
shamanic knowledge is created among other kinds of knowledge, and to understand its agency in worlds conceived as fields of distinctive energies and
powers. Shamans' distinctive abilities were not separated off from those of
other social actors, like rulers or Buddhist lamas, but contended with them.
The final part of the book relates the disjunctive character of shamanic practices
to the decline of some earlier traditions and the emergence of new 'modernist'
ones in the context of early twentieth-century politics.

The issues tackled in this book are not irrelevant to understanding
'shamanism' today. From descriptions of North Asian shamanic practices
and those of many other parts of the world, pared-down models have been
abstracted and worked on by shamanic practitioners in California and
elsewhere. 'Shamanic workshops' of New Age movements, 'shamanic coun-
selling', and so forth are now being re-exported back to the Siberian lands of
their origin (Hoppal 1992). Here they are encountering self-conscious,
marketed, and sometimes even licensed, revivals of shamanism. These
globalized practices recognize that the magic of the acting-out (mimesis) of
reality, so transforming it, is not simply 'primitive'. They assume there is a
'shamanic' possibility of self-transformation available to anyone, and this is
something Urgunge would agree with. But the workshops too are an active
element in the cultural politics of our time—a fact that is mostly ignored.
Their apparent de-contextualization of their content from any social specificity,
in order to produce a universal technique, is in the end illusory. This book
has shown how a knot of relations is produced in shamanic practice, and how
this invariably produces an art and a politics of representation. In Urgunge's
youth too shamanic visions rendered an objectification of ontologies of
various powers, and this was both active, mirroring and confronting Buddhism
and Communism, and self-reflexive, creating a plagiarism of the shaman's
own experience. It is because this has still not been adequately described
that our book aims to provide a historically aware, nuanced account of that

time, as well as a sense of the way in which one person, Urgunge, *believes in* shamanism.

I now briefly attempt to place this account of shamanism in relation to some other recent interpretations. We would agree with Overing (1990) about the creativity of shamans, their use of previous images to build new ones, and their use of moral-emotional categories to establish the identity of spirits and explain their vengeful activities. But Urgunge agrees with me in querying her formulation of the idea that shamans are 'worldmakers', constantly taking apart and putting together versions at hand which are through-and-through unique and *sui generis*. Overing quotes Goodman (1978) to the effect that 'there is no solid bedrock of reality to such worldmaking' (1990: 605). However, not only is reality exactly what shamans and other practitioners are aiming to discover, but they proceed from basic concepts of the nature of human, animal, and material existence in the world, which might well be shared by anyone anywhere. These are never entirely lost sight of in the contentious or mythic versions discovered by shamans, since one finds that the latter are not entirely random but are related to salient aspects of the everyday concepts (cf. Boyer 1994). So when the relevant aspect of trees, for example, is their capacity to grow healthily, flourish, reproduce themselves, and die, these aspects are the ones upon which the shamanic imagination dwells in its exploration of further dimensions or analogies of tree-like existence. The basic concepts remain at issue even when the shaman yells her poetic calls to deny, subvert, or destabilize them.

Our account accords most closely with Severi's illuminating series of articles (1982, 1985, 1987, 1993) on Cuna shamanism. Shamanism is understood here as a certain way of conceiving the invisible aspect of reality, and as a particular style of world-view related to it. In Cuna traditional thought all things, rocks, trees, stars, clouds, or people, owe their perceptible 'face' to the invisible presence of *purpa*, the immaterial life-giving double which can never be seen. The function of the shaman is to represent these invisible energies. This is an anxiety-making *terra incognita*, in which traditional thought places the foreign, the new, and the incomprehensible, and it is from this domain that suffering comes to people. Severi's most notable contribution (1987, 1993) is to show how the shaman constructs a paradigm in his ritualized songs to relate two negatively defined dimensions of existence: an invisible landscape within the body and an external, inaccessible world located at the limits of human perception. The first is too close (inside oneself) to be known only in ordinary ways, and the latter is too distant, since it consists of natural or foreign processes that human faculties cannot ordinarily comprehend. The making of this relationship, the explaining of the one by the other, and vice versa, does indeed seem to lie at the centre of shamanic practice. Many examples from Inner Asia have been described in this book, such as the songs for Baglain Udagan and Niang-Niang.

I would suggest that the need felt by Daurs to make this relation between two such widely separated aspects of the not-yet-known is the reason why shamanic thought does not make use of 'replication' (the constant reproduction of similarity); instead it employs 'substitution', which recognizes difference in the elements of knowledge but constructs a passage, that of metamorphosis, between them. Inner, via metamorphosis, becomes outer and vice versa.

Shamanship commonly, perhaps always, coexists with other religious practices. This situation is analysed in a further series of publications, Thomas (1988), Atkinson (1989), Mumford (1989), and the authors in Thomas and Humphrey (1994). Shamans, through the 'trance' and the incorporation of spirits, have a peculiarly immediate relation with unseen forces, and this constitutes a different style which is in competition with those religious relations mediated by rituals like sacrifice. As the studies mentioned show, the agency of shamans waxes and wanes, and can change in its style and content, in relation to the effectiveness of political rule. Frequently the erosion of the religious potency of rulers enables that of shamans to rise. This book has attempted to link the kind of ideas Overing and Severi are discussing—the cultural creativity of shamans—with the constitutive actions of shamans in the political arena. Atkinson's excellent study of the Wana shamans in Indonesia (1989) is the most complete existing account of such a relation. Locating the Wana in the relatively egalitarian and dispersed periphery of the Dutch colonial (later the Indonesian) state, she documents a homology between Wana ideas of the person, their community, and the cosmos. Wana see all three as oscillating historically between concentration and dissipating, unhealthy dispersal. The shaman's role as 'mediator' is understood in Atkinson's book not just in the simple sense of a go-between from humans to spirits, but as mediating different levels of meaning, the personal, the social, and the cosmological-political. It seems to me that this interpretation is illuminating. A similarly many-layered shamanic practice is evident in the Holieri performance.

The shamanic song of Holieri and the story of Nishan Shaman produced integrating visions. However, an anthropological understanding can see them only as partial, since the conditions of the production of shamanic knowledge—the existence of various types of shamans with their own distinctive abilities at knowing—were inherently 'dispersive'. Nevertheless, it is argued by Urgunge that this very fact is what gave 'shamanism' its unity from the point of view of someone inside. For someone 'working shamanism' only his or her own way among the possibilities presented by living experience was what mattered. This perspective gave ultimate agency to the individual as the locus of singular moments of accident, decision, and fortitude. Perhaps it owed much to the immediacy and singular vividness of the shaman's activity. But in the end such a consciousness distanced all shamans or magicians, as it did the structures of clans and political rituals, since the individual saw himself as acting through them in accordance with his own fate, rather than being constituted only as an element of one or another of these systems.

8.2 Reflections of an Elder

This book ends with Urgunge's voice. It is the essence of 'shamanism' that it has its existence in the people who believe in it, rather than in texts to be mulled over by scholars. As Gudeman has written (1990: 189),

Ultimately, the intellectual historians, contextualists, verificationists, falsificationists, and literary critics in economics (and anthropology as well) focus upon inscriptions. But the text is only part of the story, because it leaves out practices. By 'practice' we do not mean something by which to verify or 'falsify' theory, for this serves only to subjugate practices to the hegemony of the theorist and writer; instead, practice refers to the actions and voices of people in history, that are sometimes inscribed in texts and of which the inscription itself is an example.

Urgunge had a partial, intentional, engaged view of 'shamanism'. But, as I have tried to show, who could not have a partial view, since the 'whole thing' was not in fact a single thing? An insider's view is sustained by a whole life of practice, and if it might be objected that Urgunge's life has made his view no longer 'genuine', then I can only reply that it is much more genuine than mine. In Manchuria I was faced squarely with political, moral, and intellectual limits to anthropological questioning (see 4.3). At various points in this narrative I have been absolutely dependent on Urgunge to understand what some Daur action could be said to mean. If my anthropological training has led me to search more widely, to verify, to bring out themes Urgunge had forgotten or thought unimportant, that must find its place alongside the voice of someone who has not rejected the ideas and feelings acquired in early childhood. Although Urgunge 'became an elder' in England, it is not for this reason that he speaks to us as a contemporary; if this book has succeeded at all in its strategy, the readers will understand his reflections not as a voice from an archaic outside (Fabian 1983), but as the truthful expression of a positioned imagination, ranging over the world in the same way that our readers also ponder the world from their situations. At the same time we can see that Urgunge's life-course has relieved him of the oppressive *double fearfulness* recalled by other Daurs still in China, many of whom saw themselves as liberated by atheism (that is, fear of the ancestral spirits present in the land-scape and fear of the state's punishment for taking part in shamanic activities). The following is my understanding of what Urgunge means, why he feels 'shamanism' to be a unity, and why he thinks it is the religion of the future.

'Up to now human civilizations have been ruled by the logics,' Urgunge said, 'Now it is time for us to rule the logics.' By 'logics' he means not only abstract

reasoning but all those ideologies which explain the world by means
of a universal system. The paradigm for this, in his mind, is Buddhism, which
has a comprehensive philosophy and ethics explaining every component of
the human being and its relation to action. Although there is much to admire
in Buddhism, the Buddhist 'logic' is ultimately repressive, subordinating
people to its tenets in such a way that, once caught, you can never escape its
construction of causality.[1] One great fault of the 'logics' is that they invariably
construct some people, or some social positions, as being superior. For this
reason, Urgunge was deeply shocked when he first went south to Chahar and
saw his revered Prince De prostrating himself before a reincarnate lama. 'I
thought of De as a great man. It was as though my father had kowtowed before
Du Yadgan, the shaman. It is all right to kowtow to your genealogical senior,
because you yourself will be senior one day. But not to a lama or shaman.'
This was why, Urgunge said, Merse had never introduced a great lama like
the Panchen Bogd to lead his movement, even if he had seen it might be
expedient.

'We should respect all of the people all the time, not some of the people
some of the time,' was another of Urgunge's aphorisms. He saw both the
Buddhist clergy and the Communist Party as only 'some of the people',
and both were temporary and historical phenomena. But shamanists, all of
them, feel themselves to be the centre of their own universe. Above is *tengger*,
who is beyond time, and each human being has also a part of *tengger*
in themselves. This is their consciousness. It is both at the centre of each
person and far away, out in the cosmos. Urgunge's universe is coloured, a vast
expanse of blueness, deeper blue the further away, and in the blue there are
two points representing the self, an outer cosmic one, which is like a bright
star in the sky, and an inner one, which is red. 'Astronomers analyse
the universe through maths and physics,' he said, 'But we do it through
our consciousness, which I feel to be like a hole, that red hole which is
nothing but itself, that is me, my heart, sensing and alive. It is breathing
(*amisaj bain*), pulsating with a barely perceptible noise. Don't you sometimes
hear that beat in yourself? That pulse is my power (*kuch*).' Consciousness
leaping outwards gives each person their own orbit and their own independence—'*ooriin tenggertei, ooriin terguultei*'—'your own sky, your own cart-
track.'

'Shamanism gives me the sense of being very, very free,' Urgunge said,
'because you have a clear sense of your own space. Between yourself and
tengger, that is a vast space and that is where you can fly (*derdeu*). We were born
with the feeling of flying out, flying far. Remember the shaman's *onggor* bird:
that is his consciousness.'

This is why the *yadgan* shamans kept their ancient views, Urgunge said. To
them shamanizing—the empowerment by *onggor*s in the trance—was their
freedom, their ability to penetrate in disguise the stoutest ramparts (see Intro-

duction). They had no need of any other views, and indeed another way would no longer be theirs.

Forgetting time, but conscious of stellate space, each person will feel free to move along their own orbit. Once Urgunge and I had disagreed about the role of time in 'shamanism'. I had argued that shamans accepted time in the sense of the life-span and its end, death. Urgunge said,

> You have not understood. Death is a change of form. In shamanism there is no such thing as the past, because everything continues to be, only in different forms. Everyone has to act at a given time, and that is *now*, this season [*erin*]. But even 'now' will soon be 'then', so ultimately it is pointless even to consider time. In my childhood, no one had a clock or a watch. To my mind 'time' means 'limit', but space is freedom.

The people moving along their paths are not separate from one another, but interact in amity and discord in an unpredictable mingling which is given by the order of the universe.

Once I asked Urgunge suspiciously if the idea of balance in the universe was really a Daur idea or whether it was not borrowed from Chinese ideas of *yin* and *yang*.[2] His reply starts off straightforwardly, but becomes more difficult to explain. 'The balance of diversity in the world is not an idea,' he said.

> It is a fact. You might as well ask whether Einstein invented relativity or not—he did not invent it, he discovered it. Personally I do not believe in invention, only in discovery. The fact is: all the things in the world and the people exist in their own way. We cannot and must not win over everything, but we must fight. Fighting is balancing. *Shurkul*s [devils] were never killed. You don't get the idea? If a shaman could completely get rid of *shurkul*, everything would lose balance. *Shurkul* has to be there.

Urgunge ruminated further:

> Merse's view was not the same as mine because he was educated and I only had about five years of high school.[3] The fact is: there were shamans and spirits, but how Merse and I would analyse them would be different. It is almost impossible for me to say how my father would think, or other Daurs; even a fish tastes different to you and me. A dog sees the world from a dog's point of view. But whatever ideas we have, or the Chinese have, we all know the universe is composed of an infinite number of different things. If we understood them all then we would not need a shaman. He was our messenger and our ambassador. He could see further and journey further. But in the end he was like us. The Daurs had shamans for the same reason that made me so happy when I was young: we needed to be able to distinguish [perceive] the many things in the world and then make our own tracks.

I ventured, 'Was that perhaps why so much of what Daurs say about shamans is half like a joke—they believe it, and they don't believe it?' 'Ah, my sister, you understand it now. A Daur only believes something for himself. Even the shaman will introduce us only to his universe. But the question is—why did the

Daurs have this attitude? It is because the balance of the universe is *tengger*, and what do any of us really know about him? We know the *tengger* that is in our heads. I don't know what my ancestors thought about this, but I'll bet they thought their consciousness *was tengger*.'

I think Urgunge did not mean anything inscrutable by this. He continued talking of *tengger* as an intelligence in ourselves and also out among the things in the world and merged with them. I came to see that a dispersed religion like 'shamanism' is unified for each individual by their choices and empathies, which establish their actions as path-making events in their various landscapes. 'The first is to understand yourself. Then what is around you. Any animal, or thing, or person, if I see, or feel, or touch it, I can understand it, what it is thinking, and what it will do, its next step. Then I take my next step.' This is Urgunge's feeling about the religion that lies behind the surfaces, practices, and segments described in this book.

Notes

1. Urgunge was once deeply impressed by Buddhism in his life. It was not the doctrines which influenced him (he says he knows little about them, which is true) but the sight of a stone statue when he was in Japan as a young man. 'When I looked at the Buddha's face I became very quiet,' he said.
2. *Yin* and *yang*, in Urgunge's view, were taken from early shamanism, not the other way around.
3. Curiously Urgunge forgot the time he spent at a Japanese university here. While in Japan he studied politics, so he considered this indoctrination rather than true education.

REFERENCES

Abayeva, L. L. (1986), 'Traditsionniye obryady predbaikal'skikh rodov selenginskikh buryat' (Traditional Rituals of the Cis-Baikal Clans of the Selenga Buryat), in K. M. Gerasimova (ed.), *Traditsionnaya kul'tura narodov tsentral'noi azii* (Nauka: Novosibirsk).

——(1992), *Kul't gor i buddizm v buryatii* (The Cult of Mountains and Buddhism in Buryatia) (Nauka: Moscow).

Aberle, David (1952), '"Arctic Hysteria" and Latah in Mongolia', *Transactions of the New York Academy of Sciences*, series II, 14/7: 291–7.

Akiba, Takashi, and Akamatsu, Chijo (1941), *Man Mo no minzoku to shukyo* (Examination of the Manchu and Mongol Nationalities) (Osaka Press: Osaka).

Alekseyev, A. A. (1993), *Zabytyi mir predkov: Ocherki traditsionnogo mirovozreniya evenov Severo-zapadnogo Verkhoyan'ya* (The Forgotten World of the Ancestors: Studies in the Traditional World-View of the Even of North-West Verkhoyan) (Sitim: Yakutsk).

Appadurai, Arjun (1990), 'Topographies of the Self: Praise and Emotion in Hindu India,' in Catherine A. Lutz and Lila Abu-Lughod (eds.) *Language and the Politics of Emotion* (Cambridge University Press: Cambridge), 92–112.

——(1991), 'Global Ethnoscapes: Notes and Queries for a Transnational Anthropology', in R. G. Fox (ed.), *Recapturing Anthropology: Working in the Present* (School of American Research Press: Santa Fe), 191–210.

Asad, Talal (1994), *Genealogies of Religion: Discipline and Reasons of Power in Christianity and Islam* (Johns Hopkins University Press: Baltimore and London).

Atkinson, Jane Monnig (1989), *The Art and Politics of Wana Shamanship* (University of California Press: Berkeley and Los Angeles).

Atran, Scott (1987), 'Ordinary Constraints on the Semantics of Living Kinds: A Commonsense Alternative to Recent Treatments of Natural-Object Terms', *Mind and Language*, 2: 27–63.

——(1989), 'Basic Conceptual Domains', *Mind and Language*, 4: 5–16.

——(1990), *Cognitive Foundations of Natural History: Towards an Anthropology of Science* (Cambridge University Press: Cambridge).

——(1990 n.d.), 'Speculations on the Structure, Development and Integration of Basic Conceptual Domains', paper prepared for the conference on 'Cultural Knowledge and Domain-Specificity', University of Michigan, October 1990.

——(1993), 'Wither the New Ethnography?', in Pascal Boyer (ed.), *Cognitive Aspects of Ritual Symbolism* (Cambridge University Press: Cambridge).

Atwood, Christopher (1992), 'National Party and Local Politics in Ordos, Inner Mongolia (1926–35)', *Journal of Asian Studies*, 26/2: 1–30.

Badaranga *et al.* (eds.) (1957), *Daudagu Biteg* (Daur Writings) (Ubur Mongoly Irgeny Keblely Kore: Hohhot).

Baddeley, Alan (1982), *Your Memory: A User's Guide* (Penguin Books: London).

Baldayev, S. P. (1961), *Izbrannoe* (Selected Works) (Buryatskoe Knizhnoye Izdatel'stvo: Ulan-Ude).

Balzer, Marjorie M. (1993), 'Two Urban Shamans: Unmasking Leadership in Fin-de-Soviet Siberia', in George E. Marcus (ed.), *Perilous States: Conversations on Culture, Politics and Nation* (Chicago University Press: Chicago and London), 131–64.

Bann, Stephen (1989), *The True Vine: On Visual Representation and Western Tradition* (Cambridge University Press: Cambridge).

Banzarov, Dorzhi (1955), 'Chernaya Vera, ili shamanstvo u mongolov' (The Black Faith, or Shamanism among the Mongols) [1846], in G. D. Sanzheyev (ed.), *Dorzhi Banzarov: Sobraniye Sochinenii* (Izdatel'stvo Akademii Nauk SSSR: Moscow).

Baranov, A. (1907) and (1911), 'Materialy po Man'chzhurii i Mongolii' (Materials on Manchuria and Mongolia), vyp. 11 and 36, *Slovar' mongol'skikh terminov* (Dictionary of Mongolian Terms) (Akademia Nauk: Harbin).

——(n.d.), 'Barga: istoricheskii orcherk' (Barga: A Historical Study), undated unpublished typescript held in Cambridge University Library.

Barlow, Tani E. (1994), 'Theorising Woman: *Funnu, Guojia, Jiating* (Chinese Woman, Chinese State, Chinese Family)', in A. Zito and T. E. Barlow (eds.), *Body, Subject & Power in China* (University of Chicago Press: Chicago), 253–90.

Barth, Frederick (1975), *Ritual and Knowledge among the Baktaman of New Guinea* (Yale University Press: New Haven).

——(1987), *Cosmologies in the Making: A Generative Approach to Cultural Variation in Inner New Guinea* (Cambridge University Press: Cambridge).

——(1993), *Balinese Worlds* (University of Chicago Press: Chicago and London).

Basilov, V. N. (1992), *Shamanstvo u narodov Srednei Azii i Kazakhstana* (Shamanism among the Peoples of Central Asia) (Nauka: Moscow).

Bastien, Joseph W. (1978), *Mountains of the Condor: Metaphor and Ritual in an Andean Ayllu* (West Publishing Co.: St Paul, New York, Los Angeles, San Francisco).

Batubayin, Daur (1990), *Da wu er zu feng su zhi* (Ethnography of the Daur People) (Press of the Central University of the Nationalities: Beijing).

Bayanbatu, H. (1990), *Mongolchuud-un modon-u sitülge* (Worship of Trees by the Mongols) (Inner Mongolia Cultural Publishing House: Hohhot).

Beffa, Marie-Lise, and Hamayon, Roberte (1985), 'Introduction au renard: Tours, détours, retours', *Études Mongoles . . . et Sibériennes*, 15 (1984): 9–16.

Bender, Mark, and Su, Huana (1984), *Daur Folktales: Selected Myths of the Daur Nationality* (New World Press: Beijing).

Berlin, B., Breedlove, D., and Raven, P. H. (1966), 'Folk Taxonomies and Biological Classification', *Science*, 154: 273–5.

Billingsley, Phil (1988), *Bandits in Republican China* (Stanford University Press: Stanford, Calif.).

Bird-David, Nurit (1990), 'The Giving Environment: Another Perspective on the Economic System of Gatherer-Hunters', *Current Anthropology*, 31: 1894–6.

Birrell, Anne (1993), *Chinese Mythology: An Introduction* (The Johns Hopkins University Press: Baltimore and London).

Blacker, Carmen ([1975] 1986), *The Catalpa Bow: A Study in Shamanistic Practices in Japan* (George Allen and Unwin: London).

Bloch, Maurice (1987), 'Descent and Sources of Contradiction in Representations of Women', in J. Collier and S. Yanagisako (eds.), *Gender and Kinship* (Stanford University Press: Stanford, Calif.), 324–40.

——(1989), *Ritual, History and Power: Selected Papers in Anthropology* (Athlone Press: London).

——(1991), 'Language, Anthropology and Cognitive Science', *Man*, 26/2.

——(1992*a*), *Prey into Hunter: The Politics of Religious Experience* (Cambridge University Press: Cambridge).

——(1992*b*), 'What Goes without Saying: The Conceptualization of Zafimaniry Society', in A. Kuper (ed.), *Conceptualizing Society* (Routledge: London).

——(1993), 'La Mort et la conception de la personne', *Terrain* 20 (20 Mar.): 7–20.

Boyer, Pascal (1980), 'Les Figures du savoir initiatique', *Journal des Africanistes*, 50/2: 31–57.

——(1991 n.d.), 'Universal Features of Intuitive Knowledge and the Variability of Religious Ideas', Wenner-Gren Foundation for Anthropological Research Symposium (Ocho Rios, Jamaica).

——(1993), 'Introduction: Cognitive Aspects of Ritual Symbolism: A Critical Survey of Issues and Directions', in Pascal Boyer (ed.), *Cognitive Aspects of Ritual Symbolism* (Cambridge University Press: Cambridge), 4–47.

——(1994), *The Naturalness of Religious Ideas: A Cognitive Theory of Religion* (University of California Press: Berkeley and Los Angeles).

Brown, R. (1973), *A First Language: The Early Stages* (Penguin: Harmondsworth).

Carey, Susan (1985), *Conceptual Change in Childhood* (MIT Press/Bradford Books: Cambridge, Mass).

——(1991), 'Knowledge Acquisition: Enrichment or Conceptual Change?', in S. Carey and R. Gelman (eds.), *The Epigenesis of Mind: Essays on Biology and Cognition* (Lawrence Erlbaum Associates: Hillsdale, NJ).

Carrithers, M., Collins, S., and Lukes, S. (eds.) (1985), *The Category of the Person: Anthropology, Philosophy, History* (Cambridge University Press: Cambridge).

Chabros, Krystyna (1992*a*), *Beckoning Fortune: A Study of the Mongol dalalga Ritual* (Otto Harrassowicz: Wiesbaden). →

——(1992*b*), 'An East Mongolian Ritual for Children', in G. Bethenfalvy (ed.), *Altaic Religious Beliefs and Practices* (Research Group for Altaic Studies: Budapest), 59–63.

Chaussonnet, Valerie (1988), 'Needles and Animals: Women's Magic', in William Fitzhugh and Aron Crowell (eds.), *Crossroads of Continents: Cultures of Siberia and Alaska* (Smithsonian Institution Press: New York), 209–26.

Cheng, Shu (1987), 'Shi lun Da wu er de zu yuan wen ti' (On the Question of the Origin of the Daur Nationality), in Meng Zhi-dung, A. Engkebatu, and Wu Twan-ying (eds.), *Daur Nationality Researches*, i (Daur History, Language and Literature Association: Hohhot).

Chesnov, Ya. B. (1986), 'Drakon: metafora vneshnego mira' (Dragon: Metaphor of the External World), in N. L. Zhukovskaya (ed.), *Mify, Kul'ty, Obryady narodov zarubezhnoi azii* (Nauka: Moscow), 59–72.

Chimitdorzhiev, Sh. B. (1991), *Kto my—Buryat-Mongoly?* (Who are we—Buryat-Mongols?) (Assotsiatsiya litertorov Buryatii: Belovo).

Chingel, G. (ed.) (1991), *Mongol yos zanshlyn dund tailbar tol'* (Middle Encyclopaedia of Mongol Custom) ('Süülenhüü' hüühediin hevleliin gazar: Ulaanbaatar).

Chomsky, Naum (1972), *Language and Mind*, enlarged edn. (Harcourt Brace Jovanovich: New York).

Classen, Constance (1991), 'Creation by Sound/Creation by Light: A Sensory Analysis of Two South American Cosmologies', in D. Howes (ed.), *The Varieties of Sensory Experience* (University of Toronto Press: Toronto), 239–56.

Clifford, James (1992), 'Traveling Cultures', in Lawrence Grossberg, Cary Nelson, and Paula Treichler (eds.), *Cultural Studies* (Routledge: London and New York), 96–112.

Collier, Jane, and Yanagisako, Sylvia (eds.) (1987), *Gender and Kinship: Essays Toward an Unified Analysis* (Stanford University Press: Stanford, Calif.).

Connerton, Paul (1989), *How Societies Remember* (Cambridge University Press: Cambridge).

Cowie, Elizabeth (1978), 'Women as Sign', *m/f* 1: 49–63.

Crossley, Pamela (1987), '*Manzhou yuanliu kao* and the Formalization of the Manchu Heritage', *Journal of Asian Studies*, 46/4: 761–90.

——(1990), *Orphan Warriors: Three Manchu Generations and the End of the Qing World* (Princeton University Press: Princeton).

Czaplicka, M. A. (1914), *Aboriginal Siberia: A Study in Social Anthropology* (Oxford University Press: London).

Dagur Ündüsten-ü Tobchi Teüke-iin Naiiragulun Bichihu Duguiilang (1989), *Dagur Ündüsüten-ü Tobchi Teüke* (A Short History of the Daur People) (Inner Mongolia People's Publishing House: Hohhot).

Dalai, Ch. (1959), *Mongolyn boogiin mørgøliin tovch tüüh* (A Short History of Mongolian Shamanism) (Shinjleh Uhaan Erdem Shinjilgeenii Gazar: Ulaanbaatar).

Damdinsüren, C. (1959), *Monggol-un uran zokiyal-un degezi zagun bilig orusibai* (One Hundred Paradigms of Mongolian Literature) (Corpus scriptorum mongolorum, 14; Academy of Sciences: Ulaanbaatar).

Danilin, A. G. (1932), 'Burkhanizm na Altai i ego kontr-revolyutsionnaya rol'' (Burkhanism in the Altai and its Counter-Revolutionary Role), *Sovetskaya Etnografia*, no. 1: 63–91.

Daur Cultural Heritage Series (eds.) (1988), *Dagur-un Ulamzilaltu Uran Zokijal* (The Traditional Literature of the Daurs) (Inner Mongolia Cultural Press: Ulaanhad).

Daur Folktales (1982), *Daur Folktales: Selected Myths of the Daur Nationality*, tr. Mark Bender and Su Huana (New World Press: Beijing).

Daur Hel' Bitegy Azily Komiss (1957), *Daudagu Biteg* (Oral Literature) (Inner Mongolian People's Publishing House: Hohhot).

Daur History Writing Team (1986), *Da wo er zu jian shi* (A Brief History of the Daur People) (Inner Mongolia People's Publishing House: Hohhot).

Daur Social and History Investigations (*DSHI*) (1985), see Inner Mongolia A. R. Editorial team, *Da wo er zu she hui li shi diao cha* (Inner Mongolia People's Publishing House: Hohhot).

Day, Clarence Burton (1940), *Chinese Peasant Cults: Being a Study of Chinese Paper Gods* (Kelly and Walsh, Ltd.: Shanghai–Hong Kong–Singapore).

de Heusch, L. (1981), 'Possession and Shamanism', in de Heusch, *Why Marry Her? Society and Symbolic Structures* (Cambridge University Press: Cambridge).

Dennett, Daniel C. (1991), *Consciousness Explained* (Penguin Books: London).

Digby, Bassett (1928), *Tigers, Gold and Witch-doctors* (John Lane the Bodley Head Ltd.: London).

Dioszegi, V. (1961), 'Problems of Mongolian Shamanism', *Acta Etnographica*, X, fasc. 1–2, Budapest: 195–206.

——(1963), 'Ethnogenic Aspects of Darkhat Shamanism', *Acta Orientalia*, 16/1: 55–81.

——(1967), 'The Origins of the Evenki "Shaman-Mask" of Transbaikalia', *Acta Orientalia*, 20: 171–210.

——(1972), 'Tunguso-Man'chzhurskoye zerkalo shamana' (The Tungus-Manchu Shaman's Mirror), *Acta Orientalia* 25: 359–83.

——and Sharakshinova, N. O. (1970), 'Songs of Bulagat Buryat Shamans', in Louis Ligeti (ed.), *Mongolian Studies* (Akademia Kiado: Budapest).

Dmytryshin, A. P., Crowther-Vaughan, A. P., and Vaughan, T. (eds.) *Russia's Conquest of Siberia, 1558–1700*, i (Western Imprints, Press of Oregon Historical Society: Oregon).

Drury, Nevill (1989), *The Elements of Shamanism* (Element Books: Shaftesbury).

Duara, Prasenjit (1988), 'Superscribing Symbols: The Myth of Guandi, Chinese God of War', *Journal of Asian Studies*, 47/4: 778–95.

——(1991), 'Knowledge and Power in the Discourse of Modernity: The Campaigns against Popular Religion in Early Twentieth-Century China', *Journal of Asian Studies*, 50/1: 67–83.

Dugarov, D. S. (1991), *Istoricheskiye Korni Belogo Shamanstva: Na materiale obryadovogo fol'klora buryat* (The Historical Roots of White Shamanism: On the Material of the Ritual Folklore of the Buryat) (Nauka: Moscow).

Dulam, S. (1989), *Mongol domog zuin dur* (The Form of Mongol Mythology) (Ulsyn Khevleliin Gazar: Ulaanbaatar).

——(1992), *Darhad boogiin ulamjlal* (The Tradition of Darhat Shamans) (MUIS-iin Hevlel: Ulaanbaatar).

Dunn, Judy (1988), *The Beginnings of Social Understanding* (Blackwell: Oxford).

Durkheim, E., and Mauss, M. (1963), *Primitive Classification*, trans. R. Needham (University of Chicago Press: Chicago).

Durrant, Stephen (1979), 'The Nisan Shaman Caught in Cultural Contradiction', *Signs*, 5/2: 338–47.

D'yakonova, V. P. (1984), 'Nekotoryye etnokul'turnyye paralleli v shamanstve tyurkoyazychnykh narodov Sayano-Altaya' (Some Ethno-Cultural Parallels in the Shamanism of the Turkic-Language Peoples of the Sayano-Altai), in Ch. M. Taksami (ed.), *Etnokul'turnyye kontakty narodov sibiri* (Nauka: Leningrad).

Einstein, A., and Infeld, L. (1938), *The Evolution of Physics* (Simon and Schuster: New York).

Eliade, Mircea ([1951] 1964), *Shamanism: Archaic Techniques of Ecstasy*, trans. from French by W. R. Trask (Routledge & Kegan Paul: London).

Ellen, Roy (1993), *The Cutural Relations of Classification: An Analysis of Nuaulu Animal Categories from Central Seram* (Cambridge University Press: Cambridge).

Endicott, Kirk (1979), *Batek Negrito Religion* (Clarendon Press: Oxford).

Engkebatu, A. (1983), *Daor Niakan Bulku Biteg* (A Daur–Chinese Little Dictionary) (Inner Mongolia People's Publishing House: Hohhot).

——(1984), *Dagur kelen-ü ügs* (Daur Vocabulary) (Inner Mongolia People's Publishing House: Hohhot).

——(1985), *Dagur kelen-ü üge kelelge-iin materiyal* (Daur Linguistic Materials) (Inner Mongolia People's Publishing House: Hohhot). (in Daur and Mongolian)

——(1987), 'Zheng-guo-gong Chengde lue zhuan' (A Brief Biography of Zheng-guo-gong Chengde), in Meng Zhi-dung, Wu Twan-ying, and A. Engkebatu (eds.), *Da wo er zu yan ju* (Daur Nationality Researches), i (Inner Mongolia Daur History, Language and Literature Association: Hohhot), 153–8.

——and Erkembayar (1987*a*), 'Wo men suo liao jie de guo dao fu' (The Guo Da-fu We Know), in Meng Zhi-dung, Wu Twan-ying, and A. Engkebatu (eds.), *Da wo er zu yan ju* (Daur Nationality Researches), i (Inner Mongolia Daur History, Language and Literature Association: Hohhot), 159–82.

————(1987*b*) 'Fan ru minzu yinxong—Lingsheng' (An Anti-Japanese National Hero—Lingsheng), in Meng Zhi-dung, Wu Twan-ying, and A. Engkebatu (eds.), *Da wo er zu yan ju* (Daur Nationality Researches), i (Inner Mongolia Daur History, Language and Literature Association: Hohhot), 183–92.

Esherick, Joseph W. (1987), *The Origins of the Boxer Uprising* (University of California Press: Berkeley and Los Angeles).

Evans-Pritchard, E. E. (1937), *Witchcraft, Oracles and Magic among the Azande* (Clarendon Press: Oxford).

Even, Marie-Dominique (1992), *Chants de chamanes mongols* (Études Mongoles . . . et sibériennes, Cahier 19–20; Labethno: Nanterre).

Fabian, Johannes (1983), *Time and the Other: How Anthropology Makes its Object* (Columbia University Press: New York).

Fei, Hsiao-tung (1980), 'Ethnic Identification in China', *Social Sciences in China*, 1, Beijing: 94–103.

Feuchtwang, Stephan (1974), *An Anthropological Analysis of Chinese Geomancy* (Vithagna: Vientiane).

Firth, Raymond (1959), 'Problem and Assumption in an Anthropological Study of Religion', *Journal of the Royal Anthropological Institute*, 89: 129–48.

Flaherty, Gloria (1992), *Shamanism and the Eighteenth Century* (Princeton University Press: Princeton).

Fortes, Meyer (1953), 'The Structure of Unilineal Descent Groups', *American Anthropologist*, 55: 17–41.

Freeman, N. H., and Cox, M. V. (1985), *Visual Order: The Nature and Development of Pictorial Representation* (Cambridge University Press: Cambridge).

Fu, Yuguang (1993), 'The Worldview of the Manchu Shamanism', in Mihaly Hoppal and Keith D. Howard (eds.), *Shamans and Cultures* (Istor Books, 5; Akadémiai Kiado: Budapest), 240–8.

Galdanova, G. R. (1987), *Dolamaiskiye verovaniya buryat* (Pre-Lamaist Beliefs of the Buryat), (Nauka: Novosibirsk).

——(1981), 'Evolutsiya soderzhaniya okhotnich'ego kul'ta' (Evolution of the Content of the Hunting Cult), *Buddizm i Traditsionnyye Verovaniye Narodov Tsental'noi Azii* (Nauka: Novosibirsk), 46–55.

Gell, Alfred (1974), 'Understanding the Occult', *Radical Philosophy*, 9: 17–26.

Gelman, Rochel (1990), 'First Principles Organize Attention to and Learning about Relevant Data: Number and Animate–Inanimate Distinction as Examples', *Cognitive Science*, 14: 79–106.

Gelman, Susan (1992 n.d.), 'Traits and Essences'.

Gemuyev, I. N. (ed.) (1998, 1989, 1990), *Traditsionnoye mirovozzreniye tyurkov* (Traditional world view of the Turks of Southern Siberia) (Nauka: Novisbirsk), 3 vols. see also under L'vova and Sagalayev.

Gerasimova, K. M. (1970), 'Lamaiskaya transformatsiya animisticheskikh predstavlenii' (The Lamaist Transformation of Animist Conceptions), in B. V. Semichev (ed.), *Materialy po Istorii i Filologii Tsentral'noi Azii*, iv (BION: Ulan-Ude), 21–34.

Gibson, J. J. (1979), *The Ecological Approach to Visual Perception* (Houghton Mifflin: Boston).

Gilberg, Rolf (1989), 'Nogle troldmaend kalder man shamaner', *Nationalmuseets Arbejdsmark*, 48–56.

Goodman, Nelson (1955), *Fact, Fiction, and Forecast* (Harvard University Press: Cambridge, Mass.).

—— (1978), *Ways of Worldmaking* (Harvester Press: Brighton).

Goodrich, Anne S. (1991), *Peking Paper Gods: A Look at Home Worship* (Monumenta Serica Monograph Series, 23; Steyler Verlag: Nettetal).

Gudeman, Stephan, and Rivera, Alberto (1990), *Conversations in Colombia: The Domestic Economy in Life and Text* (Cambridge University Press: Cambridge).

Hacking, Ian (1992), 'World-Making by Kind-Making: Child-Abuse for Example', in Mary Douglas and David Hull (eds.), *How Classification Works: Nelson Goodman among the Social Sciences* (Edinburgh University Press: Edinburgh), 180–238.

Hallpike, C. R. (1980), *The Foundations of Primitive Thought* (Clarendon Press: Oxford).

Hamayon, Roberte (1977), 'Il n'y a pas de fumée sans dieu', *L'Ethnographie*, NS 74–5: 171–88.

——(1984), 'Is There a Typically Female Exercise of Shamanism in Patrilinear Societies such as the Buryat?', in M. Hoppal (ed.), *Shamanism in Eurasia*, pt. 2 (Edition Herodot: Göttingen), 307–18.

——(1990), *La Chasse à l'âme: Esquisse d'une théorie du chamanisme sibérien* (Société d'ethnologie: Nanterre).

——(1992), 'Game and Games, Fortune and Dualism in Siberian Shamanism', in M. Hoppal and J. Pentikainen (eds.), *Northern Religions and Shamanism* (Akademiai Kiado: Budapest; and Finnish Literature Society: Helsinki), 134–7.

——(1993), 'Are "Trance", "Ecstasy" and Similar Concepts Appropriate in the Study of Shamanism?', in *Shamanism and Performing Arts*, papers and abstracts for the 2nd Conference of the ISSR (Ethnographic Institute Hungarian Academy of Sciences: Budapest), 147–9.

——(1994), 'Shamanism in Siberia: From Partnership in Supernature to Counter-Power in Society', in N. Thomas and C. Humphrey (eds.) *Shamanism, History and the State* (University of Michigan Press: Ann Arbor), 76–89.

Hangin, Gombojab (1986), *A Modern Mongolian–English Dictionary* (Indiana University Research Institute for Inner Asian Studies: Bloomington, Indiana).

Harnod, Hakanchulu, and Alhal, Høgjintai (1980), *Comparative Study of Dagur Mongolian, Classical Mongolian and Manchu* (glossary, in Chinese) (Shue Hai Press: Taibei).

Harris, P., *et al.* (1991), 'Monsters, Ghosts and Witches: Testing the Limits of the Fantasy–Reality Distinction in Young Children', *Br. Jour. Dev. Psychol.* 9: 105–23.

Hasartani, Namcharai (1983), *Dagur Hele Monggol Helen-ü Harichagulul* (Comparison of the Daur and Mongolian Languages) (Inner Mongolia People's Publishing House: Hohhot).

Haslund, Henning (1946), *Mongolian Journey* (Routledge & Kegan Paul: London).

Haslund-Christensen, Henning (1944), 'Mongolske Trøldmaend', *Nationalmuseets Arbejdsmark*, 5–20.

Hattori, Shiro (1972), 'Mongolian Ghost Stories', *Analecta Mongolica*, Mongolia Society Occasional Papers, 8: 101–14.

→ Heissig, Walther (1980), *The Religions of Mongolia*, trans. from German by Geoffrey Samuel (Routledge & Kegan Paul: London).

——(1992), *Schamanen und Geisterbeschwörer in der Östlichen Mongolei* (Otto Harrassowitz: Wiesbaden).

Hevia, James L. (1994), 'Sovereignty and Subject: Constituting Relations of Power in Qing Guest Ritual', in A. Zito and T. E. Barlow (eds.), *Body, Subject and Power in China* (University of Chicago Press: Chicago and London), 181–200.

Hirschfeld, Lawrence A. (1988), 'On Acquiring Social Categories: Cognitive Development and Anthropological Wisdom', *Man* NS 23: 611–38.

——(1991 n.d.), 'Crossing Domains: The Elaboration of Causality in the Acquisition of Biological, Social and Psychological Understandings', to appear in Hirschfeld and S. Gelman (eds.), *Domain Specificity in Cognition and Culture* (Cambridge University Press: Cambridge).

Hobsbawm, Eric (1972), *Bandits* (Harmondsworth: London).

Holmberg, David H. (1989), *Order in Paradox: Myth, Ritual, and Exchange among Nepal's Tamang* (Cornell University Press: Ithaca, NY).

→ Hoppal, M. (1992), 'Urban Shamans: A Cultural Revival in the Postmodern World', in A.-L. Siikala and M. Hoppal (eds.), *Studies on Shamanism* (Finnish Anthropological Society and Akademiai Kiado: Helsinki and Budapest), 197–209.

Howell, Signe (1994), 'Singing with the Spirits and Praying to the Ancestors: A Comparative Study of Chewong and Lio Invocations', *L'Homme*, 132, 34 (4), 15–34.

Howes, David (ed.) (1991), *The Varieties of Sensory Experience: A Sourcebook in the Anthropology of the Senses* (University of Toronto Press: Toronto).

Hull, David (1992), 'Biological Species: An Inductivist's Nightmare', in Mary Douglas and David Hull (eds.), *How Classification Works: Nelson Goodman among the Social Sciences* (Edinburgh University Press: Edinburgh), 42–68.

Humphrey, Caroline (1971–2), 'Shamans and the Trance', *Theoria to Theory*, 4 (1971) and 1 (1972) (Pergamon).

——(1973 n.d.), 'Magical Drawings in the Religion of the Buryats', Ph.D. thesis (University of Cambridge).

——(1974), 'On Some Ritual Techniques in the Bull Cult of the Buriat Mongols', *Proceedings of the Royal Anthropological Institute for 1973* (London).

——(1976), 'Omens and their Explanation', *European Journal of Sociology*, 17: 320–54.

——(1978), 'Women, Taboo and the Suppression of Attention', in S. Ardener (ed.), *Defining Females, the Nature of Women in Society* (Croom Helm: London), 89–108.

——(1979), 'The Uses of Genealogy: A Historical Study of the Nomadic and Sedentarised Buryat', in *Pastoral Production and Society*, ed. L'Équipe écologie et anthropologie des sociétés pastorales (Cambridge University Press and Maison des Sciences de l'Homme: Cambridge and Paris).

—— (1983), *Karl Marx Collective: Economy, Society and Religion in a Siberian Collective Farm* (Cambridge University Press: Cambridge).

——(1994a), 'A Daur Myth about the Bear and the Boy who Became a Man', in E. H. Kaplan and D. W. Whisenhunt (eds.), *Opuscula Altaica: Essays Presented in Honour of Henry Schwarz* (Western Washington University Press: Bellingham), 322–32.

——(1994b), 'Shamanic Practices and the State in Northern Asia: Views from the Centre and Periphery', in Nicholas Thomas and Caroline Humphrey (eds.), *Shamanism, History and the State* (University of Michigan Press: Ann Arbor), 191–228.

——(1995), 'Chiefly and Shamanist Landscapes in Mongolia', in E. Hirsch and M. O'Hanlon (eds.), *The Anthropology of Landscape: Perspectives on Place and Space* (Oxford University Press: Oxford).

——and Laidlaw, James (1994), *The Archetypal Actions of Ritual: A Theory of Ritual Illustrated by the Jain Rite of Worship* (Clarendon Press: Oxford).

Humphrey, Nicholas (1986), *The Inner Eye* (Faber & Faber: London).

Husile and Xue Yin (1981), *Da wo er zu min jian gu shi ji* (Collected Folk Stories of the Daur People) (Inner Mongolia People's Publishing House: Hohhot).

Ides, Izbrant, and Brand, Adam (1967), *Zapiski o russkom posol'stve v kitai (1692–95)* (Notes on the Russian Embassy to China 1692–95) (Glavnaya Redaksiya vostochnoi literatury: Moscow).

Ikeshiri, N. ([1943] 1982), *Da wo er zu* (The Daur Nationality), trans. from Japanese to Chinese by Odongowa (Daur History, Language and Literature Society: Hohhot).

Inagaki, Kayako (1989), 'Developmental. Shift in Biological Inference Processes: From Similarity-Based to Category-Based Attribution', *Human Development*, 32: 79–87.

——and Hatano, Giyoo (1987), 'Young Children's Spontaneous Personification as Analogy', *Child Development*, 58: 1013–20.

Ingold, T. (1986), *The Appropriation of Nature: Essays on Human Ecology and Social Relations* (Manchester University Press: Manchester).

——(1992a), 'Culture and the Perception of the Environment', in E. Croll and D. Parkin (eds.), *Bush Base: Forest Farm. Culture, Environment and Development* (Routledge: London), 39–56.

——(1992b), 'Technology, Language, Intelligence: A Reconsideration of Basic Concepts', in K. R. Gibson and T. Ingold (eds.), *Tools, Language and Cognition in Human Evolution* (Cambridge University Press: Cambridge), 449–72.

——(1993a), 'From Trust to Domination: An Alternative History of Human–Animal Relations', in A. Manning and J. Serpell (eds.), *Animals and Society: Changing Perspectives* (Routledge: London).

——(1993b), 'Hunting and Gathering as Ways of Perceiving the Environment', in K. Fukui and R. Ellen (eds.), *Beyond Nature and Culture* (Berg: Oxford).

——(1993 n.d.), 'The Temporality of the Landscape', unpublished.

Inner Mongolia A. R. Editorial Team (1985), *Da wo er zu she hui li shi diao cha* (Daur Social and History Investigations) (Inner Mongolia People's Publishing House: Hohhot).

Jacobson, Esther (1984), 'The Stage with Bird-Headed Antler Tines: A Study in Image Transformation and Meaning', *Bulletin of Far Eastern Antiquities* (Stockholm), 56: 113–80.

Jagchid, Sechin (1988a), 'An Interpretation of "Mongol Bandits" (*Meng-Fei*)', in S.

Jagchid, *Essays in Mongolian Studies*, vol. 3 in Monograph Series of the David Kennedy Center for International Studies (Brigham Young University: Provo, Ut.).
——(1988*b*), 'Shamanism among the Dakhur Mongols', in S. Jagchid *Essays in Mongolian Studies*, vol. 3 in Monograph Series of the David Kennedy Center for International Studies (Brigham Young University: Provo, Ut.).
Jahunen, Juha (1988), 'A Revival of Dagur Studies', *Finnisch-Ugrischen Forschunen*, 48: 309–16.
——(1990), *Material on Manchurian Khamnigan Mongol* (Castrenianumin toimitteita, 37; Helsinki).
——(1991), *Material on Manchurian Khamnigan Evenki* (Castrenianumin toimitteita, 40; Helsinki).
James, H. E. M. (1888), *The Long White Mountain or a Journey in Manchuria* (Longmans & Co.: London).
Jernakov, V. N. (1974), 'Dagurs in Northeast China', *Zentralasiatische Studien*, 8: 407–22.
Jian Xian Shun (1993), 'Shaman Singing and Dancing and Invoking God in the Imperial Palace of Qing Dynasty', in M. Hoppal and Pal Paricsy (eds.), *Shamanism and Performing Arts* (Ethnographic Institute Hungarina Academy of Sciences: Budapest), 96–7.
Johnson-Laird, P. N. (1983), *Mental Models* (Cambridge University Press: Cambridge).
Kabzinska-Stawarz, Iwona (1991), *Games of Mongolian Shepherds* (Institute of the History of Material Culture (Polish Academy of Sciences): Warsaw).
Kaluzynski, S. (1969, 1970), *Dagurisches Wörterverzeichnis* (Nach F. V. Muromskis handschriftlichen Sprachaufzeichnungen bearbeitet und herausgegeben, Rocznik Orientalyzny, xxxiii/1, 1969 (101–44); xxxiii/2, 1970 (33–67)).
Kapferer, Bruce (1983), *A Celebration of Demons: Exorcism and the Aesthetics of Healing in Sri Lanka* (Indiana University Press: Bloomington, Ind.).
Karatygina, M. E. (1989), 'Zvuk i kosmos: Mir glazami kochevnika i ego otrazheniye v zvukhakh mongol'skoi myzyki' (Sound and the Cosmos: The World in the Eyes of the Nomad and its Reflection in the Sounds of Mongolian Music), in *Istoriya i Kul'tura mongoloyazychnykh narodov: Istochniki i traditsii* (Akademiya Nauk ANSSSR: Ulan-Ude), 94–7.
Keesing, Roger (1985), 'Conventional Metaphors and Anthropological Metaphysics: The Problematic of Cultural Translation', *Journal of Anthropological Research*, 41: 210–17.
Keil, Frank C. (1979), *Semantic and Conceptual Development* (Harvard University Press: Cambridge, Mass.).
——(1987), 'Conceptual Development and Category Structure', in Neisser (1987), 175–200.
——(1991), 'The Emergence of Theoretical Beliefs as Constraints on Concepts', in S. Carey and R. Gelman (eds.), *The Epigenesis of Mind: Essays on Biology and Cognition* (Lawrence Erlbaum Associates: Hillsdale, NJ).
Khangalov, M. N. (1958), *Sobraniye Sochinenie* (Collected Works), i (Buryatskoye Knizhniye Izdatel'stvo: Ulan-Ude).
Kormazova, V. A. (1929), 'Kochevaya Barga: Legendy', *Vestnik Manchzhurii*, 2: 35–42.

Kosokov, I. K. (1930), *K Voprosu o Shamanstve v Severnoi Azii* (On the question of Shamanism in North Asia) (Moscow, publisher unknown).

Ksenofontov, G. V. (1992), *Shamanizm, izbrannyye trudy* (Shamanism: Selected Works) (Sever-Yug: Yakutsk).

Kuo Tao-fu [Merse; Guo Dao-fu] (1930), 'Modern Mongolia', *Pacific Affairs*, August 1930: 754–62.

Kuriyama, Shigehisa (1994), 'The Imagination of the Winds and the Development of the Chinese Conception of the Body', in A. Zito and T. E. Barlow (eds.), *Body, Subject and Power in China* (University of Chicago Press: Chicago and London), 23–41.

Lakoff, George (1987), 'Cognitive Models and Prototype Theory', in Neisser (1987), 63–100.

——and Johnson, M. (1980), *Metaphors We Live By* (Chicago University Press: Chicago).

Langer, S. K. (1942), *Philosophy in a New Key* (Harvard University Press: Cambridge, Mass.).

——(1972), *Mind: An Essay in Human Feeling*, iii (Johns Hopkins University Press: Baltimore and London).

Lattimore, Owen (1934), *The Mongols of Manchuria: Their Tribal Divisions, Geographical Distribution, Historical Relations with Manchus and Chinese and Present Political Problems* (John Day Co.: New York).

——(1942), *Mongol Journeys* (Travel Book Club: London).

——(1990), *China Memories: Chiang Kai-shek and the War Against Japan*, compiled by F. Isono (University of Tokyo Press: Tokyo).

Lessing, Ferdinand, *et al.* (1982), *Mongolian–English Dictionary* (Mongolia Society: Bloomington, Ind.).

Lévi-Strauss, Claude (1949), *The Elementary Structures of Kinship* (Eyre & Spottiswoode: London).

——([1949] 1967), 'The Effectiveness of Symbols', in C. Lévi-Strauss, *Structural Anthropology* [1958], trans. C. Jacobson and Brooke Grundfest Schoepf (Anchor Books: New York), 186–205.

——(1971), *L'Homme nu* (*Mythologiques*, 4; Plon: Paris).

——(1977), 'Avant-propos', in *L'Identité: Séminaire dirigé par Claude Lévi-Strauss* (Grasset: Paris), 9–12.

Lewis, I. M. (1971), *Ecstatic Religion: An Anthropological Study of Spirit Possession and Shamanism* (Penguin: London).

——(1989), 'South of North: Shamanism in Africa, a Neglected Theme', *Paideuma*, 35: 181–8.

Li, Wei-tsu (1948), 'On the Cult of the Four Sacred animals (*Szu-ta-men*) in the Neighbourhood of Peking', *Folklore Studies*, 7, Peking: 1–94.

Li, Yao-hua, *et al.* (1955), 'Findings on the Daur Clan and Kinship Relations', *Collected Papers on Chinese Minorities Studies*, i (Beijing), 460–93.

Liang, Bing (1983), 'La ma jiao zai e erduosi de chuan bo ji ying xiang' (The Spread and Influence of Lamaism in Ordos), in vol. 3 of the collective series *E Erduosi shizhi yan ju wen gao* (Yike zhao meng di fang zhi bian chuan wei: Dongsheng).

Lindgren, E. J. (1930), 'Northwestern Manchuria and the Reindeer Tungus', *Geographical Journal*, 75: 518–36.

——(1935a), 'The Shaman Dress of the Dagurs, Solons and Numinchens in N. W. Manchuria', *Geografiska Annaler*, 17, Stockholm: 365–78.

——(1935b), 'The Reindeer Tungus of Manchuria', *Journal of the Royal Central Asian Society*, 22 (Apr.): 221–31.

——(1935c), 'Field Work in Social Psychology', *British Journal of Psychology (General Section)*, 26/pt. 2: 174–82.

Liu, Mau-tsai (1972), 'Der Niang-Niang Kult in der Mandschurei', *Oriens Extremus*, 19.

Lloyd, G. E. R. (1990), *Demystifying Mentalities* (Cambridge University Press: Cambridge).

Lu, Ming-Hui (1980), *Menggu 'zizhi yundong' shimo* (The Beginning and the End of the Mongolian Autonomy Movement) (Zhong Hua Shu Ju: Beijing).

L'vova, E. L., Oktyabr'skaya, I. V., Sagalyev, A. M., and Usmanova, M. S. (1988, 1989), *Traditsionnoye mirovozreniye Tyurkov Yuzhnoi Sibiri* (Traditional World View of the Turks of Southern Siberia (Nauka: Novosibirsk) 2 vols.

Ma Ho-t'ien (1949), *Chinese Agent in Mongolia*, trans. John De Francis (Johns Hopkins Press: Baltimore).

McCormack, Gavan (1977), *Chang Tso-lin in Northeast China, 1911–1928* (Dawson: Folkestone).

Macintyre, John (1887), 'Roadside Religion in Manchuria', *Journal of the China Branch of the Royal Asiatic Society*, NS 21 (1886), Shanghai: 43–66.

Manduertu (1991), *Da wo er zu* (The Daur Nationality) (Nationality Publishing House: Beijing).

Manzang, Taichigudai (1991), *Monggol bøge mørgül* (Mongol Shamanism) (Inner Mongolia People's Publishing House: Hohhot).

Manzhigeyev, I. A. (1978), *Buryatskiye shamanisticheskiye i doshamanisticheskiye terminy* (Buryat Shamanist and Pre-Shamanist Terms) (Nauka: Moscow).

Mathieu, Remi (1985), 'Aux origines de la femme-renarde en Chine', *Études Mongoles . . . et Sibériennes*, 15 (1984): 83–109.

——(1991), 'Croyances des Toungouses de Chine', *Anthropos*, 86: 111–25.

Mauss, Marcel ([1938] 1985), 'A Category of the Human Mind: The Notion of Person; the Notion of Self', trans. W. D. Halls, in M. Carrithers, S. Collins, and S. Lukes (eds.), *The Category of the Person* (Cambridge University Press: Cambridge), 1–25.

Mead, Margaret (1932), 'An Investigation of the Thought of Primitive Children, with Special Reference to Animism', *Journal of the Royal Anthropological Institute*, 62: 173–90.

Mendüsürüng, M. (1983), 'Dagur-un bøge mørgül-ün tuhai torsin ügülekü ni' (Attempt at a Study of Dagur Shamanism), *Colmon* 3: Køkehota (Hohhot).

Meng Zhi-dung, Engkebatu, A., and Wu Twan-ying (eds.) (1987), *Da wo er zu yan ju* (Daur Nationality Researches), i (Inner Mongolia Daur History, Language and Literature Association: Hohhot).

Mergendi (1981), 'Da wo er zu zhi zong jiao xin yang' (The Religious Beliefs of the Daur Nationality), *Neimenggu Shehui Kexue*, 3 (1981): 192–7.

——(1987), 'Da wo er zu zhi zong jiao xin yang' (The Religious Beliefs of the Daur Nationality), in Meng Zhi-dung, Wu Twan-ying, and A. Engkebatu (eds.), *Da wo er zu yan ju* (Daur Nationality Researches), i (Inner Mongolia Daur History, Language and Literature Association: Hohhot).

Merleau-Ponty, M. (1962), *Phenomenology of Perception*, trans. Colin Smith (Routledge & Kegan Paul: London).

Mervis, Carolyn B. (1987), 'Child-Basic Object Categories and Early Lexical Development', in Neisser (1987), 201–33.

Middleton, Nick (1992), *The Last Disco in Outer Mongolia* (Sinclair-Stevenson: London).

Mikhailov, T. M. (1976), 'Animisticheskiye predstavleniya buryat' (Animist Conceptions of the Buryat), in I. S. Vdovin (ed.), *Priroda i Chelovek v Religioznykh Predstavleniyakh Narodov Sibiri i Severa* (Nature and Humanity in the Religious Conceptions of the Peoples of Siberia) (Nauka: Leningrad), 292–319.

——(1979), 'Vliyaniye lamaizma i khristianstva na shamanizm buryat' (The Influence of Lamaism and Christianity on the Shamanism of the Buryat), in I. S. Vdovin (ed.) *Khristianstvo i Lamaizm u Korennogo Naseleniya Sibiri* (Christianity and Lamaism among the Native Populations of Siberia) (Nauka: Leningrad), 127–49.

——(1980), *Iz Istorii Buryatskogo Shamanizma, s drevneyshikh vremen po XVIII v.* (From the History of Buryat Shamanism, from the Earliest Times to the 18th Century) (Nauka: Novosibirsk).

——(1987), *Buryatskii Shamanizm: Istoriya, struktura i sotsial'nyye funktsii* (Buryat Shamanism: History, Structure and Social Functions) (Nauka: Novosibirsk).

Moerman, Michael (1988), *Talking Culture: Ethnography and Conversation Analysis* (University of Pennsylvania Press: Philadelphia).

Molidawa Dawoerzu Zizhiqi gaikuang (1986), 'Molidawa Dawoerzu Zizhiqi gaikuang bianxiezu' (A Description of the 'Molidawa Daur Autonomous Banner'), in *Zhongguo shaoshu minzu zizhi difang gaikuang congshu.* (Inner Mongolia People's Publishing House: Hohhot).

Mongolyn ard tümnii 1911 ony undesnii erkh choloo, tusgaar togtnolyn toloo temtsel: barimt bichgiin emkhtgel (1900–1914) (1982). (Ulsyn Hevleliin Gazar: Ulaanbaatar). (Collection of documents 1900–1914 concerning the Mongolian people's struggle for autonomy and national sovereignty in 1911)

Mumford, Stan R. (1989), *Himalayan Dialogue: Tibetan Lamas and Gurung Shamans in Nepal* (University of Wisconsin Press: Madison and London).

Namcharai and Hasartani (1983), *Dagur kele Monggol kelen-ü harichagulul* (A Comparison between Daur and Mongolian Languages (Inner Mongolia People's Printing House: Hohhot).

Naquin, Susan (1985), 'The Transmission of White Lotus Sectarianism in Late Imperial China', in David Johnson, Andrew Nathan, and Evelyn Rawski (eds.), *Popular Culture in Late Imperial China* (SMC Publishing Inc.: Taipei).

Nei Menggu Tongji Nianjian (1990) (Statistical Yearbook of Inner Mongolia Autonomous Region) (China Statistics Bureau: Beijing).

Neisser, Ulric (ed.) (1987), *Concepts and Conceptual Development: Ecological and Intellectual Factors in Categorization* (Cambridge University Press: Cambridge).

——and Winograd, Eugene (eds.) (1988), *Remembering Reconsidered: Ecological and Traditional Approaches to the Study of Memory* (Cambridge University Press: Cambridge).

Neklyudov, S. Yu. (1992/3), 'Polistadial'nyi obraz dukha-khozyaina, khranitelya i sozdatelya ognya v mongol'skoi mifologicheskoi traditsii' (The Multi-Layered Image of the Spirit-Master, Protector and Creator of Fire in the Mongolian Mythological Tradition), *Acta Orientalia*, 26/2–3 (1992–3): 311–21.

Nelson, Richard K. (1983), *Make Prayers to the Raven: A Koyukon View of the Northern Forest* (University of Chicago Press: Chicago).

Novik, E. S. (1984), *Obryad i fol'klor v sibirskom shamanizme: Opyt sopostavleniya struktur* (Ritual and Folklore in Siberian Shamanism: Experiment in a Comparison of Structures) (Nauka: Moscow).

Nowak, Margaret, and Durrant, Stephen (1977), *The Tale of the Nishan Shamaness* (University of Washington Press: Seattle).

Obeyesekere, Gananath (1977), 'Psychocultural Exegesis of a Case of Spirit Possession in Sri Lanka', in V. Crapanzano and V. Garrison (eds.), *Case Studies in Spirit Possession* (John Wiley: New York), 235–94.

——(1981), *Medusa's Hair: An Essay on Personal Symbols and Religious Experience* (University of Chicago Press: Chicago).

Odonggow-a [Odongowa] (ed.) (1987), *Dagur-un Ulamzilaltu Uran Zokijal* (Daur Traditional Literature) (Inner Mongolia Culture Publishing House: Hohhot).

——(1991), 'Ancient Daur Shamanism', *The Northern Ethnic Groups*, 7: Hohhot (in Chinese).

O'Hanlon, R. (1988), 'Recovering the Subject: Subaltern Studies and Histories of Resistance in Colonial South Asia', *Modern Asian Studies*, 22/1.

Ohnuki-Tierney, Emiko (1976), 'Shamanism and World View: The Case of the Ainu of the Northwest Coast of Southern Sakhalin', in A. Bharati (ed.), *The Realm of the Extra-Human: Ideas and Actions* (Mouton: The Hague), 175–99.

——(1980), 'Shamans and *Imu*: Among Two Ainu Groups', *Ethnos*, 8/5: 204–28.

——(1981), *Illness and Healing among the Sakhalin Ainu: A Symbolic Interpretation* (Cambridge University Press: Cambridge).

Omachi, Tokuzo (1949), 'Hairaru Dauru zoku no ujizoku miko' (The Clan Shamans of the Daurs of Hailar), *Minzokugaku Kenkyu*, 14/1: 17–26.

——(1982), *Complete Works* (in Japanese), vi (Future Press: Tokyo).

Onon, Urgunge (1990), *The History and the Life of Chinggis Khan (the Secret History of the Mongols)*, trans. and annotated by Urgunge Onon (Brill: Leiden).

Ots, Thomas (1994), 'The Silenced Body—the Expressive Leib: On the Dialectic of Mind and Life in Chinese Cathartic Healing', in Thomas Csordas (ed.), *Embodiment and Experience: The Existential Ground of Culture and Self* (Cambridge University Press: Cambridge), 116–38.

Overing, Joanna (1990), 'The Shaman as Maker of Worlds: Nelson Goodman in the Amazon', *Man*, 25/4: 602–19.

Palladius, Arkhimandrit (1871), 'Dorozhnyya zametki na puti ot Pekina do Blagoveshchenska chrez Man'chzhuriyu v 1870 godu' (Travel Notes on the Way from Pekin to Blagoveshchensk through Manchuria in 1870), *Zapiski Imp. Russk. Geog. Obshchestva*, vol. 4, St Petersburg.

Poppe, N. N. (1930), *Dagurskoye Narechiye* (the Dagur Dialect) (Izdatel'stvo Akademiya Nauk SSSR: Leningrad).

——(ed.) (1940), *Letopisi Khorinskikh Buryat: Khroniki Tuguldur Toboyeva i Vandana Yumsunova* (Annals of the Hori Buryats: The Chronicles of Tuguldur Toboev and Vandan Yumsunov) (Trudy Instituta Vostokovedeniya, 33; Akademiya Nauk SSSR: Moscow and Leningrad).

Popper, K., and Eccles, J. C. (1984), *Self and its Brain* (Routledge & Kegan Paul: London).

Potanin, G. N. (1881–3), *Ocherki Severo-Zapadnoi Mongolii* (Sketches of North-West Mongolia) (Karshbaum: St Petersburg).

Potapov, L. P. (1991), *Altaiskii Shamanizm* (Altaian Shamanism) (Nauka: Leningrad).

Purev, Otgony (1993), 'The Problem of Knots of Mongolian Shaman's Garment', in Zhang, Jun-yi (ed.), *International Symposium of Mongolian Culture* (Taipei, Taiwan), 85–108.

Qiu Pu (ed.) (1985), *Sha man jiao yan jiu* (Researches on Shamanism) (Shanghai People's Publishing House: Shanghai).

Richards, Paul (1994), 'Natural Symbols and Natural History: Chimpanzees, Elephants and Experiments in Mende Thought', in Kay Milton (ed.), *Environmentalism* (Routledge: London).

Ridley, M. W. (1983), 'The Mating System of the Pheasant *Phasianus colchicus*', D. Phil. thesis (University of Oxford).

Rinchen, B. (1962), 'Doma dukhov u shamanov prikosogol'ya' (Houses of the Spirits of the Shamans of the Cis-Kovsgol Region), *Acta Orientalia*, 15/1–3: 249–58.

Rinchen, Yongsiyebu (1977), 'Noms des chamanes et des chamanesses en mongol', *L'Ethnographie*, 74–5: 148–53.

Rival, Laura (1993), 'The Growth of Family Trees: Understanding Huaorani Perceptions of the Forest', *Man*, 28/2: 635–52.

Rosaldo, R. (1980), *Ilongot Headhunting, 1,883–1974: A Study in Society and History* (Stanford University Press: Palo Alto, Calif.).

Roseman, Marina (1991), *Healing Sounds from the Malaysian Rainforest: Temiar Music and Medicine* (University of California Press: Berkeley and Los Angeles).

Rouget, Gilbert (1980), *La Musique et la transe* (Gallimard (Bibliothèque des sciences humaines): Paris).

Sagalayev, A. M., and Oktyabr'skaya, I. V. (1990), *Traditsionnoye mirovozraniye Tyurkov Yuzhnoi Sibiri: Znak i ritual* (Traditional World View of the Turks of Southern Siberia: Sign and Ritual) (Nauka: Novosibirsk).

Sahlins, M. (1985), *Islands of History* (University of Chicago Press: Chicago and London).

Sain Tanaa (1987a), 'Da wo er zu de shen hua he sa man jiao' (The Mythology and Shamanism of the Daur People), in Meng Zhi-dung, Wu Twan-ying, and A. Engkebatu (eds.), *Da wo er zu yan ju* (Daur Nationality Researches), ii (Daur History, Language and Literature Association of Inner Mongolia: Hohhot), 287–315.

——(ed.) (1987b), *Da wu er zu feng shu zhi* (Collected Folk-Tales of the Daur People) (Inner Mongolia People's Publishing House: Hohhot).

Saladin d'Anglure, Bernard (1986), 'Du foetus au chamane: La Construction d'un "troisième sexe" inuit', *Études/Inuit/Studies*, 10/1–2: 25–113.

Sangren, P. Steven (1983), 'Female Gender in Chinese Religious Symbols: Kuan Yin, Ma Tsu, and the "Eternal Mother"', *Signs*, 9/1: 4–25.

Schwarz, Henry G. (1984), 'The Daurs of China: An Outline', *Zentralasiatische Studien*, 17: 154–71.

Schwartz, T. (1978), 'The Size and Shape of a Culture', in F. Barth (ed.), *Scale and Social Organization* (Universitetsforlaget: Oslo).

Severi, Carlo (1982), 'Le Chemin des métamorphoses: Un modèle de connaissance de la folie dans un chant chamanique cuna', *Res* (Spring): 31–67.

——(1985), 'Penser par séquences, penser par territoires', *Communications*, 41: 160–90.

——(1987), 'The Invisible Path: Ritual Representation of Suffering in Cuna Traditional Thought', *Res*, 14: 66–85.

——(1988), 'L'Étranger, l'envers de soi et l'échec du symbolisme: Deux representations du Blanc dans la tradition chamanique cuna', *L'Homme*, 106–7: 174–83.

——(1993), 'Talking about Souls: The Use of a Complex Category in Cuna Ritual Language', in Pascal Boyer (ed.), *Cognitive Aspects of Ritual Symbolism* (Cambridge University Press: Cambridge), 165–81.

Shelton, Anthony (1994), 'Huichol Prayer: Image and Word in Sacred Communication', *Journal of the Anthropological Society of Oxford*, 25/1: 77–89.

Shirokogoroff, S. M. (1933), *Social Organization of the Northern Tungus* (Commercial Press, Ltd: Shanghai).

——(1935), *Psychomental Complex of the Tungus* (Kegan Paul, Trench, Trubner & Co., Ltd: London).

Siikala, A.-L. (1987), *The Rite Technique of the Siberian Shaman* (Academy of Science: Helsinki).

——(1985), 'Comment on Noll "The Role of Visions in Shamanism"', *Current Anthropology*, 26/4: 445–6.

——(1992), 'Two Types of Shamanic Songs: A Chukchi Case', in Anna-Leena Siikala and Mihaly Hoppal, *Studies on Shamanism* (Finnish Anthropological Society and Akademiai Kiado: Helsinki and Budapest), 41–55.

Smolyak, A. V. (1976), 'Predstavleniya Nanaitsev o mire' (Nanai Concepts of the World', in I. S. Vdovin (ed.), *Priroda i chelovek v religioznykh predstavleniyakh narodov Sibiri i Severa* (Nauka: Leningrad).

——(1991), *Shaman: Lichnost', funktsii, mirovozreniye (narody Nizhnego Amura)* (The Shaman: Person, Function and World-View (Peoples of the Lower Amur)) (Nauka: Moscow).

Sneath, David (1991), 'Post-Revolutionary Social and Economic Changes among the Pastoral Population of Inner Mongolia', Ph.D. thesis (University of Cambridge).

Spence, Jonathan D. ([1966] 1988), *Ts'ao Yin and the K'ang-hsi Emperor: Bondservant and Master* (Yale University Press: New Haven and London).

Sperber, Dan (1985a), *On Anthropological Knowledge* (Cambridge University Press: Cambridge).

——(1985b), 'Anthropology and Psychology: Towards an Epidemiology of Representations', *Man*, NS 20/1: 73–89.

——(1990), 'The Epidemiology of Beliefs', in Colin Fraser and George Gaskell (eds.), *The Social Psychological Study of Widespread Beliefs* (Clarendon Press: Oxford).

Stary, G. (1990), 'A New Altaistic Science "Nishanology"', *Altaica Osloensis: Proceedings of the 32nd Meeting of the Permanent International Altaistic Conference, Oslo, June 1989* (Oslo), 317–23.

State Statistical Bureau of the People's Republic of China (1985), *China: A Statistics Survey in 1985* (New World Press: Beijing).

Steadman, Philip (1979), *The Evolution of Designs* (Cambridge University Press: Cambridge).

Stern, D. N. (1985), *The Interpersonal World of the Infant* (Basic Books: New York).

Stewart, Michael (1993), 'Mauvaises morts, prêtres impurs et pouvoir récupérateur du chant', *Terrain*, 20 (20 Mar.): 21–36.

Strathern, Marilyn (1988), *The Gender of the Gift: Problems with Women and Problems with Society in Melanesia* (University of California Press: London).

Suritai, E. (1987), 'A Discussion of Daur Folk Plastic Arts', in Meng Zhi-dung, Wu Twan-ying, and A. Engkebatu (eds.), *Da wo er zu yan ju* (Daur Nationality Researches), ii (Daur History, Language and Literature Association of Inner Mongolia: Hohhot), 260–70.

Szynkiewicz, Slawoj (1984), *Herosi Tajgi: Mify, Legendy, obyczaje Jakutow* (Warsaw).

Takho-Godi, A. (1989), 'Aleksei Fedorovich Losev', *Soviet Anthropology and Archaeology*, Fall 1989: 72–84.

Tambiah, Stanley Jeyaraja (1985), *Culture, Thought and Social Action* (Harvard University Press: Cambridge, Mass).

Tannen, Deborah (1989), *Talking Voices: Repetition, Dialogue and Imagery in Conversational Discourse* (Cambridge University Press: Cambridge).

Tao Yang and Mu Zhong-xiu (1989), *Zhongguo chuangshi shenhua* (Cosmological Mythologies of China) (Shanghai People's Press: Shanghai).

Taussig, Michael (1987), *Shamanism, Colonialism and the Wild Man: A Study in Terror and Healing* (University of Chicago Press: Chicago and London).

Thomas, Nicholas (1988), 'Marginal Powers: Shamanism and the Disintegration of Hierarchy', *Critique of Anthropology*, 8: 53–74.

——(1989), *Out of Time: History and Evolution in Anthropological Discourse* (Cambridge University Press: Cambridge).

——and Humphrey, Caroline (eds.) (1994), *Shamanism, History and the State* (University of Michigan Press: Ann Arbor).

Todayeva, B. Kh. (1960), *Mongol'skiye yazyki i dialekty Kitaya* (Mongolian Languages and Dialects of China) (Izd. Vost. Lit.: Moscow).

——(1986), *Dagurskii Yazyk* (Dagur Language (Nauka: Moscow).

Toren, Christina (1993), 'Making History: The Significance of Childhood Cognition for a Comparative Anthropology of Mind', *Man*, 28/3: 461–78.

Tugutov, I. E. (1978), 'The Tailagan as a Principal Shamanistic Ritual of the Buryats', in V. Dioszegi and M. Hoppal (eds.), *Shamanism in Siberia* (Akademiai Kiado: Budapest).

Vitebsky, Piers (1993), *Dialogues with the Dead* (Cambridge University Press: Cambridge).

Vladimirtsov, B. Ya. (1927), 'Etnologo-lingvisticheskiye issledovaniye v Urge, Urginskom i Kenteiskom raionakh' (Ethnological-Linguistic Research in Urga, Urga Province and Kentei Province) (*Severnaya Mongolia*, 2: Akademiya Nauk SSSR: Leningrad).

Volkova, M. P. (ed.) (1961), *Nisan'samani bitkhe* (Legend of the Nishan Shaman) (Academy of Sciences: Moscow).

Vreeland, Herbert Harold III ([1954] 1962), *Mongol Community and Kinship Structure* (HRAF Press: New Haven).

Weiner, James F. (1991), *The Empty Space: Poetry, Space and Being among the Foi of Papua New Guinea* (Indiana University Press: Bloomington and Indianapolis).

Wellman, Henry M., and Gelman, Susan A. (1992), 'Cognitive Development: Foundational Theories of Core Domains', *Annual Review of Psychology*, 43: 337–75.

Whitehouse, Harvey (1992), 'Memorable Religions: Transmission, Codification and Change in Divergent Melanesian Contexts,' *Man*, NS 27/4: 1–21.

Wolf, M. (1992), *A Thrice-Told Tale: Feminism, Postmodernism and Ethnographic Responsibility* (Stanford University Press: Stanford).

Wu, Bing-an (1989*a*), *Shen mi de sha man shi jie* (The Mysterious World of Shamanism) (Shanghai San Lian Shu Dian: Shanghai).

——(1989*b*), 'Shamans in Manchuria', in M. Hoppal and O. von Sadovsky (eds.), *Shamanism: Past and Present*, ii (Hungarian Academy of Sciences and Los Angeles/ Fullerton International Society for Trans-Oceanic Research: Budapest), 263–70.

Yablonskaya, M. N. (1900), *Women Artists of Russia's New Age, 1900–1935* (Thames and Hudson: London).

Yakhontova, K. S. (1990), 'Man'chzhurskoye i dagurskiye rukopisi iz sobraniya V. A. Starikova' (Manchurian and Dagur Manuscripts from the Collection of V. A. Starikov) (*Vostochnyi Sbornik*, 4: Leningrad), 92–51.

——(ed.) (1992), *Kniga o shamanke Nisan'* (Book about Nisan' Shaman) (Tsentr 'Peterburgskoye Vostokovedeniye' i Izd. 'Vodolei': St Petersburg).

Yamomoto, H. (1971), 'On the Cries of the Green Pheasant (*Phasianus colchicus*) concerned to the Earthquake', *Tori* 20: 239–42.

Yusefovich, Leonid (1993), *Samoderzhets pustyni: Fenomen sud'by barona R. F. Ungern-Shternberg* (Autocrat of the Desert: The Fate of Baron R. F. Ungern-Shternberg) (Ellis Luck: Moscow).

Zhambalova, S. G. (1991), *Traditsionnaya okhota buryat* (The Traditional Hunt of the Buryat) (Nauka: Novosibirsk).

Zhang, Jun-yi (ed.) (1993), *International Symposium on Mongolian Culture* (Mongolian and Tibetan Commission, Taipei: Taiwan).

Zhukovskaya, N. L. (1986), 'Prostranstvo i vremya v mirovozrenii mongolov' (Space and Time in the World-View of the Mongols), in N. L. Zhukovskaya (ed.), *Mify, Kul'ty, Obraydy Narodov Azii* (Nauka: Moscow).

Zito, Angela (1994), 'Silk and Skin: Significant Boundaries', in A. Zito and T. E. Barlow (eds.), *Body, Subject and Power in China* (University of Chicago Press: Chicago and London), 103–56.

INDEX

Bold-face page references indicate illustrations or figures.

partiality 11–12, 39, 204, 360–1
pastoralism 67 n., 72 n.
patricharchy 23–7, 29, 37, 61, 151–2, 168, 242–3
  contrast with shamanic thinking 60–3, 188, 280, 284, 300, 310–11, 352
  and banditry 45
perception 87–8
personality 100, 105
pheasant 56, 102–3, 155, 333, 353 n.
  as analogy for women 157, 180 n., 333
  harbinger of doom 333
  hunted 172
  were-pheasant 334
physical strength 34, 336
pig 153–4, 165, 331
Pingguo Yadgan 133, 183–4, 185, 228–30, 243, 268, 313 n.
  knife repertoire of 133, 229–30
  spirits mastered by 252 n.
plants 85, 95, 179 n., 303
  as metaphor for ancestry 274–5
  and regeneration 131, 176–8, 292, 347
poetics 59–61, 303–4
politics 3, 13, 40, 275
  and discourse of ancestry 274–5
  of everyday life 112–13, 304, 358
  and ideologies 344–7
  leaders 27, 273–4
  and *oboo* cults 349–50, 351
  politics of anthropology of shamanism 204, 358
  principle of *arag bilig* 348
  and shamanism 6, 45, 63, 104, 127, 204, 280, 360
  and were–animal cult 335–6
  see also empire, Manchu Empire, power, revolution, state
pollution 131, 170–1, 302–3, 323
  acted upon by women 172–6
  female pollution objectified 172–6
  as weapon 173, 181 n.
Poppe, N. 64 n., 115 n., 117 n., 139 n., 167, 169, 186–8, 203, 251 n., 336, 351
possession (by spirits) 70–1 n., 102, 156–7, 216, 219–20, 220–3, 235–7, 281, 339–41
poverty 44–5
power 76
  conflictual 106, 172, 211
  discourse of 8, 85, 106, 128, 190–1, 280, 283, 338–9, 358
  distribution in Mongolian families 347–8

imperial versus shamanic 8, 281–2
  and knowledge 3, 227, 320, 324, 357–8
  of natural entities 85–6, 88–9, 95, 108, 115 n., 117 n.
  of order 233–5
  and religion 348
  seniority and 25–6
  of spirits 8, 25–6, 108, 128, 138 n., 190–1, 271
  spiritual power of persons 25, 106, 362
  state 95, 282–3, 338
  subjection to 283
  techniques of 329, 333–4
  transformative 193
prayer 57, 80, 124, 135, 142, 144–6, 153–4, 324
predicate restrictions 54, 77
procreation 286–7, 300
projectability 74 n.
prophesy 130
propitiation 145, 152–5, 230, 258 n., 331
  as representation of love 263–4
protocol 24–5, 35
psychology 219–23, 318–19 n.
  cognitive 4, 54–5, 85, 107–8, 359
  domain specificity 55, 321
  human 61, 192–3, 222–3
purification 141, 172–3, 299–300, 316 n., 318 n., 319 n.
  of *oboo* from spirit power 355 n.
  see also New Year

Qidan *see* Khitan
qigong (Chinese spiritual technique) 355 n.
Qiqihar (Tsitsihar) 14, 22, 162–3, 186, 188, 329, 351

railways 7, 40, 329, 340, 335
  shaman fights influence of 337, 434
rain 139 n., 147, 151, 155, 158, 254 n.
  and fertility 155–6
  in origin myths 294
rainbow 131
rank 23, 25, 202
  family 24–5, 26–7
  in Manchu Empire 95
  of shamans 70 n.
  of spirits 67 n.
  see also aristocracy, bondsmen
ransom 42, 72 n.
reality, ideas of 49, 304–5, 357, 359, 363
redress 262–3

shamans (*cont.*)
  asexual form of 185–6, 203–4, 248
  assistants of 73 n., 200, 229, 231, 307, 309,
    352 n.
  authority of 112–13, 350
  and *bagchi* (ritualist) 30, 325–6
  'burial' of 27, 130, 212, 253 n.
  constitution of 31
  costume 7, 34, 200, 202–9, 210–22, 288
  curing by 213, 301–4
  death 31, 130–1, 138 n., 198–202
  on delegation to Tsar 139 n.
  do not hunt 29–39, 324
  do not officiate at sacrifice 26, 147, 154–5
  feed spirits with blood 241–2
  foreign shamans mistrusted 325–6
→ and gender 176, 183, 185, 188, 245, 306
  identity and 6, 235, 302–3
  individuality of 5, 183–4
  initiate as chrysallis 185, 251 n.
  initiation 32–4, 237
  journey of 120, 122–4, 125, 236, 260 n.,
    296–300, 317–18 n.
  limitations of 104, 324–5, 350
  mistakes of 240
  mortuary sites of 132–3, 138 n., 198–202,
    348–50
  need for 363
  and psychological knowledge 34, 61–3,
    190, 192–3, 212–14, 216, 222–3, 263,
    271, 357
  relationships and 261–71, 350
  sexually active 34, 261, 310, 319 n.
  social duality of 5, 39, 351
  songs of 37, 183, 230, 272, 295–301, 304
  spirits and 31, 33, 36–9, 130, 185–93, 324
  teacher 31, 185–6, 189, 239
  techniques 49, 228–30, 235–7, 315 n.,
    317 n., 324, 358
— terms for 64 n., 74 n., 251 n., 322
  tests of fortitude of 257 n.
  trance 30–1, 229–30, 234, 257–8 n.
  undermines 'natural' order of elders 33,
    38, 60–2, 193, 245, 249, 309–11
  wary of mastering new spirits 324
  weakness of 34, 37–9, 201, 211–12
  wealth and poverty of 34, 270
  white and black 73 n., 123, 138 n., 315 n.
  as 'wounded healer' 191, 304
  see also Du Yadgan, Fukan Yadgan,
    Huangge Yadgan, *otoshi*, Pingguo

Yadgan, specialists
shamanship 49, 73 n., 113, 185–6, 227–37,
  237
  compared with prayer 325–6
  compared with were-animal cults 343
sharing 35, 92, 219–20
Shenyang (Mukden) 94, 116 n., 276,
  313–14 n., 346
Shirokogoroff, S. 65 n., 99, 101–4, 117 n.,
  123, 137 n., 181 n., 195, 219, 221, 251 n.,
  255–6 n., 260 n., 273, 283, 290, 302, 310,
  313 n., 324–6, 333–6
shurkul, *see* devils
signification 301–2
Siikala, A.-L. 4, 48, 143, 235–6
singing 187, 195, 342
skills 36, 329, 339
  copying of 334
sky (*tengger*) 16, 29, 33, 37, 50, 70 n., 78–84,
  108, 109–10, 119, 272, 280, 310–11, 333
  alternative vision of 299–301
  ascent to 122–3, 125, 207, 247–50
  aspects of 74 n., 82
  and consciousness 362, 364
  father and 81, 299–301
  female aspect of 174–5
  gender and 80, 81
  'heavenly hair' 208–9, 254 n.
  propitiation of 152–5
  representation of 80
  sky deities 82, 122–3, 125
  'small sky' in head 88, 144, 214, 362
  support of 175–6, 182 n., 290–1
  and weather 78
  women's view of 173–6, 301
  worship of 26, 29, 53, 55, 142, 146–7,
    154–5
smoke offering 27, 141, 146–7
snake 38, 204, 220, 260 n., 269–70, 278, 293,
  313 n.
  and bone-setter 324
  as *kiant* spirit 330
sociality 221–3, 271, 357
society 4
  dissolution of clan society 236–7, 350–1
  fissures in 302–3
  like grove of trees 98, 116 n.
  not constrasted with individual 194
  'social structure' 151
Solon 13, **32**, 65 n., 68 n., 244, 269, 277, 337,
  343